Contents

2   Map of principal sights

6   Map of touring programmes

10   Map of places to stay

13   Introduction

14   Description of the region

32   Prehistory

34   Historical table and notes

39   Art

54   Traditions

59   Food and drink

63   Sights

371   Practical information

382   Sport and leisure

389   Getting to know the region

391   Calendar of events

393   Admission times and charges

418   Useful French words and phrases

420   Index

D031749C

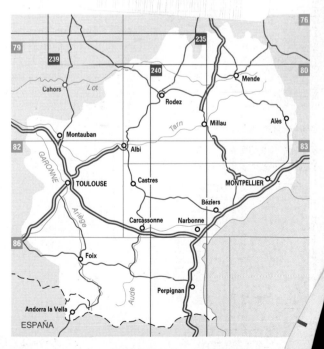

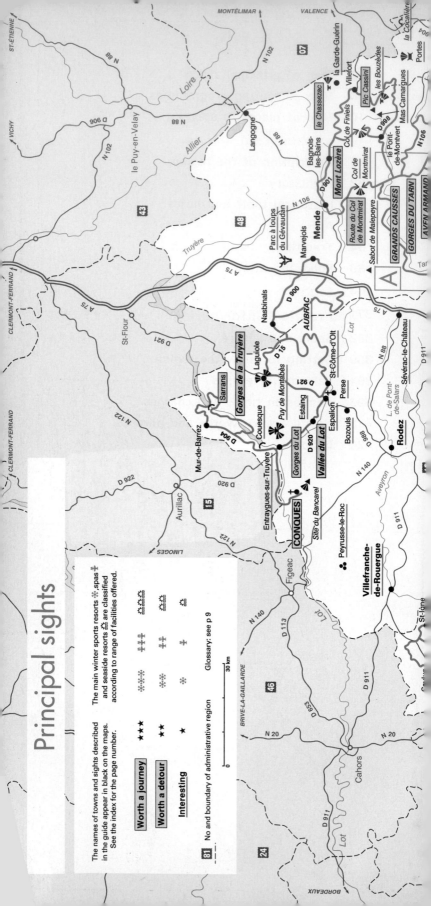

Principal sights

The names of towns and sights described in the guide appear in black on the maps. See the index for the page number.

The main winter sports resorts ❄ spas ♨ and seaside resorts ☼ are classified according to range of facilities offered.

Worth a journey	★★★	❄❄❄	♨♨♨	☼☼☼
Worth a detour	★★	❄❄	♨♨	☼☼
Interesting	★	❄	♨	☼

Glossary: see p 9

81 No and boundary of administrative region

0 ───── 30 km

MONTÉLIMAR   VALENCE
la Cocalière
la Garde-Guérin
07
Villefort
Pic Cassini
les Bouzèdes
Mas Camargues
Portes
le Chassezac
Col de Finiels
Bagnols-les-Bains
Mont Lozère
le Pont-de-Montvert
D 998
N 106
ST-ÉTIENNE
Loire
88 N
D 906
VICHY
N 102
le Puy-en-Velay
Allier
Langogne
88 N
Col de Montmirat
Route du Col de Montmirat
Mende
Sabot de Malepeyre
GRANDS CAUSSES
GORGES DU TARN
AVEN ARMAND
A
Tarn
43
Truyère
48
Parc à loups du Gévaudan
Marvejols
N 106
D 901
N 88
A 75
CLERMONT-FERRAND
St-Flour
D 921
D 922
Nasbinals
D 900
AUBRAC
St-Côme-d'Olt
Sévérac-le-Château
Lot
N 88
D 911
D 15
Gorges de la Truyère
Laguiole
Puy de Montabès
D 921
Estaing
Espalion
Perse
Bozouls
Gorges du Lot
Vallée du Lot
Sarrans
Couesque
D 904
L. de Pont-de-Salars
N 140
D 988
Rodez
Mur-de-Barez
D 920
D 922
CLERMONT-FERRAND
Aurillac
15
N 122
LIMOGES
Entraygues-sur-Truyère
CONQUES
Site du Bancarel
Peyrusse-le-Roc
Aveyron
D 911
Villefranche-de-Rouergue
Figeac
N 140
D 113
46
BRIVE-LA-GAILLARDE
N 20
D 653
Lot
St-Igne
Cahors
24
BORDEAUX
D 911
N 20

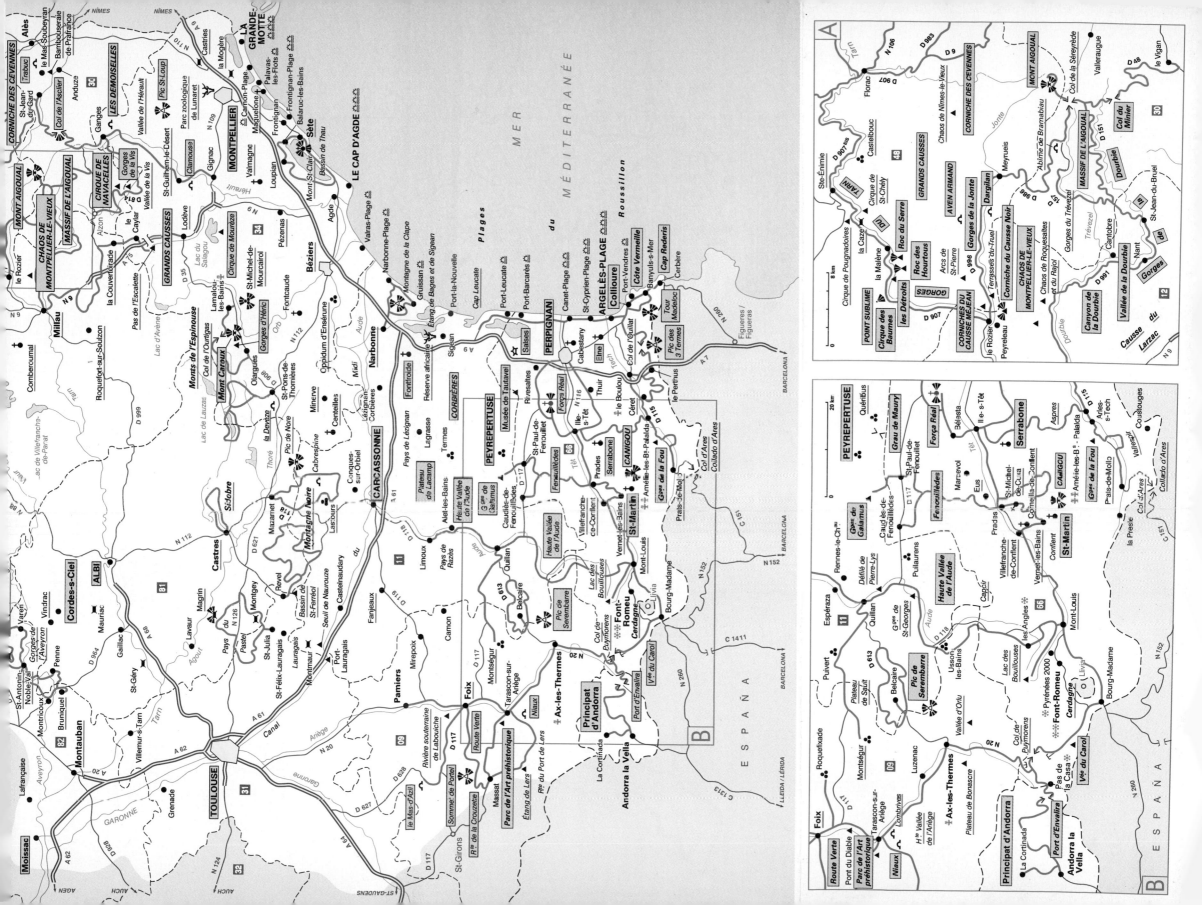

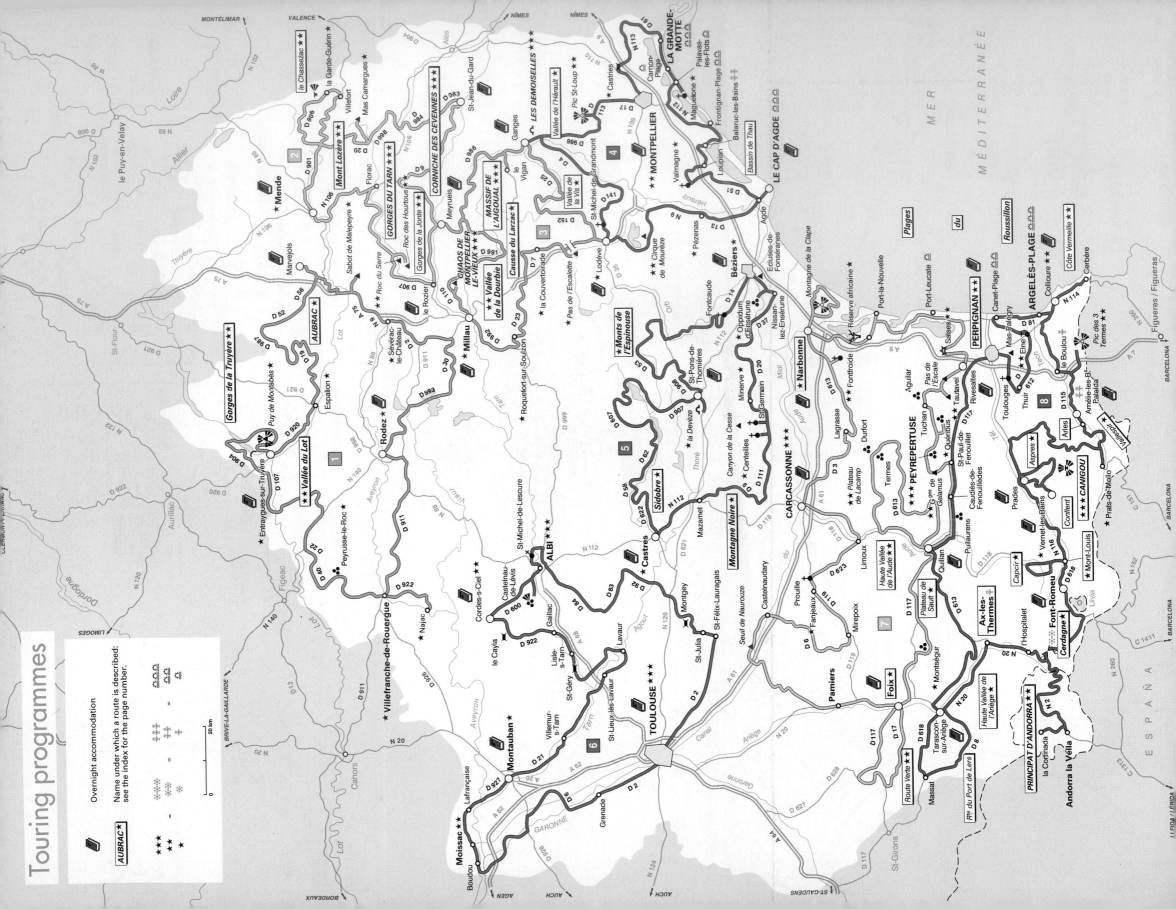

Touring programmes

1. Lot Valley-Aubrac-Rodez: 600 km – 372 miles (4 days)

2. Northern Cévennes-Tarn Gorge: 550 km – 340 miles (4 days)

3. Southern Cévennes-Causse du Larzac:
   400 km – 250 miles (4 days)

4. Languedoc Coast and Hinterland: 400 km – 250 miles (4 days)

5. Monts de l'Espinouse-Minervois-Montagne Noire:
   500 km – 310 miles (3 days)

6. Toulouse-Montauban-Albi: 450 km – 279 miles (3 days)

7. Carcassonne-Corbières-Foix: 800 km – 500 miles (7 days)

8. Perpignan-Roussillon-Principat d'Andorra-Ariège:
   900 km – 560 miles (7 days)

Abîme	Chasm	
Aven	Swallow-hole, chasm	
Bambouseraie	Bamboo plantation	
Bassin	Lagoon, lake	
Belvédère	Viewpoint	
Cap	Cape	
Cascade	Waterfall, falls	
Causse	Limestone plateau	
Chaos	Group of scattered rocks or rock formations	
Château, Ch^au	Castle, château	
Cirque	Cirque, corrie	
Col	Pass	
Corniche	Ledge, overhang	
Côte	Coast	
Défilé	Narrow gorge, defile	
Écluse	Lock (canal)	
Étang	Lake, pool	
Forêt	Forest	
Gorges, G^ges	Gorge	
Gouffre	Swallow-hole, chasm	
Grotte	Cave	
Haute, H^te	Upper	
Lac	Lake	
Mas	Farmhouse (S France)	
Massif	Massif, mountain rouge	
Mont, M^t	} Mount, mountain	
Montagne		
Musée	Museum	
Parc	Park	
Parc de l'art préhistorique	Museum of prehistoric art	
Pays	Country, region	
Pic	Peak, summit	
Plage	Beach	
Plateau, Pl^au	Plateau	
Port	Harbour, port	
Puy	Hill formed by a volcanic cone	
Ravin	Ravine, gully	
Rivière souterraine	Underground river	
Route, R^te	Road	
Site	Site (archeological)	
Sommet	Peak, summit	
Terrasses	Terraces, banks	
Tour	Tower	
Vallée, V^ée	Valley	
Viaduc	Viaduct	

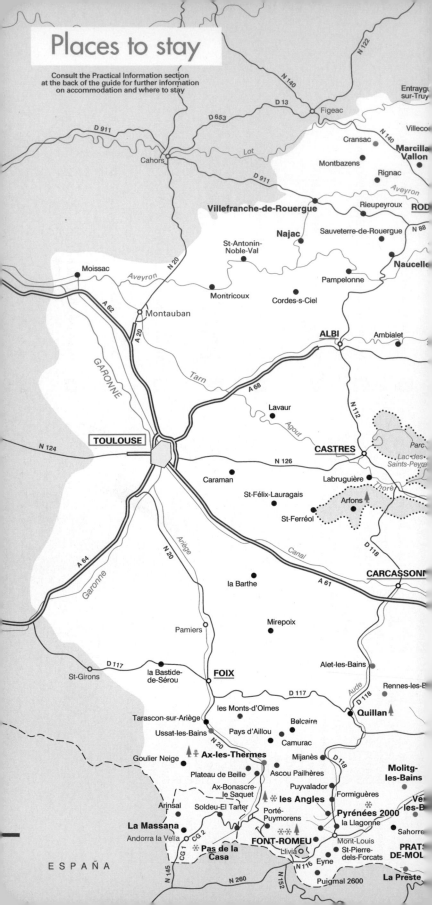

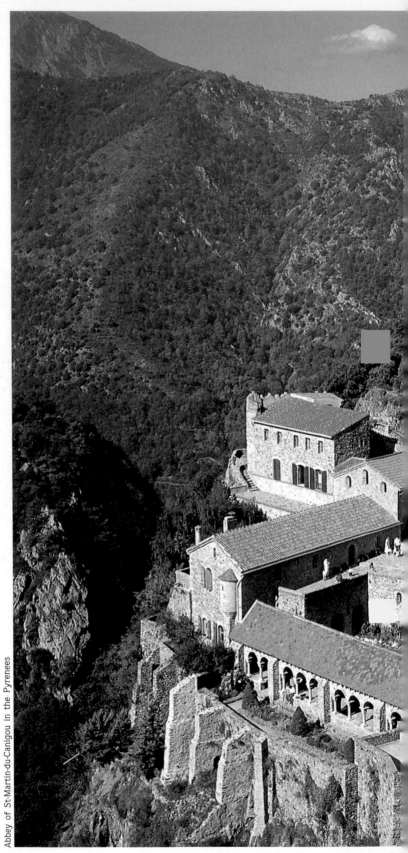

Abbey of St-Martin-du-Canigou in the Pyrenees

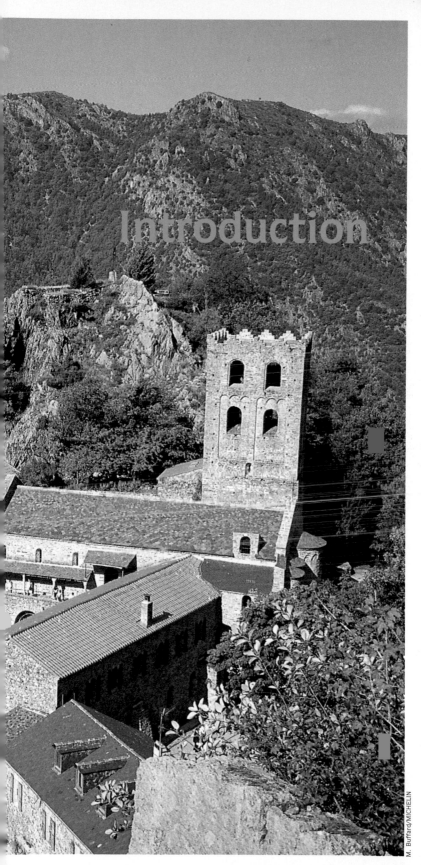

Introduction

Description of the region

The regions described in this guide encompass a wealth of incomparable natural features. To the northeast lie the rounded hills of the Auvergne. The empty rolling green expanses of the Aubrac are essentially given over to pasture. The region really comes to life during the cattle fairs of Laissac and Nasbinals. In the winter, a covering of snow intensifies the region's prevailing sense of isolation, broken only by cross-country skiers in search of silence and pure fresh air. Further east lie the undulating plateaux of the Margeride, chequered with pastureland and forests which provide vital resources for the local economy.

As we approach the river Lot to the south, the countryside changes dramatically. Vast limestone plateaux, delineated by sheer cliffs, stretch away, separated by deeply incised river gorges. These limestone plateaux, with their often arid, rocky surfaces devoid of water, are known as the **Causses**. The spectacular river gorges cutting between them, at the bottom of which a seemingly innocuous thread of water is capable at any time of becoming a raging torrent, are known as *canyons*.

To the east of this breathtaking landscape of *causses* and river gorges rise the **Cévennes**, rugged mountains characterised by a complicated network of ridges and gullies, with numerous, tortuous ramifications. For centuries, this region was impenetrable, and even now it retains something of an air of mystery, offering those who do decide to explore it the increasingly rare sense that they are treading where no one has trodden before.

The somewhat harsh landscape of the Grands Causses gives way, to the west, to the *ségalas* (literally "rye fields"), where fertile valleys rub shoulders with gentle hills.

The Causses and the Cévennes do not lead directly into the wine-growing plains of the Bas Languedoc. The transition is made by the **Garrigues**, limestone hills scorched by the sun, bristling with white rocks and isolated clumps of holm-oak, broom or aromatic plants (wild thyme or rosemary, for example). These, with the types of vegetation predominantly cultivated here (olive trees, mulberry bushes, vines), form a truly Mediterranean landscape.

Between the *garrigues* and the long straight Languedoc coast, lined with a glittering string of lagoons, vineyards stretch as far as the eye can see over the plains and hillsides. This slightly monotonous landscape is enlivened in the summer months by noisy, colourful crowds of holidaymakers who flock to the **Languedoc Coast** and, at the start of autumn, by the cheerful bustle of the grape harvest.

Moving further south, we come to the Pyrenees, forming a natural frontier between France and Spain, which is not easily crossed. The steep slopes on the French side drop quite sharply down into France. They are scored by a series of

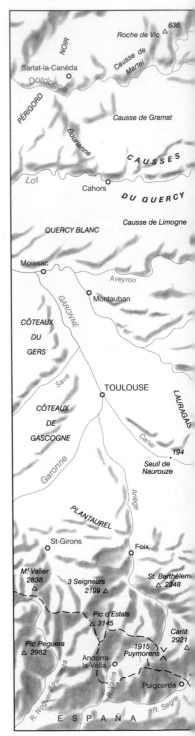

valleys, separated by high ridges, which link the Pyrenees to the inland plains and the coast. From the Montcalm summit (3 078m/10 098ft) to the Albères massif (1 256m/4 120ft at the Neulos peak), the Pyrenean range drops gradually until it finally sinks into the Mediterranean.

The formation of the Pyrenees began at the end of the Secondary Era and continued during the Tertiary Era, when massive folding motions in the earth's crust disturbed the old Hercynian layers. Erosion then played its part, levelling the mountain range to reveal primary sedimentary rock formations and even, along the axial crests, the granite core itself.

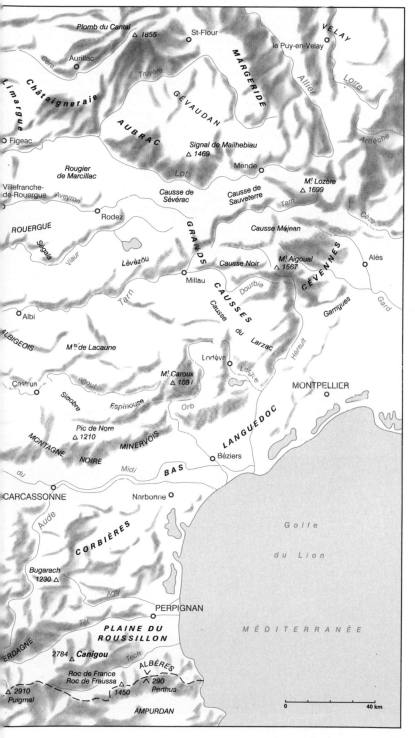

THE CAUSSES, THE CÉVENNES AND THE TARN GORGES

The Aubrac and the Margeride

The **Aubrac** mountains run from northwest to southeast, between the Truyère and Lot valleys. They are made up of formidable streams of solidified basalt, several hundred metres thick, the product of volcanic activity in the Tertiary Era, which cover a granite core. The asymmetric mountain range slopes gently down to the Truyère in the northeast, never going lower than about 1 000m/3 280ft above sea level. The steeper slopes to the southwest are scored by ravines.

Above 850m/2 788ft, the Aubrac is one vast pasture, with, however, a wide variety of flora. Daffodils and narcissi flourish in the spring. Beech woods, moorland and the occasional lake are to be found in the west. Hardly any crops are grown, for they would not thrive, in this, one of the most sparsely populated regions in France (14 inhabitants per km², compared to an average in France of 96 per km²). Winters are long and arduous; the plateau is buried beneath snow for several months every year. Stock rearing is the principal livelihood of those who live here. Traditionally, huge flocks of sheep from the Bas Languedoc would spend the summer in the Aubrac; nowadays, it is cattle that graze on all the pastures. At the end of May, following tradition, cows that have wintered at the foot of the mountain slopes move up to the meadows, where they remain until mid-October, without returning to the cowsheds. One or two local cheesemakers still produce *fourme de Laguiole* in their dry-stone huts. The livestock fairs of Laissac and Nasbinals, especially those in spring and autumn, are major events rich in local colour. All over the Aubrac massif, you will come across *drailles*, a kind of track running between low dry-stone walls, along which herds are moved from one pasture to the other.

The **Margeride**, a granite massif running parallel to the volcanic mountains of the Velay to the north, stretches between the Allier, to the east, and the high volcanic plateaux of the Aubrac, to the west. It reaches its highest point at the Randon beacon *(signal)*, 1 551m/5 088ft above sea level.

The high-lying ground, known as the **"Montagne"**, has an average altitude of 1 400m/4 593ft. It consists of undulating plateaux covered by vast stretches of pastureland, the monotony of which is broken by forests of pine, fir and birch. North of Mende, the plateaux (Palais du Roi, La Boulaine) are littered with granite rocks eroded into columns, obelisks or rounded blocks, here and there poised somewhat precariously on top of one another.

Below the "Montagne" lie rolling plains (the **"Plaines"**) scattered with numerous rocky outcrops. More people live down here, in large farmhouses which are either isolated or grouped in little hamlets. The main sources of income in the Margeride are timber, livestock and uranium.

West of the mountain range lies the **Gévaudan**, a lower-lying plateau (alt 1 000-1 200m/3 280-3 937ft) and kind of corridor lying in the shadow of the Aubrac. *For more details on the northern part of the Margeride, consult the Michelin Green Guide Auvergne Rhône Valley.*

The Causses

The vast limestone plateaux of the *causses*, south of the Massif Central, constitute one of the most unusual natural regions in France. They are bordered by the Cévennes to the east, by the Lot valley to the north and by the plains of the Hérault and Bas Languedoc to the south. To the west they stretch as far as the Lévézou and Ségala plateaux, and beyond to the *causses* of Quercy which form the eastern limit of the Aquitaine basin.

H. Van Ingen/EXPLORER

Off to pastures new in Aubrac's *Fête de la Transhumance*

A *lavogne*

The limestone rock gives rise to a landscape rich in contrasts: the arid tablelands of the *causses*, the colossal depths of the river gorges, and the natural wells formed by swallow-holes. Villages and hamlets consist of white drystone dwellings which accentuate the rugged atmosphere of their surroundings. Since 1995, the *causses* have been incorporated in part into the Parc naturel régional des Grands Causses for the conservation of the natural, architectural and cultural heritage of this unique region.

In contrast to the deep, but generally fresh and green ravines, the *causses* stretch away as a seemingly endless expanse of grey, rocky semi-desert. The austere grandeur of these vast plateaux, with barely a dip to break their flat surface and no sign of water, is nevertheless impressive. The dryness of the ground is due to the limestone rock of which it is formed which soaks up rainwater like a sponge; beneath this surface aridity however lies a hive of subterranean aquatic activity *(see Caves and chasms overleaf)*. The plateaux, at around 1 000m/3 280ft above sea level, have a harsh climate, with dry, scorching summers and long, cold winters when deep snow covers the ground and violent gales sweep unobstructed across the countryside.

To the west, at the edge of the cliffs, beside new plantations of black Austrian pine, grow groves of beech, oak and Scots pine, all that remain of the ancient forest cover which, already sparse, was denuded during the Middle Ages by flocks of grazing animals. To the east, on the moorland, rocky outcrops are dotted with thistles or tufts of lavender which form soft blue splashes of colour. Here and there grow clumps of juniper, either as stunted bushes or small trees up to almost 10m/33ft high. These plants require a lot of light, but are also resistant to frost. They have sharp, spiny leaves and produce small blueish-black berries as fruit, which add a unique flavour to many local dishes (especially game).

Traditionally, the *causses* have always been the preserve of sheep, whose meagre needs are satisfied by the sparse local vegetation. For many years, flocks of sheep were kept for their wool which supplied the textile industries in the towns (serge and caddis) and for their droppings which were used to fertilise the soil. Nowadays, sheep – about 500 000 head in the Roquefort area – are reared for their ewe's milk *(lait des brebis)* which is transformed into the famous cheese and matured underground in caves. Lambskin is processed in Millau, the capital of the Causses, situated at the confluence of the Tarn and the Dourbie. *Bleu des Causses*, a blue cheese, is manufactured from cows' milk not far from Millau.

Limestone relief landscapes (known also to geographers as karstic relief, from **Karst**, a limestone region in northern Slovenia) have a vocabulary all of their own *(see Local words and special terms on p 23)*.

Lavognes – This the local name for special ponds used as watering holes by the flocks. They are a feature unique to the *causses* region (they are particularly numerous around Roquefort), and generally take the form of an oval or teardrop-shaped pool in which water is prevented from soaking into the limestone by an underlying layer of clay or stone paving.

Eroded rock formations – Here and there, in a vast dip in the *causses* or out-lined against the sky on the edge of an escarpment, strange landscapes of bizarrely shaped rocks can seen. The size and arrangement of the rock strata, with protruding ledges and sheer sides, combine to resemble abandoned cities complete with streets, monumental doorways, ramparts and strongholds all falling into ruin.

These fantastic natural phenomena are due to the presence of a rock known as **dolomite** (named after Dolomieu, the geologist who discovered it) comprising carbonate of lime, which is soluble, and carbonate of magnesium, which is far less so. The chemical action of water streaming down the rocks, causing erosion, has chiselled them in part into these "ruins" with rounded crests, often as high as 10m/33ft, forming pillars, arcades, towers, animal shapes and weird cliffs for which imagination, given its head, can invariably find a name.

The clay residues formed by the erosion of the rock have helped to sustain a vegetation that enhances the scenic beauty of these areas. Particularly interesting examples of this are to be found at Montpellier-le-Vieux, Nîmes-le-Vieux, Mourèze, Les Arcs de St-Pierre, Roquesaltes and Le Rajol.

The river gorges

Known also as *canyons*, from the Spanish *cañon*, these are river valleys sunk amidst massive, limestone outcrops either on the crest of slopes, or in the depths of hollows in the *causse*. The Tarn gorges between Les Vignes and Le Rozier, and the Jonte and Dourbie gorges are magnificent examples of *canyons*.

Suddenly, at a bend in the road, the ground seems to fall away; the sweeping horizons of the Causses are replaced by a vertiginous landscape of vertical cliff faces. A deep gorge, sometimes dropping 500m/1 640ft or more, opens up, as if someone had gashed the plateau with an enormous saw. The valley sides are crowned with magnificent jagged cliffs, up to 100m/328ft tall, in shades of colour ranging from black to rust.

The cliff walls are peppered with caves formed by the erosive action of draining water. The large number of these caves (or *baumes*, from the local word *balma* used even before the arrival of the Romans) is reflected in the name of many a local village or hamlet: Cirque des Baumes and Les Baumes-Hautes in the Tarn gorges, Baume-Oriol on the Causse du Larzac, St-Jean-de-Balmes on the Causse Noir, and so on.

Caves and chasms

The caves *(grottes)* and chasms *(avens)* on the surface of the *causses* or in the hollow of a valley reveal a strange subterranean world, in which flowing water contrasts with the aridity of the plateaux.

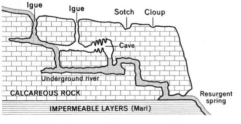

Development of a resurgent spring

Water infiltration – Instead of simply flowing across the limestone plateaux of the Causses, rainwater infil-trates them. The carbonic acid with which it is charged dissolves the carbonate of lime in the limestone to form small depressions, known as **cloups**, or larger ones, known as **sotchs**. Where rainwater percolates down the numer-ous fissures in the plateau, the hollowing out and dissolution of the limestone layer produces wells or natural chasms which are called **avens** or **igues**.

Gradually, these swallow-holes increase in size, extending into underground tunnels which branch out, link up with each other and widen into caves.

Underground rivers and resurgent springs – The disappearance of a water course into a chasm in the *causse*, or the accumulation of infiltrated water reaching non-porous strata (marl or clay) creates a network of underground rivers, sometimes covering several hundred miles. These then drain, following the line of the strata, and join up into larger rivers which bore tunnels, widen-ing their course and often gushing along as cascades. When the impermeable rock strata break through onto the side of a hill, the water emerges once more above ground, with a varying degree of force, as a resurgent spring. Where the underground rivers flow slowly, they form little lakes above natural dams, known as **gours**. These low natural walls are built up gradually by depos-its of lime carbonate on the edge of the pools of water, which are saturated with it, and subsequently impede the river's flow. There are good examples of *gours* in the Grotte de Dargilan.

Although underground rivers are not easily accessible (entrance is either via the resurgent spring or the chasm), they are thought to be quite numerous. Some have been located by speleologists: on the Causse du Larzac, the underground river Sorgues was discovered through the **Aven du Mas Raynal**; on the Causse du Comtal north of Rodez, the Salles-la-Source stream can be visited via the **Gouffre du Tindoul de la Vayssière**. Similarly, the Bonheur, which gushes into the open air at the Bramabiau "Alcôve", is a further example of an underground river.

In some cases the dissolution of the limestone crust continues above these subterranean streams; blocks of stone fall from the roof, leaving domes curving upwards towards ground level. When the roof of the dome wears thin it may suddenly cave in, revealing the cavity and forming a chasm.

Speleology – The first speleologists probably date from the Paleolithic Age (the age of flint knapping). They may have been looking, some 50 000 years ago, for the entrance of caves and shelters beneath the rocks in order to inhabit them. Later, in the Neolithic Age (the age of polished stone), humans used the caves as burial places.

During Antiquity, one or two bolder types braved the dangers of this underworld in the hope of finding precious metals, whereas in the Middle Ages the caves were thought to be inhabited by demons and therefore studiously avoided.

In the 18C, systematic explorations were undertaken. However, it was not until 1890 and Édouard-Alfred Martel that speleology won acclaim and recognition as a science. Knowledge of this subterranean world is still incomplete, and numerous chasms remain to be discovered.

Édouard-Alfred Martel (1859-1938) – The name of this famous speleologist is linked with the history of the exploration of the Causses. An attorney at the Paris courts (Tribunal de Commerce), Martel had been keenly interested in geography since adolescence and turned to geology and travel as a relaxation from his legal career. An intrepid explorer and mountaineer, he toured Italy, Germany, Austria, the United Kingdom and Spain, visiting famous caves, discovering new ones and giving his name to numerous caves and tunnels hitherto undiscovered.

However, it was in France that he concentrated his efforts. In 1883, he undertook a methodical study of the Causses region, about which nothing was known at the time. A series of underground explorations, at some risk to his own life, brought to light hundreds of amazing natural features – hidden marvels beyond people's wildest dreams.

Martel was also fascinated by the Pyrenees, the Vercors and the Dévoluy. His daring expedition along the Grand Canyon of the river Verdon opened the way for the general public to be able to explore in their turn what is undoubtedly one of the most breathtaking natural features in France *(see Michelin Green Guide Alpes du Sud in French)*.

Stalactites adorned with crystals in the Grotte de Clamouse

Martel was also a scientist at heart. Having made a wealth of observations, he devoted himself to the study of the laws of erosion in limestone soils and founded a new branch of scientific study, underground geography or **speleology**. His numerous publications made him world-famous.

In his writings, he summarised the work he had done, which provided an invaluable resource for those explorers who came after him. His style successfully imbues the reader with his enthusiasm.

Martel's work was also of great benefit to the inhabitants of the Causses. Perhaps his most important contribution was that his studies of the network of underground rivers in the region directly influenced the creation of a more hygienic public water supply, which up until then had been prone to all sorts of life-threatening contamination. Furthermore, his discoveries and the publicity surrounding them attracted tourists to this otherwise impoverished area, giving local economy a much needed boost.

Journey into the realm of shadows – A speleologist must first find a way of getting underground. In winter, the misty vapour caused by warm air rising from underground caverns can be a useful indication of their whereabouts. The presence of animals that frequent caves, such as bats or jackdaws, can also often point the way. Some explorers prefer to look out for resurgent springs.

Once this preliminary fieldwork has been carried out, the expedition can begin. Speleologists should be equipped with a helmet with a lamp attached to shield them from falling stones, a set of waterproofs and boots for crossing rivers and as a protection against waterfalls which might drench them at any moment. At times they will be making their way along tunnels so narrow that they have to crawl along on their belly like a snake to make any progress. Other obstacles they may have to contend with include sumps, for which diving suits may be needed, lakes with indistinct edges, or rocks made slippery with wet clay. Then there are sudden underground floods, due to storms, or the natural dams formed by underground lakes or **gours**. To combat the fatigue of particularly long expeditions, there have been successful attempts at underground camping. In most caves, the carbon dioxide content in the air is no higher than that at ground level; apart from the psychological unease aroused by staying underground, the main problem is caused by the humidity in the air.

Speleology is both a sport and a discipline, leaving no room, for reasons of facilities and safety, for individual exploits. Numerous sciences have benefited from its discoveries: prehistory, archeology, geology, biology, physics, chemistry, and, more recently, psychology.

In 1962, Michel Siffre spent two months in the Scarasson chasm, west of Tende pass, where he completely lost all track of time.

Fauna – Since the Upper Paleolithic Age, "cave bears" have disappeared. Nowadays, a badger, stone marten or polecat might occasionally get lost underground, or fish might be swept along by rivers in spate, but they are only there by chance. However, caves are pretty much without exception the permanent residence of bats. These sinister little creatures leave the cave only at night to go hunting and return at dawn.

They can cover the entire roof of a cave, making deep scratches in the domed ceiling with their claws. Armed with their own inbuilt radar system, they have no problems moving around in the dark. Their excrement, guano, can build up into gigantic cones on the cave floor – a speleologist's nightmare. Besides bats, caves are inhabited by a huge variety of invertebrates, such as beetles, millipedes etc. The underground laboratory of Moulis in Ariège *(not open to the public)* is devoted to the study of these cave dwelling animals.

The Cévennes

Lying to the southeast of the Massif Central, the Cévennes cannot really be called a mountain range in the true sense of the term. These schist and granite peaks stretching from the Tarnague to the Aigoual appear as a succession of almost flat, rather dreary plateaux, clad in peat bogs – the Aigoual *Pelouse* (or "lawn") and the Mont Lozère *Plat* ("dish").

There is a sharp contast between the very steep Mediterranean side, and that towards the Atlantic, which slopes more gently on either side of a watershed at the eastern end of the Mont Lozère, at the Col de Jacreste *(pass on N 106, east of Florac)* and at the Col du Minier.

The crests – The crests of the Cévennes are not very high; Mont Lozère, with its long granite ridges, has an altitude of 1 699m/5 574ft. Similarly, Mont Aigoual, from which there is a wonderful panorama on a clear day, does not exceed 1 567m/5 141ft.

The crests are covered by meagre pastureland, only suitable for sheep. Pastoral hamlets, with houses made from granite blocks, built very low to resist the wind, are scattered here and there. Lower down, there are holm-oaks, heather and the *châtaigneraie* (chestnut grove) together with little villages.

Cévennes landscape

And still it was perhaps the wildest view of all my journey. Peak upon peak, chain upon chain of hills ran surging southward, channelled and sculptured by the winter streams, feathered from head to foot with chestnuts, and here and there breaking out into a coronal of cliffs. The sun, which was still far from setting, sent a drift of misty gold across the hilltops, but the valleys were already plunged into a profound and quiet shadow.

Robert Louis Stevenson: *Travels with a donkey*

The upper valleys – Numerous streams flow along deep ravines with steep though by no means sheer sides, created by erosion of a rock which bears no relation to the limestone of the *causses*; this is real granite and schist relief, with its impermeable ground.
Some of these ravines, with their surging streams full of trout and grassy slopes studded with apple trees, are reminiscent of the Alps.

The lower valleys – These all face south and they mark the transition between the Cévennes and Mediterranean country. As the sun is already quite strong, green meadows rub shoulders with sheltered slopes given over to terraced cultivation: vines, olive trees, mulberry bushes. Throughout the region, lavender is distilled. As a reminder of the once flourishing intensive silkworm breeding, numerous old silkworm farms *(magnaneries)*, large usually three-storey buildings easily recognisable by their narrow windows, and spinning mills can still be seen.

The Cévennes landscape – The population of the upper valleys of the Cévennes has become increasingly sparse, with only meagre crops to support it. Alongside small streams, meadows planted with apple trees are interspersed with fields. The predominant tree, however, is the sweet chestnut, which occupies most of the slopes, leaving only a little room for vines trained to grow on trees, vegetable gardens and fruit trees scattered at the bottom of the valleys and near water sources.
In certain villages, on the periphery of Mont Lozère and in the Margeride, owners of sheep who have agreed to group their sheep together gather them into a communal flock which is led by a single shepherd to graze by day on the mountain. By night, they return to enclosures where they fertilize the soil.

The Ségalas and the Lévézou

The Grands Causses are separated from the Quercy Causses by the Lévézou massif and by a group of plateaux named the Ségalas because for a long time they were devoted to the cultivation of rye *(seigle)*.

The Lévézou – This is a large rugged massif of crystalline rock, situated between Millau and Rodez, rising to 1 155m/3 789ft at the Puech del Pal, its highest point. The uplands around Vezins are much bleaker than the lowlands, featuring clumps of undergrowth and moorland mainly inhabited by flocks of sheep. The lowlands are more hospitable with patchworks of woodland and meadows dotted with large lakes. Since it is some distance away from the main railway lines, the Lévézou has not enjoyed the same revival as the Ségalas. Its rivers, which have been developed for the production of hydroelectric power and tourism (the lakes of Pont-de-Salars, Bage, Pareloup and Villefranche-de-Panat), nonetheless encourage new economic activity.

The Ségalas – During the 19C, the Ségalas, traditionally poor in comparison to Fromental, the wheat-producing region of Aquitaine, began to prosper. At that time, it was decided to take advantage of the proximity of the Carmaux coal basin and the Aquitaine limestone rocks to produce lime. The development of railway lines (Carmaux-Rodez, Capdenac-Rodez) made it possible to transport this precious soil conditioner. Thus, moorland and rye fields were replaced by the cultivation of clover, wheat, maize and barley. Stock rearing also developed: cattle and pigs in the west, and sheep in the east and in the southeast, particularly around Roquefort. Nowadays the gently undulating landscape of the Ségalas is covered with green pastures, copses and meadows hedged with hawthorn. There are often chapels on the hilltops *(puechs)*. Anyone exploring the Ségalas will be struck by the rich red colour of the local soil, particularly in the Camarès or Marcillac regions, caused by the high percentage of iron oxide in the sediments. This extremely fertile soil is ideal for growing fruit. The main town in the Ségalas is Rodez, followed by Villefranche-de-Rouergue on the boundary of the Ségalas and the Quercy Causses.

Forests

The Causses and the Cévennes were once thickly covered by forests, in which wild beasts roamed. In the 18C, the "Bête du Gévaudan" terrorised the region for three years, devouring more than fifty people (seeming to show a preference for young girls and children) and successfully evading all attempts to hunt it down. Superstitious speculation abounded, with the general consensus being that the "beast" was some kind of Divine scourge. Finally, a huntsman shot down what was most probably a wolf, and the "beast" passed into local folklore, particularly effective as a means of subduing uncooperative offspring...

The *Bête du Gévaudan*

The dangers of deforestation – The majority of the beech forests were destroyed by glass-makers, who used them to manufacture the charcoal they required for their trade. The consequences of deforestation have been particularly severe in the Cévennes, a region prone to violent storms (98cm/38in of rainfall in 48 hours in Valleraugue in September 1900, that is about 40cm/15in more than the average annual rainfall in Paris). The water, which cannot be contained by the remaining plant cover, streams downhill and gushes into the valleys, causing flood waves up to 18-20m/59-65ft high. These inundations destroy everything in their path.

Sheep: an enemy of the forest – All along the **drailles** (tracks) taken by flocks moving to and from mountain pastures, and on the ridges and plateaus where they grazed, sheep feeding on young leaves and shoots also contributed to the destruction of the forest. Towards the middle of the 19C, only tiny areas remained of the immense forests which once covered the countryside. At this point Georges Fabre, the forest's benefactor, undertook to reafforest the massif.

Reafforestation – Afforestation by sowing seed directly on the ground is a method hardly ever used nowadays. Much more common is the method of afforestation by planting out seedlings. This involves transporting seedlings, raised in nurseries for a year, in the case of cedar, or three or four years, in the case of most other species, to the designated area where they are then planted out. Nowadays, the area between the valleys, home to beech trees, a good fire break, is planted with pine, firs and spruce. About 14 000ha/34 594 acres have been reafforested by Fabre and his successors. The French National Forestry Commission is justly proud of this achievement.

However, much still remains to be done; other areas which have become denuded of trees need to be replanted, and areas in which the forest cover consists largely of pine trees need to be replanted with hardier species of tree less susceptible to fire and better adapted to the conditions of the environment.

The chestnut – Even if the chestnut no longer features as part of the staple diet for the inhabitants of the Cévennes, chestnut trees nonetheless continue to adorn the Cévennes region. They can be seen growing at an altitude of 600m/1 968ft, sometimes even as high up as 950m/3 116ft on well-exposed slopes. In order to flourish, the chestnut needs to anchor its powerful

Chestnut tree

roots into schist, granite, sandstone or sand; however it does not thrive in limestone soils. From May, leaves cover the tree; it flowers in June and towards the middle of September produces the first chestnuts, grouped in threes and enclosed in a shell bristling with spines.

Unfortunately, chestnuts are a threatened species. After any felling, new shoots require considerable care and attention. Pruning, trimming and grafting are necessary to combat the damage caused by grazing flocks of animals. The havoc wrought by cryptogamic diseases such as canker makes the preservation of chestnut groves very difficult.

Local words and special terms

Aven: swallow-hole or chasm
Balme, baume: cave, natural shelter
Buron: small stone hut used by cowherds on pasture land
Can: small *causse*
Causse: limestone plateau with an arid, rocky surface
Cazelle, chazelle: dry-stone hut
Clède: small dry-stone construction in which chestnuts used to be left to dry
Cros: small valley or glen, hollow
Devèze: land grazed by flocks
Draille: track once used for moving herds of animals from one pasture to another, often along mountain ridges
Gour: small subterranean lake formed when calcite deposits build up into a dam
Grau: channel through which a river or lagoon runs into the sea
Lauze: flat schist or limestone slab used as roofing material
Lavogne: man-made water-hole
Masse (dimin. mazet): country house or farmstead
Ombrée: slope shaded from the sun (in the Pyrenees)
Planèze: basalt plateau bordered by converging valleys
Puech: hilltop, knoll
Ségalas: ryefields
Serre: long, narrow ridge stretching between two deep valleys
Soulane: slope exposed to the sun (in the Pyrenees)

AND NOW FOR THE WEATHER FORECAST...

The climate in the Languedoc region is basically Mediterranean, with summer temperatures soaring towards 30°C (over 80°F) in Perpignan – one of the hottest places in France in season. The region has its own version of the Provençal *mistral* in the shape of the **tramontane**, which periodically whistles through the Languedoc corridor from the northwest. July and August are hot and, as elsewhere in France, can tend to be crowded, especially towards the coast, although the Languedoc coast is nowhere near as bad as the Côte d'Azur at this time of year. Those seeking respite from the blistering heat of the coastal plain should head up to the mountains... or down into some of the numerous caves which pepper the region. June and September are generally good months to visit, as the weather is fine and warm (apart from the odd outbreak of rain).

Autumn on the Mediterranean coast remains relatively mild, making this a good time of year for a tour of the Corbières vineyards and neighbouring ruined Cathar strongholds. Rainfall in the Pyrenees and over Mont Aigoual is heavy, in particular in the autumn. However this is also the harvest season, which adds a splash of colour, amidst the rain, to the Cévennes and the Montagne Noire.

The first snow falls from late October, and by Christmas the resorts are alive with keen skiers, both downhill and cross-country in the Pyrenees, Andorra, and the Capcir and Cerdagne mountain plateaux, and predominantly cross-country in the Aubrac, Mont Lozère and Aigoual massif.

The coming of milder spring weather brings a burst of colour to the Pyrenees, with the blossoming of mountain flora, and to the orchards of Roussillon in full bloom. Spring and summer are the best seasons to visit the Causses, as temperatures are rarely oppressively hot. It is the ideal time of year for exploring the gorges by canoe, or for pot-holing, rock-climbing and hiking.

Regional nature parks

Parc naturel régional du Haut Languedoc

The Haut Langue-doc regional nature park was founded in 1973 to preserve the natural wealth of the region, which comprises the Caroux-Espinouse massif, the Sidobre, part of the Montagne Noire and the Lacaune mountains. It injected new life into these breathtakingly beautiful, but isolated regions, which are too remote for any economically stimulating industrial development to be viable.

Facilities – Depending on the time of year, numerous sporting activities can be undertaken, such as canoeing on the Orb and the Agout, sailing on the lakes (Lac des Saints-Peyres, Lac de la Raviège, Lac de Lauzas), rock climbing on the Caroux massif, speleology, hiking throughout the park, cross-country cycling, cross-country skiing etc.

Particularly interesting natural features include the Caroux, inhabited by wild sheep, the Mediterranean garden at Roquebrun, and Devèze cave.
The tourist offices and "Maisons du parc" have many suggestions for tours, walks and excursions.

Parc national des Cévennes

The Cévennes national park covers an area of 91 500ha/ 226 101 acres, surrounded by a peripheral zone of 237 000ha/ 585 639 acres. It was founded in September 1970 and is the largest of the seven French national parks.

The region displays great variety. Depending which face of the mountain you are on, the climate may be Mediterranean or more typical of northern France. Landscape ranges from snowy summits (the Lozère and Aigoual peaks, the Bougès range) to low-lying valleys in which mimosa flourishes. Soil types include schist southeast of Florac and on the foothills of the Bougès range, granitic on Mont Lozère and the Lingas mountains, and limestone on the Causse Méjean. The park can boast forest cover over almost two thirds of its surface area, including the peripheral zone.
One of the most characteristic, although not at all well known, landscapes is that of Mont Lozère, a mountain ridge with flattened contours which stretches for nearly 30km/18mi, more than 1 500m/4 921ft above sea level, a vast windswept fell bereft of trees.

One of the aims of classifying the central zone as a national park is the preservation of the landscape, the flora and the fauna, which includes some magnificent birds of prey. Various deer, including roe deer, as well as beavers, wood grouse and wild vultures have been reintroduced into the region. However, the main objectives are to sustain local agriculture and stem the gradual deterioration of the local environment, in which hamlets were falling into rack and ruin as the local inhabitants left the area to seek a living somewhere less punishing. It is now the only French national park with a resident population in its central zone.

Tourist facilities, for activities well-suited to large expanses, such as all forms of hiking, with accommodation in renovated rural dwellings, are contributing to demographic and economic revival.

Since 1984, the Cévennes national park has been twinned with the Saguenay national park (Quebec, Canada – *see Michelin Green Guide Quebec*), and as part of a programme of scientific cooperation the Cévennes park (made a biosphere reserve by UNESCO in 1985) was twinned with the Montseny Reserve in Catalonia in Spain in 1987.

Reception and information – The map shows the whereabouts of the Cévennes national park information centres, which are also the point of departure, in season, for day-long guided tours. The largest of these is in the Château at Florac, which houses the administrative headquarters and an exhibition on the park.

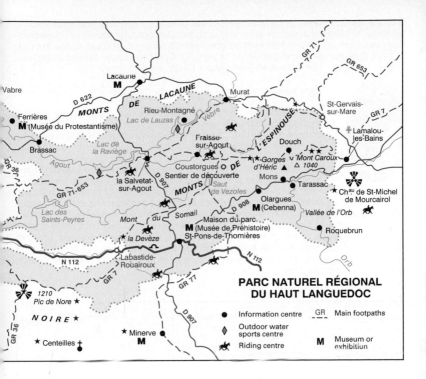

PARC NATUREL RÉGIONAL DU HAUT LANGUEDOC

- ● Information centre
- ◆ Outdoor water sports centre
- 🏇 Riding centre
- GR Main footpaths
- M Museum or exhibition

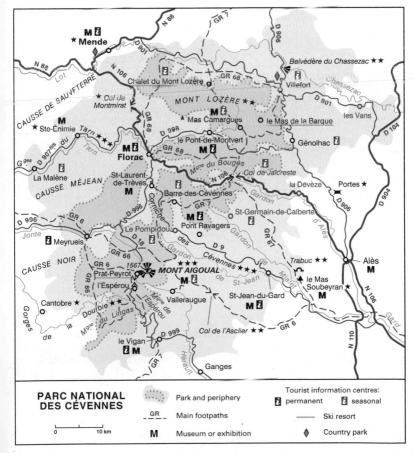

PARC NATIONAL DES CÉVENNES

- Park and periphery
- GR Main footpaths
- M Museum or exhibition
- 0   10 km

Tourist information centres:
- 🄸 permanent
- 🄸 seasonal
- Ski resort
- ◆ Country park

25

Besides these, further efforts to encourage people to discover the local natural heritage, traditional activities and rural architecture, open-air museums (écomusées) have been set up with exhibitions or observation trails of interest to the tourist, for example the *écomusées* of Mont Lozère, La Cévenne *(under construction)* and the Causse Méjean *(plans under way)*.

Parc naturel régional des Grands Causses

This regional park was founded in 1995 and covers 315 640ha/779 963 acres, roughly the whole of the southern part of the Aveyron *département*. It incorporates 94 towns or villages with a total population of more than 64 000.

The park's charter sets out various aims: enhancement of the region's natural and architectural heritage, support for agricultural methods designed to make best use of available land and local economy (conservation of local breeds of sheep threatened with extinction, development of accommodation facilities such as bed and breakfast offered by farms), promotion of locally grown foodstuffs and traditional crafts. As far as the preservation of the local architectural heritage is concerned, projects are already under way to save typical features which testify to the region's past way of life, such as village ovens, dry-stone shepherds' huts, village ponds, dovecots, washhouses and fountains.

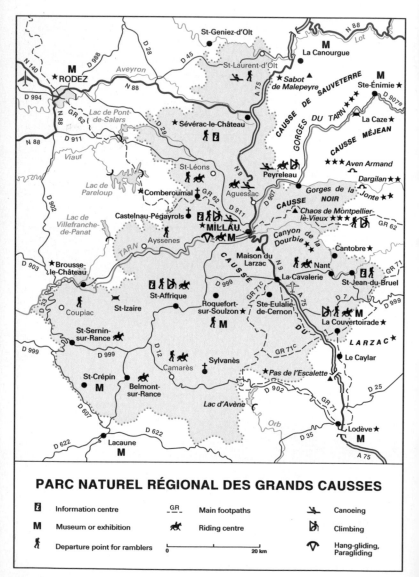

PARC NATUREL RÉGIONAL DES GRANDS CAUSSES

🛈	Information centre	GR	Main footpaths	🚣	Canoeing
M	Museum or exhibition	🏇	Riding centre	🧗	Climbing
🚶	Departure point for ramblers	0 — 20 km		⩗	Hang-gliding, Paragliding

Lagoon near Maguelone

LANGUEDOC

Bas Languedoc

Languedoc is the region stretching from the Rhône to the Garonne, with Toulouse as the capital of Haut Languedoc and Montpellier as the capital of Bas (Mediterranean) Languedoc. Bas Languedoc is a strip, about 40km/25mi wide, along the Mediterranean coast. South of the Cévennes, the Garrigues stand about 200-400m/600-1 400ft above sea level. Below the Garrigues stretches a sandy plain, covered with vineyards, with a necklace of lagoons dotted along the coast. The line of the plain is broken only by the odd limestone outcrop (La Gardiole mountain at Montpellier, Mont St-Clair at Sète, La Clape mountain at Narbonne) and the mountains of Agde (Pic St-Loup), a prolongation of the solidified lava flow of Escandorgue. Bas Languedoc lies sandwiched between mountains which are part of the outlying primary deposits of the Massif Central, from the Cévennes, the Espinouse, Minervois and Lacaune mountain ranges as far as the Montagne Noire, and the first limestone foothills of the Pyrenees, the Corbières.

The Languedoc vineyards, which for centuries concentrated on the production of table wine, are now putting the emphasis on quality, not quantity, and efforts including detailed studies of the soil and climate and a judicious selection of grape varieties are paying off with the region's wines being ranked among the fine wines of France.

The Garrigues – This is the name given to a region of limestone plateaux and mountain ranges, through which flow the Hérault, the Vidourle and the Gard. The mountains of St-Loup and Hortus are rare outcrops in an otherwise flat landscape. Formed, like the *causses*, by marine deposits from the Secondary Era, the Garrigues (this name is derived from the Occitan *garric*: kermes oak) are covered by stunted, fragrant scrubland vegetation: dwarf shrubs of kermes oak, tufts of thyme and lavender, rockroses and pasture land scorched by the sun.

In spring, this arid countryside, much frequented by hunters, is scattered with brilliantly coloured flowers. The *garrigues* remain the preserve of sheep.

The coast – The Mediterranean coast in the Languedoc is lined with lagoons. The sand bars separating these lagoons from the sea were created by the waves and currents. Gravel and sand carried by the Rhône to the sea were washed towards the Languedoc coast, eventually forming barriers of sand at the mouth of the bays. The sand bar, as it gradually increased in size, transformed each bay into a shallow lagoon isolated from the open sea. These salt water lagoons are filled with eels, grey mullet, sea perch, sea bream and clams. The Aude and the Orb did not form such lagoons, however, nor did they succeed in creating deltas, because the coastal currents constantly swept away their alluvial deposits.

The invasive sand left the old ports of Maguelone and Agde stranded inland. Only the Thau lagoon, virtually an inland sea, is navigable; it is noted for its oyster and mussel farms. Two little fishing ports, Marseillan and Mèze, have adapted to modern demands by developing marinas.

Sète, built in the 17C, has continued to expand since then, but only by a ceaseless struggle against silting up has it been able to maintain its position as the second largest French port on the Mediterranean.

The Garonne corridor

The Garonne is a capricious river, with an irregular rate of flow and frequent spates. Together with its tributaries, it cuts a vast corridor linking Aquitaine and Languedoc.

On either side stand ranges of hills moulded from the thick **molassic** substratum typical of the Toulouse region. Molasse is a product of the accumulation of layers of debris churned up from the Pyrenees in the middle of the Tertiary Era – sand, marl, clay, easily eroded limestone – a soft assortment of material in which a network of rivers had no trouble becoming established.

At the edges of the corridor, the relief becomes undulating: to the south, tiny beaches at the foot of the Pyrenees are shored up by gravel; to the north, the ancient plateau and the sedimentary hills intermingle (Tarn region).

The geographical area around Albi encompasses some of the plateaux situated southeast of the Aquitaine basin. The landscape alternates between molassic hills (soft yellow sandstone broken by intermittent strata of limestone and marl) and small limestone plateaux (Cordes, Blaye) or rocky outcrops *(puechs)* often with a village perched on top.

Canal du Midi

Haut Languedoc, between the Aude and the Garonne

Agricultural regions – Traditional mixed cultivation (wheat, maize, vines) was perfectly suited to the capacity of small-scale concerns. These, pressurized by the need for technical innovation and increased specialisation, are now expanding. The land under cultivation is divided between the **terreforts**, heavy fertile clay soils on which cereals are grown, and the **boulbènes**, lighter, poor quality terrain consisting of sand, clay, silt and pebbles.

The Toulouse and Lauragais regions are considered to be the "granary" of the south of France, with a prospering agricultural industry, despite a massive rural exodus. On the other hand, the alluvial plains of the Garonne and the Tarn are the region's orchard (apples, pears, peaches, strawberries). Market gardening also plays an important part in agricultural life, and it is easily combined with poultry farming. Apart from the Gaillac slopes to the west, vineyards are mainly found in the areas around Carcassonne and Limoux.

The appearance of rural houses changes with the landscape. In the Lauragais and Toulouse regions, low brick houses are built, in which the various parts of the building (living quarters, stable, barn, cart shed) are covered by the same gently sloping roof. In contrast, houses in Bas Languedoc are taller: the stable and cellar *(cave)* are on the ground floor, the living quarters (which once consisted of a single room) on the first floor, and the hay loft above.

Industrial modernity – A number of small enterprises have grown up around the aerospace industries of Toulouse. Chemical, electrometallurgical, textile, leather, farm-produce and granite industries further contribute to the economic growth of the area. In the Carmausin, coal-mining at the Découverte Ste-Marie pit is restricted to open-cast only.

The Canal du Midi in itself does not play a particularly vital role in the local economy; however, it is becoming increasingly important as a tourist attraction.

The conurbation of Toulouse (with about 600 000 inhabitants) is the focal point of the Midi-Pyrénées region. With its considerable resources for research, its state of-the-art industries and its public facilities, Toulouse exerts an influence far beyond regional boundaries.

THE PYRENEES AND ROUSSILLON

The Central Pyrenees

The structure of the Pyrenean range is characterised by the juxtaposition of large geological formations arranged running longitudinally.

The Pre-Pyrenees - The "Petites Pyrénées" and the Plantaurel ridge were caused by Jurassic folding movements which created this landscape of rows of limestone ridges, intersected by transverse valleys (ravines of Boussens on the Garonne, and of Labarre on the Ariège) cutting a path through to the plain for the rivers.

The foothills - These consist of strata dating from the Secondary Era, Cretaceous or Jurassic, which were folded more violently. The deeply grooved limestone or sandstone ridges give way, around Foix, to crystalline massifs of dark rock detached from the axial zone, such as the St-Barthélemy massif.

The axial zone - This section constitutes the very backbone of the Pyrenees. From among the primary sediments rise towering crags of the granite core, recognisable by the outline of their crests, which are jagged from glacial erosion. The granite massifs are home to the greatest number of mountain lakes in the Pyrenees.

Peaks and valleys - The absence of a valley running the length of the chain, downhill from and parallel to the line of the axial ridge, which would thus have linked the transverse valleys, has remained an obstacle to communications within the chain. These are dependent on mountain passes which are impassable in winter. For years the transverse valleys have been affected by this enforced segregation, which has encouraged the survival of various local ways of life, as if each valley were a miniature country in itself.

The massive, fortress-like mountains of **Andorra** and the **upper Ariège valley**, carved out of hard gneiss, seem to stand guard over a bleak and rugged landscape (rocks and scree). Gorges gouged out by glaciers during the Quaternary Era, which frequently end in a mountain lake, stand out dramatically amidst the surrounding landscape. These isolated regions link the Central and Mediterranean Pyrenees.

The Mediterranean Pyrenees

The Mediterranean Pyrenees, perhaps the section of the chain most open to the outside world, rub shoulders to the north with the Corbières massif. This stretches as far as the Montagne Noire, the furthest southern outpost of the Massif Central, and separates the Aquitaine basin from the plains of Mediterranean Languedoc.

The mountains - Between the Corbières and the axial ridge of the Pyrenees lie limestone foothills, which differ in various aspects of their relief and landscape from the northern sedimentary surface of the Central Pyrenees. The **Plateau de Sault**, a

J.-D. Sudres/SCOPE

The Canigou

sort of *causse* covered with forests, gives way to rows of crests whose jagged silhouettes tower above the deep furrow of the **Fenouillèdes**. The river Aude, which rises in the axial zone, cuts through this crust in a series of breathtaking gorges. The eastern Pyrenees, which were pushed the furthest upwards by the ancient folding movements of the earth's crust, have nonetheless been reduced to a lower altitude than that of the Central Pyrenees. The first peaks to emerge, they were exposed to wear and tear by erosion for a longer period. They underwent only a relatively short period of glaciation, centred around the Carlit summit, which briefly boasted a thick ice cap.

The **Cerdagne** and the **Capcir**, high-altitude valleys (1 200m/3 937ft and 1 600m/ 5 249ft above sea level) formed by erosion in the flanks of the Pyrenees, are filled with an assorted debris of clay, marl and gravel accumulated towards the end of the Tertiary Era. The valleys are home to villages and cultivated land.

East of the Canigou (alt 2 784m/9 133ft), the Pyrenean range drops into the trench occupied by the Mediterranean. The **Albères**, the chain's final set of peaks, formed of crystalline rock, cut between two sections of subsided ground: the Roussillon, to the north, and the Ampurdan, to the south (in Spain).

The Roussillon – The parallel valleys of the Têt and the Tech enhance the majestic Canigou peak, by allowing Mediterranean influences to penetrate to the heart of the mountain range. Resorts in these valleys are renowned for their exposure to sunlight, their dry climate and their vegetation (orange trees and pink oleander). The mountain rivers are subject to dramatic variations in rate of flow. The floods in autumn 1940 are fresh in the memories of local inhabitants; between 16 and 19 October, rainfall recorded in Amélie was as great (758mm/29in) as the usual annual average. It was estimated that during those three days the Tech swept along, in the space of a few miles, one third more water than the total volume transported by the Rhône in one year.

The Roussillon plain, which stretches for 40km/24mi, was originally a gulf which was filled in (at the end of the Tertiary/beginning of the Quaternary Era) with debris from the mountain range. Arid rocky terraces (**Les Aspres**), pocked with wide valleys and dotted with hillocks, are cultivated with fruit trees and vines. An offshore sand bar separates the sea from the **salanques** marshes, where alluvial deposits from the Têt and the Agly have accumulated to a depth of several hundred metres.

Tradition and Modernity

Straddling two regions (Midi-Pyrénées and Languedoc-Roussillon), the Pyrénées-Roussillon-Albigeois area is characterised by contrasts where tradition rubs shoulders with modernity.

The Mountains

Traditional rural life – Mountain countryside can be divided into three zones: the lower slopes with cultivated fields and villages, an intermediate level with forests and hay meadows, and right up on high mountain pastures. Wheat, rye and maize are still grown in Haut Vallespir, Cerdagne and Conflent. The vines and olive trees which once grew in abundance in the Mediterranean valleys have now all but disappeared.

Hay meadows are grown exclusively on the wetter slopes. Groves of holm-oak, Scots pine and beech, on the outskirts of the villages, have been somewhat reduced by felling and have now given way to scrubland of broom or *garrigues*. These mountain valleys make a pretty sight with their groups of villages and chessboard fields separated by hedges and trees. Flocks are still transferred from winter to summer pastures, and large flocks of sheep can be seen grazing in the summer, making the upkeep of the pastures economically viable.

Traditional rural life no longer plays that important a role in the activities of modern mountain dwellers. The areas worst hit by rural depopulation are the little dead-end valleys, or isolated villages on the slopes of the mountain which are not exposed to the sun where cultivated land and meadows have been gradually left to go fallow or revert to heathland.

Renewed growth – The industrial potential of the Pyrenees depends on exploitation of its energy sources. The old Catalan forges were fuelled with charcoal. But from 1901, hydroelectric schemes were set up in the mountains, which are still being developed today (the Hospitalet plant dates from 1960).

Besides hydroelectricity, a great variety of industrial concerns (French chalk mines at Luzenac, cement works, textile manufacturing, aluminium works, various metallurgy and timber industries etc) boost the economic activity of the valleys. Nevertheless, industrialisation is somewhat limited here; it has not been sufficient to stem the rural exodus and, because of its age, it has great difficulty in adapting to modern conditions.

The liveliest valleys are crisscrossed by busy roads; they are densely populated, well developed, and place great emphasis on tourism as a means of supporting their economy. In spas and winter sports resorts, accommodation is steadily increasing. All this has brought about a new mix in the population. The departure of the local inhabitants has been offset by the arrival of French or foreign newcomers come to settle here.

Vineyards near Banyuls

The Roussillon Coast

The garden of Roussillon – With its orchards, market gardens and vineyards, Roussillon resembles an enormous allotment. A well-designed irrigation system and the use of greenhouses and plastic cloches and tunnels have helped improve vegetable production.

Vegetables grown here are mainly tomatoes, new potatoes, winter lettuce and endive, while local fruit is principally peaches, nectarines and apricots. These plant varieties are now established in the Roussillon plain, but they can also be cultivated on the intermediate mountain slopes up to an altitude of 600m/1 968ft. Other crops include early cherries from the Céret orchards and apples from Vallespir and central Conflent.

In Roussillon, houses are mostly grouped in villages, but in some areas, the presence of the odd *mas* (isolated farmhouse) amidst acres of cultivated land is evidence of farming on a larger scale. The towns of Perpignan, Elne and Ille-sur-Têt are geared to wholesale markets.

Vineyards – Vineyards cover the banks of the Agly, the rocky terrace of Les Aspres and the sweep of land along the Côte Vermeille, which is the most typical region of the Roussillon coast. The grape varieties cultivated have resulted in the production of a vast range of *vins de coteaux*, including young white wines, rosés and robust, heady reds.

The **Côtes du Roussillon** covers the sun scorched marl and schist of the southern slope of the Corbières as well as the arid terraces of Les Aspres as far as the Albères range.

The majority of wine produced locally is still the *vins doux naturels* (dessert wines), such as Rivesaltes, Banyuls and Maury. The production of local table wines is giving way to the development of better quality vintage wines. The wine-growing industry has also branched out into new sidelines, such as apéritifs (Thuir), vermouths (Noilly Prat at Marseillan) and liqueurs.

Sea fishing – The fishing fleets in the harbours along the Côte Vermeille and coast of the Aude delta have diversified into four different areas.

Lamparo or lamplight fishing, mainly for sardines or anchovies, requires the installation of powerful lamps on an adjacent vessel. Powerful deep-sea fishing vessels are used for red tunny fishing. The fish are caught with a huge net which is wound mechanically. Trawling, mainly from Port-Vendres, Port-la-Nouvelle and St-Cyprien, uses huge pocket-shaped nets which are dragged along the sea bed. Small-scale fishing with mesh nets, trammel nets or floating lines is a method used at sea and in the coastal lagoons (for eels).

At the same time, oyster-farming on the Leucate lagoon and mussel-farming in the open sea near Gruissan and Fleury-d'Aude is on the increase.

Beaches – From the mouth of the Aude, the coast of the Golfe du Lion comprises 70km/43mi of flat shore terminating in the jagged rocky cliffs of the Côte Vermeille, towards the Spanish border. As a result of the development of the Languedoc-Roussillon coast, modern tourist seaside resorts have been built along the sandy shore, in contrast to the old fishing ports on the rocky coast, tucked in narrow bays and still reminiscent of their traditional role as tiny maritime cities.

Prehistory

During the Quaternary Era, which began about 2 million years ago, glaciers developed, spreading over the highest mountains (Günz, Mindel, Riss and Würm Ice Ages). A much more significant event, however, was the advent of humans in Europe, and particularly in the Pyrenees.

Various phases of evolution, subdivisible into periods, can be classified thanks to archeology and scientific methods of dating – Paleolithic (Old Stone Age), Mesolithic (Middle Stone Age), Neolithic (New Stone Age). *See table.*

Lower Paleolithic – The Lower Paleolithic period is represented in the Pyrenees by **Tautavel man**, who came to light when the remains of a human skull were discovered in a layer of ancient sediment in the **Caune de l'Arago** by a team led by Professor H de Lumley in 1971 and 1979. Tautavel man belongs to the "Homo erectus" genus, which inhabited Roussillon 450 000 years ago. He was 20-25 years old, able to stand upright and about 1.65m/5ft 6in tall. He had a flat, receding forehead, prominent cheekbones, and rectangular eye sockets beneath a thick projecting brow. Since no trace of any hearth has been found, it is assumed that this intrepid hunter, who had not mastered the use of fire, ate his meat raw. He used caves for several purposes: as a look-out to keep track of the movements of animals, as a temporary place to set up camp and dismember prey, and as a workshop for manufacturing tools.

Palynology (the analysis of fossilised pollen grains) has helped to determine the specific characteristics of flora and fauna from different prehistoric periods. Although the alternation of climates produced changes (from grassy steppes to deciduous forests), Mediterranean plant species (pines, oaks, walnut trees, plane trees, wild vines etc) have been present. Large herbivores to be found in the area included various types of deer and mountain goats, prairie rhinoceros, bison, musk ox and an ancient species of wild sheep. Carnivores (bears, wolves, dogs, polar foxes, cave lions, wild cats) were hunted for their fur. Small game comprised rodents (hares, voles, beavers, field mice) and birds still found nowadays (golden eagles, lammergeyer vultures, pigeons, rock partridges, red-billed choughs). The tools found are in general quite small (scrapers, notched tools). The largest are stones, measuring on average 6-10cm/2-4in, made into choppers, or flat two- or more-sided implements of varying degrees of sharpness.

Middle Paleolithic – The presence of numerous Mousterian deposits is evidence that Neanderthal man was present in the Pyrenees. Taller than "homo erectus", he had a well developed skull (1 700cm³/103in³). He produced more sophisticated, specialised tools, fashioning numerous double-sided implements, stone knives with curved edges, chisels, scrapers, pointed tools and all kinds of notched implements. His evolution is also evident in the construction of vast dwelling and burial places.

Upper Paleolithic – With the advent of "homo sapiens", there was now a significant human presence in the Pyrenees. During the Aurignacian period, stone implements were supplemented with tools made of bone and horn, and technical evolution progressed still further during the Solutrean and Magdalenian periods. Towards the end of the last Würm Glacial Period (Würm IV), landscape and fauna were transformed, with boar and deer predominating from now on. Humans both hunted and fished. However, the most revolutionary change was the birth of art, reflected by sculpted human figures (the Aurignacian "Venuses") and cave paintings of exceptional interest.

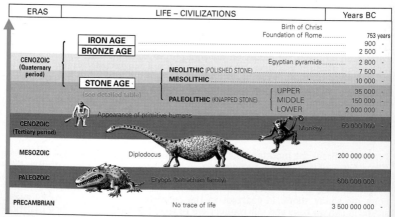

ERAS	LIFE – CIVILIZATIONS		Years BC
		Birth of Christ	
		Foundation of Rome............	753 years
	IRON AGE		900 -
	BRONZE AGE		2 500 -
CENOZOIC (Quaternary period)		Egyptian pyramids............	2 800 -
	NEOLITHIC (POLISHED STONE)............................		7 500 -
	MESOLITHIC .... *		10 000 -
	STONE AGE (see detailed table)	UPPER	35 000 -
	PALEOLITHIC (KNAPPED STONE)	MIDDLE	150 000 -
		LOWER	2 000 000 -
	Appearance of primitive humans		
CENOZOIC (Tertiary period)		Monkey	60 000 000 -
MESOZOIC	Diplodocus		200 000 000 -
PALEOZOIC	Eryops (batrachian family)		600 000 000 -
PRECAMBRIAN	No trace of life		3 500 000 000 -

Read this table from bottom to top

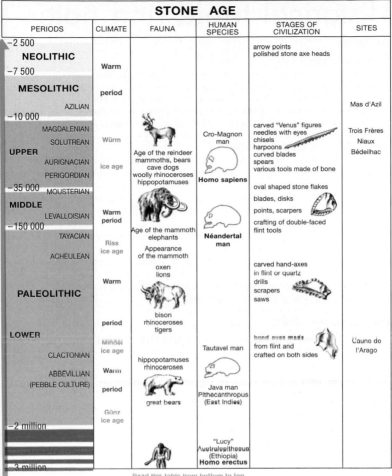

STONE AGE					
PERIODS	CLIMATE	FAUNA	HUMAN SPECIES	STAGES OF CIVILIZATION	SITES
−2 500 **NEOLITHIC** −7 500	Warm period			arrow points polished stone axe heads	
MESOLITHIC AZILIAN −10 000					Mas d'Azil
MAGDALENIAN SOLUTREAN **UPPER** AURIGNACIAN PERIGORDIAN −35 000 MOUSTERIAN	Würm ice age	Age of the reindeer mammoths, bears cave dogs woolly rhinoceroses hippopotamuses	Cro-Magnon man **Homo sapiens**	carved "Venus" figures needles with eyes chisels harpoons curved blades spears various tools made of bone	Trois Frères Niaux Bédeilhac
MIDDLE LEVALLOISIAN −150 000 TAYACIAN ACHEULEAN	Warm period Riss ice age	Age of the mammoth elephants Appearance of the mammoth	**Néandertal man**	oval shaped stone flakes blades, disks points, scarpers crafting of double-faced flint tools	
PALEOLITHIC LOWER	Warm period	oxen lions bison rhinoceroses tigers		carved hand-axes in flint or quartz drills scrapers saws	
CLACTONIAN ABBEVILLIAN (PEBBLE CULTURE)	Mindel ice age Warm period	hippopotamuses rhinoceroses great bears	Tautavel man Java man Pithecanthropus (East Indies)	hand-axes made from flint and crafted on both sides	Cauno de l'Arago
−2 million −3 million	Günz ice age		"Lucy" Australopithecus (Ethiopia) **Homo erectus**		

Read this table from bottom to top

Mesolithic Age – At the end of the Ice Age, the historical landscape of the Pyrenees settled down. The Mesolithic Age is, in fact, an intermediary phase during which a multitude of civilizations appeared. During the Azilian culture (named after the **Mas d'Azil** cave), which began at the end of the Upper Paleolithic period, the harpoon became an increasingly important weapon. Art, however, was restricted to enigmatic pebbles with symbolic markings.

Neolithic Age – The Neolithic Age is characterised by polished (rather than chipped) stone tools and the use of earthenware. However, in the eastern Pyrenees and the Ariège, the local post-Paleolithic population continued to live in caves, and earthenware came into use only sometime later.
Further north, valuable ethnological information was discovered in the Font-Juvénal shelter, between the river Aude and the Montagne Noire. As early as the 4th millennium, agriculture and cattle-rearing had become a means of subsistence, with wheat and barley being cultivated. At the same time, dwellings became more elaborate, illustrated by the discovery of flat hearths for cooking, air vents to raise the combustion temperature, supporting structures (posts and slabs) and silos for storage.
In the Narbonne region, rural communities with specialised activities, using complex implements, started to barter and trade with each other. Megalithic constructions (dolmens and tumuli) were introduced to the Pyrenees from the western zone during the 3rd millennium. The middle mountain slopes were the most densely populated. Activities included stock-rearing and, increasingly, the making of weapons (arrows, axes and knives). Jewellery (necklaces and bracelets) and earthenware (bowls and vases) became more widespread. In the Catalan region, the Megalithic culture lasted until the Bronze Age.

The Pyrenean dolmens (2500-1500 BC) – The majority of **dolmens** lie at altitudes ranging from 600-1 000m/1 968-3 280ft. They were originally covered by a **tumulus** of earth or a heap of stones, which might measure anything up to 20m/65ft, with perhaps a circle of stones around it. The largest dolmens, erected in areas with a stable population, contain the remains of hundreds of people. On the higher pastures, they are smaller and were later replaced by **cists** (stone chests), individual burial chests for shepherds who had died during the summer.

Historical table and notes

Antiquity

BC 1800-50	Metal Age.
1800-700	Bronze Age. End of Pyrenean Megalithic culture.
1000-600	End of Bronze Age and first Iron Age. Penetration of external influences, first continental, then Mediterranean.
600-50	Foundation of Massalia (Marseille) by the Phoceans. Development of metallurgy in ancient Catalonia (Catalan forges). The eastern Pyrenees are composed of numerous small clans.
6C	The Celts invade Gaul.
214	Passage of Hannibal across the Pyrenees and into Roussillon.
2C	Roman Conquest. The Romans occupy the region later known as Bas Languedoc.
118	Foundation of Narbonne, capital of Gallia Narbonensis, at the crossing of the Via Domitia and the road to Aquitaine.
58-52	Conquest of Gaul by Caesar.
27	Bas Languedoc becomes part of Gallia Narbonensis. This marks the start of a long period of prosperity.
AD 3C and 4C	Christianity arrives in the region. Decline of Narbonne and Toulouse.
313	Edict of Milan. Emperor Constantine grants Christians freedom of worship.
356	Council of Béziers, Arian heresy.

Invasions, the Middle Ages

3C-5C	Invasions of the Alemanni, the Vandals, then the Visigoths. Toulouse becomes the capital of the Visigothic kingdom.
507	Battle of Vouillé: Clovis's defeat of the Visigoths, whose kingdom is now restricted to seven cities (Carcassonne, Narbonne, Béziers, Agde, Nîmes, Elne and Maguelone).
719	Capture of Narbonne by the Saracens.
732	Charles Martel defeats the Saracens at Poitiers.
737	Charles Martel recaptures the seven cities from the Visigoths.
759	Pépin the Short recaptures Narbonne.
801	Charlemagne marches into Spain; Catalonia is integrated into his Empire, but remains autonomous.
843	Under the Treaty of Verdun, Charlemagne's Empire is divided: the territories extending from the west of the Rhône to the Atlantic Ocean are given to Charles the Bald.
877	On the death of Charles the Bald, most of the great princely houses who will rule the south of France until the 13C are established. The counts of Toulouse own the old kingdom of seven cities and the Rouergue; the Gévaudan belongs to the Auvergne family.
10C	Religious revival and pilgrimages to St James's shrine in Santiago de Compostela, Spain.
987	Hugues Capet is crowned king of France.
11C	Renewed economic and demographic growth in the West. The counts of Toulouse assert their power. Wave of construction of ecclesiastical buildings. Tour of Languedoc by Pope Urban II.
1095	First Crusade
1112	The count of Barcelona becomes viscount of Béziers, Agde, Gévaudan and Millau.

Union with the French crown

12C-13C	Flowering of the art of the troubadours. First appearance of *bastides* (fortified towns).
1140-1200	Spread of the Cathar doctrine.
1152	Marriage of Henry II Plantagenet with Eleanor of Aquitaine.
1204	The king of Aragon gains sovereignty of Montpellier, Gévaudan and Millau.
1207	Excommunication of Raymond VI, count of Toulouse.

Seal of Count Raymond VI
of Toulouse

1208	Assassination of Pierre de Castelnau, legate to Pope Innocent III.
1209	Albigensian Crusade (further details in the section on The Cathars below). Capture of Béziers and Carcassonne by Simon de Montfort.
1213	Battle of Muret.
1226	A new crusade: Louis VIII seizes Languedoc.
1229	The war against the Albigensians ends with the Treaty of Paris. St Louis annexes the whole of Bas Languedoc. Foundation of Toulouse University.
1250-1320	The last strongholds of Catharism are quelled by the Inquisition.
1270	Death of St Louis.
1276-1344	Perpignan is capital of the kingdom of Majorca and the Balearic Islands founded by Jaime I of Aragon, which also includes the Cerdagne, Roussillon and Mont-pellier.
1290	The counts of Foix inherit the Béarn.
1292	Annexation of Pézenas, the Rouergue and the Gévaudan.
1312	Dissolution of the Order of the Templars by Philip the Fair: the Templars' considerable estates in the Causses are handed over to the Knights Hospitallers of St John of Jerusalem (or of Malta).
1331-91	Life of Gaston Fébus.
1337	Beginning of the Hundred Years War (which lasts until 1453).
1348	A third of the population of Languedoc perishes from the Black Death.
1349	The king of Majorca sells the seigneury of Montpellier to Philip of Valois.
1350-1450	The Pyrenees and Languedoc endure a lengthy period of war, unrest, epidemics and famine.
1360	Treaty of Bretigny: end of the first part of the Hundred Years War. Saintonge, Poitou, Agenais, Quercy, Rouergue and Périgord are ceded to the king of England. Languedoc is then divided into three seneschalsies: Toulouse, Carcassonne and Beaucaire.
1361	The countryside is plundered by outlaws.
1420	Charles VII enters Toulouse.
1462	Intervention of Louis XI in Roussillon.

Battle of Muret
Victory of Simon de Montfort over the Albigensians

Arch. Snark/EDIMEDIA

Wars of Religion and Union with France

1484	The princes of Albret, "kings of Navarre", gain ascendancy in the Gascon Pyrenees (Foix, Béarn, Bigorre).
1512	Ferdinand the Catholic monarch divests the Albrets of their territory.
1539	Under the edict of Villers-Cotteret, French is decreed the legal language.
1560-98	Wars of Religion between the Protestants and the Roman Catholics.
1598	Edict of Nantes. Protestants obtain freedom of worship and guaranteed strongholds (Puylaurens, Montauban).
1607	Henri IV unites his own royal estate (Basse-Navarre and the fiefs of Foix and Béarn) to the French Crown.
1610	Assassination of Henri IV and renewal of religious strife.
1629	Treaty of Alès. The Protestants keep their freedom of worship, but lose their strongholds.
1643-1715	Reign of Louis XIV
1659	Under the Treaty of the Pyrenees, Roussillon and the Cerdagne are united with the French Crown.
1666-80	Construction of the Canal du Midi by Riquet.
1685	Revocation of the Edict of Nantes. Numerous Protestants flee the country.
1702-04	War of the Camisards

1746	The thesis of De Bordeu on the mineral springs of Aquitaine plays an important role in the setting up of spa resorts and the rise in popularity of taking cures.
1787	Ramond de Carbonnières, first enthusiast of the Pyrenees, stays in Barèges.
1790	The Languedoc is divided into new administrative districts (*départements*).
1804-15	First Empire. Discovery of new thermal springs in the Pyrenees.
1852-1914	Second Empire and Third Republic. Development of spa resorts, rock climbing and scientific study of the Pyrenees.
1875	Destruction of the Languedoc vineyards by phylloxera.
1901	First hydroelectric schemes set up.
1907	Uprising of the wine-growers ("Mouvement des gueux") in Bas Languedoc, in protest against overproduction, competition from imported Algerian wines and falling prices.
1920	The Pyrenees convert to hydroelectric power.
1940-44	The Pyrenees prove to be of vital importance to the French Résistance. The Massif de l'Aigoual is a major headquarters for the *maquis*.
1955	Inauguration of the Compagnie Nationale d'Aménagement du Bas-Rhône-Languedoc, to develop an irrigation system in the region.
1963	Plans for the development of the Languedoc-Roussillon coastline.
1969	Maiden flight of "Concorde 001".
1970	Designation of the Parc National des Cévennes. Founding of Airbus Industrie.
1973	Designation of the Parc naturel régional du Haut Languedoc.
1992-97	Opening in progessive sections of the new motorway (A 75) linking Clermont-Ferrand with Béziers.
1993	Toulouse underground railway (*métro*) begins operation.
1994	Puymorens tunnel is opened in the Pyrenees.
1995	Designation of the Parc naturel régional des Grands Causses.
1996	Opening of a high-speed rail link (TGV) between Paris and Perpignan (*journey time: 6hr*)

THE CATHARS

The repression of the Cathar sect, in the 13C, profoundly affected the history of the Languedoc, which then became linked with that of the French kingdom.

The Cathar doctrine – The origins of Cathar doctrine are lost in a labyrinth of complex and distant Eastern influences (including the powerful Bogomiles in Bulgaria), which were propagated in Europe during the 11C and 12C and became rooted in Languedoc towards 1160.

The basic tenet of Cathar doctrine is the dualistic separation of "Good" from "Evil"; God, who reigns over a spiritual world of beauty and light, is opposed by the material world governed by Satan, and man is no more than a spirit trapped in the material world by a Satanic ruse. The Cathars (from the Greek "kathari" or "pure ones") were obsessed with a fear of evil and so sought to free man from the material world, restoring him to divine purity. They interpreted biblical texts in the light of their doctrine and came into head-on confrontation with the orthodox Christian church, for example by denying the divinity of Christ, whom they nonetheless strove to emulate.

The Cathar Church – This breakaway Church was headed by four bishops: Albi (which earned the Cathar Church the name "Albigensian"), Toulouse, Carcassonne and Agen. A significant feature of the Cathar Church was its hierarchy of vocations, distinguishing between **Parfaits** ("Perfect ones") and **Croyants** ("Believers").

As a reaction against the obvious laxity of the Roman Catholic clergy, the Parfaits had to lead an austere life, following the ascetic ideals of poverty, chastity, patience and humility. They were considered men of God who had already seen the light and, as such, were venerated and cared for by the Croyants.

The Cathar Church administered only one sacrament, the **Consolamentum**, which varied according to the occasion, be it the ordination of a Parfait, or the blessing of a Croyant on the point of death as a means of admission into the world of light. The faithful gathered together for other liturgical events, such as prayer meetings, public confessions etc.

Cement-clad *Cathar Warriors* by the side of the motorway

The beliefs, way of life and religious rituals of the Cathars conflicted with Roman Catholic thought. Their rejection of the traditional sacraments of baptism and marriage, and their toleration of different customs and attitudes (particularly in financial and commercial matters) gave rise to violent disputes with the clerics.

A favourable environment – The Cathar heresy reached the towns, centres of culture and trade, and then spread into the lowlands of Languedoc. It has been pointed out that it may be no coincidence that the area where the Cathar Church flourished, between Carcassonne and Toulouse, Foix and Limoux, corresponded exactly with that dominated by the Languedoc cloth industry, which exported from Narbonne to the Levant. Indeed, the "**Bonshommes**" (Parfaits) were very often textile manufacturers or merchants. Powerful lords, such as Roger Trencavel, viscount of Béziers and Carcassonne, and Raymond, count of Foix, supported the heresy. Women, far from being excluded from the Cathar church, founded their own communities of Parfaites.

The war against the Cathars – In 1150 St Bernard arrived in the Albigeois region on a mission to convert the Cathar heretics. In view of his minimal success, the Third Lateran Council (1179) drew up plans to enlist some secular muscle to further their cause. In 1204, Pope Innocent III sent three legates to preach against the Cathars and persuade the Count of Toulouse, **Raymond VI**, to withdraw his protection of them. This the count refused to do and was consequently excommunicated in 1207.

In January 1208, Pierre de Castlenau, one of the papal legates, was assassinated. Raymond VI was immediately accused of his murder. The incident sparked off the **First Albigensian Crusade**, preached by Pope Innocent III in March 1208. Knights from the Paris region, Normandy, Picardy, Flanders, Champagne and Burgundy, as well as noblemen from the Rhineland, Friesland, Bavaria and even Austria rallied forces

---

From military stronghold to religious refuge

The castles now associated with the Cathars were originally built as defensive outposts. They were built c 1000 by local noblemen seeking to protect their lands from the armed forces of the King of Aragon. In this way, the fortresses at Aguilar, Termes, Quéribus, Puilaurens and Peyrepertuse were built to defend Carcassonne. At the beginning of the 13C, these bastions of Occitan independence transformed themselves quite naturally into entrenched camps for Cathar refugees, earning them the label "châteaux cathares" in French annals.

After the Albigensian Crusades, they were rebuilt and modified to participate in the defence of the new French territory, once more against attack from Aragonese troops. However, the Treaty of the Pyrenees in 1659 annexed Roussillon to France, depriving the citadels of their defensive function, now that the French border was pushed south to the Pyrenees. They were left to fall into ruins, until a regional programme of economic renewal set up in the 1980s converted the castles into a major tourist attraction. Nowadays, the Châteaux Cathares have a new defensive role to play, against rural impoverishment of the Aude region.

under the command of Abbot Arnaud-Amaury of Cîteaux and then under **Simon de Montfort**. The "Holy War" was to last for more than 20 years. In 1209, 30 000 residents of Béziers were massacred. Carcassonne was besieged in 1209 and fell because of lack of water. Viscount Raymond-Roger de Trencavel was taken prisoner and his place taken by Simon de Montfort, who continued his crusade, capturing one Cathar fortress after another: Lastours, Minerve, Termes and Puivert (1210). By 1215, the whole of the Count of Toulouse's territory was in the hands of Montfort. Raymond VII avenged his father by waging a war of liberation which lasted eight years. Simon de Montfort died in 1218 but was succeeded by his son, Amaury.

Strongholds might fall, but the Cathar doctrine was not so easily quashed. In 1226, a **Second Albigensian Crusade** was preached, under the leadership this time of the King of France himself, Louis VIII. The Holy War very rapidly became a political struggle, however. In the Treaty of Meaux-Paris in 1229, Blanche of Castille effectively annexed a vast territory, to become the Languèdoc a century later, to the French Royal estate. The battle against heresy was not over; this time the **Inquisition** intervened. Pope Gregory IX entrusted it to the Dominican Order in 1231. In 1240, the Crusaders captured Peyrepertuse. The governor of the main Cathar stronghold at Montségur, Pierre-Roger de Mirepoix, undertook an expedition to Avignonet in 1242, with the intention of killing off the members of an Inquisition tribunal. Six thousand Crusaders promptly installed themselves at the foot of his castle, where they remained for a siege which lasted ten months. At the end of it, in March 1244, the fortress capitulated and the besiegers built an enormous pyre on which they burned alive 215 unrepentant Cathars. Those still espousing the Cathar doctrine took refuge in the fortress at Puilaurens, where they were butchered shortly after the fall of Montségur. The war against the Cathars reached its final bloody conclusion in 1255 with the siege and fall of Quéribus, the last remaining Cathar stronghold.

Henry James on the basilica of St-Sernin, Toulouse

My real consolation was an hour I spent in Saint-Sernin, one of the noblest churches in southern France, and easily the first among those of Toulouse. This great structure, a masterpiece of twelfth-century romanesque, and dedicated to Saint Saturninus – the Toulousains have abbreviated – is, I think, alone worth a journey to Toulouse. What makes it so is the extraordinary seriousness of its interior; no other term occurs to me as expressing so well the character of its clear grey nave. As a general thing, I do not favour the fashion of attributing moral qualities to buildings; I shrink from talking about tender porticos and sincere campanili; but I find I cannot get on at all without imputing some sort of morality to Saint-Sernin. As it stands today, the church has been completely restored by Viollet-le-Duc. The exterior is of brick, and has little charm save that of a tower of four rows of arches, narrowing together as they ascend. The nave is of great length and height, the barrel-roof of stone, the effect of the round arches and pillars in the triforium especially fine. There are two low aisles on either side. The choir is very deep and narrow; it seems to close together and looks as if it were meant for intensely earnest rites. The transepts are most noble, especially the arches of the second tier. The whole church is narrow for its length, and is singularly complete and homogeneous. As I say all this, I feel that I quite fail to give an impression of its manly gravity, its strong proportions, or of the lonesome look of its renovated stones as I sat there while the October twilight gathered. It is a real work of art, a high conception.

Henry James: *A Little Tour in France* (1884)

Art

ABC OF ARCHITECTURE

Religious architecture

CORNEILLA-DE-CONFLENT – Ground plan of the church of Ste-Marie (11-12C)

This church originally had a basilical ground plan with three aisles, a very common layout in Roussillon in the 11C. The transept was added in the 12C.

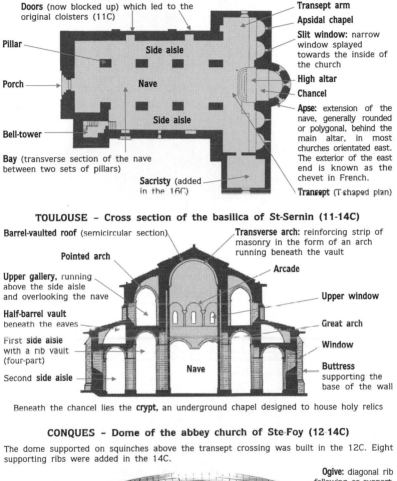

Doors (now blocked up) which led to the original cloisters (11C)

Pillar

Porch

Bell-tower

Bay (transverse section of the nave between two sets of pillars)

Sacristy (added in the 16C)

Side aisle

Nave

Side aisle

Transept arm

Apsidal chapel

Slit window: narrow window splayed towards the inside of the church

High altar

Chancel

Apse: extension of the nave, generally rounded or polygonal, behind the main altar, in most churches orientated east. The exterior of the east end is known as the chevet in French.

Transept (T-shaped plan)

TOULOUSE – Cross section of the basilica of St-Sernin (11-14C)

Barrel-vaulted roof (semicircular section)

Pointed arch

Upper gallery, running above the side aisle and overlooking the nave

Half-barrel vault beneath the eaves

First side aisle with a rib vault (four-part)

Second side aisle

Transverse arch: reinforcing strip of masonry in the form of an arch running beneath the vault

Arcade

Upper window

Great arch

Window

Buttress supporting the base of the wall

Nave

Beneath the chancel lies the **crypt,** an underground chapel designed to house holy relics

CONQUES – Dome of the abbey church of Ste-Foy (12-14C)

The dome supported on squinches above the transept crossing was built in the 12C. Eight supporting ribs were added in the 14C.

Quarter or **cell** (segment of vault between ribs)

Keystone

Basket-handle arch

Splayed window

Sculpted **pendant**

Double curve arch

Ogive: diagonal rib following or supporting the pointed arch of the vault

Drum: cylindrical (or polygonal) wall supporting a dome

Squinch: small series of corbelled arches bridging the gaps at the corners between a square plan structure, such as a tower, and a circular or polygonal superstructure (dome etc). In this case it is decorated by figures sculpted in **high relief.**

R. Corbel

39

ST-MICHEL-DE-CUXA – Bell-tower of the abbey church (11C)

The Romanesque churches in Roussillon and Catalonia nearly all feature one or two Lombard bell-towers. This style was probably imported from Italy in the 11C, making its earliest appearance at St-Michel-de-Cuxa, and later became typical of the architecture of this region. The bell-tower at Cuxa stands at the far south end of the transept (originally, there was a matching tower at the far north end).

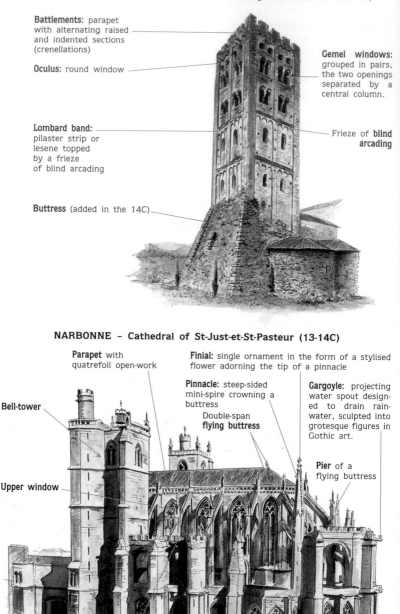

Battlements: parapet with alternating raised and indented sections (crenellations)

Oculus: round window

Lombard band: pilaster strip or lesene topped by a frieze of blind arcading

Buttress (added in the 14C)

Gemel windows: grouped in pairs, the two openings separated by a central column.

Frieze of **blind arcading**

NARBONNE – Cathedral of St-Just-et-St-Pasteur (13-14C)

Parapet with quatrefoil open-work

Bell-tower

Upper window

Buttress

Watch-path with **battlements**

Finial: single ornament in the form of a stylised flower adorning the tip of a pinnacle

Pinnacle: steep-sided mini-spire crowning a buttress

Double-span **flying buttress**

Gargoyle: projecting water spout design-ed to drain rain-water, sculpted into grotesque figures in Gothic art.

Pier of a flying buttress

Tracery: stone open-work decorating the upper part of the windows

Lanceolate or spearhead motif in the undulating ornamentation of a Flamboyant Gothic window

R. Corbel

40

ELNE – Cloisters of the cathedral of Ste-Eulalie-et-Ste-Julie (12-14C)

The cloisters are a set of four roofed galleries around a central quadrangle, enabling monks to walk under cover from the conventual buildings to the church.

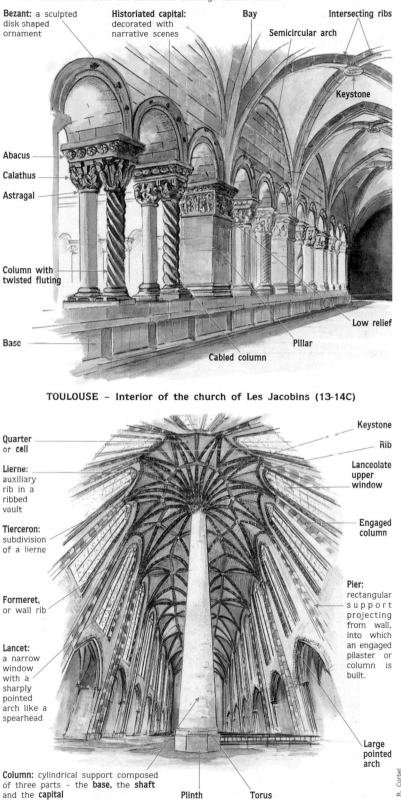

Bezant: a sculpted disk shaped ornament

Historiated capital: decorated with narrative scenes

Bay

Semicircular arch

Intersecting ribs

Keystone

Abacus

Calathus

Astragal

Column with twisted fluting

Base

Low relief

Pillar

Cabled column

TOULOUSE – Interior of the church of Les Jacobins (13-14C)

Keystone

Rib

Quarter or cell

Lierne: auxiliary rib in a ribbed vault

Lanceolate upper window

Tierceron: subdivision of a lierne

Engaged column

Formeret, or wall rib

Pier: rectangular support projecting from wall, into which an engaged pilaster or column is built.

Lancet: a narrow window with a sharply pointed arch like a spearhead

Large pointed arch

Column: cylindrical support composed of three parts – the **base**, the **shaft** and the **capital**

Plinth

Torus

R. Corbel

CARCASSONNE – East gateway of the Château Comtal (12C)

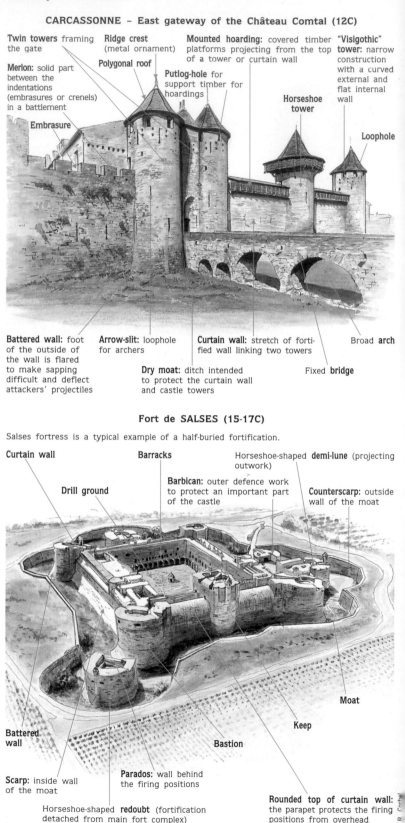

Twin towers framing the gate

Ridge crest (metal ornament)

Polygonal roof

Merlon: solid part between the indentations (embrasures or crenels) in a battlement

Embrasure

Putlog-hole for support timber for hoardings

Mounted hoarding: covered timber platforms projecting from the top of a tower or curtain wall

"Visigothic" tower: narrow construction with a curved external and flat internal wall

Horseshoe tower

Loophole

Battered wall: foot of the outside of the wall is flared to make sapping difficult and deflect attackers' projectiles

Arrow-slit: loophole for archers

Dry moat: ditch intended to protect the curtain wall and castle towers

Curtain wall: stretch of fortified wall linking two towers

Broad **arch**

Fixed **bridge**

Fort de SALSES (15-17C)

Salses fortress is a typical example of a half-buried fortification.

Curtain wall

Barracks

Drill ground

Barbican: outer defence work to protect an important part of the castle

Horseshoe-shaped **demi-lune** (projecting outwork)

Counterscarp: outside wall of the moat

Moat

Keep

Bastion

Battered wall

Scarp: inside wall of the moat

Parados: wall behind the firing positions

Horseshoe-shaped **redoubt** (fortification detached from main fort complex)

Rounded top of curtain wall: the parapet protects the firing positions from overhead.

TOULOUSE – Hôtel d'Assézat (16C)

The Hôtel d'Assézat, designed by Nicolas Bachelier, is the earliest example of Palladian style architecture in Toulouse, with its characteristic superposition of the Classical decorative orders – Doric, Ionic and Corinthian.

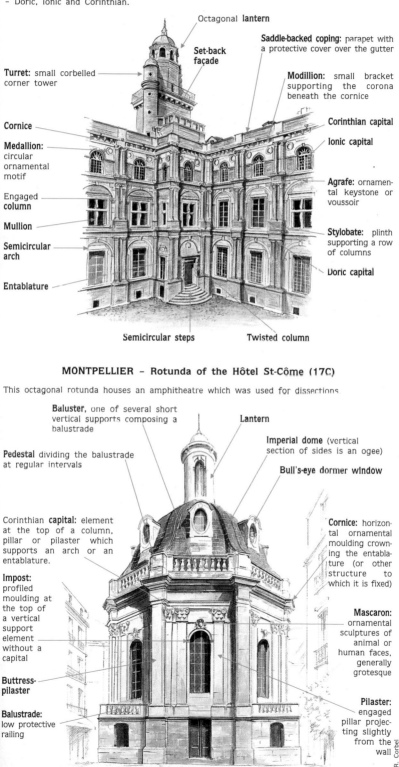

Octagonal **lantern**

Saddle-backed coping: parapet with a protective cover over the gutter

Set-back façade

Modillion: small bracket supporting the corona beneath the cornice

Turret: small corbelled corner tower

Cornice

Medallion: circular ornamental motif

Engaged column

Mullion

Semicircular arch

Entablature

Corinthian capital

Ionic capital

Agrafe: ornamental keystone or voussoir

Stylobate: plinth supporting a row of columns

Doric capital

Semicircular steps

Twisted column

MONTPELLIER – Rotunda of the Hôtel St-Côme (17C)

This octagonal rotunda houses an amphitheatre which was used for dissections.

Baluster, one of several short vertical supports composing a balustrade

Lantern

Pedestal dividing the balustrade at regular intervals

Imperial dome (vertical section of sides is an ogee)

Bull's-eye dormer window

Corinthian capital: element at the top of a column, pillar or pilaster which supports an arch or an entablature.

Cornice: horizontal ornamental moulding crowning the entablature (or other structure to which it is fixed)

Impost: profiled moulding at the top of a vertical support element without a capital

Mascaron: ornamental sculptures of animal or human faces, generally grotesque

Buttress-pilaster

Balustrade: low protective railing

Pilaster: engaged pillar projecting slightly from the wall

R. Corbel

ART AND ARCHITECTURAL TERMS USED IN THE GUIDE

Altarpiece: vertical part of the altar above the altar table; the painted or carved altarpiece often comprises several hinged panels. A triptych is an altarpiece with three panels.

Antefix: decorative upright stone roof tile.

Apse: an extension of the eastern end of a church, behind the altar.

Archstone: one of the stones forming an arch or vault.

Arrow slit: narrow slit, splayed on the inside, through which archers shot their arrows.

Barbican: defensive gatehouse.

Bas-relief: sculpture in which the forms project slightly from the background.

Basket-handled arch: depressed arch, common to late medieval and Renaissance architecture.

Bond: an arrangement of stones or bricks.

Boss: rounded protuberance projecting from a wall and framed by deeply carved ornamentation. They were very fashionable during the Renaissance.

Claustra: stone railings with vertical bars.

Cloisonné: design made by filling in with enamel small compartments formed by the insertion of wafer-thin strips of metal. This process is the reverse of champlevé.

Colonnette: small decorative column.

Comb belfry: belfry consisting of a hollow wall containing the bells.

Console: projecting moulded bracket supporting a cornice or balcony.

Crown: segment of a cross vault.

Diagonal arch: arch supporting a vault.

Flamboyant: last phase (15C) of French Gothic architecture; name derived from the undulating (flame-like) lines of the window tracery.

Flight: rise of a staircase; section of a staircase between two floors.

Foliated scrolls: sculptures and paintings depicting leaves, flowers etc, often forming part of a frieze.

Fresco: mural painting executed on wet plaster.

Gable: triangular part of an end wall carrying a sloping roof.

Gemel window: window with two openings or bays.

Glacis: embankment in front of a fortress, sloping so that the attackers are in the line of fire.

Half-timbered: timber-framed construction, having the exposed framework filled with light masonry.

High relief: sculpture in which the forms project sharply from the background, without however becoming detached from it (intermediate between bas-relief and sculpture in the round).

Jacquemart: figure of a man with a hammer striking the hours on a clock.

Keystone: topmost stone in an arch or vault.

Knot-work: interlaced design.

Lancet arch: narrow pointed arch, resembling the point of a lance.

Leaf of door: door panel.

Lombard arcades (strips): decorative blind arcading consisting of arches and intervening strips of shallow projecting pilasters; typical of Romanesque art in Lombardy.

Misericord: a narrow ledge, in the shape of a bracket, projecting from the underside of a hinged seat of a choir stall, on which the occupant can support himself while standing.

Mitre arch: opening pointed at the top, shaped like a bishop's mitre.

Modillion: an ornamental bracket on a wall, supporting a bust, an urn etc.

Mozarab: used to describe Christians living or having lived in Moorish Spain. They brought Arab influences to Christian countries.

Mullion: a vertical stone post dividing a window.

Ogee arch: arch formed by four sections of a circle.

Panelling: cladding of walls (in wood, stucco, marble etc) used both for protection and as decoration.

Peristyle: a range of columns surrounding or on the façade of a building.

Pier: engaged post on which rest the mouldings and ornamentation of an arch.

Pilaster: engaged rectangular column.

Recess (tomb): niche set in the wall of a church for accommodating a tomb.

Rood screen: transverse gallery separating the nave from the chancel in some churches.

Stalls: high-backed wooden pews on either side of the choir of a church, for the use of the clergy.

Stele: a vertical stone slab decorated with inscriptions or figures commemorating a victory or mourning a death.

Terra sigillata: red glazed earthenware.

Triforium: a storey immediately above the arcade of the nave or the choir, and below the clerestory, sometimes called a blind storey, because there are no windows.

Triptych: painted or carved panels hinged together, chiefly used as an altarpiece.

Triumphal arch: large arch at the entrance to the chancel of a church.

Twinned or paired: columns or pilasters grouped in twos.

Tympanum: space between the door lintel and arch or pediment above.

Volute: spiral carved ornament on a capital; the centre of the spiral is called the "eye".

The artistic heritage of prehistory and Antiquity

The Causses and the Cévennes are rich in vestiges of the art of Neolithic civilizations.

Megaliths – These large (Gr *mega*) stone (Gr *lithas*) monuments comprise dolmens, menhirs, covered alleyways, alignments of menhirs and "cromlechs" (groups of menhirs serving as boundary markers). The Aveyron *département* has the greatest concentration of dolmens in France. Menhirs, which are rarer, are nevertheless found both in the Gard and the Aveyron. Scientists consider the first megaliths to date from slightly earlier than the Bronze Age (which began approximately 1 800 BC).

Menhirs – These colossal standing stones, deeply embedded in the ground, probably had some sort of symbolic significance. In the south of the Aveyron *département* numerous statue-menhirs, or menhirs carved to depict a human figure, have been found. Features include a face (with eyes and nose, although the mouth is always missing), arms, hands, short lower limbs and jewellery (necklaces or patterns tattooed on the face). It is not known whether these figures represent people or some sort of protective goddess.

Dolmens – Consisting of a horizontal slab supported by several vertical stones, these are thought to have been tombs. Originally some were buried beneath a tumulus, or mound of earth or stones.
The craftsmen behind these mysterious megalithic monuments may well have been a seafaring people who had come and taught the local inhabitants how to erect such massive blocks. Team work and innovative techniques would have been required; use of an inclined ramp, a plumb line, rollers capable of transporting stones weighing up to 350 tonnes, and the construction of roads presupposes quite advanced technical prowess. By way of comparison, the installation (in 1836) of the Luxor obelisk, which weighs "only" 220 tonnes, on Place de la Concorde in Paris was considered a tremendous feat.

The Bronze and Iron Ages – The fine, elegantly shaped bowls and jewellery on display in the Musée Ignon-Fabre in Mende date from these periods.

The Gallo-Roman period – Ceramic ware from the Graufesenque pottery, near Millau, was renowned throughout the Roman Empire. At about the same time, Banassac was reputed for the high quality of its earthenware.

Military architecture in the Middle Ages

The intense military activity of the Middle Ages has left many traces throughout the Languedoc. The Albigensian Crusade, the bands of outlaws pillaging the country during the Hundred Years War, and the proximity of Guyonne, which remained under English rule until 1453, prompted feudal lords to have well-organized defences. They built their castles at the mouths of canyons or upon rocky pinnacles. The southern face of the Montagne Noire once bristled with fortresses; reduced to ruins, they lend a note of austere grandeur to the landscape.
The collapse of public power and the crumbling authority of the princes and counts in the 10C and 11C led to a significant rise in the number of fortified strongholds built. During the 12C and 13C, the castles were once again in the hands of the king and great feudal lords; they were a source of frequent rivalry in Languedoc, which was always seething with border disputes.

Castles – Cities could be defended by the consolidation and reinforcement of the Gallo-Roman city walls (as at Carcassonne). Outside the city limits, fortresses were built on high ground. Originally somewhat crude, the 10C **mounds** (natural or man-made hillocks), which were large enough for a simple shelter, multiplied rapidly on flat land. They were subject to constant improvement, eventually becoming impregnable citadels, in the same mould as Cathar castles which were purely military in purpose.
The end of the 11C marked the advent of stone **keeps** *(donjons)*, either rectangular (Peyrepertuse) or rounded (Catalonia) in shape, with thick walls and narrow window slits. The interior was divided into several storeys: the dark and vaulted ground floor was a store room; the upper floors could be used as reception or living rooms. The only means of access was on the first floor, via a ladder or a retractable gangway.
Most of the keeps had limited facilities as residences. Many were merely defensive towers, which housed a garrison. The lords preferred to live in a larger building in the **lower courtyard**, either adjacent to or detached from the keep.
During the 13C and 14C, the main castle building was extended, making it more comfortable as a residence. The keep then became incorporated with the other buildings and acquired one or several enclosing walls, interrupted at intervals by towers. **Puilaurens** castle, with its fortified wall and four corner towers, is a fine example of this new trend, whereas the keep at **Arques** is a remarkable specimen of 13C military construction.

Watchtowers – These are a common feature in the Corbières, Fenouillèdes, Vallespir and Albères. They transmitted signals, using fire by night and smoke by day, and employing a specific code to convey the nature or gravity of the danger. It has been possible to reconstitute this visual telecommunications link in the Catalan mountains; it ended up at **Castelnou** castle in Les Aspres during the Catalan earldoms of the early Middle Ages, and at Perpignan during the reign of the kings of Aragon.

Fortified churches – Towards the end of the 10C, the custom of fortifying churches became widespread in southern France. Traditionally a place of asylum – the areas of immunity, as defined in the Truce of God, extended as far as 30 paces all around the building – the church, with its robust architecture and its bell-tower ideally suited for keeping watch, provided a refuge for the local inhabitants in times of warfare. **Machicolations**, either mounted on corbels or supported on arches between buttresses, as in Beaumont-de-Lomagne *(see Michelin Green Guide Atlantic Coast)*, were first seen in France at the end of the 12C on Languedoc churches.

However, strict regulations on the fortification of churches were prescribed at the time of the Albigensian Crusade. The count of Toulouse and his vassals were accused of abusing their privilege in this regard. Thus the bishops regained a monopoly which had long evaded them.

The 13C, which for Languedoc marked the union with the French crown and the triumph of orthodoxy over heresy, was a time when large brick churches in the Gothic style of Toulouse were constructed, with a layout and height appropriate for the potential part of a system of fortifications.

In 1282, Bernard de Castanet, Bishop of Albi, laid the first stone of the cathedral of Ste-Cécile. The severity of its mighty walls, 40m/131ft high, give it the appearance of a massive fortress at the heart of the subjugated Cathar country. Well preserved fortified churches and villages are still to be seen in the upper valleys of the Pyrenees; the church of Stes-Juste-et-Ruffine in Prats-de-Mollo is a curious blend of roofs and fortifications. One of the finest sights is Villefranche-de-Conflent with its ramparts refurbished by Vauban. Languedoc abounds with fine examples of fortified churches – the cathedral at Maguelone, the church of St-Étienne in Agde, the cathedral of Notre-Dame in Rodez and the cathedral of St-Nazaire in Béziers, to name but a few.

Bastides – In 1152, Eleanor of Aquitaine took as her second husband Henry Plantagenet, Count of Anjou and Lord of Maine, Touraine and Normandy. Their joint estates were as great as those of the King of France. Two years later, Henry Plantagenet inherited the throne of England which he ruled as Henry II. The balance of power was destroyed and the Franco-English wars which broke out were to last for the next three hundred years or more. Bastides, or fortified "new" towns, were built in the 13C by kings of France and England in the hope of consolidating their position and justifying their territorial claims.

The bastides, both French and English, were mostly built to an identical grid street layout – in so far as the local terrain allowed. Their straight streets intersect at right angles. At the centre of town is a square surrounded by covered arcades, called *couverts* (Mirepoix). Carcassonne's "Ville Basse", Montauban and Villefranche-de-Rouergue are particularly fine examples of these "new towns" (13C and 14C).

Siege warfare

When it was not possible to take a castle by surprise attack, lengthy sieges often ensued. Cathar fortresses undoubtedly presented the greatest challenge to any assailant. Perched on rocky outcrops, surrounded by steep, vertiginous rock faces, they confounded all the conventional techniques of siege warfare.

In 1210, it was thirst and sickness rather than any skill on the attackers' part which forced the fortress of **Termes** to succumb, and in 1255 the fall of **Quéribus**, last bastion of the Cathars, was only accomplished by treacherous means.

When laying a siege, the attackers first had to surround the stronghold. To this end they would build fortifications (trenches, stockades, towers, blockhouses etc) designed not only to prevent those under siege from making a possible sortie, but also to counter any attack by a relief army.

During lengthy sieges, which could go on for months if not years, an entire fortified town would be built round the besieged fortress.

To break through the stronghold's curtain wall, sappers would dig tunnels into the foot of it, shoring up the cavity with wooden props which were then set alight so that the tunnel and part of the curtain wall above collapsed. Slings, mobile siege towers and battering rams would be pressed into service. Military engineers supervised the construction of the various siege devices, for which the Crusades had provided the most recent testing ground.

The age of the cannon – Early methods of bombardment increased in effectiveness. Towards the middle of the 15C, under the inspiration of two talented gunners, the Bureau brothers, the French royal artillery became the most effective in the world. No feudal fortress could withstand French attacks. In one year, Charles VII recaptured from the English 60 positions which until then resisted sieges lasting four to six months.

Military architecture therefore underwent a complete transformation: towers were replaced by low, thick bastions, and curtain walls were built lower but much thicker (up to 12m/40ft thick). In the 17C, **Vauban** perfected these new defence systems. The **Fort de Salses** is a perfect example of the changes brought about in the face of improved artillery. Half-buried, and well protected with the ingenious device of curtain walls with rounded tops, the fortress is shielded both from bullets and against the possibility of attackers scaling the walls.

Religious architecture

Romanesque architecture

Languedoc, the crossroads of many civilizations, has been exposed to a variety of influences: from Auvergne, in the church of Ste-Foy in Conques; from Provence, in the abbey of St-Victor in Marseille, which had numerous dependent priories by the end of the 11C; from Aquitaine, in the basilica of St-Sernin in Toulouse and the church of St-Pierre in Moissac. Red or grey sandstone was employed in the Rouergue region in preference to schist, which is very difficult to carve, whereas, further south, brick and stone were combined harmoniously.

Early Romanesque churches – These appeared at the beginning of the 11C, when the prosperity of the Church stimulated a dramatic increase in the construction of ecclesiastical buildings. They are characterised by rustic masonry consisting of rough-hewn stones mixed with mortar. Around the outside of the apse, the walls are often adorned with Lombard bands, vertical pilasters projecting only slightly from the wall of the apse and linked at the top by a series of small arcades.

Inside, naves were roofed with barrel vaulting and ended in an oven-vaulted apse (quarter sphere). The ribbed vault, adopted some time later, is formed by the intersection of two barrel vaults; it was often used for crypts and side aisles.

The overall appearance of these churches is quite austere. They feature only a few, very narrow and deeply splayed windows. The heavy stone vaulting tended to put far too heavy a load on the supporting walls, so it was necessary to reduce windows to a minimum and to build the side aisles, designed to buttress the nave, up to the level from where the arch of the vaulting sprang. The abbey church at St-Guilhem-le-Désert is just one example from this period.

The Romanesque churches of Gévaudan in Haut Languedoc – The churches in this area encompass a wide range of layouts. Nonetheless, the single nave predominates and, at the end of the 11C, it was even made a feature of some of the larger churches (Maguelone cathedral, St-Étienne in Agde).

On the exterior of such churches, massive, sturdy walls reinforced by arcades and a sober architectural style reflect Provençal influence. Inside, the ambulatories and radiating chapels characteristic of great pilgrimage churches, such as Ste-Foy in Conques or St-Sernin in Toulouse, are rarely seen in the less wealthy country churches. Further features inherited from neighbouring Provence were the polygonal apse and twin columns.

A magnificent example of the sculpted decoration of churches of this period can be seen at Ste Foy in Conques, a jewel of 12C Romanesque sculpture.

J.L. Barde/SCOPE

Detail on the tympanum of the west doorway of the church of Ste-Foy at Conques

Catalan architecture – An original architectural style combining Mozarabic and Carolingian influences appeared in the Catalan Pyrenees towards the middle of the 10C. The abbey church of **St-Michel-de-Cuxa**, in Conflent, exhibits a variety of features – a low, narrow transept, an elongated chancel with an apse, side aisles, barrel vaulting throughout – which lend it the complex appearance typical of early Romanesque architecture. The simpler style of **St-Martin-du-Canigou** was widely copied during the 11C. Numerous local churches of this period have a vaulted nave supported by pillars, for example.

The next stage in architectural evolution was the construction of churches with barrel vaulting supported by transverse arches (Arles-sur-Tech, Elne) and the use of richer decorative motifs. Nor should one forget one of the most remarkable achievements of Catalan architecture, the introduction of domes on pendentives. Mountain sanctuaries, often situated some way away from main communications routes, and built somewhat crudely from roughly hewn rock, are most notable for their fine square towers, decorated with small arcades and with their otherwise forbidding appearance alleviated somewhat by Lombard bands, which were constructed until the 13C.

Sculptural elements were frequently made of the grey or pink marble from the Conflent and Roussillon quarries. Capitals embellished with simple floral motifs and later with narrative scenes, and altar tables were produced in ever larger numbers by Pyrenean craftsmen. The 12C decoration of **Serrabone** priory, particularly the tribune used as a choir by the monks, is one of the finest examples of Romanesque art in Roussillon.

Painted mural decoration, usually a feature of smooth walls with only a few narrow window openings, is an important characteristic of the architecture of this period. Apses were decorated with the image of Christ in Majesty, or of the Apocalypse, or of the Last Judgment, urging the faithful to work hard for their salvation, as on the doorways of Languedoc churches.

J. Dieuzaide

Moissac cloisters

Moissac – A major stopping place on the road to Santiago de Compostela, Moissac abbey exerted a considerable influence throughout Languedoc in the 11C and the 12C. Its doorway and cloisters are masterpieces of Romanesque art.

The **tympanum**, a rendering in stone of an illumination from a book, gave rise to a whole school of imitations. It represents Christ in Majesty surrounded by the symbols of the four Evangelists. The composition, and particularly the face of Christ, with its harsh and somewhat disturbing expression, suggests a latent Eastern influence which would have come via Spain. Similarly, the trefoil and poly-lobed arcades are reminiscent of Mozarabic art.

Rich decorative elements are also evident in the harmonious sculpture of the cloisters. The Apostles carved on the corner pillars (on white marble facings) are depicted standing with their body facing forwards and their head in profile. The capitals on the galleries display a great variety of geometrical and floral motifs, animals and narrative scenes. The decorative style at Moissac bears some relation to that of Toulouse, another cradle of medieval Romanesque sculpture.

Toulouse – Toulouse flourished as the centre of the Languedoc Romanesque school at the peak of its glory.

A major pilgrimage church, the basilica of **St-Sernin** – the largest Romanesque basilica in western Europe – was designed on a grandiose scale. A subtle blend of stone and brick, it is vaulted throughout and features a number of typical Romanesque techniques: semicircular barrel vaulting on transverse arches in the main nave, half-barrel vaulting in the galleries, ribbed vaulting in the side aisles, and a dome over the transept crossing. The sculpted decoration was completed in less than 40 years (from 1080 to 1118) by Bernard Gilduin's workshop. The symbolism and logical ordering of the scenes depicted on the church doorways point to a deep and well-informed faith, drawing on imagery from the Old and New Testaments. The **Porte Miègeville**, leading into the south side aisle of the basilica, was completed in 1100; it reflects interesting Spanish influences from the workshops of Jaca and Compostela (the figure of King David depicted on the left on the lintel is identical to that on the Goldsmiths' Doorway in the cathedral at Santiago de Compostela, as is the figure of St James to the left of the tympanum).

The shape of the capitals is interesting, as it is obviously influenced by the classical Corinthian order, to which decorative motifs of animals or narrative scenes have been added. Unfortunately, the cloisters of St-Sernin abbey, La Daurade monastery and St-Étienne cathedral were destroyed in the 19C (fragments of the capitals are exhibited in the Musée des Augustins).

Southern French Gothic architecture

The south of France did not adopt the principles of Gothic architecture used in the north of France, instead developing its own new architectural style closely linked with the Romanesque tradition. The chancel of Narbonne cathedral is virtually the only construction in the northern French (read as French) Gothic style.

Languedoc Gothic – In the 13C, a specifically southern French Gothic style, known as Languedoc Gothic, developed. It is characterised by the use of brick, and by the presence of a belfry wall or a bell-tower decorated with mitre-shaped arched openings, as in the church of Notre-Dame-du-Taur or the upper storeys of the bell-tower of the basilica of St-Sernin, both in Toulouse. In the absence of flying buttresses, the load of the roof vault was supported by massive buttresses between which chapels were inserted.

Toulouse – Bell-gable of Notre-Dame-du-Taur

Inside churches in this style, the single nave is relatively dark, stands almost as wide as it is high, and terminates in a polygonal apse. Its vast size was designed to accommodate the large congregations sought after by preachers in the wake of the Albigensian Crusade. The empty wall surfaces were adorned with painted decoration.

The light weight of brick made it possible to build vaulted roofs instead of the earlier timber roofing.

Albi cathedral – The cathedral of Ste-Cécile at Albi is a magnificent example of southern French Gothic art at its best. The cathedral comprises a single nave, 100m/328ft long and 30m/98ft high, with twelve bays, supported by massive buttresses and lit through very narrow window openings. Despite the cathedral's strong resemblance to a fortress, it exhibits great purity of line. The absence of side aisles, transept or ambulatory resulted in a better structural balance. The cathedral was begun in 1282, but not finished until two centuries later. In 1500, the Flamboyant Gothic style made its first appearance, in the shape of the choir screen and **rood screen**, and in the last three storeys of the bell-tower added to the square tower. In 1533, the addition of an ornate canopy porch completed the impressive appearance of the building.

The mendicant orders – The Dominican friars, known as "Jacobins" in France, built their first monastery in Toulouse, in 1216. It was occupied by the Franciscan Order, during the lifetime of their founder St Francis of Assisi, in 1222 (the church was destroyed by fire in 1871).

The vaulting of the church of **Les Jacobins** with its audacious "palm-tree" ribbing supported on a single pillar to overcome the problem of vaulting a semicircular space (the apse) and the restrained cloisters with their delicate twin colonnettes contribute to the overall grace of this marvellous architectural ensemble which radiates spirituality.

The bastide churches – The *bastides*, or "new towns", gave rise to numerous construction projects for churches on the edge of or close to the single central market place surrounded by covered arcades *(couverts)*. The southern French Gothic style was particularly suitable, since the churches had to be fitted into a confined space.

Although it has been modified a number of times over the centuries, the church of St-Jacques in Montauban is a good example of the Languedoc school, with its single nave and octagonal brick bell-tower. The church at Grenade was inspired by Les Jacobins in Toulouse.

49

Catalan Baroque

Catalan Baroque art, Spanish in origin and inspiration, developed at a time when Catalonia was embroiled in a critical territorial dispute (1640-60) which resulted in its being divided between Spain and France (Cerdanya, hitherto part of Catalonia, was annexed to Roussillon under the Treaty of the Pyrenees in 1659). Catalan Baroque art, primarily religious, was to become to some extent a manifestation of the unification in artistic expression achieved by a people otherwise torn asunder.

Altarpieces – By far the most significant work of art produced in the Catalan Baroque style is the altarpiece. From 1640, even the smallest parishes were commissioning their own. The necessary materials were right at hand: marble from Caune (Aude) and Villefranche-de-Conflent, pine from the forests of the Canigou and Spanish gold imported from America. The Catalan Baroque altarpiece might almost qualify as a work of architecture, so much do the two art forms have in common. It is in fact quite impressive to see how the altarpiece, built to increasingly huge dimensions and incorporating architectural elements such as the column, entablature, cornice, baldaquin or niche, ultimately becomes an architectural feature in its own right. The art of making these altarpieces evolved over the years. During the early decades of the 17C, they remained a sensible size with fairly restrained ornamentation. Between 1640 and 1675, altarpieces entirely covered in sculpture and gilding gained in popularity. They followed a strictly uniform design: two or three tiers embellished with increasing numbers of pinnacle turrets, broken pediments and canopies, accompanied by a wealth of ornamentation using geometric motifs, winged cherubs and fluted columns. From 1670 to 1730, the

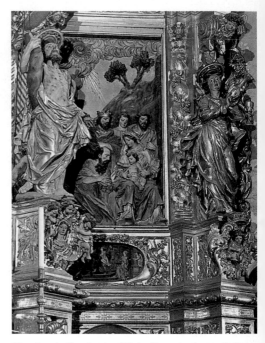

Altarpiece in the church of Notre-Dame-des-Anges, Collioure

style became unreservedly Baroque. Architectural order was swamped by a profusion of decorative elements: pediments were invaded by crowds of angels; every available space was covered with floral motifs (bouquets, garlands, foliage); and the fluted column was replaced by the twisted one. The best example of a Catalan Baroque altarpiece at the height of the style's exuberance is that at Notre-Dame-des-Anges (1699) in Collioure.

Masters of Catalan Baroque – Numerous workshops flourished throughout Roussillon with the advent of Catalan Baroque. After 1640, several schools sprang up around **Lazare Tremullas**, a Catalan sculptor who introduced the carved altarpiece to France. It is to this artist that we owe the altarpiece in Notre-Dame-du-Rosaire (now on display in the church of St-Jacques at Perpignan). **Lluis Generès** was very productive during the second half of the 17C. His works include the high altar at Espira-de-Conflent *(18km/11mi east of Prades)* and the altarpieces at Prats-de-Mollo and Baixas *(13km/8mi northwest of Perpignan)*. Much more everyday figures were introduced by Jean-Pierre Geralt, sculptor of the high altars at Pallalda and Trouillas and the altarpiece at Notre-Dame-du-Rosaire. However, the incontestable master of late 17C and early 18C Catalan Baroque extravagance was **Joseph Sunyer**, whose talent gave rise to the high altar of St-Pierre at Prades (1695), that of Notre-Dame-des-Anges at Collioure and one of the altarpieces at Vinça. The decoration of the high altar and "camaril" in the hermitage at Font-Romeu are also his work.

Sculpture – Catalan Baroque altarpieces make enormous recourse to sculpture. Lazare Tremullas introduced the use of sculpture to decorate altarpieces and this continued to evolve until the 18C. The Rosary altarpiece in the church at **Espira-de-Conflent** is a masterpiece of its kind. It was sculpted in 1702 by an anonymous artist, the "Master of Espira". The low reliefs on this altarpiece in particular are characteristic: profusion and animated line of the figures; attention given to detail; rounded forms; and faces with smooth features. In the same church, there is a sculpture group of the Entombment by Sunyer with quintessentially

Baroque theatricality. The sculpted figures, both those that are part of and those separate from the altarpiece, are of course painted and gilded. The treatment of the statues of the saints to whom the altarpieces are dedicated evolves in true Baroque fashion also: the dignified figures well tucked into their niches in the mid 17C literally seem to have taken flight by the end of the same century.

Secular architecture

In the "triangle" between Albi, Toulouse and Carcassonne, the centre of production of dyer's woad, wealthy merchants had beautiful Renaissance mansions built for themselves during the economic boom in the textiles and dyeing industries, from the mid 15C to mid 16C. In the 17C and 18C, private mansions – or *hôtels particuliers* – inspired by the Italian Renaissance were built, particularly in Montpellier and Pézenas.

The façades overlooking the courtyard feature loggias and superimposed colonnades, crowned with balusters or pediments. Interior decoration is lavish, and monumental staircases abound.

At the end of the 17C, the architect **D'Aviler** revolutionised the appearance of such mansions; decoration was transferred to the exterior, particularly the porches. D'Aviler replaced lintels with heavily depressed arches, which came to be called *davilerte* arches. Above these was a triangular pediment with a certain amount of ornamentation. Magnificent openwork staircases with balusters were reminiscent of the preceding period. Towards the end of the century, pilasters and superposed orders of columns were no longer a feature, and windows were built without any decorative frame. However, façades were adorned with sculptures and wrought iron balconies.

Montpellier – Hôtel de Mirman

D'après photo Lauros/GIRAUDON

The school of architecture in Montpellier is represented by D'Aviler, the Girals and Jacques Donnat. It also numbered in its ranks master craftsmen in wrought iron and carved wood. The school of painting includes such famous names as: Antoine Ranc, Hyacinthe Rigaud, Jean de Troy (17C), Jean Raoux and Joseph-Marie Vien (18C). Pretty fountains, and the Peyrou water tower *(château d'eau)* and aqueduct show another aspect of the artistic creativity of this fertile period.

Traditional rural architecture

Built primarily for practical, rather than aesthetic, purposes, rural houses can be particularly revealing about local rural industry. Their layout, construction and materials are often evidence of a traditional way of life deeply rooted in its region of origin. Thus in the Causses, the Cévennes and the Aubrac, where stock raising is the main livelihood, sheepfolds are a significant architectural feature, while in the plains of Bas Languedoc, the wine cellar *(chai)* is of primary importance.

Construction materials nearly always come from local sources, forging a further link between the house and its surrounding landscape. The following materials are used for roofing: volcanic lava, slate and schist slabs from the Cévennes, generally referred to as **lauzes**, as are the limestone slabs used in the Causses.

Nowadays, rural houses are adapting to new ways of life, showing the influence of new construction methods, and frequently suffering from the lack of craftsmen trained to rebuild or restore traditional constructions. Similarly, the evolution of agricultural techniques has had an impact on the appearance of the traditional rural cottage: there are fewer large lofts, now that grain is stored in silos.

Aubrac – A typical construction of this region is the **buron**, a solidly built hut of lava and granite with a single opening, found in the middle of pastureland generally standing on sloping ground near a spring. *Burons* are used as temporary living quarters by cowherds from May to October, while the cows are in their summer pastures. The huts are roofed in heavy stone *lauzes*, and inside they have a room used for both accommodation and cheesemaking, leading to a cellar, entirely hollowed out of the slope on which the *buron* stands, in which the cheese is left to mature. A few of these huts are still in use.

Causses – On the limestone *causses*, houses are grouped in hamlets on the banks of rivers or else scattered singly to be as close as possible to land suitable for cultivation. They are robust buildings, with thick walls and an outside staircase leading to the upper floor. The cistern, near the kitchen, is always an important feature in these areas where water is scarce. Dry, white limestone is used for both the walls and the roof. The house and the sheepfold, usually a vast low-lying rectangular building of rough-hewn stone, are two distinct buildings, sometimes quite far removed from one another. The house comprises a cellar and a tool room on the ground floor and living quarters on the first floor. In these regions where wind and lack of rain result in there being no trees of any great height, the traditional timber frame roof is replaced with a stone vault.

Cévennes – Typical of this area are solid mountain houses, built halfway down the valley sides and designed to withstand the rigorous climate. The walls and roofs are built of unevenly shaped schist, and the walls feature small window openings.
Depending on the region, the lintels, window frames and corner stones are built of sand- or limestone, which create a decorative contrast in colour. Timberwork is made from the wood of the chestnut tree.
The first floor, where the living quarters are located, is reached up a flight of stone steps which can sometimes look more like a bridge, if the house stands on sloping ground. The stable and barn are on the ground floor. The second floor was sometimes reserved for silkworm breeding. On the roofs covered with rough schist slabs *(lauzes)*, the only decorative feature is the chimneys. The roof ridge sometimes features schist slabs arranged on the slant (*à lignolets*).
East of the Cévennes, towards the Vivarais mountains, houses are more Mediterranean in style, with roofs of half-cylindrical brick tiles, or pantiles, and the characteristically wavy-edged cornices formed when such tiles are laid.
On the Lozère and Sidobre slopes, granite becomes a feature in walls and around window openings.

Espinouse range – Between the Lacaune mountain range and the Montagne Noire lie the Monts de l'Espinouse, cloaked in forests of beech, oak and chestnut, with intermittent patches of pastureland and broom-covered heath. The farmhouses typical of this region are protected by large slate tiles on the walls exposed to the prevailing, rainladen northwesterly winds. In Fraisse-sur-Agout, there are still one or two houses thatched with broom. The barn of the Prat d'Alaric farmstead is a large two-storey building (cowshed below, barn above), with walls built of granite and gneiss, a timber framework and a roof thatched with broom. Local barns typically feature gable walls with stepped edges. Each step is covered by a *lauze* laid so as to drain rainwater off to the sides.

Languedoc – Bas Languedoc, orientated towards its capital Montpellier and the sea, is the land of vineyards, exposed to the Mediterranean climate. Houses here are inhabited by wine-growers, and are characterised by their tiny windows designed to keep the inside of the house cool. The walls are traditionally plastered with a sand-based material, usually in shades of pink or ochre.
Haut Languedoc, with Toulouse as its capital, is a region of cereal crop farming. Its rich clay soils are reflected in the fact that buildings here are almost exclusively made of brick.
A feature shared by all Languedoc houses is their gently sloping roof, covered by curved brick pantiles.

Bas Languedoc – The main façade of houses in this region often has a triangular pediment. The residential part of the building is separated from the stable and the barn. The rectangular wine cellar *(chai)*, lit through semi-circular dormer windows, occupies the whole of the ground floor. There are two doors in the façade: a large round-arched doorway leading into the wine cellar, and a smaller entrance opening onto the staircase which leads to the first floor living quarters.

Haut Languedoc – In the Castres region, as in the region around Albi, walls are built entirely of brick, whereas in the eastern parts of Haut Languedoc brick is used only for framing doors and windows, and sometimes also decoratively arranged in horizontal bands beneath the cornice.
Many farms in Haut Languedoc boast a **dovecot**. Some are attached to the main farmhouse, but in most cases they are situated close by in some choice spot. In past centuries, pigeons were valued for their droppings, which were used to fertilise poor soils, and they were therefore a sign of special wealth or privilege.

Mediterranean Languedoc – Small dry-stone huts, known locally as **capitelles** or **cazelles**, can be seen dotted amidst the *garrigue* and vineyards of this region. The walls, generally circular, are built of blocks of schist or limestone, with a break for the doorway. The roof is formed by laying *lauzes* to overlap like the scales of a fish, and shifting them gradually inwards to meet, forming a corbelled roof vault capped by a single flat slab. These huts were used as shelters by shepherds or as stores for farming implements.

Mountain house in the Cévennes

House on the Causses

Farmhouse with balcony in the Rouergue

Barn thatched with broom (Monts de l'Espinouse)

Buron in the Aubrac

Wine-grower' houses (Hérault)

Small, square-shaped, dry-stone constructions known as **mazets**, with two-sided or pyramidal roofs, are to be found in wine-growing areas, in the Hérault *département*. They are used as shelters by those tending the vineyards, at lunchtime, during storms and sometimes overnight.

Rouergue – The walls are built of schist or granite rubble masonry. On the roof, covered with schist or slate *lauzes*, are dormer windows which make the main façade look as if it has pediments, thereby adding interest to the line of the roof. The houses are again laid out on several floors: on the ground floor, are the wine cellar and tool room; on the first floor, the living quarters. The attic is used for drying chestnuts. The space beneath the outside staircase leading to the living quarters is sometimes converted into a pigsty. If the farmer is comfortably off, his house will comprise several buildings (living quarters, stable, barn and a turret serving as a dovecot) standing round a courtyard which is entered through a gateway with a sloping roof.

Dotted here and there in the fields, are isolated small round dry-stone huts with conical roofs. These strange little buildings, which resemble the *bories* of Haute Provence, are used as shelters, barns or toolsheds. Dry-stone huts such as these are a common architectural feature of Jurassic limestone regions in general (although they are known by a wide variety of local names), where it was necessary to clear the ground of blocks of limestone to be able to cultivate it. The rocks were then used to build low stone walls and temporary shelters from the elements.

In the Lot valley, some of the barns feature roofs shaped like the keel of an upturned boat, thus increasing the amount of storage space available inside.

D. Hée/MICHELIN

Sculpted face and lion's head on Mirepoix's covered arcades

Traditions

The "Langue d'Oc"

The fusion of Vulgar Latin with the old Gallic language gave rise to a group of "Romance" languages, including in France the "langue d'Oïl" (in the north) and the "langue d'Oc" (in the south), depending on how *oui* was pronounced in each region. The border between the two lay north of the Massif Central. **Occitan** thus comprises several major dialects: those spoken in Languedoc, Gascony, Limousin, Auvergne and Provence.

The language of the troubadours – The language of Oc is above all the language of the troubadours, who flourished during the 11C to 13C. These were poets who composed their own songs and, together with jugglers, travelled round the courts of southern France, entertaining the nobility with their plaintive songs of unrequited love.

This poetry of "courtly love" evolved from the earthy, even faintly erotic lyrics of the 12C into a purely spiritual celebration of love, often embellished with references to the Virgin Mary. Famous troubadours include Bernard de Ventadour from the Limousin, who sang at the court of Raymond V of Toulouse, Peire Vidal, a lyricist given to extravagant images whose reputation stretched from

TALLANDIER

Peire Vidal

Provence to the Holy Land, Jaufré Rudel and Guiraut Riquier. The influence of the troubadours made itself felt as far away as Germany and Italy, where Dante is even said to have hesitated between Provençal and Tuscan when choosing in which language to write his *Divine Comedy*. At the same time, political satire, directed almost exclusively against Rome and the clergy, held a special place in Occitan literature.

Included in the tide of destruction unleashed by the Albigensian Crusade was the beginning of the decline of the Occitan tongue. There was an attempt to revive it in the early 14C, when a group of poets from Toulouse initiated the Jeux Floraux medieval poetry competition, but the Edict of Villers-Cotterêts in 1539, imposing Parisian French as the official language throughout France, dealt Occitan a heavy blow.

The reforms introduced to Provençal by Frédéric Mistral and the Félibrige in the 19C gave renewed impetus to the interest in reviving Occitan. Two organisations were founded in the early 20C (Escola Occitana in 1919 and the Institut d'Études Occitanes in Toulouse in 1945) with the aim of standardising as well as disseminating the language. A law was passed in 1951 allowing Occitan to be taught in schools and since 1969 it has been on the list of languages which it is possible to submit for examination at *baccalauréat* level.

Catalan – The Catalan language is very close to Occitan. It comes from the geographical area extending from Salses in Roussillon to Valencia in Spain, bounded to the west by Andorra and Capcir. Catalan was at its height during the 13C, a time when it became renowned through the writings of the poet and philosopher Ramon Llull. Like the language of Oc, it began to decline in the 16C, when the centralised monarchy of Philip II imposed Castilian Spanish, to the detriment of the other regional dialects. While Catalan is still spoken in everyday life, the literary renaissance begun in the 19C is contributing to the establishment of Roussillon's cultural identity.

Traditional crafts

The Cévennes, Rouergue, Causses and Languedoc, home to a host of tiny isolated villages in enchanting settings and quaint old town centres, in which traditional ways of life can still be upheld. have attracted numerous craftsmen who have set up their workshops here.

Revel has been famous for its fine furniture and marquetry ever since the cabinet-maker Alexandre Monoury went there from Versailles in 1889. It is also home to a variety of other craftsmen: weavers, gilders, lacquerers, sculptors on wood, bronze-smiths and blacksmiths. Wool-making and associated crafts have been centred around **Mazamet** since the middle of the 19C. From the late Middle Ages **Durfort** specialised in beating copper. Of the numerous hydraulic hammers set up along the River Sor, two dating from the 15C are still in operation. Traditionally the beaten copper is used to make pots and cauldrons. **Laguiole** is renowned for its elegant pocket-knives, with curved handles made of horn or some other natural material.

Fine kid gloves are made in and around **Millau**, while the **Cévennes** are the place to go for silk items since the revival of silk-farming in the region. The wood of the nettle tree is also used to make various items, such as pitchforks at **Sauve** (Gard). Glazed vases produced in **Anduze**, which adorn many a garden, have been renowned since the 17C. The sheep-bells which can be heard tinkling as the flock makes its way to the pastures in the mornings are more often than not the product of village workshops at Castanet-le-Bas or Hérpian in the Hérault valley.

Craft workshops remain numerous as we head south. From Albi to the Pyrenees, amid the diversity to be found as local natural resources change, the use of brick for both civil and religious architecture remains constant. Brickworks abound on the river plain of the Garonne, as well as along the Roussillon coast where there is a plentiful supply of red clay.

In the Albi region, **Graulhet** specialises in the production of leather for lining shoes, so there are a number of tanning workshops and other activities associated with the leather and shoe-making trades in the area. Dyer's woad *(Isatis tinctoria)* is still cultivated around **Magrin** and the resulting dye used to colour clothes and textiles shades of blue. Stone has been cut and polished in the Ariège region since the end of the 19C and **Saurat** is home to the last operational sandstone quarry as well as the last producer of mill-stones in France.

The **Bethmale valley** is a centre of production for traditional wooden *sabots*, made out of locally grown beech or birch, marked with a heart shape linked with the somewhat macabre legend of a local shepherd betrayed by his fiancée who returned from a confrontation with her and her new lover with their hearts nailed to his clogs. Horn combs are made in **Lavelanet**, near Foix, and the quality of their craftsmanship means that they retain their hold on the luxury end of the market against cheaper plastic competition.

In French **Catalonia**, typical crafts include the making of whips from the wood of the nettle tree at Sorède in the lower Tech valley, corks from the cork-oak in Roussillon, notably at Céret and Le Boulou, espadrilles at St-Laurent-de-Cerdans, the brightly coloured (predominantly red and yellow) Catalan textiles in cheerful geometrical designs, and the cutting and setting of garnets at Perpignan.

Rugby

The game of rugby was born in England in 1823 during a game of football at Rugby College when William Webb Ellis broke the rules in a moment of heightened tension and grabbed the ball with both hands. Rugby was not introduced to France until the early 20C and only really caught on in the southwest, perhaps because it strikes a particular chord with the robust Occitan temperament. It is now both played and followed with equally huge enthusiasm throughout the Pyrenees, where the strong sense of solidarity needed to make a successful team is to be found in every town and village community, with the result that defending the local team colours has become a matter of pride and honour. Despite the rough physical nature of the game, which is played to the full in true Occitan *"jusqu'au bout"* spirit, rivalry between teams lasts for the length of the match only and is laid aside immediately afterwards during the "third half", or lavish meal that the players eat together to round off the event.

Rules of the game – Rugby is played between two teams of 15 players, using an oval-shaped ball which can be carried or kicked. The aim is to score as many points as possible during two 40-minute halves with a break of five minutes at half-time. Each team consists of a full-back, four half-backs, a fly-half, a scrum-half and eight forwards. A **try** (5 points) is scored when a player succeeds in touching the ball down past the opposing team's goal line and a **goal** (3 points) is scored if a player kicks the ball over the cross-bar (3m/10ft high) of the opposing team's goal. A try can be "converted" by scoring a goal from a free kick to earn an extra 2 points. Players must only pass the ball back; if it is passed forward, the opposing forwards form a **scrum**, into which the scrum-half of the non-offending team throws the ball which the forwards then have to try to get into their team's possession by shoving and kicking. If the ball goes offside, there is a throw-in, when the players from both teams line up perpendicular to where the ball went off and have to try to catch the ball when it is thrown back into play.

In the region centred around Carcassonne, **rugby league**, a variation of rugby with teams of 13 players *(jeu à XIII)*, is played, earning itself the nicknames "heretic rugby" or "the Cathar sport".

Star teams – There is fierce competition for the French national rugby championships. Since they were first held in 1892, the **Championnats de France** have been won:
- 12 times by Toulouse (star player Jean-Pierre Rives)
- 11 times by Béziers
- 6 times by Perpignan
- 3 times by Castres
- twice by Narbonne (star players the Spanghero brothers)
- once each by Montauban, Carmaux and Quillan

The fact that rugby is much more popular and widespread a sport in the southwest than elsewhere in France is reflected in the French international rugby team (victor 10 times of the Five Nations Tournament and 4 times of the Grand Slam) which is made up almost entirely of players from southwest France. The most famous of these include Spanghero (Narbonne), Rives (Toulouse), and at the moment Castaignède and Christian Califano (both from Toulouse).

Recognising the teams:
- Toulouse   red and black strip
- Béziers   red and blue strip
- Perpignan   blue and white strip
- Narbonne   orange and black strip

Folklore and religious festivals

Local legends – There are numerous megalithic monuments to be found throughout the Languedoc region, many in the middle of nowhere. Their presence has often given rise to local superstitions reflected by the names they have been given: Planted Stone, Giant's Tomb, Fairies' Dwellings etc. The unusual shapes of many natural rock formations have also resulted in folk tales on their origins *(see the goose of the Sidobre, p 325)*.

Most villages have tales of animals that have been mysteriously bewitched – cows which no longer give milk, dogs which apparently lose their sense of smell. To guard against malevolent spirits, local people have frequently developed practices such as wearing clothes back to front or throwing salt on the fire. Myths such as that of the Bête du Gévaudan *(see p 22)* abound in regions where wild beasts preyed on livestock and even occasionally people.

Wild animals particular to a region, such as the Pyrenean bears, have had festivals dedicated to them, in this case the Fête de l'Ours held in the Vallespir region (Arles-sur-Tech, Prats-de-Mollo and St-Laurent-de-Cerdans) in late February/early March and again during the summer for the benefit of tourists.

Carnival time – In the Aude, carnival time traditionally begins during winter with the slaughtering of the pig. Children with masked or blackened faces go from house to house to ask for food. During this season when the status quo is thrown to the

Rugby

The tackle –
*Perpignan
vs Narbonne*

The throw-in –
Montauban vs Graulhet

The hand-off –
*Colomiers vs
Villefranche-
de-Lauragais*

The scrum pass –
Stade Toulousain

The drop goal –
Pamiers vs Albi

The try – *Argelès-
sur-Mer*

The penalty kick or
conversion – *Carcassonne*

R. Corbel

57

winds people dress back-to-front, or cross-dress, or dress up as babies or old people. A straw dummy is paraded round the village and made the scapegoat for all the misfortunes which have befallen the villagers, for which it is sentenced before a mock court held in the local *patois* before being hanged or burnt as punishment. The children dance around the fire.

One of the most famous carnivals in the region covered in this guide is that celebrated in Limoux. Every Sunday from January to March, as well as Shrove Tuesday and Ash Wednesday, people dressed as Pierrot figures dance slowly round Place de la République, beating time with sticks decorated with ribbons. They are followed by revellers in various disguises all acting the clown. The festivities last until nightfall, when the square is lit by resin torches. The climax of the carnival is the Nuit de la Blanquette, during which the Carnival King is burned.

Religious festivals – The most common religious festivals are those held in honour of the local patron saint or saints. For example, St Peter the patron saint of fishermen is honoured in Gruissan on 29 June. A bust of the saint is paraded around town behind a splendid float and the fishermen's standard. A Mass is celebrated with local fishermen at the local church, then the procession continues to the harbour where a floral wreath is cast into the water in memory of those lost at sea.

In Perpignan, on Good Friday, a procession is held by the Pénitents de la Sanch, a religious brotherhood dedicated to the Holy Blood, founded in the 15C by Spanish Dominican friar St Vincent to accompany people about to be executed along the final stage of their journey. These rather bizarrely dressed penitents, in long black or red robes with pointed hoods covering their faces, process to the sound of hymns through the streets of Perpignan to the cathedral, carrying *misteris* – painted or sculpted images of Scenes of the Passion of Christ.

Sardana – This dance is one of the most colourful of Catalan traditions. It is set to the music of an accompanying **cobla**, a special orchestra with a dozen or so original instruments (brass, wind and percussion) capable of evoking a range of emotions, from the most gentle to the most passionate. The dance itself involves different sequences of long and short steps and some fairly complicated footwork. The sight of the whirling dancers flourishing garlands during festivals or local competitions is one to be remembered (the *sardana* festival at Céret is the most famous). The grand finale of any such event is traditionally the *sardane de la fraternité* in which all the various teams join together to dance in circles.

Sardana competition at Argelès

Food and drink

ON THE MOUNTAIN PLATEAUX

Far from the coast, the region stretching from the Aveyron *département* to the Cévennes has developed a rich and flavoursome local cuisine, based largely around the livestock bred on the *causses*. The region is particularly famous for its cheeses: Fourme de Laguiole, a type of Cantal, which is used to make the local dish *aligot*; Bleu de Causses, a blue cheese also made from cow's milk; Pérail, small and strong, and the well-known Roquefort, both from ewe's milk; and Cabécou or Cévennes *pélardons* from goat's milk. Lamb from the *causses* is a delicious, but pricey, option for the main course. On the whole, local recipes use mutton or pork, as is usual in traditional peasant cooking. Offal (variety meat), such as tripe, also features widely on local menus: *tripoux de Naucelles* (tripe stewed in white wine with ham and garlic); *charcuterie* from Entraygues; sausages from St-Affrique and Langogne; *trénels de Millau* (sheep's tripe stuffed with ham, garlic, parsley and egg); *alcuit* from Villefranche-en-Rouergue (stewed chicken livers). Visitors to the Tarn should be sure not to miss *charcuterie* from the Montagne Noire, *bougnettes* from Castres (small, flat pork sausages) and cured hams and sausages from Lacaune. Fresh fish is hard to come by, apart from river trout, but recipes featuring salted or dried fish are common, such as *estofinado* (stockfish stew). Chestnuts are another traditional local ingredient, used in soups and stews or roasted and eaten whole with a glass of cider. For those with a sweet tooth, there are a number of interesting local sweetmeats such as *soleils* from Rodez (round yellow cookies flavoured with almonds and orange blossom), *fouaces* from Najac (*brioches* flavoured with angelica), Cévennes *croquants* (hard almond cookies) and *nènes* (small aniseed biscuits) from St-Affrique.

LANGUEDOC

The cuisine of the Languedoc is typical of the Mediterranean, using herbs from the *garrigues* (rosemary, thyme, juniper, sage, fennel), garlic and olive oil, with fresh vegetables such as aubergines, tomatoes, courgettes and peppers. There is a local garlic soup called *aigo boulido*, made with garlic, olive oil and thyme. Sometimes dishes will include snails, delicious wild mushrooms *(cèpes, morilles)* or even – as a special treat – truffles, found growing at the foot of the holm-oaks on the slopes of the Hérault and the Gard.

Most commonly, meat dishes involve mutton or pork, occasionally veal. Local game, which has fed on fragrant wild herbs, juniper berries and thyme all its life, has a delicious flavour, as do the lambs and sheep raised on the *causses*. They can be served in pies or stews. Cheeses from this region are mainly from goat's milk, very tasty when heated and served on a bed of lettuce. Near the coast, menus reflect the variety of seafood at hand: oysters and mussels from Bouzigues, *bourride sétoise* (fish stew from Sète), *gigot de mer de Palavas* (fish baked with garlic and vegetables), seafood pasties and the famous spicy little Clive Pies *(petits pâtés)* from Pézenas. In Montpellier, fish dishes are accompanied by *beurre de Montpellier*, a sauce of mixed herbs, watercress, spinach, anchovies, yolks of hard boiled eggs, butter and spices. Sweets include *oreillettes* (orange biscuits fried in olive oil), eaten in Montpellier at Epiphany and on Shrove Tuesday, or *grisettes* (candy made from honey, wild herbs and liquorice).

FROM TOULOUSE TO THE PYRENEES

Further west, towards Toulouse, and stretching from here south towards the Pyrenees, the rich local cuisine is that associated with the Périgord or southwest France in general. Goose and duck feature in many forms on local menus, either preserved as *confits*, or as *foie gras*, or in stews. Assorted *charcuterie* includes the delicious *saucisson sec* (a sort of local salami). Meat dishes are usually stews which have been allowed to simmer gently for hours. Undoubtedly the most famous dish from this region is **cassoulet** *(see CASTELNAUDARY)*. Vegetables include sweetcorn, olives, asparagus from the Tarn valley and the fragrant purple garlic from Lautrec. The Pyrenees produce a tasty ewes' milk cheese called *brebis*. Those with a sweet tooth should sample nougat from Limoux, *marrons glacés* (candied chestnuts) from Carcassonne or rosemary-scented honey from the Corbières.

Catalan cuisine – This is a typically Mediterranean cuisine, with its use of olive oil, and specialities such as garlic mayonnaise (*ail y oli* in Catalan, *aïoli* in French) and a paste made of anchovies, olive oil and garlic (*el pa y all*, or *anchoïade*). **Bouillinade**, the Catalan version of *bouillabaisse* (fish soup), and *civet de langouste au Banyuls* – spiny lobster stewed in Banyuls wine (dry Banyuls is very good for cooking, while the sweet variety goes well with creamy sweets and fruit salads) – make a delicious follow-up to a starter of Collioure anchovies. In Les Aspres,

escalade is a fragrant soup made with thyme, garlic, oil and egg. Mushrooms fried in oil with an olive sauce are eaten with game (partridge and hare). Catalan *charcuterie* includes such delicacies as black pudding (*boutifare* or *boudin*), pig's liver sausage, and cured hams and salami from the Cerdagne mountain. **Cargolade**, snails from the *garrigue* grilled over burning vine cuttings, frequently feature in the open-air meals which follow prayer retreats at the hermitages.

Sweets include *crème catalane* (*crème brûlée* with caramel), *bunyettes* (orange-flavoured doughnuts), *rousquilles* from Amélie-les-Bains (small almond biscuits) and the variety of fresh fruit from Roussillon's many orchards (peaches, pears, cherries and melons).

Nimetz/IMAGES PHOTOTHÈQUE

WINE

Coteaux du Languedoc – Wine-growers in the Languedoc vineyards, the main area for production of French table wine *(vins de table* and *vins de pays)*, are nowadays concentrating on improving grape varieties and the way they are blended, efforts which have been rewarded with an increase in the number of designated AOCs (Appellations d'Origine Contrôlée) in the region. Prime advantages of the Languedoc as a wine-growing region are the variety of its soil types (layers of schist, pebble terraces and red clay) and its Mediterranean climate.

Promoted to AOC in 1985, the **Coteaux du Languedoc** *appellation* includes red, rosé and white wines produced in the Hérault, Gard and Aveyron *départements*. Besides Faugères and St-Chinian, whose heady, powerful wines have won these areas their own AOC designations, the AOC has been awarded to particular vintages; for red and rosé wines: Cabrières, La Clape, La Méjanelle, Montpeyroux, Pic-St-Loup, St-Christol, St-Drézéry, St-Georges-d'Orques, St-Saturnin and Vérargues; for white wines: Picpoul-de-Pinet, aged in oak casks. The main grape variety cultivated in the region is the Carignan grape.

The Cabrières region also produces **Clairette du Languedoc**, a dry white wine made from the Clairette grape which has won an AOC.

Local table wine is sold under the label "Vins de pays d'Oc" or "Vin de Pays" followed by the name of the *département* it comes from.

Notable *vins doux naturels* from the Coteaux du Languedoc include Muscat de Frontignan, Muscat de Mireval and Muscat de Lunel.

Minervois – The vineyards of the Minervois AOC are situated on terraces clinging to the flanks of the Montagne Noire as the mountain range gradually drops down into the Aude valley. The Minervois region is reputed for its fine fruity red wines which are robust and well-balanced with a deep rich red colour. The St-Jean-du-Minervois vineyard, which occupies the limestone *garrigues* on the uplands in the northwest, produces a fragrant muscat dessert wine.

The vineyards of the Aveyron – Once a source of great wealth to the region, thanks to the work put in by the monks from Conques, the Aveyron vineyards are characteristically located on steep slopes where they stand out from the surrounding mountain landscape. The red wines of **Marcillac** (AOC) are well balanced with a hint of raspberry and go well with the tripe dishes of the Rouergue region.

The red wines from **Entraygues** and **Fel**, classified as VDQS (Vin Délimité de Qualité Supérieure – one step down from AOC), have plenty of substance and a good fruity flavour; the whites from these designations are lighter with more finesse. In the

Lot valley, the **Estaing** VDQS vineyards are cultivated on the valley sides up to an altitude of 450m/1 476ft and produce subtle, fragrant red wines and pleasant dry whites.

The sheltered sides of the Tarn valley between Peyreleau and Broquiès are home to the **Côtes de Millau** VDQS vineyards, which produce mainly red and rosé wine; **Cerno** is a local aperitif made from Côtes de Millau wine and herbal extracts.

Gaillac – The wines produced from the Gaillac vineyards, to the west of Albi, are officially classified as *Appellation d'Origine Contrôlée*. White wines are made using local grape varieties Mauzac, Len de Lel and Ondec which produce dry wines with a fragrant bouquet. There are three types of Gaillac white: sweet *(moelleux)*, very slightly sparkling *(perlé)* and sparkling *(mousseux)*. Gaillac red is made from traditional grapes such as Gamay, Syrah, Merlot and Cabernet, mixed with typically local varieties such as Braucol or Duras, for a robust wine, or Négrette. These wines are fruity and can be laid down.

Slightly further west, just north of Toulouse, **Côtes du Frontonnais** wines are produced from a very old grape variety, the Négrette, mixed with Cabernet, Syrah, Fer Servadou and Cot to give supple, fruity wines, which are best drunk young. Around Carcassonne, there are two AOCs: Cabardès, well-balanced with plenty of body, and Malepère, a fruity red wine. Both complement game and red meat perfectly.

Corbières and Roussillon wines – The **Fitou** *Appellation d'Origine Contrôlée* is reserved for a red wine from a certain area in the Corbières. Its alcohol content must be at least 12°, output is limited to 30hl per hectare/330gal per acre, and the wine must have been aged in a cellar for at least nine months. Fitou wines, produced from high quality grapes, are strong and full-bodied.

The **Corbières** *Appellation d'Origine Contrôlée* covers an area with a mixture of soil types, producing a varied range of wines. Besides red wines with a fine bouquet, production includes fruity rosés, and some dry white wines.

The Roussillon vineyards are noted for their high quality *vins doux naturels* (dessert wines), the **Côtes du Roussillon** and **Côtes du Roussillon Village** wines classified as *Appellation d'Origine Contrôlée*, and their robust, earthy local wines. Just north of Agde, the tiny village of Pinet produces a dry white wine called Picpoul de Pinet (from the Picpoul grape) which makes the perfect accompaniment to a dozen or so oysters from the nearby Bassin de Thau.

The *vins doux naturels* produced in this region represent the majority of French production of wines of this type. The grape varieties – Grenache, Maccabeu, Carignan, Malvoisie, among others – add warmth and bouquet to these wines. The warm local climate and the vineyards well-exposed to sunlight mean that these wines mature perfectly and have a high natural sugar content. The most famous examples are **Banyuls**, **Maury**, **Muscat de Rivesaltes** and **Rivesaltes**.

Blanquette de Limoux – This sparkling white wine is made from the Mauzac and Clairette grapes ripened on the slopes around Limoux, and is much in demand due to its fine quality.

Aligot

This tasty cheese and potato dish comes from the regions of Rouergue and Aubrac. Rub a casserole dish with garlic, then melt 150g/6oz butter and 150g/6oz cream over a high heat and gradually stir in 400g/14oz *tomme* or Cantal cheese cut into thin strips and 600g/1lb 4oz mashed potato. Using a strong, long-handled wooden spoon keep stirring the mixture *(quite hard work, can take up to 45min)*, always in the same direction so as not to break the strings of cheese. When the mixture is smooth and no longer sticks to the sides of the casserole, the *aligot* is ready to be eaten.

J. Blues/TOP

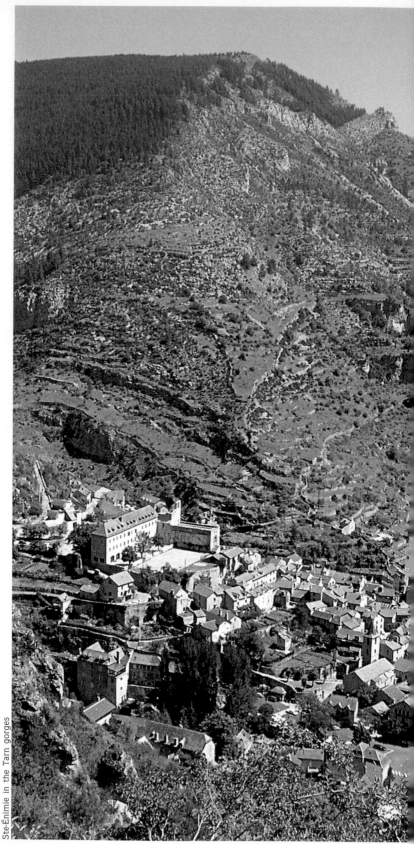

Ste-Énimie in the Tarn gorges

Sights

AGDE

Population 17 583
Michelin map 83 folds 15 and 16 or 240 folds 26 and 10

Agde, an ancient Ligurian settlement, was founded by the Phoenicians 2 500 years ago, and known initially as Agatha ("the good"). Trade with the Levant and the cultivation of vines and olive trees brought the town prosperity, and evidence suggests that it developed an advanced civilization. In the 5C, it was made an episcopal seat.

Trade through the town's port continued to thrive until the 12C, despite periods of economic setback (in the wake of Barbarian and Saracen invasions), but towards the end of the 18C it declined in the face of competition from Montpellier, Aigues-Mortes and, most of all, Sète. A more recent blow to the port has been the buildup of alluvial silt from the river Rhône, which means that nowadays boats have to travel 4km/2.5mi upriver to get to Agde harbour.

Agde is characterised by the dark grey (almost black) lava used in many of its buildings, which comes from the nearby Mont St-Loup, an extinct volcano. Against this somewhat sombre setting, the town's inhabitants, for the most part farmers, wine-growers or fishermen, go about their daily activities. Tourist trade blossoms during the summer months. Agde shares with neighbouring Sète the tradition of *joutes nautiques*, or jousting in boats, and the annual tournaments are enthusiastically followed by the townspeople.

SIGHTS

★ **Ancienne cathédrale St-Étienne** ⊙ – *Entrance via the chapel in Rue Louis-Bages.*
This fortified church was rebuilt in the 12C, probably to replace an earlier 9C Carolingian building. It was damaged during the Wars of Religion, after which it was restored in the 17C and again at the end of the last century. The rather forbidding appearance of the church, which looks more like a fortress, is emphasised by the black lava blocks from which it is built. The church walls are 2-3m/6.5-10ft thick and are crowned with crenellations and machicolations above small decorative arches. The 35m/113ft high bell-tower is a solid square machicolated keep, with a turret and bartizans at each corner (14C). In the 19C, the houses which concealed the west front, on the banks of the Hérault, were demolished, and a main doorway was added to the newly revealed façade.

The **interior** of the church consists of a nave covered with pointed barrel vaulting supported on a single transverse arch. Note the small round window in the vault through which those defending the church in times of siege could haul food and ammunition on a rope. The rectangular chancel is wider than the nave, making the ground plan of the church T-shaped. The chancel contains a 17C polychrome marble altarpiece. The two capitals on the columns supporting the triumphal arch carved into the marble are thought to have served originally for some other purpose. One of the most interesting of the church furnishings is the 18C marble pulpit.

Follow the signposts to the "Musée" through the old town of Agde.

Musée agathois ⊙ – This museum of local folk art and traditions occupies a Renaissance mansion which was converted to a hospital in the 17C – the hospital's old dispensary forms part of the exhibition. The extensive display of various artefacts, paintings, glazed earthenware and costumes (including a collection of local lace head-dresses known as *sarrets*) illustrates traditional livelihoods (seafaring, fishing, viticulture, crafts etc) and aspects of daily life in Agde.

The diversity of local history comes across well in this exhibition, which also incorporates reconstructions of the interiors of local houses, model boats, works by local artists, memorabilia of local seafarers, liturgical exhibits, votive offerings and a sizeable collection of amphorae from the ancient Greek port.

EXCURSIONS

Le Grau-d'Agde – *4km/2.5mi south. Take Quai des Chantiers, along the southeast bank of the river, leading into D 32.*
The road runs alongside the mouth of the river Hérault, which forms a sheltered harbour. Where the river flows into the Mediterranean, there is a fine sandy beach.

≜≜≜ **Le Cap d'Agde** – *5km/3mi southeast. Take Rue Ernest-Renan east from the town centre, then Rue de Brescou and continue on D 32ᴱ. Description of resort under CAP D'AGDE.*

The length of time given in this guide
- *for **touring** allows time to enjoy the views and the scenery*
- *for **sightseeing** is the average time required for a visit.*

Massif de l'AIGOUAL★★★

Michelin map 80 folds 5, 6, 15 and 16 or 240 folds 10 and 14

The Aigoual mountain massif is crisscrossed by a number of scenic roads, cuttir.
through the young forests which cloak the mountainside, or running along ridge.
from which there are splendid views. On the summit of the mountain is an
observation post with a tremendous panoramic view, weather permitting.
Breathtaking river gorges, such as those of the Dourbie, the Jonte and the Trévezel,
carve their way across the slopes of the massif, part of which falls within the
boundaries of the Parc national des Cévennes *(see p 24).*
From July 1944 onwards, the Aigoual massif played a role as the centre of the
important "Aigoual-Cévennes" resistance movement, which had its headquarters
at L'Espérou.

Salles/CAMPAGNE CAMPAGNE

Massif de l'Aigoual

GEOGRAPHICAL NOTES

A gigantic water tower – The Aigoual, a 1 567m/5 093ft high granite and schist
outcrop, is the highest peak in the southern Cévennes. It is also one of the major
water catchment areas in the Massif central, as clouds rolling in from the chilly
Atlantic converge with warm Mediterranean air currents right above the summit.
The resulting rainfall has earned the mountain its name: "Aiqualis" or "the watery
one". In an average year rainfall can measure up to 2.25m/over 7ft.
This rainwater drains off the mountain into two very different regions – the south
face towards the Mediterranean is riddled with deep river gorges and jagged rocky
ridges, whilst the gentler western slopes towards the Atlantic link the Aigoual
massif with the vast limestone plateaux known as the Causses.

Reafforestation on the Aigoual – Only a century ago, the mountain massif was
a sorry spectacle, bare of trees or any other vegetation. A reafforestation scheme
was launched in 1875 by **Georges Fabre**, head warden of the French Rivers Authority
and Forestry Commission. To add weight to his cause, he proved that much of the
sand clogging up the port of Bordeaux had been washed down from the Aigoual.
He obtained legal authorisation to purchase both communal and privately-owned
plots of land, on which he planted large stands of trees to replace the existing
straggly rows of trees along the river banks designed to prevent soil erosion. Despite
the hostility of some towns and villages which refused to part with their pasture
land, and the at times incendiary opposition of certain shepherds not averse to
setting fire to the young trees, Fabre gradually managed to restore the Aigoual to
its former forested glory.
Fabre did not content himself only with reafforestation, but developed the network
roads and footpaths which now covers the Aigoual, restored foresters' lodges,
up arboretums (such as that at l'Hort-de-Dieu – *see below*) for the study of
vth patterns in trees and built an observatory for meteorological research.

65

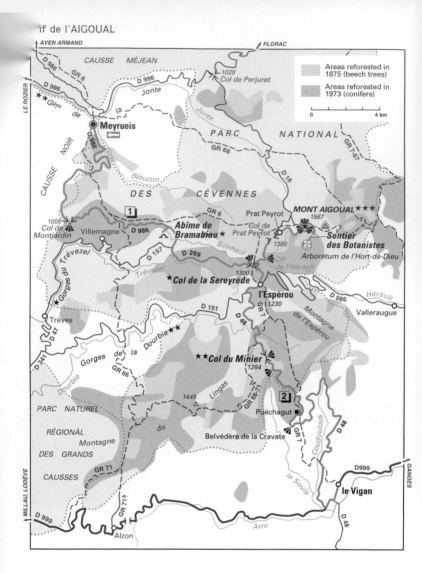

Map legend:
- Areas reforested in 1875 (beech trees)
- Areas reforested in 1973 (conifers)

0   4 km

Tour – The Aigoual lends itself ideally to exploration on foot. Two long-distance footpaths (Grande-Randonnée), the GR 6, from the Alps to the Atlantic, and the GR 7, from the Vosges to the Pyrenees, converge on the massif, where they branch off into numerous other paths. One of these, the GR 66 which runs right round the Aigoual, has a ramblers' guide devoted to it *(the Topo-Guide "Tour du Mont Aigoual"; see the Practical information section at the back of the guide for addresses of ramblers' associations).*

The route described below for travellers by car covers the whole Aigoual massif and leads to the summit itself. We recommend following it from Meyrueis to Le Vigan, as the particularly spectacular stretch of road across the Minier pass and down to the Arre valley is best appreciated when travelling downhill.

NB Between November and May the roads may be blocked by snow.

1 THE WESTERN SLOPES

From Meyrueis to the Aigoual summit *32km/20mi - allow 3hr*

Meyrueis – This small town on the confluence of the rivers Bétuzon, Brèze and Jonte perches at the mouth of the Jonte river gorge, where the Causse Noir, the Causse Méjean and the Aigoual massif all converge. Its clear mountain air (due to its altitude of 706m/2 316ft) and the many and varied attractions which surround it make the town a popular holiday destination. Strolling along Quai Sully beneath the plane trees by the river bank and exploring the network of smaller streets, look out for the Maison Belon, with its elegant Renaissance windows, and the **Tour de l'Horloge**, a clock tower once part of the town's fortifications.

Leave Meyrueis on D 986 south.

Just after leaving Meyrueis take a small road on the left as far as a car. A 15min walk along a forest path brings you to the 15-16C **Château de Roqued**, a massive square castle flanked by four round towers. The pink and ochre t of the stone stand out against the green backdrop of the Bétuzon valley. Ins there is a lovely Renaissance staircase and some fine antique furniture, as v as old horse-drawn carriages and a model of the Aigoual. The château is t property of the Parc national des Cévennes and houses an **information centr** overlooking the main courtyard.

Return to D 986.

The road up to the Col de Montjardin initially runs through forest along the west bank of the Bétuzon, before climbing along the edge of the Causse Noir. From the pass there is a good view of this plateau and that of Larzac and, shortly afterwards, of the Aigoual and Espérou peaks. The road then enters a forest, largely of larch trees, and follows a dizzying course cut into the rock face, offering delightful views *(right)* of the old mines for silver-bearing lead ore in Villemagne. Further along on the right is the curious rocky cirque known as "l'Alcôve" in which the Bramabiau tumbles down as a waterfall, having flowed across the Camprieu plateau underground.

★ **Abîme de Bramabiau** - *See Abîme de BRAMABIAU.*

Just past the "Alcôve" is the junction with the D 157, which leads off to the **Gorges du Trévezel**★ *(see Vallée de la DOURBIE).* Carry straight on, across the small Camprieu plateau, to the north bank of the Trévezel, where the road plunges into the reafforested area on the Aigoual slopes (beeches and conifers).

★ **Col de la Sereyrède** - This pass is situated 1 300m/4 265ft above sea-level, astride the Atlantic-Mediterranean watershed. Beneath the pass lies the valley of the Hérault, which flows east towards the peaks of the Cévennes towering in the distance. From the back of the Maison de l'Aigoual information centre there is a good view of the Bonheur valley.

The Col de la Sereyrède was once part of the great **"draille du Languedoc"**, or wide sheep trail used for transferring flocks from summer to winter pastures, which until not so very long ago would be milling with sheep every June making their annual trip from the Languedoc *garrigues* up to summer pastures on the Aubrac plateau, or the slopes of Mont Lozère or La Margeride. *(The path of the old "draille" can be followed to the north along D 18 and to the south along the GR 7 as far as the town of L'Espérou, where the track turns off towards Valleraugue.)* Such sheep tracks, some of which are still in use, are much in evidence, recognisable by the deep channels they cut into the Cévennes ridges. Nowadays, most of the 25 000 head of sheep are taken up to their summer pastures by lorry. Some herds are still driven up to L'Espérou on foot on the occasion of the Fête de la Transhumance every summer in mid-June.

The road leading from the Col de la Sereyrède to the Aigoual summit offers some spectacular views over the Hérault valley, along which runs the winding road to Valleraugue. Nearer the summit, the road re-enters the forest.

Sentier des Botanistes - *1.5km/1mi below the summit, a signpost indicates the start of the trail; 20min walk.*

This trail loops round the Trépaloup peak for 1km/0.6mi and overlooks the **Hort-de-Dieu** (literally, "God's garden"), an arboretum founded by the botanist Charles Flahault, assisted by Georges Fabre, to study growth patterns in tropical trees. From the footpath there are some marvellous views of the south face of the Aigoual with its craggy ridges, the Cévennes peaks beyond, and the forest-covered east slopes of the Aigoual. From the summit itself, the view takes in the Cévennes range and the Causse Méjean.

★★★ **Mont Aigoual** - The view from the summit is at its clearest during the winter months (January) – some people have reported seeing both Mont Blanc and the Maladetta on the same visit. In the summer, the panorama is often obscured by haze, so tourists are advised not to visit the summit during the hottest hours of the day. Particularly intrepid visitors might like to make their ascent in the early hours of the morning in time to see the sunrise from the summit. Weather permitting, this is a breathtaking spectacle; the view at daybreak is generally best in September.

The **meteorological observatory** built on the summit (alt 1 567m/5 141ft) in 1887 by the French Rivers Authority and Forestry Commission is currently occupied by the French meteorological office (Météo France). The site, overlooking the Gard, Hérault and Tarn valleys, is ideal. Increasingly sophis-ticated instruments enable researchers to record, among other things, the peed and direction of winds which herald either torrential Mediterranean wnpours, flattening anything in their path, or the kinder Atlantic rainfall ponsible for the region's lush green vegetation. A centre for testing all the pment under extreme conditions has just been set up in the observatory.

de the observatory is an interesting exhibition, **Exposition Météo-France** ⊙, on
ather forecasting past and present, with a section on the French Météotel
stem, which processes satellite images for weather reports.
om the viewing table at the top of the observatory tower the **panorama**★★★
encompasses the Causses and the Cévennes and, in fine weather, the Cantal
range, Mont Ventoux, the Alps, the Languedoc plain, the Mediterranean and the
Pyrenees.
In the summer, the Parc national des Cévennes organises guided walks *(1hr)*
round the summit.

② THE SOUTH FACE

From the Aigoual summit to Le Vigan
39km/24mi – allow 1hr 30min local map p 66

Return to the Col de la Sereyrède.

Just before the pass, to the left of the road, the waterfall formed by the sprightly
young Hérault can be seen in a ravine on the far side of the valley.

L'Espérou – This small, south-facing town lies amidst wood and pasture land.
Its picturesque mountain setting (alt 1 230m/4 035ft), well-protected from
northerly winds, and the ski slopes at **Prat-Peyrot** make it a popular holiday
destination in both summer and winter.

★★ **Col du Minier** – This pass is 1 264m/4 147ft above sea-level. In fine weather,
you can see as far as the Mediterranean. A memorial stone commemorates **Général
Huntziger** (Commander of the French IIe Armée in Sedan) and his colleagues killed
in an air crash in November 1941.
As the vertiginous cliff road begins its long, steep drop down the south face of
the Aigoual, it overlooks the deep Souls ravine, giving a magnificent view of the
Montdardier plateau and the Séranne range further south. It then passes through
a broken and chaotic granite rock formation.
The road passes the **Puéchagut** forester's lodge to the right, surrounding which
there is another arboretum for the study of tropical forest species. Then the
road curves sharply left, round the Belvédère de la Cravate, from which can be
seen a panoramic view of the Arre valley in the foreground, the Larzac plateau,
the Séranne range, the St-Loup peak and beyond towards the Mediterranean.
Further on, the road overlooks the Coudoulous valley, its sides thick with
chestnut trees, before crossing countryside more Mediterranean in character
(vines, mulberry bushes, olive and cypress trees) to reach Le Vigan.

Le Vigan – *See Le VIGAN.*

ALBI★★★

Conurbation 64 359
Michelin map 80 fold 11 or 82 fold 10 or 235 fold 23
Plan of the conurbation in the current Michelin Red Guide France

Albi's enormous cathedral-cum-fortress towers above the rooftops of the red-brick
town, dwarfing all else. Albi "la rouge" lies on the banks of the Tarn, which flows
at a sedate pace now that it has left the last foothills of the Massif Central. This
charming, friendly town is at its most appealing when seen from the 11C **Pont Vieux**★
(**Y**), or when strolling around the old town, along narrow, winding streets lined with
attractive old houses.
Next to Old Albi, the modern city is clearly laid-out, with wide, busy roads. The lively
squares, Places du Vigan and Jean-Jaurès, testify to Albi's commercial role as an
agricultural market town, which was at the height of its importance during the
mid-15C to mid-16C, the golden age of dyer's woad (the blue dyestuff obtained
from the leaves of the *Isatis tinctoria* plant). Albi, with Carcassonne and Toulouse,
formed the triangle which delimited the "Pays de Cocagne" (land of milk and honey)
in which dyer's woad was produced, and the many beautiful Renaissance mansions
in the old town are evidence of the economic and artistic boom created by the textiles
and dyeing industries. Modern industries (steel, man-made textiles, glass ware,
electronics) were linked for many years with the coal seams north of the town
around Carmaux.

River Tarn – On its way through the Albigeois region, the river Tarn waters th
vineyards from which Côtes du Tarn wines are produced. Downstream of Rabaster
it flows into the Bas-Quercy region, in which the Aveyron, Tarn and Garonne riv
characterised by their broad valleys, all converge. The alluvial plain of the
spreads generously between the hills on either side of the valley, its rich, f
soil cultivated with a wide variety of crops: wheat, corn, tobacco, early vege
and orchards.

OUT AND ABOUT IN ALBI

Tourist information – There are three tourist walks around Albi: the Purple Walk *(circuit Pourpre)* explores the heart of medieval Albi with its wealth of historical sites, personalities and monuments; the Gold Walk *(circuit Or)* retraces Albi's evolution over 20 centuries of history; and the Blue Walk *(circuit Azur)* leads along the banks of the Tarn to admire the views of the town from there. Details from the tourist office: Palais de la Berbie, place Ste-Cécile, ☎ 05 63 54 22 30.

Bars and restaurants – The centre of Albi for socialising is Place du Vigan, which remains lively day and night with its terrace-cafés (**Le Pontié** and **Le Grand Café de la Poste**). **Café de la Préfecture** attracts a younger clientele. Traditional local cuisine can be found in restaurarunts along rue Toulouse-Lautrec, for example at **Vieil Alby** where tripe cooked to an Albi recipe is on the menu.

Entertainment – Albi has a **Carnival** in March, which is when a post card fair (**Salon de la Carte postale**) is also held. **Albi-jazz** takes place in May, and the **Festival de musique** (classical, opera, jazz) in July (☎ 05 63 49 48 80). A motor rally (**Grand Prix Automobile d'Albi**) is held in September.

Markets – There is a large market held in Place Ste-Cécile on Saturdays, with fruit, vegetables, poultry, *foies gras* (in season), wild mushrooms, pink garlic from Lautrec, *charcuterie* from Lacaune and wines from the Gaillac region. A health-food market is held on Tuesdays from 5pm to 7pm in the Jardin National.

Shopping – A number of streets in Old Albi are for pedestrians only and are home to antiques shops and smart boutiques (rue de l'Hôtel de Ville), or more everyday shops and restaurants (rue Ste-Cécile). Food shops are concentrated around Place du Marché. Besides *foies gras* and *confits*, visitors should try **jeannots** (aniseed cookies), **gimblettes** and **briques albigeoises** (types of confectionery), on sale at Boulangerie-pâtisserie J.-P. Galy, rue Toulouse-Lautrec, among other places.

HISTORICAL NOTES

An ecclesiastical centre – In the Middle Ages, the temporal power of the Roman Catholic bishops and the influence of Catharism grew apace.
In the wake of the Council of Lombers, which had been convened in 1176 to condemn Cathar doctrine, the Albigensian Crusade launched in 1209, the Treaty of Meaux in 1229 and the setting up of the Inquisition, the bishops became lords in all but name, constantly involved in legal or military wrangles. They did, however, find time to patronise the arts as well. **Bernard de Combret**, bishop from 1254-71, began construction of an episcopal residence, the Palais de la Berbie, and **Bernard de Castanet** (1276-1308) undertook that of the cathedral of Ste-Cécile, at least until he was forced to retire to a monastery because his abuse of power was so blatant it outraged the pope. **Louis d'Amboise** (1473-1502) was compelled to step down in his turn, after a lengthy and luxurious period in office, because of incessant quarrels with members of his flock.
Albi was elevated to an archbishopric in 1678.

The "Albigensians" – This was the name given in the 12C to followers of Catharism – an academic term not used at the time – since Albi was the first place to offer them refuge. The name may also derive from an episode that took place in Albi, when the townspeople saved some of the heretics from the stake. *For further information on the Cathars, see the Introduction.*

The Albigensian crusade – When Giovanni Lotario became Pope **Innocent III** in 1198, he resolved to stamp out this heresy of "the pure ones", which he saw as a threat to established Roman Catholic doctrine and institutions. Representatives of the Holy See travelled the length and breadth of the country in their efforts to denounce Catharism. Moves were made to defrock priests and bishops whose dissolute lifestyles were driving their disillusioned congregations to convert to Catharism. St Dominic went round preaching, performing miracles and renouncing worldly goods, like the Cathar "Parfaits". However, Cathar influence continued to spread throughout the Languedoc, as people from all walks of life, from labourers to landlords, embraced it. Things came to a head in 1208, when the Papal Envoy, Pierre de Castelnau, was assassinated near St-Gilles. Innocent III promptly excommunicated the Count of Toulouse, accusing him of having been an accomplice, and raised crusading army to rid the country of its heretics.
1209, **Simon de Montfort** was put in charge of the crusade. First Béziers was pillaged its townspeople massacred, Carcassonne was next to fall, followed by Bram, erve and Lavaur in turn. Finally, in 1229, the **Treaty of Meaux** (or Paris) declared nd to the crusade and placed the Languedoc region under the aegis of the French

arch. However, twenty years of bloody slaughter failed to stamp out the gensian heresy altogether; it took the Inquisition and the massacre at ntségur in 1244 to finish it off once and for all.

enri de Toulouse-Lautrec – The famous artist was born son of Comte Alphonse e Toulouse-Lautrec Montfa and Adèle Tapié de Celeyran, a German cousin, at the Hôtel de Bosc in Albi in 1864. Two childhood accidents, in 1878 and 1879, left him crippled for life, a diminutive figure on stunted legs.

In 1882, Toulouse-Lautrec set up home in Montmartre, where he immersed himself in the seamier side of Parisian life. He frequented bars, nightclubs, brothels and racecourses, and quickly developed a unique artistic style as he sketched the scenes around him, capturing the atmosphere of a social milieu of poverty and loose living remarkably vividly. From 1891 onwards, his posters appeared on more and more Parisian walls, as his skill as a lithographer won him fame. By 1899, his alcoholism and debauched lifestyle had reduced him to such a state, that he was interned for a while in a sanatorium in Neuilly. Once he had recovered, he was released but soon fell back into his old ways, despite the vigilance of his friend Paul Viaud. On the verge of collapse, he left Paris in 1901 and died in the family château at Malromé, near Langon in the Gironde, on 9 September of that year. He is buried at the cemetery in Verdelais.

★★★ CATHÉDRALE STE-CÉCILE ⊙ (Y) *45min*

The Catholic church had to move fast to reestablish its authority in the wake of the Albigensian crusade. Bishop Bernard de Combret began the construction of an episcopal palace in 1265, and Bernard de Castenet began that of the cathedral in 1282. This was intended to symbolise the church's newly found grandeur and power, since events had shown that faith occasionally needs to be backed up with physical force. For this reason, the cathedral of Ste-Cécile was designed as a fortress. The great monument was structurally completed in a century, with successive bishops then contributing to the finishing touches.

To get a better idea of the massive proportions of the cathedral, take a look at it from a distance, from the bridge across the Tarn (the Pont du 22-Août), or from one of the streets of Old Albi which open onto the cathedral square.

Exterior

In the immediate vicinity of the cathedral, it is hard to stand back sufficiently to appreciate its enormous dimensions; it is, quite simply, huge. The sheer, red brick walls, once crowned by a tiled roof resting on the vaulting at the level of the windows (where there is now a row of white stone gargoyles), have been surmounted since 1849 by a band of false machicolations, a rampart walk and bell turrets. The architect, César Daly, designed this new roof, as the weight of the old one was too much for the vaulted roof structure of the nave, with its magnificent painted ceiling. The severity of the sheer brick walls is mitigated to a degree by the curve of the engaged half-turrets, extensions of interior buttresses, between the windows.

Doorway and canopy porch – The main entrance is in the south side of the cathedral, through a 15C doorway (built by Bishop Dominique de Florence, depicted kneeling), linking the building to an old defence tower, and up a grand flight of steps to an elaborate, carved stone canopy which forms the porch. This work of art was added under Louis I of Amboise, and the extravagant, intricate decoration contrasts markedly with the austerity of the brick façade. The six statues in niches, two on each side of the canopy, are representations of local saints: above the entrance stairway are St Carissime *(above)* and St Salvy *(below)*; facing south are St Ségolène and St Amarand; and facing west are St Martiane and St Eugène.

Bell-tower – The original tower was a square, keep-like structure about the same height as the nave. Between 1485 and 1492, Louis I had three more storeys added. The corners on the east side of the tower, where it adjoins the church, are adorned by two turrets running to the full height, while those on the west side have decorative turrets only up to the level of their first storey, giving the tower a somewhat lop-sided appearance.

Interior

Turn left as you enter the cathedral and go and stand to one side of the organ at the west end, looking towards the east end. To picture what the original cathedral looked like, imagine the building without the ornate rood screen halfway down, or the gallery added in the 15C which cuts across the line of the side chapels. This would leave a vast nave with pointed vaultin no transept and supported by interior buttresses with side chapels betwe them.

ALBI – Rood screen in the cathedral of Ste-Cécile (16C)

The **rood screen** was designed to separate the chancel (reserved for the clergy) from the nave (where the congregation gathered) and carry the Crucifix (rood). This example in Albi is typical of the Flamboyant Gothic style.

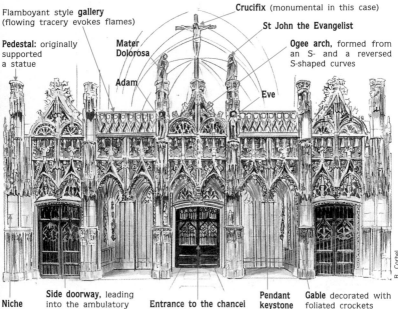

Flamboyant style **gallery** (flowing tracery evokes flames)

Crucifix (monumental in this case)

St John the Evangelist

Pedestal: originally supported a statue

Mater Dolorosa

Ogee arch, formed from an S- and a reversed S-shaped curves

Adam

Eve

Niche

Side doorway, leading into the ambulatory

Entrance to the chancel

Pendant keystone

Gable decorated with foliated crockets

R. Corbel

Chancel – The church was consecrated in about 1480. At around the same time, Louis I of Amboise decided to build the chancel, closed off by a carved stone rood screen★★★. The resulting magnificent work of art, a consummate example of late Flamboyant Gothic decoration, has often been compared with a piece of lacework. It is a mass of skilfully interlaced motifs, pinnacles and arches, with richly ornate pendant keystones.

Just above the central doorway in the rood screen, on the ceiling vault, note the representations of St Cecilia *(north side)* and her husband St Valerian *(for further details on the ceiling, see "Cathedral vault" below).*

The central and side doorways are elegantly carved from wood, with remarkably intricate iron doorlocks, beautifully wrought by hand. Of the 96 statues which adorned the rood screen until the French Revolution, only 6 remain: Christ crucified, with the Virgin Mary to his right and St John to his left, and further down Adam and Eve. Behind the central crucifix, on the side of the rood screen facing into the choir *(only visible from inside the choir),* is a statue of St Cecilia, holding an organ and the palm of martyrdom.

Go through the south door in the rood screen to the ambulatory.

The great choir takes up half the chancel, entirely in keeping with the pomp and ceremony with which the chapter carried out its religious offices. The carved stone screen running round the outside of the choir consists of ornate ogee arcading with Flamboyant tracery and the Chi-Rho Christogram. Against each of the pillars between the arches stands the polychrome statue of an Old Testament figure (33 statues in all – the age of Christ when he died) including the major and minor prophets, kings of Judah and other characters. These statues in the chancel of Albi cathedral are one of the best examples of the naturalism of Gothic sculpture in France. A comparison of the style of the various statues suggests that they are the work of at least two different schools. The influence of the Burgundian school can be seen in the realistic facial expressions, the slightly heavy folds of the clothing and the sturdiness of the figures. Particularly interesting statues include those of Judith (**1**), the prophets Zephaniah (Sophonias) (**2**), Isaiah (**3**) and Jeremiah (**4**), and, in the north ambulatory, Esther (**5**).

Inside the choir, the statues of Charlemagne (**6**) and the Emperor Constantine (**7**) look down from above the entrance doorways. If you stand facing the high altar, the rich colours of the paintings on the walls of the ambulatory chapels can be seen through the openwork of the choir screen. The statues inside the choir (on the inside of the pillars from the Old Testament figures) depict characters from the New Testament; the Virgin Mary (**8**) occupies place of honour

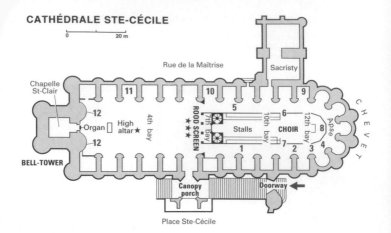

CATHÉDRALE STE-CÉCILE

0   20 m

Rue de la Maîtrise

Sacristy

Chapelle St-Clair

11   **10**   **9**

5

12

4th bay

High altar★

Organ

12

ROOD SCREEN

7th bay

Stalls

CHOIR

6

10th bay

12th bay

Apse

8

1

7

2   **3**   **4**

C H E V E T

BELL-TOWER

Canopy porch

Doorway ←

Place Ste-Cécile

behind the high altar, with St Paul on her right and St John the Baptist on her left, and then the 12 Apostles, holding bands inscribed with the Creed, distributed on either side. There are two rows of magnificently carved oak choir stalls, beneath a frieze of cherubim alternating with red or blue painted stone panels decorated with gilded arabesques. *(See "Cathedral vault" below for details of the ceiling decoration.)*

The five stained glass windows around the apse date from the 14C and were restored in the 19C. Note the chapel of the Sainte-Croix (**9**), in the north of the ambulatory, which contains frescoes depicting scenes from the lives of the Emperor Constantine and St Helena.

Return to the main body of the church.

Above the west end of the cathedral, the monumental **organ**, built 1734-6 by Christophe Moucherel and last restored in 1981, is best admired from level with the rood screen. It consists of two distinct levels, one above the other, supported by a pair of atlantes. The elegant wooden organ loft is beautifully decorated with statues of cherubs playing musical instruments and, above them, St Cecilia and St Valerian.

Below the organ stands the new **high altar★** (consecrated in 1980), a black marble creation by Jean-Paul Froidevaux. It is decorated with brightly coloured enamels, depicting a vine on three sides and St Cecilia on the fourth. A text from St Matthew's Gospel, on the mystery of the Eucharist, is inscribed around the altar.

The side chapels are of mixed interest. Note in particular the chapel by the north entrance to the ambulatory (**10**), which contains a 16C painting of the Holy Family *(right wall)*, and the chapel "du Rosaire" (**11**), in which there is an ornate triptych by the Sienese school. The monumental pulpit on the south side of the church was built by Mazetti and Maderni in 1776.

The Last Judgment (**12**) – This enormous mural painting at the west end of the cathedral, decorating the plaster wall beneath the organ, was executed in the late 15C, but was unfortunately stripped of its entire central panel, and most importantly of the focal image of Christ, when the chapel of St-Clair was added to the cathedral in 1693.

The scene was painted in tempera, that is colour pigment ground and mixed with egg yolk and glue, unlike the fresco scenes painted on the cathedral vault. The brick wall beneath the painting, caught in the play of light from time to time, adds to the delicacy of touch and clarity of detail of the whole. It is possible that this painting was intended to compensate for the lack of sculpture on the west front, which is traditionally reserved for scenes of the Last Judgment in cathedral design.

The composition is in three tiers. Across the top, Heaven is represented by a band of angels. In the centre and to the right of where Christ would have been *(ie to the left as you look at it)* are the heavenly elect in three rows: on top, the Apostles wearing white robes and crowned with golden haloes; beneath them the saints, some of whom are obviously of quite high rank, who have been judged already and allowed to enter Heaven; and below them, those newly resurrected dead judged fit to join the ranks of the blessed, who are still facing the Judge Eternal holding out the books of their life story. In contrast to this serene group the cringing damned *(to the right as you look)* are being hurled into the darkne of Hell. Above them, between them and the angels representing Heaven, th is only a dark, cloudy void, symbolising the unbreachable gap that their sins h created between them and the Heavenly Father. The bottom tier of the pair depicts, in vivid detail, the various punishments Hell has to offer those who have broken any of the Seven Deadly Sins. The hideous tortures are clearly devised to reflect the particular vice to which the sinners were prone. From left to right, we see the proud, the envious, the angry, (the slothful disappeared when the opening to the chapel was made), the greedy, the gluttonous and the lustful. Once this masterpiece was completed, the French artists left the cathedral of Ste-Cécile, so Louis II of Amboise called in Italians to decorate the walls and ceiling vault.

Cathedral vault – The Bolognese artists who embellished the austere nave of the cathedral with dazzling paintings drew on the splendours of the golden age of the Italian Renaissance, the Quattrocento (15C). The effect of the white and grey ornamental foliage, highlighted in gold, on an azure background is most striking.

Many portraits of saints and Old Testament figures adorn the vault, which consists of twelve bays, each divided by the ribbing into four concave triangular sections (a real challenge to the artists' techniques of perspective). In the fourth bay along from the bell-tower, the triangular section to the west depicts Christ showing his wounds to Thomas, while that to the east contains the Transfiguration. In the seventh bay along *(above the rood screen)*, to the east of St Cecilia and St Valerian, there is the Annunciation. The tenth bay along *(above the great choir)* is sumptuously decorated with the Parable of the Wise and Foolish Virgins *(west)* and the Coronation of the Virgin against the backdrop of a magnificent gold glory surrounded by cherubim and seraphim *(east)*. Finally, above the beginning of the apse *(twelfth bay along)* the Christ of the Apocalypse is depicted in a gold mandorla, surrounded by angels, cherubim and seraphim and the symbols of the four Evangelists.

★PALAIS DE LA BERBIE (Y) *2hr*

The initiative to build an episcopal palace near the 12C cathedral (no longer extant) was taken by Bernard de Combret in about 1265. The name "Berbie" is derived from *bisbia* or "bishopric" in local dialect. Bernard de Castenet transformed the original building into a fortress, adding a massive keep and a fortified curtain wall. The size of this is best appreciated from the terrace on the banks of the Tarn. Although designed initially to protect the entrance to the keep, the wall has undergone alterations over the centuries. In the late 17C, the old parade ground was turned into a flower garden, and a hexagonal roof was added to the west tower. The rampart walk was transformed into a shaded path lined with marble statues of Bacchus and the Four Seasons (18C). The eastern wing of the building, with a slate roof, dates from the end of the 15C. Louis I of Amboise added pepperpot roofs to the turrets, with elegant stone dormer windows to let in the light. All but one of these have disappeared. After the proclamation of the Edict of Nantes in 1598, there was no further need for a fortress. The towers of the Berbie palace were levelled, the west curtain wall demolished and the north tower of the keep reduced in height. Prelates subsequently concentrated on the interior. Since 1922, the palace has housed the Musée Toulouse-Lautrec, a museum founded by a lifelong friend of the painter, Maurice Joyant.

★★ **Musée Toulouse-Lautrec** ⓥ – A grand 17C staircase leads *(left)* to a gallery of archeological exhibits (**20**) on the first floor; note the tiny, 20 000 year old *Vénus de Courbet* (Upper Perigordian era) discovered at Penne in the Tarn *département (3rd display case on right).*
The 13C chapel of Notre-Dame (**2**) has ribbed vaulting and colourful décor by the Marseille artist Antoine Lombard. Bishop Le Goux de la Berchère (1687-1703) commissioned the seven panels bearing his coat of arms.

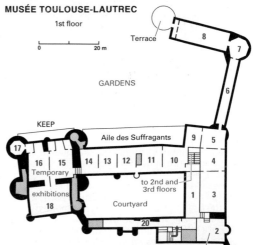

MUSÉE TOULOUSE-LAUTREC

1st floor

Terrace

GARDENS

KEEP

Aile des Suffragants

Temporary

to 2nd and
3rd floors

exhibitions

Courtyard

Chapelle Notre-Dame

The following series of rooms were fitted out in the 17C. Gallery (1) contains copies of works by Georges de la Tour. The spacious Salon Daillon du Lude (3) has a handsome French style ceiling, where the beams and rafters are left visible and are enhanced with painted decoration, and contains among others a painting by Guardi and works by La Tour.

The exhibition of the **Toulouse-Lautrec collection** itself begins in room (4), given over to portraits of the artist by his contemporaries; note in particular the full-face portrait by Javal, which captures the dignity in Toulouse-Lautrec's gaze, and the full-length portrait by Vuillard, which shows clearly his stunted physique. The museum at Albi houses the most comprehensive collection of the artist's works, bequeathed to the city by the Comtesse Alphonse de Toulouse-Lautrec, his mother, in 1922 and augmented by donations from other members of his family. Room (5) and the long gallery (6) contain early works, which bear witness to the artist's overriding interest in animals and people. *Artilleur sellant son cheval*, of a soldier saddling his horse, is an outstanding example of work executed by Toulouse-Lautrec at the age of only 16. Many of the works evoke his mother's estate at Celeyran (near Narbonne), where the artist often went to stay. During the course of the visit, notice the variety of signatures he used: Henri de Toulouse-Lautrec, Montfa, monograms like HL or HTL, Tréclau (anagram of Lautrec) written in an elephant, a mouse or a cat. The circular room at the end of the gallery (7 – drawings) and the following large room (8 – paintings) contain famous portraits and works, mainly evoking Toulouse-Lautrec's life in Montmartre. Subjects include Suzanne Valadon, mother of Utrillo, as *La Buveuse ou "Gueule de Bois"*. *L'Anglaise du Star*, one of Toulouse-Lautrec's most famous portraits, is a reminder of one occasion in Le Havre, when the artist had to send to Paris for his painting materials in order to capture the smile of blonde "Miss Dolly", a pretty English barmaid he had met in one of the bars by the port, before catching his usual boat to Bordeaux. The portrait of *La Modiste* (Mlle Louise Blouet d'Enguin) is an interesting departure from Toulouse-Lautrec's usual work with its use of an almost chiaroscuro technique. The artist's friend and cousin, Dr Gabriel Tapié de Celeyran, who kept a watchful eye on him, is also depicted. The drawings of circus scenes are reproductions of those executed from memory by Toulouse-Lautrec while he was being treated at the sanatorium at Neuilly in 1899. At the end of the room, a door leads onto a terrace *(closed out of season)* from which there is a pretty view of the river Tarn, the Pont Vieux and the formal, French style gardens of the Palais de la Berbie.

Au salon de la rue des Moulins by Toulouse-Lautrec

Room (9) contains a number of sketches of "le jeune Routy", a labourer at Celeyran, showing the amount of preparation Toulouse-Lautrec put into his portraits.

In rooms (10) to (14), along the north wing of the palace where visiting bishops were lodged, several famous works stand out. Room (10) contains a study for the poster for *La Revue blanche* (1895), a charcoal sketch given added depth by the use of colour, which pays homage to the beauty of Missia Godebski, wife of one of the Natanson brothers who edited *La Revue blanche*.

Room (11) is dominated by one of Toulouse-Lautrec's most famous works: *Au Salon de la rue des Moulins*. The pastel study and finished painting of 1894 are displayed on opposite walls. The artist's supreme skill as a draughtsman a his keen observational powers are well illustrated in pictures such as this, in which he relentlessly records the often harsh reality of the scenes he saw. The pencil lines are left visible beneath the paint.

Other subjects are taken from the world of Parisian music halls and theatres, where Toulouse-Lautrec would go every night and draw numerous portraits: Valentin "le Désossé" ("boneless") who used to come and dance with La Goulue at the Moulin de la Galette; the singer-songwriter Aristide Briant, who would perform numbers in slang at his cabaret Le Mirliton; Caudieux, a café-concert artiste; Jane Avril, whose wild dancing earned her the nickname "La Mélinite", and whose delicate features and elegant posture are captured in several of Toulouse-Lautrec's works; and the singer Yvette Guilbert, who was passionately pursued by the artist but who forbade him to publish his portraits of her as she found them unflattering. Numerous drawings, lithographs and posters are displayed on the second floor of the museum. Room (**23**) contains the hollow walking cane, complete with miniature glass, used by Toulouse-Lautrec during and after his cure in Neuilly; he could fill it with brandy, thus deceiving Paul Viaud, the friend looking after him.

On the third floor is a collection of modern and contemporary art, including drawings by Louis Anquetin of Verlaine, sculptures by Maillol, Bourdelle and P Belmondo, and paintings by Yves Brayer, Marie Bermond, Matisse, Bonnard, Vuillard, Marquet and Dufy.

From the rotunda there is a good **view** of the Tarn, with the bridges and old mills.

★★OLD ALBI *1hr*

From Place Ste-Cécile, take Rue Ste-Cécile and then the Rue St-Clair (2nd on the right).

Hôtel Séré de Rivières (Z N) – This 15C-18C mansion was the residence of a family of dyer's woad merchants who were ennobled in the 17C. The most distinguished member of the family was General **Raymond Séré de Rivières** (1815-95), who designed the defensive system based on a string of half-buried polygonal forts along the new borders of France after the loss of the eastern provinces to Prussia in 1870-1.

Maison du vieil Alby (Z B) – This brick and timber house, restored to the medieval design, stands at the forked junction between the pretty streets of Croix-Blanche and Puech-Berenguier (good view of the bell-tower of Ste-Cécile from the end of the latter). The first floor is corbelled out over the street, and there is a *solelhièr*, or woad drying room, beneath the eaves. The house hosts local craft exhibitions and contains various literature on the town of Albi.

Rue Henri de Toulouse-Lautrec (Z 60) – On the right as you follow this street are the Maison Lapérouse, named after a famous French seaman (1741-88) *(see also Musée Lapérouse below)*, which houses a **waxworks museum (M¹,** *see below*), and the Hôtel du Bosc (**D**), where Toulouse-Lautrec was born. This house was built on the site of the 14C fortifications, part of which can still be seen (two towers and a section of rampart walk). At no 8, the **Hôtel Decazes (R)** features a handsome courtyard in a transitional architectural style from Renaissance to Classicism, with a balustraded staircase and galleries with basket-handle arches. Take the Rues des Nobles, du Palais (the Palais de Justice – **J**, or law courts, is housed in a 16C Carmelite convent), and des Pénitents. Note the lovely Renaissance Hôtel de Ville (**H** – town hall).

★ **Pharmacie des Pénitents (or Maison Enjalbert) (Z E)** – This 16C house (now a chemist's shop) features timbering and crisscross pattern brickwork typical of the Albi region.

★ **Hôtel de Reynès (Z C)** – *Headquarters of the local chamber of commerce.* This Renaissance stone and brick mansion once belonged to a wealthy merchant family. The courtyard is decorated with two galleries one above the other, next to a 14C corner tower. The mullions of the windows on the inner façade are ornately decorated with mermaid figures. The courtyard also features two busts of François I and Eleanor of Austria.

Take the Rue Mariès towards the cathedral, noticing no 6 (**Y F**) on the right, an attractive 15C timber and brick building.

Église St-Salvy (YZ) – St Salvy began his working life as a lawyer, before taking holy orders and finally becoming Bishop of Albi in the 6C. He introduced Christianity to the region and is now buried on the site of this church, which has a turbulent history. Its layout and foundations date from the Carolingian period. In the 11C a church and Romanesque cloister were built, then work was interrupted by the Albigensian crusade and not restarted until the 13C, when it was continued in the Gothic style. The bell-tower on the north of the building reflects the different stages of construction: the Romanesque stone tower (11C) with Lombard bands has a Gothic storey (12C) on top of it, and there is a 15C brick construction on top of that. The crenellated turret known as "la Gacholle", on one side of the main tower, is decorated with the coats of arms of the city of Albi and the chapter. It originally served as a watchtower.

ALBI

Lices G. Pompidou .... **YZ**
Malroux (R. A.) .... **Y** 25
Mariès (R.) .... **Y**
Ste-Cécile (R.) .... **Z** 47
Timbal (R.) .... **Z** 58
Verdusse (R. de) .... **Z** 64
Vigan (Pl. du) .... **Z**

Archevêché (Pl. de l') .. **Y** 3
Castelviel (R. du) .... **Y** 7
Choiseul (Quai) .... **Y** 8
Croix-Blanche (R. de la) . **Z** 9
Croix-Verte (R. de la) ... **YZ** 12
Dr-Camboulives (R. du) .. **Z** 14
Empeyralots (R. d') ..... **Z** 15
Genève (R. de) .... **Z** 18
Hôtel-de-Ville (R. de l') .. **Z** 19
Nobles (R. des) .... **Z** 28
Oulmet (R. de l') .... **Z** 29
Palais (Pl. du) .... **Z** 30
Palais (R. du) .... **Z** 31
Pénitents (R. des) ...... **Z** 33
Peyrolière (R.) .... **YZ** 34
Porte-Neuve (R.) .... **Z** 35
Puech-Bérenguier (R.) .. **Z** 37
Rivière (R. de la) .... **Y** 40
Roquelaure (R.) .... **Z** 41
St-Afric (R.) .... **Z** 42
St-Antoine (R.) .... **Y** 43
St-Clair (R.) .... **Y** 44
St-Julien (R.) .... **Y** 45
Ste-Cécile (Pl.) .... **Y** 46
Ste-Claire (R.) .... **Y** 48
Savary (R. H.) .... **Z** 51
Sel (R. du) .... **Z** 52
Séré-de-Rivières (R.) ... **Z** 53
Toulouse-Lautrec (R. H. de) **Z** 60
Visitation (R. de la) ..... **Y** 67

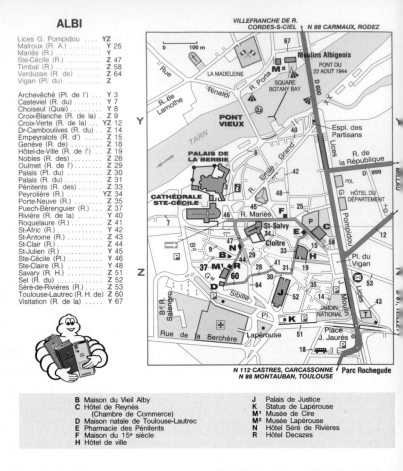

B   Maison du Vieil Alby
C   Hôtel de Reynès
    (Chambre de Commerce)
D   Maison natale de Toulouse-Lautrec
E   Pharmacie des Pénitents
F   Maison du 15e siècle
H   Hôtel de ville

J   Palais de Justice
K   Statue de Lapérouse
M¹ Musée de Cire
M² Musée Lapérouse
N   Hôtel Séré de Rivières
R   Hôtel Decazes

Enter the church by the north door. All that remains of the Romanesque doorway, rather spoiled by a classical style appendage, is the archivolt, the arch mouldings and two capitals. The first four bays inside are Romanesque and still have their 12C capitals. Two apsidal chapels in the chancel also remain from the first stage of construction, offset from the line of the side aisles.

The chancel and the remaining bays of the nave are in the Flamboyant Gothic style. In the chancel is a group of Christ surrounded by six statues depicting priests, scribes and elders of the Sanhedrin (the supreme court of justice in Jerusalem). In the first south side chapel, note the 15C statue of Christ chained to a pillar, and a beautiful, primitive painting on wood of the Entombment. The sacristy houses a 15C stone Pietà and a 12C wooden statue of St Salvy, copies of which are to be found above the entrance doorway of the church and above the high altar.

The **cloisters** *(access via a doorway in the south side)* were rebuilt by Vidal de Malvesi in the 13C. All that is left is the east gallery, in which there are Romanesque historiated capitals and Gothic ones decorated with plant motifs. The artist and his brother are buried in a mausoleum with a funerary niche backing onto the church.

Return to Place Ste-Cécile.

ADDITIONAL SIGHTS

Moulins albigeois (Y) – The brick buildings of the **old mills** have been successfully restored and now house a hotel, the local tourist board, private residences and a museum in honour of Lapérouse. From the terrace in Square Botany Bay there is a pretty **view**★ of the Tarn, the Pont Vieux and the part of town on the south bank, with the cathedral towering on the skyline.

Musée Lapérouse ⊙ **(Y M²)** – *Entrance in Rue Porta.*
Set out in a series of handsome vaulted rooms, this museum recalls the naval expeditions of Admiral Jean-François de Galaup de Lapérouse, who was born in the Manoir du Go on the outskirts of Albi in 1741. In 1785, Lapérouse set off on a scientific expedition on board two frigates, the *Boussole* and the *Astrolabe,* but perished when the latter was shipwrecked off the island of Vanikoro, north of the New Hebrides. His last port of call had been Botany Bay in Australia in 1788.

Navigational instruments, maps, charts and scale models of ships give an insight into what it was like to sail the seas in the 18C. A video film covers four centuries of maritime adventures in the Pacific. The last investigations of the wreck of the *Astrolabe* were carried out by an international team of experts in 1986.

Musée de Cire ⊘ (Z M') – The waxworks museum occupies the cellars of a house which was once the property of Lapérouse. Tableaux with wax characters evoke famous Albi residents – Toulouse-Lautrec, St Salvy and Lapérouse inter alia – and significant episodes in the town's history. Once-important local activities such as mining or the cultivation and extraction of dyer's woad are also depicted.

Statue of Lapérouse (Z K) – This memorial to the famous seaman stands in the square which bears his name.

► ► **Parc Rochegude** – *South of town.* Pleasant park with an ornate 16C lead and bronze fountain.

EXCURSIONS

★ **Lescure: Église St-Michel** ⊘ – *5km/3mi northeast towards Carmaux-Rodez, then right at the signpost to Lescure.*
The old priory church in Lescure cemetery was built by Benedictine monks from Gaillac abbey in the 11C. The Romanesque doorway, which dates from the 12C, is one of the most interesting features. Four of the capitals are decorated with narrative scenes, depicting the Temptation of Adam and Eve and Abraham's Sacrifice of Isaac, to the left, and the Damnation of the Moneylender and two scenes featuring Lazarus the beggar in heaven and the rich man in hell, to the right. There is a marked similarity between these capitals and those of the basilica of St-Sernin in Toulouse and the church of St-Pierre in Moissac.

Notre-Dame-de-la-Drèche – *5km/3mi north on the road to Carmaux-Rodez, then left towards Cagnac-les-Mines.*
Perched on a little plateau in the Tarn countryside is a strikingly large shrine with warm rose-coloured brick walls. It was built in the 19C, on the site of a 13C church, and consecrated to the "Vierge d'Or de Clermont", a mid-10C gold statue of the Virgin Mary in Majesty from the Auvergne which inspired a number of imitations. The name of the church means "Our Lady of the sunny hillside" (*adrech* is the local dialect for a slope exposed to the sun). The upper walls of the interior of this octagonal rotunda are decorated with mural paintings depicting the Life of the Virgin Mary, designed by Bernard Bénézet and executed by Father Léon Valette.
A small museum, the **musée-sacristie** ⊘, contains among other things a remarkable altar hanging in gold brocade on the same theme as the murals, made by nuns of the Order of St Clare in Mazamet.

Castelnau-de-Lévis – *7km/4.5mi northwest. Leave Albi on the road to Cordes-sur-Ciel, then take D 1 left.*
All that remains of the 13C fortress is a narrow square tower and some ruins. There is a good view of Albi, with the cathedral's silhouette towering above it, and the surrounding Tarn valley.

ALÈS

Conurbation 76 856
Michelin map 80 fold 18 or 240 fold 11

Alès, situated at the heart of an old mining and silkworm farming region, is a typical town of the Cévennes plain, with broad, bustling streets and esplanades. In high season, the town offers a full festival programme.
Alès is also the departure point of the long-distance footpaths, GR 44C and GR 44D, which form part of the network covering the Cévennes from Mont Lozère to Mont Aigoual.

HISTORICAL NOTES

Origins of Alès – The town (known as "Alais" until 1926) derives its name from Alestum, probably of Celtic origin. Founded at the junction of roads linking Nîmes and the Auvergne region, it spread out from a hillock enclosed in a meander of the Gardon. The hillock is now the site of Fort Vauban. There was once an oppidum on the hill to the southwest, the Colline de l'Ermitage.

The Peace Treaty of Alès – Alès is where the Edict of Grace between Louis XIII and the Protestants was signed in 1629. After Richelieu captured La Rochelle for Louis XIII in 1628, as part of their drive to create a united French kingdom, the Duc de Rohan, great leader of the Protestants and son-in-law of Sully, fell back to the Cévennes, where Anduze *(see p 87)* was his base. He was hotly pursued by the King and his forces, who captured and torched Privas. The duke rallied resistance at Alès, made the residents swear on oath that they would defend the town to the death, and then returned to Anduze. The royalists forced Alès to surrender after nine days of siege. Rohan, realising his cause was lost, entered into negotiations with Richelieu. Under the terms of the treaty of Alès, the Protestants were deprived of their right to play an active political role in the state, and they were stripped of their fortresses. The freedom of worship granted in the **Edict of Nantes** was, however, confirmed. Rohan was awarded compensation of 300 000 *livres*, which he shared out among his collaborators.

Louis Pasteur at Alès – In 1847, an epidemic disease called pebrine, about which little was known at the time, attacked the silkworms which were the region's traditional source of income *(see p 308 for information on silkworm breeding)*. The epidemic worsened from year to year, until people began cutting down their mulberry bushes in despair. The famous chemist, J-B Dumas, who came from Alès, was commissioned to study this scourge, but he met with no success. By 1865, 3 500 silkworm breeders were sending out distress signals loud and clear, at which point Dumas appealed to Pasteur, who took up the task for the public good. The four years he spent studying the silkworm disaster at Alès were among the most exciting, but also emotionally charged, of his illustrious career.

The great scientist set about gathering information from the farmers about the disease and all the remedies that had been tried so far. He had barely arrived at Alès, when he learned of the death of his father, and in the course of the following year, two of his daughters died. Pasteur nonetheless managed to continue his studies, despite his great personal grief, and by January 1867 he had found a remedy: all the farmers had to do was to examine the breeding butterflies under a microscope and destroy any eggs which exhibited certain characteristics typical of the disease. Tests were set in train to check the theory, and in 1868 results showed Pasteur's preventive method to be a resounding success. Pasteur continued to oversee the work of his colleagues at Alès, despite suffering a stroke, until he was sure the problem had been resolved definitively.

The town of Alès put up a **statue (A B)** in the Bosquet gardens to mark its gratitude to the great scientist.

Industrial development – From as early as the 12C, Alès prospered from textile manufacturing and the cloth trade. In the 19C, the town became a major industrial centre fed by coal mines in Alès itself, the Grand'Combe and Bessèges, as well as mining for iron, lead, zinc and asphalt.

Nowadays, coal is only mined in open-cast mines. The Alès conurbation is still a major industrial centre in the Languedoc region, specialising in metallurgy, chemistry (Rhône-Poulenc at Salindres) and mechanical engineering. The local economy, though, is beginning to branch out into other sectors, influenced by the presence in Alès of the national college of engineering, the École Nationale des Mines. The town attracts small and medium size businesses, and an industrial estate, including a science and technology park, has been founded there.

SIGHTS

Cathédrale St-Jean-Baptiste ⊙ **(A)** – The west front of the cathedral is Romanesque, with a Gothic porch dating from the 15C. The rest of the building dates from the 17C (nave) and 18C (great choir). There are some interesting paintings in the transept: *Assumption of the Virgin Mary* (1694) by Antoine Ranc, *St Peter Chastises Sapphira* (18C) by J-B Regnault and *Education of the Virgin Mary* (19C) by Deveria.

Ancien Évêché (AB F) – The old episcopal palace dates from the 18C.

Musée du Colombier ⊙ **(B)** – This museum occupies the Château du Colombier, in a pretty public park, next to the dovecot *(Fr.: colombier)* after which the château and museum are named.

The art collection housed here covers the 16-20C, and some of the more notable works include a triptych of the Holy Trinity by Jean Bellegambe (early 16C), and paintings by Van Loo, Mieris, Bassano, Velvet Brueghel, Masereel, Mayodon, Marinot, Benn and others. There is also an interesting collection of local archeological exhibits, and ironwork and other items from old Alès.

Fort Vauban (A) – The fort, a disused prison with a courtyard open to the public, stands at the top of a hill laid out as a public park. There is a good view of Alès and its outskirts.

★ **Musée minéralogique de l'École des Mines** ⊙ – *6, Avenue de Clavières, in the Chantilly district. Leave the town centre via Avenue de Lattre-de-Tassigny and Avenue Pierre-Coiras.*

This museum, housed in one of the buildings belonging to the École Nationale des Mines, has a collection of more than 1 000 minerals from all over the world. Some of the exhibits are quite outstanding (opal from Australia

ALÈS

Avéjan (R. d')	B	Audibert (R. Cdt)	A 3	Rollin (R.)	A 14		
Docteur-Serres (R.)	B	Barbusse (Pl. Henri)	B 4	Semard (Pl. Pierre)	B 16		
Edgar-Quinet (R.)	B	Hôtel-de-Ville (Pl. de l')	A 5	Soleil			
Louis-Blanc (Bd)	B	Lattre de Tassigny		(R. du Faubourg-du)	B 17		
St-Vincent (R.)	B 15	(Av. de)	B 6	Stalingrad (Av. de)	B 18		
Taisson (R.)	B 19	Leclerc (Pl. Gén.)	B 8	Talabot (Bd)	B 20		
		Martyrs-de-la-Résistance					
Albert-1er (R.)	B 2	(Place des)	B 9				
		Michelet (R.)	B 10	B	Statue de Pasteur		
		Paul (R. Marcel)	B 12	F	Ancien Évêché		

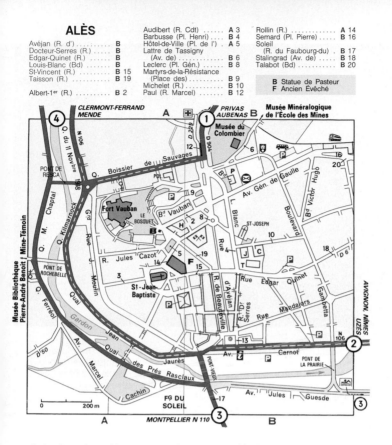

chalcedony from Morocco, morion quartz - black cairngorm - from Aveyron in France). A 3-D audiovisual presentation sets off the brilliance of the stones and the diversity of their shapes and colours to good effect. Other interesting sections include a paleontological collection, with fossils and local rock specimens, and a display on the natural resources of the Languedoc-Roussillon region.

★ **Musée-Bibliothèque Pierre-André Benoît** ⊘ – *Montée des Lauriers, Rochebelle. Take the Rochebelle bridge over the Gardon, then follow the signposted route.* The restored 18C Château de Rochebelle, once the residence of the bishops of Alès, houses a gift from Pierre-André Benoît to his native town and to the Bibliothèque Nationale. Benoît (1921-93) was a printer, publisher, writer, painter and draughtsman. He built up these interesting collections in the course of his encounters and correspondence with famous people, for example Char, Claudel, Tzara, Seuphor, Braque, Picasso, Miró, Jean Hugo, Villon etc.

Benoît published illustrated books, often in small format and limited editions. At the same time he collected works of art and books by his friends.

To save them from wear and tear, the graphic art works and the books are displayed in rotation or during temporary exhibitions, which are held on the ground floor, or in the library decorated by Benoît *(2nd floor)*. The rooms on the 1st floor house the art collection: beautiful oil paintings on canvas by Camille Bryen, paintings from the years 1946-53 by Picabia, compositions with birds by Braque, landscapes by L Survage and miniatures.

★ **Mine-témoin** ⊘ – *3km/2mi west. Take the Rochebelle bridge over the Gardon and carry on north on the Rue du Faubourg de Rochebelle. Turn left onto Chemin de St-Raby, then right onto Chemin de la Cité Ste-Marie. Temperature: 13-15ºC/55-59ºF. 20min audiovisual presentation on the formation of coal and mining technology.*

The mining museum comprises 650m/710yd of shafts hollowed out of the hillside, from which Benedictine monks extracted coal as early as the 13C. The exhibition covers the history of mining in the Cévennes region from the beginning of the Industrial Revolution to the present. Machinery, tools and the backdrop of the mine shafts themselves are used to illustrate changes in the various working practices within the mines: coal cutting (pickaxes give way to pneumatic drills and then to a coal-cutting machine which drills into the base of the seam and collects the coal automatically), transporting ore (in baskets or carts pushed

Mine-témoin/PH. DELGADO

by men or pulled by animals, before the installation of rails, then locomotives and even overhead monorails), pit props (mine shafts initially supported by timber vaulting, in which logs were chopped into shape by axe and fitted without rivets, then rounded or ogival metal frames, followed by a moving support system which keeps pace with work at the coal face), and safety practices (ventilation, helmets, warning signals, monitoring of miners' movements) etc.

EXCURSIONS

L'Ermitage – *3km/2mi west. Leave Alès on D 50 to the southwest, towards St-Jean-du-Pin, then turn right.*
To the right of the road to the chapel are the ruins of the old oppidum. From the chapel *(viewing table)* there is a panoramic view of Alès, Mont Lozère and the Cévennes to the northwest and north, and of the *garrigues* country around Nîmes to the south, beyond the valleys of the two river Gardons (which flow into each other a little south of Alès to form the river Gard or Gardon).

★ **Château de Portes** ⊙ – *20km/12.5mi north. Leave Alès on D 904, ① on the town plan, towards Aubenas, then turn left onto D 906. Park the car at the pass to explore the castle ruins on foot.*
The old stronghold of Portes is perched on the ridge separating the Gardon and Luech valleys, overlooking a wide expanse of surrounding land. For many years it provided protection for pilgrims travelling to St-Gilles through the Cévennes. The medieval fortress, now in ruins, has a square ground plan. The lords of Budos, to whom the castle belonged from 1320 to the 17C, had an extra building added during the Renaissance, which gave the whole a slightly strange outline. The polygonal layout and carefully shaped projection shaped like the prow of a ship are architectural feats of note.
The castle was used as a prison during the Revolution. It began to crack up towards the end of the 19C, because of the mine shafts beneath it. Since 1969, an association ("Renaissance du Château de Portes") has taken charge of conservation of the castle and organisation of entertainment there. Inside the Renaissance building (used for exhibitions and concerts) are some beautiful monumental chimneypieces with mantelpieces formed of a single slab of stone. From the top of the castle, the **panorama★** stretches to the north over the Chamborigaud valley, beneath Mont Lozère and the Tanargue foothills.

Rousson – *10km/6mi northeast. Leave Alès on D 904, ① on the town plan, then take the third road on the right after Les Rosiers.*
Château de Rousson ⊙ – The fief of Rousson was bought in 1588 by Jacques d'Agulhac de Beaumefort, who built the château there between 1600-15. The robust castle, protected by four corner towers, has not undergone any substantial modifications since it was built. The Bary family, who bought it in 1910 and undertook its restoration, made only minor alterations to one or two windows and extended the northeast wing into the central courtyard. The main façade faces southeast and features a series of mullioned windows and an impressive Louis XIII door with bosses. Inside, there are various well-preserved

old **tiled floors** which are most attractive. The kitchen on the ground floor has a huge fireplace and bread oven. The gallery on the first floor contains an old sea chest.

The castle terraces give good views of the Aigoual and Ventoux ranges.

Carry on to Rousson-les-Blés and turn left into a small road leading up to Rousson.

From the village of **Rousson** itself, halfway up the slope of a rock spur on which the original fortress once stood, there are lovely views of the Cévennes.

Drive downhill and turn left onto D 904 and then almost immediately turn right.

Préhistorama ⊙ – This centre retraces the evolution of life on earth (mouldings of fossils) and of man in particular with tableaux peopled by fairly subjective reconstructions of the earliest human beings.

Parc ornithologique des Isles ⊙ – *20km/12.5mi northeast. Leave Alès on D 904, ① on the town plan. In Les Mages, take D 132 to the right. The bird sanctuary is 800m/870yd beyond the turn-off to St-Julien-de-Cassagnas.*

The sanctuary is home to hundreds of birds from all over the world: wild fowl, web-footed species, waders, birds of prey, climbing birds (good collection of parrots and budgerigars) etc.

★ **Bambouseraie de Prafrance** – *17km/10.5mi southwest. Leave Alès on N 110, ③ on the town plan, and then take D 910A to the right, then D 129, also to the right. Description of the bamboo grove under Bambouseraie de PRAFRANCE.*

Vézénobres – *11km/7mi southeast. Leave Alès on N 106, ② on the town plan.*
Vézénobres occupies a pleasant site on a hillside overlooking the confluence of the Gardon d'Alès and the Gardon d'Anduze. There is still some evidence of the medieval town: the Sabran gateway, remains of the old ramparts, ruins of a fortress and several houses dating from the 12C, 14C or 15C. Take the flights of steps up to the top of the village, from where there is a great **panorama**★ of the surrounding area against a backdrop of the Cévennes to the west *(viewing table).*

AMÉLIE-LES-BAINS-PALALDA‡‡

Population 3 239
Michelin map 86 folds 18 and 19 or 235 fold 56 or 240 fold 45
Town plan in the current Michelin Red Guide France

Amélie was originally called Bains-d'Arles and then renamed after Queen Marie-Amélie, wife of Louis-Philippe. It owes its development to Général de Castellane, who opened a military hospital there in 1854 and had footpaths laid out on the surrounding hillsides.

The most southerly spa town in France – The sulphur-rich spa waters at Amélie-les-Bains-Palalda, 230m/748ft above sea level in the Vallespir region, are widely renowned for their effective treatment of rheumatic complaints and diseases of the respiratory tract (people come all year round to take the waters). Mediterranean plantlife, such as mimosas, oleanders, palm trees and agaves, in the local gardens reflects the mild climate. The air here is particularly pure, there are hardly any strong winds and the sun shines brightly for much of the time. Amélie has one military spa centre and two for the public: the baths at Le Mondony, at the mouth of the Mondony gorge, and the Roman baths, in which there is a restored Roman swimming pool.

★ **Palalda** – *3km/2mi from the centre of Amélie.*
The medieval town of Palalda, overlooking the Tech, is twinned with the spa town for administrative purposes. It is a fine example of a Catalan village. The tiny, often quite steeply sloping streets, bright with flowers, below the *mairie* are well worth exploring. The little square surrounded by the church of St-Martin, the museum and the town hall is particularly pretty.

St-Martin – The church contains a lovely altarpiece depicting the life of St Martin.

Museum ⊙ – The museum is divided into two sections.

The **museum of folk arts and traditions** displays tools used in professions which either are no longer practised or have been mechanised. One room is devoted to the manufacture of espadrilles. Twenty metres *(just over 20yd)* further down the hill on Place de la Nation are two rooms reconstructed as an early 20C kitchen and bedroom - note the Catalan card game known as *truc* and the *cargolade,* a local dish of grilled snails, eaten with *aïoli* (garlic mayonnaise) and washed down with *vins doux naturels* (sweet wine) such as Rivesaltes or Banyuls.

The **Roussillon postal museum** exhibits pictures, literature and other items tracing the history of the local postal service. There is a reconstruction of a late 19C post office, and a display on the Roussillon lighthouse system *(tours à feu),* a code based on smoke signals which could alert the entire region within 15min to the threat of enemy invasion.

Among the machines on display note the rare example of a "Daguin" franking machine. Finally, pause to admire the postman's uniform, in particular his smart boots.

Gorges du Mondony – *30min there and back on foot. Leave from the Roman baths and walk past the Hôtel des Gorges as far as the terrace which overlooks the mouth of the gorge. Take the cliff path and the galleries clinging to the rock face.*
The gorge is a cool, pleasant place for a walk.

EXCURSION

★ **Vallée du Mondony** – *6km/3.5mi as far as Mas Pagris. Spectacular cliff road (passing places over the last 2km/1.2mi).*
The road to Montalba leads off from the Avenue du Vallespir to the south of the town, before climbing the rocky spur of Fort-les-Bains and leading along the clifftops overlooking the Mondony gorge. It then crosses a series of stepped terraces, in full view of the jagged Roc St-Sauveur and of the deserted valley below, uniformly carpeted with green oak trees. Leaving the Montalba aerial tower to the left, it carries on through the granite gorge as far as the small valley of Mas Pagris. This is a good departure point for walks in the upper valley of the Terme.

The annual **Michelin Guide Camping Caravaning France**
offers a selection of camp sites and up-to-date information
on their location, setting, facilities and services.

Principat d'ANDORRA★★

Michelin map 86 folds 14 and 15 or 235 folds 50, 51 and 54

Andorra, which has a total area of 464km²/179sq mi (about one and a third times the area of the Isle of Wight), lies at the heart of the Pyrenees and has remained curiously apart from its neighbours, France and Spain. Visitors are attracted by its beautiful rugged scenery and picturesque villages.

In less than half a century, the Andorran way of life has evolved remarkably rapidly; the first roads suitable for vehicles linking it with the outside world were not opened until 1913, on the Spanish side, and 1931, on the French. The development of hydroelectric power and tourism, with the construction of special holiday villages ("urbanitzacio") and the influx of foreign visitors, is having a profound impact on the Andorran economy and traditional way of life.

Andorran relief is defined by two main valleys, the Valira del Orient and the Valira del Nord, from which the rivers converge to form the Gran Valira flowing south into Spain. The country is separated from France by a ring of mountain peaks varying in altitude from 2 500-3 000m/8 000-10 000ft. The road across these has to scale the Envalira pass (2 407m/7 897ft).

The small independent state shows signs of a somewhat haphazard development; the mushrooming of residential and office blocks in the Gran Valira is balanced by the peaceful atmosphere on the high plateaux and tributary valleys, served by narrow mountain tracks, which seem almost to be suspended in a previous age. The population of Andorra numbered 62 400 in 1995, most of whom speak Catalan. The state is divided into 7 "parishes" or administrative units: Canillo, Encamp, Ordino, La Massana, Andorra la Vella, Sant Juliá de Lòria and Escaldes-Engordany.

ONLY DAUGHTER OF CHARLEMAGNE

"Charlemagne the great, my father, will deliver me from the Arabs" begins the Andorran national anthem, which then continues proudly, "I alone remain the only daughter of Charlemagne. Christian and free for eleven centuries, Christian and free I shall carry on between my two valiant guardians, my two protecting princes."

From co-principality to independent sovereignty – Until 1993, Andorra was a co-principality under a regime of dual allegiance, a legacy from the medieval feudal system. Under such a contract, two neighbouring lords would define the limits of their respective rights and authority over a territory that they held in common fief. Andorra was unusual, however, in that its two lords came to be of different nationality, but left the status of the territory as it was under feudal law, with the result that neither of them could claim possession of the land. This dual allegiance to two co-princes was established in 1278 by the Bishop of Urgell and Roger Bernard III, Count of Foix. However, while the Bishops of Urgell remained co-price, the Counts of Foix passed their lordship on to France (when Henri IV, Count of Foix and Béarn, became king in 1589) and thus eventually to the President of the French Republic.

Visitors' tips to Andorra

Customs and other formalities – Visitors need a valid passport and, for those driving a car, a green card and current driving licence. There are customs checkpoints on the borders.

Money matters – Both Spanish and French currencies are accepted. The Caisse d'Épargne at the post office in Andorra la Vella allows cash withdrawals on a credit card (you will need to know your PIN).

Postal service – Andorra has both Spanish and French postal services, with full-time post offices in Andorra la Vella and local offices elsewhere. Only Andorran stamps (with face values in either francs or pesetas) are valid. There are plans to create an Andorran mail service at an as yet unspecified future date.

Telephoning – The code for Andorra is 376, followed by 8, followed by the five-digit correspondent's number.

Shopping – Andorra has long held a reputation as a shopper's paradise, due to its duty-free status. A wide variety of products are on offer at very reasonable prices (food, luxury items, clothes, electronic goods etc.). Shops are generally open from 9.30am to 1.30pm and 4.30pm to 8pm.

Health cures – Andorra's favourable climate (sunny, dry, pure mountain air) makes it an ideal place for a relaxing break. There are numerous health resorts and spas, such as Caldea *(described below)*, offering health cures, massages, bathing etc.

Out on the town – Andorra has numerous restaurants offering a variety of cuisines. Visitors should be sure not to miss those set up in *bordes*, typical Andorran buildings of stone and timber, once used as barns or stables.
The Andorra National Auditorium (in Ordino) organises a number of classical music concerts, and there is a jazz festival held annually in July at Escaldes-Engordany.

Tourist information – Andorran Government Tourist Office, ☎ (376) 82 93 45; local tourist offices in Andorra la Vella, ☎ (376) 82 02 14 and ☎ (376) 82 71 17; Andorran hotels association, ☎ (376) 82 06 25/ 82 06 02.

On 14 March 1993 the Andorrans voted in a referendum to adopt a new democratic constitution making the principality a fully independent state. The official language of the country is Catalan. The principality has signed a treaty of cooperation with France and Spain, the first countries to officially recognise its independence. It has also become a member of the U.N.

A taste for liberty – Andorrans pride themselves above all on seeking and fiercely defending their liberty and independence. A longstanding system of representative government and eleven centuries of peace have given them little incentive to alter the country's administration. The country is governed by a General Council, which holds its sessions at the "Casa de la Vall" and ensures the proportional representation of the various elements of the Andorran population and the seven parishes. The councillors (of whom there are at least 28 and no more than 42) are elected by universal suffrage and hold office for 4 years. The General Council elects the chief representative, the Sindic General, and his deputy. After each renewal of the General Council, elections are held to find a new head of government. Each parish has a council, or *Comu*, to represent its interests and take charge of day-to-day administration. Legal authority is exercised by three tribunals, one for *bayles*, one for *corts* and one a supreme court.
Andorrans do not pay any direct taxes, nor do they have to do military service. They also have free postal services within their country. Most of the land is communally owned, so there are very few private landowners.

Work and play – Until recently this essentially patriarchal society traditionally made a living from stock rearing and crop cultivation. In between the high summer pastures and the hamlets you can still see the old *cortals*, groups of barns or farmhouses, which are gradually becoming more accessible as the tracks leading up to them are made suitable for vehicles. The mountain slopes exposed to the sun are cultivated in terraces. Tobacco, the main crop in the valley of Sant Juliá de Lòria, is grown up to an altitude of 1 600m/5 200ft.
The choice of the solemn festival of Our Lady of Meritxell (8 September) as the national feast day bears witness to the deeply ingrained religious faith here. Mass is celebrated, attended by the country's clergy and officials, and then like every Catalan *aplech* (pilgrimage) it is followed by open-air feasting in the surrounding meadows.

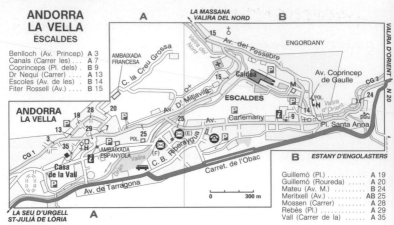

ANDORRA LA VELLA

ESCALDES

Benlloch (Av. Princep) ... A 3
Canals (Carrer les) ... A 7
Coprinceps (Pl. dels) . B 9
Dr Nequi (Carrer) .... A 13
Escoles (Av. de les) . B 14
Fiter Rossell (Av.) .... B 15

Guillemó (Pl.) .... A 19
Guillemó (Roureda) ..... A 20
Mateu (Av. M.) .... B 24
Meritxell (Av.) .... AB 25
Mossen (Carrer) .... A 28
Rebès (Pl.) .... A 29
Vall (Carrer de la) ...... A 35

ANDORRA LA VELLA

The capital of the Andorran valleys, huddled on a terrace (alt 1 209m/3 967ft) above the Gran Valira valley, is a bustling commercial town. Once away from the busy main axis, however, the heart of Andorra la Vella has kept its peaceful old streets. The town has spread to the east, beyond the bridge over the torrential river, to merge with the no less lively town of Escaldes, which occupies the small plain at the confluence of the two upper reaches of the Valira.

Casa de la Vall ⊘ (A) – The Casa is both Andorra's Parliament building and its Law Courts. The General Council holds session here. The massive stone building owes its overall appearance to the period of its construction, in the 16C, but it was heavily restored in 1963, when a second watch turret was added to the south corner. The main doorway is framed by long heavy archstones, characteristic of Aragon architecture. The façade is adorned with the coats of arms of the co-princes, added in 1761: to the left, the mitre and crozier of the Bishop of Urgell and the four vertical red bands of Catalonia; to the right, the three vertical bands of the Count of Foix and the two oxen "passant" of Béarn. The interior owes its elegance chiefly to the ceilings and wood panelling. The reception room, once a refectory, on the first floor is decorated with 16C murals. The council chamber still has the famous "cupboard with the seven keys", fitted with seven different locks to which the seven parishes each had one of the keys, in which the national archives are kept.

Caldea

Caldea is a major water sports complex, designed for keeping fit and having fun, which is located 1 000m/3 250ft above sea level and is fed by the Escaldes-Engordany spa waters pumped from the ground at 68°C/155°F. The complex, designed by French architect Jean-Michel Ruols, takes the form of a gigantic futuristic cathedral entirely of glass. The total area is 25 000m²/269 000sq ft, of which 6 000m²/64 560sq ft are given over to water-based leisure activities. There is a wide range of activities available: Indo-Roman baths, Turkish baths, jacuzzis, bubble beds, hot marble, spray fountains etc. Restaurants, snack bars, shops and a panoramic bar some 80m/260ft above the ground all contribute to the happy atmosphere of this aquatic paradise. *For information, telephone* ☎ *(376) 86 57 77.*

Caldea – Central pool

J. Boyer/IMAGES TOULOUSE

★ 1 VALIRA D'ORIENT VALLEY

From Andorra la Vella towards the Puymorens pass
36km/22.5mi – allow 1hr 30min – see local map

The Envalira pass can be blocked by snow, but it is always reopened within 24hr. In bad weather, the Puymorens pass road may be open only in the direction of Porté and the Cerdagne.

The road leaves the outskirts of Escaldes and climbs the increasingly steep and rugged valley, leaving behind it the Andorra radio station with its startling neo-Romanesque bell-tower.

After Encamp, the road negotiates a sharp defile before reaching the hamlet of **Les Bons**, which occupies an eye-catching **site★** perched on a rocky spur beneath the ruins of its once-protective castle and the chapel of Sant Roma. A little further on to the right stands the striking black and white form of Andorra's national shrine, the **chapel of Our Lady of Meritxell**, rebuilt in 1976.

Canillo – The church in this village has the tallest bell-tower in Andorra (27m/88ft). Not far off stands a white charnel house, in which the cells are funerary niches; such buildings are a common sight in countries of Iberian culture.

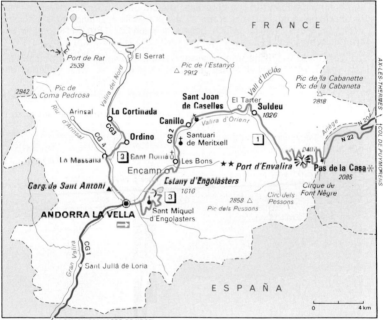

LA SEU D'URGELL/ SEO DE URGEL

Sant Joan de Caselles ⊙ – This lone church, with its three-storeyed bell-tower, is a particularly fine example of Romanesque Andorran architecture. The altarpiece (1525) behind the attractive wrought-iron parclose screen separating it from the chancel is the work of the Master of Canillo and depicts the Life of St John and his apocalyptic visions. During the last restoration (in 1963) a Romanesque **Crucifixion★** was found; the stucco fragments of the Christ figure were fixed back onto the wall in its original setting, where a fresco completing the Calvary scene was also found (sun, moon, Longinus, the soldier with the lance, and Stephaton, the soldier who offered the sponge soaked in vinegar).

The road makes a brief detour up part of the pretty, rural valley of the Inclès.

Soldeu El Tarter – This ski resort is 1 826m/5 935ft above sea level.

As the road climbs up to the Envalira pass, the Pessons cirque is visible away to the right of the road and, a little further on, the ski resort of Grau Roig.

★★ **Port d'Envalira** – Alt 2 407m/7 823ft. This is the highest pass in the Pyrenees which has a good road over it. It marks the watershed between the Mediterranean (Valira) and the Atlantic (Ariège). There is a **panorama** taking in the Andorra mountains, which reach an altitude of 2 942m/9 653ft, stretching away to the west as far as the Coma Pedrosa.

As the road drops down to the Pas de la Casa, it offers spectacular views of the **Font-Nègre** cirque and lake.

✻ **Pas de la Casa** – Alt 2 091m/6 861ft. This frontier village, the highest in Andorra, has become a major ski resort.

The N 22 runs through a desolate landscape as far as the N 20, which leads to the Puymorens pass.

★ ② VALIRA DEL NORD VALLEY

From Andorra la Vella to La Cortinada *9km/5.5mi*

The old Andorran way of life and traditions are still to be found in this isolated upper valley. The road climbs quickly up out of Andorra-Escaldes.

Gargantas de Sant Antoni – From a bridge across the Valira del Nord you can see over to the right the old hump-backed bridge, once used by muleteers. The valley narrows before opening out dramatically onto a bleak mountainous backdrop. The Coma Pedrosa peaks loom in the distance beyond the Arisinal valley.

Go through the pleasant holiday village of La Massana to Ordino.

Ordino – *Leave the car in the upper village in the square near the church.*
Downhill from the church this village has a network of picturesque streets well worth exploring. The church has attractive wrought-iron gates, which are commonly found in churches near the old Catalan forges. Near the church is another example of this craft, in the erstwhile residence of a blacksmith, "Don Guillem's" house, which boasts a splendid, 18m/59ft long wrought-iron balcony.

La Cortinada – Village in a pleasant setting. Downhill from the church and graveyard with charnel house is an attractive house with galleries and a dovecot.

The road continues northwards. There are plans to link it up eventually with Vicdessos, via the Port de Rat (alt 2 539m/8 330ft).

Engolasters – Church of Sant Miguel

③ ESTANY D'ENGOLASTERS

9km/5.5mi, then 30min there and back on foot

Leave Escaldes east of Andorra, on the road to France, and at the outskirts of the village turn right, doubling back slightly, to follow the Engolasters mountain road.

On the Engolasters plateau, where there are pastures as well as sports grounds used by the residents of Andorra la Vella, the outstanding landmark is the lovely Romanesque bell-tower of **Sant Miguel**.

At the end of the road, cross the crest under the pine trees and start downhill *(on foot)* to the dam, which has raised the level of the lake (alt 1 616m/ 5 272ft) by 10m/33ft. The waters of the lake reflect the dark forest which lines its shores. In the distance, opposite, stand the aerials of the Andorra radio station.

ANDUZE

Population 2 913
Michelin map 80 fold 17 or 240 fold 15

The picturesque little town of Anduze lies in a small valley in which the greenery of the plantlife contrasts strongly with the aridity of the surrounding mountain peaks. A narrow, deep gorge, known as the "gateway to the Cévennes" **(Porte de Cévennes** or **Pas du Portail)**, commands the entrance into the valleys of the Gardon de St-Jean and the Gardon de Mialet. There is a good view of Anduze and its setting from the D 910 to Alès, from a bend half a mile out of town.

Anduze has won nationwide renown over the last four centuries for the huge glazed earthenware vases made here, some of which were to be seen until quite recently decorating the orangery at Versailles.

HISTORICAL NOTES

Calvinism gained a foothold in Anduze in 1557 and spread rapidly. The town, almost all of which had converted to Protestantism, was chosen as the head-quarters of the Protestant General Assembly of Bas-Languedoc in 1579. Religious strife, which had died down during the reign of Henri IV, flared up again on his death. In 1622 Anduze, known as the Geneva of the Cévennes, became the hub of the resistance organised by the great Protestant leader, the **Duc de Rohan**. Rohan's support was especially strong in the Cévennes, as the region was entirely won over to the Protestant cause. He had the ramparts at Anduze reinforced with outworks and built fortresses on the higher ground. When Louis XIII and Richelieu mounted their campaign in 1629, Anduze's fortifications were sufficiently daunting for them to opt to attack Alès instead, which surrendered almost immediately. Anduze was thus not subjected to a siege, but after the Treaty of Alès *(see p 77)*, all Protestant strongholds were demolished and Anduze was stripped of its fortifications, including the section of ramparts which protected it from the turbulent spates of the Gardon.

In the early 18C, the old stronghold became the main operations centre for Royalist troops during the Camisard uprising *(see p 220)*. Once the turmoil of this period was over, the town prospered. In 1774, the États de Languedoc built a dike, the "quai", along the bank of the Gardon. The town expanded considerably, devoting itself to textile industries (wool, silk and hat-making). For many years Anduze rivalled Alès, until the latter's rich mineral resources enabled it to put on an economic spurt in the 19C.

SIGHTS

Clock tower (Tour de l'Horloge) – The clock tower on the elongated square which was once part of the castle dates from 1320 and is all that remains of the town's fortifications. It was spared in 1629 because of its clock.

Protestant church (Temple protestant) – The Protestant church was built in 1823 on the site of an old barracks. The rather severe façade can be seen not far from the clock tower. A peristyle with four columns shelters the entrance to the building, one of the largest Protestant churches in France.

Old town (Vieille ville) – The narrow, winding streets of the old town, such as Rue Bouquerie, are a joy to explore. The doorway next to the château leads to Place Couverte, a square containing the old corn market and an

Anduze - Pagoda-fountain

unusual **pagoda-fountain**, decorated with glazed tiles made specially by local ceramicists in 1649.

Ancien parc du couvent des Cordeliers - The park, in the grounds of the old Dominican monastery, contains a number of beautiful Mediterranean species of tree and an avenue lined with bamboos. From beneath the shade of the chestnut trees on the terrace at the top end of the park, there is a good view of the Gardon valley.

Musée de la Musique ⊘ - *Route d'Alès, on the east bank of the Gardon.* This museum collection comprises over 1 000 musical instruments of all ages from all over the world, displayed by family: percussion with stretched membrane heads (drums) and without (bells, gongs, scrapers etc); wind instruments and instruments operated by bellows, with reeds (clarinets, reed-stop organs or bombardes, mouth-organs) or with a mouthpiece (flutes, horns); and finally string instruments, played by plucking (guitars, harpsichords, zithers), bowing (violins), or striking (pianos). Demonstration performances illustrate the huge variety of musical techniques and sounds possible.

EXCURSIONS

* **Bambouseraie de Prafrance** - *2km/1.2mi along D 129. See Bambouseraie de PRAFRANCE.*

* **Musée du Désert; Grotte de Trabuc**★★ - *11km/7mi north, beyond Générargues and the valley of the Gardon de Mialet, along D 50 as far as the turn-off to the right just after Luziers. See Le MAS SOUBEYRAN and Grotte de TRABUC. Allow 1hr 30min.*

Tourist steam train (Train à vapeur des Cévennes) from Anduze to St-Jean-du-Gard - *See ST-JEAN-DU-GARD: Excursions.*

Dolmens de la Grande Pallière - *5.5km/3.5mi along the road to St-Félix, then turn right at the bridge onto the old road to the mines.*
A waymarked footpath *(details from Anduze tourist office)* leads along the ridge to a megalithic necropolis consisting of two dozen dolmens, one of the largest sites of its kind in east Languedoc.

Haute vallée de l'ARIÈGE★

Michelin map 86 folds 4, 5 and 15 or 235 folds 38, 42, 46 and 50

The Ariège rises on the Andorra border, in the Font-Nègre cirque, and flows into the Garonne just south of Toulouse, having covered 170km/106mi.
In its upper reaches, the river flows along a glacial channel which widens out and changes direction at Ax. The traces of the old glacier are much in evidence around Tarascon. The Ariège then flows through the Labarre ravine, cutting across the limestone Plantaurel range to reach the Pamiers plain, laid down by the river's own alluvial deposits, where it finally leaves the Pyrenees.

A mineralogical museum - Thanks to its wide range of geological deposits and mineral seams, the *département* of Ariège has been over the years a mining region with resources that have been worked or left abandoned depending on demand in world markets. Quantities of iron, bauxite, zinc, manganese and, more recently, tungsten (ⁱ Salau) have been mined here. At present only the talc (French chalk) mined at Luzer is a mineral resource of any national significance (10 % of world production).

★ FROM THE COL DE PUYMORENS TO TARASCON-SUR-ARIÈGE

54km/34mi – about half a day

The Puymorens pass road links the Cerdagne, Catalonia, the part of the Pyrenees in the Ariège region, Foix and Toulouse.

The Puymorens tunnel

Since 20 October 1994, a tunnel has enabled traffic to avoid the trip across the Puymorens pass itself, which tends to be a difficult journey in the winter. The building of the Puymorens tunnel, 4 820m/almost 3mi in length, was welcomed by local residents, although it was less well received by ecologists. The tunnel was a physical realisation of the economic and cultural opening up of the Ariège region to Catalonia. The improved communications between France and Spain are expected to be greatly helped by a road which is planned to link Toulouse and Barcelona. This highway between Toulouse and the Spanish border will not be completed, however, until 2010. Moreover, the proposed link is already causing problems as the volume of heavy goods traffic has increased considerably since the opening of the tunnel.

Above the entrance to the tunnel, on the French side, there is a 16m/52ft-high sculpture in coloured glass, the *Cascade de Lumière* (Cascade of Light), by Josette Rispal.

★ **Col de Puymorens** – Alt 1 920m/6 300ft. The snowfields and ski slopes can be reached via the road, at least the south section of which is cleared, or the ski lifts up from **Porté-Puymorens**. From the pass, take the old road *(one-way)* down to **L'Hospitalet** (alt 1 436m/4 667ft), the first village in the Ariège valley after the pass, keeping careful watch for the troops of wild horses that frequently follow this route. The bleak and rugged landscape becomes less and less harsh as the road descends.

Centrale de Mérens – Alt 1 100m/3 575ft. This automated power plant is the middle stage of the hydroelectric project of the same name, made possible by the raising of the level of Lanoux lake. This reservoir, fed by redirecting the tributary waters of the river Segre (and so also the river Ebro) in Spain into the Garonne valley, is the object of an agreement between the French and Spanish governments, to compensate Spain for the loss of water.

There is a viewing table to help you identify the mountain peaks at the far end of the valley.

Mérens-les-Vals – The village was rebuilt along the roadside after the fire that destroyed Mérens-d'en-Haut in 1811 in an arson attack by the "Miquelets" (Spanish mercenaries feared since the 16C), during the Franco-Spanish Napoleonic war. The road runs alongside some of the bridges – remarkable engineering feats – of the trans-Pyrenean railway line, one of the highest in Europe. Then it enters the Mérens gorge, before carrying on down the upper valley of the Ariège in between magnificent forests. On the right is the peak called "Dent d'Orlu".

✣ **Ax-les-Thermes** – *See AX-LES-THERMES.*

Just past Ax, the road crosses the river Ariège to run along the southwest bank. On the other side of the river, the lovely Romanesque bell-tower of the church at Unac can be seen.

Luzenac – *See AX-LES-THERMES: Excursions.*

The contrast between the slope facing the sun, covered with fields of crops and farmhouses, and the slope in the shade, clad in forests, is particularly striking along the next stretch of road. On the closer outcrops to the right of the road the ruins of first the Château de Lordat and then the Ermitage de St-Pierre can be seen, against the towering backdrop of the Pic de St-Barthélemy (alt 2 348m/7 631ft). Beyond the dip in which the village of Les Cabannes lies, where the river Aston flows into the Ariège, the road enters the Sabarthès region. The steep valley sides, riddled with caves, make up the Val d'Ariège at this point – once a glacial valley, as its deep, symmetrical cross-section suggests.

The caves of the Sabarthès region – *See TARASCON-SUR-ARIÈGE. Local map under FOIX: Excursions.*

Tarascon-sur-Ariège – *See TARASCON-SUR-ARIÈGE.*

FROM TARASCON-SUR-ARIÈGE TO PAMIERS

37km/23mi – allow half a day – local map under FOIX: Excursions

Tarascon-sur-Ariège – *See TARASCON-SUR-ARIÈGE.*

Leave Tarascon north on the road to Mercus-Garrabet, along the east bank of the Ariège.

As the road sets off down the valley from Tarascon, note the great piles of terminal moraine on the left, bristling with erratic boulders marking the retreat of the glacier. Two of these boulders are well within view of the road just before it reaches Bompas. On the left is the Roc de Soudour (alt 1 070m/3 478ft). Further on at **Mercus-Garrabet**, there is a Romanesque church set apart on a rocky outcrop in the middle of its graveyard. Other spurs further down the valley on the opposite bank give the countryside a rugged, untidy appearance.

Le Pont du Diable – *Keep following the road along the east bank of the Ariège. Leave the car just after the level crossing.*

This pretty bridge spans the Ariège at a point where the river flows fast but calmly. The lower projection of the main arch suggests that the height of the bridge was raised at least once in the 14C. Take a look at the bridge's system of fortification on the side of the west bank (door and lower chamber). The bridge struck terror into the hearts of the people of the region; building was restarted more than a dozen times as, legend has it, all the work done each day collapsed during the night... hence the bridge's name (*diable* = "devil").

After the Pont du Diable, the edge of the moraine comes into sight on the opposite bank. The river has carved out a 50m/150ft deep course for itself into the ledge of moraine. Further on, there are more traces of the old Ariège glacier, which could have been anything between 100 and 400m/325 and 1 300ft deep at this point. Beyond the turn-off to Lavelanet, a rocky outcrop called the **Pain de Sucre** ("sugarloaf") looms into view ahead, with the village of Montgaillard at its foot.

★ **Foix** – *See FOIX.*

In Foix, take the road to Vernajoul (D 1), where you turn left.

★ **Underground river of La-bouiche** – *See Rivière sou-terraine de LABOUICHE.*

The road from Foix to Varilhes runs alongside the Ariège as it flows through the Plantaurel hills, before cutting across the plain to Pamiers.

Pamiers – Pamiers, the largest town in the Ariège, is situated on the east bank of the river of that name, at the edge of a fertile plain well-protected from floods. Its name is derived

Mérens horses

These small, bearded horses belong to an ancient local breed as depicted in the paintings on the walls of Niaux cave, which were painted over 10 000 years ago! The good-tempered, hardy little horses used to be put to work in the fields. An association (Syndicat hippique d'élevage de la race pyrénéenne ariégeoise, or SHERPA) set up in 1933 has been promoting the role these horses can play in the tourist economy of the Ariège. Their gentle character makes them ideal for riding and pony-trekking holidays, of which there are many to choose from in this region. From May to October, they can be seen grazing at liberty in the mountain pastures of the upper Ariège valley. There is an information centre about the breed at La Bastide-de-Sérou.

from that of a town in Asia Minor, in memory of the part played by the Count of Foix, Roger II, in the First Crusade. It became a bishopric in 1295 and has since been home to four monastic communities. The **Cathédrale St-Antonin**, in the Place du Mercadel, has a handsome bell-tower in the Toulouse style, resting on a fortified base. All that remains of the original 12C church is the doorway. The church of **Notre-Dame-du-Camp** ⊙, in Rue du Camp, features a monumental brick façade with crenellations and two towers, and a 17C single nave inside. Pamiers has several interesting **old towers**: the Clocher des Cordeliers *(Rue des Cordeliers)*, similar to the tower of this name in Toulouse; the Tour de la Monnaie *(near Rambaud school)*; the square Tour du Carmel *(Place Eugène-Soula)*, originally a keep built by Count Roger-Bernard III of Foix in 1285; the tower of the Couvent des Augustins *(near the hospital)*; and the brick and stone Porte de Nerviau *(near the town hall)*. The **Promenade du Castella** is a walkway which follows the line of the old castle, the foundations of which are still visible between the Porte de Nerviau and the Pont-Neuf. At the top of the hill is a bust of the composer **Gabriel Fauré**, born in Pamiers in 1845.

Pamiers is a good departure point for trips to the rest of the Ariège and the Pyrenees.

ARLES-SUR-TECH

Population 2 837
Michelin map 86 fold 18 or 235 fold 56 or 240 fold 45

Arles grew up around an abbey built on the banks of the Tech in around 900, of which the church and cloisters have survived. The village has been the focal point of religious and folk traditions in the Haut-Vallespir region and is now a centre of production of traditional Catalan fabrics.

★ **Church** – *30min.* The tympanum depicts Christ in majesty, set in a Greek cross with medallions on the arms bearing the symbols of the four Evangelists (dating from the first half of the 11C, as does the whole of the west front). To the left of the main door, just before entering the church, note a 4C white marble sarcophagus behind a wrought-iron grille. This is the **Sainte Tombe** ("holy tomb") from which several hundred litres of pure clear water seep every year. To date, no scientific explanation has been found for this phenomenon. Above it there is a fine, early 13C funerary statue of Guillaume Gaucelme de Taillet.

Interior – The nave has a surprisingly high vault (17m/55ft). As you walk down the aisle, look at the layout of the arches, which points to their being the work of two different groups of craftsmen. The lower arches were part of the 11C building, which had a roof of relatively light rafters. When a vault was added to the church in the 12C, the weight of the vaulting meant that the supporting structure had to be reinforced. A second pillar was added on the inside of all the existing ones, and a row of taller, blind arches along the walls of the nave. In the first chapel on the south side is a great Baroque altarpiece dedicated to Saints Abdon and Sennen, once venerated throughout Roussillon as protectors in time of disaster. In a series of 13 panels it depicts the martyrdom of these young Kurdish princes and the transporting of their relics, first by boat, then in barrels loaded on the backs of mules. The second chapel contains three images of Christ (awaiting death, on the cross and laid out in a glass tomb) executed with a realism which brings to mind nearby Catalonia and its influence. These effigies, known as *misteris*, are carried by Penitents in the night-time procession on Good Friday.

Cloisters – *(Via door at the far end of the north aisle).* The cloisters date from the 13C.

El Palau Santa Maria ⊙ – This is the old abbot's lodgings. Some features of the façade bear the hallmark of the 13C. This privately-owned residence, still inhabited, contains a collection of paintings by Spanish artist Pallarès-Lleó, depicting the lives of Saints Abdon and Sennen, and that of Abbot Arnulfe.

EXCURSIONS

Coustouges – *20km/12.5mi south – allow 45min – leave Arles west on D 115 and take D 3 to the left.* The road crosses the Tech and climbs the river's west bank, through chestnut groves, before turning into the fertile Quéra valley. To the right, the Cos tower (1 116m/3 627ft tall) stands atop a strange, pyramidal mountain. A bend in a ravine reveals a clear view of Montferrar and Corsavy to the right. The road passes through the town of **St-Laurent-de-Cerdans**, the most populated of the southern Vallespir region, which specialises in the production of espadrilles and the weaving of traditional Catalan fabrics (**museum** ⊙). The small mountain village of **Coustouges** stands close to the Franco-Spanish border, on the site of an Ancient Roman sentry post (reflected in its name). It is home to an interesting 12C fortified **church** which has weathered well over the years. A decorative crenellated

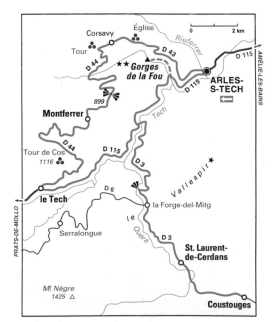

moulding runs under the eaves, beneath which there is a dainty scalloped motif around the east end of the church. The same pattern adorns the tower, below the parapet. Inside the south porch is a Romanesque door carved - most unusually for Roussillon - in soft stone (rather than marble) and decorated with numerous sculptures. The chancel is closed off by a beautiful wrought-iron grille, featuring the scroll motifs so often found in Vallespir on the hinges of old doors. The vaulting of the side chapels in the chancel is supported by two very archaic, sausage-shaped ogival ribs.

Round tour west of Arles - *36km/22mi - allow 2hr*
From Arles, the D 43 climbs steeply between the pleasant Riuferrer valley and upper reaches of the Fou gorge, winding its way along the crest of a ridge.
The ruins of the old parish church of **Corsavy** soon come into view. The road runs gently downhill, through the village and past an old watch turret on the right. Take the D 44 which heads uphill again and then crosses the river Fou *(good view)*. In a bend to the right, at the highest point along the road (899m/2 922ft), the panorama sweeps from west to east across the Canigou peak, the Albères mountains, Roussillon and the Mediterranean.

Montferrer - Church with a delightful bell-tower; to the left, the ruins of a castle.

Carry on along D 44 to Le Tech.

Le Tech - The lower section of this village, situated on a spur at the confluence of the Tech and the Coumelade, was wiped out by the floods in 1940. The 1914-18 War Memorial was replaced in 1964 by a plain memorial. The church was rebuilt on the promontory.

Take D 115 to the left. Shortly before Arles, park the car near the footpath off to the left which leads to the pretty gorge of the river Fou.

★★ **Gorges de la Fou** ⊘ - *1hr 30min there and back on foot (just under a mile, along well-maintained footbridges).* The gorge was explored for the first time in 1928. The crevice cut by the river is less than 3m/10ft wide in some places, despite being over 100m/328ft deep. Stretches where cataracts can be seen thundering down from one deep pool to the next alternate with calmer, more open reaches. There are a number of large boulders which have tumbled down and got wedged below.

Col de l'ASCLIER★★

Michelin map 80 folds 16 and 17 or 240 fold 15 - northeast of Le Vigan

The trip described below crosses a ridge of the Cévennes between the valleys of the Gardon and the Hérault, at the foot of Mont Aigoual.

FROM ST-JEAN-DU-GARD TO PONT-D'HÉRAULT
44km/27mi - allow 1hr 30min

The road from St-Jean-du-Gard to Peyregrosse is very tortuous and quite narrow in some places, so should be approached with caution, especially between L'Estréchure and the Asclier pass. Passing places have been built to help traffic conditions. The Asclier pass is generally snowbound between December and March.

St-Jean-du-Gard - *See ST-JEAN-DU-GARD.*

Northwest of St-Jean-du-Gard the road (D 907) climbs along the course of the Gardon de St-Jean, following the river's every twist and turn.

Before L'Estréchure, turn left onto D 152 towards the Asclier pass.

After Milliérines, the countryside becomes extremely rugged. The road overlooks the several tributary valleys of the Gardon de St-Jean, then skirts the Hierle ravine. A road to the left leads to the Asclier pass.

★★ **Col de l'Asclier** - Alt 905m/2 941ft. The road passes beneath a bridge used during the driving of flocks of sheep from the Margeride area to new pastures. From the pass, there is a magnificent **panorama**★★ to the west: in the foreground is the ravine of Notre-Dame-de-la-Rouvière; further off, to the left, are the Anjeau peak and the Tude rocks; beyond the Anjeau peak, along the horizon, looms the limestone ridge of the Séranne range; to the right stretches the limestone plateau of Blandas, with its steep scarp slopes dropping down in the valley of the Arre; further right still stand the mountains of Le Lingas and L'Espérou (part of the Aigoual range).

Col de l'Asclier

After the Asclier pass, the road (D 20) gives a good view of the deep chasm of Notre-Dame-de-la-Rouvière and the Aigoual range. The Sereyrède pass, with its forester's lodge, and the observatory on the summit of the Aigoual can be seen.

Col de la Triballe – Alt 612m/1 989ft. From the pass, there is a broad view over the Cévennes, with the village of St-Martial down below.

Take the picturesque road (D 420) down to the Hérault valley, with hamlets dotted about its slopes in quite improbable settings.

At Peyregrosse, just after the bridge over the Hérault, turn left onto D 986.

The road runs alongside the Hérault as far as the confluence with the river Arre at **Pont-d'Hérault.**

Les ASPRES*

Michelin map 86 fold 18 or 235 folds 52 and 56 or 240 folds 41 and 45

This is the name of the area bordered to the north by the Têt valley, to the south by the Tech valley, to the east by the plain around Perpignan and to the west by the Canigou range. It is a rugged region, where inhabitants are few and far between and nothing breaks the overall stillness. A major part of the attraction for visitors lies in the beauty of an essentially Mediterranean landscape, covered mainly by olive groves and cork oaks, against a backdrop of schist or granite rocks, and in the discovery of Serrabone priory standing in solitary splendour against this somewhat unforgiving backdrop.

FROM ILLE-SUR-TÊT TO AMÉLIE-LES-BAINS
56km/35mi – allow 3hr

Ille-sur-Têt – *See PERPIGNAN: The Roussillon Plain.*

Leave Ille-sur-Têt south on D 2, then turn right onto D 16 to Bouleternère.

The D 618 *(turn left in Bouleternère)* leaves the orchards in the valley of the Têt for the *garrigues* (scrubland) along the Boulès gorge.

After 7.5km/4.5mi turn right to Serrabone.

★★ **Prieuré de Serrabone** – *See Prieuré de SERRABONE.*

Col Fourtou – Alt 646m/2 100ft. The view looking back from the pass is of the Bugarach, the highest point in the Corbières (1 230m/3 998ft), and looking forward is of the Vallespir mountains on the Franco-Spanish border – the Roc de France and, further to the right, the Pilon de Belmatx with its jagged crest. To the right of these is the Canigou range.

Prunet-el-Belpuig – The **Chapelle de la Trinité** ⊘ has a door with scrolled hinges. Inside, there is a 12C robed Christ and a Baroque altarpiece depicting the Holy Trinity, with the Holy Ghost as a youth, Christ as an adult and God the Father as an old man.

Château de Belpuig – *30min walk (there and back) from the Chapelle de la Trinité.*
Across the moor, the brooding ruins of this castle occupy a prime site on a rocky spur overlooking a wide **panorama★**, taking in the Canigou, the Albères, the Roussillon and Languedoc coasts and the Corbières (Bugarach).
After the Xatard pass the road drops down to Amélie, passing only two villages on its way – St-Marsal and Taulis – and skirting the upper valley of the Ample. Holm oaks and chestnut trees grow on the surrounding slopes.

‡‡ **Amélie-les-Bains** – *See AMÉLIE-LES-BAINS.*

L'AUBRAC★

Michelin map 76 folds 13 and 14 and 80 folds 3 to 5 or 240 folds 1, 2, 5 and 6

L'Aubrac is the most southerly of the volcanic uplands of the Auvergne. It is a region of ponderous, rolling hills, with vast stretches of countryside covered in pastureland on which herds of cattle graze during the summer. While travelling through the area, keep an eye out for the **drailles**, trails occasionally lined with low drystone walls along which animals are herded from one seasonal pasture to another.
In winter, cross-country skiers arrive at the resorts of the **Espace Nordique des Monts d'Aubrac**, set up in 1985 (Aubrac, Bonnecombe, Brameloup, Lacalm, Laguiole, Nasbinals, St-Urcize).

① WESTERN AUBRAC

Round tour leaving from Nasbinals
117km/73mi – allow 4hr – see local map

Nasbinals – Nasbinals is an active livestock market, with an interesting little Romanesque church. There are several lively agricultural **fairs** during the year. The village is also a ski resort, with facilities for both downhill and cross-country skiing. At the end of the last century one of the village's inhabitants, a certain **Pierre Broude** nicknamed "**Pierrounet**", acquired quite a reputation for his skill in healing broken or dislocated limbs. News of his amazing medical prowess spread rapidly, and soon invalids of all kinds, not only the lame, were travelling from far and wide to consult him. He is said to have been seeing around 10 000 clients a year at the height of his fame. Nasbinals has a monument to him, the base of which is decorated with crutches.

Leave Nasbinals on the D 987 southwest.

The road crosses vast tracts of pasture land interspersed with the forests of Aubrac and Rigambal (state-owned) on the outskirts of Aubrac.

Aubrac – Situated at 1 300m/4 225ft above sea level, Aubrac is a small holiday resort which offers plenty of sunshine and fresh air during the summer months, but which is popular also with winter sports enthusiasts. Parisians with roots in the Auvergne return here to enjoy local treats such as *aligot*, a potato dish made with lashings of local *tomme* cheese. After a few days of good cooking and fresh air, they depart homewards sufficiently revitalised to cope with city life again.
A great square tower, a Romanesque church and a 16C building which has been turned into a forester's lodge are all that remain of the estate of the Brothers Hospitaller of Aubrac, an order of monastic knights who, from the 12C to the 17C, took it upon themselves to escort and protect pilgrims crossing these desolate regions on their way to Rocamadour or Santiago de Compostela.

Take D 533 down into the delightful Boralde de St-Chély valley, then turn left onto D 19 to Bonnefon.

Bonnefon – This hamlet is dwarfed by a 15C square granary tower built by the monks of Aubrac.

On leaving Bonnefon, take D 629 left and then keep right.

The road twists its way uphill offering beautiful views of the Lot valley and the Sévérac plateau. Just past a forester's lodge, it enters the forest of Aubrac, a tall beech wood dotted with pines.

Brameloup – This small winter sports resort has a number of wide pistes through the forest.

Turn back and take D 19 to the left.

Winter in the Aubrac

Prades-d'Aubrac – The 16C church in this village features a sturdy octagonal bell-tower. From the far side of the village there is a view of the Lot valley. As the road drops down towards the Lot, giving views over the Rouergue plateaux, it passes through a rapid succession of different landscapes. The vast pastures of the plateaux, with here and there a stunted beech tree, give way to moorlands, a few meadows and the odd field of crops. The valley of the Boralde cuts off to the right. More and more land is given over to crops, and the road begins to go through groves of chestnut trees, and then orchards. The vineyards that once covered the south-facing slopes, which are really too steep for growing vines, have almost all now been abandoned.

★ **St-Côme-d'Olt** – The houses of this small fortified town have now spread beyond the limits of the old curtain wall. Any one of the three former town gateways leads inside the wall, where 15C and 16C houses line the streets. The **church** features an unusual spiral bell tower in the Flamboyant style (16C) and a panelled door sculpted in the Renaissance style. The **château**, once the residence of the lords of Calmont and Castenau, is now the town hall.

★ **Espalion** – See ESPALION.
Leave Espalion on D 921 north.
The road climbs towards Laguiole giving views of the Aubrac mountain range to the right and the Viadène plateau to the left.

Laguiole – See LAGUIOLE.
Take D 15 from the entrance to Laguiole.
To the east of Laguiole, the road crosses expanses of pasture land and the odd beech wood. The views of the Viadène and Rouergue plateaux give way to that of the Margeride. This is one of the highest roads in the Aubrac region.
From Aubrac, take D 987 back to Nasbinals.

② EASTERN AUBRAC

Round tour from Nasbinals *97km/60mi – allow 4hr – local map overleaf*

The Bonnecombe pass is snowbound from December to April.

Nasbinals – See ① above.
Leave Nasbinals on D 900 southeast, then take D 52 to the right.

Grotte et Cascade de Déroc – *30min there and back on foot. Park the car by D 52 and take a rough path lined with dry-stone walls to the left, towards a farm.*

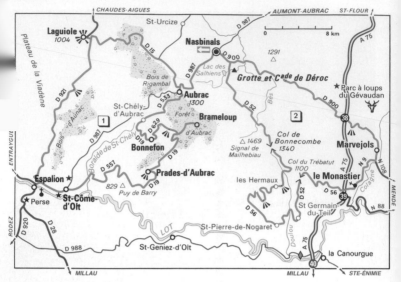

The path leads to a stream and carries along its bank for a while, before crossing it to get to the edge of a gully down which a tributary of the Bès plunges. The waterfall tumbles over a granite ledge in front of a cave in which rock prisms form the ceiling vault.

Before long the D 52 reaches a barren region with lakes. It runs along the shores of Salhiens lake, before cutting across pasture land to the **Col de Bonnecombe**. After the pass, the road drops down through Les Hermaux to St-Pierre-de-Nogaret, giving pretty **views★** of the Lot valley and the entire Causses region as it goes. It then follows a winding, scenic route through woodland and the Doulou valley to St-Germain-du-Teil.

Take D 52 to the left to the Col du Trébatut. Turn right at the crossroads onto D 56, which leads to the Colagne valley.

Le Monastier – The 11C church, which was restored in the 16C, contains an interesting set of sculpted capitals, embellished either with narrative scenes or decorated with foliage motifs.

Marvejols – *See MARVEJOLS.*

As it climbs, the D 900 offers a broad view of Marvejols, La Margeride, Mont Lozère, the Causses and the Cévennes on the horizon, before passing through pine forests, then fields and meadows, and finally the pasture land so typical of the Aubrac region. It then reaches Nasbinals.

Haute vallée de l'AUDE★★

Michelin map 86 folds 7, 16 and 17 or 235 folds 43, 47, 51 and 55

The Aude rises on the east slope of the Carlit peak and flows parallel with the Têt for a while, before heading north. The river crosses the watershed between the Atlantic and the Mediterranean, marked by the Col de la Quillane (alt 1 714m/ 5 571ft), before flowing across the Capcir plain, high above sea level and cut off from its surroundings by forested peaks which retain their snow caps for most of the year. The Capcir is more exposed to northerly winds than nearby Cerdagne and temperatures during the winter can be bitter. However, the pure, clear air and bright sunshine during the season make this an ideal mountain holiday resort.

Water levels in the river Aude fluctuate; rainfall and melting snow can swell its flow by up to a thousandfold. The river washes an enormous volume of alluvial silt down the mountain with it. The power of the river in spate when the snows melt has proved sufficient to merit the construction of two dam and reservoir installations – at Matemale and Puyvalador – to regulate its flow and supply a chain of hydroelectric power stations down to the plants at Nantilla and St-Georges in the lower reaches. In September 1993, the Couiza area around the confluence of the Aude and the Sals suffered serious flood damage.

Forests in the upper Aude valley – The Pyrénées-Orientales *département* is home to some beautiful forests. There are relatively few in the Cerdagne, and those that there are occupy mainly the shady slopes, with Scots pines lower

96

down and passing through various other species of pine as one approaches the mountain summits. At the heart of these forests, clearings have been converted into ski-slopes.

The Capcir, on the other hand, has much more dense forest cover, in particular in the forest of La Matte where the Scots pines are among some of the most beautiful specimens in France. The other woodlands in the Capcir, in which a variety of species of pine and fir trees grow, cover slopes of all angles, crisscrossed by forest roads, some of which are properly surfaced, others more precarious, but all of them providing interesting itineraries for day trips. Beauty spots include the lakes of Balcère, in Les Angles forest, or of Campoureils, more than 2 200m/7 150ft above sea level, and the roads over the passes of Col de Creu and Col de Sansa, through the Matemale forest.

Further north, beech and pine grow majestically side by side in the forests of Carcanet and Hares, in the Donézan region, and those around Quillan and on the Plateau de Sault.

Hat-making – In 1804, a few people from Bugarach in the Corbières returned from captivity in Upper Silesia, where they had learned about the hat trade, and decided to set up their own branch of the industry in their homeland. They moved to Espéraza in 1820, attracted by the plentiful water supply there, and soon new factories had been founded at Quillan, Couiza and Chalabre. Initially there were adequate resources of wool and rabbit fur locally, but before long the hat-making centres were importing their raw materials from elsewhere and exporting finished and semi-finished *(cloches)* hats.

Production had to bow to a drop in demand once the younger generations stopped wearing hats so much. There is now only one factory left, in Montazels, while most of the others have switched to making shoes, furniture, plastic foam (at Espéraza) or decorative laminates (such as Formica).

★**CAPCIR** – *See Le CAPCIR.*

★★ RIVER GORGES

From Usson-les-Bains to Quillan *30km/18.5mi – allow 1hr (not including the tour of the Ayuzou caves)*

Usson-les-Bains – *See Le CAPCIR.*

This pretty stretch of road runs along the edge of the Sault plateau.

Grottes de l'Ayuzou ○ – This complex network of caves was discovered in 1965. On the tour, visitors can see a large number of crystals and some wonderful examples of aragonite.

In the **Aude gorge**, a reach of some 10km/6mi, the river surges along between high cliffs thickly covered with plant life. Nantilla power station, supplied by water through pressure pipes, marks the lower level of the most powerful hydroelectric scheme in the upper Aude valley.

★ **Gorges de St-Georges** – This river gorge, cutting straight down through bare rock, is the narrowest in the upper Aude valley.

★ **Défilé de Pierre-Lys** – This is an impressive stretch of road between the ravine's sheer cliff walls, to which the odd bush clings tenaciously. The final tunnel is known as the **Trou du Curé** ("priest's hole") in memory of Abbot Félix Armand (1742-1823), parish priest of St-Martin-Lys, who cut the passage through the rock using a pick and pickaxe.

Quillan – This town is a major tourist centre for the upper Aude valley and is one of the best points of departure for forays into the forests of the Pyrenean foothills. Rugby has enjoyed a passionate following locally since the period between the two world wars, the hat-making industry's swansong. Modern local industry includes laminates (Formica), luxury and garden furniture, trousers and shoes. On the esplanade in front of the station there is a quaint little monument to Abbot Armand. On the east bank of the Aude stand the ruins, sadly being left to fall into disrepair, of a medieval fortress with a square ground plan – most unusual in this region.

RAZÈS REGION

From Quillan to Limoux *35km/22mi – allow 2hr 30min*

This is a lovely stretch of road, lined with plane trees, but one which carries a lot of traffic.

Quillan – *See above.*

Downstream of Quillan, the river flows through a somewhat cheerless region – the old Razès region.

Espéraza – This small town on the banks of a tight meander in the Aude was once an important hat-making centre, a past which is commemorated by a museum, the **Musée de la Chapellerie** ⊘, in the old goods depot. The museum is laid out like a factory, showing the twenty or so stages involved in the making of a felt hat. An exhibition of various types of head-dress and a film add to the interest of the visit.

Espéraza's other claim to fame, the discovery locally at the end of the 19C of the fossils of prehistoric reptiles, also has a museum dedicated to it, the **Musée des Dinosaures** ⊘, next to the hat-making museum. The display includes panels retracing the discovery of the fossils, a reconstruction of one of the local digs, bone fragments (mostly remoulds) and semi-fossilised eggs, a video and the enormous skeleton of a dinosaur related to the tyrannosaurus species, unearthed locally.

Couiza – This town, essentially devoted to the shoe-making industry, is home to the old **château** ⊘ of the Dukes of Joyeuse. This well-preserved mid-16C building, flanked by round towers, is in a style typical of many buildings in the Languedoc and Cévennes regions. It has been turned into a hotel. A pitted rustic work doorway leads into an austere Renaissance courtyard. The arcade on the inside of the entrance façade is decorated with superimposed columns divided by an entablature.

Rennes-le-Château – *4km/2.5mi off D 118, to the right up a steep narrow road with a view of Coustaussa and the ruins of its 12C castle.*

The village of Rennes-le-Château stands on a plateau more than 25m/80ft above the Aude valley. From the car park near the water tower there is a view to the west of the upper Aude valley dotted with the red rooftops of tiny towns such as Espéraza and Campagne-sur-Aude.

Rumour abounds in Rennes-le-Château about the enigmatic figure of Father Béranger Saunière, parish priest here from 1885 to his death in 1917. How was the abbot suddenly able to fund from 1891 onwards the complete restoration of his church, which was in rack and ruin, the construction of a sumptuous mansion (the Villa Bétania), a bizarre, semi-fortified library-tower (the Tour Magdala) and a tropical greenhouse for himself, and in general a lifestyle fit for a prince for the next 20 years? Speculation has tended to agree that the secret of the abbot's wealth must have been the discovery of some hidden treasure, which has led to all sorts of hypotheses about the Knights Templar (despite the fact that they were never based locally), the Cathars, and even the treasure brought back from the Holy City itself by the Visigoths. The **Domaine de l'abbé Saunière** ⊘, regrouping the priest's garden, his private chapel, the Villa Bétania and the Magdala tower, contains a museum on what is known of the life of the priest.

The **local museum** ⊘, in the presbytery, gives more details about the history of the town, and contains among other things an 8-9C Visigothic pillar which once supported the high altar table in the church and in which Father Saunière is said to have discovered some mysterious parchments just before his fortunes took a sudden turn for the better. The little parish church of Ste-Marie-Madeleine also attracts the curious, who are generally left somewhat bemused by the unorthodox interior décor in dubious aesthetic taste which was added at the end of the 19C at the priest's behest.

Alet-les-Bains – This small town lies in a sheltered spot at the mouth of the Défilé d'Alet, the final gorge along the Aude valley, and as a result it enjoys a mild climate.

The town grew up around a sizeable Benedictine abbey, which was made the seat of a bishopric by Pope John XXII in 1318. Not far from the road are the **ruins** ⊘ of the 11C Romanesque abbey church which was raised to the status of cathedral from 1318. This was when the Romanesque chancel was replaced by a Gothic one complete with a vast ambulatory. Work was left unfinished, however, and what with the destruction of the cathedral by the Huguenots in 1577 and the construction of the road in the 18C, which cut off the ambulatory chapels, all that remains of the Gothic elements of the building is the north tower *(to the right as you look at the east end)*. The polygonal **Romanesque east end**, built of beautiful red and ochre sandstone, has five buttress columns around the outside with Corinthian capitals incorporated into a wide, ornate cornice. A narrower, less ornate cornice runs right round the inside of the apse, linking the two Corinthian capitals supporting a triumphal archway. The door and windows of the chapter-house feature some interesting Romanesque capitals, while the south door of the abbey church *(in the nearby cemetery)* is decorated with haut-reliefs.

The **old town** of Alet, surrounded by 12C ramparts, is a charming place to explore with many interesting old houses.

On leaving Alet, the Aude valley cuts across a fold in the Corbières mountain massif, before narrowing down again into a gorge, the **Étroit d'Alet**.

Carnival-time in Limoux

Limoux – Part of this town is still enclosed within a fortified wall built in the 14C after the damage inflicted by the Black Prince, son of King Edward III of England.

Limoux has gained quite a reputation for its carnival, which runs from January to March, during which processions of masked people dance along, accompanied by musicians, beneath the arcades on the Place de la République, and great fun is had by all.

The town's skyline is dominated by the distinctive outline of the Gothic spire and east end of St-Martin church overlooking the river. Limoux is the hub of production of **blanquette** ⊘, a sparkling AOC wine made from the Mauzac, Chenin and Chardonnay grapes, using the *méthode champenoise*.

To plan a special itinerary:
- *consult the **Map of Touring Programmes** which indicates the recommended routes, the tourist regions, the principal towns and main sights*
- *read the descriptions in the **Sights** section which include Excursions from the main tourist centres.*

Michelin Maps nos 235, 239 and 240 indicate scenic routes, interesting sights, viewpoints, rivers, forests...

AVEN ARMAND★★★

Michelin map 80 fold 5 or 240 fold 10 – Local map see Les GRANDS CAUSSES

The Aven Armand is undoubtedly one of the wonders of the underground world. The vertical entry shaft or chimney leads beneath the Causse Méjean *(see p 189)*, a vast tract of deserted heathland stretching away on all sides as far as the eye can see.

Discovery of the Aven Armand – The famous speleologist E-A Martel *(see p 19)* began his exploration of the Causses in 1883, going underground to explore in detail every pot-hole he discovered. He was accompanied on these dangerous expeditions by **Louis Armand**, a locksmith from Le Rozier. On 18 September 1897 Armand returned from an outing to the Causse Méjean in a state of great excitement, claiming to have discovered one of the most promising chimneys he had ever come across, which he believed might lead to a more tremendous underground cavern than any they had yet discovered. An expedition set off the very next day to investigate the enormous crevice, known by local farmers as *l'aven* ("the swallow-hole"). Initial soundings revealed a depth of 75m/244ft, but Armand got to the bottom without any problems and was enraptured at the forest of rock formations he found down there. Martel and another colleague, Armand Viré, went down the following day in their turn. Immediately after the discovery, Martel acquired ownership of the chimney for his devoted assistant, and named it the "Puits Armand" ("Armand's well-shaft") after him. A consortium was set up to oversee the refitting and commercial exploitation of the underground chasm. Work on it began in June 1926 and a year later Aven Armand was opened to the public.

FORMATION OF THE AVEN ARMAND

Preliminary phase: as water drains underground to join the water table, the carbon dioxide it contains dissolves the limestone. The water table, which joins the river Jonte, gradually sinks to a lower level, as the Jonte hollows out its river bed. As increasingly large fissures appear in the rock, it starts to disintegrate and chunks of it fall off. Eventually chimneys are formed, linking the underground cavern with ground level.

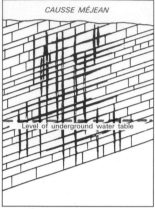

1st phase

Cracks widen in the underground water table, which is situated in a zone of fractures. Vertical cracks, or chimneys, appear to balance the horizontal fissures, and grooves, or *lapiés*, are worn in the rocks at surface level as the water runs down them.

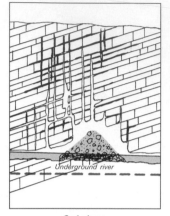

2nd phase

A circular gallery is formed underground. Draining water erodes the rock strata making up the roof of the gallery until part of it collapses, forming a pile of scree.

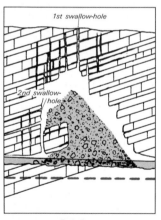

3rd phase

Water continues to erode the limestone, and the pile of scree on the floor of the gallery grows. A chimney is formed underground between the scree and an outcrop of solid rock.

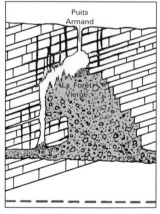

Current phase

Water deposits some of the calcium carbonate it is carrying on the roof and floor of the gallery, forming concretions.

TOUR ⓥ *45min; temperature: 10°C/50°F*

Viewing platform – A 200m/220yd long tunnel has been excavated for easier access to the cavern and leads almost to the foot of the 75m/244ft deep chimney down which the first explorers came. Subtle electric lighting gives a fairy-tale atmosphere to this land from the Arabian Nights. The tour takes you round the vast subterranean gallery. From the viewing platform *(accessible to everyone)* at the end of the tunnel there is an impressive view of the gallery below, which measures 60m by 100m/195ft by 325ft and is 45m/146ft high (in comparison, Blackpool tower is 48m/158ft and the Statue of Liberty 46m/151ft high).

The "Forêt Vierge" – Some spectacular concretions have built up on the scree that has fallen from the roof of the cavern, forming a sort of petrified forest. These fantastically shaped rock trees, in stands of varying density, can have bases measuring up to 3m/10ft in diameter, and some have grown up to 15-25m/50-80ft in height. Their "trunks" resemble those of palm trees or cypresses, and large, jagged "leaves" sprout from their crowns, some measuring two or three feet across. The stalagmites are no less intriguing, as they explode into a riot of arabesques, needles, palm branches and elegant pyramids topped with fat domes. In all there are 400 of them, a strange burgeoning over the centuries into this luxuriant virgin jungle glistening with calcite crystals.

As you walk through the gallery *(the steps have handrails, but some steps are slippery)*, you can appreciate the variety of concretions it contains: elegant candles many feet high; bizarre figures with monstrous, club-shaped heads; curly cabbages and delicately engraved fruit; and most magnificent of all, the 30m/97ft high corbelled column supported by a narrow pedestal, in the shadow of the great stalagmite.

A new lighting system has recently been installed, which picks out the various concretions in better detail and makes still more of the surprises that the Aven Armand has in store for visitors easier to see.

AX-LES-THERMES✝

Population 1 488
Michelin map 86 fold 15 or 235 folds 47 and 51

Ax lies in the valley at the point where the rivers Oriège and Lauze flow into the Ariège. It is a spa town, both a summer holiday destination and a winter sports resort.

Its eighty mineral springs, at temperatures ranging from 18-78°C/64-172°F, supply three pump rooms: the Couloubret, the Modèle and the Teich. The main afflictions treated here are rheumatism, respiratory disorders and some skin problems. The focal point of the resort is the Promenade du Couloubret.

Bassin des Ladres – On the Place du Breilh, a jet of steam marks the site of this hot water basin which is filled in the morning and can be used as a public wash-house. St Louis had it built for soldiers returning from the Crusades suffering from leprosy – hence its name "Lepers' Basin". The hospital of St-Louis (1846), easily recognised by its bellcote, is a typical example of 10C "spa town" architecture.

EXCURSIONS

★ **Vallée d'Orlu** – *8.5km/5mi – see local map. Leave Ax on the road to Puymorens and turn off left just before the bridge over the Oriège; stay on the north bank of the river.*
The road runs along the shore of the reservoir contained by the Orgeix dam, with Orgeix manor-house reflected in the waters. The old Orlu ironworks is surrounded by rocky slopes riddled with streams.

★ **Plateau de Bonascre** – *8km/5mi – see local map. Leave Ax on N 20 to Tarascon and turn off left almost immediately onto D 820.*
The road climbs steeply in a series of hairpin bends, giving a good view of the three river valleys which converge on Ax: the Ariège (towards Tarascon); the Orlu, with the Dent d'Orlu peak towering on the skyline, and the upper Ariège valley. At the top is the Bonascre plateau, home to the ski resort of **Ax-Bonascre-le-Saquet**, equipped with the basic facility of a **cable-car** ⊙ leading to the **Plateau du Saquet** (alt 2 030m/6 598ft).

The izard

About 40 years ago, the izard, a variety of wild goat found in the Pyrenees, had been all but killed off by hunters' bullets. Nowadays it is a protected species. There are over a thousand in the Orlu valley, which has consequently been designated a nature reserve since 1981. The izard is usually to be found between 1 600-2 500m/5 250-8 200ft above sea level, but it does venture below 900m/2 950ft. It is gradually taking over those areas which have been abandoned by man. The izard's coat changes colour depending on the season: it is red-gold in the summer and dark brown with patches of white in the winter, when it also becomes much thicker to combat the cold. The animals are not that timid and can be observed quite easily, especially during spring or autumn. The summer heat and winter cold force them to take refuge in the undergrowth. Izards are perfectly suited to their environment and can climb up and down even quite steep slopes with an impressive agility.

Drive on past the "Sup-Aéro" holiday home and turn off left across the mountain side, on the Route forestière des Campels. Follow this road for about a mile, taking in the superb **view**★★ stretching from the valley cut by the upper reaches of the Ariège as far as the mountains on the border with Andorra. In the valley the main road and the railway line run side by side, crisscrossing one another from time to time.

ANDORRA LA VELLA ↓ COL DE PUYMORENS

★ **Col du Pradel** – *30km/ 18.5mi – see local map.*
Leave Ax to the east on the road to Quillan. 3.5km/2mi out of town, turn left onto D 22. The narrow pass road is closed from 15 November to 14 May.
The Dent d'Orlu (alt 2 222m/7 222ft), with its distinctive pointed outline making it the best known of the mountain peaks in the upper Ariège valley, can be seen to the southeast. The road leads up the pass (alt 1 680m/5 460ft) along a series of tight hairpin bends. There is a lovely view of the mountains surrounding the upper reaches of the Ariège.

From the Col du Pradel, it is a 1hr 30min walk there and back to the Pic de Serembarre summit.

★★ **Pic de Serembarre** – Alt 1 851m/6 016ft. From the summit there is a panorama south of the Pyrenees range from Pic Carlit on the left, over the Andorra mountains and the central Pyrenees (Massif de la Maladeta), to the Pic du Midi de Bigorre on the right. To the east and north stretch the Corbières region and the Plateau de Sault.

★ **Signal de Chioula** – *Round tour of 38km/24mi – allow 3hr. Leave Ax on D 613 north, following the Ariège valley in a series of hairpin bends.*
At the Chioula pass, a wide footpath leads to the beacon (alt 1 507m/4 898ft; *45min there and back on foot*), from where there is a view of the peaks framing the upper Ariège valley.
At the Marmare pass, take D 2 left. From the Cos bend the Ariège valley comes into view once more. Near Caussou, a village set amidst terraced fields, note the iron crosses which are products of the old local ironworking industry.

Carry on along D 2, which takes you straight down to Luzenac on the valley floor, unless you choose to visit the quarry at Trimouns (see below) on the way, in which case turn right into D 20 just after Caussou, then right again at the Lordat crossroads (add on 32km/19mi).

Luzenac – This village has been famed since the end of the 19C for the nearby deposit of French chalk, which is quarried at the **Carrière de Trimouns**★ ⊙, cut into the middle of the St-Barthélemy mountain massif between 1 700-1 850m/5 577-6 070ft above sea level. The raw French chalk is transported in skips to the factory in the valley, where it is dried, crushed and packaged. The quarry at Trimouns, which is one of the largest operations of its kind in the world, is open to visitors *(take D 2 back towards Caussou, turn left onto D 20 towards **Lordat**, where there are some interesting castle ruins, and then right into the quarry road; round tour of 39km/24mi).* Not only is the **view**★ of the huge white seam of French chalk itself impressive, but there is a magnificent **panorama**★★ of the upper Ariège mountains from the quarry. *Drive back to Luzenac via **Vernaux**, where there is a small Romanesque church built from tufa.*

Take N 20 back to Ax.

*Michelin Maps (scale 1: 200 000)
which are revised regularly show at a glance:*
- *main roads linking the main towns and sights*
- *regional roads*
- *side roads for a quiet drive.*
*Keep current **Michelin Maps** in the car at all times.*

BALARUC-LES-BAINS‡‡

Michelin map 83 fold 16 or 240 fold 27

Built on flat land on the shores of the Bassin de Thau this lively resort has many amenities to offer, especially for those keen on outdoor activities and water sports. In the evenings, the floodlit shoreline around Sète and the Mont St-Clair provides a sparkling backdrop to the resort's night-life.
The application of sea mud thinned down with chlorinated spa water, rich in sodium, has been shown to help in the treatment of bone disorders and rheumatism. Balaruc is the third most popular spa resort in France.

Balaruc-le-Vieux – *4km/2.5mi north.* The old village of Balaruc, on a hill overlooking the lagoon, still has its original, defensive circular layout and typically Languedoc atmosphere. Some of the houses feature striking arched doorways.

BANYULS-SUR-MER⌂

Population 4 662
Michelin map 86 fold 20 or 240 fold 46

Banyuls, the most southerly seaside resort in France, has a delightful yachting harbour. The resort is developing without detriment to its charm, set against a pretty backdrop of vineyards around a bay divided into two coves by the promontory on which the old town stands. This site is sheltered from the harsh northwesterly gusts of the *tramontane*, with the result that a number of tropical plants have been introduced here (carob, eucalyptus, and various palm trees), originally by the biologist Charles-Victor Naudin (1815-99), and propagated along the Mediterranean coast as far as the Riviera.
A sea-water cure (thalassotherapy) centre has recently been opened.

The sea – The coastal waters along the Côte Vermeille are deep and clear and well-stocked with fish. They have attracted the attention of scientists, because of their wealth of biological interest, to the extent that the Laboratoire Arago (Université de Paris VI), has been established at Banyuls, a research and teaching centre specialising in oceanography, marine biology and land ecology. A nature reserve has been set up between Banyuls and Cerbère.
The main beach lies in the shelter of the cove which is closed off to the east by a pair of islands, the Ile Petite and the Ile Grosse (on which there is a war memorial by Maillol), linked to the mainland by a dike.

Aquarium ⊙ – Clearly presented display of Mediterranean fauna.

Vineyards and mountains – Vineyards reign supreme over the last slopes of the Albères, covering the final outcrops of the Pyrenees and the steep hillsides of the Baillaury valley. The schist slopes have been cut into terraces, supported by low stone walls, and reinforced to prevent the more exposed slopes being washed away by rainwater with a system of crisscrossing ditches.
The grapes are vinified according to traditional methods developed by the Knights Templar. After a lengthy maturing process in oak casks in cellars or in the open air, the result is the famous **Banyuls**, a dry, medium or sweet wine capable of gracing the best of tables. It can be drunk as an apéritif, or with dessert, and is the ideal accompaniment to *foie gras,* strongly-flavoured cheeses and game, among other things.
Several cellars, or **caves** ⊙, are open to the public, including two on the vertiginous cliff road (route des Crêtes). The **Grande Cave** ⊙ shows a video on the history of Banyuls and organises a guided tour of the place where the oak barrels are kept, where the wines are left to mature in the sun and the cellars with their antique casks. The **Cave du Mas Reig** ⊙ is also open to the public. This wine cellar dates from the days of the Knights Templar (13C), whose feudal castle and sub-commandery (Mas Reig) are next door *(closed to the public)*.

Métairie Maillol – *4km/2.5mi southwest. Leave Banyuls towards Les Arènes and turn sharp left after a craft centre.* The road runs along the Baillaury valley. **Aristide Maillol** (1861-1944) was born in

La Méditerranée by Aristide Maillol

D. Lerrault/DIAF

103

Banyuls. At the age of 20 he "went up" to Paris, where he began learning painting and more importantly, in line with the trend set by the "Nabis", interesting himself in the revival of crafts such as pottery and tapestry. He was over 40 by the time he had established himself as a sculptor of great talent, basing his groups of sturdy nude figures on earlier sketches. While as a painter and draughtsman he may have worked from models, as a sculptor he is distinguished by his unwavering observation, his quest for fluid movement and by his sense of the grandiose, which led him to produce some outstanding works, in which his figures exude both grace and power. The artist liked to retire to his little country house at the bottom of a valley which gets scorching hot and dusty in the summer. This now houses the sculptor's workshop and some memorabilia (sculptures, photographs). The artist was buried on his request in the garden (bronze: *La Méditerranée*).

Abbaye de BEAULIEU-EN-ROUERGUE★

Michelin map 79 fold 19 or 235 fold 19 – 10km/6mi southeast of Caylus
Local map see ST-ANTONIN-NOBLE-VAL

The charming Seye valley on the border of the Quercy and Rouergue regions was the place where a group of monks sent by St Bernard founded an abbey in 1144. They called the abbey Beaulieu (*Belloc* in Occitanian).
In the wake of the French Revolution, the abbey was partly demolished and converted into a farm. It was not until 1960 that a programme of restoration was begun by the abbey's new owners, which continued until the abbey was donated to the French Historic Buildings Commission (Caisse des Monuments Historiques) in 1973. The result is remarkable, especially in the case of the church, which is a magnificent example of Cistercian architecture. The abbey is now a **contemporary art centre** which holds exhibitions and concerts in the summer.

TOUR ⊘

★ **Abbey church** – This fine building dating from the mid 13C exemplifies a pure Gothic style with its vast single nave beneath pointed vaulting, lit through rose and lancet windows. The transept ends in an elegant heptagonal apse and there is an interesting octagonal **dome** on squinches above the transept crossing. A square chapel opens off each transept. The church houses exhibitions of contemporary art.

Conventual buildings – The **chapter-house**, the oldest part of the abbey, opened onto the cloisters (no longer extant) through three pointed arches. It is composed of two bays, each covered with three pointed vaults resting on two massive columns. The **cellar**, on the ground floor of the lay-brothers' building (Bâtiment des Convers), has ten cross-ribbed vaults supported on four columns decorated with capitals carved with leaf motifs in low relief. The beauty of this room and the restraint and refinement of details such as the pendant keystones illustrates the careful attention that the Cistercians paid to the construction of every building in their abbeys, even annexes.

A Map of Touring Programmes
is given at the beginning of the guide.
To plan a special tour
use the preceding Map of Principal Sights.

BÉZIERS★

Conurbation 76 304
Michelin map 83 folds 14 and 15 or 240 fold 26
Plan of conurbation in the current Michelin Red Guide France

Capital of the Languedoc vineyards and home town of Pierre-Paul **Riquet** (who designed the Canal du Midi), Béziers was already a thriving city when the Romans arrived and colonised it in 36 or 35 BC. It was renamed Julia Baeterrae and fell within the Narbonensis province. Modern Béziers still occupies the original site on a plateau on the east bank of the Orb, overlooking the river, which it occupied before the arrival of the Romans. The Roman forum was probably located in front of the present town hall, where it would have been surrounded by temples and a market. Between the Rue St-Jacques and the Place du Cirque, the old houses are laid out in an elliptical pattern which reflects the presence, beneath the neat urban gardens and garages, of Béziers' Roman amphitheatre. The site is currently being excavated. In the 3C, under threat of Barbarian invasion, stones from the amphitheatre were used to build a fortified wall around the city.

Béziers is a city which takes festivals and merry-making very seriously, and the year is punctuated by numerous events, such as the Feria d'Été (summer festival) or the Festival de Béziers en Languedoc *(for details, see the Calendar of events at the end of the guide)*. The oldest of the festivals is held in honour of Aphrodise, the first Bishop of Béziers and patron of the city, to which he bequeathed his heraldic device – a camel (legend attributes Egyptian origins to the saint).

The Béziers rugby team (ASB) and its achievements have also helped to spread the city's name abroad.

The cost of backing the Cathars – During the Albigensian Crusade, the Crusaders laid siege to Béziers in 1209. The resident Roman Catholics were given the chance to leave the town before battle commenced, but they refused. Side by side with their Cathar neighbours, they fought outside the city walls to defend Béziers from the intruders, but eventually they were routed. The Crusaders pursued them into the town, and the ensuing massacre was bloody in the extreme, sparing neither old nor young. Even those who sought refuge in the churches were butchered, and Béziers itself was finally pillaged and put to the torch until not a creature there remained living.

The city did eventually manage to rise from its ashes, but for many years it was a sleepy, backward community. It was not until the vineyards were developed in the 19C that it rediscovered its old wealth and vigour.

OUT AND ABOUT IN BÉZIERS

Guided tour of the town – Tours are organised from July to mid-September by the tourist office. ☎ 04 67 62 30 59.

Out on the town – Try the Allées Paul-Riquet, which is lined with numerous brasseries with pleasant shaded terraces, cinemas (to the east) and bars (to the west), or Place Jean-Jaurès, where the fountains are illuminated in the evening.

Entertainment – Around 15 August Béziers hosts a particularly lively summer festival, the Féria de Béziers.

Arènes (Amphitheatre): avenue Émile-Claparède, bullfighting events.

Palais des Congrès et des Expositions (Exhibition and conference centre): concerts, exhibitions.

Théâtre municipal: theatre, classical music, dance, opera.

Théâtre des Franciscains: plays and exhibitions.

Théâtre de Verdure: variety shows, concerts, theatre, in summer at the heart of the Plateau des Poètes.

Markets – The central covered market (*halles*) is open Tuesday to Sunday. Other foodstuff markets are held on Tuesday mornings in Place Émile-Zola, on Wednesday mornings in the Iranget district, and on Friday mornings in Place David-d'Angers.

★ANCIENNE CATHÉDRALE ST-NAZAIRE (BZ)

Perched on a terrace above the river Orb, the cathedral symbolised the might of the Bishops of Béziers between 760 and 1789. The Romanesque building was badly damaged in 1209 *(see above)*, and repairs were carried out on it from 1215 until the 15C.

In the west front, which is flanked by a pair of fortified towers (late 14C), there is a beautiful rose window 10m/32ft in diameter. The fortifications on the east end are also a decorative feature: the arches between the buttresses are in fact machicolations. A few of the windows feature some lovely examples of 13C ironwork. The base of the bell tower is a remnant from the Romanesque building.

Interior – *Enter through the doorway in the north transept.* The bay directly in front of the chancel contains some 11C sculpted capitals. The colonnettes on top of them, decorated with crocketed capitals, and the cross-ribbed vaulting were added in the 13C, when this part of the cathedral was made higher. Note the lovely chancel apse which was built in the 13C and modified in the 18C. To the left, and set down slightly, is the sacristy, with a beautiful 15C stellarvaulted roof.

Cloisters – *Go round the south side of the cathedral.* The corbels supporting the ribs of the vaulting are decorated with beautiful 14C sculptures. Take a flight of steps into the Jardin de l'Évêché, from which there is a pretty view of the church of St-Jude and the river Orb spanned by a 13C bridge, the Pont Vieux (the Pont Neuf dates from the 19C).

Cathedral of St-Nazaire and the Pont Vieux

★ **Viewpoint** (BZ) – The terrace near the cathedral gives an interesting view of the region around Béziers. In the foreground you can see the Orb flowing through vineyards, the Canal du Midi between tree-lined banks and the hillfort of Ensérune. In the distance are the Mont Caroux, the Pic de Nore to the west and, on a clear day, the Canigou.

ADDITIONAL SIGHTS

★ **Musée du Biterrois** ⊘ (BZ M¹) – This museum, in the old St-Jacques barracks built in 1702 to designs by Charles d'Aviler, contains substantial collections on local archeology, ethnology and natural history.

In the vast entrance foyer, roofed with metal beams, there is a display of fauna from land, sea and lake, presented in the form of dioramas. There is also a collection of Greek, Iberian and Roman amphorae discovered on the seabed nearby at Cap d'Agde, site of many a shipwreck. There is an interesting reconstruction of a *capitelle*, a dry-stone shelter used by shepherds in the *garrigues*. Various galleries covering a range of topics lead off from the main foyer *(begin to the right of the entrance)*; the first ones look at geology and volcanic activity in the Languedoc region, and life during the Bronze and Iron Ages.

A major part of the museum is given over to the region's Gallo-Roman heritage, in the form of numerous finds made during excavation digs in the city. There is sigillated pottery from the workshops at La Graufesenque *(see MILLAU)*, large earthenware amphorae called *dolia*, and milestones which once lined the Via Domitia *(see p 370)*. The high spot of the exhibition is the "Trésor de Béziers", consisting of three large chased silver platters discovered in 1983 in a vineyard on the outskirts of the city. Exhibits such as cippi, steles and votive altars give an insight into 1 and 2C funerary rites.

A special place is reserved for the local saint, Aphrodise. Medieval Romanesque and Gothic artefacts include 12C historiated capitals and 14C low reliefs. Various aspects of local economy are also illustrated, eg fishing, wine-growing and the construction of the Canal du Midi. A collection of Greek vases embodies the 19C revival of interest in Antiquity. Another display recalls the operas that were performed in the amphitheatre between 1898 and 1926.

Musée des Beaux-Arts ⊘ (BYZ) – The museum of fine art occupies two old private mansions near the cathedral. The **Hôtel Fabrégat** (M²) contains works by Martin Schaffner, Dominiquin, Guido Reni, Pillement, Languedoc painter

J Gamelin, Géricault, Devéria, Delacroix, Corot, Daubigny, Othon Friesz, Soutine, Chirico, Kisling, Dufy and Utrillo, among others. There are also a hundred or so drawings by J-M Vien, the complete collection of Jean Moulin's drawings, and a large bequest by Maurice Marinot (paintings, drawings, glassware).

The **Hôtel Fayet** (**M³**) houses 19C paintings, a bequest by J-G Goulinat (1883-1972) and the contents of the workshop of Béziers sculptor **J-A Injalbert** (1845-1933).

Allées Paul-Riquet (**CYZ**) – This broad, 600m/650yd long avenue, shaded by plane trees, positively bustles with life.
In the centre of the avenue stands a statue of Riquet by David d'Angers. The theatre (**T**) was built in the mid-19C and its façade is decorated with allegorical low reliefs, also the work of David d'Angers.

Plateau des Poètes (**CZ**) – This delightful, hilly landscaped park runs on from Allées Paul-Riquet. It was laid out by the Bühler brothers in the 19C and contains tree varieties such as the Caucasian elm, the Californian sequoia, the magnolia and the Cedar of Lebanon. The busts of poets which line the paths are what earned the park its name. The fountain is by Injalbert (Fontaine du Titan).

Basilique St-Aphrodise ⊙ (**BY**) – The original church was a cathedral until 760. Inside, beneath the gallery, is the font, a handsome 4-5C **sarcophagus** on which the scene of a lion hunt has been carved. Opposite the pulpit is a 16C polychrome wood Crucifix. In the pre-chancel, to the left, there is a bronze Crucifix by Injalbert. The Romanesque crypt houses a lovely sculpture of the head of Christ.

►► **Église de la Madeleine**; **Église St-Jacques**

BÉZIERS

Flourens (R.)	**BY** 23	Drs-Bourguet (R. des)	**BZ** 13	Tourventouse (Bd)	**BZ** 65
Péri (Pl. G.)	**BYZ** 49	Dr-Vernhes (R. du)	**BZ** 16	Victoire (Pl. de la)	**BCY** 68
République (R. de la)	**BY** 55	Estienne-d'Orves (Av.)	**BZ** 22	Viennet (R.)	**BZ** 69
Riquet (R. P.)	**BY** 58	Garibaldi (Pl.)	**CZ** 26	4-Septembre (R. du)	**BY** 72
		Joffre (Av. Mar.)	**CZ** 32	11 Novembre (Pl. du)	**CY** 74
Abreuvoir (R. de l')	**BZ** 2	Massol (H.)	**BZ** 43		
Albert-Ier (Av.)	**CY** 3	Moulins (Rampe des)	**BY** 44		
Canterelles (R.)	**BZ** 6	Orb (R. de l')	**BZ** 47	**M¹** Musée du Biterrois
Capus (R. du)	**BZ** 7	Puits-des-Arènes (R.)	**BZ** 54	
Citadelle (R. de la)	**BZ** 9	Révolution (Pl. de la)	**BZ** 57	Musée des Beaux-Arts :
		St-Jacques (R.)	**BZ** 60	**M²** Hôtel Fabrégat
		Strasbourg (Bd de)	**CY** 64	**M³** Hôtel Fayet

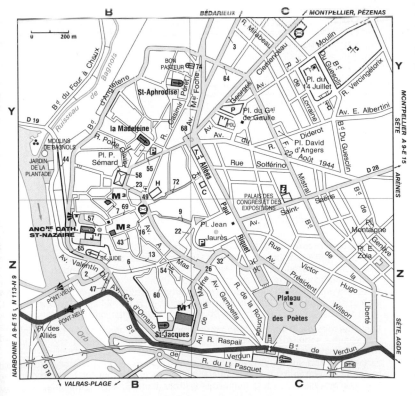

EXCURSIONS

Écluses de Fonsérancs – *Take N 9 southwest towards Narbonne, then follow the signposts for "les Neuf Écluses".* A sequence of eight locks makes up a sort of 312m/338yd long staircase, which enables river craft to negotiate a drop in level of 25m/81ft. Nowadays the locks have been replaced by a single lock, lying parallel to the original system. Since 1857, a canal-bridge downstream, carrying the Canal du Midi over the Orb, provides an alternative to the somewhat daunting stretch of river *(for further details on the Canal du Midi, see Seuil de NAUROUZE).*

★ **Oppidum d'Ensérune** – *13km/8mi southwest. Leave Béziers on N 9. 10km/6mi further on, at Nissan-lez-Ensérune, turn right onto D 162ᴱ which leads to the hillfort. See Oppidum d'ENSÉRUNE.*

Sérignan – *11km/7mi south on D 19 towards Valras.* The old **collegiate church**, dating from the 12, 13 and 14C, stands on the southwest bank of the Orb. There are still traces of the fortifications visible on the exterior, including loopholes, machicolations and the remnants of watch turrets. Inside, the nave has a coffered ceiling and on either side of it a side aisle with ribbed vaulting. It ends in an elegant heptagonal apse. In a small chapel to the north of the chancel there is an ivory Crucifix attributed to Benvenuto Cellini.

⌂ **Valras-Plage** – *15km/9.5mi south on D 19.* This fishing port and yachting harbour at the mouth of the Orb has a fine sandy beach stretching as far as the Grau de Vendres at the mouth of the Aude to the west. The Théâtre de la Mer hosts various shows during the summer.

Abbaye de Fontcaude ⊙ – *18km/11mi northwest. Leave Béziers towards Narbonne, and turn right onto N 112 and then D 14. Turn left after Cazouls-les-Béziers onto D 134ᴱ.*

The ruins of this Romanesque Premonstratensian abbey, founded in 1154, make a pretty sight nestling at the bottom of a valley. The abbey's name means "hot spring" *(fontaine chaude)* and is derived from a nearby resurgent spring. Fontcaude reached the peak of its influence during the Middle Ages, but was destroyed during the Wars of Religion. It has been the object of a number of restoration projects, having been abandoned in the wake of the French Revolution, and the abbey buildings are now used to host concerts. All that remains of the **abbey church**, since the ravages wrought by fire in the 16C, are the transept and the east end, which is best appreciated by walking round the church. The apsidal chapel is oven-vaulted and has three large windows framed by colonnettes with capitals. There are also some pretty remnants of the **cloisters** and chapter-house. In the large scriptorium, where the monks copied out and illuminated manuscripts, there is a museum containing fragments of the **capitals** from the cloisters, executed with remarkable craftsmanship in the 13C to depict a variety of scenes. The old foundry, in which the original 12C bell was cast, has also been discovered on this site.

Le BOULOU ⚜

Population 4 436
Michelin maps 86 fold 19 or 240 fold 41

Le Boulou, spa resort and ideal point of departure for exploring the Roussillon, lies at the foot of the Albères mountains on the north bank of the Tech, at the intersection of the main routes between Perpignan – Spain and Argelès – Amélie-les-Bains.

To the east, not far from the river Tech, the town still boasts remnants of its medieval past, in the shape of a quadrangular tower, part of the 14C curtain wall, and the early 15C chapel of St-Antoine.

Located on the fringes of a cork-oak wood, Le Boulou has two sizeable cork-making factories.

Église Notre-Dame d'El Voló – Of the original 12C Romanesque church, the beautiful white marble **portal** by the Master of Cabestany has survived. Above the arch decorated with knot-work, seven carved corbels support a frieze illustrating scenes from Christ's childhood.

Note, inside, the Baroque altarpiece adorning the high altar and, on the north wall of the nave, a 15C predella surmounted by two panels (15C) depicting St John the Baptist on the left and St John the Evangelist on the right.

Les Thermes du Boulou – The spa waters of Le Boulou have a high mineral (potassium, sodium and magnesium) and oligo-element content and are used for the treatment of liver complaints and metabolic illnesses. They are hgihly carbonated and so are also effective in the treatment of circulatory problems in the legs. Water from two of the five springs is suitable for bottling.

The nearby casino attracts numerous visitors from Spanish Catalonia.

MONTS ALBÈRES

The Albères mountain range is the last outcrop of crystalline rocks on the eastern flank of the Pyrenees. Before it sinks into the Mediterranean trench, this barely indented massif separates two areas of subsidence – to the north Roussillon, and to the south (in Spain) the Ampurdan, old gulfs which were filled in with alluvial deposits in the Tertiary Era up to several hundreds of metres deep (800m/2 500ft in Roussillon). The highest peak, the Pic Neulos, towers 1 256m/4 120ft above sea level.

① **Via the Pic de Fontfrède** *49km/30mi - allow half a day*

Leave Le Boulou west on D 115.

★ **Céret** – *See CÉRET.*
Leave Céret heading southwest on D 13 towards Fontfrède.

This pleasant road climbs through chestnut groves, offering many pretty views. Turn right off the Las Illas road at the Col de la Brousse (alt 860m/2 820ft) into a very winding road through undergrowth to the Col de Fontfrède (June 1940-June 1944 stele – it was through these mountains that people escaped from France to join the Liberation Army). There is a fountain and picnic area at the pass.

A wide hairpin track, unsurfaced but accessible to vehicles, leads to the top of the Pic de Fontfrède.

Pic de Fontfrède – Alt 1 093m/3 585ft. The summit offers a good **view**★ either side of the backbone of the Albères, of Roussillon to the left and the Mediterranean to the right (with Rosas bay in Spain), as well as the Canigou, with its triple peak, and the rampart-like Corbières massif.

Return to the Col de la Brousse and turn right towards Las Illas.

The road winds through dense vegetation initially, followed by terraced gardens and farmhouses scattered over the hillside, each with its own private access. The tinkle of goat bells at every turning is a reminder of an unseen human presence. The Case Nove *mas* or farmhouse, to the left of the road, in a wide bend, followed almost immediately by the Mas Liansou, to the right, are characteristic examples of traditional Albères dwellings.

After passing through Las Illas, the road follows the river of the same name, clinging to the rock face and affording excellent views of the river gorge. The rocks themselves are scarcely visible beneath the dense vegetation, making the countryside appear very green.

Maureillas-Las-Illas – In this pleasant holiday village in the midst of cork-oak groves and orchards, a group of former cork-cutters have set up a cork museum, **Musée du Liège** ⊙, which explains the transformation of this material from when

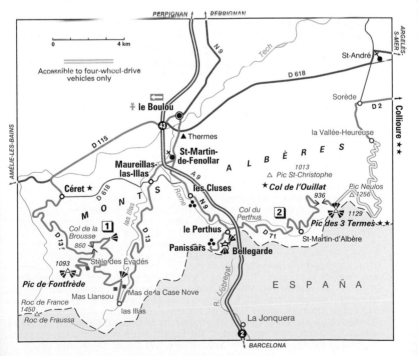

it is stripped from the tree to the marking of the finished corks. The exhibition is enhanced by some astonishing cork sculptures and six magnificent oak casks acting as a show-case for local handicrafts.

Chapelle St-Martin-de-Fenollar ⊘ – This modest chapel has a pre-Romanesque layout, with a single nave and trapezoidal chevet. The nave, originally with a timber-framed roof, has since been vaulted with transverse arches.

The chapel was founded in the 9C by Benedictines from Arles-sur-Tech and contains some interesting 12C **mural paintings**★ in the chancel, illustrating the mystery of the Incarnation. The lower tier depicts the Annunciation, the Nativity, the Adoration of the Magi and the Return of the Magi to their own country; the tier above this, the 24 old men of the Apocalypse; and the vault, Christ in Majesty, surrounded by the four Evangelists, shown as angels each holding a book and the appropriate symbol. This painted decor, executed with bold strokes in refreshing ochres, reds, greens and blues, captivated artists such as Picasso and Braque.

N 9 leads back to Le Boulou.

② Via the Vallée de la Rome and Pic des Trois Termes
53km/33mi – allow half a day

Leave Le Boulou on N 9 south towards Perthus.

The **Vallée de la Rome** ⊘, traversed for more than 2 000 years by the Via Domitia (built between 118 and 117 BC), is still a very important communication route between France and Spain. Leaving behind the "Catalane" motorway, the amateur historian and archeologist will discover a series of megalithic, Gallo-Roman and medieval sites in a superb landscape, against a background of vegetation composed of every possible shade of green.

Chapelle St-Martin-de-Fenollar – *See above.*

Go back to N 9.

Les Cluses – This name is given to a series of hamlets on either side of the narrow gorge (or *clusa* in Latin) followed by the Via Domitia and the valley of the Rome. There are a number of remains of 3C-4C Roman fortifications: on the west bank, **Château des Maures** or "Castell dels Moros" and on the east bank, **Fort de la Cluse Haute**. The viewing platform that has been set up on the "Dressera" (the old Roman crest road) overlooks the ruins of a gateway, perhaps an old toll gate where the "Gaul's one-fortieth levy" was collected on goods in transit between the Narbonensis and the Tarraconensis regions.

Next to the fort, the **church of St-Nazaire** ⊘ is a pre-Romanesque construction with three naves (late 10C-early 11C), ending in oven-vaulted apses, the central one of which still bears traces of frescoes depicting Christ Pantocrator in a mandorla with a winged angel. The composition and colours used have led to the frescoes being attributed to the Master of Fenollar. In front of the south façade, with its gemel window, and slightly set back stands a large archway, all that remains of the old porch.

Le Perthus – Since prehistoric times, Le Perthus (from the Latin for "hack open with a pick") has been the scene of continual comings and goings of nomadic hordes, armies, refugees and, most recently, tourists. The original tiny village of customs huts finally expanded into a fully-fledged town in the late 19C.

Until the "Catalane" motorway was opened in 1976, the main street, Avenue de France, which for a couple of hundred yards forms the border between France and Spain, would be teeming with millions of tourists every year.

The vital strategical importance of this pass (alt 290m/951ft) in the Albères mountains was fully recognized after the Pyrenees Treaty.

From the centre of Le Perthus, turn left towards the Fort de Bellegarde.

Fort de Bellegarde ⊘ – This powerful fortress, which stands in proud isolation on the top of a rock overlooking the town of Le Perthus from 420m/1 380ft above sea level, was rebuilt by Saint-Hilaire, and then by Vauban between 1679 and 1688 on the site of a Spanish fort. Lower downhill to the south, a smaller fort guards the route up to the fort facing towards Spain. The main fort is reached over a drawbridge, from which a slope leads up to the "Place d'Armes", a vast inner courtyard. The renovated buildings contain various exhibitions, one of which is devoted to the history of the fort. The others cover the Via Domitia and Pompey's trophies. The lower room of the stronghold of St-André still contains the system for drawing water used by the garrison from the 18C onwards. The well (62m/203ft deep and some 6m/19ft in diameter) was entirely dug out of the rock and is surfaced for 50m/165ft of its depth.

To the east, a stele commemorates the deeds of General **Dugommier** (1738-94) who, after being appointed head of the French army in the eastern Pyrenees, recaptured Bellegarde from the Spanish. He was buried there until 1800.

From the large terrace, a vast **panorama**★★ encompasses to the west the Canigou and Fontfrède peaks, to the north the Rome valley and its bottleneck through Les Cluses, Ricardo Bofill's pyramid on the edge of the motorway (symbolising the meeting here of the two Catalonias) and the sprawling village of Le Perthus, and to the south the Panissars archeological site and (in Spain) the Rio Llobregat valley, with the town of La Jonquera in the background.

Site archéologique de Panissars – In the days of the Roman occupation, the Panissars pass, or "Summum Pyrenaeum" as it was then called, was the main route over the Pyrenees. The pass marks the Atlantic-Mediterranean watershed, the Franco-Spanish border and the junction of the Via Domitia and the Via Augusta (which leads to Cadiz in Spain). In 1984, the large-scale masonry foundations of a Roman monument, which would once have straddled the road cut out of the rock, were discovered on the site; they are thought to be the remains of the Trophy of Pompey, erected when he returned from his victorious compaign in Spain against Sertorius (71 BC). Above them are the ruins of the priory of Ste-Marie (11-17C), of which the church and outbuildings have been uncovered. To the west of the site, the ruins of a village have also been found on the ridge. Border post no 567 dates from the 18C.

Turn back and, north of Le Perthus, turn right onto D 71 to the Col de l'Ouillat.

Initially shaded by chestnut trees, the road lingers a while on the cultivated terrace (rye) of St-Martin-de-l'Albères (magnificent oaks). There is a good view of the Canigou and the southern slopes of the Albères; to the north, the St-Christophe summit looks like a human face lifted skywards.

From a right-hand bend, there is a view of Trois Termes peak.

★ **Col de l'Ouillat** – Alt 936m/3 070ft. A cool stopping place on the edge of the carefully maintained forest of Laricio pines from Laroque des-Albères *(viewing terrace)*.

The road winds through beeches and pines to the foot of the rocky outcrop of Trois Termes.

★★ **Pic des Trois Termes** – Alt 1 129m/3 703ft. **Panorama** of the gullies and ridges of the Albères mountains, the plain of Roussillon with its string of coastal lagoons, and the valleys of the Confluent and Vallespir.

Towards Spain, there is a view of the Costa Brava, beyond Cape Creus, as far as the sweeping bay of Rosas.

Turn back.

It is also possible to get to the Roussillon plain via Sorède, but the unsurfaced road between the Pic des Trois Termes and Sorède is accessible to four-wheel-drive vehicles only.

BOZOULS★

Michelin map 80 fold 3 or 240 fold 5

Bozouls, famous for its canyon *(trou)*, can be distinguished from afar by its modern church (1964), south of the D 20. The sanctuary, in the shape of a ship's prow, houses a statue of the Virgin Mary by local sculptor Denys Puech.

★ **Trou de Bozouls** – The terrace just next to the war memorial, both works by Denys Puech, affords the best view of this 800m/2 600ft canyon, hollowed out of the Comtal *causse* by the river Dourdou. The sheer cliffs are pitted with caves. On the promontory encircled by the river, a Romanesque church and the convent of St-Catherine are perched on the very edge of the precipice.

Ancienne Église Ste-Fauste – Inside this old church are a number of rather curious capitals. The 12C nave, with its raised, semicircular barrel vaulting, was originally roofed with heavy limestone slabs *(lauzes)*, made heavier still by a thick layer of earth. Under this enormous weight, the pillars sagged and in the 17C, the old roof had to be replaced by a timber-frame one.

From the shady terrace to the left of the church, there is an attractive view of the Dourdou gorge.

Join us in our constant task of keeping up-to-date.
Please send us your comments and suggestions.

Michelin Tyre PLC
Tourism Department
The Edward Hyde Building
38 Clarendon Road
WATFORD – Herts WD1 1SX
Tel: 01923 415000

Abîme du BRAMABIAU★

The river Bonheur, which rises at the foot of Mont Aigoual at the Sereyréde pass (see p 67), used to flow across the small *causse* of Camprieu, before cascading into its lower reaches.

CAUSSE DE CAMPRIEU

"Alcôve"   Swallow-hole   Entrance

Resurgent spring   Waterfalls

Subterranean course of the river Bonheur

The Bonheur left its surface bed to bury itself in the *causse*. After a subterranean course of more than 700m/2 300ft, it emerges through a high, narrow cleft and bursts into a rocky cirque called the "Alcôve" as a glorious waterfall. When the river is in spate, the deafening noise of the waterfall is not unlike the bellowing of a bull – hence the name "Bramabiau" (*Brame-Biâou*: singing bull) given to the river from its resurgence until it flows into the Trévezel further downstream. The river's underground course was first followed, with enormous difficulty, by E-A Martel and his companions on 27-28 June 1888 while water levels were low. As well as the 700m/2 300ft of the main river course, they discovered more than 1 000m/3 300ft of secondary galleries. From 1890 to 1892, and then again in 1924, 7km/4mi of new subterranean ramifications were explored.

This labyrinth, nearly 10km/6mi in length, consists of galleries 20-40m/65-130ft in diameter, at times up to 50m/165ft high, linked by extremely narrow passages and numerous cascades. E-A Martel declared Bramabiau to be a remarkable example of still active subterranean erosion. As the fast-flowing water gradually increases the size of the galleries, the cave roofs will fall in, transforming caverns into canyons, and, perhaps in thousands of years time, the Bonheur will once again find itself flowing in the open air, at the bottom of a deep gorge.

D. Faure/SCOPE

Resurgent spring of the Bonheur

TOUR ⊙

allow 1hr 30min, including the return trip; temperature: 8ºC/46ºF

For some years now, the site has been developed vertically, to prevent the damage caused annually by the sometimes very violent action of the river in spate.

From the kiosk signposted "Bramabiau", follow the gently sloping path down through the undergrowth to the river. There are lovely views of the opposite bank, carved out by the old canyon of the Bonheur on the edge of the *causse*. On arriving at the river bank, cross the bridge and climb up to the **Alcôve** at the foot of the cliff, where a spectacular waterfall gushes forth.

Visitors enter the underground world at the point where the river emerges from it. After crossing the Bramabiau between the first waterfall (in the open) and the second (underground), called the "Échelle" (ladder), the path leads along an impressively high gallery, with deep crevices caused by subterranean erosion, to the "Salle du Havre" (harbour chamber).

From this gallery, a recent modification gives access to the "Grand Aven" (swallow-hole), where visitors can admire the work of cave painter Jean Truel. A path along a ledge more than 20m/65ft above the river, leads back up the Martel gallery, overlooking the "Pas de Diable" (devil's footprint), to a mineral seam. At this point some 200m/220yd of the cavern's length are dug out of a whitish barite seam, opening up into the "Petit Labyrinth". A few steps lead to the "Salle de l'Étoile" (star chamber), with an unusual roof made up of rocks bound together with calcite.

From some steps leading out of the chasm, there is a magnificent view from a height of more than 50m/160ft against the light down onto the river.

BRUNIQUEL★

Population 469

Michelin map 79 fold 19 or 235 fold 22 – Local map see ST-ANTONIN-NOBLE-VAL

Bruniquel, the bold outline of its castle rising like a crown above the town, lies in a picturesque **setting**★ at the mouth of the great gorges that the Aveyron has cut through the limestone of the Limogne *causse*.

According to Gregory of Tours (bishop, theologian and historian 538-594), Bruniquel has its origins in the founding of a fortress on this site by **Brunhilda**, daughter of the king of the Visigoths and wife of Sigebert, King of Austrasia. The memory of this princess is perpetuated by the castle tower that bears her name. The bitter rivalry between her and her sister-in-law Fredegund caused war to break out between Austrasia and Neustria in the 6C. The brutality of Brunhilda's own death is legendary: she was bound by her hair, an arm and a leg to the tail of an unbroken horse and smashed to pieces.

★ **Old town** – Bruniquel is a pleasant place for a stroll, past the remains of its fortifications, town gateways and the old belfry, along steep and narrow streets lined with old houses roofed in half-cylinder tiles. Look out for Rues du Mazel, Droite de-Trauc and Droite-de-la-Peyre which are particularly pretty.

Château ⊘ – The various parts of the castle, built in attractive yellow stone on foundations said to date from the 6C, were built from the 12C to 18C. The barbican, which defended the approaches to the castle from the side of the village, stands on the esplanade in front of the main buildings. The massive 12C square tower is named after Brunhilda.

Inside, the decor of the 12-13C Knights' Hall features colonnettes with capitals. There is a good view of the valley from a little terrace near the castle chapel. Stairs lead to the first floor where the guard-room boasts a beautiful 17C chimneypiece with Baroque ornamentation.

In the seigneurial wing of the castle, a Renaissance loggia overlooks the sheer cliff-face, in which numerous rock shelters have been hollowed out, giving an open **view**★ of the bend in the river below.

Maison Payrol ⊘ – This town house, the property of influential local family the Payrols, was built over several centuries, from the 13C to the 17C. Upstairs, the imposing Renaissance ceiling is supported by relieving arches and carved brackets. Collections of locally made objects on display include cards, candlesticks, glass ware and faience.

EXCURSION

Montricoux – *6km/3.5mi northwest.* Montricoux is built on terraces above the north bank of the River Aveyron where it broadens out into a wide plain. The town's old curtain walls are still standing. Place Marcel-Lenoir and some of the streets contain picturesque medieval half-timbered houses with over-hanging upper floors (13-16C).

Musée Marcel-Lenoir ⊘ – Inside the château at Montricoux is an exhibition of most of the œuvre of painter Marcel Lenoir, born in 1872 in Montauban. This local artist became one of the leading lights of the Montparnasse art scene in Paris after the First World War, admired by Giacometti, Braque and Matisse. However, he chose to marginalise his talent, alienating critics and refusing to adhere to any one style. As a result he failed to achieve the same degree of fame as his erstwhile admirers and ended his days in obscurity at Montricoux. His original and powerful work deserves to be rediscovered.

CANAL DU MIDI

See Seuil de NAUROUZE

Le CANIGOU★★★

Michelin map 86 folds 17 and 18 or 235 fold 51, 52 and 55

The Canigou, a mountain peak revered by Catalonians from France and Spain alike, who still come to light the first of their Midsummer Eve bonfires on its summit, towers above the orchards of Roussillon. The peak, which is snow-capped for most of the year, is clearly delineated on three sides by the ravine of the Têt (Conflent), the Roussillon subsidence plain, and the Tech valley (Vallespir).

Even in the time of Louis XIV, the geographers responsible for determining the Paris meridian were aware that Mont Canigou was only a few minutes of a degree out (7'48" to the east) from it and had thus calculated its altitude above sea level. In the absence of such precise data for the other massifs, the Canigou was for a long time thought to be the highest peak in the Pyrenees.

One feat after another – Ever since the very first ascent of the Canigou, reputed to have been in 1285 by King Peter of Aragon, Catalonian sportsmen have vied with each other to conquer the peak in every imaginable manner. The Chalet des Cortalets was reached by bicycle in 1901, and on skis and then on board a Gladiator 10 CC automobile in 1903. In 1907, a lieutenant of the military police reached the summit on horseback without setting foot to the ground. The project to build a rack-and-pinion railway had to be discarded on the outbreak of the First World War. Vernet-les-Bains and Prats-de-Mollo are linked only by forest roads.

★★★ CANIGOU MOUNTAIN ROADS

① From Vernet-les-Bains to Mariailles *12km/7.5mi – allow 45min*

The only possible way of travelling to the summit on this route is by private car and then on foot. Take D 116 to the Col de Jou via Casteil and park the car at the pass. Follow GR 10 footpath to the summit, via **Mariailles**, where there are facilities for accommodation and refreshment, ☎ 05 68 96 22 90 *(10hr there and back for an experienced hiker).*

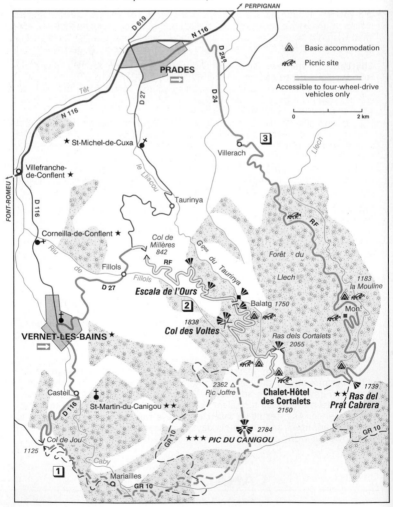

② From Vernet-les-Bains to the Chalet-hôtel des Cortalets

23km/14.5mi – about 1hr 30min

The old Cortalets road, built for the Club Alpin by the Water and Forestry Department in 1899, is a picturesque but very uneven mountain road, accessible only in summer and dry weather, in a four-wheel drive or Jeep. *Excursions in Jeeps or Land-Rovers are organized from* **Vernet-les-Bains** ⊙ *or from* **Corneilla-de-Conflent** ⊙. *Beware the poor condition of the road. The trickiest part, a very narrow 21% gradient, is protected by a parapet. There are 31 hairpin bends.*

★ **Vernet-les-Bains** – *See VERNET-LES-BAINS.*

Take D 27 in the direction of Prades. After Fillols, turn right.

After Col de Millères: alt 842m/2 762ft, the road winds in tight hairpins along the rocky crest separating the Fillols and Taurinya valleys. On the left, there are views of Prades and St-Michel-de-Cuxa. The road follows a switchback route through larch trees and between rocky outcrops. A sweeping left bend affords a stunning view of the Cerdagne and Fenouillèdes regions. The road climbs steeply through magnificent undergrowth (beautiful tree trunks).

Escala de l'Ours – This vertiginous cliff road is the most spectacular on the trip. It cuts a narrow tunnel through the rock itself, overlooking the Taurinya gorges several hundred metres below *(viewpoints at various stages along the tunnel)*. After the Baltag forest hut, the increasingly bare trees (Arolla pines) thin out considerably. The surrounding countryside becomes a pastoral one with open meadows.

Col des Voltes – Alt 1 838m/6 029ft. From the pass there is a view of the northern slopes of the Canigou and the Cady basin.

At the Ras dels Cortalets (alt 2 055m/6 740ft; picnic area), turn right.

Catalan midsummer celebrations

Every summer on the feast of St John, or Midsummer Day, the Canigou is the venue for celebrations in honour of the continuing brotherhood between French and Spanish Catalans. On 24 June a flame is lit in the Castillet at Perpignan and then carried to the Canigou summit where Catalans from Spain gather to receive it. The same evening, the flame is used to light fires all over Catalonia. It is then returned to the Castillet, via other parts of Perpignan where fires are to be lit. Celebrations continue all through the night until dawn, when people go to gather flowers associated with St John in the foothills of the Canigou (Les Aspres) – vervain, St John's wort, walnut flowers – which they arrange in the form of crosses. These are hung on the doors of their homes to bring good luck and protection.

For details of the St-Jean celebrations, contact Perpignan tourist office: ☎ 05 68 66 30 30.

Chalet-hôtel des Cortalets – Alt 2 150m/7 050ft. Hotel-chalet at the mouth of the cirque formed by the Canigou, Joffre and Barbet peaks.

From the Chalet-hôtel des Cortalets to the Canigou summit

3hr 30min on foot there and back

West of the hotel-chalet, follow the path waymarked by red and white flashes along the banks of a lake and then up the eastern face of the Joffre peak. Leave the path when it starts going back down to Vernet and continue the ascent on the left below the ridge. A zigzag path winding between the rocks leads to the summit.

★★★ **Pic du Canigou** – Alt 2 784m/9 131ft. The Canigou summit is crowned by a cross and the remains of a stone hut used in the 18C and 19C for scientific observations. To the south, the tinkling of bells can be heard from the animals grazing in the Cady valley below. From the viewing table, there is an immense **panorama** to the north-east, the east and the south-east, towards the Roussillon plain and the Mediterranean coast. The Canigou has been seen from as far away as the church of Notre-Dame-de-la-Garde in Marseille, 253km/157mi as the crow flies, when the mountain peak stands out clearly against the setting sun at certain times of the year *(around 10 February and 28 October)*. Even with the much lower Albères range forming a slight barrier in the foreground, the Costa Brava in Catalonia can still be seen in the distance. To the northwest and west the view takes on a sort of layered effect, with the ponderous secondary chains of the crystalline foundations of the eastern Pyrénées (Madrès, Carlit etc), contrasting with the more rugged limestone ridges of the Corbières (Bugarach).

3 From Prades to the Chalet-hôtel des Cortalets via the Llech gorge *20km/12.5mi – allow 1hr 30min*

The road, which is accessible only during the summer in dry weather, is very rough along the Llech gorge; a 10km/6mi stretch of the road is cut into the rock face. Excursions by Jeep or four-wheel drive are organised from **Prades** ⊙*.*

Prades – *See PRADES.*

Leave Prades on N 116, towards Perpignan, then turn right onto D 24ᴮ.

After Villerach, the D 24 goes through the Conflent orchards and then drops down into the gorge. The road, cut into bare rock, overlooks the Llech gorge 200-300m/700-1 000ft below. It then continues over more rugged ground as far as the La Mouline forest hut (alt 1 183m/3 880ft; *picnic area).*

★★ **Ras del Prat Cabrera** – Alt 1 739m/5 704ft. This is a delightful stopping place *(with a bench seat)* above the unspoiled valley of La Lentilla. The ridges of the Serra del Roc Nègre block the upstream view. Panorama of the Roussillon plain, the Albères mountains and the Mediterranean.

The road opens out in the upper cirque of the Llech valley which is thick with silver pines. The **views**★★★ are stupendous; to the north lies the southern border of the Corbières, with the deep gash made by the Galamus gorge clearly evident. The road leads through the orchards of the Lower Conflent to the foothills of the Canigou.

For the ascent to the Pic du Canigou, see 2 *above.*

Le CAPCIR★

Michelin map 86 fold 16 or 235 fold 51

Forming a plateau at an altitude of 1 500m/4 920ft, the Capcir is the highest region of Northern Catalonia. Its mountains – covered with pine forests and spangled with lakes – provide many ski runs as well as numerous paths for walking or horse riding. Moreover, the Capcir has the largest course for cross-country skiing in the Pyrenees. The forest of La Matte has really beautiful Scots pines, with long and even trunks that often reach over 20m/65ft at their highest. They can be admired from the D 118 and the D 52, between Formiguères and Les Angles.

Between France and Spain – The two border countries, which used to fight over Catalonia, divided the Capcir between them for a long time, as they did Cerdagne, a region with which the Capcir shares much of its history. During the Middle Ages, the Capcir used to be governed by Catalan administration, but it was united with the archdiocese of Narbonne, then with the diocese of Alet (from the 14C to the 18C). It became an annexe of Roussillon in the 17C, with the Treaty of the Pyrenees. However, its Catalan customs and traditions have survived over the centuries and are still very much alive today.

FROM MONT-LOUIS TO USSON-LES BAINS
44km/27mi – allow half a day

★ **Mont-Louis** – *See MONT-LOUIS.*

Leave Mont-Louis heading north on D 118.

As it climbs gently, the road offers an attractive view of the citadel, emerging from a wreath of trees with the Cambras d'Azé mountains in the foreground, in which an old glacial cirque was hollowed out.

La Llagonne – Located at a crossroads, this village of the Haut-Conflent (alt 1 680m/ 5 511ft) takes its name from an old Catalan term that means "the lagoon". We can still see the signal-tower with its surrounding wall. The fortified church of St-Vincent houses an outstanding Romanesque-Byzantine Christ made of wood.

From the Col de la Quillane, the pass which marks the watershed and the mouth of the Capcir, take D 32ᶠ to the left.

The landscape opens out, but the mark of the harsh climate can be seen in the villages with their low-lying houses roofed in rust-coloured, weathered schist. However, much of the land is nonetheless cultivated. The Matemale reservoir lies in the bottom of the valley.

At the southern end of the village of Les Angles, a road leads off to the Pla del Mir, where a **zoological park** ⊙ has been laid out. Two tours of the park (3.5km/2mi and 1.5km/1mi) enable you to meet various examples of the wildlife unique to the Pyrenees, in their mountain surroundings (moufflons, wild boars, ibexes, brown bears etc).

❋ **Les Angles** – This important Pyrenean resort, overlooking the Capcir plateau, was created in 1964 around an old village that has preserved its bell-tower. The skiing area, which lies on the slopes of Le Roc d'Aude and Le Mont Claret, provides sportsmen with 40km/25mi of downhill ski runs, accessible thanks to an extensive system of skilifts, and 115km/71.5mi of cross-country ski runs marked out around the Matemale lake.

Formiguères - Passing along the forest of La Matte, you can reach this little winter sports resort, in which the church houses a Romanesque Christ.

Take D 32ᴮ to the left and follow the signposts for "Grotte de Fontrabiouse".

Grotte de Fontrabiouse ⓥ - This cave was discovered in 1962 during the excavation of an onyx quarry, from which comes the floor covering that decorates the Palais de Chaillot in Paris and the Palais des Rois de Majorque in Perpignan. Well laid-out *(the disabled have access to a part of the route)*, the tour of the cave reveals tubular structures, clusters of "organ pipes", frozen falls, cascades of "jellyfish" and disc-columns, as well as finer forms resembling cauliflowers or bunches of flowers made of aragonite. A butterfly-shaped piece of aragonite stands for the logo of the cave.

Puyvalador - This village (a winter sports resort) which watches over the Aude gorge well deserves its Catalan name, which means "mountain sentinel".

Leave the road that snakes through the Carcanet forest (fir and beech trees, elms) to the right and take D 32 to the left, towards Quérigut.

Le Donézan - The Donézan region, one of the wildest areas of the Pyrenees, where villages lie at an altitude of about 1 200m/3 936ft, is set in a hollowed-out basin in the granite plateaux of the Quérigut, from which the rivers flow into the Aude. The Donézan used to belong to the County of Foix, which has become the *département* of Ariège.

Usson-les-Bains - The imposing ruins of the castle set high up on an isolated rock to the left of the road stand guard over the confluence of La Bruyante, which has flowed down from the Donézan region, and the Aude.

For any further information on the Capcir, available accommodation, recommended hiking and winter sports resorts, contact:
–La maison du Capcir, 66210 Matemale, ☎ 05 68 04 49 86
–L'Office de tourisme, 66210 Les Angles, ☎ 05 68 04 32 76
–L'Office de tourisme, 66210 Formiguères, ☎ 05 68 04 47 35

CAP D'AGDE⚐⚐⚐

Michelin map 83 fold 16 or 240 fold 30

This promontory, formed by a lava flow from Mont St-Loup, has been lengthened by the Richelieu breakwater, which was originally intended to connect Cap d'Agde to the island of Brescou to form one long roadstead. This enterprise was abandoned on the death of Richelieu.

Since 1970, the modern seaside resort of Cap d'Agde, designed in line with the region's coastal development scheme, occupies one of the best sites on the Languedoc coast. Dredging has opened up a vast, sheltered harbour, with no fewer than eight marinas, both public and private, along its shores, giving a total capacity of 1 750 berths. The architectural style of the town centre is inspired by traditional Languedoc architecture. The pastel walls and tiled roofs of some of the three or four storey blocks of holiday apartments are reflected in the waters of the harbour, while others line shady, winding streets leading to "piazzas".
Part of the resort has been given over to *les naturistes*, forming one of the largest nudist colonies in Europe.

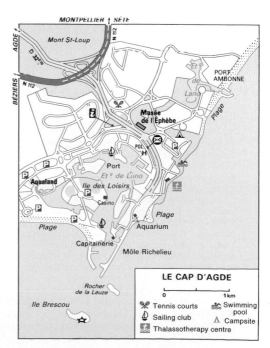

117

Musée de l'Éphèbe ⓥ **(Underwater archeology museum)** – This museum contains the finds of excavations carried out for more than 25 years both out at sea in the Mediterranean and in the coastal lagoons of the Hérault delta.

In the entrance is a display on the techniques used in underwater archeological excavation work. This is followed by an exhibition of Ancient Greek and Roman boats and Antique amphorae (displayed according to type and date) illustrating maritime trade during Greek and Roman occupation of the area.

The display of Antique works of art is dominated by the magnificent **Éphèbe d'Agde★★**, a bronze statue of a young Greek man, in the Hellenistic style, found in the Hérault in 1964.

The visit ends with a look at a Roman shipwreck and studies of seafaring in the Middle Ages and from the 16-18C.

Aqualand ⓥ – This 4ha/10 acre aquatic leisure park, includes swimming pools with wave machines into which breathless daredevils are shot from the mouths of giant water chutes.

The park offers a wide range of aquatic entertainment for young and old alike, as well as shops, a cafeteria, a snack bar etc.

Éphèbe d'Agde

Henry James on Carcassonne

Carcassonne is moving, beyond a doubt. (...) Perched on its solid pedestal, the perfect detachment of the Cité is what first strikes you. (...) It is almost too perfect – as if it were an enormous model, placed on a big green table at a museum. A steep, paved way, grass-grown like all roads where vehicles never pass, stretches up to it in the sun. It has a double enceinte, complete outer walls and complete inner (these, elaborately fortified, are the more curious); and this congregation of ramparts, towers, bastions, battlements, barbicans, is as fantastic and romantic as you please.

(...) Our peregrinations made it very clear that Carcassonne was impregnable; it is impossible to imagine, without having seen them, such refinements of immurement, such ingenuities of resistance. We passed along the battlements and *chemins de ronde*, ascended and descended towers, crawled under arches, peered out of loop-holes, lowered ourselves into dungeons, halted in all sorts of tight places, while the purpose of something or other was described to us. It was very curious, very interesting; above all, it was very pictorial, and involved perpetual peeps into the little crooked, crumbling, sunny, grassy, empty Cité. In places, as you stand upon it, the great towered and embattled enceinte produces an illusion; it looks as if it were still equipped and defended.

Henry James: *A Little Tour in France* (1884)

CARCASSONNE★★★

Population 43 470
Michelin maps 83 fold 12 or 235 fold 39
Town plan of Carcassonne Ville Basse in the current Michelin Red Guide France

To visit the fortified town of Carcassonne is to be transported back seemingly to the Middle Ages. One of the most memorable events held here is a dramatic annual fireworks and illuminations display, in which the entire citadel appears to go up in flames, in honour of Bastille Day (14 July). It is hardly surprising that the romance and excitement conjured up by this impressive, lovingly restored fortress tend to eclipse the more day-to-day businesslike lower town, the Ville Basse, on the west bank of the Aude. Carcassonne is in fact the commercial centre of the Aude *département*'s wine-growing industry. The famous clothmaking industries of the past have given way to the manufacture of synthetic rubber and vehicle accessories. The town is also home to workshops for the assembly of agricultural machinery, clothing manufacture and food processing.

Carcassonne is the home town of Philippe Fabre d'Églantine (1755-94), dramatist, poet and Revolutionary pamphleteer who met his end under the guillotine with his companions Danton and Desmoulins, and Général Sarrail, who won renown for his performance in the Battle of the Marne in 1914.

MEDIEVAL STRONGHOLD

The outcrop on which the fortified city of Carcassonne is built commands the main communication route between the Mediterranean and Toulouse. In the 1C, the Romans set up an entrenched camp in Carcassonne, at the heart of the Narbonensis. The Visigoths captured it in the 5C and organised their conquest of first the kingdom of Toulouse, then of Septimania, from within the safety of its walls. Having become an important stronghold, the city even boasted a bishopric after the conversion of the Visigoths to Catholicism. In the 8C, the fortress fell to the Franks.

The crusaders arrive – For 400 years, Carcassonne remained the capital of a county, then of a viscountcy under the suzerainty of the Counts of Toulouse. Its prosperity was interrupted in the 13C by the Albigensian Crusade.

The crusaders from the North, who came down the Rhone valley, arrived in Languedoc in July 1209, to stamp out the Cathar heresy. Since Count Raymond VI of Toulouse was bound by his excommunication and the public penitence he had undergone in St-Gilles-du-Gard, following the assassination there of the Papal Legate preaching the crusade, the weight of the invasion fell on the shoulders of his nephew and vassal **Raymond-Roger Trencavel**, Viscount of Carcassonne, who had publicly offered his protection to all those being hounded by the northern invaders.

After the sacking of Béziers, the crusading army, led by Papal Legate Arnaud-Amaury, besieged Carcassonne on 1 August. At that time, the town's defences amounted to a single rampart. Despite the dynamic leadership of the youthful Trencavel, only 24, lack of water forced the town to surrender after two weeks. The Army Council then appointed Simon de Montfort Viscount of Carcassonne in place of Trencavel. Before the year was out, Trencavel was found dead in the tower in which he was being held prisoner.

Rebellion – In 1240, Trencavel's son tried in vain to recapture his inheritance by laying siege to Carcassonne. However, although his missiles and mines breached the walls, the royal army forced his retreat. St Louis IX then had the small towns which had grown up around the foot of the ramparts razed, and the town's inhabitants paid for their rebellion with seven years of exile, at the end of which they were allowed to build a town on the opposite bank of the Aude – the present Ville Basse. The walled city was repaired and reinforced – work which was continued by Philip the Bold. From then on the town was so well fortified that it was considered to be impregnable.

Decline and restoration – After the annexation of Roussillon under the Treaty of the Pyrenees, Carcassonne's military importance dwindled to almost nil, as some 200km/125mi separated it from the new border, over which Perpignan stood guard in its stead. It was abandoned and left to decay. There was even talk of demolishing the fortifications altogether.

However, the Romantic movement brought the Middle Ages back into fashion. **Prosper Mérimée**, appointed general inspector of Historical Monuments, made a particular study of ruins in his travel document, *Notes d'un voyage dans le Midi de la France – 1835*. A local archeologist, Jean-Pierre Cros-Mayrevieille, was passionately committed to defending the interests of his native town and persistently demanded its restoration from the authorities. **Viollet-le-Duc** was sent to visit Carcassonne and returned to Paris with such an enthusiastic report that the Commission of Historical Monuments agreed to undertake the restoration of the Cité in 1844.

CARCASSONNE

★★★ THE CITÉ *2hr*

The "Cité" of Carcassonne, on the east bank of the Aude, is the largest fortress in Europe.

It consists of a fortified nucleus, the Château Comtal, and a double curtain wall: the outer ramparts, with 14 towers, separated from the inner ramparts (24 towers) by the outer bailey, or lists *(lices)*.

There is a resident population of 139, with facilities such as a school and a post office etc, which saves Carcassonne from becoming a ghost town, entirely dependent on tourism for animation.

Getting there – Leave the car in one of the car parks outside the walls in front of the gateway to the east, the Porte Narbonnaise.

Alternatively, if coming on foot from the Ville Basse, cross the Pont Vieux *(good view of the illuminated Cité at night)* and bear right, through some residential streets, past the church of St-Gimer, to climb the zigzag footpath which leads up to the west gateway, the Porte d'Aude *(see description under "Les lices" below)*.

Porte Narbonnaise – This is the main entrance, the only one wide enough to admit carts. A crenellated redoubt, built on the bridge across the moat, and a barbican peppered with arrow-slits stand in front of the two massive Narbonne towers, on either side of the gateway, with beak-shaped spurs designed to deflect missiles and to enable the defending soldiers to repel attackers more easily. Between the towers, above the archway, there is a 13C statue of the Virgin Mary.

Inside, the 13C rooms restored by Viollet-le-Duc house the tourist information centre *(to the right)* and **temporary exhibitions** of modern art.

Rue Cros-Mayrevieille (**D 24**) – This street leads directly to the castle, although visitors might well prefer to take a less direct route through the medieval town, with its narrow, winding streets and many interesting shops (crafts, souvenirs, etc). To the right of the Place du Château is a large well, nearly 40m/145ft deep.

Carcassonne by night

Château Comtal ⊙ *(Can only be visited as part of a guided tour.)*

Built in the 12C by Bernard Aton Trencavel, with its back to the Gallo-Roman fortified wall, the castle was originally the palace of the viscounts. It was converted to a citadel after Carcassonne was made part of the royal estate in 1226. Since the reign of St Louis IX, it has been protected by a large semi-circular barbican (typical of Gallo-Roman architecture, but nonetheless known here as "Visigothic") and an immense moat which make it a formidable internal fortress. From the drawbridge, note the wooden hoardings protecting the walls to the right.

The tour begins on the first floor of the castle, which has been converted into an archeological museum (this part of the visit is unaccompanied).

Musée lapidaire – Archeological remains from the fortified town itself and the local region are exhibited: 12C marble lavabo from the abbey of Lagrasse, a late-15C stone **calvary★** from Villanière, the recumbent figure of a knight killed in battle, beautiful Gothic windows from a Franciscan convent, small, finely carved figures, alabaster low relief plaques, commemorative stone tablets, disc-shaped stone crosses from the Lauragais, commonly though not always accurately called Cathar tomb stones, etc. There is a collection of old prints of the fortified town, showing it as it was before Viollet-le-Duc's restoration.

Cour d'honneur – The main courtyard is large, with its surrounding buildings largely restored. To the south, the building has an interesting façade in which the three window levels reflect the different styles and periods of its construction: Romanesque below, Gothic in the middle and Renaissance above. The brick and timber façade to the left dates, surprisingly enough, from the 1950s. To the right are doors to the dungeons. The doorway leading to the Cour de Midi was built wide enough for horses to pass through.

Cour du Midi – In the southwest corner of the southern courtyard stands the tallest of the fortress's towers, the Tour Pinte, a very well preserved watchtower, which is the only remaining unrestored part of the castle. From the top, which was reached by a single wooden staircase, it was possible to see up to 30km/19mi away. The Cour du Midi is being set up as an open-air theatre.

IMAGES PHOTOTHÈQUE

Inner western ramparts *(Can only be visited as part of a guided tour.)*

Besides the Château Comtal, which forms an integral part of them, the western ramparts also incorporate other defensive towers.

Tour de la Justice – The Trencavels, as viscounts of Béziers and Carcassonne and protectors of the Cathars *(see above)*, sought refuge here with the Count of Toulouse during the Albigensian Crusade to escape the army of Simon de Montfort. This tower, rebuilt under St Louis in place of a Gallo-Roman tower, is circular, with round-arched doorways and brick inlays to level out the stone courses. The window openings were protected by tilting wooden shutters which enabled those inside the tower to see (and drop things on) anybody trying to attack the foot of the walls, without themselves being seen.

Tour de l'Inquisition – As its name indicates, this tower was the seat of the Inquisitor's court. A central pillar, with chains, and a cell on the floor below bear witness to the tortures inflicted upon heretics.

Tour carrée de l'Évêque – This square tower is built across the outer bailey, thus blocking any communication between its northern and southern parts. Since, with the exception of the upper watchpath, it was reserved for the bishop, it was fitted out more comfortably. There is a good view of the castle from the second room.

Construction dates of fortifications

– Gallo-Roman era (3C-4C): the walls were made of small bond with rows of brickwork to level out the masonry courses. The bases with their alternate layers of rubble and mortar are plainly visible when the foundations are bared.

– The period between both sieges (1209-40) and the reign of St Louis: the high, defensive walls are made of rectangular grey stones laid in regular, medium bond. In the 13C, the Gallo-Roman constructions along the inner ramparts, reinforced and in many cases underpinned by more modern sections of wall (this inversion of the different periods of construction can be clearly seen in the various layers of masonry), were modified to create what are known as "**Visigothic**" structures. These are narrow, with a rounded, apse-like external wall and a flat internal wall, and lend themselves not only to defence, but also to use as double storey storerooms.

Along the outer ramparts, numerous towers with horseshoe ground plans were built, some open on the inside, so that attackers who captured them would be exposed to fire from defenders on the inner ramparts, and others completely closed to form redoubts, from which a few defenders could harass any attackers who made it over the outer ramparts into the outer bailey.

– Reign of Philip the Bold (1270-85): characterised by rustic masonry and beak-like projections on the towers, for the deflection of missiles. Some of the most beautiful of the buildings were constructed during this period – the redoubt at the Porte Narbonnaise, the Tour du Trésau (Treasury), and the Tour de l'Inquisition, for example.

"Les lices"

This is the name given to the **outer bailey**, enclosed within the inner and outer ramparts. Notice how the levels of the watch-paths, curtain walls, crenellations and hoardings vary to follow the slope of the ground outside.

You can get into the outer bailey through the Tour St-Nazaire or the Porte d'Aude.

Tour St-Nazaire – This handsome square tower was built to protect the church, located at the far end of the fortified town, away from the entrance. The tower's postern, masked by a corner bartizan, was only accessible up ladders. There are still a well and an oven in evidence on the first floor, and a viewing table has been installed at the top of the tower.

Porte d'Aude – This is the main feature of the outer bailey. A fortified path, the Montée d'Aude, weaves its way from the church of St-Gimer at the bottom of the hill *(on the side of the Ville Basse)* up to this gateway, which is heavily defended on all sides: various gates, large and small fortified buttresses, and a completely enclosed central space in which any attackers who had managed to penetrate that far would have been easy targets for those defending from the surrounding battlements.

The "lices basses" – This is the name given to the west and north section of the outer bailey. To the west, the *lices* run from the Tour Mipadre on the corner, getting narrower and narrower until the dead end at the Tour carrée de l'Évêque.

CARCASSONNE

Château (Pl. du) C
Combéléran
  (Mtée G.) .... D 21
Cros-Mayrevieille (R.) ... D 24
Gaffe (R. de la) C
Grand-Puits (R. du) .. CD
Marcou (Pl.) .... D
Médiévale (Voie) .... D 36
Nadaud (R. G.) ...... CD
Plô (R. du) .... CD
Pont (Pl. A.-P.) C
Porte-d'Aude
  (Mtée de la) C
Porte-d'Aude (R.) C
Prado (Pl. du) .... D
St-Jean (Pl.) C
St-Jean (R.) .... C 46
St-Louis (R.) C
St-Saëns (R. C.) ...... D 48
St-Sernin (R.) .... D 49
Trencravel (R. R.-R.) ... C
Trivalle (R.) .... CD
Viollet-le-Duc (R.) ...... C 56

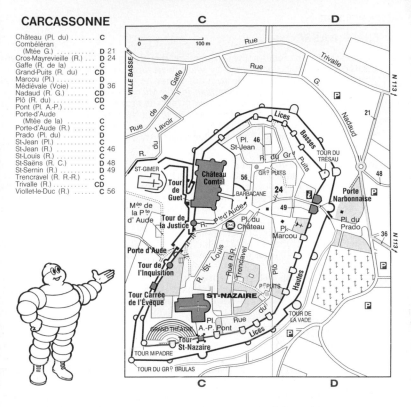

From the Porte d'Aude, the outer bailey leads past the Château Comtal and along the northern, or Visigothic, inner curtain wall, which is the oldest stretch of the ramparts. The curtain walls and towers are very high at this point (note the later underpinning), and the original flat, Mediterranean tile roofs can be clearly seen on the towers of the outer curtain wall (whereas those rebuilt by Viollet-le-Duc are pointed and slate-covered, as in northern France).

The "lices hautes" – This is the name given to the stretch of outer bailey to the east of the fortified Cité, heading south from the Tour du Trésau. The gap between the inner and outer ramparts is very wide here (it was used for weapons practice and jousting), and it is edged with moats. Some way past the Porte Narbonnaise, note the Tour de la Vade on the outer curtain wall to the left; this three storey tower, almost entirely projecting outside the curtain wall, is a fortified keep in itself, designed to keep watch on the whole of the eastern ramparts. Carry on along the southern part of the bailey as far as the Tour du Grand Brulas, which stands on the corner opposite the Tour Mipadre.

★ Basilique St-Nazaire ⊙

All that remains of the original church, the building materials for which were consecrated by Pope Urban II in 1096, is the Romanesque nave; the Romanesque apse and apsidal chapels were replaced by a Gothic transept and east end in 1269-1320. The west front was modified by Viollet-le-Duc, who, in the mistaken belief that the church was part of a fortified "Visigothic" curtain wall, took it upon himself to add a row of crenellations along the top of the wall-belfry. Once inside the church, it is easier to appreciate the contrast between the central nave, typical of Mediterranean French Romanesque architecture with its simple, austere lines beneath a barrel vault, and the much more ornate east end, all openwork and stone dappled with coloured light through the windows of the apsidal chapels and six transept chapels. The perfect proportions, uncluttered delicacy of line and tasteful decoration make this a remarkable piece of architectural design. The side chapels north and south of the Romanesque nave were added at a later date.

The basilica's **stained-glass windows**★★ (13-14C) are considered the most impressive in the south of France. Remarkable **statues**★★ – reminiscent of those in Reims and Amiens – adorn the pillars in between the windows around the chancel walls. There are a number of eye-catching bishops' tombs, in particular that of Pierre de Roquefort (14C) in the chapel on the left, and that of Guillaume Razouls (13C) in the south transept chapel.

VILLE BASSE

The heart of the modern town of Carcassonne is the *bastide* (fortified town) created by St Louis, delineated by wide boulevards along the line of the old ramparts. It has the geometric layout of a "new town" *(and a ferocious one-way system to go with it – see town plan in the Michelin Red Guide France)*. The monotony of the grid of grey, narrow streets is broken in the centre of town by Place Carnot, a spacious square adorned with a Neptune fountain (1770) and enlivened by the stalls of market gardeners on Tuesdays, Thursdays and Saturdays. Above the rooftops, the tall tower (15C) of the church of St-Vincent is etched against the skyline.

Musée des Beaux-Arts ⊙ – *Entrance: Rue de Verdun.*
17C and 18C paintings (principally French, Flemish and Dutch masters) are displayed together with a varied collection of faience (from Moustiers, Marseille and elsewhere). A collection of the work of Carcassonne painter Jacques Gamelin (1738-1803) adds local flavour. Note the painting by Chardin, *Les Apprêts d'un déjeuner.*
The museum has a collection of memorabilia of the Chénier family, Languedoc by adoption: portraits of André Chénier, and of his mother in her Greek national costume – André Chénier's father was consul in Constantinople, and married there.
19C painting is also well represented, with works by Corot and a number of artists from the French Academy. Finally, there is a room of 20C art, containing among other things several paintings by pointilliste Achille Laugé (1861-1944) from the Aude region.

Interested in fortresses?
Don't miss the "five sons of Carcassonne" – Aguilar, Peyrepertuse, Puilaurens, Quéribus and Thermes – along with the ruins of other Cathar strongholds and the better-preserved Fort de Salses in the neighbouring Corbières region.

Excursions

Conques-sur-Orbiel – *8km/5mi north on D 201.*
This pretty village still boasts traces of its earlier fortifications, such as the 16C south gateway surmounted by a statue of the Virgin Mary. The **church** belfry-porch, which spans a street, has all the air of a fortified building. Inside, the church's heptagonal Gothic apse flanked by two apsidal chapels has very pure lines. To the right of the chancel is a 16C altarpiece.

Montolieu: Ancienne abbaye de Villelongue – *23km/14.5mi northwest. Leave Carcassonne on N 113 towards Toulouse. After Pezens, turn right onto D 629.*
Montolieu – This village in the Cabardès region, overlooking the confluence of the rivers Dure and Alzeau, is devoted to books and their related industries. It is home to 20 or so bookshops, craft workshops (bookbinder's, copyist's, engraver's) and a museum of graphic arts and crafts. There is an 18C **paper mill** ⊙ open to the public at Brousses-et-Villaret. A book fair is held every third weekend from July to October.
A small road (D 54) south of the village leads to Villelongue abbey.
Ancienne abbaye de Villelongue ⊙ – Originally founded at Compagnes near Saissac, the abbey was transferred to Villelongue in the Vernassonne valley. It flourished in the 13C but then fell into decline. One or two interesting parts of the monastery complex have survived: the refectory, a large room roofed with ribbed vaulting and with three windows surmounted by an oculus in the south wall; the south gallery of the cloisters; and the chapter-house with the ribbed vaulting supported on two central pillars.
The old abbey church was built to a Cistercian design and was rebuilt in the late 13C and early 14C. Of the original building, the chancel with its flat chevet, flanked with rectangular chapels, two transepts and the square of the transept crossing remain. The sculpted decoration reveals that Cistercian architectural methods were abandoned during the second phase of construction. Note the keystone depicting the Paschal lamb and the heads on the southwest pillar in the nave.
From the garden there is a view of the fortified wall, the lay-brothers' wing and the dovecot.

Gourmets...
The annual Michelin Red Guide France offers a selection of good restaurants.

CASTELNAUDARY

Population 10 970
Michelin maps 82 fold 20 or 235 folds 35 and 39

Castelnaudary's location on the banks of the Canal du Midi made it a busy trade centre for many years. Nowadays, the port's commercial role has been replaced to a large extent by **pleasure boating**.

Castelnaudary is famous in particular for its *cassoulet* factories, and also for its pottery and earthenware workshops and brick works.

/leussens/IMAGES TOULOUSE

Cassoulet

This local gastronomic delight, a thick sumptuous stew of haricot beans, sausage, pork, mutton and preserved goose, is popular throughout France with those of a traditional, hearty appetite. Whilst the recipe is based on these ingredients, it varies from centre to centre throughout the Midi. The Castelnaudary purist will insist on four essential local ingredients: it should be cooked in an earthenware pot made of Issel clay, using white haricot beans grown in Lavelanet and pure Castelnaudary water, over a fire of gorse twigs from the Montagne Noire. Whichever detailed recipe is used, the cooking process is both long and complicated, so most people now settle for the commercial tinned product, of which there is a wide choice available.

SIGHTS

Église St-Michel ⊘ (**BZ**) - This church was built as a collegiate church in the early 14C, on the site of an earlier building. The most remarkable features are the 56m/200ft high belfry porch and the north façade with its two doorways (Gothic and Renaissance) and rose windows. In the second chapel off the Gothic nave, to the right, is a beautiful 16C carved stone cross. The 18C organ is the work of Cavaillé-Coll.

Présidial (**BZ**) - Built in the 16C, on the site of the castle which gave birth to the town, the Présidial - or seneschal's court - was partly destroyed under Louis XIII. The premises were subsequently rebuilt and extended, and after the French Revolution they housed, on one side, a school and, on the other, a prison which was used until 1926. The left part of the façade, with three large mullioned windows, dates from the 16C. Inside, the **Musée archéologique du Présidial** ⊘ retraces the evolution of the area's inhabitants from protohistory, through the Gallo-Roman era and the Middle Ages, to modern times (types of dwelling, necropolises and places of worship etc). A room is also devoted to the various aspects of local earthenware production.

Chapelle Notre-Dame-de-la-Pitié (**BZ**) - Inside this chapel is a lovely set of 18C gilt wooden panelling, which depicts, in no particular order, ten episodes from the life of Christ.

Grand Bassin (**BZ**) - This lake formed by the Canal du Midi constitutes a reservoir which supplies the four locks of St-Roch as well as a pleasure boating centre.

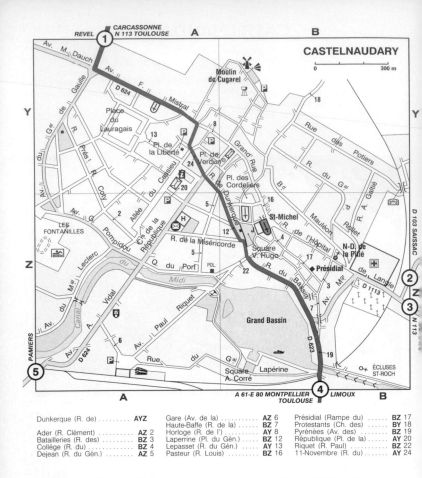

CASTELNAUDARY

Dunkerque (R. de) .... **AYZ**	Gare (Av. de la) .... **AZ** 6	Présidial (Rampe du) ...... **BZ** 17
	Haute-Baffe (R. de la) ...... **BZ** 7	Protestants (Ch. des) ...... **BY** 18
Ader (R. Clément) .... **AZ** 2	Horloge (R. de l') .... **AY** 8	Pyrénées (Av. des) .... **BZ** 19
Batailleries (R. des) .... **BZ** 3	Laperrine (Pl. du Gén.) .... **BZ** 12	République (Pl. de la) ...... **AY** 20
Collège (R. du) .... **BZ** 4	Lepasset (R. du Gén.) ..... **AY** 13	Riquet (R. Paul) .... **BZ** 22
Dejean (R. du Gén.) .... **AZ** 5	Pasteur (R. Louis) .... **BZ** 16	11-Novembre (R. du) .... **AY** 24

Moulin de Cugarel ⊘ (**BY**) – At the beginning of the 20C, a dozen or so windmills were still operating on the hills around Castelnaudary. From the Moulin de Cugarel, on Pech hill, there is a pretty view of the Lauragais plain around Castelnaudary. The mill was built in the 17C and restored in 1962. The sliding roof and, inside, the old milling machinery have been reconstructed.
Elsewhere, Castelnaudary also had a number of flour-mills driven by water from the canal.

►► **St-Papoul** – *5km/3mi east.* Romanesque **abbey** ⊘.

CASTRES★

Population 44 811
Michelin map 83 fold 1 or 235 fold 31

The busy city of Castres stands on the banks of the Agout, which is still plied by **passenger barges** ⊘ (*promenades en coche d'eau*). It is an excellent point of departure for excursions to the Sidobre region, the Lacaune mountains and the Montagne Noire. The austere façades of its buildings, the constant hustle and bustle of its inhabitants and the sprawling industrial zone of Melou and La Chartreuse in the southwest all add to the day-to-day, hard-working atmosphere of the city.
Local economy is dominated by the wool industry. With Mazamet and Labastide, Castres has kept up the tradition of *peyrats* which started in the 14C. These weavers, who also worked on the land, used the wool from their own sheep and the dyers used the madder and woad cultivated on the neighbouring plains. The industry's evolution was interrupted during the Wars of Religion and the turbulent period which followed the revocation of the Edict of Nantes, but in the 18C the Languedoc Fairs led to renewed growth.
Nowadays, Castres and the surrounding area is the leading centre in France for carded wool and the second most important centre for the wool industry after Roubaix-Tourcoing. It encompasses a large number of textile mills, specialised

spinning-mills, dying and dressing workshops. With 59 000 spindles and 830 looms clacking away, annual production amounts to more than 7 000 tonnes of yarn and almost 15 million metres of cloth.

The traditional textile and timber industries have been joined by the mechanical engineering, chemical, pharmaceutical, cosmetics and robotics industries.

To the north of the town lies a leisure park, the Parc de loisirs de Gourjade, with camp sites and golf courses.

HISTORICAL NOTES

Castres grew up on the west bank of the Agout, around a Benedictine monastery founded c 810. At the end of the 9C veneration of the relics of St Vincent, one of the preachers who took the Gospel to Spain, made Castres a stopping place on the pilgrim route to Santiago de Compostela. In the 10C, the town came under the rule of the Viscounts of Albi and Lautrec. In the 11C, the Viscount of Albi granted Castres the right to self-government by a college of "consuls" or *capitouls*.

The town managed to keep out of trouble during the Cathar heresy by submitting to Simon de Montfort. From 1563, the Reformation attracted numerous followers. Once the city's *capitouls* had renounced Roman Catholicism, Castres became one of the strongholds of Calvinism in Languedoc. It was caught up in the Wars of Religion, which the peace treaty of Alès, Henri IV's ascent to the throne and the promulgation of the edict of Nantes eventually brought to an end. In the 17C, the city hosted one of the four chambers set up by the Edict of Nantes to regulate differences between Protestants and Roman Catholics. This was a prosperous period during which local magistrates and merchants built luxurious town houses and the bishopric a magnificent episcopal palace.

However, the confrontations between Protestants and Roman Catholics persisted after the Revocation of the Edict of Nantes until the French Revolution, forcing numerous Huguenots to flee into exile.

Jean Jaurès – The famous Socialist leader was born in Castres on 3 September 1859 and spent part of his childhood in Saïx, a little village on the banks of the Agout, southwest of Castres. He was a student at the *lycée* that now bears his name, and went on to train as a teacher at the École Normale Supérieure in Paris, after which he taught philosophy at the *lycée* in Albi and at the University of Toulouse. Attracted by politics, he was elected Republican Member of Parliament for the Tarn in 1885, then Socialist Member for Carmaux, where he took up the miners' cause in 1893. At the next elections, however, Jaurès was defeated, largely because of his support for Dreyfus, victim of what was eventually proved to be a military conspiracy which led to his being falsely convicted of selling sensitive information to the Germans, an affair which provoked bitter controversy between those of right and left wing political persuasion with accusations of religious prejudice, social factionalism and infringement of human rights being hurled thick and fast. Jaurès nonetheless became head of the United Socialist Party (S.F.I.O.) not long after its foundation in 1905. As war approached, he put his influential voice to the service of promoting peace and devoted himself to the cause of international brotherhood. He was assassinated at the Café du Croissant in Paris on 31 July 1914. In 1924, his remains were transferred to the Panthéon, Paris.

★ MUSÉE GOYA ⊙ (BZ) *1hr*

This museum is located on the second floor of the Hôtel de Ville *(see Old Castres below)* in the former bishops' palace. It specialises in Spanish painting and is particularly famous for its exceptional collection of **works by Goya★★**, bequeathed in 1893 by the son of the collector Marcel Briguiboul, a painter from Castres. A vast room, its ceiling decorated with a frieze of medallions featuring the coats of arms of the bishops of Castres, contains 16C tapestries and a beautiful red marble fireplace by Caunes-Minervois.

The next room contains the works of 14C Spanish Primitives, followed by three rooms given over to the Spanish "Golden Age", the 17C, represented by Murillo, Valdès Leal and Ribera.

Goya's works are displayed in three rooms. Francisco de Goya y Lucientes was born in Fuendetodos, south of Zaragoza, in 1746, and was appointed court painter in 1786. He was commissioned to paint the portraits of numerous high ranking figures. The paintings and engravings on display here correspond to specific periods of his development as an artist.

The first room is dominated by *The Junta of the Philippines presided over by Ferdinand VII*, a painting of exceptional dimensions, painted in about 1814, with a composition bathed in an atmosphere of dust. By emphasizing the oval shape of the chair backs, the painter has frozen the king and his councillors in attitudes devoid of any sign of humanity; the impression of heavy immobility is accentuated even more by large, coldly geometric spaces, while the assembly dozes, yawns with boredom and tries to look important. Goya's self-portrait with glasses and the portrait of Francisco del Mazo illustrate the expressiveness of Goya's painting. Two small rooms contain his etchings.

Show cases display Goya's series of etchings entitled *Los Desastres de la Guerra* (The Disasters of War), inspired by the Spanish war of independence (1808-14).

On the walls the second edition of his 1799 series of etchings reinforced with aquatint, *Los Caprichos* (Caprices), expresses the isolation and inward contemplation provoked by the onset of the artist's deafness in 1792. The ephemerality of youth and beauty, the vanity of feminine coquetry, the

Goya – Self-portrait

injustice of a society in which fools trample over the poor, the alienation of men hounded by the Inquisition, chained to all sorts of superstitions – these are the themes depicted by Goya in his drawings peopled with witches and monsters. As such audacity could have been detrimental to the career of the court painter, Goya gave the copper plates for *Los Caprichos* to Charles IV, thus preventing the sale of the etchings.

OLD CASTRES *1hr 30min*

Start from the theatre.

Opposite are the superb **formal gardens** (Jardin de l'Évêché) designed by Le Nôtre in 1676.

Hôtel de Ville (BZ H) – The town hall occupies the **former bishops' palace** (Castres was the seat of a bishopric from 1317 to 1790), built in 1669 following Mansart's designs. To the right on entering the courtyard stands the **Tour St-Benoît**, a massive Romanesque tower with an elegant main doorway. It is all that remains of the former abbey of St-Benoît.

Cathédrale St-Benoît (BZ) – This cathedral, dedicated to St Benoît de Nursie, was built on the site of an abbey church founded in the 9C by the Benedictine Order. It was designed by the architect Caillau in 1677; after completion of the chancel, Eustache Lagon took charge of construction work in 1710.

The most striking thing about this Baroque edifice is its enormous size. Above the high altar, which has a baldachin supported on Caunes marble columns, is a painting depicting the Resurrection of Christ by Gabriel Briand (1626-1777). Around the chancel are four late 17C marble statues. The side chapels contain a rich collection of paintings from the charter-house in Saïx. Most are the works of the Chevalier de Rivalz, an 18C painter from Toulouse.

Cross Place du 8-mai-1945.

Quai des Jacobins (BY 19) – The Pont Neuf and the quay afford attractive **views** of the houses lining the banks of the Agout. These used to be the homes of weavers and dyers in the Middle Ages and are built over vast stone cellars which open directly onto the water. Their bright colours reflected in the water make an attractive scene, particularly pretty when seen from a passenger barge.

Place Jean-Jaurès (BY 20) – The houses around this square feature classical façades carved from sandstone (most of the buildings date from the first half of the 19C) and form an attractive group. The statue of Jean Jaurès by Gaston Pech dominates the square, and the fountain opposite is a scaled-down reproduction of one of the fountains at Place de la Concorde in Paris. A lively and colourful market is held here Thursdays to Sundays and also on Tuesdays.

Cross Place Jean-Jaurès and turn right into Rue Henri-IV, then left into Rue du Consulat.

Centre national et musée Jean-Jaurès 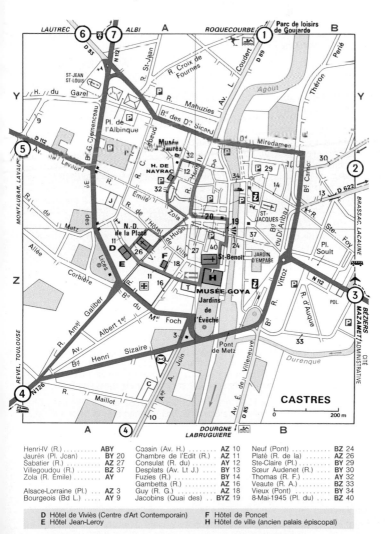 (AY) – This museum devoted to the life and work of the politician, as well as society in the late 19C and early 20C, also has an information centre with literature on the history of socialism. Seminars and temporary exhibitions are held here.

★ **Hôtel de Nayrac (AY)** – *12, rue Frédéric-Thomas.* This beautiful brick and stone mansion dating from 1620 is typical of 16C Toulouse civil architecture. The façades on three sides of the courtyard have mullioned windows and are connected by two corner towers on pendentives.

Take Rue Emile-Zola and Rue Victor-Hugo.

Église Notre-Dame-de-la-Platé (AZ) – This Baroque style building was rebuilt between 1743 and 1755. In the centre of the high altar is a very beautiful Assumption of the Virgin in Carrara marble, which was executed by the Italian artists Isidora and Antonio Baratta (Bernini school). In the chapel containing the font there is a Baptism of Christ. Opposite the altar is a fine 18C organ.

Retrace your steps and turn left into Rue de l'Hôtel-de-Ville.

At no 31, admire the doorway with its round arch on fluted columns surmounted by a carved pediment depicting various types of weapon (pistol, sabre, cannon, and so on).

Turn left into Rue de la Platé.

Hôtel de Viviès (AZ D) – *35 rue Chambre-de-l'Edit.* A monumental door leads to a courtyard surrounded by a 16C building with a square corner tower. It houses the **Centre d'Art contemporain** .

Rue Chambre-de-l'Edit goes back to the theatre.

Henri-IV (R.) .... **ABY**	Cassin (Av. H.) .... **AZ** 10	Neuf (Pont) .... **BZ** 24
Jaurès (Pl. Jean) ...... **BY** 20	Chambre de l'Edit (R.) . **AZ** 11	Platé (R. de la) .... **AZ** 26
Sabatier (R.) .... **AZ** 27	Consulat (R. du) .... **AY** 12	Ste-Claire (Pl.) .... **BY** 29
Villegoudou (R.) ...... **BZ** 37	Desplats (Av. Lt J.) .... **BY** 13	Sœur Audenet (R.) .... **BY** 30
Zola (R. Emile) .... **AY**	Fuziès (R.) .... **BY** 14	Thomas (R. F.) .... **AY** 32
	Gambetta (R.) .... **AZ** 16	Veaute (R. A.) .... **BZ** 33
Alsace-Lorraine (Pl.) .. **AZ** 3	Guy (R. G.) .... **AZ** 18	Vieux (Pont) .... **BY** 34
Bourgeois (Bd L.) ..... **AY** 9	Jacobins (Quai des) .. **BYZ** 19	8-Mai-1945 (Pl. du) .... **BZ** 40

D Hôtel de Viviès (Centre d'Art Contemporain)	**F** Hôtel de Poncet
E Hôtel Jean-Leroy	**H** Hôtel de ville (ancien palais épiscopal)

➤➤ **Hôtel Jean-Leroy** (AZ **E**; 16C) and **Hôtel de Poncet** (AZ **F**; 17C).

Purple garlic from Lautrec

Purple garlic has been cultivated for centuries in and around Lautrec *(15km/9.5mi northwest of Castres)* and is widely considered to be the best garlic in the world, with a particularly pleasant flavour and long storage-life. It is said to have been brought to Lautrec by Spanish pedlars in the 17C. Nowadays, purple garlic from Lautrec carries a quality label, the Label Rouge, and annual production exceeds 4 000 tons. Besides growing it, local people hold celebrations in its honour: on the first Friday in August every year there is a competition of sculpture using garlic as medium, followed by the tasting of a special garlic soup, then the culmination of the festivities with local residents gathering round at the end of the day to enjoy an enormous pot of cassoulet accompanied by *confit de canard*.

Naturally, garlic plays a leading role in local cuisine. It is crushed into sauces, used to stud meat, rubbed onto croutons and added to soups, vegetable dishes and stews. Even so, this represents something of a come-down compared with the prominence it once assumed in the local diet: in its heyday, the most popular packed lunch with local workers was a handful of raw garlic cloves eaten with a chunk of bread.

CASTRIES

Population 3 992
Michelin map 83 fold 7 or 240 fold 23 – 12km/7mi northeast of Montpellier

The village of Castries and its imposing castle are built on a hill in the middle of the *garrigue*, at the foot of which flows the river Cadoule.

★ **Château de Castries** ⊘ – The present château was built in the 16C by Pierre de Castries (pronounced Castres) on a hillock which had previously been the site of a Roman encampment and a Gothic castle. It is still owned by the Castries family. The Renaissance château includes a vast main courtyard decorated with a bust of Louis XIV by Puget. Sadly, one of the wings was destroyed during the Wars of Religion and its stones used to make a series of terraces providing access to gardens designed by Le Nôtre.

Inside, the main staircase, lined with paintings from the Boucher school (1760), leads to the great hall of the États de Languedoc which contains a painting evoking the huge assemblies held there in the past. It also has a remarkable Nuremberg earthenware stove and a Meissen porcelain table top (late 18C, early 19C) depicting the Judgement of Paris.

The library contains some handsome family portraits and fine bookbindings. In the dining room is a Louis XV Provençal olive wood sideboard and a painting of Cardinal de Fleury by Rigaud. The kitchen contains a linen display.

After visiting the château, if you take the D 26 to Guzargues, off the N 110, there is a very interesting **view** of the **aqueduct** built by Riquet (creator of the Canal du Midi) to supply water to the château.

Le CAYLAR

Population 339
Michelin map 80 fold 15 or 240 fold 18 – Local map see Les GRANDS CAUSSES

The name of this village means "rock", and it is indeed crowned by extremely jagged crumbling rock formations. From some distance away, it looks as though the village has impressive ramparts and fortified towers. As you get closer, however, you can see that the supposed "fortress" is actually rocks eroded by water.

Church – Inside, there is a 17C Christ Wounded in wood and, in the Lady Chapel, a beautiful 14C carved stone altarpiece depicting scenes from Christ's childhood.

Tour de l'Horloge – The clock tower is all that remains of the ramparts which surrounded the medieval town.

Picturesque old houses – Some still have their 14C and 15C doors and windows.

Chapelle Notre-Dame-de-Roc-Castel ⊘ – This small Romanesque chapel, built on the side of the Roc-Castel among the rocks overlooking the village, contains a 12C stone altar. A lone section of wall reminds us that the chapel was part of the fortress demolished on Richelieu's orders.

The highest of the rocks gives a very pretty view over the dolomitic rocks.

CAYLUS

Population 1 308
Michelin map 79 fold 19 or 235 fold 18

This little village of Bas Quercy is set in a picturesque spot above the west bank of the Bonnette, a tributary of the Aveyron. The best view of the old town, clustered around the church with its tall bell-tower and overlooked by the ruins of a 14C fortress, is from the southwest along D 926.

Covered market (Halle) – The great size of the market is evidence of Caylus's long-standing commercial importance. The old grain-measures can still be seen cut into the stone.

Church – As might be surmised from the sturdy buttresses topped by machicolations, this was once a fortified church.
Inside, near the chancel on the north side of the 14C nave, stands a gigantic figure of **Christ**★ carved in wood, by sculptor Zadkine in 1954. It is a striking and deeply poignant work. This artist, who was born in Smolensk in 1890 and died in Paris in 1967, was profoundly influenced by Cubism and his friends Braque and Fernand Léger. The 15C stained-glass windows (restored) in the chancel are worth a closer look.

Rue Droite – The main street leads off from the church and contains several medieval houses, notably a 13C gable-fronted house known as the Wolves' Lair (**Maison des Loups**), adorned with corbels and gargoyles in the form of wolves, from which the house derives its name.

UPPER SEYE AND BONNETTE VALLEYS
Round trip of 40km/25mi – allow 2hr

Leave Caylus north on D 19.

There are good views of the River Bonnette from the road, which soon passes a path on the left leading to the pilgrimage chapel of **Notre-Dame-de-Livron**. The road runs along a picturesque and somewhat vertiginous route overlooking the valley.

Notre-Dame-des-Grâces – This little pilgrimage chapel with its roof of thickcut stone tiles is Gothic in style with a fine sculpted doorway.
From nearby, at the tip of the promontory on which the chapel is built, there is a sweeping view of the Bonnette valley in its setting of hills dotted with woods and meadows.

Continue along D 19,

Lacapelle-Livron – This old village with its stone roofed houses has a group of buildings, mostly in ruins, which used to be a commandery of the Order of Knights Templars. After 1307, it passed into the hands of the Order of St John with the Knights of Malta until the Revolution. There now remains a fortified manor-house overlooking the Bonnette, with a central courtyard preserving the original layout of the commandery. To the south, towering over the small Romanesque fortified church, is a powerful belfry-keep with a few surviving brackets left of the watchpath. The church is opposite the refectory, which was converted into the guard-room.

Rejoin D 97 as far as Puylagarde. Turn right onto D 33, then right again onto D 926 to Parisot.

In a valley to the east of the village lies **Parisot lake** *(swimming)* surrounded by poplar trees.

Leave D 33 south of Parisot and head straight on (via Le Cuzoul).

St-Igne – Near this village there is an unusual and striking monument, the "Phylloxera cross", dating from 1882 in memory of the devastating effects of the phylloxera aphid on local vines. The inscription means "We are struck down by the hand of God."

Return towards Parisot and, shortly before the junction with D 33, turn left onto a little road along the river (via Labro and Cornusson).

Château de Cornusson – This castle was largely rebuilt in the 16C and is flanked by numerous towers. It is well situated on a wooded hill overlooking the Seye.
A small road linking the two valleys leads back to Caylus, giving a good view at the crest of the ridge dividing them.

The star ratings are allocated for various categories:
- *regions of scenic beauty with dramatic natural features*
- *cities with a cultural heritage*
- *elegant resorts and charming villages*
- *ancient monuments and fine architecture*
- *museums and picture galleries.*

La CERDAGNE★

Michelin maps 86 folds 15 and 16 or 235 folds 50, 51, 54 and 55

The Cerdagne region, *meitat de Franca, meitat d'Espanya* (half French, half Spanish), in the eastern Pyrenees lies in the upper valley of the Sègre, a tributary of the Ebre, between St-Martin gorge (alt 1 000m/3 300ft) and La Perche pass (alt 1 579m/5 179ft).

The floor of this sheltered rift valley, as often as not bathed in golden sunlight, is a peaceful rural idyll, chequered with fields of crops and pasture between streams lined with alders and willow trees. Majestic mountains frame this valley, which was occupied by a lake during the Tertiary Era: to the north, on the **sunny** side *(la soulane)*, towers the granite massif of Le Carlit (alt 2 921m/9 581ft); to the south, the **shady** side *(l'ombrée)*, lies the Puigmal chain (alt 2 910m/9 545ft), with dark pine forests tucked into deep parallel ravines.

The region earns its livelihood from stock breeding and winter sports (Font-Romeu).

Cradle of the Catalan State – After the Arabs had been driven out of Roussillon and Catalonia, the Cerdagne became essentially a small independent highland state, less and less subject to the Frankish administration of the Spanish border country.

In 878, one of the lords of the Cerdagne, **Wilfred le Velu** ("the hairy"), was invested with the counties of Barcelona and Gerona. By the 10C, his heirs, who had assumed overall rulership of their county, controlled the upper valley of the Sègre, Capcir, Conflent, the Fenouillèdes and the upper Roussillon plain. The dynasty died out in 1117 and the Cerdagne state, thereafter administered from Barcelona by the Catalan kings of Aragón, lost its original highland character.

The memory of the counts of Cerdagne has lived on in local religious and monumental history: Wilfred le Velu founded the abbeys of Ripoll and Sant Joan de les Abadesses and the bishopric of Vic *(see Michelin Green Guide Spain)*; in the 11C, Count Guifred extended the abbey of St-Martin-du-Canigou, and his brother, Abbot Oliva, a great builder and spiritual leader, turned Ripoll and St-Michel-de-Cuxa into incomparable centres of culture.

As a mark of their past as civil "capitals", Corneilla-de-Conflent, Hix and Llivia still have their beautiful churches.

French Cerdagne – The 1659 Treaty of the Pyrenees did not define the new Franco-Spanish border precisely in Cerdagne, since an agreement had not yet been reached as to which mountains were to serve as natural borders. In 1660, experts signed a treaty for the division of the Cerdagne in **Llivia**, recognizing Spain as owner of the county, except for the Carol valley and a strip of land which would enable French subjects to travel between the Carol valley and the Capcir and Conflent regions. In all, 33 villages were annexed to France under the treaty. These were chosen from those closest to the border, but Llivia, with its official status of "city", was not included and remained under Spanish rule. It has formed a Spanish enclave on French territory ever since.

★★ 1 VALLÉE DU CAROL

From the Col de Puymorens to Bourg-Madame
27km/16.5mi – allow 1hr

After leaving the upper valley of the Ariège, with its relatively gentle slopes, the road enters a valley which gets deeper and deeper.

★ Col de Puymorens – *See Haute vallée de l'ARIÈGE.*

The landscape changes after the pass, which lies on the Atlantic-Mediterranean watershed between the Ariège, a tributary of the Garonne which flows towards the Atlantic, and the Sègre, a tributary of the Ebre which flows towards Spain. The road crosses a bridge over a gully scored by the passage of an avalanche, and leads down into the Carol valley, which shows more signs of human presence. There is a good view of the village of Porté-Puymorens, well-placed to catch the sun, and of the glacial threshold beneath the reddish-brown ruins of the Tour Cerdane.

The road drops steeply into Font-Vive valley, dominated by the peaks of Col Rouge and the foothills of the Carlit summit (alt 2 921m/9 581ft).

After Porté, the road runs through a narrow ravine, the Défilé de la Faou. To the left there is an attractive view of the hamlet of Carol and two ruined towers beyond the viaduct. A stretch of road between tall, sheer valley walls brings you to the outskirts of Enveitg. In front stretches the Cerdagne, widening into a fertile mountain plateau (average altitude: 1 200m/3 400ft) which makes the surrounding peaks seem lower than they really are.

Before Bourg-Madame, the Grand Hôtel de Fort-Romeu can be seen on the left, with the Spanish enclave of Llivia in the foreground. To the right, on the Spanish side of the border, Puigcerdà is perched on top of a hill.

Bourg-Madame – The name Bourg-Madame was given to this village in 1815 by the Duke of Angoulême, the last Dauphin, in honour of Madame Royale his wife. On the fall of the Empire, the Duke had returned to France from his exile in Spain along this route. Before this promotion, the hamlet was home to the open-air cafés and dance-floors *(guinguettes)* which provided the nightlife for nearby Hix, besides making the most of its border location on the banks of the river Rahur to develop such activities as industry, peddling and smuggling.

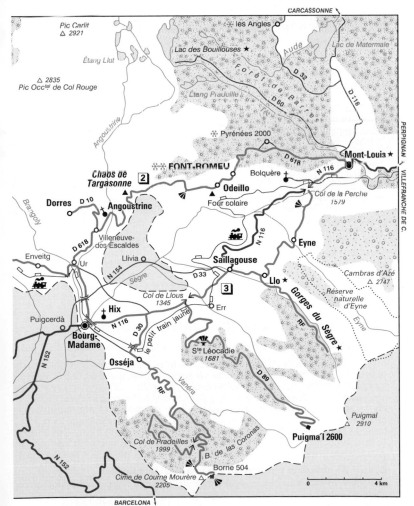

★ ☑ **THE SUNNY SIDE OF THE VALLEY** ("LA SOULANE")

From Bourg-Madame to Mont-Louis *36km/22.5mi – allow 2hr*

Bourg-Madame – *See above.*

Leave Bourg-Madame to the north (N 20). At Ur, turn right onto D 618 and at Villeneuve-des-Escaldes take D 10 to the left.

Dorres – In the church *(only rarely open to the public)*, the north side altar features a typical example of the Catalans' enduring penchant for dressing up their statues: an Our Lady of Sorrows *(soledat)*. In the south chapel, closed off by a grille, is an impressive, somewhat bony-looking Black Madonna.
The cemented path below Hôtel Marty leads to a sulphur spring (41°C/106°F) *(30min there and back on foot)* where the locals and summer holiday makers indulge in open air hydrotherapy.
Go back to D 618.

Angoustrine – Walk up to the Romanesque church ⊘ at the top of the village to admire the **altarpieces**★, particularly that dedicated to St Martin, which depicts a knight in the central alcove and, on the painted panels, some of the saint's miraculous feats (rescuing a sailor, a hanged man etc).
The horizon seems to open out as the road, running along slightly higher ground than the level of the plain, winds its way uphill overlooking the plain all the way.

Chaos de Targasonne – This gigantic heap of granite boulders, of fantastically contorted shapes, was deposited by glaciers in the Quaternary Era.
A short distance (2km/1.2mi) on from the Chaos de Targasonne, there is a view of the border mountains from the Canigou to the Puigmal, and of the more jagged Sierra del Cadi. The close-cropped slopes of the sunny side of the valley provide pastureland for flocks of sheep.

Odeillo – The church contains a 13C Virgin and Child, known as the Madonna of Font-Romeu, for most of the year (except during the grazing season from June to September). In the summer months, a 15C Virgin of the Hermitage takes its place.
Not far from the village stands the huge concave mirror of the **four solaire** ⊘, or solar furnace, which was inaugurated in 1969. The sunny slopes of this side of the valley can be seen reflected in the mirror's enormous parabolic surface (1 800m²/19 400ft²), consisting of 9 500 smaller mirrors. The sun's rays are focused onto the mirror by 63 heliostats (flat mirrors which can be positioned at various angles) arranged in rows up the hillside in front of the mirror. Solar energy (1 000 thermal kW) is thus concentrated into an 80cm/31in diameter space in which the temperature can exceed 3 500°C/6 300°F. The installation is used to process refractory and mineral ore components and to test materials for resistance to thermal shock.
The countryside gives way to a built-up area as the road reaches the outskirts of Font-Romeu. The monument of Christ the King and the imposing Grand Hôtel come into view. Ahead, beyond La Perche pass, the Canigou peak can be seen clearly, towering at the far end of the mountain chain which runs along the south side of the Têt valley.

✳✳ **Font-Romeu** – *See FONT-ROMEU.*

The road runs through the pine forest just above **Bolquère**, a picturesque village with a little church perched on a promontory, to the Mont-Louis plateau, leading into the Aude valley and the Conflent region. At the junction with N 116, there is a monument to Emmanuel Brousse, a former member of parliament for Cerdagne.

★ **Mont-Louis** – *See MONT-LOUIS.*

③ **THE SHADY SIDE OF THE VALLEY** ("L'OMBRÉE")

From Mont-Louis to Bourg-Madame *112km/70mi – allow half a day*

After Mont-Louis, the N 116 climbs steadily to the wide grassy threshold of La Perche pass (alt 1 579m/5 179ft) linking the valleys of the Têt (Conflent) and the Sègre (Cerdagne). To the south rises the Cambras d'Azé, with a very regular glacial cirque scooped out of it. Driving through the high moorland on the road to Eyne, there is an ever-broadening **panorama**★ of the Cerdagne: from left to right are the ragged outline of the Sierra del Cadi, Puigcerdà rising out of the bottom of the valley on its morainal base, the mountains on the Andorra border (Campcardos summit) and the Carlit massif. From now on the road more or less follows a line joining the mouths of the four river valleys which drain off the Puigmal massif: the Eyne, the Llo, the Err and the Osseja.

Eyne – An attractive terraced village in a shell-shaped site.
The more rugged site of Llo comes into view from a hairpin bend as the road leads downhill.

★ **Llo** – This picturesque village is built on steep slopes at the mouth of a ravine through which a tributary of the Sègre flows. A watchtower dominates the scene. Further downhill is a Romanesque church, which features a doorway with the middle arch moulding decorated with bosses shaped like, inter alia, faces and spirals.

★ **Gorges du Sègre** – Leave from the church in Llo. The Sègre flows down from the Puigmal massif through a gorge which can be followed back up as far as the third bridge over the torrent. On the way, admire a beautiful rock which is needle-shaped when seen from downstream.

Saillagouse – One of the production centres for the famous Cerdagne *charcuterie*.

After the Col de Llous, turn left onto D 89 leading to the Puigmal ski resort (centre de ski); when you come to the edge of the forest, take the surfaced forest road to the right just after a hairpin bend.

Table d'orientation de Ste-Léocadie – Alt 1 681m/5 513ft. The viewing table is on the left, at the beginning of a bend, below road level. There is a **panorama★** of Cerdagne, opposite the gap formed by the Carol valley through which Fontfrède summit can be seen.

Go back to D 89 and turn right.

The mountain road leads up the Err valley.

Centre de ski Puigmal 2600 – Alt 2 221m/7 285ft. Winter sports centre.

Go back to N 116, turn left and a little further on left again (D 30).

★ **Routes forestières d'Osséja** – Picnic areas are provided along these forest roads.

Osséja – Mountain health resort.
Just above Osséja, leave the Valcebollère road to follow the *route forestière*, which forks at the edge of one of the largest forests of mountain pines in the Pyrenees. Take the right fork, which, after crossing the Col de Pradeilles on the brow of the Puigmal, leads to boundary-post 504 (Courne Mourère summit, about 2 205m/7 232ft above sea level). There are **views★** of the Cerdagne, the mountains on the Andorra border and, to the south, the sierras of Catalonia.

Go back down to Osséja via the other branch of the fork in the road (completing a loop) and turn left onto N 116.

Hix – Once the residence of the Counts of Cerdagne and commercial capital of the region until the 12C, Hix declined to the rank of simple hamlet when King Alfonso of Aragón had the town transferred to the less vulnerable site of "Mont Cerdan" (Puigcerdà) in 1177, and more particularly once the collection of *guinguettes* nearby had been made the centre of local administration under the name of Bourg-Madame in 1815.

The little Romanesque church  houses two interesting works of art. On the right, the large altarpiece painted in the early 16C and dedicated to St Martin incorporates a 13C seated Madonna. On the predella are depicted, from left to right: St Helen, the Virgin Mary, Christ of Pity, St John and St James the Great. The Romanesque Christ with dishevelled hair exudes a certain air of gentleness.

Bourg-Madame – *See* [1] *above.*

The **petit train jaune** *: one way of seeing more of the Cerdagne is by taking the "little yellow train", which runs along a local metric track between Latour-de-Carol and Villefranche-Vernet-les-Bains, a trip of 62km/39mi. The stretch from Mont-Louis to Olette (Haut Conflent) is particularly pretty (includes Gisclard bridge and Séjourné viaduct). This little tourist train in the Catalan colours (red and yellow) has been in service since 1895.*

The Petit train jaune crossing the Séjourné viaduct

J.-D Sudres/SCOPE

135

CÉRET★

Population 7 285
Michelin maps 86 fold 19 or 235 fold 56 or 240 fold 45
Local map see Le BOULOU

The town of Céret in the Vallespir region is the lively hub of Catalan tradition in the northern Pyrenees, with activities such as bullfights and *sardana* dancing. It is a major fruit growing area thanks to well-irrigated orchards – local cherries ripen in mid-April and are among the earliest to reach the French markets.
The town is becoming increasingly popular as an arts and crafts centre.

The "Céret school" – At the beginning of the 20C, the Catalan sculptor, Manolo Hugué (1872-1945), a friend of Picasso, came to live in Céret. He was joined by the composer Déodat de Séverac (to whom there is a monument with a medallion by Manolo next to the tourist office), Picasso himself, Braque, Juan Gris, Herbin, Kisling and Max Jacob, the poet and painter.
After an interruption due to the First World War, Manolo, Pierre Brune and Pinkus Krémègne encouraged visits from other artists; among many others, Masson and Soutine came in 1919 and Chagall in 1928-29. Brune was responsible for founding a museum of modern art, which opened in 1950 with an exhibition of works donated by artists who had stayed in the town. Since 1966, it has hosted important exhibitions of contemporary art, making Céret something of a Mecca for artistic creativity.

SIGHTS

Old Céret – Huge majestic plane trees offer plenty of often welcome shade to those strolling between Place de la République and Place de la Liberté. Remnants of the original ramparts include a fortified gateway, the Porte de France, in Place de la République and a restored section of another gateway, the Porte d'Espagne, in Place Pablo-Picasso. A monument has been erected opposite the bullring *(arènes)* in honour of Picasso – *Sardane de la Paix* (1973) is made of wrought iron welded to stainless steel and based on a drawing by the artist.
Like several towns in Roussillon, Céret commissioned Aristide Maillol to design its First World War Memorial.

★★ **Musée d'Art moderne** ⊘ – This modern building, with a sober main façade off Boulevard Maréchal-Joffre, was designed by Barcelona architect Jaime Freixa. The entrance doorway is flanked on either side by a mural diptych by Antoni Tàpies on enamelled lava blocks.
Inside, spacious galleries are harmoniously arranged around patios which let in the beautiful Mediterranean light to enhance the works on display. As well as temporary exhibitions, the ground floor is home to ceramics by Picasso, works from the Céret period (1909-50) and contemporary works of art from 1960 to 1970.
The 1st floor is given over to contemporary art: Tony Grand, Joan Brossa, Perejaume, Viallat, Tàpies, Dominique Gauthier, Jean-Louis Vila, Susana Solano and Jean Capdeville.

CÉRET

Clemenceau (Av. Georges)
Commerce (R. du) 4
Joffre (Bd Mar.) 16
Picasso (Pl. Pablo) 23
St-Férréol (R.) ....

Arago (Bd) 2
Aribaud (Av. M.) 3
Cosmonautes
  (Allées des) 7
Déodat de Séverac (Av.) 9
Évadés de France (R. des) 12
Fusterie (R. de la) 13
Jardins fleuris (R. des) 14
Jaurès (Bd Jean) 15
Liberté (Pl. de la) 18
République (Pl. de la) 25
Résistance (Pl. de la) 28
Tarris (R.) 29
Tilleuls (Av. des) 30
Tilleuls (Pl. des) 33

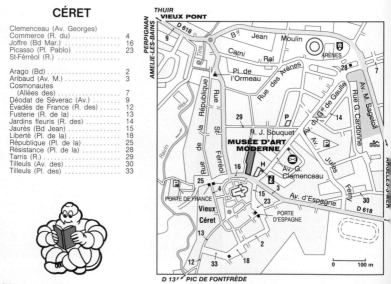

A library, an auditorium and an educational department provide back-up for the museum's activities, which include a policy of on-going acquisition of works by artists from the south of France and, particularly, of Catalonia.

★ **Old Bridge (Vieux pont)** – The old bridge more than holds its own in comparison with the nearby modern road and railway bridges. The 14C "devil's leap" spans the Tech in a single 45m/150ft arch, 22m/72ft above the river. There is a lovely view on one side of the Canigou massif and, on the other, the Albères range, sloping down to the Perthus pass.

Walk downstream to the sawmill for a good view of the bridge.

Corniche des CÉVENNES★★★

Michelin map 80 folds 6, 16 and 17 or 240 folds 6, 10 and 11
Local map see FLORAC

The scenic road known as the "Corniche des Cévennes", running from Florac to St-Jean-du-Gard along the ridge between the two rivers Gardon ("Entre deux Gardons"), is quite spectacular. It was built in the early 18C to enable Louis XIV's troops to penetrate the Cévennes more easily in their fight to quell the Camisard *(see p 220)* Protestant uprising.

Écomusée de la Cévenne – This open-air museum, part of the Cévennes national park, was founded to emphasize the value of the historical, natural and cultural heritage of the Cévennes region. It includes various sites of interest *(access to some can be quite difficult):* paleontological site at St-Laurent-de-Trèves; Barre-des-Cévennes footpath; silk museum at St Hippolyte-du-Fort; and the local museum at St Jean-du-Gard.

FROM FLORAC TO ST-JEAN-DU-GARD
53km/33mi – allow 1hr 30min

To get the best out of this beautiful road, you should make this trip in the late afternoon on a fine day, when the low-lying sun's rays throw the jagged outline of the ridges and the depth of the valleys into vivid relief. However, the landscape can leave an even stronger impression when seen beneath a stormy sky.

Florac – See FLORAC.

Leave Florac heading south on D 907.

At first, the road follows the Tarnon valley, at the foot of the escarpments of the Causse Méjean, before climbing to St-Laurent-de-Trèves.

St-Laurent-de-Trèves – On a limestone promontory overlooking this village, the remains of 190 million year old **dinosaurs** have been discovered. At that time, the area was covered by a lagoon, inhabited by dinosaurs of about 4m/13ft in height which walked on two legs. Inside the old church, there is a display (**spectacle audiovisuel** ⊙) on dinosaurs in general and this site in particular.
There is also a splendid **view★** of the Causse Méjean, as well as of Mont Aigoual and Mont Lozère. The Corniche des Cévennes proper actually starts from the Col du Rey, leading through the wind-swept limestone plateau of **Le Can de l'Hospitalet**, dotted with rocks, which was one of the assembly points of the Camisards in the 18C. The road then follows the edge of the plateau overlooking the Vallée Française through which the Gardon de Ste-Croix flows.

Col des Faïsses – A *faïsse* is a local term for a bank of cultivated land. The mountain drops away steeply either side of the pass, from which there is a good view of the Cévennes.
The road crosses the Can de l'Hospitalet plateau, a bare and rocky stretch of land with a stunning view of Mont Lozère, the little town of Barre-des-Cévennes, the Vallée Française and the Aigoual massif.
At Le Pompidou, limestone gives way to schist. The road then follows a ridge through chestnut groves and sparse meadows where daffodils bloom in the spring. As far as St-Roman-de-Tousque, the road overlooks the Vallée Française, beyond which are the long, narrow ridges and deep valleys of the Cévennes. The view is marvellous. In fine weather, you can see as far as Mont Ventoux in Provence.

Corniche des Cévennes

St-Roman-de-Tousque – This pretty little village lies in the middle of meadows and chestnut groves.

The road now runs along the other side of the ridge overlooking the valley of the Borgne. In the foreground lies the old silk town of **St-André-de-Valborgne**. At the Col de l'Exil, the road swaps back to the other side and the vallée Française comes into sight once more, as well as magnificent views of the Cévennes and Mont Lozère. At the Col de St-Pierre, the road begins a spectacular, winding descent to St-Jean-du-Gard.

St-Jean-du-Gard – *See ST-JEAN-DU-GARD.*

Grotte de CLAMOUSE★★

Michelin map 83 fold 6 or 240 fold 18
3km/2mi south of St-Guilhem-le-Désert – Local map see Vallée de l'HÉRAULT

The Clamouse cave is hollowed out of the south Larzac *causse*, near where the Hérault river gorge opens onto the Aniane plain. It was explored in 1945, during an exceptional summer drought, and opened to tourists in 1964.

The cave takes its name from the resurgent spring which bubbles out below the road, cascading noisily into the Hérault after very heavy rain, amply justifying its dialect name of Clamouse ("howler"). However, there is a poignant popular legend according to which the origin of the name is a mother's cry of grief. The story goes that there was once a peasant family living in the Hérault gorge. The parents sent their eldest son up onto the *causse* to work as a shepherd. One day when the youth was visiting his family, he recognised to his surprise a carved stick he had thrown into a swallow-hole out on the *causse*. His mother had found it in the hole from which she regularly came to collect water, and they deduced it must have been carried along by an underground river. After this, the shepherd boy regularly sent things to his parents using this route. But one day, he was pulled into the swallow-hole by a more than usually vigorous sheep, and his poor mother saw the body of her son come floating down on the peaceful waters of the stream.

TOUR ⊙ *allow 1hr; temperature: 17ºC/62.5ºF*

The guided tour leads through various natural galleries to the Gabriel Vila chamber, also called the sand chamber because of the layers of sand the river deposits on it each time it floods. At first the route leads through various caverns, following the old river bed, along which water still runs when the river is in spate. These initial galleries, in which the chiselled, jagged rock forms a ghostly backdrop, are a good illustration of the effects of the slow corrosive action of water on the easily dissolved dolomitic limestone of which the cave is made.

The cave deposits formed at a time when the upper cave galleries were completely submerged with water. Then the Hérault scoured out a deeper bed for itself, the flow level of underground water dropped and the galleries through which the tour leads dried out and became fossilized. This was when the first rock deposits formed – several million years ago.

The next galleries contain two types of formation: the classic calcite stalagmites, stalactites, columns, discs and draperies, in some cases coloured by mineral deposits; and **delicate crystallizations**, relatively

> **Delicate crystallizations**
>
> The Grotte de Clamouse is renowned for the great number and variety of delicate crystalline formations it features. Unlike the calcite formations usually found in caves, those at Clamouse are made of aragonite, calcite or a mixture of these two different forms of calcium carbonate crystallization. Their clear white colour, another particularity, indicates that they contain hardly any impurities or mineral deposits.
>
> The underground network at Clamouse provides a set of conditions well-suited to the development of such crystallizations: dolomitic rocks which lend themselves to the formation of aragonite; porous rock walls; plentiful supply of water; above average temperatures; and a permanent slight draught.

young formations (several thousands of years old), sparkling white and much more rarely found in caves than the former: crystalline "flowers" of aragonite arranged in "bouquets"; showers of tube-like formations which sway in the slightest draught; weird and wonderful eccentrics; crystalline dams transforming subterranean lakes into beautiful jewellery caskets containing "cave pearls" (pisolites). The Couloir blanc (White corridor) and Cimetière (Graveyard) feature a particularly impressive number and variety of formations. At the exit of the Cimetière is a huge translucent white concretion made of several discs run together, known as the "Méduse" (jellyfish).

A man-made exit tunnel leads back to the open. There is a picturesque view of the Hérault valley and an exhibition on life in prehistoric times at Clamouse.

Grotte de la COCALIÈRE*

Michelin map 80 fold 8 or 240 fold 7

This cave, northwest of St Ambroix on the Gard plateau, contains a network of explored galleries, running for over 46km/29mi underground. In addition, the site of La Cocalière has shown itself to have been a densely populated prehistoric settlement between the Mousterian period (45 000 BC) and the Iron Age (400 BC).

Turn left off D 904 coming from Les Vans, 300m/330yd past the right turn to Courry.

TOUR ⊙ *1hr 15min; temperature: 14ºC/57ºF*

At the end of the entrance tunnel, a path leads for about 1 200m/1 310yd along the bottom of a horizontal gallery linking the various chambers.

The cave contains a remarkable number and variety of deposits and formations. These are reflected in pools of water, some fed by tiny waterfalls, on either side of the path. Numerous discs – concretions with impressive diameters whose formation continues to mystify experts – are suspended from or attached to the overhanging rockface often growing upwards in an irregular way. Some of the rocky roofs feature a sort of geometric coffering of fragile stalactites which are white, if made of pure calcite, or of varying colours, if bearing metal oxides. A small underground lake enclosed by a natural dam contains some cave pearls still in the process of being formed. After the speleologists' camp, walk through the Chaos chamber beneath roofs covered with evidence of erosion to get to a gallery of frozen falls and eccentrics which overlooks an imposing, sparkling waterfall and wells linked to the lower levels where underground rivers flow. Pass a prehistoric deposit before taking a small train back to the entrance. Outside, in the immediate surroundings of the cave, note: a dolmen; some tumuli (piles of earth or stones built above graves); small dry-stone constructions like the *bories* of Provence, prehistoric shelters and a variety of karstic phenomena (caves, sinkholes, faults).

For a quiet place to stay.
*Consult the annual **Michelin Red Guide France** which offers a selection of pleasant and quiet hotels in a convenient location.*

COLLIOURE★★

Population 2 726
Michelin maps 86 fold 20 or 240 fold 42 – Local map see La CÔTE VERMEILLE

Collioure is an extremely attractive small town on the Côte Vermeille, against the backdrop of the foothills of the Albères range. It has much to offer, in terms of both charm and amenities, and attracts huge crowds of tourists every year.

The town is well known for its anchovies (factories for salting and semi-preserving on site) caught in Port-Vendres.

★★ **Setting** – Collioure, built in unspoiled natural surroundings, occupies an idyllic site made even more charming by the sun and the blue of sky and sea. With its fortified church, so close to the coast that it seems to be actually in the Mediterranean, its old royal castle separating the two little ports, with their fishing nets, brightly coloured Catalan boats and characteristic masts, its old streets with colourful, flower-bedecked balconies and picturesque flights of steps, its seaside promenade and its terrace cafés and boutiques with their inviting window displays, this little fortress town has a very distinctive character. Numerous painters, attracted by its colourfulness, have chosen to immortalise it on their canvases. As early as 1910, the first of the "**Fauves**" had made it their meeting place – Derain, Braque, Othon, Friesz, Matisse etc. Later, it was the turn of Picasso and Foujita.

Boramar beach is still a favourite subject for numerous modern artists.

Origins of the town – Medieval Collioure was first and foremost the trading port for Roussillon, from where the famous "ornate" cloth from Perpignan was exported. This was when the Catalan naval forces ruled the Mediterranean as far as the Levant.

In 1463, the invasion of Louis XI's troops marked the beginning of a turbulent period for the town. The castle was built on the rocky spur separating the port into two coves, around the square keep built by the kings of Majorca. Charles the Fifth and Philip II converted it to a citadel, reinforced by Fort St-Elme and Fort Miradou. After the Peace Treaty of the Pyrenees, Vauban put the finishing touches to the defences – the enclosed town was razed to the ground in 1670 to make way for a vast glacis. The lower town then became the main town.

SIGHTS

Walk to the old port or "Port d'Amont" via the Quai de l'Amirauté on the banks of the "Ravin du Douy", which is usually dry, then along Boramar beach.

Chemin du Fauvisme – A waymarked route has been laid out through the streets of Collioure, leading past some of the views painted by Henri Matisse and André Derain. Each stage (20 in all) is indicated by the reproduction of the relevant painting on a panel. *(Guided tours are also available, contact the tourist office for details: ☎ 05 68 82 15 47).*

Catalan fishing boats at Collioure

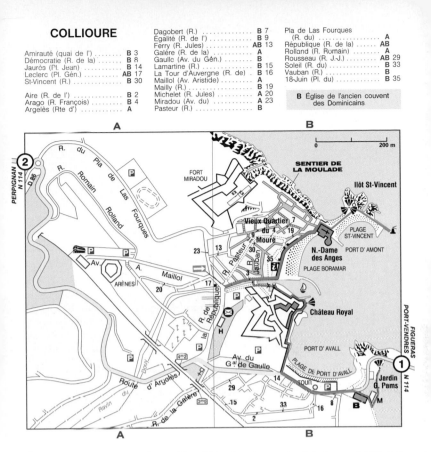

COLLIOURE

Amirauté (quai de l') . . . . **B** 3
Démocratie (R. de la) . . . . **B** 8
Jaurès (Pl. Jean) . . . . **B** 14
Leclerc (Pl. Gén.) . . . . **AB** 17
St-Vincent (R.) . . . . **B** 30

Aire (R. de l') . . . . **B** 2
Arago (R. François) . . . . **B** 4
Argelès (Rte d') . . . . **A**

Dagobert (R.) . . . . **B** 7
Égalité (R. de l') . . . . **B** 9
Ferry (R. Jules) . . . . **AB** 13
Galère (R. de la) . . . . **A**
Gaulle (Av. du Gén.) . . . . **B**
Lamartine (R.) . . . . **A**
La Tour d'Auvergne (R. de) . **B** 15
Maillol (Av. Aristide) . . . . **B** 16
Mailly (R.) . . . . **A**
Michelet (R. Jules) . . . . **B** 19
Miradou (Av. du) . . . . **A** 20
Pasteur (R.) . . . . **A** 23
                                                B

Pla de Las Fourques
  (R. du) . . . . **A**
République (R. de la) . . . . **AB**
Rolland (R. Romain) . . . . **A**
Rousseau (R. J.-J.) . . . . **AB** 29
Soleil (R. du) . . . . **B** 33
Vauban (R.) . . . . **B**
18-Juin (Pl. du) . . . . **B** 35

B Église de l'ancien couvent
      des Dominicains

Église Notre-Dame-des-Anges ⊘ – This church was built between 1684 and 1691 to replace the church in the upper town which had been razed on Vauban's orders. The distinctive bell-tower with its pink dome used to be the lighthouse for the old port.

The dark interior houses nine surprisingly ornate carved wooden, gilded **altarpieces★** *(explanation provided on the left of the chancel)*. That of the high altar is the work of Catalan artist Joseph Sunyer and dates back to 1098. It is an immense three-storey triptych occupying the whole of the retrochoir and, as a result, completely hiding the apse, in the style of Churriguera altarpieces (the Churrigueras were a family of 17C and 18C Spanish architects) in the Spanish churches of this period.

In the centre is the Blessed Virgin of the Assumption, and above is the Eternal Father between Justice and Charity. All the statues are finely carved and well worth admiring. Also by Joseph Sunyer, note the Holy Sacrament altarpiece on the left of the chancel, more modest in size, but just as delicately carved.

Treasury – The sacristy houses a beautiful Louis XIII vestment cupboard, 15C paintings, a 16C reliquary and a 17C Madonna, which is thought to have belonged to the older church.

Îlot St-Vincent – The former island is connected to the church by two beaches back to back. Behind the little chapel, a vast panorama encompasses the Côte Vermeille. A sea wall leads to the lighthouse.

Go back, passing behind the church.

★ **Sentier de la Moulade** – *45min on foot there and back from the foot of the old Château St-Vincent.* This is a very pleasant footpath between the cliff and the sea. To the north there is a clear view of Argelès-sur-Mer, St-Cyprien and Canet-Plage.

Old district of Mouré – This old district near the church is a very pleasant place for a stroll with its steep, flower-filled back streets.

Cross the Douy, at the end of the marina.

The path along the quayside skirts the impressive walls of the Château Royal.

Château Royal ⊘ – The imposing bulk of this castle, built on a former Roman site, juts into the sea between the Port d'Amont and the Port d'Avall. It was the summer residence of the Kings of Majorca from 1276 to 1344 before

141

being taken over by the Kings of Aragón. Vauban had the outer wall added and the village sprawling at its feet demolished to make room for a glacis. The visit includes the underground passages, the parade ground, the 16C prison (in which there is a Catalan forge), the 13C chapel, the main courtyard, the Queen's bedchamber, the upper rooms and the ramparts with their sentry path. The 17C barracks house exhibitions on grape vines, cork, the manufacture of Sorède whips and espadrilles (rope-soled sandals), Catalan boats etc. Several rooms are reserved for temporary exhibitions.

From the western car park, towards the Douy, there is an excellent **view** of the town and port; in the background are the Albères mountains, towering above the sea.

Continue to the Port d'Avall beach called the "Faubourg".

On the way, admire the delightful coloured boats. It is also pleasant to stop for a while beneath the palm trees, perhaps to watch one of the many lively games of *boules* taking place.

► ► **Église de l'ancien couvent des Dominicains (B B)** – This old church now houses the local wine cooperative.

► ► **Jardin Gaston-Pams** – A terraced park which has a Moorish shelter giving a view over the bay and the town.

Anchovies from Collioure

Anchovies, a speciality from Collioure, have been preserved in the same way for generations. Once brought to harbour, the anchovies – minus heads and guts – are left to pickle in vats of brine for a few months (May to August). They are then rinsed, their backbones removed and they are left to drain. Finally, the anchovies are put into glass jars or tins filled with oil, either arranged flat or carefully rolled around a caper.

To compete with foreign competition, anchovies imported from Morocco for example, local producers have diversified, adding tubes of anchovy paste and olives stuffed with anchovies to their product lines. Collioure anchovies feature prominently in many Catalan dishes. *Anchoïade*, a paste of anchovies mashed with olive oil, garlic and basil, is delicious spread on French toast as an accompaniment to apéritifs.

Prieuré de COMBEROUMAL ★

Michelin map 80 fold 13 or 240 fold 9 – 3km/2mi west of St-Beauzély

Park the car at the end of the path leading to the priory.

The Prieuré grandmontain de Comberoumal, founded at the end of the 12C and suppressed in 1772, is one of the best preserved priories owned by the Grandmont order. The solitude and renunciation of worldly goods sought by the hermit and founder, Étienne de Muret, and his disciples, can still be felt. Their vow of poverty and life of contemplation resulted in an architectural design no less beautiful for its sobriety (note the quality of the bonding).

TOUR ⊙ *allow 1hr*

The priory, from the Romanesque period, consists of four buildings forming a square around a small cloister which unfortunately has been destroyed. To the north is the church, with its very slightly pointed barrel-vaulted nave. The nave is lit by a single window, at the back, while the chancel is wider and pierced with three very splayed windows, flooding it with light. The west wing, which has been altered, was reserved for guests (Romanesque fireplace with a circular duct). The south wing, altered during construction of the first floor, still has its ground floor refectory and kitchen (a service hatch can be seen in the passageway leading to the cloisters). To the east, there is a covered passageway leading to the cemetery, a chapter-house with a triple window surmounted by a relieving arch on the side of the cloisters, and a common room – or stillroom – now divided by a wall. Outside, the buttresses, the regularity of the windows with their monolithic lintels and the slight difference in the height of the roofs, reveal the interior organisation of this wing, against which the projecting polygonal apse of the church has been built.

Michelin Maps Red Guides and Green Guides are complementary publications – to be used together.

Le CONFLENT

Michelin maps 86 folds 16 to 18 or 235 folds 51, 52 and 55

This is the part of Roussillon through which the Têt flows, alongside the N 116. The region is rich and fertile thanks to its many rivers, which supply water to market gardens and orchards. It lies parallel to the Tech valley, from which it is separated by the Canigou massif – visible from Mont-Louis at the gateway to the Cerdagne region.

FROM MONT-LOUIS TO VILLEFRANCHE-DE-CONFLENT
30km/19mi – about 4hr

The road forming a corniche between Mont-Louis and Olette is extremely busy, particularly at the weekend.

★ **Mont-Louis** – *See MONT-LOUIS.*

The N 116, taken in the direction of Prades on leaving Mont-Louis, winds through shady trees concealing the town and fortress. On the way downhill, the mountain summits on the south bank of the Têt can be seen at each bend in the road – the Cambras d'Aze, the Pic de Gallinas and Pic de Redoun. These gentle peaks frame the perfect curve of the Col Mitja, with the Canigou towering in the background.

Pont Gisclard – This remarkably sturdy suspension bridge bears the name of its creator, an officer in the French equivalent of the Royal Engineers *(le Génie)*, killed accidentally during testing *(roadside monument)*.

The road drops steeply and becomes more winding. There is an open view as far as the skyline. On the right, in the middle of terraced fields of crops, are the hillside hamlets of St-Thomas and Prats-Balaguer. The road leads through the village of Fontpédrouse, built into a sheer rock face.

Pont Séjourné – A sturdy but elegant viaduct, dedicated to its builder, the engineer Paul Séjourné (1851-1939). The charm of the scene is considerably enhanced for those lucky enough to see the "Little Yellow Train" crossing the viaduct *(photograph p 135)* on the Villefranche-Bourg-Madame line.

The foliage is much less dense along this stretch of road, revealing glimpses of various feats of civil engineering on the railway line which the road follows closely.

Thuès-les-Bains – This small spa resort includes a thermal physiotherapy and functional rehabilitation centre for the handicapped.

The valley becomes more angular and rugged. The well delineated road passes through Graüs gorge. On the right, a small, narrow valley has been hollowed out by the river Mantet. The last vineyards and aloes are left behind.

Olette – This charming one-street village has three- and four-storey houses built against the rock face. The factory and ruins of the Château de la Bastide soon come into sight. As far as Serdinya, the countryside takes on a different character, with terraced hamlets.

★ **Villefranche-de-Conflent** – *See VILLEFRANCHE-DE-CONFLENT.*

FROM VILLEFRANCHE-DE-CONFLENT TO ILLE-SUR-TÊT
41km/26mi – allow 5hr

★ **Villefranche-de-Conflent** – *See VILLEFRANCHE-DE-CONFLENT.*
Leave Villefranche south on D 116.

Corneilla-de-Conflent – Corneilla, the last seat of the Counts of Cerdagne and Conflent, has an interesting Romanesque church, the **Église Ste-Marie**★ ⊙, once a priory of Augustinian canons. The tall square church tower, made of rough granitic ashlar, is visible as you approach the village. The church has some beautiful carved decoration; note in particular the 12C doorway (marble columns) and the three attractive windows on the east end (sawtooth bands, ornate arch mouldings and capitals on the colonnettes). Inside, there are two Romanesque statues of the Virgin Mary seated – one in wood, the Notre-Dame-de-Corneilla *(left of the high altar)*, characteristic of the 12C Catalan school, and a 14C Virgin and Child in marble *(south transept chapel)* – and the original beautifully sculpted white marble altarpiece from the high altar (1345).

The road, shaded with plane trees, climbs up the broad valley of the Cady, with its apple and pear orchards. The torrent gushes along on a bed of pebbles.

★ **Vernet-les-Bains** – *See VERNET-LES-BAINS.*

On the descent towards the Col d'Eusèbe, the D 27 offers very attractive views of the valley of the Cady, framed first with apple trees, then with oaks. After Fillols comes the Col de Millères, which marks the beginning of the road to the Canigou. The descent becomes steeper in the valley of the Taurinya, with lovely glimpses of St-Michel-de-Cuxa and Prades.

★ **Abbaye de St-Michel-de-Cuxa** - *See Abbaye de ST-MICHEL-DE-CUXA.*

Prades - *See PRADES.*

Drive through Prades and take N 116 to the right.

The road now takes you through the orchards of the Conflent plain. There is a pretty **view**★ of the village of Eus, perched on a spur on the opposite bank of the river, as the road runs between the Têt and the railway line. After **Marquixanes**, a fortified village built around a church with a bell-tower which was crowned with decorative turrets in the 17C, the N 116 runs alongside the **Barrage de Vinça** (1977), a reservoir built to provide irrigation, regulate the autumn floods of the Têt and form a supply of drinking water.

Vinça - This town, also fortified, has an 18C church built in the southern French Gothic style, with surprisingly rich interior decoration: 9 Baroque altarpieces, a 15C Pietà and Entombment, and an imposing high altar dedicated to the Assumption of the Blessed Virgin.

After Vinça, the road crosses an arm of the reservoir, the south bank of which has bathing facilities, before reaching Ille-sur-Têt.

Ille-sur-Têt - *See PERPIGNAN: The Roussillon Plain.*

CONQUES★★★

Population 362
Michelin map 80 north of folds 1 and 2 or 235 folds 11 and 12

Conques is a peaceful little village occupying a stunningly beautiful **site**★★ on the steep slopes of the Ouche gorge. It is home to a splendid Romanesque church with a magnificent treasury, the remains of an abbey which for many years offered shelter to the interminable stream of pilgrims on their way to Santiago de Compostela.

Housed in an underground complex on the hillside overlooking the site of Conques, the new **Centre européen d'Art et de Civilisation médiévale** is a cultural reference centre for the historical period from 476 to 1453. Its unique documentary collection forms the basis for a complete programme of cultural activities (seminars, national heritage classes, presentations, concerts) aimed at researchers, the general public and any one else interested in western medieval civilization.

St Faith - The abbey only became famous after the relics of St Faith, known to the French as Sainte Foy, came into its possession in a rather dubious manner. This young Christian girl, no more than 13 years old, was martyred in about 303 in Agen, where her relics were subsequently kept and jealously guarded. In the 9C, the legend goes, one of the monks from Conques held them in such veneration that he decided to steal them. He left for Agen, where he passed himself off as a pilgrim and joined the community of St Faith. Over a period of ten years, he won the confidence of the community to the extent that he was put in charge of guarding the relics, whereupon he promptly stole them and took them back with him to Conques. Once there, the saint doubled the number of miracles she performed – at the time, they were known as the "japes and jests of St Faith".

Pilgrimages - Construction of the present church began in the 11C. Its architecture is similar to the other famous sanctuaries of the day – Santiago de Compostela, St-Sernin in Toulouse, St-Martin in Tours and St-Martial in Limoges (the last two of which have been destroyed). Between Le Puy and Moissac, Conques was the stopover recommended in the guide book written for pilgrims on their way to Santiago de Compostela.

From the 11C to the 13C, the endless stream of pilgrims to Santiago de Compostela made this the Golden Age for Conques. It is quite extraordinary to think how popular this long, difficult journey was, but it was practically the only equivalent of modern tourism available in the Middle Ages. People went to absolve themselves of their sins or were motivated by simple devotion. Jugglers and tumblers followed the route taken by the pilgrims and, in the evening, in the hostelry of some monastery, would entertain the weary travellers. When the pilgrims arrived at their journey's goal – not without one or two potentially life-endangering adventures on the way – they would gather large quantities of the scallop shells to be found in plenty on the coasts of Galicia (still known in French as *coquilles St-Jacques*), which are one of the symbols of St James the Great. They would return home absolved of their sins and having considerably broadened their experience.

The monastery was eventually converted into a collegiate church of canons. In 1561, the Protestants reduced it to ruins. The church was partly burned down, then sank into obscurity. It was on the point of complete collapse when Prosper Mérimée, during one of his tours of inspection of historic buildings, discovered it and gave such a heart-rending account of its plight that he saved it.

The towers of the abbey church at Conques

★★ ABBATIALE STE-FOY ⊘ *allow half a day*

Exterior – This magnificent Romanesque abbey church was begun in the middle of the 11C, but most of it dates from the 12C. Two towers, which were rebuilt during the 19C level with the façade, and an octagonal lantern tower over the transept crossing, rise above the church's roofline.

★★ **Tympanum above the west door** – The tympanum *(best seen in the late afternoon towards sunset)* is in a remarkable state of repair. Its originality and dimensions make it a masterpiece of 12C Romanesque sculpture. Any pilgrim arriving on the parvis in front of the church could not fail to be impressed by this image of the Last Judgement, made up of 124 figures representing the dramatic juxtaposition between souls at peace and souls in torment described in St Matthew's Gospel. This iconographical scene arranged around the figure of Christ is carved in yellow limestone, and a few remaining traces of paint remind us that it used to be painted in bright colours.

Bands reserved for inscriptions delimit three superposed tiers divided into sections. On the left of the figure of Christ (1) is Hell, and on his right Paradise, clearly indicated by his left hand pointing downwards to the condemned, while his right hand is raised towards the Elect. Christ sits enthroned in a mandorla surrounded by five layers of clouds. In the tier above (2), two angels carved on the spandrels are blowing their horns to herald the Last Judgement while two others are carrying the Cross. In the middle tier, the procession of the Elect (3) is making its way to the Lord, led by the Virgin Mary followed by *(right to left)* St Peter, then important figures in the history of Conques, including Charlemagne, a legendary benefactor of the abbey.

On the other side of the figure of Christ, angel knights are fending off the hordes of the damned (4), who are pursued by the fires of hell; the sinners include errant monks captured in a net and a drunken man hung by the feet. The central and upper section (5) of the lower tier is devoted to the weighing of souls; the Archangel St Michael is opposite a devil who is trying to tip the scales. To the left of this, angels are opening coffins in an image of the resurrection of the dead (6) and, further still to the left (7), tiny arcades represent the church of Conques next to which St Faith is prostrating herself to receive God's blessing. Beneath her, on the bottom tier, is Paradise (8) with Abraham welcoming the Holy Innocents into his arms, surrounded by wise Virgins, martyrs and prophets. The entrance (9) to this celestial Jerusalem is guarded by an angel reaching out his hands to greet the Elect, while to the right, the antechamber of Hell (10) is marked by a devil

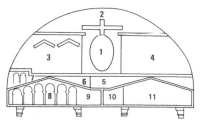

pushing the damned into the gaping jaws of Leviathan. On the far right, Satan is seen presiding over the chaos of Hell (11) where mortal sins are being punished; Pride is shown being unseated from its horse, Greed being hung high and dry, and Slander having its tongue pulled out by a devil.

All this must have made quite a strong impression on pilgrims making their way to Santiago de Compostela. The stern face of the Eternal Judge must have struck fear into many a heart. The peace of Paradise (once painted blue), emphasised by the almost monotonous alignment which is designed to convey order and serenity, contrasts strongly with the violence and confusion of hell (painted red), which is treated altogether differently. The sculptors at Conques achieved an exceptional degree of mastery which never fails to amaze those who visit this example of Romanesque genius.

The medieval sculptors were not without a sense of humour, however – if you take a closer look at the outside edge of the archivolt, curious little faces can be seen peeping over the rim of the moulding *(les curieux de Conques)*.

Go round the church to the right, along the south façade with its 12C funerary niches, one of which still bears the epitaph of Abbot Bégon (1087-1107), and enter the church through the door in the south arm of the transept.

Interior – The inside of the church makes a striking impression because of its enormous height (22m/72ft) and general simplicity of line, which verges on the austere. In contrast to the overall lack of ornamentation, several of the capitals are beautifully carved to show scenes from the Bible *(a leaflet is available for a small charge, explaining what these are)*. As in other churches frequented by pilgrims the chancel is wide and surrounded by an ambulatory to allow the faithful to process past the relics of St Faith, which used to be displayed there. On the walls of the sacristy are traces of frescoes (15C) depicting the martyrdom of St Faith. The ornate 12C railings in front of the choir replaced a screen which was said to have been made from the fetters of prisoners released by St Faith. Above the passage which connects the galleries, in the central bay of the north transept, there is a beautiful sculpture group of the Annunciation. All the windows are gradually being fitted with a brand new type of translucent glass (uncoloured) which diffuses light entering the church, lending it an interesting quality. They are the work of Pierre Soulages, from Aveyron. *(See also illustration of the cupola above the transept crossing, p 39)*.

Cloisters – In 1975, the ground plan was reconstructed with paving stones. All that is left of the cloisters themselves is a series of arcades opening onto what used to be the refectory and a very beautiful serpentine marble basin which was once part of the monks' lavabo.

Six twin windows open into the refectory where a number of lovely capitals from the original arcades are now on display.

★★★ **Trésor de Conques** ⊘ **(Treasury)** – The treasury of the abbey of Conques houses a collection of silver and gold plate which is the most comprehensive display of the evolution of church plate in France from the 9C to the 16C. It includes a particularly interesting set of reliquaries, produced by a goldsmithing workshop set up in the abbey in the 11C. Listed below, in chronological order, are the most important exhibits *(some of which have a switch beneath them so that they can be rotated and admired from all sides)*.

9C – Reliquary of Pepin, gold leaves embossed on a wooden core – thought to be a gift from Pepin, this exhibit is inlaid with numerous precious stones, including an antique intaglio depicting the god Apollo.

10C – Reliquary statue of St Faith (**Statue-reliquaire de Sainte Foy**), the main piece in the collection, gold and silver gilt plating on a wooden core – over the years the statue has had numerous precious stones added to it as well as, in the 14C, the monstrance through which the relic can be seen (in the middle of her chest, just behind the head of the little figure in her lap). This unique piece of craftsmanship is also adorned with cameos and antique intaglios. The figure of the saint is holding tiny tubes designed to take flowers between her fingers.

11C – Portable alabaster altar, known as the *autel de Sainte Foy*, featuring embossed silver and enamel work; reliquary thought to be of Pope Pascal II, in silver on a wooden core, reworked several times; the *A de Charlemagne*, in gold-plated silver on a wooden core – tradition has it that the Emperor, wishing to assign all the abbeys in Gaul with a letter of the alphabet, according to their order of importance, awarded Conques the letter "A".

12C – St Faith's reliquary chest – this leather chest decorated with 31 enamel medallions still contains the remains of the saint; portable altar of the Abbot Bégon, consisting of a red porphyry plate in an engraved, niello silver mounting; reliquary known as the *Lanterne de Bégon III* or "St Vincent" reliquary, silver on a wooden core; five-and six-sided silver, gilt and enamel reliquaries, made in the 12C with much older fragments.

13C – Arm reliquary thought to be of St George, in silver on a wooden core, the hand making a sign of blessing; embossed and gold-plated silver triptych; Virgin and Child, in silver on a wooden core – this type of reliquary statue was very popular during the reign of St Louis.

14C – Head-reliquaries of St Liberate and St Marse, silver and painted canvas – small silver shrine of St Faith.

16C – Gilt gospel book-binding; processional cross, made from embossed silver leaf on a wooden core with a relic of the true cross beneath the figure of Christ.

Trésor II (Musée Joseph-Fau) – *Entrance through the tourist office.* This old house, located opposite the pilgrims' fountain, contains 17C furniture, statues, neo-Gothic reliquaries and Felletin tapestries from the abbey *(ground and 1st floors)*. The basement contains a lapidary museum with a beautiful collection of Romanesque capitals and abaci, which are remains of the old cloisters.

★VILLAGE

The steep little streets are lined with lovely old houses in red stone which harmonizes with their limestone roof slabs *(lauzes)*.
Above the church of Ste-Foy, the village is spread out on the hillside along Rue Charlemagne, the path once climbed by the pilgrims on their way to the abbey. From this street, a rocky path leads to a hillock topped by the chapel of St-Roch and a calvary. From here there is a beautiful view of Conques clustered around the abbey church. Above the church, more streets lead to the remains of old fortifications.
At the war memorial, turn left into Place du Château.
In the square stands the fine Château d'Humières (15C-16C) with its carved consoles. Further on is one of the three remaining 12C gates, the Porte de Vinzelle.
From the cemetery, a corner of which is occupied by the funerary chapel of the abbots of Conques, there is a pretty view of the Ouche.

► ► **Pont Romain** – Roman bridge over the Dourdou.

► ► **Site du Bancarel★** *(3km/2mi southeast)* and **Le Cendié** *(2km/1mi south)* – **Views★** of Conques.

Les CORBIÈRES★★

Michelin maps 86 folds / to 10 or 235 folds 39, 40, 43, 44, 47 and 48 or 240 folds 29, 30, 33, 34, 37 and 38

The Corbières massif, which lies between the sweeping, almost right-angle bend in the river Aude (to the west and north), the Mediterranean (to the east) and the Agly valley with surrounding mountains, known as the Fenouillèdes (to the south), forms a roughly square plateau sloping gently northwards from the eastern Pyrenees. At the heart of the massif, a core of primary deposits in the Orbieu valley has resulted in a dramatically jumbled relief with colour contrasts heightened by the uniquely luminous Mediterranean light. Much of the countryside is covered in the spiny and sweet-smelling scrub known as *garrigue*.
The Corbières massif attracted numerous **monastic institutions** with their various associated outbuildings – priories, granaries, oil and wheat mills, almshouses etc. The Benedictines settled in Alet, St-Polycarpe, St-Hilaire (northeast of Limoux; Romanesque church remains of what was an 8C Benedictine abbey) and Lagrasse; the Cistercians in Fontfroide while their sisters went to Rieunette *(see below and index)*. The large number of sanctuaries, easy to spot because of the cypress trees growing in their graveyards, is striking in such a depopulated area. In such spread-out communities as Les Moulines near Fourtou and Caunette-sur-Lauquet, the church stands in splendid isolation at the bottom of a small valley.
However, it is above all for two of its features that the Corbières is best known: ruined castles and wine.

The battlefield of the Languedoc – Towering above the Fenouillèdes on rocky limestone ridges (such as the Pic de Bugarach – alt 1 230m/4 030ft) are numerous vertiginous feudal fortresses, almost all of which are now in ruins. The Corbières region was initially a fall-back position for the Visigoths after they had been driven south from the Haut-Languedoc, then later a battlefield bloodied by epic combats between the Franks and the Saracens, before finally becoming border territory under the Carolingian Empire, subject to the vicissitudes stemming mainly from rivalries among neighbouring vassals. However, after integration of the region into the French royal estate in 1229, capture of the fortresses which had supported the Cathar cause, and the King of Aragon's renunciation of his feudal rights over the territories north of the Agly in 1258, the border between France and Spain settled down. For the next five centuries the "five sons of Carcassonne" – Puilaurens, Peyrepertuse, Quéribus, Termes and Aguilar – served as royal garrisons ready to confront any threat of invasion posed by the Spanish. They were deprived of their strategic importance by the annexation of Roussillon to France and subsequently for the most part fell into disuse.

The perfect spot for a vineyard – The *garrigue* has been ousted increasingly by vines, which have taken over every available clay dip and valley east of the Orbieu and, around Limoux, the slopes of the small region that produces *blanquette* (a sparkling white wine). The sight of vines stretching as far as the eye can see, and a sudden proliferation of wine cooperatives tells you that you have arrived in the Corbières "wine country". For many years dismissed as a region which concentrated on quantity not quality, the **Corbières** has relatively recently been awarded the *Appellation d'Origine Contrôlée* for its fruity, full-bodied wines (mainly red, some white and rosé) with their bouquet so evocative of the fragrant local flora. The widely differing soil types in the region (ranging from Primary era gneiss and schists to Jurassic or cretaceous limestones) dictate that a corresponding variety of grape types is cultivated (the grape varieties most commonly used in Corbières wines are carignan, cinsaut and grenache). This has the happy result that any tour of *dégustation* taken in the region turns into a real voyage of discovery, as local wines can vary enormously even between neighbouring vineyards.

The wines (red only) of neighbouring **Fitou**, also an *Appellation d'Origine Contrôlée* (one of the first in the region to receive this accolade), come from vines (grape varieties: carignan, syrah, grenache) grown in an area with the ideal type of soil and climate (dry and sunny) and reflect this in their degree of finesse; dark, robust wines with a hint of spiciness.

Many of the local villages have their own wine cooperative *(cave coopérative)* and these, with many local private wine-growers, are only too willing to allow potential customers to taste their wares (some private producers require prior reservation, however, so a wine guide listing telephone numbers comes in useful).

Harvesting grapes in the Corbières

CATHAR CASTLES *listed alphabetically*

Numerous castles and castle ruins dot the landscape of the Corbières region. Whether military strongholds or places of refuge for Cathar refugees of the Inquisition *(see Introduction p 36 for details of Catharism)*

Aguilar (Château d') – *2.5km/1.5mi along the road from Tuchan to Narbonne, turn right just after a service station onto a narrow surfaced road through the vineyards. From the end of the road, 30min on foot there and back through vines and scrub.*
The Château d'Aguilar stands on a very exposed site on top of a small rounded hill, the only outcrop for some distance around. The fortress was reinforced in the 13C, on the orders of the King of France, with the addition of a hexagonal curtain wall flanked by six round towers open to the gorge. Besides the wall, a Romanesque chapel with its interior architecture remains intact, apart from the vault which has caved in.
There is an attractive view of the vineyards in the Tuchan basin.

Arques (Donjon d') ⊘ – *From Arques, 500m/550yd along the road to Couiza.*
This keep, used as living quarters since the end of the 13C, stands inside a quadrangular wall now in ruins. It is built of beautiful gold-coloured sandstone and features a large number of arrow slits and a curious arrangement of corner

turrets mounted on hollow bases. The upper section of the walls is of rusticated masonry. Inside, two rooms, one above the other, and a room with a high ceiling and the corners cut off, are open to the public. In Maison Déodat Roché in the village there is an audio-visual exhibition on the Cathar doctrine.

Padern - *East of Peyrepertuse.*
The Château de Padern, owned by the abbots of Lagrasse until 1579, was completely rebuilt in the 17C. The now ruined castle overlooks the village and the Verdouble. East of Padern, the river flows through a narrow gorge in between weathered rockfaces. The road to Tuchan runs alongside a ravine overlooking a deep gorge in which shelters in the rock protected by stone walls were built as early as in prehistoric times.

★★★ **Peyrepertuse (Château de)** - *See Château de PEYREPERTUSE.*

Puilaurens (Château de) ⊘ - *From Lapradelle on D 117, take the small road south (D 22) and then the uphill road to the right a little after Puilaurens. Then 30min on foot there and back.*
The castle high above the Boulzane valley has remained more or less intact; the crenellated curtain wall with four towers and projecting battlements defending the approach to the keep can be seen from some way off. From the treaty of Corbeil in 1258, Puilaurens was the most advanced position held by the King of France towards the Kingdom of Aragon, and it was still in use as a fortress in the 17C, finally falling to the Spanish in 1636. A zigzag path leads up to the main gateway and into the lower courtyard. Go through a postern at the foot of the eastern tower to a rocky spur from which the strength of the fortress's site can best be appreciated; it is impregnable from the north. Note also the embossed stonework. There is a view of the Pic de Bugarach to the northeast and the Canigou to the south.

★ **Quéribus (Château de)** - *See Château de QUÉRIBUS.*

A combined ticket is available, priced 65F, covering entrance to the following castles: Arques, Lastours (see MONTAGNE NOIRE), Quéribus, Termes and Villerouge-Termenès.

Termes (Château de) ⊘ - *Take a steep track up from the village bridge, then 30min on foot there and back, climbing a succession of tiers which mark the curtain walls.* The castle was held by Ramon de Termes, a notorious heretic, and only succumbed to Simon de Montfort after a four month siege (August to November 1210), the hardest of the first stage of the Albigensian Crusade. The site, on a promontory defended by the huge natural trench of the Sou valley (Terminet gorge), is more interesting than the ruins of the fortress itself, which once covered 16 000m²/172 224ft². There are good views of the Terminet gorge from near the northwest postern *(dangerous slopes)* and the top of the rock.

Villerouge-Termenès - *10km/6mi north of Mouthoumet along D 613.*
At the heart of this village stands the castle (12C-14C) flanked by four towers. It was owned by the bishops of Narbonne and in 1321 was the scene of the burning at the stake of the last Cathar Parfait, Guilhem Bélibaste. The three floors of the east wing, which has been restored, house audio-visual exhibitions on Bélibaste's life and works *(ground floor)*, on the archbishop of Narbonne, Bernard de Farges, and the administration of his diocese *(first floor)* and on the daily life of Villerouge and its inhabitants in the Middle Ages *(second floor)*. From the sentry walk there is a view of the village and its surroundings. The south wing is home to the great banqueting hall and the west wing to a medieval spitroast.
Every year during the summer months Villerouge is the scene of medieval banquets and various other events evocative of life in Languedoc in the Middle Ages.

ADDITIONAL SIGHTS

Alet-les-Bains - *See Haute vallée de l'AUDE.*

Auriac (Château d') - *Southwest of Mouthoumet.*
Below the village, clinging to a rocky spur, the ruins of a castle overlook a sheer drop.

Bages et de Sigean (Étang de) and excursions - The Bages and Sigean lagoon is linked to the sea only by the Nouvelle channel. From Antiquity to the 14C, it formed a single huge lagoon with that of Gruissan, into which the river Aude was diverted by a dike. In those days Narbonne was still a busy port. Numerous archeological finds around the lagoons reflect the economic importance of this stretch of coast during the Roman occupation. Later, the lagoons and their shores became infested with malarial mosquitoes and remained deserted for centuries.

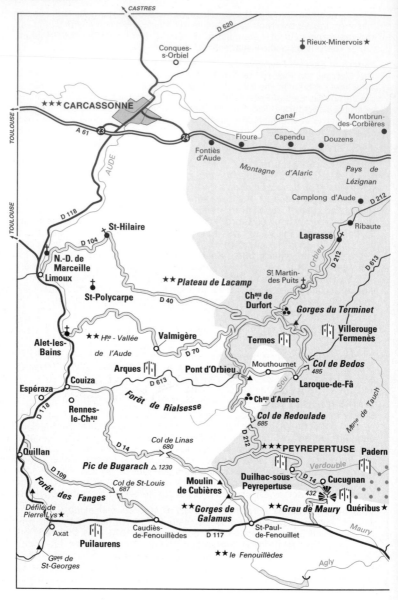

Heading south along the coast from Narbonne to Port-la-Nouvelle the road takes you through the tiny village of **Bages** perched on a rocky spur protruding into the lagoon. Further along the shores of the lagoon lies **Peyriac-de-Mer** where there is a **archeological museum** ⊙ containing artefacts discovered during excavations at the ancient township of Moulin. Just south of here is a game park, the **Réserve africaine de Sigean**. Excavations at the oppidum of Pech de Mau have revealed that nearby **Sigean** was occupied by the Greeks. Finally, **Port-la-Nouvelle** at the mouth of the Canal de la Robine from Narbonne is the only town on this part of the Mediterranean coast, apart from Sète and Port-Vendres, to have preserved some degree of economic activity outside the tourist season. The commercial port here handles the distribution of fuel oil for the whole of southwest France. The comings and goings of freighters and tankers make an exciting scene. The harbour at Port-la-Nouvelle also has yachting facilities.

Bedos (Col de) – *On D 613 northeast of Mouthoumet.*
Bedos pass is located on the D 40, a **ridge road★** winding through wooded ravines. In the dip formed by the lower gorge of the Sou, the ruins of the Château de Termes are clearly visible on their rock.

Bugarach (Pic de) - The Bugarach summit (alt 1 230m/4 030ft) can be seen from a number of charming yet virtually deserted valleys which surround it, giving good views of the different faces of the mountain with its rugged slopes. The ascent to the Col du Linas, winding through the valley of the upper Agly, is particularly impressive. Looking back (east) from the pass, the ruins of St-Georges - the western spur of the citadel of Peyrepertuse - seem to merge with the rocks on which they stand.

Couiza - See Haute vallée de l'AUDE.

Cubières (Moulin de) - Near the old mill, some private land has been set out as a rest area with picnic tables in a cool site on the shady banks of the Agly. Behind the mill, Bugarach summit stands out with the waters of the feeder channel in the foreground.

Cucugnan - This pretty village is perched on a small rise in the valley between the fortresses of Peyrepertuse and Quéribus. The village is well known from the tale of Le Sermon du curé de Cucugnan, presenting an anthology of Oc folklore in the form of a sermon by Cucugnan's parish priest, which was adapted into French by Alphonse Daudet in the second half of the 19C. A Provençal version by Roumanille and an Occitan version in verse by **Achille Mir** (the original) are also extant. The tiny Achille-Mir theatre on place du Platane hosts a virtual theatre performance on the theme of the "**Sermon du curé de Cucugnan** ⊘" following Achille Mir's version, with the voice of writer Henri Gougaud.

Duilhac-sous-Peyrepertuse – As you leave the upper town to the north, note the village fountain, which is fed by a spring with a surprising volume of flow for the region.

Durfort (Château de) – *South of Lagrasse.*
The ruins of the castle *(no entry)* rise from a sea of vineyards in a tight loop in the river, just after the confluence of the Orbieu and the Sou.

Escale (Pas de l') – *On D 12, northwest of Rivesaltes.*
This is the name given to a rocky indentation in the ridges of the eastern Corbières. The view★ stretches as far as the Canigou and Puigmal peaks.

Espéraza – *See Haute vallée de l'AUDE.*

Fanges (Forêt domaniale des) – *Southeast of Quillan.*
This forest massif covers an area of 1 184ha/2 924 acres and is home to some exceptional Aude firs. The **Col de St-Louis** (alt 687m/2 253ft) is a good departure point for ramblers *(rocky, often very uneven ground).*

★★ **Fontfroide (Abbaye de)** – *See Abbaye de FONTFROIDE.*

★★ **Galamus (Gorges de)** – *See Gorges de GALAMUS.*

★★ **Grau de Maury** – There is a fine **panorama** from this little pass, the southern gateway to the Corbières. The mountain chains stretch back in steps from the jagged ridge which overlooks the dip formed by the Fenouillèdes to the south. A path leads up from the Grau de Maury to the ruined fortress of Quéribus.

★★ **Lacamp (Plateau de)** – *Southwest of Lagrasse.*
Between Caunette-sur-Lauquet and Lairière, the Louviéro pass on the D 40 gives access to the "forest track" of the western Corbières. The Plateau de Lacamp, at an average altitude of 700m/2 300ft, forms a breakwater towards the Orbieu. For about 3km/2mi, the track runs along the southern edge of the *causse*, giving sweeping **views** of the Orbieu valley, the Bugarach and Canigou peaks, St-Barthélemy, the threshold of the Lauragais and the Montagne Noire.

Lagrasse – *See LAGRASSE.*

Laroque-de-Fâ – *East of Mouthoumet.*
The village occupies a picturesque site on a fortified spur, watered by the Sou which can be seen dropping towards the Orbieu in the distance.

Limoux and surrounding area – *See Haute vallée de l'AUDE.*

★ **Narbonne and surrounding area** – *See NARBONNE.*

Pont d'Orbieu – *West of Mouthoumet.*
The village stands on a crossroads on the banks of the Orbieu. The D 212 leads north along the river gorge. To the east, the D 613 climbs up to the *garrigue* on Mouthoumet plateau, while to the west, it joins the Aude valley at Couiza.

Quillan – *See Haute vallée de l'AUDE.*

Redoulade (Col de) – *South of Mouthoumet.*
This pass on the picturesque D 212 links up the Agly and Orbieu valleys.

Rennes-le-Château – *See Haute vallée de l'AUDE.*

Rialsesse (Forêt de) – *East of Couiza.*
This forest was planted a century ago. The transition from Austrian pines to deciduous trees can be seen clearly from the opposite side of the valley on the D 613 which leads up to the Col de Paradis from the west.

Rivesaltes – *See PERPIGNAN: The Roussillon Plain.*

Roussillon (Plages du) – The Roussillon coast from Cap Leucate to Port-Barcarès. *See Plages du ROUSSILLON.*

St-Polycarpe – *Southeast of Limoux.*
The **fortified church** ⊘ here was part of a Benedictine abbey which was dissolved in 1771. The Romanesque apse, with Lombard bands forming part of the building's actual framework, can be seen from the graveyard. Beneath the high altar various items from the treasury are on display: head reliquary (bare head) of St Polycarp, head reliquary of St Benedict and a reliquary of the Holy Thorn, all 14C works; fabrics from the 8C. The two side altars feature Carolingian decoration carved with knot-work and palm leaves. On the walls and vault are the remains of 14C frescoes (restored in 1976).

★★ **Salses (Fort de)** – *See Fort de SALSES.*

★★ Tautavel (Musée de) – *See Musée de TAUTAVEL.*

Terminet (Gorges du) – *North of Mouthoumet.*
Follow the D 40 north of the Col de Bedos. Just past the Château de Termes, before coming to two tunnels, the road hugs a loop in the river, giving a good view of the fortress.

Tuchan – Production centre for Fitou wines (AOC). The picturesque D 39 winds through the Tuchan valley, between the vibrant splashes of colour formed by the vineyards – green or bronze, depending on the season – at the foot of the imposing, but desolate, Tauch mountain.

Valmigère – *14km/8.5mi east along D 70 from where it leads off D 118, the Aude valley road between Couiza and Limoux.*
South of the village there is a beautiful **panorama★**: in the foreground, the Arques valley in which the forest of Rialsesse stands out against a backdrop of red gullys; in the background, the jagged crest of the Pic de Bugarach; on the horizon, the Canigou.

CORDES-SUR-CIEL★★

Population 932
Michelin maps 79 fold 20 or 235 fold 23

Cordes-sur-Ciel occupies a remarkable **site★★**, perched on top of a rocky outcrop, the Puech de Mordagne, overlooking the Cérou valley. On a sunny day, it looks quite charming seen from the approach roads. The village may owe its name to the textile and leather industry which prospered there in the 13C and 14C, as in the case of Córdoba in Spain.

In 1222, during the Albigensian Crusade, the Count of Toulouse, Raymond VII, decided to build the fortified town of Cordes in response to destruction of the stronghold of St-Marcel by Simon de Montfort's troops *(see Introduction: Bastides)*. The charter of customs and privileges enjoyed by the inhabitants of Cordes included, among other things, exemption from taxes and tolls. The town-cum-fortress rapidly became a favourite haunt of heretics, and the Inquisition found rich pickings during its work here.

The end of the Cathar disturbances ushered in a period of prosperity. In the 14C, the leather and cloth trades flourished; craftsmen wove linen and hemp cultivated in the surrounding plains, while the dyers on the banks of the Cérou used the *pastel* (blue dyer's woad) and saffron which grew so abundantly in the region. The beautiful houses built during this period bear witness to the wealth of the inhabitants.

The quarrels among the bishops of Albi, which affected the entire region, the resistance of Cordes to the Huguenots during the Wars of Religion and two plague epidemics put an end to this golden age in the 15C. After a brief burst of life at the end of the 19C, due to the introduction of mechanical embroidery looms, Cordes, which had originally been designed to be isolated, finally fell into decline, cut off as it was from the main communication routes. Fortunately, the threatened demolition of its Gothic houses spurred the population into action and a number of measures to classify some of its buildings as historic monuments were taken in 1923. But those most susceptible to the charm of Cordes were the artists and craftsmen who rallied to the cause and helped to put the town back on the map. Restoration is still being carried out, preserving the original character of Cordes. In 1970 the town also became a venue for musical entertainment.

The winding, steeply sloping, stone streets are home to an ironmonger, an enameller and a sculptor of figurines, not to mention weavers, engravers, sculptors and painters, who practise their crafts in the beautiful old houses whose original appearance has been so successfully conserved.

★★ UPPER TOWN *2hr*

The upper town can be reached by shuttle bus, particularly recommendable in the summer when traffic is banned in the upper town and parking nearby is severely limited.

Arched windows – The main attraction of Cordes, besides its exceptional setting, is undoubtedly its beautiful **Gothic houses★★** (13-14C), in particular, the **sculpted decoration of the façades**. The largest and best preserved houses line the Grand-Rue (or Rue Droite). The façades, built of warm pinkish Salles sandstone with hints of grey, open through great arches at street level, surmounted by two storeys with ogive windows, some of which have unfortunately been replaced by simple rectangular openings.

In several houses, iron bars ending in a ring project from the façade at the level of the second floor. These were to support a wooden or iron rod, placed horizontally through each of the rings, on which material was probably draped to act as blinds, following a medieval custom popular in Italy and Provence. However, since the sun does not penetrate too far into the narrow streets, the rings may have been used to hang banners during festivals.

You can park the car (fee charged) near the Porte de la Jane or at the bottom of Grande Rue de l'Horloge, but expect problems finding a space in season. The climb to the old town is not so steep from the former as it is from the latter.

Cordes, which is laid out in a diamond-shape, had two curtain walls built around it in 1222. These had the strongest fortifications at their weakest points of access open to attackers, the east and west ends.

Porte de la Jane – This portcullis gateway, a remnant of the second curtain wall, doubled the Porte des Ormeaux.

Porte des Ormeaux – Assailants thinking they had penetrated the town's defences, having fought their way past the Porte de la Jane, were surprised to find themselves confronted by the massive towers of this second fortified gateway.

Chemin de Ronde – The southern wards (le Planol haut), and those of the Rue du Planol (**17**), offer attractive views of the surrounding countryside.

Porte du Planol or du Vainqueur (D) – This gateway is the eastern counterpart of the Porte de la Jane.

Barbacane – This barbican, below the Porte du Planol, is part of a third curtain wall which was built around Cordes when the town was extended at the end of the 13C.

Maison Gorsse (E) – The façade of this house features some beautiful Renaissance window frames.

Portail peint (F) – The name of this gateway – painted gate – probably comes from the painted Madonna which once adorned it. It is the partner of the Porte des Ormeaux to the east.

★ **Musée d'Art et d'Histoire Charles-Portal** ⊙ **(M¹)** – The museum is named in honour of Charles Portal, keeper of public records for the Tarn *département* and great historian of Cordes. It is located inside the Portail peint and contains items of local historical interest.

On the ground floor are some antique grain measures, a rather unusual sarcophagus from the Merovingian necropolis (6C) in Vindrac *(5km/3mi west of Cordes)*, the beautiful studded door from the Maison du Grand Fauconnier and the falcons *(faucons)* to which this house owes its name.

A room on the first floor is entirely devoted to the various styles of architecture in Cordes (military, religious, civil).

The second floor houses interesting collections of local prehistorical exhibits, a set of earthenware typical of the end of the Bronze Age and some opulent Gallo-Roman furniture which belonged to the temple at Loubers.

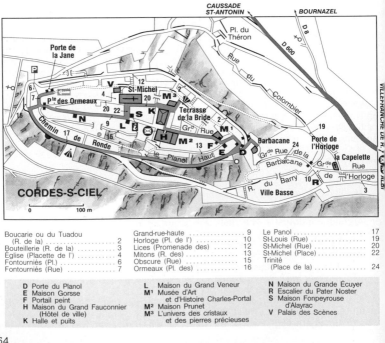

Boucarie ou du Tuadou (R. de la) ... 2	Grand-rue-haute ... 9	Le Panol ... 17
Bouteillerie (R. de la) ... 3	Horloge (Pl. de l') ... 10	St-Louis (Rue) ... 19
Église (Placette de l') ... 4	Lices (Promenade des) ... 12	St-Michel (Rue) ... 20
Fontourniès (Pl.) ... 6	Mitons (R. des) ... 13	St-Michel (Place) ... 22
Fontourniès (Rue) ... 7	Obscure (Rue) ... 15	Trinité (Place de la) ... 24
	Ormeaux (Pl. des) ... 16	

D Porte du Planol	**L** Maison du Grand Veneur	**N** Maison du Grande Écuyer
E Maison Gorsse	**M¹** Musée d'Art et d'Histoire Charles-Portal	**R** Escalier du Pater Noster
F Portail peint	**M²** Maison Prunet	**S** Maison Fonpeyrouse d'Alayrac
H Maison du Grand Fauconnier (Hôtel de ville)	**M³** L'univers des cristaux et des pierres précieuses	**V** Palais des Scènes
K Halle et puits		

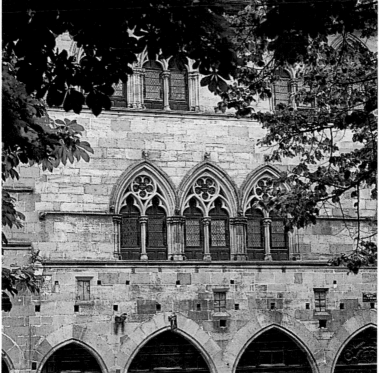

Maison du Grand Fauconnier

The Vieux Cordes room contains the *libre ferrat* or iron book, so-called because its binding incorporated an iron chain. This record-book contains the town's regulations from the end of the 13C to the 17C. New consuls were sworn in on the Gospel extracts inside it.

The third floor displays objects found during excavation of the Vindrac necropolis: jewellery, buckles, a set of antefixes and earthenware from Gallo-Roman times.

The Grand-Rue, which is cobbled and very steep, leads to the heart of the fortified town.

Maison Prunet (M²) – This lovely rose-coloured mansion contains the **Musée de l'Art du sucre** ⊙, an unusual museum in which works of art made entirely of sugar are displayed, mostly in glass cases.

In the second room, a 2.60m/8.5ft high "arbour of a hundred roses" greets the visitor. The museum display also includes, at intervals, various paintings, reproductions of cars, trains and planes and miscellaneous exhibits (stamp album, Provençal market, musical instruments).

★ **Maison du Grand Fauconnier (H)** – This beautiful old mansion, in warm golden stone, now houses the town hall. The roof corbels were once decorated with falcons, which earned the mansion its name.

The remarkably elegant façade with its lovely regular bond was restored in the 19C. Inside, which has been refurbished, a 15C spiral staircase leads to the 1st floor and the **Musée Yves-Brayer** ⊙, home to some of the painter's works: drawings, lithographs, etchings and watercolours.

In the cellar, the **Musée de la Broderie cordaise** ⊙ organises embroidery demonstrations on a tambour frame. These mechanical embroidery frames, from St-Gall in Switzerland, brought Cordes prosperity in the late 19C and early 20C.

Covered market and well (K) – Twenty-four octagonal wooden pillars (renovated several times since the 14C) support the roof structure (reconstructed in the 19C) over the market place which once rang to the sound of cloth merchants. Fixed to one of the pillars, behind a handsome 16C wrought iron cross, a marble plaque commemorates the assassination of three inquisitors (an episode dismissed as hearsay by scholars). Nearby there is a **well** 113.47m/372ft deep. North of the market place is a small gemstone museum, **L'univers naturel des cristaux et des pierres précieuses** ⊙ **(M³)**.

Terrasse de la Bride – This terrace forms a welcome rest area shaded by trees. There is a sweeping view of the peaceful valley of the Cérou to the northeast, against the slender silhouette of the Bournazel belfry to the north.

Église St-Michel ⊙ – This church, which has been refurbished many times over the centuries, still has its original 13C chancel and transept, with pointed intersecting rib vaulting, and a splendid 14C rose window set in the wall. The interior buttresses separating the side chapels are similar to those in the cathedral at Albi. Likewise, the 19C paintings are an imitation of the decoration on the vault of Ste-Cécile. The organ (1830) comes from Notre-Dame in Paris (the cathedral's first choir organ).

There is a vast panorama from the top of the watchtower adjoining the belfry.

North of Place de l'Église, the **Palais des Scènes** ⊙ (**V**) houses giant animated tableaux recounting the history of the fortified town.

Maison Fonpeyrouse d'Alayrac (**S**) – The inner courtyard of this recently renovated late 13C house has a particularly interesting layout. Two timber galleries, reached by a narrow spiral staircase, give access to the upper storeys. The mansion now houses the Tourist Office.

★ **Maison du Grand Veneur** (**L**) – This mansion, named for the Master of the Royal Hunt, has a distinctive three-storey façade, decorated at the level of the second storey with a frieze of high-relief sculptures depicting hunting scenes. They include a huntsman on the point of stabbing a wild boar which has been chased out of the forest by a dog; a hare, with a dog in hot pursuit, about to be struck by a hunter's arrow (between the windows on the left); a hunter blowing his horn while two animals are escaping into the forest (between the right hand windows). Note the protruding iron rings *(see above)*, which are particularly well-preserved.

Maison du Grand Écuyer (**N**) – The elegant façade of this mansion is built of beautiful regularly bonded Salles sandstone and adorned with highly imaginative figures, sculpted in the round.

Return to the Porte des Ormeaux.

ADDITIONAL SIGHTS

The "Ville basse" – As suburbs sprang up around the citadel, a fourth, then a fifth curtain wall were built in the 14C. East of the town the clock gateway, or **Porte de l'Horloge**, probably rebuilt in the 16C, is a picturesque remnant of the fourth wall. It can be reached from the square at the end of Rue de la Bouteillerie up a flight of steps known as the **Escalier Pater Noster** (**R**), because it has as many steps as the prayer has words.

La Capelette ⊙ – The interior of this old chapel, built in 1511, was decorated by Yves Brayer. In a niche outside stands a statue of the Virgin Mary, sculpted by Paul Belmondo.

EXCURSION

Vindrac – *5km/3mi to the west*. This attractive hamlet, bright with flowers in season, is home to an old mill in which the **Musée de l'Outil et des Métiers anciens** ★ ⊙ displays a rare collection of wrought tools vividly evoking bygone crafts.

On the first floor, there is a grain measure from the Albi area, dating from 1784, with hinges made of animal-horn. A tooth-puller and a 19C paring-iron, used to trim the horn on a horse's hoof, show two aspects of the farrier's work.

Numerous tools and objects bring to mind trades that have now disappeared: chair-making (breast-plate, or *conscience*, used to support a breast-drill), shepherding (spring shears used for shearing) and clog-making (lovely pair of mounted clogs).

In one display-case there are masonry tools used for decorative plasterwork and an 18C precision balance for weighing gold dust.

A small room off the living room contains a fine collection of moulds for making **curbelets** (also known as *oublies*) – thin wafer biscuits which are a speciality of the Cordes region.

After a brief look at how hemp is worked, the tour ends outside with a baker's oven which still operates.

► ► **Le Cayla** – *11km/7mi southwest on D 922 to Gaillac (signposted)*. **Musée du Cayla** ⊙ commemorates writers and poets **Maurice de Guérin** (1810-39) and his sister **Eugénie** (1805-48).

► ► **Monestiés** – *15km/9mi east, on D 922 to Villefranche, then D 91 to Carmaux*. The **Chapelle St-Jacques** ⊙ contains some beautiful sculpture groups, in particular a marvellous 15C **Entombment** ★★.

CÔTE VERMEILLE★★

Michelin maps 86 fold 20 or 240 folds 42 and 46

The resorts along this rocky stretch of coast, tucked inside narrow little bays, owe much of their character to their old vocation as small maritime fortresses. The "vermilion" coast is named after just one of the vivid colours which make up the natural palette of the local landscape, which is further enhanced by the bright, clear light of this region.

1 ARGELÈS-PLAGE TO CERBÈRE along the mountain road
37km/23mi – about 2hr 30min

Argelès-Plage – *See Plages du ROUSSILLON.*

After Argelès and the long flat stretch of beach to the north, the coast suddenly becomes much more dramatic. The road (N 114) climbs into the first foothills of the Albères range, continually cutting across the rocky headlands lapped by the Mediterranean.

At the roundabout just before Collioure, take D 86 left.

The road heads uphill, initially through the Collioure vineyards.

Turn left again at the first intersection, into a road downhill.

Notre-Dame-de-Consolation – This hermitage is well-known throughout Roussillon. The chapel contains numerous votive offerings from sailors.

Turn back to D 86 and turn left (NB this stretch of mountain road has no safety barriers or other protection).

Cork-oaks become more prevalent, in between patches of exposed black rock – flaky schist.

Follow the signs for the wine route – "Circuit du vignoble" – through the vineyards towards Banyuls.

This spectacular mountain road leads to a viewing table. On the roadside opposite are the ruins of some old three-storey brick and schist barracks built in 1885.

Take the steep, narrow track to the right leading up to the Tour Madeloc (NB extreme caution required: gradient of 1:4, with tight hairpin bends and no space for passing).

The road passes two more fortified constructions before reaching a small level plateau.

Tour Madeloc – *15min on foot there and back.* Alt 652m/2 138ft. An old signal tower which, together with the Tour de la Massane to the west, was part of a network of lookout posts during the reign of the Kings of Aragón and Mallorca. The Tour de la Massane surveyed the plain of Roussillon while the Tour Madeloc kept watch out to sea. In front of the tower is a postern forming a lookout point with a splendid **panorama**★★ of the Albères mountains, the Côte Vermeille and Roussillon. The tower itself is round, made of schist and crowned with machicolations.

The track back down to the D 86 gives breathtaking, unrestricted **views**★ of the sea and the town of Banyuls.

Turn right onto D 86.

The road, with its many pretty views of the surrounding slopes, leads to Banyuls. It goes past the underground wine cellar of Mas Reig, situated in the oldest vineyard in the Banyuls area, as well as the modern cellar in which wines from the Cave des Templiers are aged.

Banyuls – *See BANYULS-SUR-MER.*

★★ **Cap Réderis** – *See below.*

Cerbère – This small seaside resort lies well-sheltered in a little cove, and has a pebble beach. It is the last town on French soil before Spain and the Costa Brava, and the international railway line from Paris to Barcelona has a stop here. The railway viaduct can be seen as you arrive along the – tortuous – road. White houses, terrace cafés and narrow pedestrian streets all lend charm to the scene.

2 CERBÈRE TO ARGELÈS-PLAGE along the coast road
33km/21mi – about 2hr

Cerbère – *See above.*

After Cerbère, the clifftop road winds through vineyards – including several terraces which have been abandoned – overlooking a vast seascape. Beaches follow in quick succession, separated by sharply pointed promontories.

★★ **Cap Réderis** – Where the road is nearest to the edge of the cliff, walk a few paces towards the edge for a better view. A magnificent **panorama** encompasses the coasts of Languedoc and Catalonia, as far south as the Cabo de Creus.

CÔTE VERMEILLE

Further along, the whole of the bay of Banyuls comes into view on the left, from a wide bend in the road. This is a particularly spectacular sight at high tide. The road twists and turns along the coast, with the sea in full view close at hand. Down below, there are numerous tempting little bays and rocky coves. As the road drops down towards Banyuls, there is a clear view of the town with its schist pebble beach and palm trees.

⌂ **Banyuls** – *See BANYULS-SUR-MER.*

As it leaves Banyuls, the road goes past a seaside sanatorium specializing in heliotherapy. In the distance, on the left, the Tour Madeloc rears its proud head.

Just before you reach Port-Vendres, there is an excellent view of the port complex on the right.

Turn right towards Cap Béar then, after the Hôtel des Tamarins, cross the railway line and drive round to the south of the bay.

Cap Béar – The narrow cliff top road climbs steeply in a series of tight bends. From the lighthouse at the tip of the headland, the coast can be seen all the way from Cap Leucate to Cabo de Creus.

⌂ **Port-Vendres** – Port-Vendres – the Port of Venus – grew up around a cove which offered excellent shelter for galleys. The town's development as a naval port and stronghold really took off in 1679, under Vauban's influence.

In the 19C, activity shifted from the old port to the Castellane docks.

Port-Vendres was once a major port for trade and passengers to and from Algeria, a role which finished with the end of French rule there. However, the well-sheltered bay has become increasingly popular for pleasure boating, and the fishing fleet is the most active on the Roussillon coast.

★★ **Collioure** – *See COLLIOURE.*

The road leaves the foothills of the Albères before reaching Argelès.

⌂⌂⌂ **Argelès-Plage** – *See Plages du ROUSSILLON.*

La COUVERTOIRADE★

Population 148
Michelin map 80 fold 15 or 240 folds 14 and 18 – 6.5km/4mi north of Caylar

This curious fortified town, with its striking military features, in the middle of the Causse du Larzac was once the property of the Knights Templar, under orders from the commandery at Ste-Eulalie-de-Cernon. The curtain wall was built in about 1450 by the Knights of St John of Jerusalem (who took over possession of the *causses* on dissolution of the order of the Templars).

La Couvertoirade, like other villages on the Larzac plateau, rapidly became depopulated. By 1880, the village had only 362 inhabitants. A few craftsmen now live there (enamel work, pottery, weaving).

SIGHTS

Park the car near the north gate, outside the ramparts.

Ramparts ⊙ – Go through the north gateway and take the flight of steps *(no handrail)* leading up from the foot of a Renaissance house. The tall, square north tower would appear to have been used as a watchtower.

Following the watch-path round to the left as far as the round tower, there is an interesting view over the town and its main street, the Rue Droite.

Return to the foot of the north tower and go into the village, bearing left.

Church ⊙ – This fortified church built on the edge of the parade ground was an integral part of the town's defences. Inside, at the entrance to the chancel, there are two disc-shaped steles showing different representations of the cross. The tiny graveyard by the entrance to the church contains some unusual disc-shaped gravestones.

Many of the doors in La Couvertoirade and other villages in the area are adorned with a curious dried plant, resembling a sunflower surrounded by ragged spiny leaves – this is the *Carlina acanthifolia*, a type of thistle known locally as the **cardabelle**. It has the characteristic of opening or closing according to the degree of humidity, making it the local equivalent of seaweed hung outside to forecast the weather.

Château – This fortress was built by the Templars in the 12C and 13C; the two upper floors have since disappeared.

Keep left until you reach a large square, once a village pond, where you walk round a block of houses to the right to reach Rue Droite.

Rue Droite – The houses in the main street are very attractive, with straight flights of stone steps outside leading up to a balcony and the door into the living area, beneath which a vault protected the ground floor where the sheep were kept. The street leads to a square in which an exhibition hall has been built. Go through the south gateway, bereft of its tower which collapsed. To the left, just past the corner of the town wall, there is a fine example of a *lavogne*, or village sheep pond, a common feature in the *causses*.

Walk along the outside of the ramparts, round to the right, to get back to the car.

La Couvertoirade

Grotte de DARGILAN**⋆⋆**

Michelin map 80 south of fold 5 or 250 fold 10
Local map see Les GRANDS CAUSSES

In 1880, a shepherd called Sahuquet was chasing a fox when he saw it slip between a crack in the rocks. The shepherd enlarged the crack to follow his quarry and found himself in a huge dark underground chamber. Thinking it to be the antechamber to hell, he fled. A young geographer heard about his adventure, and in 1884 he made an initial exploratory foray into the cave which was subsequently named after the neighbouring hamlet of Dargilan. However, the first complete exploration was not carried out until 1888, when E-A Martel and six companions took four days to examine it. Once "officially" discovered, it was not long before the cave began to attract visitors, but little was done to adapt it for them. Dargilan then became the property of the Société des Gorges du Tarn which, under the management of Louis Armand, fitted iron steps, ramps and railings so that the cave could be visited safely. In 1910, electric lighting was installed in all the galleries.

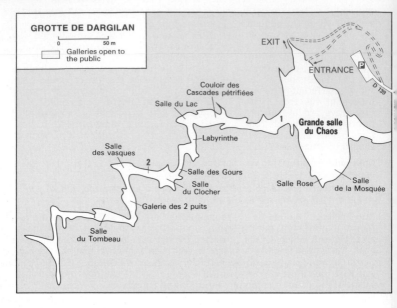

GROTTE DE DARGILAN

0 — 50 m

☐ Galleries open to the public

EXIT

ENTRANCE

P

D 139

Couloir des Cascades pétrifiées

Salle du Lac

Labyrinthe

Grande salle du Chaos

1

Salle des vasques

2

Salle des Gours

Salle du Clocher

Salle Rose

Salle de la Mosquée

Galerie des 2 puits

Salle du Tombeau

TOUR ⏱ *allow 1hr; temperature: 10°C/50°F*

Visitors first enter the **Grande Salle du Chaos**, a gallery 142m/465ft long, by 44m/114ft wide and 35m/115ft high. This sinkhole was formed later than the rest of the cave. It looks like a chaotic underground heap of rocks on which concretions are slowly building up.

At the back of the Grande Salle, the smaller Salle de la Mosquée contains a large number of beautiful stalagmites *(see chapter on Caves in Introduction)*. The "Mosque", a mass of stalagmites with glints of mother-of-pearl, is flanked by the "Minaret", a lovely column 20m/66ft high.

The "Salle Rose" adjoining the "Mosque" takes its name from the colour of its concretions (pink). Go back into the Grande Salle, from where a number of staircases lead down into the depths of the cave.

A natural shaft (**1**) leads to the "corridor of petrified cascades" in which there is a magnificent calcite drapery, reddish-brown flecked with yellow ochre and white, stretching 100m/330ft long and 40m/130ft high.

The Salle du Lac owes its name to a shallow stretch of water. It is decorated with thin, folded translucent draperies. After going through the "labyrinth" and a chamber of *gours* (natural underground lakes), left as a mark of its passage by the water that once flowed here *(see Introduction)*, the visitor reaches the Salle du Clocher with, in its centre, a slender pyramid 20m/66ft high – the "Belfry". Beyond this, the Salle du Cimetière (**2**) leads to the Salle des Vasques (hand basins) and then the "gallery of the two wells". The visit ends in the Salle du Tombeau, which contains a fine stalagmitic frozen falls.

Visitors retrace their steps to leave the cave via a semi-artificial gallery and an overhang path from which there is a beautiful panorama of the valley of the Jonte.

Grotte des DEMOISELLES★★★

This cave was discovered in 1770, and properly examined and documented ten years later. E.-A. Martel, who explored it in 1884, 1889 and 1897, revealed the cave to be in fact an old swallow-hole, the mouth of which opens onto the **Plateau de Thaurac**. In the imagination of the local rural community, this gaping chasm was home to fairies or *demoiselles*.

At St-Bauzille-de-Putois, take the hairpin road (one-way) up to two terraces (parking facilities) near the entrance to the cave.

From the terraces there is an attractive view of the Séranne mountain and Hérault valley.

TOUR ⏱ *allow 1hr; temperature: 14°C/57°F*

"Organ pipes"

From the upper funicular station, hollowed out of the mountain on a level with the roof of the cave, a series of chambers leads to the natural mouth of the swallow-hole. The most striking thing about the cave is the number and size of the concretions thickly covering its walls. The magnificent "architecture" of their surroundings cannot fail to impress visitors throughout the tour. From the swallow-hole, a series of narrow corridors leads to a sort of platform overlooking the central part of the cave itself: an immense chamber, 120m/394ft long, 80m/262ft wide and 50m/164ft high. The huge space, the enormous columns seeming to support the roof, the awesome silence and the light mist which seems to hang in the air from time to time, all combine to give the impression that one is in a gigantic cathedral.

Walkways lead all round this spectacular chamber, gradually dropping down to the elegant stalagmite resembling a Virgin and Child, perched on a white calcite pedestal. At this point look back to admire the fantastic set of "organ pipes" adorning the north wall of the cave.

The walkway leads on through beautiful draperies, some of which are translucent, while others form mini-stages for the strangest performers.

A number of viewpoints above the cavern enhance the impression of passing through some dream world of rock right until the end of the tour.

Grotte de la DEVÈZE★

This cave was discovered in 1886, when a tunnel was being drilled through Devèze mountain to carry the Bédarieux-Castres railway line, and explored in 1893 by a team including Louis Armand, Martel's faithful assistant. From 1928 to 1930, it was explored in more detail by Georges-Milhaud and his team and, in 1932, part of the cave was opened to visitors. It lies beneath the railway station at Courniou and is a trace of the old course of the Salesse, a tributary of the Jaur.

TOUR ⏱ *allow 1hr; temperature: 12°C/54°F*

The tour begins on the middle level, from where there is a view of some fine mineral draperies of various shapes and colours. All along the cave walls are slender, white concretions forming delightful bouquets of aragonite flowers. At the end of the chamber is a large frozen waterfall dropping down onto the lower level.

Grotte de la DEVÈZE

In the middle of a pile of boulders resulting from a rockfall are a number of rocks of varying shapes and forms, the most impressive of which is a huge stalagmite known as the "Cenotaph" or "Bridal Cake", an architectural structure on a pedestal beneath a roof covered with tubular shapes and draperies.
The upper chamber 60m/195ft above *(access via a flight of steps)* is full of eccentrics, draperies and discs.
The tour ends in the Georges-Milhaud chamber which is dotted with dazzling white crystallisations.

Musée français de la Spéléologie ⊘ – The museum contains a collection of documents and objects relating to pot-holing in France and to famous French speleologists such as Édouard-Alfred Martel, Robert de Joly, Norbert Casteret, Guy de Lavaur de la Boisse etc. Several different topics are covered, including the history of the science, genesis, paleontology, protection of the underground environment and cave-dwelling animals.

Vallée de la DOURBIE★★

Michelin map 80 folds 14, 15 or 240 folds 10, 14

A trip along the banks of the river Dourbie from its source to Millau where it flows into the Tarn is a superb drive. The entire valley is picturesque, narrowing in two places to form magnificent gorges with very differing appearances.
The river rises in the Aigoual mountains south of L'Espérou. It begins by gouging a path out of the schist and granite where its wild, untamed gorge reaches a depth of 300m/975ft before flowing on down to St-Jean-du-Bruel and crossing the vast, lush dip that separates the Grands Causses from the outcrops of the Cévennes. Downstream from Nant, the landscape changes again. The river slips between the Causse Noir and the Causse du Larzac, digging a very deep canyon into the limestone rocks. The canyon is flanked by scarp slopes dotted with rocks shaped like ruined buildings.

FROM L'ESPÉROU TO MILLAU *96km/60mi – about 2hr 30min*

There are numerous sharp bends and road junctions that are, in many places, difficult to cross, especially between the hamlet of Les Laupies and the village of Dourbies.

L'Espérou – *See Massif de l'AIGOUAL*
A few miles from L'Espérou lies the Dourbie river. The upper reaches of its valley are difficult to see among the pastures but gradually the river valley deepens and becomes covered with woodland. There are also more hamlets and villages.
Beyond Dourbies, the road, which is narrow and winding in places, runs high above the **Gorges de la Dourbie★★** (300m/975ft at the rock known as the Cade, or Juniper Bush, 5km/3mi from Dourbies).
This is a splendid drive along a cliff road that is impressive in many places, with breathtaking views over the wooded abyss bristling with granite and schist rocks. Far down on the valley floor is the river.
Switching onto the other side of the ridge, the road overlooks the deep Trévezel valley lying in the shadow of tall limestone cliffs.

Col de la Pierre Plantée – Alt 828m/2 691ft. There is an extensive view from the pass over the lower Dourbie valley and beyond to the Lingas mountain range and the Causse du Larzac.

162

★ **Gorges du Trévezel** – The river Trévezel flows between the Aigoual range and the Dourbie valley, over a bed strewn with rocks and boulders. The valley gradually narrows to become a ravine between scarp slopes topped by tall cliffs 400m/ 1 300ft high of varying colours. The narrowest part, which is no more than 30m/ 97ft wide, is known in local dialect as the *Pas de l'Ase* ("Donkey's Step").
Beyond the Col de la Pierre Plantée, there is a superb scenic road down to St-Jean-du-Bruel cut into the side of the small Causse Bégon.

St-Jean-du-Bruel – This summer holiday resort, in the region known as the "garden of Aveyron" which stretches from here to Nant *(see below)*, is a fruit-growing centre specialising in apples and plums. Wooden barrels for grape harvesting are made here. An old **humpbacked bridge** spans the Dourbie, while near the new bridge is an attractive 18C covered market.
Between St-Jean and Nant, the Dourbie valley is wide and cultivated. To the south are the ruins of the Château d'Algues; to the north, the scarp slopes of the Causse Bégon creating a spur of rock above Nant known as the Roc Nantais.
On the right are the four towers of Castelnau castle, now a farm.
Leave the car at the "St-Michel" signpost to the left of the road and climb the narrow path to the chapel.

St-Michel-de-Rouviac – This delightful Romanesque chapel, set against a background of trees and fields, blends in well with the graveyard and presbytery. In the 12C, this was a priory and a daughter-house of Nant Abbey and the decorative features are similar in both buildings, for example, capitals with knotwork and palmettes.

Nant – This old market town stands on the banks of the Dourbie at the mouth of the river gorge. A monastic community founded in the 7C was largely responsible for converting the swampy region into a well-drained, fertile valley with vineyards and meadows. The original Benedictine community prospered and built vast monastery buildings and the church of St-Pierre in the valley. In 1135, the monastery was promoted to the status of abbey by Pope Innocent II and the **church of St-Pierre** was rebuilt. It is very austere from the outside, dominated by a square keep topped by a spire (renovated in 1960) above the transept crossing, to replace the bell-tower demolished in 1794. The central arch leading into the narthex has a Gothic doorway and is surmounted by a trefoil arch moulding. Inside the church, which has several interesting features, note in particular the decoration on the **capitals**★.
The town that grew up around the abbey was well-fortified and became a bastion for the Roman Catholics during the Wars of Religion. In the 16C, the abbey was placed *in commendam* and became a mere source of income for the abbots, who were rarely seen in Nant. It prospered nonetheless until the Revolution. The college at Nant, founded in 1662, specialises in literature and philosophy and has the highest student intake in the Rouergue area. The main town square contains the remains of the covered market, or **vieille halle**, which was once part of the monastery – a squat, sturdy gallery with five arcades (14C). From the Chapelle du Claux (Wars of Religion memorial) there is a good view of the attractive span of the 14C **Pont de la Prade**. Downstream from Nant, the valley narrows again between the limestone rocks of the Grands Causses.

Les Cuns – Interesting 12C church of Notre-Dame.

★ **Cantobre** – This picturesque village at the confluence of the rivers Trévezel and Dourbie stands on a rocky outcrop of the Causse Bégon. It is an extraordinary sight and the village fully deserves its name of *quant obra*, meaning "what a masterpiece".

★★ **Canyon de la Dourbie** – The sides of the ravine bristle with limestone rocks that have been worn away into strange shapes by erosion.
Level with **St-Véran**, a hilltop village in a picturesque setting, the road provides a superb **view**★ of the village with its renovated houses and tower, all that remains of the old castle which was once the property of the **Marquis de Montcalm** (1712-59) who died in Quebec in Canada while defending the town during a siege laid by the English. Below the castle is the church of Treilles.

Moulin de Corps – This watermill is powered by a resurgent spring. The setting is delightful.

La Roque-Ste-Marguerite – This village, nestling at the foot of the machicolated tower of a 17C castle, is built in terraces at the entrance to the Riou Sec ravine. The Romanesque castle chapel, now used as the village church, stands at the end of narrow, winding streets. High above the village are the ruin-shaped rocks of Le Rajol and Montpellier-le-Vieux.
The road runs on along the banks of the Dourbie, through its magnificent canyon. On each side of the river upstream from Millau are the tall, vividly-coloured cliffs of the Causse Noir and Causse du Larzac, topped by jagged rocks.

★ **Millau** – *See MILLAU.*

ELNE*

Population 6 262
Michelin maps 86 folds 19, 20 and 240 fold 41

Elne was known, during the days of the Iberians, as "Illiberis" and was named after the Empress Helen, Constantine's mother. At the end of the Roman Empire, it was the true capital of the Roussillon area. Its status of bishopric from the 6C to 1602 entitled it to call itself a "city", the term originally applied to administrative divisions of Roman provinces. Its wealthier rival, Perpignan, on the other hand, was never more than a "town".

Set 6km/3.5mi from the coast between apricot and peach orchards lining the roads east and west (D 4 and D 612), Elne is a major stopping point on the road to Spain.

CATHÉDRALE STE-EULALIE-ET-STE-JULIE *1hr*

Building work began on the cathedral in the 11C. The six chapels in the south aisle were built from the 14C to mid 15C; their ribbed vaulting reflects the three stages in the evolution of Gothic architecture. The original plans provided for two bell-towers but only the square, stone tower on the right was built. The other one, on the left, is a small tower erected at an unknown date. The chevet is surrounded by foundations that are the remains of a Gothic chancel with radiating chapels. From the terrace behind the cathedral, the Mediterranean can be seen in the distance.

Interior – The Romanesque marble altar-table has been returned to its rightful place after the "post-conciliar" refurbishment of the high altar. In the chapel beside the south entrance (chapel 3), there is an altarpiece painted by a 14C Catalan artist depicting the visions and miracles of St Michael. Opposite the southeast entrance beneath the Passion Crucifix known as the "Improperia Cross", there is an interesting fluted marble stoop made out of an ancient basin decorated with a large acanthus leaf. The last span of the north aisle (baptismal chapel) contains a 14C statue of Christ giving His Blessing.

★★ **Cloisters** ⊘ – *To enter the cloisters, walk round the chevet to the left.*
The south cloister backing onto the cathedral was built in the 12C; the other three date from the 13C and 14C. Nevertheless, there is a high level of architectural uniformity since the Gothic construction copied its Romanesque predecessor.
The superb **capitals** on the twin columns supporting the rounded arcades are decorated with narrative carvings, imaginary animals, Biblical and evangelical figures, and plants. The carvings are particularly descriptive beneath the abaci of the quadrangular pillars. The sophistication and harmony of the carvings themselves and the minutely observed, realistic details bear witness to the skills of the

Cloisters seen from the north gallery

artists. The Romanesque south gallery is the most outstanding of all. Capital 12, depicting Adam and Eve, is the most remarkable work in the cloisters.
From the east cloister (where some 6C and 7C sarcophagi are on display), a spiral staircase rises to a terrace from which there is a view over part of the cloisters, the towers (note the larger of the two) and the cathedral roof. On the horizon is the Albères range.

Musée d'archéologie – *Entrance up the staircase at the end of the east cloister.*
The archeological museum occupies the old chapel of St-Laurent and exhibits 15C, 16C and 17C earthenware, Attic ceramics (4C BC) and sigillated ceramic

ware from Illiberis (Elne under Roman rule). At the back there is a display on Véraza culture (Aude region) with reconstructions of huts made of wood and reeds.

Musée d'Histoire – *Entrance via the west cloister.* The historical museum occupies the old chapter-house, now the Salle Louis Bessède, and contains archives, various literature and the town seals. In one of the display cases are two statues of the Virgin Mary, the Vierge des Tres Portalets (13C) and the Vierge du Portail de Perpignan (14C).

Musée Terrus ⊙ – This museum, in a modern building, is named after a local artist, Étienne Terrus (1857-1922) and displays works by him and by the artists whose company he kept, such as Luce, Maillol and G. de Monfreid (woodcuts). Terrus was influenced by the Impressionists and the Fauves but nonetheless developed a style of his own which is evident in his Roussillon landscapes (View of Espira-de-Conflent or Mas d'Adel) and his still-life pictures.

Oppidum d'ENSÉRUNE★

Michelin map 83 fold 14 or 240 fold 30 – 14km – 9 miles southwest of Béziers

The Ensérune hillfort stands 120m/390ft above the Béziers plain. Its decidedly Mediterranean geographical location and wonderful pine wood are quite out of the ordinary, and its archeological site is also of particular interest. It was here, in 1915, that traces of Iberian-Greek settlement and a crematorium dating from the 4C and 3C BC were uncovered.

Ensérune was a settlement from the 6C BC until the beginning of the Christian era and its remains are an indication of the type of civilization that preceded the arrival of the Romans. In the 6C BC, huts probably built of *pisé*, or mud, were strung out across the hilltop. Nothing remains of this period except the food stores dug into the tufa stone. Ensérune had trading links with Greece via Marseille and enjoyed an economic boom. The old village evolved into a town with stone houses set out in a checkerboard pattern. A large earthenware jar *(dolium)* was sunk into the floor of every house to serve as a pantry. A town wall was built and to the west of the town there lay a vast area used for funeral pyres.

From the middle of the Second Iron Age, Ensérune underwent further change. It expanded and the hillsides were laid out in terraces. A grainstore was built to the south, consisting of a number of silos. At the end of the 3C BC, the hillfort was probably razed by Hannibal. It was rebuilt and regained its erstwhile prosperity after the arrival of the Romans who, in 118 BC, founded their first colony in Narbonne. Tanks were built, a sewage system was installed, paving stones were laid, and the walls were plastered and painted. Then the population gradually moved away from the hillfort, and it finally fell into a total decline in the 1C AD when *Pax Romana* enabled people to settle safely in the plains.

TOUR ⊙ *About 1hr 30min*

★ **Museum** ⊙ (Musée) – The museum is built on the site of the old town and contains the objects found during archeological digs. They give an indication of what everyday life was like between the 6C and 1C BC.

The ground floor houses a collection of *dolia* (earthenware jars) found in the floors of houses, ceramics, drinking cups, vases, amphorae and pottery, of Phocean, Iberian, Greek, Etruscan, Roman and local origin. Note *(case 22)* the small hollowed-out cornelian representing an armed Greek slaying a woman. It is thought to depict the combat between Achilles and Penthesilea, Queen of the Amazons.

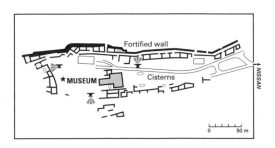

The first floor contains funerary items from the necropolis, dating from the 5C to 3C BC. They include vases and Greek wine bowls used as urns for ashes or gifts. In the Salle Mouret *(central display case)*, there is an egg which was found in one of the graves. It is a symbol of rebirth. Another outstanding exhibit is the famous Attic drinking cup decorated with Procris and Cephalus in a small case.

Panorama – Viewing tables set out at all four cardinal points of the compass around the hillfort provide an opportunity to enjoy a vast panoramic view stretching from the Cévennes to the Canigou and across the entire coastal plain. In the foreground are archeological finds that have been left in place, such as *dolia,* remains of columns, and the foundations of ancient walls.

The **view**★ is particularly unusual to the north. It takes in the **old Montady lake** which was drained in 1247. The plots of land radiate out from the centre because of the channels that drain the water off into a collector. From there, an aqueduct passes under the hill and takes the water to the floor of the old Capestang lake, which was drained in the 19C.

► ► **Nissan-lez-Ensérune** – *3km/2mi southeast.* 14C southern French Gothic church, and **archeological museum** ⊙.

ENTRAYGUES-SUR-TRUYÈRE★

Population 1 495
Michelin map 76 south of fold 12 or 240 fold 1
Local map see Gorges de la TRUYÈRE

Entraygues, which was founded in the 13C by Count Henri II of Rodez, is well situated at the confluence of the rivers Lot and Truyère, between hillsides covered with meadows, fruit trees and vines which produce an excellent wine.

The town has become a sports and leisure resort (canoeing, rambling). There is an excellent view of the village and the Truyère valley from Condat to the northwest, on the Aurillac road.

SIGHTS

★ **Gothic bridge (Pont gothique)** – *One-way traffic in summer.* The bridge dates from the end of the 13C.

Old town – To see the covered passageways known locally as "*cantous*" and the picturesque houses with overhanging upper storeys and flowers at every window, start from the tiny Place Albert-Castanié or Place de la Croix and walk down Rue Droite. On the right is a fine 16C entrance with a knocker above the door so that riders did not have to dismount (**B**). Continue left along the Rue du Collège and the **Rue Basse**★, the best-preserved of all the streets in Entraygues.

On the Place A.-Castanié, at the corner of the old Sabathier mansion (**D**), marks on the wall indicate the highest levels reached by the rivers Lot and Truyère when in spate. Continue along the water's edge (quai des Gabares) to the confluence of the two rivers. From this spot, there is a fine view of the castle *(not open to the public).* Only the two towers date from the 13C; the central section was rebuilt in the 17C.

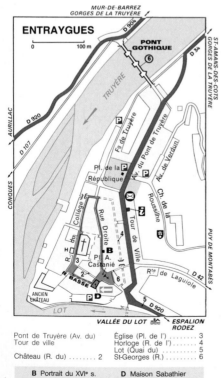

ENTRAYGUES

EXCURSIONS

Bez-Bedène; Puy de Montabès – *Head northwards from Entraygues on D 34.* The drive along the east bank of the Truyère includes a view of the Cambeyrac dam and the Lardit hydroelectric plant. These two features constitute the last downstream sections of the hydroelectric installations on the Truyère *(see Gorges de la TRUYÈRE).*

Pont de Truyère (Av. du)	Église (Pl. de l') 3
Tour de ville	Horloge (R. de l') 4
	Lot (Quai du) 5
Château (R. du) 2	St-Georges (R.) 6

B Portrait du XVIᵉ s.	**D** Maison Sabathier

In the hamlet of Banhars, turn left onto D 34. Beyond the bridge over the Selves, continue right along D 34.

The road winds through the picturesque Selves valley before reaching the tiny Volonzac plateau.

In Volonzac, turn right onto a narrow road leading to Bez-Bedène.

Bez-Bedène – This typical Rouergue-style village occupies a harsh, isolated setting and consists of a few houses strung out along a rocky ridge enclosed within a meander of the Selves. Of note are the small 12C church with a bellcote, and the 14C single-span bridge.

Continue along the same road to the crossroads with D 34, into which you turn right towards St-Amans-des-Cots. The D 97 leads to the Maury dam.

Maury dam – The dam *(barrage)* was built in 1948 at the confluence of the Selves and Selvet. Its reservoir, covering an area of 166ha/410 acres and containing 35 million m³/1 236 million ft³ of water, lies in a varied, colourful landscape.

Continue southwards along D 97 then turn right onto D 42 and right again onto D 652.

★ **Puy de Montabès** – *15min on foot there and back.* Superb **panoramic view**★ over the mountains of Cantal, Aubrac, and Rouergue (the cathedral in Rodez is visible in clear weather). Downstream from Entraygues, the view encompasses the Lot valley and Châtaigneraie plateau. *Viewing table.*

The road then runs down to the Truyère valley and back to Entraygues.

★★ **Vallée du Lot** – *See Vallée du LOT.*

★★ **Gorges de la Truyère** – *See Gorges de la TRUYÈRE.*

ESPALION★

Population 4 614
Michelin map 80 fold 3 or 240 fold 1 – Local map see L'AUBRAC

Espalion lies in pleasant surroundings in a fertile basin crossed by the river Lot. Above the town are the feudal ruins of Calmont d'Olt.

Old bridge (Vieux pont) – From the marketplace, this 11C bridge forms part of a picturesque view that encompasses the Vieux Palais and the old tanneries with timber balconies lining the river banks.

Old palace (Vieux palais) – The palace was built in the 16C and used to be the residence of the Governors of Espalion.

Musée Joseph-Vaylet ⊘ – The museum, housed in the old church of St-Jean and adjacent buildings, has a large number of collections relating to folk arts, crafts and traditions including weaponry, furniture, glassware, religious artefacts (450 holy-water stoups), pottery etc.

Old tanners' houses by the old bridge on the river Lot

There is also a museum of diving-suits in the same building. The exhibits are all on the theme of underwater diving and honour the memory of the three men from Espalion who, in 1860, invented the aqualung and the depressurizer (gas regulator).

Musée du Rouergue ⊙ – The cells of the former prison now house exhibits relating to local life and customs, including an extensive costume collection.

★ **Église de Perse** ⊙ – *1km/0.6mi southeast along Avenue de la Gare.* This fine pink sandstone Romanesque building dates from the 11C and is reminiscent of the abbey church at Conques. Indeed, this was once one of the daughterhouses of Conques abbey. It is dedicated to St Hilarian, Charlemagne's confessor, who is said in holy legend to have retired to Espalion and been beheaded by the Moors. On the south side is a **portal**★ including a tympanum depicting Pentecost. The lintel is decorated with carvings of the Apocalypse and the Last Judgement. Above and to the left are three naive carvings of the Adoration of the Magi. Inside the church, note the historiated capitals, among them a lion hunt and Christ in Majesty, either side of the apse.

EXCURSIONS

Château de Calmont d'Olt ⊙ – *3.5km/2mi south via D 920. Follow the signs to the car park.*
This medieval fortress stands on a spur of basalt from which there is a fine **view**★ of the Lot valley, the Aubrac and the Causse du Comtal. It has not been used as a military stronghold since the 17C. A historic tour backed up by an audio-visual presentation gives information on the castle and the strategy and machinery of siege warfare used here in the 15C.

St-Pierre-de-Bessuéjouls – *4km/2.5mi west via D 556 (avenue de St-Pierre).* At St-Pierre cross the bridge to the left. Then turn onto the track to the left. This unpretentious church in a rustic setting shelters beneath its bell-tower an outstanding little **Romanesque chapel**★ *(access via a worn flight of steps).* The pink chapel was built in the 11C. Each of its sides measures 6m/19ft and it is decorated with archaic motifs such as knotwork, palmettes, Maltese crosses and historiated capitals. Carved on the left side of the altar is a figure of the archangel Michael slaying the dragon, and on the right side the archangel Gabriel with an inscribed scroll.

★ **Château de Roquelaure; St Côme d'Olt** – *37km/23mi round tour – allow 2hr.* Leave Espalion on the Avenue de la Gare, pass the Église de Perse, then bear left onto the St-Côme-d'Olt road and immediately turn right into a narrow, steep road.
Further on, the road crosses a strange basalt flow known as the **clapas**★. The Mont de Roquelaure is an outcrop of basalt overlooking the Lot valley.

Château de Roquelaure – *Not open to the public.* The castle lay in ruins for many years but has been almost entirely rebuilt. From the colourful surroundings of the terrace, there is a **view**★ over the Lot valley to the north and the Causse de Gabriac to the south. In the distance are the mountains above the Lévézou plateau.
The Romanesque **chapel** at the foot of the castle contains a 15C statue of the Entombment of Christ and a 16C Renaissance Pietà.
Drive through the village and turn left onto a small road that joins D 59. Then turn left onto D 6 to St-Côme-d'Olt.
From the road, there is an interesting view of the dam at **Castelnau-Lassouts**.

★ **St-Côme-d'Olt** – *See L'AUBRAC.*

★★ **Vallée du Lot** – *See Vallée du LOT.*

Monts de l'ESPINOUSE★

Michelin map 83 folds 2, 3, 4, 13 and 14 or 240 folds 21, 22 and 25

The Espinouse uplands on the southern edge of the Massif Central stand more than 1 000m/3 250ft above the Jaur and Orb valleys and are bordered to the north by the upper Agout valley. This mountainous hinterland of the Bas Languedoc region encompasses three zones: the lush Somail to the west where the main town St-Pons lies amidst pleasantly rural countryside; the Espinouse in the centre where the land is more rugged; and the Caroux to the east gashed by ravines around Lamalou-les-Bains. The region lies within the **Parc naturel régional du Haut-Languedoc** and has developed a range of tourist amenities such as open-air leisure complexes, waymarked footpaths etc.

⬚ SOMAIL

The Somail is the most fertile part of the Espinouse uplands. It is an area of rolling hills covered with chestnut or beech groves and carpeted with heather that takes on russet tones in the autumn.

Round tour from St-Pons *76km/47mi – allow 2hr*

St-Pons-de-Thomières – This pretty mountain town in the upper valley of the Jaur, near the river's source, grew up around a Benedictine abbey founded in 936 by Count Raymond Pons of Toulouse. St-Pons is now the administrative centre for the **Parc naturel régional du Haut-Languedoc** *(13, rue du Cloître)*.
The **old cathedral** ⊘ *(allow 30min)* dates from the 12C, with modifications in the 15C, 16C and 18C. The north side retains some fortified features: two of the original four crenellated corner towers and a row of arrow slits above the windows. The richly sculpted doorway presents something of a puzzle in the shape of seven niches and four unidentified figures above the archivolt. The west front, where the main entrance used to be, has two sculpted tympana (unfortunately rather difficult to see) depicting the Last Supper and the Washing of Feet to the left, and the Crucifixion to the right (note the unusually tortuous position of the two thieves). The 18C façade through which one enters the church replaced the 16C Gothic chancel. The strikingly spacious interior has undergone numerous modifications. The choir stalls date from the 17C, while the cathedral is 19C. The chancel is closed off by a railing and contains numerous sculpted marble decorations.
A **Musée de Préhistoire régionale** ⊘ contains objects discovered on archeological digs in caves in the region (particularly that at Camprafaud).

Leave St-Pons via D 907, the Salvetat-sur-Agout road.

The road winds picturesquely uphill, providing some fine views of St-Pons and the Jaur valley before reaching the Col de Cabaretou.

Beyond the pass, turn right onto D 169 that crosses the Somail plateau. A narrow road to the right signposted Saut de Vésoles leads to the shores of a lake set in the middle of woodland.

Saut de Vésoles – *15min on foot there and back.* The Bureau, which flows through rugged countryside, used to form an impressive waterfall with a 200m/650ft drop over gigantic granite boulders before running into the Jaur as it tumbles down the steep slope on the Mediterranean side of the range. Since the building of the hydroelectric dam that supplies the power for the Riols power station, the waterfall has lost some of its power but the beauty spot has remained as impressive as ever.

Return to D 169 and head back to Fraisse-sur-Agout.

The road crosses some superb heather-clad moorland and the Col de la Bane (pass, alt 1 003m/3 260ft).

Prat d'Alaric ⊘ – This typical Espinouse farmstead has been renovated by the Haut-Languedoc regional park authority and is now used as a visitor centre *(maison du pays)*. Near the farmhouse stands the long, low barn that is so characteristic of local architectural style. Its steeply-sloping roof runs down onto side walls that are less than 2m/6ft 7in in height *(see illustrations of rural architecture in Introduction)*. The building is unusual in that the rafters do not include any crossbeams. The house is roofed with broom laid across rafters that cut across each other at the ridge and are supported by the side walls.

Fraisse-sur-Agout – This peaceful village is famous for its angling. It gets its name from its tall ash trees.

From the village, either head for the Col de Fontfroide and the tour through the Espinouse uplands or continue to Salvetat.

169

On the outskirts of the village in the Salvetat direction, there is another house with a broom roof, at the junction of the road to Le Cambaissy.

La Salvetat-sur-Agout – This is a summer holiday resort perched on a rocky promontory high above the confluence of the rivers Vèbre and Agout. Its name is a reminder of the days (11C and 12C) when prelates, abbots, and commanders of the Knights Templar founded "new towns" on their lands to increase their value. The "guests" arriving in these new towns (or *sauvetés*) were given a house and a plot of land. Later, for economic and military reasons, the ecclesiastical authorities and noblemen set up hilltop villages known as *bastides*.

From La Salvetat, there is a road running right round the Lac de la Raviège.

Lac de la Raviège – Not far from La Salvetat on the shores of this vast reservoir covering an area of 450ha/1 112 acres, there is a beach named Les Bouldouires (swimming, water sports, water skiing, sailing etc). The road crosses the dam and runs along the right bank of the reservoir, returning via the left bank. The shores are wooded and there are very few views of the lake.

From La Salvetat, return to St-Pons via D 907.

② ESPINOUSE

Separated from the Somail by the D 14 and from the Caroux mountains by the **Gorges d'Héric**★★ and the Pas de la Lauze, the Espinouse is an area of alternating ravines and scrub or woodland. There is a stark contrast between the upper northern areas lying at altitudes in excess of 1 000m/3 250ft where the countryside is lush and cool, and the bare landscape on the southern slopes in the Jaur valley below 200m/650ft.

From Olargues to the Col de l'Ourtigas *38km/24mi – allow 2hr 30min*

Olargues – This village with its steep streets occupies a promontory encircled by the river Jaur. The village skyline is dominated by a tower, the vestige of an 11C feudal fortress which was converted into a bell-tower in the 15C. A curious doorway *(opposite the Syndicat d'initiative)* opens off the Rue de la Place onto the covered stairway of the Commanderie which leads up to a **viewpoint** beside the bell-tower, from where there is a **view** of the Jaur and the old humpbacked bridge which spans it, the Espinouse, and the Caroux to the northeast. The local **museum** ⊙ contains displays on traditional crafts and agricultural practices, most of which have now disappeared in the wake of modern technology.

Take D 908 out of Olargues and head west towards St-Pons then turn right onto D 14 to Fraisse-sur-Agout and La Salvetat.

The pass road leading to the Col de Fontfroide along the western slopes of the Espinouse starts in a Mediterranean setting of vines, olive trees, holm-oaks and chestnut trees.

To the right is the Mauroul ravine leading to the hamlet of the same name visible further down the hill. From the Col du Poirier, the view extends over the mountains in the Somail to the left beyond the Coustorgues gully. There is an even wider view to the south towards the Jaur valley *(viewpoint)*.

At higher altitudes, the Mediterranean vegetation gives way to moorland dotted with beech trees.

Col de Fontfroide – Alt 971m/ 3 156ft. The Col de Fontfroide is a mountain pass set in an impressively wild spot. It marks the watershed between the Mediterranean and Atlantic sides of the range.

Turn right onto D 53 to Cambon.

The road runs along the banks of the Agout, through the village of Cambon which gets quite lively in summer, and continues through rugged, lonely, mountainous scenery where the moorland is backed by the conifers in the Espinouse forest.

Forêt domaniale de l'Espinouse – Tree-planting began in the late 19C and has continued to the present day. Now, the forest of beech, pine, and spruce covers the entire Espinouse plateau. Much of the plateau has been designated as the Caroux-Espinouse hunting ground *(réserve de chasse)*. Corsican moufflons (wild sheep), which have acclimatized themselves to the local environment, are occasionally to be seen here. Only the western part of the forest around the forest ranger's house at Le Crouzet is easily accessible and then only on foot.

Forêt du Crouzet – *Turn onto a path to the right, beyond Agoudet (signposted "pique-nique").* The 219ha/561 acres of forest include a variety of different species.

Beyond Salvergues, the scenery consists of endless stretches of windswept moorland.

At a road junction, turn right onto D 180.

From the road near the top of the Espinouse, the roof of the Espinouse farm or **Rec d'Agout** is visible further down the hill to the right. It is here that the river rises. The road then reaches the foot of the bare dome-shaped crest of the Espinouse (alt 1 124m/3 653ft) and runs on down through rugged countryside with ravines to each side, before crossing the **Pas de la Lauze**, a slender ridge linking the Espinouse and Caroux ranges.

★ **Col de l'Ourtigas** – Alt 988m/3 211ft. An observation platform provides an interesting **view★** of the rugged Espinouse range gashed by ravines. To the left is the Montagne d'Aret and to the right the two outcrops forming the Fourcat d'Héric. In the distance are the Corbières, with the Canigou closing off the horizon. On the other side of the road is a path leading to the **Plo des Brus** *(45min on foot there and back)*. Not far away are archeological digs that have revealed the existence of a Roman hillfort here. The path leads to the edge of the plateau. From there, the view extends over the Mare valley, the Causses and the Cévennes.

③ CAROUX

This mountain range, bordered to east and south by the Mare and Orb valleys, is separated from the Espinouse by the Gorges d'Héric. Its beauty spots are popular with nature lovers, climbers and walkers and are all part of nature conservation projects. Its name comes from the Celtic root *Karr* meaning "rock", an appropriate description given the stony landscape formed by the vast plateau 1 000m/3 250ft high flanked by deep, rugged gorges bristling with slender needles of rock.

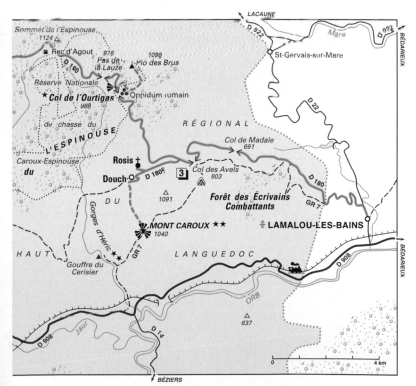

From the Col de l'Ourtigas to Lamalou-les-Bains

21km/13mi – allow 3hr, including walk up Mont Caroux

From the Col de l'Ourtigas *(see above)*, continue to the road junction with the D 180ᴱ branching off to Douch on the right.

Église de Rosis – Standing to the right of the road, this rustic church with stone bell-tower stands out against particularly fine rural countryside.

Douch – The character of this village, which is typical of the Caroux region, is fairly well preserved. The narrow streets are flanked by stone houses roofed with stone slabs *(lauzes)*.

Table d'orientation du Mont Caroux – *2hr on foot there and back. Leave the car in Douch and follow the path to the left up through the fields. Take the left fork 50m/55yd further on.*
The path climbs up through clumps of broom, then a beech forest. To the left, at the top of the hill, is the highest point on Mont Caroux itself (alt 1 091m/3 546ft). The path then runs across a vast plateau where heather and broom tremble in the breeze. In the silence that envelops this isolated spot stands a viewing table *(table d'orientation)*, with the Plo de la Maurelle to the right. The rugged, bare Caroux peak towers above the Orb and Jaur valleys. The **panorama**★★ is a magnificent sight. From west to east are the rounded summits of the Montagne Noire with its highest peak, the Pic de Nore, the Pyrenees with the Carlit and Canigou, then the plains around Narbonne and Béziers and on down to the Mediterranean. To the right of the plateau is the start of the Gorges de Colombières.

Rejoin D 180.

Forêt des Écrivains Combattants – *Get there by car via the Chemin Paul-Prévost or on foot via a flight of steps 200m/220yd further on opposite an old inn.*
After the catastrophic floods in 1930, the slopes of the Caroux range had to be reafforested. The Association des Écrivains Combattants, the Touring Club de France and the villages of Combes and Rosis replanted the 78ha/ 193 acres of forest dedicated to writers who had laid down their lives for France. The steep flight of steps leads first to a plateau where there is a memorial commemorating the 560 writers who fell during the First World War (1914-18), then to the Rond-point Charles-Péguy with its gigantic Military Cross. From the roundabout radiate avenues, each named after a writer. The forest includes some magnificent cedars, pines, chestnut trees and oaks. From it, there are several superb views of the Caroux and the eastern slopes of the Espinouse.

The picturesque D 180 leads to **Lamalou-les-Bains**‡.

ESTAING★

Population 665
Michelin map 80 fold 3 or 240 fold 1

The old houses in Estaing huddle round the foot of the castle, birthplace of the family of the same name. The Lot flows through Estaing, making it a pleasant holiday resort and an ideal centre from which to visit Entraygues and Espalion.

HISTORICAL NOTES

The **D'Estaing family**'s first step up the ladder to fame and fortune was made at the Battle of Bouvines by Dieudonné d'Estaing, who saved the life of King Philippe-Auguste. As a reward, the grateful king authorised him to include the royal fleur-de-lis on his coat of arms.
Successive generations gave birth to cardinals and warriors, all of whom won favour at the royal court, right up to the 18C when a particularly glittering branch of the family produced Charles-Hector, Comte d'Estaing. He also became a prominent figure as a seafarer who had a distinguished career in the Indies, America, and Caribbean. The Revolution brought him certain advantages after his return to France; he was appointed admiral of the fleet. However, although Charles-Hector d'Estaing had Republican tendencies, he tried to save the life of the monarch and his family, and he exchanged a few confidential letters with Marie-Antoinette. He was arrested, appeared in Court as a witness at the queen's trial, and was finally sentenced to death and executed. "When you've cut my head off," he said to his judges, "send it to the English. They'll pay you dearly for it."

A. Kumurdjian

Estaing

SIGHTS *45min*

From the Entraygues road, there is a picturesque view of the Lot, the old bridge and the castle high above the village. From the Laguiole road, there is a delightful view, especially in the morning, of the other side of the castle, the chevet of the church and the old houses of the village.

Château ⊙ – Built over successive architectural periods (15C-16C) using a variety of building materials, the castle features a curious combination of styles and is dominated by its keep. From the west terrace, there is a superb view of the old town and the river Lot. The castle is occupied by a religious Order.

Church – The 15C church opposite the castle contains the relics of St Fleuret, Bishop of Clermont, who died in Estaing in the 7C. On his feast day (1st Sunday in July), there is a procession. In front of the church are several fine Gothic crosses.

Gothic bridge – The bridge carries a statue of François d'Estaing, Bishop of Rodez, who had the superb bell-tower built on the town's cathedral.

Maison Cayron – This house is located in the old town. It still has its Renaissance windows and now houses the town hall *(mairie)*.

Chapelle de l'Ouradou – *1.5km/1mi north on D 97 to Nayrac (signposted).* Tiny 16C chapel with interesting stone altarpiece of the Baptism of Christ.

FANJEAUX★

Population 775
Michelin map 82 fold 20 or 235 fold 39

The town of Fanjeaux was considered to be a sacred spot in Roman times (its name comes from *Fanum Jovis,* meaning "Temple of Jupiter"). The continued religious significance of the town, built on a spur of rock from which there is a vast **panorama** over the Lauragais plain and Montagne Noire, is evident from the few reminders there of the early days of the preaching of **St Dominic** in an area where Catharism was rife.

In June 1206, Dominic, who was the Sub-Prior of the chapter of Osma cathedral in Old Castile, stopped in Montpellier with his bishop while travelling back to Spain from Rome. There, they gave their support to the condemnation of the Cathar heresy zealously being preached by the three legates sent by Pope Innocent III. In April 1207, after the famous debate with the Cathars in Montréal, Dominic settled at the foot of the hill at Fanjeaux, an active centre of the Cathar faith, and set up a religious community of women converts in Prouille 3km/2mi east of the town. Meanwhile, a community of monks took up residence in the hilltop town itself. They received frequent visits from their leader before he set off for Toulouse where, in 1215, he founded the Order of Preachers, otherwise known as the Dominican Order.

Maison de Saint Dominique – During his time in Fanjeaux, Dominic lived in the tack room of a castle, now no longer extant. "St Dominic's bedchamber" still has its old beams and a fireplace. It was turned into a chapel in 1948 and had stained-glass windows by Jean Hugo added to it depicting the miracles that occurred during the saint's missionary work. From the tiny garden, there is a view of the Pyrenees in clear weather.

★ **Le Seignadou** – *East of the village.* This is the viewpoint on a promontory (memorial) from which St Dominic had three visions of a fireball descending on the hamlet of **Prouille**, which led him to select that spot for his first community. His memory has been perpetuated in a Dominican convent (a contemplative order).

From the top of the hill, there are views far into the distance over the Lauragais area, Montagne Noire, Corbières and Pyrenees. In the foreground lies the village of Prouille; facing the hilltop directly east is the St-Barthélemy peak.

Church ⊙ – This is a large late-13C building in the southern French style. The elegant chancel is adorned with a fine set of six 18C paintings. Above the carved wooden high altar is a superb transparency depicting Our Lady of the Assumption. Dainty medallions decorate the vaulted roof.

St Dominic's chapel *(2nd on the left)* contains a beam that serves as a reminder of the "miracle of fire". At the end of a winter's day spent debating with the Cathars, Dominic gave one of his adversaries a document summarising his arguments. The Cathar returned to his host's house and in front of others attempted to set fire to the document. He threw it into the hearth three times, but it remained unscathed, on each occasion flying out of the flames up to the ceiling, leaving scorch marks on the beam there. The stained-glass windows and fine stoup are also particularly interesting.

Treasury ⊙ – Note the bust-reliquaries of St Louis of Anjou, one of the patron saints of the Franciscan Order (*c*1415), and of St Gaudéric, protector of peasants (1541).

Les FENOUILLÈDES★★

Michelin map 86 folds 7, 8 and 17 or 235 folds 47, 48 and 52

The Fenouillèdes is the name given to the area which lies between the southern Corbières and the Conflent. The area effectively forms the southern glacis of the Languedoc region. It was annexed to the *département* of Pyrénées-Orientales in 1790. Geographically speaking, the Fenouillèdes area links the furrow hollowed out between the Col Campérié and Estagel (the more populated area, including the vineyards of Maury and the "Côtes du Roussillon") and a more rugged crystalline mountain range that becomes particularly arid between Sournia and Prades. However, here as elsewhere, extensive land clearance indicates the advance of the vineyards into the scrubland of holm-oaks and thorn-bushes.

The northern part of the region is crossed by the river Agly. Its valley, sometimes consisting of deep ravines with steep sides, is a very impressive sight.

FROM CAUDIÈS TO PRADES *45km/28mi – about 2hr 30min*

Caudiès-de-Fenouillèdes – This village forms the gateway to the Fenouillèdes. It is also the point of departure for excursions into the Aude valley, west towards Axat via the Col Campérié and northwest towards Quillan via the Col de St-Louis.
Take D 9 south.

Notre-Dame-de-Laval – Once a **hermitage** ⊙. The Gothic church stands on an esplanade lined with olive trees, its pink-roofed body flanked by a tower with an octagonal top section surmounted by a brick roof shaped like a candle snuffer. We recommend approaching the church from the Caudiès side, up a slope. At the foot of the slope the lower gate forms a shrine. It contains a statue of Mary and Joseph (15C). The upper gate, dedicated to Our Lady "the Bread-Giver" (Madonna and Child, also 15C) has Romanesque columns and capitals that have been brought here from another building and re-used.

The road climbs to **Fenouillet**, a village in the shadow of the two ruins that has given the area its name, giving a succession of delightful views *(looking back)* of the hermitage of Notre-Dame-de-Laval and the Bugarach summit, on the horizon.

Continue through the Col del Mas to Le Vivier, where the D 9 is joined by the D 7 from St-Paul-de-Fenouillet. The road then runs up to Prats-de-Sournia. There is an extensive view of the Corbières to the north and a couple of glimpses of the Mediterranean through the Bas-Agly gap. In Sournia, the road joins the D 619, also from St-Paul-de-Fenouillet, which runs on to Prades *(remainder of the description of route below)*.

Prades – *See PRADES.*

FROM ST-PAUL-DE-FENOUILLET TO PRADES
47km/29mi – about 2hr 30min

St-Paul-de-Fenouillet – This town lies on the east bank of the Agly, a short distance before its confluence with the Boulzane. To the north, the D 7 leads to the Gorges de Galamus.

Clue de la Fou – This is a *cluse* or transverse valley gouged out by the Agly. There is always a strong wind blowing here whatever the weather. Cross the river and follow the D 619 as it hugs the river bank.

The road consists of a picturesque succession of bends in sight of the Fenouillèdes furrow and its vineyards. In the background the ruined castle of Quéribus can be seen perched on its rocky pinnacle. In the foreground, note the large rocky back of the Serre de Verges ridge, which is seen from various angles. The Canigou peak looms in the distance.

The road runs close to the Roman aqueduct at **Ansignan**, which is well-preserved and still in use, then, in an ever-increasing number of bends, it follows the course of the Matasse for a short distance, before going through Pézilla-de-Conflent and following the Desix to Sournia. It climbs from the valley floor to reach the Campoussy plateau. The panoramic view of the sea, the Roussillon plain, and the

> ### Fennel from Le Fenouillèdes
>
> As might be expected from the name (*fenouil* = "fennel"), Le Fenouillèdes is an area where fennel grows in abundance. This typical Mediterranean plant with its pretty parasol-like flowers can be found growing wild along the hedgerows, as well as being cultivated for its gastronomic or aromatic properties. The fresh, slightly aniseed flavour of fennel makes it an excellent accompaniment to fish dishes.

Corbières becomes ever vaster as the road crosses the moors dotted with huge granite boulders. The strangest rock of them all, the Roc Cornu, stands beside the road like the head of some monstrous bird.

The road then reaches its highest point (976m/ 3 172ft) and crosses the Roque Jalère, a small mountain range topped by a telecommunications station. Beyond it, the final **descent★★** provides a continuous view of the Canigou. Its sharp outline and gullies are best seen in the oblique late afternoon light. Beyond the roadmender's hut, there is a view along the upper Têt valley on the other side of the Villefranche gorge. Slightly to the right of Prades is the tower of St-Michel de-Cuxa.

Prades – *See PRADES.*

FROM ST-PAUL-DE-FENOUILLET TO CUBIÈRES
See Gorges de GALAMUS.

FLORAC

Population 2 065
Michelin map 80 fold 6 or 240 fold 6 – Local maps see overleaf and
Les GRANDS CAUSSES, Mont LOZÈRE and Gorges du TARN

This small town lies in the Tarnon valley at the foot of the dolomitic cliffs which make up the Rochefort rock. Florac is situated at the entrance to the Tarn gorges, on the edge of the Causse Méjean, the Cévennes, and Mont Lozère. Because of this location, it was chosen as the site for the head office of the **Parc national des Cévennes**. Florac, which was the capital of one of the eight baronies in the **Gévaudan** area under the direct control of the Bishop of Mende, has a very eventful history. It was subjected to a very tough feudal regime and was only too painfully aware of the truth in the saying, *pays du Gévaudan, pays de tyrans* (Gévaudan, land of tyrants). After the constant struggle against local noblemen came the Wars of Religion. Nowadays, though, this small town is a peaceful spot famous for its good food and outdoor leisure activities.

Every summer, the town hosts the *24 heures de Florac*, when riders complete a 160km/99mi trip on horseback in the area around Florac, taking in Mont Lozère, the Aigoual and the Causse Méjean.

Château ⊘ – This long 17C building flanked by two round towers now houses on the ground and first floors an interesting exhibition on the Parc national des Cévennes (landscape, flora, fauna, and activities linked with the park). The **Information Centre** provides a full range of information on hiking, guided tours, open-air museums *(écomusées)* in the park and overnight accommodation.
Nearby is the start of the "Beaver Trail" *(Sentier du Castor)* along which the explanatory signposts give a full insight into the natural environment in which the Pêcher river rises.

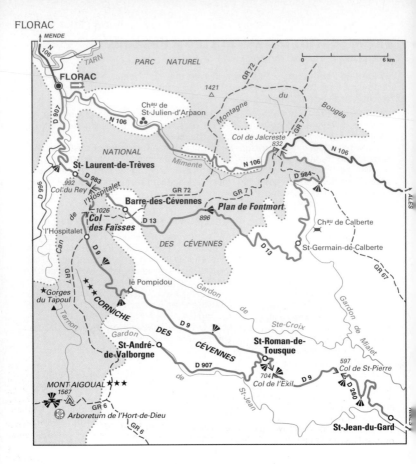

Couvent de la Présentation – This convent used to be a commandery of the Knights Templar. Note the superb façade and monumental doorway dating from 1583.

Source of the Pêcher – Situated at the foot of the Rochefort rock, this is one of the main resurgent springs on the Causse Méjean. The river bubbles and froths up from the spring during heavy rain or when the snow melts.

EXCURSIONS

★★★ **Corniche des Cévennes** – *See Corniche des CÉVENNES.*

Round tour in the Cévennes – *75km/47mi – allow 3hr.*
This trip takes visitors through the Cévennes, a region crisscrossed by deep valleys in between serrated ridges, in which houses are roofed with schist slabs, roads lined with chestnut trees, and villages steeped in memories of the Camisard uprising.

Head south from Florac on D 907 and N 106 to Alès.

The road begins by following the Mimente valley, where it is flanked by schist cliffs. Beyond the ruins of the Château de St-Julien-d'Arpaon perched on a hilltop to the left of the road, there is a view of Le Bougès, a mountain rising to an altitude of 1 421m/4 618ft, to the right.

At the Col de Jalcrests, turn right onto D 984 to St-Germain-de-Calberte.

There is an interesting view of the mouth of the Gardon de St-Germain valley. Beyond the pass, the road runs down to St-Germain-de-Calberte among chestnut trees, holm-oaks and broom. Cévennes-style houses with stone-slab roofs and decorative chimneys line the roadside.

The Château de Calberte comes into view in a bend of the road, perched on a spur of rock.

Beyond St-Germain-de-Calberte, turn right onto D 13.

Plan de Fontmort – Alt 896m/2 912ft. At a junction in the Fontmort forest is an obelisk which was inaugurated in 1887 to celebrate the signature of the Edict of Tolerance by Louis XVI. The memorial also serves as a reminder of the many battles fought by the Camisard rebels against the Maréchal de Villars in this region. There is a superb view to the east over the ridges of the Cévennes.

From the Plan de Fontmort to Barre-des-Cévennes, the road follows a narrow ridge that provides a number of fine views over the valleys of the Cévennes to the south and, in the foreground, the heather-clad moorland.

Barre-des-Cévennes – This small, austere village with its tall, bare house fronts overlooks all the roads running along the Gardon rivers. Its setting is particularly picturesque and from the village there is a superb view of the Gardon valleys in the Cévennes and Mont Aigoual areas. Its location made it a major defensive and lookout position during the Camisard uprising. The remains of entrenchments are still visible on the Colline du Castelas.

Along the 3km/2mi long Barre-des-Cévennes footpath, walkers can find out about the village's past and discover its natural environment.

Join the Corniche des Cévennes at the Col du Rey and turn right onto D 983. There are views of the Mont Aigoual range to the left and the Mont Lozère ridge to the right.

Return to Florac via St-Laurent-de-Trèves and the Tarnon valley.

For a quiet place to stay.
*Consult the annual **Michelin Red Guide France** (hotels and restaurants)*
*and the **Michelin Guide Camping Caravaning France***
which offer a choice of pleasant hotels and quiet camp sites
in convenient locations.

FOIX★

Population 9 660
Michelin map 86 folds 4 and 5 or 235 fold 42

Situated at the mouth of the old Ariège glacial valley, Foix makes a striking impression on visitors with its rugged **setting**★ against a backdrop of jagged peaks and its skyline with three castle towers, proudly standing on their rock overlooking the river's final gully as it wends its way across the folds of the Plantaurel hills.

The old town has narrow streets radiating out from the crossroads at the corner of the Rue de Labistour and the Rue des Marchands adorned with a tiny bronze fountain "de l'Oie" (goose). This part of the town forms a stark contrast to the 19C administrative area laid out around vast esplanades consisting of the Allées de la Villote and the Champ de Mars.

Château de Foix

The Foix region – The region around Foix forms the *département* of Ariège, named after the main river that tumbles down from the mountains to form a Pyrenean valley constituting the backbone of the *département*. With the Couserans (*see Michelin Green Guide Atlantic Coast*) and Donézan, this area is one of the richest in traditions, myths and legends linked in some way with Catharism.

HISTORICAL NOTES

The County of Foix – The Foix region, which was part of the Duchy of Aquitaine before becoming part of the County of Carcassonne, was raised to the status of county in its own right in the 11C. Under the terms of the Treaty of Paris (1229) putting an end to the Albigensian Crusade, which was particularly bloody in this region, the Count of Foix was forced to acknowledge his position as vassal to the King of France. In 1290, the Foix family inherited Béarn and promptly settled there, preferring to be master of its own house than to submit to royal authority.

The area was annexed to the crown by King Henri IV in 1607. The Count of Foix, co-sovereign of Andorra with the Bishop of Urgell, handed over his rights of co-sovereignty to the Crown of France.

A family covered in glory – In his day, Gaston III (1331-91), the most famous of the **Counts of Foix** and Viscounts of Béarn, was the only one of the King of France's vassals to be in a sound financial situation. He took the surname of Fébus c 1360, meaning "the Brilliant" or "the Hunter". **Gaston Fébus** was a man of many characters. He was a skilled politician who exercised absolute power, and literate to the extent that he even wrote poetry and summoned writers and troubadours to his Court. However, he also ordered the murder of his brother and killed his only son. He was an enthusiastic hunter and wrote a treatise on the art of hunting.

However, Gaston Fébus is not the only representative of the illustrious lineage of the Counts of Foix worth a mention. Gaston IV, a loyal supporter of Charles VII, negotiated the treaty signed by the King of Aragon and Louis XI in 1462. In reward, he was given the town and estate of Carcassonne.

Catherine of Foix brought the County of Foix and Navarre to Jean d'Albret in 1484, as part of her dowry. Her estates were later invaded by the King of Spain, Ferdinand the Catholic, and she died of chagrin in 1517.

Gaston of Foix, the famous "Italian thunderbolt", Louis XII's nephew, was ordered to take command of the royal army in Italy. He won the Battle of Ravenna in 1512 but lost his life, cut down by fifteen lances, at the age of only 22. Odet of Foix, his cousin, fought beside him at Ravenna and was also wounded. He survived, however, and went on to play a major role in the conquest of the Milan area (1515).

SIGHTS

Château ⊙ – The castle's history is closely linked to the history of France. In 1002, the Count of Carcassonne, Roger the Elder, bequeathed the castle of Foix and its lands to his son, Roger-Bernard, who took the title of Count of Foix.

The castle's earliest foundations date from the 10C. It is a sturdy stronghold which Simon de Montfort was careful not to attack in 1211-17 during the Albigensian Crusade. In 1272, however, the Count of Foix refused to acknowledge the sovereignty of the King of France, and Philip the Bold personally took charge of a military expedition to attack the town. With food supplies exhausted and seeing the rock beneath his castle being hacked at with pick-axes, the Count finally surrendered.

After the union of Béarn and the County of Foix in 1290, the Counts all but abandoned the town. Gaston Fébus was the last of them to live in the castle. In the 17C, the castle lost any remaining military function. It was taken over by Henri IV and turned into a prison. It remained a place of internment until 1864. Nowadays, it houses a museum. The main interest of the castle is really its geographical setting. Little now remains of the building itself apart from three towers and the museum, representing a quarter of the original complex. The apartments used to be in the lower section, in a vast building that stretched as far as the church of St-Volusien.

Of the three watchtowers, which were also part of the defence system, the most interesting are the central tower and the round tower which have both retained their 14C and 15C vaulted rooms inside. The two towers used to be encased in a double ring of curtain walls, making the castle a particularly formidable target. From the terrace between the towers or, even better, from the top of the round tower, there is a **panoramic view**★ of Foix, the Ariège valley, and the Pain de Sucre ("sugar-loaf") in Montgaillard.

Traditional crafts

For many centuries, the skill and knowledge required for certain crafts that were typical of Foix and its area were handed down from father to son.

The miners of Le Rancié – Pyrenean iron ore was highly reputed for its richness and was first extracted a very long time ago. A charter dated 1293 mentions "the right for each and every person to extract ore from the iron mines in the (Vicdessos) valley, to cut down trees and to produce charcoal in the forests".

The mine at Le Rancié was finally closed in 1931, although it was still being worked in the 19C on a long-established co-operative basis and the people living in the valley were registered with the "Office of Miners". As such, they were partners rather than salaried staff. They were limited as to the quantity of ore they could extract every day. Often, miners would work alone and, once they had filled their hods, they would carry them on their backs up to the mouth of the gallery and would then sell the ore for cash to muleteers. They in turn transported it down to Vicdessos where the managers of iron foundries would come and purchase the supplies they needed.

Blacksmiths – In 1833, seventy-four "Catalan" iron foundries were still getting their supplies from this mine. They processed the ore by means of reaction with charcoal (this was made possible by the fact that this ore, like the ore mined in Pyrénées-Orientales, contains the necessary flux) but this led to massive deforestation.

Gold-panners – The waters of Ariège contain gold dust and, from the Middle Ages to the end of the last century, there were large numbers of men called *orpailleurs* panning for gold in the sandy river beds. The Ariège river contained gold downstream from Foix; the largest nuggets were found between Varilhes and Pamiers, some of them weighing as much as 15g. This source of wealth, however, became too unreliable, and the race of professional gold-panners died out.

Musée départemental de l'Ariège ⊘ – In the large, lower room are collections of military and hunting weapons reminding visitors of the castle's original function. Archeological exhibits are evidence of the prehistoric industries found in the caves in Ariège, dating from the Paleolithic Era to the Bronze Age. These include remnants of animals (most of them castings) including cave bears, reindeer, hyenas, mammoths etc. There are also castings of human footprints from the caves of Ariège, of which 300 have been listed and 60 explored. The museum also contains the remains of capitals from the cloisters at the church of St-Volusien.

► ► **Église St-Volusien** (Gothic church); **Pont de Vernajoul** (bridge with good view of castle).

EXCURSIONS

★★ ① **Route Verte and Route de la Crouzette** *Round tour 93km/58mi – allow 5hr*

The road is usually blocked by snow from mid-December to mid-June between the Col des Marrous and the Col de la Crouzette. It may also be blocked at the Col des Caougnous.

Head westward from Foix along D 17.

★★ **Route Verte** – The "green road" climbs gently as it runs up the **Arget** (or Barguillère) **valley**, an area that was once famous for its metalworking (nails), wending its way through woodland. After La Mouline, the road becomes steeper and, in Burret, it parts company with the Arget, which rises in a small wooded corrie a little further south. The landscape either side of the road becomes more pastoral.

Col des Marrous – Alt 990m/3 218ft. From the pass, there are extensive views to the south over the Arget valley and Arize forest.

The road continues to climb through a forest where beech trees predominate. From the first bend on this stretch of the road, there are some fine views of the Plantaurel area and Labastide-de-Sérou. Beyond the Col de Jouels, the road clings to the upper slopes of the wooded Caplong cirque, in which the Arize rises, and the views of the surrounding countryside become ever more panoramic. In the background is the truncated pyramid of Mont Valier (alt 2 838m/9 223ft).

Col de Péguère – Alt 1 375m/4 469ft. From the pass, there is an uninterrupted panorama.

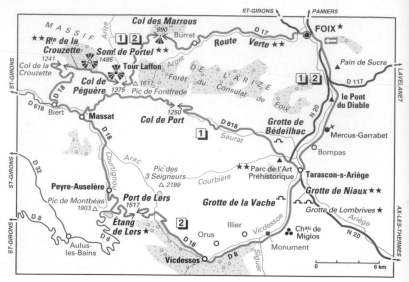

Tour Laffon – *15min on foot there and back, along the path to the right behind the hut.* Magnificent **panorama★** of the central and Ariège Pyrenees, from the Pic de Fontfrède (1 617m/5 255ft) to the Pic de Cagire (1 912m/6 214ft) beyond the Col de Portet d'Aspet.

★★ **Route de la Crouzette** – A hilltop road running along the rounded, bracken-covered crests of the Arize range. The road overlooks the forested cirques formed by the tributaries of the Arize to the north and the cool, gently hollowed out Massat valley to the south.

★★ **Sommet de Portel** – Alt 1 485m/4 826ft. *15min on foot there and back.*

Leave the car in a wide bend on the road, at a mountain pass 3.5km/2mi beyond the Col de Péguère, and climb the grassy bank to the northwest, as far as the foundations of an old beacon. **Panorama** of the peaks in the upper Couserans region, extending as far as the mountains on the border. From this pass, the old track drops down inside the line of the bend in the road, reaching the Coulat spring in just a few minutes. This attractive spot is ideal for a picnic or a stroll.

Beyond the Col de la Crouzette, during the steep descent to Massat via Biert and then the D 618 to the left, there is a view of the upper Couserans region and the entire range of peaks below the Col de Pause, Aulus and the Garbet valley.

Massat – This small local capital boasts a church with a gabled west front flanked by an elegant 15C octagonal tower. At the top level (the tower reaches 58m/190ft), the muzzles of decorative cannon project through diamond-shaped apertures. Above the entrance there is a fine wrought-iron grille. *(For description of Couserans region, see Michelin Green Guide Atlantic Coast).*

Continue along D 618.

To the east of Massat, the upper Arac basin widens out and the winding road provides some attractive views of the rural countryside around Massat. Further on, the majestic Mont Valier range looms into sight. The road then climbs up to the Col des Caougnous.

Before reaching this pass, there is the gap formed by the Col de Port. To the right, beyond the rounded hills in the foreground, towers the jagged summit of the Pic des Trois Seigneurs.

The road passes a succession of hamlets, and the view of Mont Valier becomes most impressive. Leaving the last few houses behind, along with the upper limits of the pastures and forests, the road enters an area of moorland decked in ferns and broom. To the right is a wonderful pine forest.

Col de Port – Alt 1 250m/4 100ft. This pass seems to mark a natural boundary between the "green" Pyrenees on the side of the Atlantic watershed and the "sunny" Pyrenees towards the Mediterranean where the landscape is full of contrasts.

The road runs down through the Saurat valley, an area of fertile land well-exposed to sunshine. Beyond Saurat, in line with the road, is the Montorgueil tower. The road then runs between two enormous rocks named Soudour and Calamès, the latter crowned with ruins.

Grotte de Bédeilhac – *800m/870yd from the village of Bédeilhac. See TARASCON-SUR-ARIÈGE.*

Tarascon-sur-Ariège – *See TARASCON-SUR-ARIÈGE.*

Head northwards from Tarascon on N 20. The remainder of the trip to Foix is described under Haute vallée de l'ARIÈGE.

② **Route du Port de Lers** *94km/58mi round trip – allow half a day*

For the route from Foix to Massat, see the itinerary above; for the route from Massat to Tarascon-sur-Ariège, see Route du Port de LERS; for the route from Tarascon-sur-Ariège to Foix see Haute vallée de l'ARIÈGE.

Abbaye de FONTFROIDE★★

Michelin map 86 northeast of fold 9 or 235 fold 40 or 240 fold 29
Local map see Les CORBIÈRES

The old **Cistercian abbey** of Fontfroide lies tucked almost out of sight deep in a little valley in the Corbières. This tranquil setting surrounded by cypress trees could almost be somewhere in Tuscany. The fine flame-coloured shades of yellow ochre and pink in the Corbières sandstone used to build the abbey enhance the serenity of the sight, particularly at sunset.

In 1093 a Benedictine abbey was founded on land belonging to Aymeric I, Viscount of Narbonne, which embraced the Cistercian Order in 1145. In 1150, Fontfroide sent 12 Cistercian monks to found the monastery at Poblet in Catalonia. In the 12C and 13C, the abbey enjoyed a long period of prosperity. Pope Pierre de Castelnau's legate, whose assassination sparked off the Albigensian Crusade, stayed here after his trip to Maguelone. Jacques Fournier, who was elected Pope in Avignon in 1334 and who reigned under the name of Benedict XII, was abbot here from 1311 to 1317. In later years, the abbey fell into a decline and was placed under the authority of a commendary abbot. It was abandoned in 1791, and its works of art scattered far afield.

The abbey has been private property since 1908 and has been tastefully restored. One of the oldest share-cropping farms is now the **Château de Gaussan** ☉.

TOUR ☉ *1hr*

Most of the abbey buildings were erected in the 12C and 13C. The conventual buildings were restored in the 17C and 18C. The present owners live in the buildings overlooking the north side of the cloisters.

The setting is delightful, with floral courtyards, well-maintained paths, and superb terraced gardens.

The tour begins in the Cour d'honneur, built by the commendary abbots in the 17C.

The Guard-room (13C) has ribbed vaulting, and features a fine 18C wrought-iron doorway and a monumental chimneypiece. This room was the refectory for the lay-brothers and pilgrims.

The tour then moves on to the medieval buildings which are beautiful not least because of their exceptionally regular bonding.

Cloisters – The cloister galleries have ribbed vaulting. The oldest gallery is that adjacent to the church (mid 13C). The gallery opposite underwent alteration in the 17C. All the galleries have arcades supported on pairs of slender marble colonnettes, in different colours, decorated with capitals carved with ornate plant motifs and framed by a relieving arch. The tympana of these feature several oculi or a single larger round window. As a whole the cloisters are a consummate example of architectural elegance. Terraced roofs run above the galleries.

Abbey church – Building work began on the church in the mid 12C. The spacious interior is imposing and perfectly in proportion; it is a particularly beautiful and moving example of the elegant simplicity of Cistercian architecture. The ribbed barrel-vaulted nave is flanked by side aisles

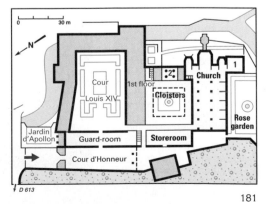

with half-barrel vaulting. Note the bases of the pillars, which have been raised in order to leave room for the choir stalls. The south chapels were added in the 14C-15C. In the funeral chapel (13C) (**1**), there is a fine stone Calvary dating from the 15C. The north transept has a gallery from which monks who were ill were able to follow services. The most surprising feature of the church, otherwise quite austere, is the modern stained glass in the windows, the work of Richard Burghstal of Nice, through which light dapples the plain walls with most un-Cistercian splashes of colour.

Chapter-house (**2**) – The chapter-house is roofed with nine Romanesque vaults supported on decorative ribs that spring from slender marble colonnettes.

Monks' dormitory – The dormitory is located above the storeroom. It is roofed with fine ribbed barrel-vaulting dating from the 12C. The stairwell leading up to the dormitory has wooden rafters.

Storeroom – A fine late-11C room separated from the cloisters by a narrow alleyway, probably given a vaulted roof in the 17C.

Rose garden – The rose garden contains about 3 000 rose bushes (11 varieties). It dates from 1990, when Fontfroide won a regional competition for designing the best layout for such a garden.

Various footpaths enable visitors to walk around the abbey and fully appreciate the charms of its setting.

FONT-ROMEU✳✳

Population 1 897
Michelin map 86 fold 16 or 235 fold 55 – Local map see La CERDAGNE

Font-Romeu is a manmade holiday resort dating from c 1920, built at an altitude of 1 800m/5 850ft on the sunny side of the French Cerdagne higher than any other mountain village.

The resort occupies a wonderful site protected from northerly winds on the edge of a pine forest. There is a superb panoramic view across the valley.

Besides its altitude, Font-Romeu's higher than average exposure to sunshine and exceptionally dry climate meant that, from the very outset, it was seen as a mountain-top health resort. Its impressive sports facilities (swimming pool, ice rink, stables etc) attract athletes from all over the world who come to follow altitude training programmes here.

Font-Romeu's ski slopes lie at altitudes of between 1 700m and 2 500m/5 525ft and 8 125ft. Thanks to the many snow cannon, the resort has never suffered from a lack of snow. Some of the pistes to the north on the slopes of Les Bouillouses are quite difficult. Between the tourist resort and the secondary school *(lycée)* lies a hermitage bearing witness to the famous Catalan pilgrimage that gave Font-Romeu its name (from *fontaine du Pèlerin* or "pilgrim's fountain").

★ **Hermitage** – The hermitage contains a statue of Our Lady known as the "Vierge de l'Invention". Legend has it that Our Lady of Font-Romeu was "discovered" (*inventé* in French) by a bull. One day the beast refused to move away from a spring, scraping the earth with its hoof and bellowing loudly. The herdsman, intrigued and in the end fed up with the noise, eventually took a closer look and found a statue of the Blessed Virgin Mary in a crack in the rock.

Hermitage at Font-Romeu – "Camaril"

During certain festivals, or *aplechs*, crowds flock to the hermitage. On 8 September, the festival *del Baixar* ("of the Carrying Downhill"), the statue of the Virgin Mary is solemnly carried downhill to the church in Odeillo where it remains until Trinity Sunday *(el Pujar:* "the Carrying Uphill"). It is then brought back to the hermitage, in a similarly solemn procession. Other *aplechs* are held on the third Sunday after Whitsun (*cantat:* "of the sick") and on 15 August (Feast of the Assumption).

The chapel dates from the 17C and 18C. The miraculous spring set into the wall to the left provides the water supply for the pilgrims' bathing pool inside the building with the gable facing the mountain.

Inside the **chapel** ⊙, there is a magnificent altarpiece by Joseph Sunyer dating from 1707. The central niche contains the statue of Our Lady of Font-Romeu or, when the statue is in Odeillo, the statue of the so-called Virgin Mary of the Hermitage (15C). On the predella are three detailed scenes depicting episodes from the "Invention".

Take the staircase to the left of the high altar leading to the **camaril★★**, the Virgin Mary's small "reception room", a typically Spanish construction that is touching for the devotion that inspired it. This is Sunyer's masterpiece. The altar has painted panels and is topped by a statue of Christ flanked by the Virgin Mary and St John. Two delicate medallions depicting the Presentation in the Temple and the Flight into Egypt adorn the wall above the door. The four corners are decorated with pretty statues of angel-musicians.

★★ **Calvary** – Alt 1 857m/6 035ft. Some 300m/325yd from the hermitage on the road to Mont-Louis, turn right onto a path lined with Stations of the Cross. From the calvary scene at the top, there is an extensive **panorama** over Cerdagne and the surrounding mountains.

EXCURSIONS

✷ **Pyrénées 2000** – Alt 1 800m/5 906ft. *2.5km/1.5mi on the road to the ski slopes (route des pistes) leading off from the Calvary.*
Above the rural village of Bolquère, Pyrénées 2000 is a winter sports resort built right at the foot of the slopes, giving easy access to numerous downhill and cross-country ski-runs.

★ **Col del Pam** – Alt 2 005m/6 516ft. *5.5km/3.5mi north on the road to the ski slopes (from the Calvary) then 15min on foot there and back.*
From the observation platform above the Têt valley, there is a **view** of the Carlit range, the Bouillouses plateau, the Capcir (upper Aude valley) and the Canigou summit.

The Pyrenees are home to some extraordinary wildlife which includes the genet (an elusive, spotted creature from the mongoose family) and the last remaining wild brown bears in Europe. The lammergeyer or great bearded vulture is also known as the bone-breaker: it drops carcasses onto rocks to smash the bones and so reveal the marrow within.

With this guide,
use the appropriate Michelin Maps (scale 1: 200 000)
shown below the contents table on page 1.
The common symbols will make planning easier.

FRONTIGNAN

Population 16 245
Michelin map 83 folds 16 and 17 or 240 fold 27 – 7km/4mi northeast of Sète

Situated between sea and *garrigues* (scrubland), on the banks of the Ingril lagoon and the Rhône-Sète canal, Frontignan has given its name to a highly-reputed Muscat wine. The Muscat de Frontignan vineyards cover nearly 800ha/1 977 acres. The local distillery, or **Cave coopérative du Muscat** ⊙ is open to visitors all year round.

Once an important oil-refining centre, Frontignan was the site where France's first catalytic cracking furnace was brought into service.

To the north of the town looms the Massif de la Gardiole, crisscrossed by waymarked tracks popular with cross-country cyclists *(V.T.T.)*, riders and hikers. To the south lies **Frontignan-Plage**≜≜, a seaside resort which boasts a marina with 600 wet-berths.

Église St-Paul – All that remains of the previous Romanesque building is the south wall (12C). In the 14C, the church was rebuilt in the southern French Gothic style, with a nave and a five-sided apse. The piers were reinforced. Then its keep-like bell tower, which was integrated into the fortifications surrounding the town, was made taller and topped with a turret.

Inside, the ceiling in the nave was restored to its 14C appearance revealing to view some fine painted beams after the removal of the false brick vaulting added in the 19C.

Musée d'Histoire locale ⊙ – *4 bis rue Lucien Salette, next to the church.*

The local museum, which includes collections on prehistory, submarine archeology and Napoleonic memorabilia, is to be found in the old chapel of the White Penitents, entered through a monumental 17C doorway. Various aspects of the local way of life, both past and present, are also evoked: cooperage; Muscat making; *joutes nautiques* etc.

GAILLAC

Population 10 370
Michelin map 82 folds 9 and 10 or 235 folds 23, 27

Gaillac lies at a crossroads on the north bank of the Tarn. For many years, its wealth came from trade based on the river boat traffic on the Tarn. The old town still has some charming squares with fountains and narrow streets lined with old houses that are a happy combination of timber and brick work.

The Gaillac vineyards –
This is one of the oldest wine-growing areas in France. As early as the 10C, the Benedictine monks of St-Michel abbey set up strict rules to ensure that the good reputation of the wines of Gaillac was maintained.

The vineyards of Gaillac cover an area of 20 000ha/49 400 acres, from which red, rosé, white and sparkling wines are produced.

The south bank of the Tarn is where the grape varieties used to make red wines are grown: Gamay, Braucol, Syrah and Duras. The better-positioned vineyards on the north bank grow not only grapes for red wine (Du-

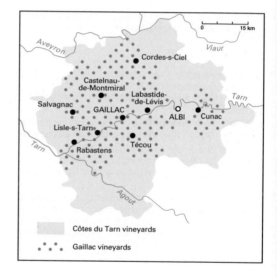

ras, Braucol, Syrah, Cabernet and Merlot) but also the Mauzac, Loin de l'oeil and Sauvignon (also found on the plain around Cordes-sur-Ciel) grape varieties used to produce white wines.

The traditional techniques used in modern wine-growing guarantee the good quality of Gaillac wines, all of which are AOC *(Appellation d'Origine Contrôlée)*. The efforts made over the last ten years in the Gaillac vineyards have ensured that they now rank among the foremost wine producers in southwest France.

SIGHTS

Abbatiale St-Michel – In the 7C, Benedictine monks founded an abbey in Gaillac and dedicated it to St Michael. Building work began on the abbey church in the 11C and went on until the 14C, with a number of interruptions. Inside the church is a fine polychrome wooden statue of the Madonna and Child (14C).

Next to the church are the abbey buildings, which now house the **Maison des Vins de Gaillac**, as well as the **Musée des Arts et Traditions populaires** ⊙ with tools and master-works illustrating the work of journeymen *(compagnons)*, displays evoking work in local vineyards, and various objects of local historical interest.

Tour Pierre de Brens – This charming brick tower dates from the 14C and 15C and underwent alterations during the Renaissance. It still has a few gargoyles, mullioned windows and a delightful bartizan.

Parc de Foucaud – The delightful terraced gardens above the Tarn were laid out by the famous 17C French landscape gardener, André Le Nôtre (whose masterpiece was the gardens at the palace of Versailles).

The château, an 18C residence belonging to the family of Counsellor de Foucaud d'Alzon, houses the **Musée des Beaux-Arts** ⊘, an art museum with works by local artists (painters and sculptors).

Musée d'histoire naturelle Philadelphe-Thomas ⊘ – This museum houses extensive mineral and paleontological collections.

EXCURSIONS

Lisle-sur-Tarn – *9km/5.5mi southwest via N 88.*
This town on the northwest bank of the Tarn boasts a vast **square** with covered arcades and a fountain in it, a reminder of the days when this was a *bastide* (1248).
The historic town centre has a few old brick and timber houses dating from the 16C, 17C and 18C. Some of them are linked to their outbuildings by *pountets*, little bridges one storey up across the narrow streets and alleyways. The church of **Notre-Dame de la Jonquière** has a Romanesque portal and a bell-tower built in the Toulouse style.
In the **Musée Raymond-Lafage** ⊘, named after a 17C draughtsman who was born in Lisle, there are not only drawings and engravings by Lafage himself, but also collections relating to Gallo-Roman and medieval architecture, and works of sacred art. Finally, there are drawings by Ingres and Horace Vernet.
From the bridge, there is a pleasant view of the town and its retaining walls.

Château de Mauriac ⊘ – *11km/7mi north of the town on D 922. Turn right just before Cahuzac.*
This castle, parts of which date from the 14C, has a beautiful, uniform façade. Two large corner towers flank a main building in which the central entrance is itself flanked by two smaller towers.
On the ground floor are a number of rooms displaying works by Bernard Bistes, painter and owner of the castle.
On the first floor is the guestroom known as the "Louis XVI Room". It has a French-style ceiling decorated with 360 panels depicting a beautifully fresh-looking **herbarium**★ *(first floor not open to the public if being hired for a private reception).*

Castelnau-de-Montmiral – *13km/8mi northwest on D 964.*
This is a picturesque village perched on a spur of rock high above the Vère valley and Grésigne forest *(outdoor leisure park)*. Castelnau-de-Montmiral is an old *bastide*, founded in the 13C by Raymond VII, Count of Toulouse, to replace the stronghold razed during the Albigensian Crusade. Its eventful past is still visible in its old houses, all of which have been enhanced by a skilful restoration programme.
The **Place des Arcades**, as its name suggests, is flanked by arcades topped with corbelled half-timbered houses. On the west and south sides are two 17C houses.
In the 15C **parish church**, note the polychrome stone statue of Christ Bound (15C), the Baroque altarpiece and, above all, to the left of the chancel the **gem-encrusted cross-reliquary** of the Counts of Armagnac known as the Montmiral Cross, a fine example of 13C religious gold and silver work.

Many camp sites have shops, bars, restaurants and laundries;
they may also have games rooms, tennis courts, miniature golf courses, playgrounds,
swimming pools...
*Consult the current edition of the **Michelin Camping Caravaning France**.*

Gorges de GALAMUS★★

Michelin map 86 southwest of fold 8 or 235 folds 47, 48 or 240 fold 37
Local map see Les CORBIÈRES

The spectacular rugged road carved out of the rock and the hermitage clinging precariously onto the hillside give this narrow gorge all the atmosphere of a fantasy world, especially when bathed in the rays of the Catalan sun.

FROM ST-PAUL-DE-FENOUILLET TO CUBIÈRES
9.5km/6mi – allow 1hr

St-Paul-de-Fenouillet – *See Les FENOUILLÈDES.*
On leaving St-Paul-de-Fenouillet, the road (D 7) leads through vineyards and soon becomes quite winding. From a wide bend, there is a view of the Canigou to the left.
Leave the car in the car park at the hermitage beyond the tunnel.

Ermitage St-Antoine-de-Galamus - *30min on foot there and back.* The path runs down from the hermitage terrace (view of the Canigou). The hermitage building *(outdoor restaurant)* conceals the chapel in the dim depths of a natural cave.

After the hermitage terrace, the road becomes very narrow (2m/6ft 6in wide) and clings to the very edge of the wall of rock. There are only occasional views of the stream because the gorge through which it flows is so narrow and sheer-sided. One particularly impressive feature is the crack flanked by sheer white rocks dotted with brush. The Agly then flows on westwards and the D 10 follows the Cubières stream to the village of the same name.

Cubières - This village marks the beginning of the upper Agly valley.

Hermitage of St-Antoine in the Galamus gorge

La GARDE-GUÉRIN⋆

Michelin map 86 fold 7 or 240 fold 7

An impressive tower is the first indication of this old fortified village lying on the Lozère plateau, at the tip of a scarp slope overlooking the Chassezac gorge. Its geographical location is interesting, situated as it is between the Gévaudan and Vivarais regions where the granite of Mont Lozère meets the schist of the Ardèche.

Road safety in the Middle Ages - The old Régordane Roman road was, for many years, the only means of communication between Languedoc and Auvergne. In the 10C, in order to free the region of its highway robbers, the bishops of Mende decided to set up a guard post in the wildest part of the plateau. It is this guard post that has given the village its name.

A community of noblemen, the *pariers*, was established here and, in return, enjoyed special civic status. There were 27 of them in all and they escorted travellers in return for a toll. Each of them had his own fortified house in La Garde and the village, encircled by a curtain wall, was defended by a fortress.

The village - The population is made up of a small number of stock breeders. The houses are built of large granite ashlar and are characteristic of an architectural style common in mountainous areas. The few taller houses with mullioned windows are the former residences of the *pariers*. The mountain church with its bellcote is particularly well-built.

Keep - The entrance is under a porch to the left of the church. This is the largest remaining section of the original fortress. From the top, there is a view of the village and the Chassezac gorge. The **panorama**⋆ stretches as far as Mont Ventoux.

Michelin Maps (scale 1: 200 000)
which are revised regularly indicate:

- *difficult or dangerous roads, steep gradients*
- *car and passenger ferries*
- *bridges with height and weight restrictions.*

*Keep current **Michelin Maps** in the car at all times.*

La GRANDE-MOTTE ☆☆☆

Population 5 016
Michelin map 83 south of fold 8 or 240 fold 23

The coastal plain southeast of Montpellier is the setting for the tall, eye-catching pyramids of La Grande-Motte, a highly original recent manmade seaside resort set in moorland and sand dunes on the Mediterranean coast.

Contemporary town planning – Thanks to the wide roads which link it to the A 9 motorway, the resort can take advantage of its proximity to Nîmes and Montpellier. Vast car parks in the town centre leave the seafront free for pedestrians. The Palais des Congrès (conference centre) overlooks the yachting marina.

The resort was built as a totally new venture in 1967. It was designed as a complete complex by a team of engineers and architects under the leadership of Jean Balladur. The main buildings, with their resolutely modern designs, form honeycomb **pyramids**, all of them south-facing.

The **villas** have been built in Provençal style or around inner courtyards.

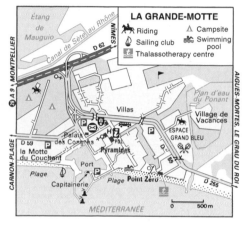

Designed for leisure – The entire complex faces the sea and has been laid out in relation with the vast fine sandy beach stretching over a distance of 6km/4mi, the marina (1 634 moorings), the golf course and the water sports amenities. The main attractions of La Grande-Motte for visitors are the water sports facilities on Ponant lake, the possibilities for angling in Mauguio (or Or) lake and at sea, and the striking architecture of the **Point Zéro** shopping centre. Among other things, the game fishing competition (tunny fish) draws crowds of people when the boats return to harbour and the catches are weighed.

The resort can accommodate up to 80 000 people. It is continuing to develop westwards into the pedestrian district of Motte du Couchant, where the buildings take the form of rounded shells facing the sea, and northwards around Ponant lake.

EXCURSION

⌂ **Carnon-Plage** – *8km/5mi.* This "lido"-style beach situated between La Grande-Motte and Palavas-les-Flots is particularly popular with people from Montpellier.

Pyramidal holiday homes at La Grande-Motte

Les GRANDS CAUSSES★★★

Michelin map 80 folds 4, 5, 6, 14 and 15 or 240 folds 2, 5, 6, 10, 13, 14 and 18

There are four Grands Causses *(see Introduction for more details)* – Sauveterre, Méjean, Noir and Larzac. They are referred to as the "Grands Causses" or "Causses majeurs" to distinguish them from the lower-lying limestone plateaux in Quercy (the "Causses mineurs"), a continuation west of the Grands Causses, and from the succession of **Petits Causses**, which are subsidiaries of their larger counterparts but which have been separated from them by water and erosion. Examples of these include the Petit Causse de Blandas, an offshoot of the Causse du Larzac from which it is separated by the Vis, the Petit Causse de Campestre, another offshoot of the Larzac but separated from it by the Virenque, and the Petit Causse Bégon separated from the Grand Causse Noir by the Trévezel etc.

The Grands Causses vary in appearance depending on their altitude, geographical location or geological composition. They are all limestone plateaux, but they may be dolomitic (dolomite is a rock consisting of a combination of limestone and magnesium) or marl-based (combination of clay and limestone). Dolomitic limestone erodes easily to form natural amphitheatres, giving rise to a type of coarse sand known locally as **grésou**. When certain areas of rock have a higher magnesia content

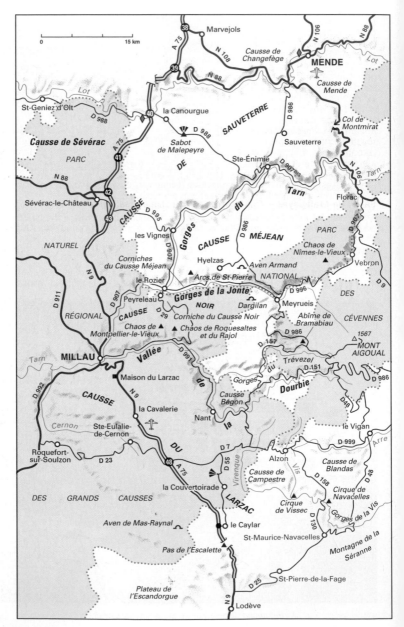

than others, they are more resistant to erosion and end up as scattered rocky outcrops which make the landscape look like a "ruined city". Marly regions have a less rugged appearance and are ideal for crop-growing. In the same way, the geological layers that make up the *causses* (which all date from the Jurassic period of the Secondary Era) determine the variety in the landscapes. Thus the Middle Jurassic saw the formation of towering cliffs, like vertical walls, among them the cliff at Le Rajol high above the river Dourbie, the cliff on which the road across the Causse Méjean has been built, high above the river Jonte upstream from Le Truel, and the Cingelgros rock, a sheer-sided cliff overlooking the river Tarn. The cliffs formed during the next stage of the Jurassic period are less impressive.

Generally speaking, the Causses feature starkly-contrasting scenery with deep, sheer-sided valleys, cool green oases of farmland, and arid upper plateaux.

The description that follows refers to the natural beauty spots in each of the Grands Causses *(see Introduction for information on the Parc naturel régional des Grands Causses)*. The routes indicated on the map follow the roads that pass from one plateau to another via a gorge and are designed to impart to visitors some of the grandeur of these unusual and breathtaking landscapes. The effect of the light reflected by the whiteness of the rocks and playing across the russet-red of the scarp slopes is particularly unforgettable. The roads run across monotonous plateaux then drop sharply down to the floor of a gorge in a series of spectacular hairpin bends, cross the river, and drag themselves up the opposite bank to the neighbouring *causse*. The routes which can be taken along the floor of the main river gorges (Tarn, Jonte, Dourbie, Vis) are described separately *(see under name of river)*.

CAUSSE DE SAUVETERRE *local map p 188*

Bordered to the north by the river Lot, this is the most northerly and least arid of the Grands Causses. Its western section (southwest of the D 998) has vast stretches of woodland and fairly steep hills.

Local people have taken advantage of even the slightest hollow; there is not a single plot of arable land that has not been carefully cultivated, with the result that the countryside is dotted with bright patches of red or green depending on the season.

★ **Sabot de Malepeyre** – This enormous clog-shaped *(sabot)* rock, 30m/98ft tall, also known as the *pont naturel* (natural bridge) *de Malepeyre* was formed by the erosive action of the water which once flowed on the surface of the *causse*. There is a huge opening right the way through it beneath a basket handle arch. You can go through the arch, which is 3m/10ft high and 10m/33ft wide. From the terrace on which the heel of the "clog" rests there is a lovely view of the Urugne valley with the Aubrac mountains in the distance.

Sauveterre – This typical *causse* village still has its drystone houses *(illustration see p 53)* roofed with limestone slabs known locally as *tioulassés*. There are some fine examples of roofs with dormer windows, old shepherds' huts with vaulted roofs, and an old village oven in perfect working order.

CAUSSE MÉJEAN *local map p 188*

This is the "middle" plateau, hence its name. The Tarn gorge separates it from the Causse de Sauveterre. The Causse Méjean is the highest of the plateaux and its climate is particularly harsh. Winters are freezing cold, summers are scorching, and there are huge differences in temperature between day and night.

The plateau is a combination of dolomite and outcrops of pure limestone, in varying degrees of thickness. In the shallow depression known as *sotchs* where the decalcification of the rock has led to an accumulation of red earth, meadows and fields produce high yields. Numerous megaliths indicate that Stone Age people had adapted very well to local conditions.

The Causse Méjean has a very low population density (fewer than two inhabitants per km² in certain places). To the east, the landscape stretches vast and arid; to the west, like the Causse de Sauveterre, wooded plateaux are interspersed with ravines several hundred feet deep. The Causse Méjean is the country of the sheep *(brebis)*. There are some 19 thousand head on the plateau and it is not unusual to come across flocks of more than three hundred. The dolomitic limestone landscape, not unlike a rabbit-warren, is also dotted with collections of ruin-shaped rocks. Local people have left areas such as these to game and coniferous forests.

The griffon vulture, a species not seen in the region for some 50 years, was re-introduced to the area in 1970. Przewalski's horses (the last surviving wild horse subspecies), which were threatened with extinction, have also been seen wild in the region recently.

Causse Méjean

★★★ **Aven Armand** – *See AVEN ARMAND.*

★★★ **Corniches du Causse Méjean** – *See Gorges du TARN.*

★ **Chaos de Nîmes-le-Vieux** – *See Chaos de NÎMES-LE-VIEUX.*

★ **Arcs de St-Pierre** – *See Arcs de ST-PIERRE.*

Hyelzas, a traditional Causse farmstead ⊙ – *Follow the signs to Aven Armand then continue on to Hyelzas.*

This restored farmhouse is an excellent example of the traditional architecture of the Causses. The farmstead is built of drystone and consists of several buildings linked by flights of steps on the outside. The cowshed is on the ground floor. The upper vaulting supports a heavy roof of limestone slabs.

The interior of the farmhouse is open to the public. The rooms are stone-flagged and the cows in the cowshed below provided the only source of heat. The tank in the scullery serves as a reminder of the importance of water in an area where it is in such short supply. The furniture and utensils have been returned to their original places. A shed contains farm machinery that shows the major stages in the development of agriculture.

A photographic exhibition describes the way of life on the Causse at the beginning of the 20C.

CAUSSE NOIR *local map opposite*

This plateau is called "Noir" ("black" or "dark") because of its old pine forests. It covers an area of 200km²/77mi², making it the smallest of the Grands Causses. It is bordered to the north by the **Jonte** river gorge and to the south by the **Dourbie** valley. Dolomitic limestone predominates, with the result that the *causse* includes some of the finest "ruined cities" of rocks in the area. The Jonte gorge can be seen in all its splendour from the cliff road which runs along its edge.

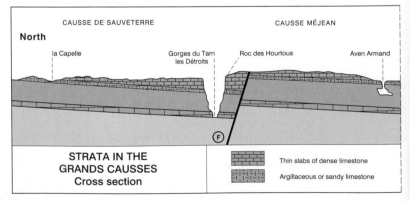

CAUSSE DE SAUVETERRE   CAUSSE MÉJEAN

North

la Capelle   Gorges du Tarn les Détroits   Roc des Hourtous   Aven Armand

Ⓕ

STRATA IN THE GRANDS CAUSSES Cross section

▨ Thin slabs of dense limestone

▨ Argillaceous or sandy limestone

*** **Chaos de Montpellier-le-Vieux** – *See Chaos de MONTPELLIER-LE-VIEUX.*

** **Corniche du Causse Noir** – The Corniche du Causse Noir consists of a network of footpaths and forest tracks that are only accessible by foot. The description below indicates a few of the views accessible to visitors in cars.

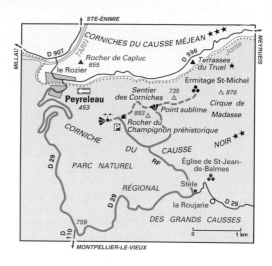

Getting there – *Via D 29 south from Peyreleau. Between the junction with the D 110 (leading to Montpellier-le-Vieux) and La Roujarie, take the rough forest track off D 29 just before the ruins of the church in St-Jean-de-Balmes. The start of the track is marked by a memorial erected by the Club Alpin Français. Approximately 2.5km/ 1mi further on, leave the car in the car park indicated on the local map, near the rock known as the "Champignon préhistorique" ("prehistoric toadstool").*

** **Views:**

1) *15min on foot there and back.* The path to the left of the "Champignon préhistorique" leads to the television mast from which there is a great view of Peyreleau in its site at the confluence of the Jonte and Tarn rivers.

2) *1hr on foot there and back.* The path to the right of the "Champignon préhistorique" is the cliff path, *waymarked in red*, which leads through woodland to the Madasse corrie, dropping down through woodland as it goes. Terraces lead right up to the edge of the cliff, from where there are delightful views of the Jonte and the peaceful village of Le Rozier. Further on, once the village has been lost to view, walkers are surrounded by the isolation and austere grandeur of the Jonte gorge.

From the ruins of St Michel hermitage (3 metal ladders to be climbed), it is possible to walk on as far as Madasse corrie.

3) Further east, a forest road open to traffic leads off from the start of the road you arrive on to a rock topped with a pine tree. From here, there is a superb view of the Jonte gorge.

** **Grotte de Dargilan** – *See Grotte de DARGILAN.*

* **Chaos de Roquesaltes et du Rajol** – *3km/2mi from St-André-de-Vézines on a surfaced road that becomes a track, followed by 1hr on foot there and back.*

Roquesaltes, meaning "tall rocks", looks for all the world like a natural fortress some 50m/162ft high overlooking the hamlet of Roquesaltes. From these rocky ramparts, the view extends over Montpellier-le-Vieux.

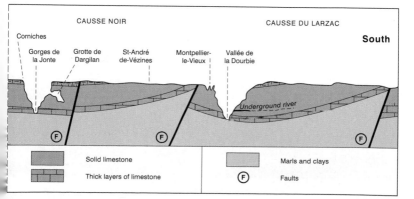

Although the area of the rocky chaos is not very large, it constitutes a remarkable set of ruin-shaped rocks including a huge natural gate-way. A one-hour walk *(there and back)* south brings you to the **Chaos du Rajol**. Visitors are greeted by a "dromedary" with its chin nonchalantly resting on a rock. Other fantastically-shaped rocks include an Egyptian Column, an Armless Statue and many more. From a natural lookout platform, the view plunges down into the extraordinary Dourbie valley.

★**CAUSSE DU LARZAC** *see Causse du LARZAC*

GRENADE

Population 5 026
Michelin map 82 fold 7 or 235 fold 26

This *bastide*, founded jointly in 1290 by Eustache de Beaumarchais and the abbey of Grandselve, is surrounded by prosperous orchards that constitute some of the most impressive new plantations made in the Toulouse area since the last war.

Church ⊙ – The most outstanding features of this majestic Toulouse-style Gothic church are the uniform layout of the three aisles, each of the same height, and the 47m/153ft tall brick bell-tower, similar in design to the one at Les Jacobins monastery in Toulouse.

►► **Bouillac** – *16km/10mi northwest.* **Treasure**★ of the abbey of Grandselve is contained in the village church.

GRUISSAN ⌂

Population 2 170
Michelin map 83 fold 14 or 86 fold 10 or 240 folds 30 and 34
Local map see Les CORBIÈRES

The **old village**, once the home of fishermen and saltpan workers, has houses set out in concentric circles around the ruins of the Barbarossa tower. Set some distance from the coast, amid the sleepy waters of inland lagoons, the village seemed to have resolutely turned its back on the sea. Yet this was once a sizeable harbour, with boats that set out to fish off the shores of Spain and Algeria. The fishermen still celebrate the festival of St Peter at the end of June.

The **new resort** of Gruissan grew up after a channel was opened linking Le Grazel lagoon with the sea. Small blocks of flats laid out around the main basin in the brand new marina (yachts, fishing boats) have formed the heart of the resort since 1975. They are characterised mainly by their yellow ochre pebble dash and their multi-ridge cradle-shaped roofs.

Old village of Gruissan

Gruissan-Plage still has a strange estate of seaside chalets (as seen in the film *Betty Blue*, shot here) built on piles to protect them from the floods that are always a possibility at the equinoxes.

There are camp sites, mainly to the north of the channel (the Aiguades du Pech Rouge), on the road to Narbonne-Plage. The popularity of the new resort lies not only in its position, wide open to the sea, but also its geographical location as an ideal centre from which to explore the Massif de la Clape, one of the lesser-known beauty spots in Languedoc.

EXCURSION

Cimetière marin – *4km/2.5mi, then 30min on foot there and back. Leave Gruissan on D 32, the Narbonne road. At the crossroads beyond the tennis courts, take the road signposted to Notre-Dame-des-Auzils into the Massif de la Clape and keep left all the way. Leave the car in the car park (in front of the Rec d'Argent nursery) and walk up to the chapel. If you prefer, you can drive the 1.5km/1mi of forest track signposted to Les Auzils, leave the car on a piece of rough ground and continue on foot (20min there and back).*

All along a stony path that winds here and there between the broom, umbrella pines, holm-oaks and cypresses are moving memorials to sailors lost at sea. From the **chapel of Notre-Dame-des-Auzils** at the top of the hill at the heart of a thicket, there is an extensive view over Gruissan and the Massif de la Clape.

Vallée de l'HÉRAULT*

Michelin map 80 fold 16 and 83 fold 6 or 240 folds 15, 18 and 22

The river Hérault rises on Mont Aigoual and cuts a steep course downhill to Valleraugue. In less than 10km/6mi, it drops from an altitude of 1 400m/4 550ft to 350m/1 138ft. Beyond Valleraugue, it flows between hillsides of schist or granite, where chestnut trees and orchards can be seen growing on terraces. On the outskirts of Ganges, these give way to vines and olive trees. Downstream from Pont-d'Hérault, the departure point for the trip described below, the landscape changes from one of metamorphic rocks to limestone scenery.

The Hérault crosses the *garrigues*, gouging out ravines and picturesque gullies or flowing into wide valleys given over to farmland, around Ganges or Brissac for example. The *garrigues*, a scrubland region with white rocks and the odd oak thicket dotted here and there, has an arid appearance.

At the "Pont du Diable" (devil's bridge), the Hérault emerges from its gorge onto the Bas-Languedoc plain.

FROM PONT-D'HÉRAULT TO GIGNAC 69km/43mi – allow 5hr

South of Pont-d'Hérault, the road (D 999) follows the winding course of the river, between hillsides covered in chestnut trees and holm-oaks. On the valley floor, vines and mulberry bushes are in evidence.

After a short distance, the road enters a spectacular limestone ravine, where the river Vis flows into the Hérault.

Ganges – The small industrial town of Ganges is situated on the confluence of the Hérault and the Rieutord and is a good base for trips into the surrounding area. The old town and the avenues lined with plane trees make a pleasant place for a stroll. Ganges made its fortune from the manufacture of fine silk stockings during the reign of Louis XIV. Natural silk was replaced by artificial silk then nylon, and cottage industry by factories, of which half a dozen or so still produce high quality stockings. The castle, of which only ruins remain, was the scene of a dastardly crime in the 17C, when the beautiful **Diane de Roussan** was murdered by her husband's brothers, who had their eye on her not inconsiderable fortune. The villains were at least subsequently caught and met a suitably sticky end. In August 1944, German troops attempted to force a passage down the Hérault valley through Ganges, but were repelled by the heroic defence of the Aigoual-Cévennes *maquis*.

Beyond Ganges, the road runs through an impressive, sheer-sided ravine, really a canyon, gouged out by the Hérault. From St-Bauzille, at the foot of the cliffs which form the edge of the Thaurac plateau, you can visit the Grotte des Demoiselles.

★★ Grotte des Demoiselles – *See Grotte des DEMOISELLES.*

Head southwards from St-Bauzille and turn right onto D 108 to cross the river Hérault. A narrow road on the right leads to Brissac.

Brissac – There is a good view of this picturesque village as you arrive. The oldest district stands in the shadow of a castle dating from the 12C and 16C.

Turn back and rejoin D 4 towards St-Guilhem-le-Désert.

The D 4 rejoins the Hérault as it flows between limestone scarp slopes. From the road, you can see the Romanesque chapel of **St-Étienne-d'Issensac** to the left and a 12C bridge spanning the river.

As the road climbs, there is a view to the left over the Lamalou ravine as it opens into the Hérault valley. The road then reaches the small Causse de la Selle and the village of the same name, after a picturesque drive along the very edge of the rockface. Shortly after Causse-de-la-Selle, the road leaves the plateau and enters a coomb hollowed out by a river that has now disappeared. On very hot days at the height of summer, this dried up rocky gully exudes an atmosphere of intense desolation.

★ **Gorges de l'Hérault** – Overlooked by steep slopes, the river gorge, which remains fairly open as far as St-Guilhem-le-Désert, gradually becomes narrower by the time it reaches the Pont du Diable. The Hérault cuts a deep, enclosed course along the floor of the valley between sheer rock faces adorned with tenaciously clinging, scrubby trees. The clear water sparkles in the light reflecting off the pale, almost white rocks past which it flows, which open out now and then into a small, inviting pebble beach. Fish and freshwater shrimp *(écrevisses)* thrive in the river. Here and there one sees a small terrace supported by a wall, a few lines of vineyard, a tiny meadow or one or two olive trees clinging onto the hillside above the river – these are the only forms of cultivation possible here. The bare countryside nonetheless exudes a certain splendour, especially when drenched in summer sunshine.

★ **St-Guilhem-le-Désert** – *See ST-GUILHEM-LE-DÉSERT.*

★★ **Grotte de Clamouse** – *See Grotte de CLAMOUSE.*

Pont du Diable – This early 11C bridge was built by Benedictine monks. It was later widened but has retained its original shape. From the modern bridge built nearby, there is a view of the Hérault gorge and the aqueduct which supplies the water for the vineyards in the St-Jean-de-Fos area.

Cross over to the east bank of the Hérault and drive down D 27 to the small town of Aniane.

Aniane – Aniane is a quiet wine-growing town which has lost all trace of the prosperous abbey founded here in the 8C by St Benedict. A stroll through the narrow streets takes in the church of St-Jean-Baptiste-des-Pénitents, built in a real mixture of architectural styles and now used to house temporary exhibitions, and also the church of St-Sauveur, with the austere west front so characteristic of French Classical architecture in the 17C, and the 18C Town Hall with rounded bay windows at the corners. The observatory, **Géospace Observatoire d'Aniane** ⊘, reached along the road (D 27) to La Boissière, is open to visitors in the high season and organises astronomy courses throughout the year.

Pont de Gignac – The road (N 109) crosses the Hérault over this bridge, which is 1km/0.6mi west of the town of the same name. Built from 1776 to 1810 to plans by architect Bertrand Garipuy, this is considered to be the finest 18C bridge in France because of its daring design and the beauty of its architectural lines. It measures 175m/190yd in length and has three arches. That in the centre is a basket-handle arch majestically spanning the river.

A flight of steps leads to a platform downstream on the east bank from where there is an admirable view of the bridge.

Gorges d'HÉRIC★★

Michelin map 83 southwest of fold 4 or 240 fold 21
Local map see Monts de l'ESPINOUSE

The Héric gorge resembles a huge sabre slash in the southern slopes of the Monts de l'Espinouse and is one of the most outstanding beauty spots in this mountain range. The walls and jagged needles of rock are composed of pink-tinged gneiss splashed with yellowish-green lichens, set high above the beech and holm-oak thickets that carpet the floor of the gorge, where the foaming waters of the Héric tumble across boulders. The river Héric rises more than 1 000m/3 250ft above sea level, in the upper Espinouse range, and tumbles down the mountainside, dropping 800m/2 600ft in just 8km/5mi until it flows into the Orb. The walls of the gorge are the finest rockfaces in the region and are therefore popular with rockclimbers, but the gorge itself is also frequented by swimmers, ramblers and people out for a picnic. In short, the Héric gorge is a much-appreciated venue for a day out. A small **scenic railway** ⊙ (tyre-mounted trains) takes visitors along a picturesque route as far as the Gouffre du Cerisier.

TOUR *3hr on foot there and back*

In Mons-la-Trivalle, take D14ᴱ to the northeast. Leave the car at the mouth of the river gorge. A track runs along the gorge to the hamlet of Héric.

The track first begins by following the course of the stream as it froths along between tall walls of rock, cascades into mini-waterfalls, and slackens its pace in natural swimming pools, the largest of which is the **Gouffre du Cerisier**. Further on, on the right, is a majestic amphitheatre, the **Cirque de Farrières**, with a fringe of jagged needles of rock round its rim. The path leads past the slopes of Mont Caroux to the right before arriving in **Héric**, a tiny hamlet with stone-slab-roofed houses.

Gorges de la JONTE★★

Michelin map 80 folds 4, 5 and 15 or 240 fold 10
Local map see Les GRANDS CAUSSES

The spectacular Jonte gorge is less impressive in size than that of the Tarn, but the great limestone cliffs that crown the valley sides or overlook the river directly lend it just as amazing an appearance.
The Jonte rises at an altitude of 1 350m/4 387ft, on the north face of the Aigoual. It then flows down through a delightful wooded valley before flowing along between the arid Causse Méjean and the Cévennes, carpeted in pastures and chestnut trees. Beyond Meyrueis, the river cuts a path between the rockfaces of the Causse Noir and the craggy, tumbledown cliffs of the Causse Méjean, scoring a magnificent canyon as far as Le Rozier, where the Jonte flows into the Tarn.

Tour – The Jonte gorge can be visited **by car** along D 996 from Meyrueis to Le Rozier, as described below, or **on foot** along the clifftop footpaths over the Causse Méjean *(see Gorges du TARN ③)* and the Causse Noir *(see Les GRANDS CAUSSES)*.

FROM MEYRUEIS TO LE ROZIER *21km/13mi – allow 1hr*

We recommend the route described below driving down, rather than up, the gorge, as the canyon becomes increasingly impressive as it nears the confluence of the Jonte and the Tarn.

Meyrueis – See Massif de l'AIGOUAL.

Downstream from Meyrueis, the road along the Jonte gorge follows the river's north bank all the way. The sides of the gorge are crowned with tall limestone cliffs worn into bizarre formations by erosion.
Some 5km/3mi from Meyrueis, the mouths of two caves in the Causse Méjean can be seen opening into the cliff on the right – the **Grotte de la Vigne** and the **Grotte de la Chèvre**. Beyond the caves, the gorge becomes narrower and, in summer months, the Jonte disappears into the crevices along the river bed.

On the outskirts of the hamlet of Les Douzes, the river reappears after flowing for some distance underground. Here it enters a second gorge which is so deep that the huge poplar trees growing in it are scarcely visible.

Roc St-Gervais – This huge isolated rock towering over the hamlet of Les Douzes is topped by the Romanesque chapel of St-Gervais.

★ **Arcs de St-Pierre** – *4.5km/3mi then 1hr 30min on foot there and back. Leave from Le Truel. See Arcs de ST-PIERRE.*

Gorges de la Jonte

★ **Les Terrasses du Truel** – *1.5km/1mi downstream from Le Truel.* There is a superb view of the Jonte gorge from two lookout platforms. The sides of the gorge consist of two levels of limestone cliffs separated by marl slopes. These are known as the *terrasses du Truel.*

Downstream of the lookout platforms tower two enormous cliffs, 190m/617ft and 160m/520ft high respectively, which are part of the Causse Noir. They are called the Rochers Fabié and Curvelié.

On the rim of the cliffs at the edge of the Causse Méjean stands a most unusual, vase-shaped boulder called the "Vase de Sèvres".

The road comes into sight of the Capluc rock, to the right, followed by the village of Peyreleau, to the left, and finally the village of Le Rozier.

Le Rozier – This little village on the confluence of the rivers Jonte and Tarn, dwarfed by the cliffs of the Sauveterre, Noir and Méjean *causses,* is inevitably the threshold for those visiting the Tarn gorges. It is an excellent point of departure for exploring the gorges on foot or by car. In autumn, Le Rozier is gripped by gourmet fever at the start of the game season. Although the species of thrush indigenous to the *causses* is no longer found here, there are wild boar, woodcock and other game in abundance. Local truffles are also a highly sought-after delicacy. Le Rozier is home to a **museum of local architecture** ⊘, containing reconstructions in miniature of local monuments and traditional stone buildings.

A great variety of birdlife is to be found inhabiting the dolomitic limestone scenery, coniferous woodland and vast empty spaces of the Causse Méjean: the rock thrush, the red-legged partridge, the jackdaw and, in winter, the alpine accentor and the snow finch. Birds of prey include the short-toed eagle, the golden eagle, the peregrine falcon, the kestrel, the hen harrier (or marsh hawk) and the griffon vulture, whose recent reintroduction into the area has been accompanied by the setting up of protected nesting sites mainly in the Jonte gorge, around the village of Le Truel.

*The chapter on art and architecture in this guide
gives an outline of artistic creation in the region,
providing the context of the buildings and works of art
described in the Sights section.
This chapter may also provide ideas for touring.
It is advisable to read it while preparing your trip.*

Rivière souterraine de LABOUICHE★

Michelin maps 86 fold 14 or 235 fold 42 – 5km/3mi northwest of Foix

The underground river of Labouiche has hollowed out a **subterranean gallery** ⊙ in the limestone of the Plantaurel range (on the northern edge of the central Pyrenees), of which 4 500m/3mi have been explored and one-third opened to the general public.

Visitors will be enchanted with the boat trip along 1.5km/1mi of this "mysterious river", which includes two changes of craft, 70m/230ft below ground level through high and low-vaulted galleries, in which the lighting varies according to the effect required. Stalactites and stalagmites, standing out clearly against the limestone background, turn into strange beasts and flowers and other fantastic objects as the imagination runs wild.

A beautiful underground waterfall marks the end of the stretch of gallery open to visitors.

LAGRASSE

Population 704
Michelin maps 86 fold 8 or 235 fold 44 or 240 fold 33
Local map see Les CORBIÈRES

On the final descent to Lagrasse, on the road (D 212) from Fabrézan, there is a sweeping view of the town, with its bridges, intermittent ramparts, historical houses and abbey.

The abbey, one of the outposts of the Carolingian civilization near the Spanish March (Frankish Catalonia) and well-endowed with large estates in both Roussillon and Catalonia, grew up in a small basin in the Orbieu valley which had been irrigated by monks of the Benedictine Order. It owes its majestic appearance to the fortifications added in the 14C and the embellishments of the 18C. Two bridges, including an 11C humpbacked bridge, link the abbey to the town, which is also fortified and has an attractive covered market.

ABBEY ⊙ 45min

Go into the main courtyard, framed by stately 18C buildings made of local flame-coloured, ochre sandstone, not unlike marble in appearance.

Cloisters – These were built in 1760, on the site of the original cloisters built in 1280, some of the remains of which are still visible. One of the chapels in the abbey church also houses a display of capitals and fragments of columns from the original cloisters.

Abbot's lodgings – These include the oldest parts of the abbey, but have been modified.

From the east cloister, an ogive doorway leads into the conventual buildings, which occupy some dark, imposing vaulted rooms. The bakehouse features a handsome fireplace. The great vaulted room, wrongly known as the "refectory", was almost certainly used as cellars, while the refectory was located running along by the south cloister, continuing the axis of the church.

A 17C straight-flight staircase leads to the dormitory (13C) via the "pre-Romanesque tower", the oldest part of the abbey.

Old cloisters – These have been charmingly, if somewhat whimsically, renovated. Two covered galleries, resting on columns with recuperated Romanesque capitals, support an upper floor beneath the timber roof frame.

In the corner of the old cloisters is the **abbot's chapel** which has some rare late-13C ceramic paving and traces of mural paintings.

Return to the cloisters and the abbey church.

Church – The abbey church, which has been altered many times over the centuries, is built on the foundations of a Carolingian church. Its present appearance dates from the 13C. In the nave, on the right, a door opens onto the Romanesque south transept, grafted onto the pre-Romanesque church in the 11C. There are three oven-vaulted apsidal chapels decorated on the outside with bands of Lombard arcading.

Bell-tower – Built in 1537, and incorporated into the 14C fortifications, the 40m/131ft bell tower is completed with an octagonal crown pierced with openings, but having no spire. A spiral staircase *(150 steps)* leads to the top from which there is an attractive view.

LAGUIOLE

Population 1 264
Michelin map 76 fold 13 or 235 fold 12

Laguiole (pronounced Laïole), once famous for its cattle fairs, is now widely reputed for its elegant pocket knives, with their distinctive handles made of horn, wood, aluminium and, more rarely, ivory.

First manufactured in 1829, the **Laguiole knife** was originally designed as an all-purpose tool, to which a corkscrew and a pointed implement (otherwise known as the "thing for taking stones out of horses' hooves") were eventually added.

Production was revived at the beginning of the 1980s, and manufacture of Laguiole knives is now the town's leading industry. Recent years have seen an explosion in the number of local knife makers, whose workshops have practically taken over the entire main street. In order to regulate a situation which is becoming somewhat confusing, an official trademark – the "Laguiole Origine Garantie" – has now been adopted.

Laguiole knife

Located more than 1 000m/ 3 300ft above sea level, Laguiole, the "capital of the mountains", is also a winter sports resort, part of the Nordic winter sports centre in the Aubrac mountains, and the producer of an excellent *tomme* cheese made of cows' milk.

> **Musée du Haut-Rouergue** ⊙ – This regional museum, on three floors, houses a display of craftsmen's tools as previously used in the Aubrac area, as well as a reconstructed *buron* or cowherd's hut.

> ►► **Château du Bousquet** ⊙ – *5km/3mi southwest.* 14C castle of volcanic basalt.

LAMALOU-LES-BAINS✦

Population 2 194
Michelin map 83 fold 4 or 240 fold 22 – Local map see Monts de l'ESPINOUSE

Most of the Lamalou springs were discovered during mining of the surrounding ore deposits in the 11C and 12C; their soothing powers were quickly appreciated and, in the following century, a bathing establishment was founded here. The present spa resort draws on the Usclade, Bourgès, Capus and Vernière springs. It specialises in treating people with illnesses affecting their motor systems, such as poliomyelitis, or other mobility problems such as the after-effects of road accidents. Lamalou can boast a number of famous patients who have come to take waters here – Mounet-Sully, Alphonse Daudet, André Gide etc.

Lamalou-les-Bains is an excellent point of departure for excursions in and around the Caroux region. Seen from the surrounding hills, its site, spread out along the Bitoulet, is very picturesque.

Lamalou lies on the route taken by the **Bédarieux to Mons-la-Trivalle tourist train** ⊙, which operates along a disused section of the Montpellier-Castres-Montauban line, also known as the Tarn-Mediterranean line. The tourist train runs through the Orb valley at the foot of the Espinouse mountains and, from Poujol-sur-Orb onwards, through the Parc naturel régional du Haut-Languedoc. Taking the train is a good way of seeing parts of the valley which are not otherwise easy to explore, and the railway itself incorporates numerous feats of civil engineering, such as the Carrel bridge just before Lamalou station and the Ste-Colombe tunnel before Colombières-sur-Orb.

> ★ **St-Pierre-de-Rhèdes** ⊙ – *200m/220yd west of town, on the side towards St-Pons.*
> Safely tucked inside the cemetery walls, this old parish church in pink sandstone was built during the first half of the 12C. It is a fine example of rural Romanesque architecture in the south of France. Outside, note the elegant apse decorated with Lombard arcades. Speculation surrounds the identity of the archaic sculpted figure which also decorates the apse; it could

be a pilgrim on the way to Santiago de Compostela, complete with staff and wallet, or, more probably, St Peter, the patron saint of the parish, with his crozier, cross and open Bible.

The lintel of the doorway on the south façade features the Chi-rho monogram worked several times in Arabic script, blossoming into a crucifix. This is surmounted by an ornate basalt tympanum. The church interior features Mozarabic capitals and two 12C low reliefs by the Toulouse school: an impressive face of Christ in Majesty and a St Peter.

EXCURSIONS

★★ **Gorges d'Héric** – *See Gorges d'HÉRIC.*

★ **Château de St-Michel de Mourcairol** – *6km/4mi southeast. Leave Lamalou heading south, cross D 908 and the Orb, then turn left onto D 160 towards Les Aires. Just past the "Moulinas" sign, turn right into a small road signposted "St-Michel" which leads almost right up to the castle.*
The ruins of the castle and its fortifications give an idea of the importance of this stronghold in the Middle Ages. From its hilltop location, there is an extensive **view**★ of the region – the Orb valley as far as Bédarieux on the right *(east)* and, directly ahead, Lamalou in its valley with the Caroux summit in the background. Notre-Dame de Capimont can be seen amidst a cluster of trees.

►► **Notre-Dame de Capimont** – *5km/3mi northeast.* Pilgrimage chapel.

►► **Gorges de Colombières** – *9km/5mi west.* Footpath along a pretty river gorge *(rockclimbing).*

LANGOGNE

Population 3 380
Michelin map 76 fold 17 or 239 fold 46

Langogne lies in an attractive setting in the upper valley of the Allier on the borders of the Lozère, Ardèche and Haute-Loire *départements.* Stock raising is the region's main economic activity. The old part of Langogne is an interesting example of medieval urban planning, with its houses arranged in a circle around the church. Some of them have been built in the towers of the old curtain wall. Along the circular boulevard is an 18C corn market.

Covered market (Halle) – Built in 1742 originally as a shelter for cattle, this later became a corn market. Its roof of heavy limestone slabs *(lauzes),* supported by 14 granite columns with Doric capitals apparently inspired by those of the temple of Ceres in Paestum in Italy, still has its original overhanging ridge course.

Église St-Gervais-et-St-Protais – The exterior of this Romanesque church (10C), altered several times between 15C and 17C, is made of sandstone ashlar mixed with volcanic material. The interior is in fine granite bond. It was originally the church of a Benedictine priory. The façade, from the late 16C and early 17C, has a portal with a basket-handle arch and coving, surmounted by a bay in Flamboyant style.

★ **Interior** – Numerous carved historiated **capitals**★, with a rich decoration of plant motifs, brighten up this austere building. The most remarkable are on the pillars in the nave, particularly the first bay on the left – guardian angels – and the third bay on the right – Lust. The first chapel on the right occupies the site of an older sanctuary, indicated by the lower floor level; it houses a statue of the Virgin and Child – Our Lady of Infinite Power. This Madonna figure, an object of secular veneration, was apparently brought back from Rome in the 11C.

►► **Filature des Calquières** ⊙ – Woollen textile museum.

Naussac reservoir – *1km/0.6mi west. Leave Langogne on D 34.* In order to control the Allier river, a dam was built which swallowed up the old village of Naussac. The resulting lake, 7km/4mi long, is ideal for water sports enthusiasts, drawn by its various facilities.

Admission times and charges for the sights described are listed at the end of the guide.
Every sight for which there are times and charges is identified by the symbol ⊙, in the Sights section of the guide.

Causse du LARZAC*

Michelin maps 80 folds 14 and 15 and 83 fold 5 or 240 folds 14 and 18
Local map see Les GRANDS CAUSSES

The Causse du Larzac rises between Millau and Lodève, for all the world like an enormous limestone fortress.

GEOGRAPHICAL NOTES

The great causse – Covering nearly 1 000km²/400mi², the Causse du Larzac is the largest of the *causses* and its altitude ranges from 560m/1 840ft to 920m/3 020ft. Broken into five blocks by a series of faults, it consists of a series of arid limestone plateaux and green valleys. On the plateaux, clayey depressions *(sotchs)* covered with red soil, are used to grow crops. The water which falls on the Causse du Larzac reappears at the bottom of the valleys which dissect it, in nearly sixty resurgent springs. Like the other *causses*, Larzac is full of "chimneys" in the limestone rock; that of **Mas Raynal**, west of the Caylar, explored in 1889 by a team consisting of E-A Martel, L Armand, G Gaupillat and E Foulquier, proved to be an "inspection chamber" for the underground river which feeds the Sorgues.

Sheep raising – Larzac's economy mainly depends on Roquefort and the production of ewe's milk for cheese making. Flocks are 300 to 1 000 strong. The farms are using increasingly modern equipment with mechanised milking rooms.
Between 1979 and 1988 – the dates of the last two general agricultural censuses – the Causse du Larzac registered a 20% drop in going concerns. However, the sheep-farming and cheese-making sectors have nonetheless expanded.

Limestone rock formations

HISTORICAL NOTES

Templars and Hospitallers – In the 12C, the Order of the Knights Templar received part of the Causse du Larzac as a gift and built a commandery, or local headquarters, at Ste-Eulalie-de-Cernon with annexes at La Cavalerie and La Couvertoirade. In 1312, after dissolution of the Order of the Knights Templar, the Hospitallers of Saint John of Jerusalem (or Malta) took over the Templars' estates, including the fortress towns on the Causse du Larzac, which consequently became part of the most powerful military order of the time. In the 15C, which was a period of instability and unrest, the Hospitallers erected many fortifications; it is to these walls, towers and fortified gates that the Causse du Larzac owes its present rugged appearance.

FROM MILLAU TO LODÈVE *79km/49mi – allow 4hr*

★ **Millau** – *See MILLAU.*

The main road (N 9) towards Béziers runs through the Tarn *département* and climbs up the northern flank of the Causse du Larzac, offering superb panoramas of Millau, the Causse Noir and the Dourbie river gorge. After a bend in the road above the cliff face, the immense bare surface of the *causse* comes into view.

Maison du Larzac ⊙ – To the right of the N 9 is an enormous sheepfold roofed with limestone slabs *(lauzes)* also called La Jasse. It contains the reception area for the open-air museum *(écomusée)* of crafts and traditions whose exhibitions provide the visitor with an excellent introduction to the Causse du Larzac. This museum was founded in 1983 with the aim of presenting the natural, historical and cultural heritage of the *causse* through various elements distributed over an area 35km/22mi long and 25km/15.5mi wide. They include a traditional farm, an ultra-modern sheepfold with a "rotolactor" which can milk 700 sheep per hour, the Blaquière sheepfold built in the 1970s, and exhibitions on local architecture, archeology, the Templars, etc.

Carry on to La Cavalerie. The road runs alongside the Larzac Military Camp.

La Cavalerie – Formerly the seat of a vice-commandery of the Templars and then the Hospitallers, this large village is a reminder of the age of chivalry, and still has its ancient ramparts. Local activity has been revived by the Larzac Military Camp whose installations can be seen from the road to Nant.

From N 9, take D 999 on the right towards St-Affrique. After 3.4km/2mi, take the road to Lapanouse-de-Cernon on the left.

Ste-Eulalie-de-Cernon – In the cool valley of the Cernon, Ste-Eulalie was the seat of the Templars' commandery to which La Cavalerie and La Couvertoirade were attached. In the 18C, the revolutionary orator Mirabeau often went there to visit his uncle, Admiral Riqueti-Mirabeau, the last of the commanders.

From its past as a medieval fortress, Ste-Eulalie has kept most of its ramparts, towers and gates (the one that opens to the east is remarkable) as well as some picturesque covered passageways. The church, with a main door surmounted by a 17C marble Virgin, looks onto a charming square graced with a fountain.

Rejoin N 9 at Hospitalet-du-Larzac, via D 77 and D 23, and follow it towards Béziers. 2.5km/1.5mi further on, turn left towards Alzon and follow the signs to La Couvertoirade.

The road passes through moorland interspersed with rocky outcrops providing views of the Dourbie valley in the far distance to the left. After the village of Cazejourdes, small valleys covered with red soil appear.

★ **La Couvertoirade** – *See La COUVERTOIRADE.*

Follow D 55 to the south and continue towards Le Caylar.

The road, which climbs slightly, offers a good view of the curious village of Le Caylar and the Aigoual massif in the distance on the left.

Le Caylar – *See Le CAYLAR.*

Leave Le Caylar south on the road past the cemetery and turn left onto a slip road parallel with and then under the A 75 motorway. Take D 155^E as far as St-Félix-de-l'Héras, where you turn left onto D 155. Where the road crosses above the motorway (the old N 9), leave the car and continue on foot to the Pas de l'Escalette.

* **Pas de l'Escalette** – Alt 616m/2 021ft. This pass, a rocky cleft between towering cliffs, gives a good **view** of the Lergue waterfall. The name of the pass derives from when there was a way down from the Larzac plateau using steps cut into the rockface.

  Retrace your steps to St-Félix and the slip road under the motorway, which you should then join heading south towards Lodève (at the Caylar-Sud junction). Leave the motorway at the next junction to get to Pégairolles-de-l'Escalette.

  Pégairolles-de-l'Escalette – This pretty little village features an old castle. It is set amid a countryside of vines, olive trees and mulberry bushes, which contrasts strongly with the bleakness of the *causse*.

  Rejoin the A 75 motorway to Lodève.

* **Lodève** – *See LODÈVE.*

LAVAUR

Population 8 147
Michelin maps 82 fold 9 or 235 northeast of fold 30

Lavaur, located on the west bank of the Agout, at a crossroads linking Toulouse, Castres and Montauban, still has the charming old districts typical of a small fortified town in Languedoc.

Lavaur was defended by the castle of Plo, the only remains of which are a few walls holding up the Esplanade du Plo, in the southern part of the town.

During the Albigensian crusade, the town was besieged by the troops of Simon de Montfort and surrendered on 3 May 1211, after two months of resistance organised by Guiraude, a lady of the town, and 80 knights who had espoused the Cathar cause. They were hanged, other heretics were burnt at the stake, and Lady Guiraude was thrown into a well which was then filled with stones.

From 1318 to 1790, Lavaur was a bishopric.

SIGHTS

* **Cathédrale de St-Alain** ⊙ – The original Romanesque building, destroyed in 1211, was rebuilt in brick in 1254. On the south façade, at the top of a Romanesque tower with a stone base, is the famous painted wood Jack-o'-the-clock which strikes the hour and half-hour. The mechanism and clock were made in 1523. Walk right round the church to admire the apse overlooking the Agout. The interior is in the southern French Gothic style with an imposing single nave (13C and 14C) and seven-sided apse (late 15C, early 16C), lower and narrower than the nave. The Romanesque door which leads to the first chapel on the right is part of the original building; the capitals on the colonnettes are decorated with scenes from Christ's childhood. In the third chapel, a funerary recess in the Flamboyant style houses a Pietà in wood and a lectern (both 18C).

  In the chancel, the 11C white marble altar table (Moissac school) comes from Ste-Foy, the oldest church in Lavaur.

  On the left side, a painting depicting Christ crucified and St Jerome is attributed to Ribera. The 16C organ was restored by Cavaillé-Coll in the 19C.

  The west side of the nave leads to the porch underneath an octagonal belfry. On the central column of the Flamboyant doorway is the statue of St Alain and, on the lintel, the Adoration of the Magi. It was damaged during the Wars of Religion and during the French Revolution.

  Jardin de l'Évêché – This garden, on the site of the former bishop's palace, forms a terrace overlooking the Agout, to the north of the church. Its ancient cedars and carefully trimmed flower beds make it a pleasant place for a quiet walk.

  Église St-François – Before the Revolution, the church of St Francis, located in the main street, was the chapel of the Franciscan convent founded in Lavaur in 1220 by Sicard VI of Lautrec, Baron of Ambres. This elegant church was built in 1328. On the right of the entrance, there is a fine brick and timber house.

EXCURSION

St-Lieux-les-Lavaur – *10km/6mi northwest on D 87 and D 631 to the left.* This charming site in the Agout valley is the point of departure for the Tarn tourist **steam train** ⊙.

*To find a hotel or a restaurant,
or to find a garage or car dealer,
consult the current edition of the Michelin Red Guide France.*

Route du port de LERS

Michelin maps 86 fold 4 or 235 fold 46 and 50 – Local map see FOIX

The Port de Lers road reveals the marked contrast between the wooded, coppiced landscape of the Atlantic watershed and the harsher, more rugged countryside towards the Mediterranean.

FROM MASSAT TO TARASCON-SUR-ARIÈGE
42km/22mi – allow 3hr

Massat – *See Haute vallée de l'ARIÈGE.*

Leave Massat on D 18 southeast.

The road runs through narrow, open-ended slate valleys. Dotted among the pastures on the valley slopes are the houses of the mountain farmers, built of the same dark slate as the valleys.

After Mouréou the road enters the mountain country, increasingly austere as the road climbs higher, facing the snow-capped peaks.

Peyre Auselère – A steep climb through woodland leads to this, the last hamlet in this sparsely inhabited valley. Leave the car in the village for a short break at the side of the torrential waterfalls of the Courtignou. A footbridge gives access to the opposite (west) bank of the river.

The road carries on round the Cirque de Lers, where horses, sheep and herds of cattle, complete with tinkling cow-bells, share the pastures.

★ **Étang de Lers** – This superb, solitary lake at the foot of the Pic de Montbéas is set in mountain scenery carved out long ago by glacier action. In the early autumn, it is brilliant with the flowering gorse and furze on the surrounding slopes.

The road goes over the Port de Lers (alt 1 517m/4 980ft) and then descends, rapidly and with many hairpin bends, into the steep, narrow Suc valley. It is here that the difference between the Atlantic and the Mediterranean vegetation can most clearly be seen. The road runs alongside the rushing stream, overlooking the many waterfalls which take it into the depths of the valley. Before reaching Vicdessos there is a good view ahead of the high valley in which the village of Goulier lies.

Vicdessos – This mountain village is built on a site carved out by glacial action below the hanging Suc valley.

The road follows the deep, rugged **vallée du Vicdessos** where the extended pasturelands play host to flocks of sheep and herds of cattle, with little sign of human habitation. To the left the villages of Orus and Illier perch on the steep mountainside.

Port de Lers

At Laramade the valley opens out to the right as it is joined by the valley of the Siguer. The Port de Siguer (alt 2 396m/7 860ft) is a pass which was frequently involved in the exchanges between France, Andorra and Spain. During the Second World War it was used by many French fleeing the country.

Ahead, high on a rocky promontory, stand the ruins of the 14C Château de Miglos. Opposite the château, on the north bank of the river and also on a rocky height, is the village of Lapège. 100m after the side road to Junac, on the left, is a monument to the dead of the 1914-18 war, sculpted by Bourdelle.

Dry-stone huts

The countryside around Auzat and Vicdessos is dotted with numerous dry-stone shepherd's huts – known as **orris** – with corbelled roof vaults covered with turfs of a particular species of local grass which keeps the water out. These huts were used by shepherds during the summer grazing season. Two footpaths have recently been marked out to enable visitors to explore the area and its huts, some of which date from the 13C. The first path leaves from Pradières and for much of its length follows the GR 10 long-distance footpath, going past the huts at La Caudière and Journosque and running above Izourt lake and the Arties valley. The second leaves from the Carla huts, which have just been restored, and leads past several more huts and the lakes of Roumazet and Soucarrane.

Further details are available from the local tourist office (rue des Pyrénées, Auzat, ☎ 05 61 64 87 53).

★★ **Grotte de Niaux** – *See Grotte de NIAUX.*

Turn left towards Alliat.

Grotte de la Vache – *See Haute vallée de l'ARIÈGE.*

Tarascon-sur-Ariège – *See Haute vallée de l'ARIÈGE.*

LÉZIGNAN-CORBIÈRES

Michelin map 83 fold 13 or 240 fold 29

Halfway between Carcassonne and the sea, between the Aude valley, the Canal du Midi and the Orbieu river, Lézignan-Corbières is a small active town which relies on vine-growing and the Corbières wine trade. Promenades lined with plane trees, tiny squares and alley-ways surround the church of St-Félix.

Between Minervois and Corbières – Grapes have been grown in Lézignan since Roman times. Throughout the centuries, they have slowly ousted the olive tree and the pastures used for sheep farming, taking root wherever they can, both on the stony hillside and the more fertile plain.

During the last 15 years, the wine-growers in this area, bent in the past on producing large quantities, have been successfully concentrating on improving the quality of their wine, paying greater attention to the selection of grape varieties and the maturation process.

Musée de la Vigne et du Vin ⊙ – This vine and wine museum has been set up in an old vineyard. The main courtyard opens onto the saddle room, the stables and a wine-press, while under an awning are displayed the tools of the now vanished cooper's trade.

The wine-making cellar contains a large vat for treading the grapes and scalding apparatus with a yoke so that it could be driven by a team of oxen.

On the first floor, the tools needed for vine-growing are displayed by season. They include swing-ploughs, pruning shears, grafting knives, back-baskets, wooden tubs, funnels and branding irons.

In the middle of the room is a display of the costumes of the Narbonne, Lézignan and Olonzac wine-drinking brotherhoods.

EXCURSION

The Lézignan region – *49km/30mi. Leave Lézignan on D 24 towards Ornaisons and then turn right in Ornaisons onto D 123.*

Gasparets – Espace Octaviana houses the **Musée de la Faune** ⊙, a museum containing a collection of stuffed animals from every continent including birds of prey, night-birds and common species as well as the Pyrenean brown bear and wild boars from the region. The most interesting exhibits in this large collection, either due to their bright colours or size, are the golden pheasant, the capercaillie and the crested eagle.

D 61, D 161 and D 611 via Boutenac and Ferrals lead to Fabrezan.

For several miles the route leaves the plain to cross the *garrigue*-covered hills.

Fabrezan – In this picturesque village with its narrow, winding streets overlooking the stony valley of the Orbieu, the town hall houses the **Musée Charles-Cros** 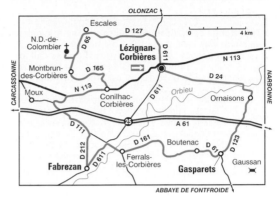, dedicated to the locally born inventer of the forerunner of the phonograph.

Take D 212, then D 111 on the left towards Moux. Just before reaching this village, turn right towards Lézignan. At Conilhac, take D 165 on the left.

The road climbs a hill, then comes to the vineyard of **Montbrun-des-Corbières**, which is spread out below. Continue towards Escales, perhaps with a brief stop at the Romanesque chapel of **Notre-Dame-de-Colombier**.

D 127 and D 611 lead back to Lézignan.

LODÈVE★

Population 7 602
Michelin map 83 fold 5 or 240 fold 18 – Local map see Les GRANDS CAUSSES

Lodève stands surrounded by graceful hills at the confluence of the Lergue and Soulondres rivers. The lookout point on the N 9 diversion coming from Millau offers a sweeping **view** of the site.

The town's main activities are the timber and textile industries and, since 1980, uranium mining. COGEMA, a nuclear fuel company, extracts uranium ore from both underground shafts and open-cast mines. Lodève's uranium deposits account for about one quarter of France's known reserves. The ore is then processed in a plant near the mines.

HISTORICAL NOTES

The bishops of Lodève – The history of Lodève goes back to Antiquity. It is here that Nero minted the coins needed for the pay and upkeep of the Roman legions. During the Middle Ages, the fortified town and diocese were ruled by the bishops. There were a total of 84 prelates between 506 and 1790. In the 10C, a certain Bishop Fulcran was renowned for his holiness. This wealthy man gave food to the poor and cared for the sick. He was also a warrior who built fortresses and defended the town against brigands.

In the 12C, one of his successors introduced industry to Lodève, founding one of the first mills used to make paper from rags. During the following century, the bishops developed the cloth trade.

After participating in the rebellion of Gaston d'Orléans and Henri de Montmorency against Cardinal Richlieu in 1632, the town was partly destroyed by the victorious Richelieu. The bishops, henceforth appointed by the king, lost all but their religious authority.

The cloth trade – Sheep raising has been the main activity of the Lodève region for many centuries. Not surprisingly, therefore, the wool industry began to prosper as early as the 13C. Later, Henri IV had cloth factories moved to Lodève from Semur, and locally produced fabrics were subsequently commissioned to clothe the royal troops. Under Louis XV, Cardinal Fleury granted his native town a monopoly in the field of military supplies.

Needless to say, this high level of protectionism had repercussions on the quality produced. The factory inspectors closed their eyes to poor workmanship and the quality of Lodève fabrics deteriorated. By the mid 18C they were already attracting criticism. Manufacture stopped in 1960. This traditional industry has now been superseded by other branches of the textile industry, particularly hosiery.

Lodève also has a carpet weaving workshop which produces copies of antiques, mainly for the State.

SIGHTS

★ **Ancienne cathédrale St-Fulcran** – The original cathedral is now the crypt. The church was rebuilt for the first time in the 10C by St Fulcran, and again in the 13C, but most of it dates from the first half of the 14C. After the Wars of Religion, it required considerable restoration, but the original style was preserved. The buttressing and the two watchtowers framing the façade show its defensive function.

The interior features a short nave with side-aisles and vast chancel. The far end of the latter, surrounded by 18C panelling and a marble balustrade, is roofed with elegant ribbed vaulting. At the opposite end is an 18C organ.

The first chapel in the south side-aisle is the final resting place for the 84 bishops of Lodève. The third chapel, devoted to Our Lady of the Seven Sorrows, has latticed vaulting which is characteristic of Late Gothic; from there, a door leads into the cloisters (14C to 17C).

Pont de Montifort – This Gothic bridge spans the Soulondres with a very pronounced humpback; there is an attractive view of it from the footbridge further downstream.

★ **Musée Cardinal-de-Fleury** ⊘ – The museum, located in what used to be the cardinal's palace (17C-18C), contains several collections concerning Lodève and its region.

The ground floor, devoted to geology and paleontology, has a rare collection of the fossilised imprints of flora and reptile (or batrician) tracks from the end of the Primary Era as well as those of huge dinosaurs from the Secondary Era. A comparison between these animal tracks and similar ones in South Africa supports the continental drift theory.

The first floor contains prehistoric remains from the Lodève area (Paleolithic and Neolithic) and a presentation of local history from Gallo-Roman times to the present (mementoes of Cardinal de Fleury). A display is also devoted to Lodève art, with engravings by Barthélemy Roger (Louis XVI-Louis XVIII), drawings by Max Théron (19C) and sculptures by Paul Darde (20C).

In a second wing of the building there is an exhibition of **disc-shaped steles** from Usclas-du-Bosc, near Lodève (12C-15C). The use of these monolithic stones, fairly popular in the southwest in the Middle Ages, dates back to Antiquity; the disc then represented the sun, but with the coming of Christianity, this symbol came to symbolise the risen Christ. Two rooms also contain a display on the traditional textile industry in Lodève.

EXCURSIONS

Prieuré St-Michel-de-Grandmont ⊘ – *8km/5mi east. Leave on N 9 towards Millau and turn right onto D 153 towards Privat.*
This priory was founded in the 12C by monks of the Grandmont order, which flourished from the 11C to 14C, and is one of the remaining examples of the 150 Grandmont monasteries *(see Prieuré de COMBEROUMAL)*.
The priory complex comprises among other things a church, Romanesque cloisters topped by a charming bell-turret, and a vast chapter-house. The priory grounds are home to some interesting dolmens and give good views of the Languedoc plain.

Cirque et grotte de Labeil – *12km/8mi north. Leave on N 9 towards Millau. Turn off west at the junction for Lauroux and take D 151 to Labeil.*
The **natural amphitheatre** of Labeil constitutes the southern foothill of Larzac plateau. From the entrance to the cave *(500m/550yd beyond Labeil)* there is a good view of Lauroux valley which stretches away from the foot of the viewpoint.

Grotte de Labeil ⊘ – A track follows the bed of an underground river for about 300m/330yd. In this very damp cave, which was once used for the production of Roquefort cheese, the main features are stalactites, stalagmites and frozen falls, of which there is a particularly spectacular example coloured ochre and grey by the metal oxides it bears.

*The annual Michelin Red Guide France
revises its selection of establishments which*

- *serve carefully prepared meals at a reasonable cost,*
- *include service on the bill or in the price of each dish,*
- *offer a menu of simple but good food at a modest price,*
- *provide free parking.*

It is well worth buying the current edition.

Grotte de LOMBRIVES*

Michelin maps 86 south of folds 4 and 5 and 235 fold 46

The main attraction of **Lombrives cave** ⊙, located south of Tarascon-sur-Ariège at Ussat-les-Bains, is its immense chambers and the stories, both fact and fiction, which surround it. The network of subterranean chambers extends over seven different levels, making Lombrives one of the largest underground sites of its kind, in terms of volume of hollowed-out space.

Geological formation – The speleologist E.-A. Martel attributes the formation of the Lombrives chambers to the waters of the Vicdessos flowing under pressure through a network of existing fissures. This hypothesis points to the conclusion that the caves of Niaux, Lombrives and Sabart were once part of the same enormous limestone plate.

A shelter through the ages – The walls of the cave are covered with inscriptions and graffiti, indicative of centuries of human occupation. In 4000 BC, it was used as both a shelter (from wild animals and bad weather) and as a place of burial. During the Middle Ages, the cave provided a refuge for outlaws. The treasure of the Cathars is said to have been hidden in the cave in 1244. In 1298, three men were beheaded there for counterfeiting coins. During the Renaissance, when rocaille drawing rooms were in vogue, its concretions were taken and used as domestic ornamentation. During the Wars of Religion, Catholics and Protestants in turn hid in Lombrives cave. Later, political refugees, brigands and freemasons sought asylum there.

TOUR

Park the car at the side of the main road (RN 20) at the entrance to Ussat-les-Bains, then walk or take the "Roucadère" small train from the reception hut.

From the viewing table just past the entrance (120m/130yd) there is a sweeping view into the upper valley of the Ariège.

A number of different tours of the cave are possible. Listed below are the "classic" one and the "extended version".

> ### The legend of Pyrene
>
> The Romans are said to have left behind the legend of Pyrene, a beautiful young princess who let herself be seduced by the young and handsome Hercules. Fleeing the anger of her father, Berbryx, King of the Bekrydes, she went to hide in the mountains where she was attacked by a bear. Hearing her screams, Hercules came running but arrived too late. Before burying her in her last resting place, Lombrives cave, he is said to have uttered these words, "So that your memory will live on forever, gentle Pyrene, henceforth these mountains in which you rest shall be called the Pyrenees."

"Circuit classique" – *1hr 30min.* Inside the cave, where the temperature remains a constant 13°C/55.4°F, the tour covers 1.8km/1mi of galleries on two levels. A fracture line running along the roof of the lower chamber gives it the appearance of the upturned hull of a boat. From here the tour brings visitors to the "cathedral", a chamber about a hundred metres (300ft) high in which concerts are held *(viewing platform)*. In the upper galleries, note the impressive rock formation shaped like a gigantic mammoth, and "Pyrene's tomb".

"Circuit longue durée" – *There are two possibilities: 3hr and 5hr. Both are within the capabilities of people used to mountain rambling. Wear sturdy walking boots. Lamps are provided.*

This tour follows the route taken by the classic circuit as far as the first lake. After this the route taken is one through parts of the cave which have been left untouched, which adds considerably to the interest of the visit. One gallery gives way to the next, past walls clad in red, blue or black marble, underground lakes, the "great chaos chamber" and a variety of fascinating rock formations such as "Solitaire", "Cascades" (frozen falls or stalagmites), "Hercules' tomb" and "Madonna". There are also more delicate formations to be admired: eccentrics, aragonite or gypsum crystals and some "cave pearls". The walk goes past E.-A. Martel's apparatus for his descent underground in 1937 and a vertiginous steel footbridge spanning the abyss, built by engineer Perpère in 1927.

*The annual **Michelin Red Guide France** offers an up-to-date selection of hotels and restaurants serving carefully prepared food at reasonable prices.*

Vallée du LOT★★

Michelin maps 76 folds 11 and 12 and 80 folds 1, 2 and 3 or 235 fold 12

Within the confines of the Auvergne and Rouergue regions, the Lot has hollowed out a deep valley from gneiss and granite.

The picturesque route described below follows the river's course closely from Espalion to Coursavy bridge.

FROM ESPALION TO CONQUES *56km/35mi – allow 3hr*

★ **Espalion** - *See ESPALION.*

From Espalion, the main road to Aurillac follows the northeast bank of the Lot. Initially the valley is wide and fertile (meadows, vineyards, fruit trees), but it later becomes narrow and wooded.

★ **Estaing** - *See ESTAING.*

Leaving Estaing, the road offers an attractive view of the Lot, the old bridge and the castle which dominates the little town.

★★ **Gorges du Lot** - After widening for a few miles, and then being flooded by the Golinhac dam reservoir, the valley narrows into some very picturesque, rugged gorges about 300m/ 1 000ft deep, and rarely exceeding 1 500m/5 000ft across at the top of the valley walls. Rocky crests or points, with jagged or forbiddingly solid silhouettes, rise up out of the woods covering the sides of the gorges.

A few miles from Estaing is the **Golinhac dam**, which stands 37m/121ft high and, a little further along on the opposite bank, stands the glass and metal structure of the hydroelectric plant, fed by the dam.

★ **Entraygues** - *See ENTRAYGUES.*

The D 107 west offers a sweeping view of Entraygues and its castle, at the confluence of the Truyère and Lot rivers.

The valley of the Lot no longer has the harsh, forbidding character of the gorges upstream of Entraygues. At first, it is quite wide and very scenic. Vineyards which produce very good wine grow in terraces on the well-exposed hillsides and the countryside is dotted with farmhouses. Further on, the vineyards become scarcer, box grows among

Lot valley (west of Entraygues-sur-Truyère)

the rocks, which are closer together, and woods cover the slopes; several times, however, the valley widens into small cultivated basins where villages with picturesque houses nestle among fruit trees.

Vieillevie - Beautiful Renaissance castle, topped with protective defence walling.

After crossing the Lot at Coursavy bridge, take D 901 to Rodez.

The road enters the valley of the Dourdou, in which the waters have the reddish tint of the sandstone through which they flow.

From **Grand-Vabre**, about 1km/0.6mi along the little road to Almon-les-Junies, there is a pretty view of the Lot and Dourdou valleys before arriving at Conques.

★★★ **Conques** - *See CONQUES.*

Mont LOZÈRE★★

Between Florac, Génolhac and Villefort, this powerful granite massif, rising majestically above the Cévennes countryside, forms a geographical unit set off by the gorges of the Tarn, the Lot, the Altier and the Cèze.

"Mont Chauve" – Mont Lozère has earned this nickname ("Bald Mountain") from its 35km/22mi of bare, high-lying plateaux. The mountain culminates at the Finiels summit (alt 1 699m/5 573ft), the highest peak in the Massif Central which is not of volcanic origin. The eroded granite of which it is made up has been weathered into curious boulders forming scattered rocky outcrops amid heathland which still bears the remains of its ancient forest cover of beech groves. The mountain slopes, replanted over the last few decades, are covered once again in pines, firs and beeches to the south (Bougès mountain), to the east (Vivarois slopes) and to the north. The robust architectural style of the houses blends in perfectly with the countryside. Granite boulders have at times been incorporated directly into the walls. Nowadays, most of the villages are deserted, as life is very harsh on these wind- and snow-swept plateaux. Storm bells, the sound of which was once the only means of finding one's way during a blizzard, are still to be found here and there. A few granite markers bearing the Maltese Cross are a reminder that part of the land was once owned by the Knights Hospitaller of St John of Jerusalem, who later became the Knights of Malta. In the past, flocks of sheep dotted the vast hillside pastures during the summer months. Estimated to have numbered about one hundred thousand head in the 19C, less than ten thousand are to be found grazing nowadays, and the sheep trails *(drailles)* of the past are slowly being overgrown. Sheep have given way to herds of cattle which come to graze on the high plateaux of Mont Lozère from villages on the southern slopes.

Écomusée du Mont Lozère – The aim of this open-air museum of local crafts and traditions, founded under the sponsorship of the Cévennes national park, is to familiarise visitors with the natural and human environment of Mont Lozère. It consists of a headquarters, the Maison du Mont Lozère at Pont-de-Montvert, and various sites of architectural and natural interest scattered throughout the massif. At the **Troubat** and **Mas Camargues** farms, the emphasis is on 19C rural architecture and everyday running of a farm. An inventory has been made of all the storm bells and markers bearing a Maltese Cross in the area. Several footpaths have been laid out.

Most of the museum's exhibits are on display at Pont-de-Montvert.

Exploring Mont Lozère on foot – The lie of the land and the scenery lend themselves well to rambling, and the area features numerous long-distance *(GR – Grande Randonnée)* footpaths. A six-day **tour of Mont Lozère**, described in the topoguide to the GR 68, keeps to the periphery of the massif, while the GR 7, which takes the old Margeride sheep trails through the centre, passes through the characteristic countryside and hamlets of Mont Lozère (particularly in the section between the Finiels pass and Aubaret farm).

Rambling on Mont Lozère

Lutra/CAMPAGNE CAMPAGNE

For further details, contact the information centre of the Cévennes national park in Florac (see the Practical information section at the end of the guide).

Cévennes biosphere reserve
As part of its Man and Biosphere programme, UNESCO designated the Parc national des Cévennes, home to Mont Lozère, a "biosphere reserve" in 1985. The reserve, which encompasses largely the same area as the park, is divided into three zones:
a central zone (14 000ha/34 595acres) of self-contained reserves and areas where hunting is forbidden; an intermediary zone (77 000ha/190 271acres) which covers the central zone of the national park; a "cooperation zone" (282 000ha/ 696 837acres) which matches the peripheral zone of the national park.

★ ⬚ COL DE FINIELS

From Le Pont-de-Montvert to Bleymard

23km/14mi – allow 1hr – see local map

This route along the D 20 winds through the heartland of Mont Lozère, offering wonderful views of the surrounding countryside.

Le Pont-de-Montvert – *See Le PONT-DE-MONTVERT.*

Leave Le Pont-de-Montvert on D 20 towards Bleymard.

The road, lined with service trees, climbs up the south face towards Finiels pass. After the village of Finiels, it crosses wide expanses of deserted countryside, punctuated here and there with granite boulders. The horizon is blocked to the south by Bougès mountain and the hilly outline of the Causse Méjean.

> *The stony skeleton of the world was here vigorously displayed to sun and air. The slopes were steep and changeful. Oak trees clung along the hills, well grown, wealthy in leaf, and touched by the autumn with strong and luminous colours. Here and there another stream would fall in from the right or the left, down a gorge of snow-white and tumultuary boulders. The river in the bottom (for it was rapidly growing a river, collecting on all hands as it trotted on its way) here foaming a while in desperate rapids, and there lay in pools of the most enchanting sea-green shot with watery browns. As far as I have gone, I have never seen a river of so changeful and delicate a hue; crystal was not more clear, the meadows were not by half so green; and at every pool I saw I felt a longing to be out of these hot, dusty, and material garments, and bathe my naked body in the mountain air and water.*
>
> **Robert Louis Stevenson:** *Travels with a donkey*

★ **Col de Finiels** – Alt 1 548m/5 077ft. From the area around the pass, and particularly from the peaks on either side of the road, the **view**★ in fine weather stretches as far as the Aigoual summit and the Causses.

At the beginning of the descent, the Tanargue massif (the Cévennes part of the Vivarais region) is visible ahead and to the right. The Mont Lozère ski resort and a modern chapel appear on the left.

Chalet du Mont Lozère – Newly planted fir trees surround the refuge chalet, a hotel, **information centre** ⊘ for the Cévennes park and a large UCPA (French open-air sports centres association) building which welcomes ramblers and horse-riders in summer. From December to April, it is also a centre for skiing, particularly for cross-country skiing. A waymarked footpath leads to Finiels peak.

★ **Sommet de Finiels** – *3hr on foot there and back.* From Mont Lozère chalet, take the waymarked path between the D 20 and the chapel, which follows a row of stones right up to the top of the ridge. Turn right towards the remains of a stone hut. From there, a sweeping **view**★★ to the south-east reveals a series of rounded peaks on the high plateaux as far as Pic Cassini, while to the north the horizon is hidden by the granite plateau of La Margeride. Follow the line of the ridge to the 1 685m/ 5 527ft marker and then join the "Route des Chômeurs" on the way down which leads back to the point of departure. After the Mont

Lozère chalet, where the D 20 leaves the ravine of the Altier to cross over to the side of the Atlantic watershed, the mountains of La Margeride can be seen stretching away to the north.

Le Mazel – Home to the buildings of a now disused lead and zinc mine which was worked here from the beginning of the century to 1952.

Le Bleymard – This village has solidly built houses with roofs of limestone slabs (*lauzes*) and a 13C church.

② TOUR OF MONT LOZÈRE

From Mende to Florac via Villefort and Génolhac
137km/86mi - see local map

★ **Mende** – *See MENDE.*
Leave Mende on N 88 heading east towards Le Puy.
The road follows the Lot valley beneath the limestone cliffs of the Causse de Mende.
At the Col de la Tourette, take D 901 towards Villefort.

Bagnols-les-Bains – This cure resort specialising in the treatment of rheumatism and ear, nose and throat complaints is built in a semicircle around the slopes of the Pervenche mountain, and stretches downhill to the banks of the Lot. The waters of the mineral spring were first exploited by the Romans.
Bagnols is first and foremost a place for holiday and relaxation. Its altitude (913m/2 995ft) and the nearby pine forests contribute to the fresh, healthy mountain air. It is a particularly good remedy for the effects of overwork or stress, with its peaceful atmosphere and steady climate.
The valley sides draw in, becoming steep rocky gorges, cloaked in woods. The ruins of Tournel castle can be seen perched proudly on a rocky spur around the foot of which surges the river.

Le Bleymard – *See ① above. At this point it is possible to take the Finiels pass road.*
After Le Bleymard, the scenery becomes increasingly bleak and rugged. The road leaves the Lot valley, having crossed the Col des Tribes, to follow the winding, wooded valley of the Altier. The towers of the **Château de Champ** (15C) can be seen downhill from the road on the right. A few miles past Altier, once a stronghold, the road reaches the shores of Villefort lake.

Taiscaire/IMAGES PHOTOTHÈQUE

Taking sheep up to summer pastures

Château de Castanet ⊘ – This square granite castle, flanked with three round towers truncated at roof level, stands on a peninsula at the edge of Villefort lake. It narrowly escaped destruction when the lake was flooded in 1964.
This Renaissance castle, built in 1578, still features many of the characteristics of fortified castles built in the Middle Ages. Inside, Renaissance influence is evident in the chimneypieces and French-style ceilings. The top floor, with its fine timber roof frame, houses exhibitions by contemporary artists.

Villefort – This pleasant town at the mouth of the Phalère valley has much to offer the holidaymaker, with its nearby reservoir, well equipped for water sports enthusiasts, and its ideal location as a base for trips on foot or by car into the Cévennes, Bas Vivarais and Mont Lozère. In season, the Syndicat d'initiative at Villefort houses an **information centre** ⊘ on the Cévennes national park.

Villefort reservoir and dam – *1.5km/1mi north.* When the Villefort dam was put into service, the Altier gorge and a nearby ravine were flooded to form a vast curved reservoir with a number of little side bays. The dam, which is 190m/623ft long at the level of its crest, rises to a height of 70m/230ft above the river bed. The reservoir supplies the Pied-de-Borne plant 9km/6mi downstream. The hydroelectric scheme in the Chassezac basin – four dams and energy plants have been set up – produce 420 million kWh. The various installations also provide irrigation for the lower valley.

On leaving Villefort, take D 66.

The road rises above a ravine shaded by chestnut trees, offering splendid views of Villefort and its valley. It goes through the villages of Paillères and Costeilades, surrounded by small terraced gardens. The houses are roofed with limestone slabs *(lauzes)*, with finials on the roof ridges.
Gradually, to the northeast, the plateaux formed by the Borne and Chassezac gorges come into view. As the road passes through a stretch scattered with granite outcrops, the Tanargue and Mézenc massifs can be seen, with the Alps on the horizon.
The road reaches the Pré de la Dame ledge, covered with large granite boulders.

Mas de la Barque ⊘ – *Just after Pré de la Dame, the road to Mas de la Barque leads off to the right.*
This forester's hut, an overnight stop for ramblers, stands in a peaceful setting of meadows and coppices surrounded by forest. In winter, it is also a ski centre. An **observation trail** *(45min)*, laid out by the Parc national des Cévennes as part of the Écomusée du Mont Lozère to give visitors the opportunity of exploring the forest environment, leads off from the hut. A second path leads up to the Cassini summit from where there is a wonderful **panorama**★★, as far as the Alps and Mont Ventoux in clear weather *(2hr there and back).*

Return to Pré de la Dame and carry on towards Génolhac.

Almost all the way down towards Génolhac, the road is surrounded by beech trees and conifers.

★ **Belvédère des Bouzèdes** – Alt 1 235m/4 051ft. At this viewpoint, the road makes a hairpin bend on open ground on the brow of a steep hill overlooking Génolhac, 800m/2 600ft below. This little village looks surprisingly Mediterranean with its tiled roofs.

Génolhac – Génolhac is a charming little town, bright with flowers in season, in a pleasant setting in the Gardonnette valley. The Maison de l'Arceau houses an **information centre** ⊙ on the Cévennes national park and offers overnight accommodation.

Take the road to Alès, then turn right onto D 998 towards Florac.

The road along the Luech valley is particularly scenic as far as St-Maurice-de-Ventalon.

2km/1mi after Les Bastides, a road on the right leads to Troubat farm-house.

Le Pont-de-Montvert – *See Le PONT-DE-MONTVERT. At this point it is possible to take the Finiels pass road described under ① above.*

After Le Pont-de-Montvert, the road follows the upper valley of the Tarn which later narrows into rugged gorges. Miral castle, with the remains of its 14C fortifications, can be seen perched on a promontory.

Florac – *See FLORAC.*

★★③ MONTMIRAT PASS ROAD

This road linking Florac and Mende is described in the opposite direction under Route du Col de MONTMIRAT.

MAGRIN

Population 106
Michelin map 82 folds 9, 10 and 19 or 235 fold 31

This little village in the Tarn valley is famous for its castle (12-16C) which has housed the only museum on dyer's woad in France since 1982.
Perched on top of a hill 330m/1 080ft high, the Château de Magrin offers a splendid **panorama**★ of the Montagne Noire and the Pyrenees.

DYER'S WOAD COUNTRY ("LE PAYS DU PASTEL")

Dyer's Woad

Known for its medicinal properties since ancient times, and still used today for fodder and as a source of nectar for honey bees, dyer's woad or *Isatis tinctoria* (*pastel* in French) is the plant traditionally used by dyers to obtain varying shades of blue dye.

"Pays de Cocagne" (Land of Milk and Honey) – Mainly grown around the Mediterranean, dyer's woad was cultivated particularly intensively in the triangle formed by Albi, Toulouse and Carcassonne. The 14C marked the beginning of an astonishing boom in woad production and trade in the Albi area. Results were so successful that the cultivation of dyer's woad gradually spread further south until it reached the Lauragais region.

IMAGES PHOTOTHÈQUE

Shades of blue

In the 15C, a few wealthy inhabitants of Toulouse began growing dyer's woad more intensively on their estates. They built woad mills which ground up the leaves to obtain an almost homogeneous pulp. This was then divided into piles and left to ferment for two weeks, giving rise to the *cocagnes*, or rounded heaps of blue dye material. Four months further treatment produced the finished dye ready for export.

Toulouse, which was a financial capital, became aware of the importance of its geographical location between the dyer's woad-growing areas and the Atlantic ports. The town's leading merchants first took control of local dye production, then of regional and European trade. This was the golden age of dyer's woad in the "Pays du Cocagne" which, despite a large number of cultural and economic initiatives, was only to last about sixty years. Decline was rapid, due to the Wars of Religion and the arrival on the scene of indigo (or dye from the "Indies").

Dyer's woad makes a comeback – There has been a revival of interest in dyer's woad in recent years as a result of various initiatives, mainly of a scientific nature, due to research conducted by the École nationale de Chimie (national college of chemistry) in Toulouse, but also agricultural, with 60ha/148 acres given over to the cultivation once more of dyer's woad in the Lauragais area.
The cosmetics industry is being envisaged as a potential outlet, while the possibility of using woad as a blue dye for tapestry thread is under investigation.

TOUR OF DYER'S WOAD COUNTRY *73km/47mi - about 1 day*

Take D 12 north to the Château de Magrin.

★ **Château-musée du Pastel** ⊙ – The dyer's woad museum in the Château de Magrin contains a woad mill and drying rack and presents the various stages involved in making blue dye from dyer's woad, including the history of the *Isatis tinctoria* plant, traditional objects and documents and samples of woad at various stages during the manufacturing process. An audio-visual presentation completes the tour.

Woad mill – The mill, which comes from an old farm in the village of Algans, has been completely restored. It comprises an enormous, two-tonne granite millstone (1.40m x 0.40m/4ft 6in x 1ft 3in), a solid oak crossbeam resting on iron axles and two wooden drive shafts.

Woad drying rack – Only four of the eight original racks, on which the piles of dried, fermented woad were piled, separated by wicker-work, still remain. Each can be used to store nearly two tonnes of woad.

Leave the Château de Magrin on D 12 and turn left onto D 40.

Château de Roquevidal ⊙ – The body of the castle is flanked by four corner towers, one storey of each of which was removed during the years following the Edict of Nantes. The main façade shows the influence of the Renaissance.

On leaving the castle, take two right turnings.

En Olivier – This little hamlet is home to the **Musée Nostra Terra Occitana** ⊙, devoted to agricultural tools and machinery. Various objects and family souvenirs adorn this reconstruction of the interior of a rural dwelling at the beginning of the 20C.

Go back to N 126 and follow the direction of Toulouse.

Loubens-Lauragais – This charming village, bright with flowers in season, is tucked up against a **château** ⊙.

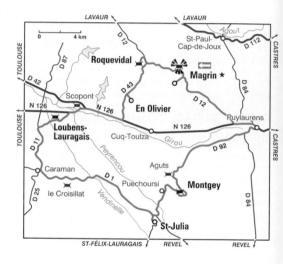

A tour round this follows the story of the Loubens family, which gave the French State a number of fine civil servants. In the 16C, Hugues de Loubens was a cardinal, prince, and sovereign of the Order of Malta. His brother Jacques rebuilt the castle at the end of the 16C.

The façade, with its two large protruding towers, looks out onto a peaceful park. Inside, there is a lovely Gothic library and a series of nine Flemish tapestries (16C).

Head towards Caraman, then, take D 1 to Revel.

St-Julia – *See ST-FÉLIX-LAURAGAIS.*

Go north towards Aguts. Turn right just after Puéchoursi to get to the Château de Montgey.

Château de Montgey – *See ST-FÉLIX-LAURAGAIS.*

Return to Magrin via Aguts and Puylaurens.

Michelin Maps (scale 1: 200 000),
which are revised regularly,
  – highlight towns cited in the Michelin Red Guide France
    for their hotels or restaurants;
  – indicate which towns in the Red Guide
    are accompanied by a town plan.

Michelin makes it so easy to choose where to stay
and to find the right route.

Keep current Michelin Maps in the car at all times.

MAGUELONE*

Michelin map 83 fold 17 or 240 folds 23 and 27
16km/10mi south of Montpellier

Maguelone, in an unusual site on a sand spit which lies between the Golfe du Lion and the Pierre Blanche and Prévost lagoons, and linked by a narrow road to the seaside resort of Palavas-les-Flots, has a peaceful charm no doubt due to its setting. The vestiges of its cathedral stand on a slight hill, framed by umbrella pines, cedars and eucalyptus.

The Rhône-Sète canal, which passes through the lagoons between the sandspits and the Languedoc coast proper, cut across the road which, up until 1708, linked Maguelone to dry land. A gigantic arch was erected in the 19C to mark the boundaries of the Maguelone territory.

Historical trials and tribulations – The oldest remains found in Maguelone date from the 2C and are not much help in confirming any one of the numerous hypotheses about the origins of Maguelone; some believe it was a Phoenician trading post, others that it was a colony of Greek navigators. In any case, in the 6C Maguelone was made a bishopric, but the prosperity of the episcopal town was rudely interrupted in the 8C when it fell to the Saracens. At that time, the harbour, south of the cathedral, was connected to the sea by a channel.

Charles Martel recaptured the town from the infidels but, afraid that they would use it as a home base again, he immediately destroyed it (737). In 1030, Bishop Arnaud I rebuilt the cathedral on the site of the old church and added extensive fortifications. He built a path from Maguelone to Villeneuve, and a 2km/1.2mi bridge, and closed off the channel joining the Saracen harbour to the sea in order to protect it from attack.

In the 12C, the church was rebuilt to make it bigger and its fortifications strengthened. During the quarrel between the Church and the Empire, a number of popes sought asylum here. They made the cathedral a major basilica. The papal envoy, Pierre de Castelnau, whose assassination triggered the Albigensian Crusade, was a member of the Maguelone chapter.

For Maguelone, the 13C to 14C was a period of expansion. A community of sixty canons lived there, reputed for their generosity and hospitality.

However Montpellier, which continued to thrive and improve its trade structures, attracted numerous inhabitants from the island. In the 16C, the bishopric was transferred to Montpellier.

Like all the strongholds in the region, Maguelone, which found itself in the hands of the Protestants and Catholics in turn during the Wars of Religion, was finally demolished in 1622, on the orders of Richelieu. Only the cathedral and bishop's palace still remain.

During construction of the canal, Maguelone was bought and sold several times, its ruins dispersed or swallowed up by the surrounding lagoons. In 1852, Frédéric Fabrège bought the estate and set out to restore it. The church became a religious building again in 1875.

★FORMER CATHEDRAL ⊙
30min

Getting there – *Out of season, via a road (cul-de-sac), 4km/2.5mi long, which begins at Palavas-les-Flots, at the end of Rue Maguelone.*
During the summer season, park in the car park 2km/1.2mi away and take the little train to the cathedral, or take the ferry, and then the little train ⊙. from Villeneuve.

Exterior – The church was attached to a continuous curtain wall, with fortified gatehouses and turrets, demolished under Richelieu at the same time as the

St Paul on Maguelone cathedral façade

F. Gégot/MICHELIN

215

three large towers. The high, very thick walls (the southern wall is 2.5m/8ft thick) have a small number of narrow arrow slits, placed asymmetrically. All that is left of the crenellated parapet which once surmounted the building are a few machicolations. A remarkable sculpted doorway leads into the church. The lintel is an antique Roman military column on which fine foliage was later sculpted and the date 1178 inscribed.

The white and grey tympanum with its slightly pointed arch and marble archstones is thought to date from the 13C; in the centre is the figure of Christ with his hand raised in benediction surrounded by St Mark, represented by a lion, St Matthew by a winged man, St John by an eagle and St Luke by a bull.

The low reliefs on the engaged piers, depicting Saints Peter and Paul, and the heads of two Apostles holding up the lintel, date from the middle of the 12C.

Interior – On the left of the entrance is a walled-up door which used to lead to the chapter-house. Fragments of tombstones have been set into the wall on the right; some are from the Roman era, while others from the 11C come from the burial places of wealthy Montpellier citizens. At that time, Pope Urban II absolved the sins of all those who asked to be buried in Maguelone.

Two bays of the rectangular nave, made of limestone blocks, are covered with a vast gallery which cuts it in half vertically and masks the pointed barrel vaulting.

The marks on the floor of the third bay were traced by Frédéric Fabrège to mark the ground plan of the pre-Romanesque building; those in the transept crossing indicate the limits of the cathedral built by Arnaud I.

The chancel is soberly decorated. The small apse, polygonal on the outside and semi-circular on the inside, is flanked by two apsidal chapels cut into the thickness of the wall. It is decorated with blind arches and three semi-circular windows and is surmounted by a thin band of cog teeth patterning.

The arms of the transept are covered with ribbed vaulting. On the south side is the Lady Chapel with two Roman tombs and some 14C tombstones, while on the north side, the Chapel of the Entombment of Christ contains a finely sculpted marble sarcophagus.

La MALÈNE

Michelin map 80 fold 5 or 240 fold 10 – Local map see Gorges du TARN

Located at the junction of the roads which wind through the Sauveterre and Méjean *causses*, La Malène has always been a thoroughfare. In the spring and autumn, huge flocks of sheep on their way to new pastures used to cross the Tarn here and drink from the river's waters. In the 12C, the barons of Montesquieu built their first castle and, up until the 18C, their prestigious name lent importance to this little town. Throughout the region of the Tarn gorges, the Revolution spread fire and bloodshed in its wake. The nobles, brutally persecuted, took refuge in caves in the cliff walls of the canyon. In 1793, a detachment of revolutionary troops shot 21 inhabitants and set fire to La Malène. This incident left an indelible black mark on the Falaise de la Barre, a cliff overlooking the village, said to be caused by the oil-filled smoke from a house full of walnuts.

Tourists should visit the 12C Romanesque **church**, the little street lined with historical houses beneath Barre rock, and the 16C castle which is now a hotel.

CLIFFTOP VIEWS

Round tour of 34km/21mi, allow 2hr. Cross the bridge over the Tarn out of La Malène and take D 43.

Just off the road to the right stand a cave chapel and a statue of the Virgin Mary from where there is a fine view of the village and its surroundings. The climb up the south bank of the Tarn is spectacular – ten hairpin bends offer a splendid view of La Malène tucked in its hollow.

At Croix-Blanche, take D 16 to the right; 5km/3mi further on, turn right again. After passing through the village of Rieisse, take the road signposted "Roc des Hourtous-Roc du Serre" near a café.

★★ **Roc des Hourtous** – *Follow the signs along the surfaced track off to the left. Car park.* This cliff overlooks La Momie cave, just upstream from the Détroits gully, which is the narrowest section of the Tarn canyon. From here there is a superb **view**★★ of the Tarn gorge, from the hamlet of L'Angle to the Cirque des Baumes and the Point Sublime.

Go back to the fork in the road; leave the car and take the track on the right to the Roc du Serre.

★★ **Roc du Serre** – *30min on foot there and back.* This is the only place which gives this marvellous **view**★★ of the narrow river gorge as it squeezes between the Sauveterre and Méjean *causses*, with, further off, Mont Lozère, the Aigoual range, the village of La Malène and the hairpin bends of the D 16 as it winds its way up the *causse.*

Take the D 16 on the right across the *causse* and down to Les Vignes via an impressive cliff-face road which runs past the ruins of the **Château de Blanquefort**.

Return to La Malène on the road along the Tarn gorges (see Gorges du TARN).

MARVEJOLS

Population 5 476
Michelin map 80 fold 5 or 240 fold 2 – Local map see L'AUBRAC

Marvejols, well-situated in the pretty Colagne valley, has benefited from a favourable climate and setting which have lent themselves to the setting up of numerous medical and pedagogical centres. Appointed a "Royal City" in 1307 by Philip the Fair, Marvejols went on to play an important role in the wars in the 14C and sided with Du Guesclin against the mercenaries of the Grandes Compagnies. A Protestant fortress town, it was destroyed in 1586 by Admiral Joyeuse. Its fortified gatehouses are reminiscent of its war-torn past.

Fortified gatehouses – Consisting of two large round towers connected by a curtain wall used as lodgings, they commanded the three entrances to the old town. On the **Porte de Soubeyran**★, an inscription records how the town was rebuilt by Henri IV – to express their gratitude, the inhabitants had a highly original statue of their royal benefactor erected in the fortified square, which is closed off by the gatehouse on one side. It is the work of the sculptor Auricoste, who was also the author of the legendary "Beast of Gévaudan" on Place des Cordeliers.

The other two gatehouses, the **Porte du Théron** and **Porte de Chanelles**, once known as the "Hospital Gatehouse", also bear inscriptions recounting the good deeds of Henri IV.

THE GÉVAUDAN

Tour north of Marvejols – 52km/32mi – about 3hr 30min. Michelin map 76 folds 14 and 15.

Leave Marvejols to the north on N 9 and after 2.5km/1.5mi, take D 2 on the right up through the Colagne valley to St-Léger-de-Peyre.

The road then enters the Crueize gorge, going past Vallée de l'Enfer, spanned by an elegant viaduct, on the left. As it climbs up the plateau, the road comes to an intersection.

Turn left over the railway line. After 3km/2mi, take D 3 on the left, and after another 3km/2mi, turn left again.

Roc de Peyre – *15min on foot there and back.*
From the summit (1 179m/3 867ft, *viewing table*) of the rock, accessed by a path and a flight of steps, there is a remarkable panorama of the Aubrac, the Plomb du Cantal, the Margeride, Mont Lozère, the Aigoual and the Causses.
It is difficult to imagine, and no trace remains to suggest, that a fortress once occupied this rocky pinnacle of exceptional strategic interest. Nonetheless, no fewer than 2 500 cannon balls were needed by Admiral Joyeuse to destroy the keep of this Protestant fief in 1586. Time then took care of the rest.

Turn back and follow D 53 then D 3, keeping left all the way. After crossing Moulinet bridge, at the bottom of the Crueize valley, where the Lac du Moulinet has been equipped as an outdoor leisure centre, turn left onto N 9 then right onto D 73. After 5km/3mi, take the turnoff to Château de la Baume.

Château de la Baume ⊘ – The rugged appearance of this 17C residence, made of granite and covered with rough slates, is softened by a shady park which is quite an unexpected sight in the middle of the surrounding plateaux. Inside,

Wolves in the Gévaudan

admire the main staircase with its Louis XIV balusters. The great hall has a beautiful parquet floor with different coloured timbers forming a geometric pattern around coats of arms. The study is decorated with painted wood panelling in pastel tones. Large paintings depicting mythological scenes complete the decoration.

Return to Le Moulinet bridge and take N 9 to the right, then a little road on the left towards Ste-Lucie, then turn right immediately into a road going uphill (past a chapel).

★ **Parc à loups du Gévaudan** ⊘ – This 4ha/10 acre **wild animal reserve** is home to about a hundred wolves from Europe, Canada and Mongolia, some of which were born in Ste-Lucie. A film shot in the park, with a commentary by J.-P. Chabrol and G. Ménatory, can be viewed on request. A viewing table along the 30min walk provides an attractive vista.

In summer, it is best to take a guided tour since the wolves are less visible than in autumn or winter.

N 9 leads back to Marvejols.

The Practical Information section at the end of the guide lists:
  – information on travel, motoring, accommodation, recreation,
  – local or national organisations providing additional information,
  – calendar of events,
  – admission times and charges for the sights described in the guide.

Grotte du MAS-D'AZIL ★★

Michelin map 86 fold 4 or 235 fold 42

This cave is one of the most interesting natural sights in the Ariège. It is also a famous prehistoric milestone to the scientific world as it is here that the Azilian culture was studied and defined.

In 1887, as a result of methodical excavations, Édouard Piette discovered a new layer of evidence of human habitation dating from between the end of the Magdalenian (30 000 BC) period and the beginning of the Neolithic – this was the Azilian period (9 500 BC). Research continued under Abbé Breuil and Joseph Mandement, and others such as Boule and Cartailhac. The items excavated, representing thousands of years of prehistory (the cave was inhabited before the Magdalenian period), are exhibited in the cave and the town of Mas-d'Azil.

Cave ⊘ – The cave, hollowed out by the Arize underneath one of the Plantaurel mountain ranges, is 420m/1 378ft long with an average width of 50m/160ft. Upstream, the entrance forms a magnificent archway (65m/ 213ft high), while downstream, a flattened opening (8m/25ft or so) pierces a sheer rock

140m/460ft high. The path follows this passageway alongside a torrent, whose waters are gradually eroding the limestone walls, then under a majestic vault, shored up in the centre by an enormous pillar of rock.

Originally, the Arize went around the mountain before eventually going through it. The line of the original valley, now dry, is clearly visible where it threw a meander to the east level with the village of Rieubach.

Prehistoric collections – The 4 floors of excavated galleries run for 2km/1mi through limestone which is sufficiently homogeneous to prevent infiltration and propagation of moisture. The tour includes the Salle du Temple, a Protestant place of refuge, the intermediate floor of which was destroyed under Richelieu after the fruitless siege of 1625. Display cases contain exhibits dating from the Magdalenian (scrapers, chisels, needles, a moulding of the famous neighing horse head) and Azilian periods (harpoons made from antlers – the reindeer moved northwards as the climate became warmer – arrowheads, coloured pebbles, miniaturized tools).

The Mandement room contains the remains of animals (mainly mammoth and bear), coated in rubble and doubtless reduced to a heap of bones by subterranean flooding (the Arize, which was ten times the volume that it is today, made the water level reach the roof).

René Delon/CASTELET

Carving of fawn
with birds

Musée de la Préhistoire ⊙ – This prehistory museum contains collections from the Magdalenian period, particularly the famous carving of a fawn with birds *(Faon aux oiseaux)*.

Le MAS SOUBEYRAN★

Michelin map 80 fold 17 or 240 fold 15 – 8km/5mi north of Anduze

Le Mas Soubeyran overlooks the river Gardon. A few houses, huddled close together, stand on the small plateau surrounded by mountains. The countryside is bleak and rugged. The hamlet, with its Musée du Désert, is a Protestant Mecca. It will also interest any tourists with a love of history.

This little place is redolent with the history of the Protestant struggle, particularly in the Cévennes, from the time of the revocation of the Edict of Nantes (1685) to the Edict of Tolerance (1787).

Beneath the oak and chestnut trees near the museum, an annual "general assembly" is held in early September which attracts 10 000 to 20 000 Protestants.

Revocation of the Edict of Nantes – The peace treaty of Alès allowed Protestants to practise their religion freely. But in 1661, Louis XIV mounted a vigorous campaign against the Reformed Church. Every possible means was used to convert its members to Roman Catholicism. One of the toughest was *la dragonnade* or "dragooning" – dragoons were billetted in Protestant communities with licence to act as if they were on conquered territory.

Historical Protestant sites in Languedoc

The **Cévennes massif** is one of the main sites of the Huguenots' epic struggle, in particular the rebellion of the Camisards. The latter used the **Grotte des Demoiselles** near Ganges as a refuge. The **Mas Soubeyran**, which became a symbol of their combat, is home to the Musée du Désert. **St-Jean-du-Gard** was one of the centres of the battle against Roman Catholic power in the early 18C (Musée des Vallées Cévenoles). In **St-Hippolyte-du-Fort**, where resistance to royal troops was strong, the Roure-Sarrau library contains a large collection of Protestant books. The Musée cévenol in **Le Vigan** testifies to the Protestant faith in the Cévennes. **Alès** is where Louis XIII granted a peace treaty to the Huguenots in 1629.

Other Protestant sites in Languedoc include: the **Château de Ferrières**, which houses the Musée du Protestantisme du Haut-Languedoc; **Montpellier**, home to the Institut Protestant de Théologie; **Nîmes**, Languedoc's Protestant metropolis where the Huguenot cross was invented; and **Aigues-Mortes** with its sinister Tour de Constance, the tower in which Protestant prisoners including Marie Durand were locked up (her house is now also a museum and can be visited at Bouchet de Pransles in the Ardèche).

Le MAS SOUBEYRAN

In 1685, on the tendentious reports of the administrators, the royal court was persuaded wrongly to believe that only a handful of "heretics" remained. The Revocation of the Edict of Nantes was pronounced – Protestantism was forbidden, Protestant churches demolished and their ministers driven out of the kingdom.

These measures were greeted immediately by mass emigration, and the huge numbers involved showed that the number of Protestants who had resisted conversion had

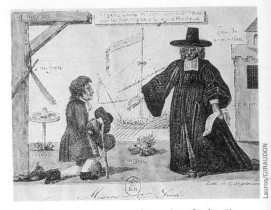

Engelmann engraving – Conversion of a heretic

been grossly underestimated. Draconian punishments were imposed to try to stop the exodus, but 300 000 to 500 000 Protestants succeeded in fleeing France, depriving agriculture, trade, industry, science and the arts of some excellent resources.

The Camisard Uprising – Dragooning was stepped up; people were thrown into prison or flogged, and children were taken from their parents. The ministers and their followers therefore sought secluded spots in the mountains for their meetings. The name "Désert" (or wilderness), adopted to designate these places, can thus be interpreted in both the literal and the figurative sense.

In July 1702, Abbot Chayla, in charge of operations in the Cévennes, arrested a small group of fugitives and locked them up in the Château du Pont-de-Montvert which he was using as a presbytery. Fifty or so peasants undertook to release the prisoners, but during the operation the abbot was killed. This sparked off general insurrection which was to last two years. The mountain dwellers, who were known as the "Camisards" (from the Languedoc *camiso* or "shirt", which Protestants wore over their clothes to identify themselves at night), set off to wage war armed with their pitchforks and scythes, but procured more sophisticated weapons for themselves by pillaging castles or taking their opponents' arms. They knew the countryside, which lent itself admirably to guerilla-type warfare, like the back of their hands, and were aided and abetted in secret by local people who kept them informed.

Cavalier and Roland – The Camisard leaders were peasants and craftsmen, fervent believers who were generally regarded almost as visionaries. The two most famous were Cavalier and Roland.

The Camisard rebels numbered no more than between 3 000 and 5 000 altogether, but it took no fewer than 30 000 men and three marshals to stamp them out. One of the marshals, Villars, was cunning enough to strike up negotiations with Cavalier and finally persuaded him to surrender. The Camisard leader was appointed colonel with a pension of 1 200 *livres*. He was allowed to form a Camisard regiment to go off and fight in Spain. Accused of treason by his companions, Cavalier went into service in England and eventually became governor of Jersey.

Roland continued the fight for the Camisard cause, but was betrayed and shot in 1704. This brought the Camisard resistance to an end.

Persecution continued, with one or two respites, until 1787 when Louis XVI signed the Edict of Tolerance. Protestants were now allowed to practise a trade, marry legally and register the birth of their children. In 1789, this "tolerance" was upgraded to full freedom of conscience.

★ MUSÉE DU DÉSERT ⊘ *allow 1hr*

The tour of the museum concentrates mainly on the Maison de Roland and the Mémorial. Illustrations of the Reformation and a video are on show in two reception rooms.

Maison de Roland – Roland's house is the same as it was in the 17C and 18C. Note the "jeu de l'Oye" (a type of snakes and ladders) designed to teach Roman Catholic principles to young Huguenots imprisoned in convents.

Various documents, declarations, orders, edicts, old maps and paintings retrace the period preceding the persecutions, the struggle of the Camisards, the restoration of Protestantism and the triumph of the ideology of tolerance.

In the kitchen is the bible owned by the Camisard leader and the hiding-place he used when the dragoons arrived. Roland's bedroom still contains its original furniture.

One room recalls the clandestine "Désert" religious meetings organised by the Protestants in remote ravines; exhibits include a Désert pulpit which could be turned into a grain barrel. The Bible room contains numerous 18C Bibles, a remarkable series of psalters and paintings by Jeanne Lombard.

Mémorial – Two rooms have been given over to the memory of the "Désert Martyrs" – executed ministers and preachers, refugees, galley slaves and prisoners. The display cases contain Huguenot crosses and an interesting collection of collapsible communion chalices.

The Salle des Galériens commemorates the suffering of the 2 500 Protestants condemned to the galleys. It also contains models of galleys and paintings by Labouchère and Max Leenhardt.

The tour ends in a reconstruction of the interior of a Cévenol home, in which the family is gathered together to listen to Bible readings, and with a memorial to the prisoners of the Tour de Constance in Aigues-Mortes.

An esplanade at the village entrance offers an attractive view of the Gardon.

Painting of a "Désert" religious meeting by Max Leenhardt

For a quiet place to stay.

*Consult the annual **Michelin Red Guide France** (hotels and restaurants) and the **Michelin Guide Camping Caravaning France** which offer a choice of pleasant hotels and quiet camp sites in convenient locations.*

MENDE★

Population 11 286
Michelin map 80 folds 5 and 6 or 240 fold 2
Local maps see Les GRANDS CAUSSES and Mont LOZÈRE

Mende, the capital of the least populated of all French *départements*, the Lozère (population 78 000), is a large rural market town dominated by an imposing cathedral inside a circle of boulevards. Its narrow winding streets are lined with lovely old houses with, here and there, a beautiful timber door, a portal or oratories. Mende's administrative, educational and commercial roles have stimulated a certain degree of development in recent years.

HISTORICAL NOTES

Beautiful mansions already graced the north bank of the Lot as early as Roman times.

In the 3C, St Privat, who converted the Gévaudan, sought refuge from the Barbarians in a cave on Mont Mimat. He was captured and killed however. The cave he had lived in and the crypt where he was buried became very popular centres of pilgrimage, around which the town developed over the centuries.

MENDE

During the Wars of Religion, a particularly gruesome episode in the history of Mende occurred when Captain **Merle**, a fanatical Protestant, attacked the town on Christmas Eve in 1579, while all the inhabitants, including those defending the town, were in church celebrating Christ's birth. A few months later, the Roman Catholics, seeking to reclaim their home town, laid siege to Mende, but Captain Merle, something of an expert at nocturnal attacks, had them all cut to pieces during their sleep. Merle was not without enemies in his own camp, however, and another Protestant leader, Châtillon, took advantage of Merle's absence to seize Mende. Merle managed to recapture the town nonetheless and was appointed Governor of it by the future Henri IV.

★ CATHEDRAL

Several churches predated the present cathedral, most of which was built in the 14C under Pope Urban V. The belfries date from the 16C. When Captain Merle seized Mende in 1579, he had the cathedral pillars blown up, leaving only the belfries, the north side walls and the apsidal chapels. The cathedral was restored in the early 17C.

Exterior – The west façade, in front of which is a porch built in 1900 in the Flamboyant style, is framed by two belfries. That on the left, the "Clocher de l'Évêque" ("Bishop's Belfry"), has a fine colonnade at the top which seems to have been inspired by the Italian Renaissance and contrasts strongly with the sobreness of the belfry on the right, known as the "Clocher des Chanoines" ("Canons' Belfry").

Interior – Side doorways lead into the cathedral which has three naves flanked by fifteen side chapels.
The remains of the rood screen currently adorn the baptismal chapel *(2nd side chapel to the north)*. The woodwork of the upper and lower chancel stalls, on either side of the bishop's throne, date from the same period (1692). They depict themes from religious history and various scenes from the life of Christ.
Above the tall stained glass windows in the chancel, eight Aubusson tapestries (1708) illustrate the main scenes from the life of the Virgin Mary.
On either side of the high altar stand large candelabra in carved wood dating from the 16C. The Lady Chapel *(by the sacristy)*, dedicated to Our Lady of Mende, houses the 11C carved Black Virgin which the Crusaders are said to have brought back from the Orient where Mont Carmel monks are reputed to have carved it out of very hard wood.
Mende cathedral once had the largest bell in Christianity, the "Non Pareille" ("Unequalled"), weighing 20 tonnes. Broken by Merle's men in 1579, all that remains is the enormous clapper, 2.15m/7ft long, which is to be found under the 17C organ, next to the door of the Bishop's Belfry.
Under the nave are the tomb and crypt of St Privat *(light switch on the left as you go down)*.

MENDE

Angiran (R.)	4
Beurre (Pl. au)	5
Droite (R.)	15
Estoup (Pl. René)	22
République (Pl. et R.)	30
Soubeyran (R. du)	34
Aigues-Passes (R. d')	2
Ange (R. de l')	3
Blé (Pl. au)	6
Britexte (Bd)	7
Capucins (Bd des)	8
Carmes (R. des)	9
Chanteronne (Rue de)	12
Chaptal (Rue)	13
Chastel (Rue du)	14
Collège (R. du)	18
Écoles (R. des)	20
Épine (R. de l')	21
Gaulle (Pl. Ch. de)	23
Montbel (R. du Fg)	24
Piencourt (Allée)	25
Planche (Pont de la)	26
Pont N.-Dame (R. du)	27
Roussel (Pl. Th.)	32
Soubeyran (Bd du)	33
Soupirs (Allée des)	36
Urbain-V (Place)	37

B   Coopérative des artisans de Lozère
D   Tour des Pénitents
M   Musée Ignon-Fabre

A. Kurnurdjian

Pont Notre-Dame

ADDITIONAL SIGHTS

★**Pont Notre-Dame** – This very narrow bridge, built in the 13C, has always managed to withstand the heavy flooding of the Lot, because of the width of its main arch.

Musée Ignon Fabre ⊘ (**M**) – *3, rue de l'Épine*. The museum, housed in a 17C mansion with a beautiful main door and staircase, is devoted to geology, paleontology, prehistory, archeology and Lozère folklore. Note the Gallo-Roman ceramics from Banassac.

➤➤ **Coopérative des artisans de Lozère** ⊘ (**B**) – Craft workshops.

➤➤ **Tour des Pénitents** (**D**) – Remaining tower from the 12C fortified town wall.

The length of time given in this guide
  *– for **touring** allows time to enjoy the views and the scenery*
  *– for **sightseeing** is the average time required for a visit.*

MILLAU★

Population 21 788
Michelin map 80 fold 14 or 240 fold 14
Local maps see Vallée de la DOURBIE and Les GRANDS CAUSSES

This bustling town in a fertile green valley at the confluence of the Tarn and Dourbie is an excellent departure point for excursions, particularly for the Causses and the Tarn gorges. Nearby, the slopes of the Borie Blanque and the Brunas and Andan peaks are very popular for paragliding and hanggliding.
From the N 9, which climbs up the Causse du Larzac *(lookout point – reached via ③ on town plan)* there is a lovely view of Millau's picturesque **setting★**.

HISTORICAL NOTES

The Graufesenque potteries – During the 1C AD Condatomagus ("the market where the rivers meet"), the predecessor to Millau, was one of the main centres for the making of earthenware in the Roman empire.
Excavations carried out since 1950 in the small Graufesenque plain at the confluence of the Tarn and the Dourbie have brought to light a lot of data on this activity and on the lives of the potters themselves.
The site offered all the resources necessary for **earthenware** making – fine quality clay, a plentiful water supply and enormous reserves of wood from the forests on the Causses. The remains of a Celtic sanctuary dedicated to the worship of water have been found which give every reason to believe that the area was considered to be "blessed by the gods".

J.-P. Séguret/Musée du Millau

Terra sigillata ware from Graufesenque

The techniques used for making earthenware were imported by the Romans and involved the methods of moulding, firing and stamping with decorative designs or potter's marks used in the production of *terra sigillata* ware, bright red pottery covered with a glaze. Some of the ware was thrown on a wheel and had a smooth surface, but on the whole it was cast in a mould and decorated with floral, geometric or historiated patterns of Hellenistic influence. The designs, in relief, had themselves been cast in moulds stamped with the required pattern. Production of *terra sigillata* ware was on a mass scale: more than 500 potters made millions of pieces which were then exported throughout Europe, the Middle East and even India.

The potters' workshops covered about 15ha/36 acres at the confluence of the two rivers. The Graufesenque archeological site is open to the public, and a large collection of earthenware is on display at the Musée de Millau.

A glove-making town – In this part of the Causses, where the traditional ewes' milk cheese-making industry is sufficiently provided for only at the expense of the lambs, it was natural that a leather industry should develop. Very early on, Millau became a centre of manufacture for lambskin gloves.

The industry was already active as early as the 12C. Every year craftsmen made a free gift of gloves to the town's councillors, who never appeared with bare hands on ceremonial occasions. The fact that gloves had been worn by all present was even written into the opening lines of official reports! However, the revocation of the Edict of Nantes and the subsequent Protestant emigration threw the glove industry into disarray, and it did not really take off again until the 19C.

The glove-making process comprises three phases: tawing or softening the lambskin, dyeing it and then making it into the actual glove. Before completion, a glove changes hands about 70 times. Glacé-kid and suede gloves, washable tanned and lined sports gloves, protective gloves – Millau produces about 250 000 pairs of gloves a year which are exported all over the world.

After the war, when wearing gloves went out of fashion, other market outlets had to be found. The leather dressing factories of Millau, which tan and dye lamb and sheepskins, now direct their production towards the manufacture of clothing (particularly haute couture), glove-making, shoe-making, leather goods and furnishing. Nowadays, Millau has diversified into activities such as printing, electronics, construction and civil engineering, lingerie, in order to boost its economy.

SIGHTS

Place du Maréchal-Foch (13) – This is the most picturesque part of the old town, with its covered square embellished with arcades (12C-16C) supported on cylindrical columns. The quadrangular stone still visible was once part of the stocks *(between the 2nd and 3rd column from the north)*, and the capital of the column next to it to the north bears the inscription (very faint) *"Gara qué faras"* or "Watch what you are doing".

Musée de Millau ⊘ – Housed in the 18C Hôtel de Pégayrolles, the museum houses displays on local paleontology, archeology and mineralogy, and on the Millau leather and glove-making industry.

The paleontology section includes numerous fossils of flora and fauna from secondary marine sediments and the almost complete skeleton of a plesiosaurus from Tournemire, a 4m/13ft long 180 million year old marine reptile...

The museum's vaulted cellars house a remarkable, extremely well-presented collection of Gallo-Roman **earthenware**, found at Graufesenque – both smooth and decorated vases from every period of manufacture, moulds, potter's chisels and

MILLAU

Ayrolle (Bd de l')
Bonald (Bd de)
Capelle (R. de la) 6
Carnot (Bd S.) 7
Droite (R.)
Jaurès (Av. Jean)
Mandarous (Pl. du) 20

Belford (R. de) 2
Bompaire (Pl. F.) 3
Capelle (Bd de la) 5
Clausel-de-Coussergues (R.) ... 9
Commandeurs (R. des) 10
Fasguets (R. des) 12
Foch (Pl. du Mar.) 13
Fraternité (R. de la) 15
Jacobins (R. des) 17
Martyrs-de-la-
   Résistance (Pl. des) 22
Pasteur (R.) 23
Peyrollerie (R. de) 24
Peyssière (R.) 26
St-Antoine (Bd) 27
Sémard (Av. Pierre) 29
Voultre (R. du) 30

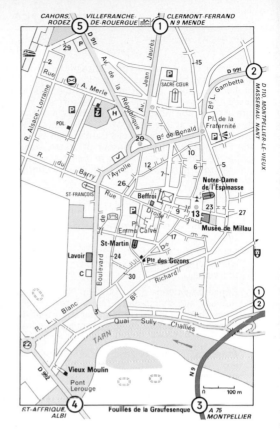

accounts books and a reconstructed kiln. In the mineralogy section, note the septarias – nodules of hardened marl with cracks in the centre which are filled with calcite, aragonite, pyrite or quartz crystals, boasting a palette of colours. There are also piles of vases which got stuck together during firing or were completely deformed. These "failures" were thrown into large pits. They have provided archeologists with a mine of information – the works of different artists were fired in the same kiln; pottery was easier to sell if standard shapes were used, etc.

The **Maison de la Peau et du Gant**, on the first floor, presents Millau's two traditional industries – tawing, by which a perishable, raw skin is converted into a high quality product which will not rot *(10min video)*, and glove-making. The exhibits include numerous tools, samples of leather and a presentation of the various stages in glove-making, from cutting out to the finishing touches.

Église Notre-Dame-de-l'Espinasse – This church once possessed a thorn from the Crown of Thorns, whence its name. An important centre of pilgrimage in the Middle Ages, the building, originally Romanesque, was partly destroyed in 1582 and rebuilt in 17C. The side chapels were added in the 18C and 19C. The frescoes which decorate the chancel (1939) are by Jean Bernard and the stained glass windows in the nave (1984) by Claude Baillon.

Belfry ⊙ **(Beffroi)** – In Rue Droite, a shopping street, this Gothic tower is all that is left of the old town hall. The square tower (12C), used as a prison in the 17C, is topped by an octagonal one (17C). Good view from Place Emma-Calvé.

► ► **Église St-Martin** (17C Flemish Descent from the Cross); **Porte des Gozons** (fortified gateway); **18C Washhouse** (Lavoir); **Old Mill** (Vieux moulin).

Fouilles de la Graufesenque ⊙ – *1km/0.6mi south of Millau. Leave on ③ on the town plan, then turn left after the bridge over the Tarn.* Covering a surface area of 2 500m/26 700ft, this archeological site contains the foundations of a Gallo-Roman potters' village with central street, canal, workshops, slaves' houses and enormous kilns used to fire up to 30 000 vases at a time.

The key on the inside front cover explains the abbreviations and symbols used in the text or on the maps.

MINERVE★

Population 104
Michelin map 83 fold 13 or 240 fold 25

Located on a *causse* at the confluence of the Cesse and the Briant, Minerve overlooks arid countryside crisscrossed by rugged gorges. The area has been inhabited since prehistoric times, as the numerous dolmens and caves discovered thereabouts testify. In the Middle Ages, a proud fortress which stood atop this spur was the site of one of the most dramatic episodes in the Albigensian Crusade. In 1210 Simon de Montfort, at the head of 7 000 men, took his stand at the gates of this stronghold in which numerous Cathars had taken cover. After five weeks of siege, the townspeople, having run out of water, were forced to capitulate. They were given the choice of converting or being slaughtered. 180 "Parfaits" nonetheless refused to deny their Cathar faith (commemorative stele by J-L Séverac on Place de la Mairie).

TOUR *allow 1hr 30min*

There are several car parks around Minerve (access to town for residents only).

Climb up to the narrow, picturesque Rue des Martyrs, lined with several craft workshops (Maison des Templiers: 13C door). It leads to the church and museums.

Église St-Étienne ⊘ – Built in the 11C and 12C, this recently restored Romanesque church has a few interesting original features. On the high altar table, there is an inscription indicating that it was consecrated by St Rustique, Bishop of Narbonne, in 456. About a hundred 5C-9C graffiti can be made out on it.

Museum ⊘ – Mainly devoted to prehistory and archeology up until the Roman and Visigoth invasions, the museum contains a moulding of human footprints discovered in 1948 in the clay of the **Grotte d'Aldène** *(see Excursions below)*. The footprints are thought to date from the Upper Paleolithic (from the Aurignacian period about 15 000 years ago). The first floor houses paleontological collections – a number of fossils found in the Cesse valley.

Musée Hurepel ⊘ – Dioramas of the main episodes in the Albigensian Crusade.

Go back down Rue des Martyrs and turn left into a narrow alley, paved with rough stones, leading down to the ramparts.

Parts of the double curtain wall which protected Minerve in the 12C still remain, including the southern postern with its pointed archway.

Follow the path to the left along the lower edge of the village.

Puits St-Rustique – Connected to the ramparts by a covered path (two ruined sections of wall still visible), this well was used to supply water to the townspeople during the siege of 1210. Simon de Montfort destroyed it with a powerful catapult from the other side of the river, forcing Minerve to capitulate.

Vallée du Briant – A narrow path skirts the village, following the steep-sided, narrow valley of the Briant. It comes up under the ruins of the octagonal keep called the **"Candela"**, all that remains of the fortress.

Natural bridges (Ponts naturels) – *Take D 147 southwest of the village.*
The road affords some attractive views of some natural bridges, which were formed at the beginning of the Quaternary Era when the Cesse abandoned the two meanders it once formed before flowing into the Briant, to attack the limestone cliff. As it forced its way through the many cracks in the wall, enlarging them gradually as it went, two tunnels were formed: the first, the **Grand Pont** spanning the river, 250m/820ft long ending in an opening about 30m/100ft high; and upstream, the **Petit Pont**, about 15m/50ft high, through which the Cesse flows for some 110m/360ft.
During droughts, it is possible to walk along the river bed.

★THE HAUT-MINERVOIS
Round tour of 35km/22mi. Take D 10^{E1} west towards Fauzan.

The road follows the narrow, steep-sided meanders of the Cesse.

Canyon de la Cesse – At the beginning of the Quaternary Era, the waters of the Cesse hollowed out a canyon, enlarging existing caves and making new ones. Upstream of Minerve, the valley gets narrower and the water, leaving the impermeable rock of the Primary Era, runs for 20km/12mi underground, only flowing along its bed at ground level during heavy storms in winter.

P. Cartier/CAMPAGNE CAMPAGNE

Minerve

Turn left onto the road to Cesseras which leads down to the plain and vineyards. Go through Cesseras and turn right onto D 168 to Siran. After 2km/1mi, turn right again.

Chapelle de St-Germain – This Romanesque chapel, nestling in a grove of pine trees, is particularly interesting for the decoration of its apse.

Return to D 168 and carry on to Siran.

After a little less than 1km/0.6mi, a hill with pine trees growing on it comes into view on the left. Stop the car after the bridge which crosses a track and take the footpath up to the top of the hill where there is an interesting **dolmen** of the covered alleyway type, called **Mourel des Fades** ("fairies' dolmen").

★ **Chapelle de Centeilles** ⊘ – *North of Siran*. Surrounded by cypress trees, holm-oaks and vines, this 13C chapel, located on the border between the Causse de Minerve and the plain, encompasses a vast panorama of vineyards, La Livinière with the unusual domed bell-tower of its basilica and, on a clear day, the Pyrenees in the distance.

Inside, beautiful 14C and early 15C **frescoes**★ depict the Tree of Jesse, St Michael and St Bruno. The transept contains a 3C Roman mosaic excavated at Siran. Around the chapel can be seen several dry stone hut constructions known locally as *capitelles*.

Return to the village of Siran and, after the water tower, take a small road on the left which skirts the St-Martin peak and rejoins D 182 to the north, overlooking the Cesse gorge. Turn right towards Minerve. Just after the hamlet of Fauzan, take a small road to the left.

After 1.5km/1mi, next to a disused factory, a vast flat stretch of land gives a view of the Cesse gorge and the **caves** which pepper the cliff face. It is in one of these caves – **Aldène** – that the human footprints from the Paleolithic were discovered *(see Musée de Minerve above)*. A small path between two rocks leads to the **Grotte de Fauzan** in which traces of prehistoric footprints were also found.

Return to Minerve along the Cesse canyon.

MIREPOIX

Population 2 993
Michelin map 86 fold 5 or 235 fold 43

The name of this ancient walled town, founded in 1279, has been linked with that of the Lévis family ever since the Albigensian Crusade. The Lévis-Mirepoix branch dates back to Guy I de Lévis, a lieutenant under Simon de Montfort who was promoted to "Marshal of the Faith".

★★ **Place Principale (Place Général-Leclerc)** – The main square is surrounded by late 13-15C houses, in which the first floor juts out over timber "**couverts**", or covered arcades. With the public gardens, olde-worlde shops and cafes, the square is a pleasant place to spend some time, particularly in the evening.
At the northwest and northeast corners, note the typical fitting together of the "valleys" where the *couverts* meet; only the smallest crack is left in the covering over the arcades below.

Cathedral – The layout of the building gives no inkling of the long drawn-out construction that went into it. Although the cathedral was begun in 1343, the ribbed vaulting was not added until 1865. The elegant Gothic spire was started in 1506, the same year as the cathedral was consecrated.

Enter through the north door.

The nave (early 16C) is the widest (31.60m/104ft) of any built for a French Gothic church. It is flanked with chapels set between the interior buttresses, following Gothic tradition in the south of France.

Mirepoix covered arcades

EXCURSION

Camon - *8km/5mi southeast, on D 625, then D 7.*
Leaving the imposing ruins of the Château de Lagarde on its left, the road enters the Hers valley. The little village of Camon, tucked close around its imposing abbey, comes into view against a backdrop of the Ariège hills.
Having visited the fortifications, enter the village through the Porte de l'Horloge (note the handsome half-timbered corner house) to see the conventual buildings renovated by Philippe de Lévis, Bishop of Mirepoix, in the 16C. There are the remains of the old cloisters, the fine spiral staircase inside the round tower and the oratory decorated with 14C mural paintings.

The church, which used to be the abbey church, houses a 17C altarpiece by the Spanish School and a 14C Crucifix.

MOISSAC★★

Population 11 971
Michelin maps 79 folds 16 and 17 or 235 folds 17 and 21

The town of Moissac lies clustered around the ancient abbey of St-Pierre, in a fresh and pretty setting on the north bank of the Tarn and either side of the Garonne branch canal. The surrounding hillsides are covered with orchards and vineyards which produce the reputed Chasselas grape variety (a white grape). This site of major interest for lovers of Romanesque art is home to the **Centre Marcel Durliat** ⊙ **(B)**, open to academics and the general public alike, offering illustrated documentation on the art of medieval illumination in southern Europe and a library specialising in the art of the Middle Ages.
In 1991 a marina was opened on the banks of the Tarn.

Golden Chasselas - The slopes of Bas-Quercy which line the north bank of the Tarn and the Garonne, between Montauban and Moissac, produce an annual yield of more than 18 000 tonnes of top quality Golden Chasselas grapes. The authentic "Moissac" variety comes in nice long bunches, with round, well-formed grapes, of a slightly translucent pale golden colour. The grapes are very sweet and fragrant and are reputed for their particularly delicate flavour. At the far end of Promenade du Moulin, a grapery sells fresh grape juice from late September to early October.

HISTORICAL NOTES

The golden age of the abbey - It was during the 11C and 12C that Moissac abbey was at its most influential. Probably founded in the 7C by a Benedictine monk from the Norman abbey of St-Wandrille, the young abbey of Moissac did not escape from the pillage and destruction wrought by Arabs, Norsemen and Hungarians.
It was struggling to right itself again when, in 1047, an event occurred which was to change its destiny. On his way through Quercy, St Odilon, the famous and influential abbot of Cluny, who had just laid down the rules at the monastery at Carennac, affiliated the abbey of Moissac to that of Cluny. This marked the beginning of a period of prosperity. With the support of Cluny, Moissac abbey set up priories throughout the region, extending its influence as far as Catalonia.

A series of misfortunes - The Hundred Years War, during which Moissac was occupied twice by the English, and then the Wars of Religion dealt the abbey some fearsome blows. It was secularised in 1628 and then suppressed altogether during the Revolution. In 1793, during the Reign of Terror, the archives were dispersed, the art treasures pillaged and numerous sculptures disfigured. In the middle of the 19C, it narrowly escaped complete destruction when there was question of demolishing the monastery buildings and cloisters to make way for the railway line from Bordeaux to Sète. The intervention of the Beaux-Arts commission saved it from ruin.

ABBEY *1hr*

★ **Église St-Pierre** - This used to be the abbey church. All that remains of the original 11C building is the belfry porch, which was fortified c 1180 with the addition of a watchpath, a crenellated parapet, loopholes and a machicolated gallery.
From the outside, the two very different periods from which the nave dates are clear to be seen - one part, in stone, is Romanesque, while the other, in brick, is Gothic. The Romanesque part is to be found at the base of the walls of the nave and in the round-arched windows in the lower part of the walls. The rest of the nave was built in 15C in the southern French Gothic style.

★★★ **South portal** – The tympanum above this doorway, executed c 1130, ranks as one of the finest examples of Romanesque sculpture in France. It is majestic in its composition, depicting a wide range of scenes and maintaining harmonious proportions between the various figures portrayed. The odd slightly awkward gesture or rigid posture in no way mars the overall beauty of this immensely moving work.

The theme of the tympanum is the Vision of the Apocalypse according to St John the Evangelist. Enthroned at the centre of the composition, Christ (**1**) dominates the other figures: wearing a crown and with a halo around his head, he holds the Book of Life in his left hand and is raising his right hand in benediction. Strongly defined features, penetrat-

The prophet Jeremiah on the doorway of the abbey church

Carcanague/IMAGES PHOTOTHÈQUE

ing eyes, and the neat arrangement of beard and hair in symmetrical curls all add to the intensity of his expression and accentuate the power and majesty which emanate from his figure.

Christ is surrounded by the symbols of the four Evangelists: St Matthew is represented by a young winged man (**2**), St Mark by a lion (**3**), St Luke by a bull (**4**) and St John by an eagle (**5**). Two abnormally tall, but nonetheless elegant seraphim (**6**) frame this magnificent scene. The rest of the tympanum is occupied by the four-and-twenty Elders of the Apocalypse (**7**), arranged in three tiers, but each depicted in an individual pose. Their faces, turned towards Christ, express amazement at the majesty of the sight. The effect of the scene on the onlooker is unusually intense, as the composition centres entirely around the main figure, who is the object of all the other figures' gazes. The beauty and elegance of form, the perfection of contour and drapery, the precision of detail and the facial expressions are remarkable.

The tympanum is supported by a remarkable lintel (**8**) decorated with eight rosettes framed in a cable moulding coming out of the mouth of a monster at either end.

The central pier (**9**), vigorous in style, is a magnificent monolithic block decorated with three pairs of rampant lions, each pair forming an X one above the other. Finally, there are two strikingly longilinear figures carved on either side of the pier: St Paul, on the left, and Jeremiah, on the right (**10**). The engaged doorposts depict St Peter (**11**), patron saint of the abbey, and the prophet Isaiah (**12**). The multifoiled doorposts and certain decorative motifs reflect Hispano-Moorish influence, which can be explained by the fact that Moissac was on the pilgrimage route to Santiago de Compostela.

The tympanum is framed by three arch mouldings (**13**) decorated with stylised foliage. On each side of the doorposts are historiated scenes carved on remnants of sarcophagi made of Pyrenean marble. On the right (**14**) are, from bottom to top, the Annunciation, the Visitation, the Adoration of the Magi, the Presentation of Jesus in the Temple and the Flight to Egypt, while the left (**15**) features scenes of Damnation: a miser and an adulteress being tortured by devils; toads and serpents; the evil rich man feasting while poor Lazarus

Moissac: south portal

lies dying of hunger, with an angel shown taking his soul to the breast of Abraham. The archivolt of the porch and the pilasters are finely decorated; on the columns flanking the portal are statues of the Abbot Roger, who was responsible for having the portal built, and a Benedictine monk.

Interior – The entrance is through the narthex, in which the four intersecting pointed ribs of the vault spring from eight sturdy engaged columns decorated with highly stylised capitals (11C and 12C). On entering the church itself, the most immediately striking aspect of the interior is the brightly coloured walls (yellow with red and blue). The nave still contains some of the original furnishings. In the second chapel on the right after entering the church, note an Our Lady of Pity from 1476 (**a**), and in the following chapel, a charming Flight into Egypt from the late 15C (**b**). There is a magnificent Romanesque **Crucifix★** (12C) (**c**) on the wall between this chapel and the next. The last chapel on the right contains an Entombment (**d**) from 1485. The chancel is enclosed by a 16C carved stone screen, behind which a Carolingian apse has recently been uncovered *(not open to the public)*. The choir stalls (**e**) date from the 17C. In an alcove beneath the organ, stands a white Pyrenean marble Merovingian sarcophagus (**f**).

★★ **Cloisters** ⊙ (**D**) – Entrance through the tourist office.

These beautiful cloisters (late 11C) have remarkably delicate arcades with slender columns, alternatively single and paired, in harmonious tones of marble – white, pink, green and grey – and a rich wealth of sculpted decoration. The four galleries, with timber roof vaults sloping down into the cloister garth, are supported by 76 arcades reinforced by piers at the corners and in the middle of each side. These piers, clad in blocks of marble taken from old sarcophagi, are decorated

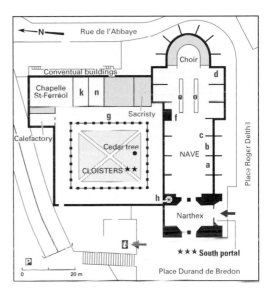

with low reliefs, including nine effigies of the Apostles and, on the pier in the middle of the east gallery (the gallery opposite the entrance), that of Abbot Durant de Bredon (**g**), Bishop of Toulouse and Abbot of Moissac, who played a decisive role in the abbey's development; his effigy, executed only fifteen years after his death, is so strikingly realistic that it is considered to be a true portrait. The decoration on the capitals includes a huge variety of motifs – animal, vegetal, geometric and historiated – all testifying to the skill of the artists who executed them. Scenes represented are taken from the Old and New Testaments and include episodes from the Life of Christ, his miracles and parables, scenes from the Apocalypse and the Life of the Saints honoured in the abbey.

A handsome cedar tree stands in the cloister garth. In the southwest corner, a staircase (**h**) leads to the first floor of the narthex in which a striking series of robust arches surrounds a ring-shaped keystone.

The conventual buildings open off the northeast corner of the cloisters and the east gallery. They include the calefactory, St-Ferréol chapel containing some 12C capitals, a room (**k**) in which a display of photographs illustrates the extent of Moissac's influence on sculpture in the Quercy region and leading off from this a room (**n**) housing religious art (gold and silver work, note the late 15C Virgin of Sorrow) and liturgical vestments.

ADDITIONAL SIGHTS

Musée Moissagais ⊙ (**M¹**) – The museum is housed in what used to be the abbot's lodgings, a large building flanked by a 13C crenellated brick tower, which was destroyed during the Revolution.

Just inside the entrance, two maps show the importance of the abbey during the Middle Ages and the spread of its influence throughout the whole of southwest France. The vast 17C stairwell is used to display items of religious historical interest.

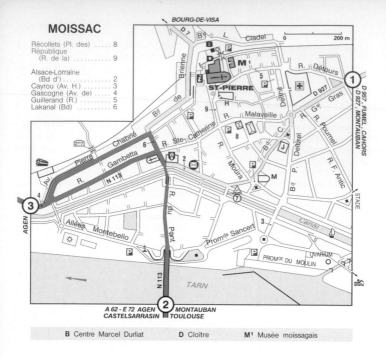

MOISSAC

Récollets (Pl. des) 8
République
(R. de la) 9

Alsace-Lorraine
(Bd d') 2
Cayrou (Av. H.) 3
Gascogne (Av. de) 4
Guillerand (R.) 5
Lakanal (Bd) 6

B Centre Marcel Durliat   **D** Cloître   **M¹** Musée moissagais

The various rooms contain collections on the history and traditions of the region – local ceramics (particularly from Auvillar), furniture, Moissac head-dresses, reconstruction of a 19C kitchen from the Bas Quercy region, various examples of local craftwork and costumes. From the top of the tower there is a broad view of the town, with its old districts clustered around the abbey, and the Tarn valley and Moissagais hills beyond.

►► **Boudou** – *7km/4.5mi west.* Village with **panorama★** of Garonne valley.

Michelin Maps (scale 1: 200 000), which are revised regularly, provide much useful motoring information.

*Keep current **Michelin Maps** in the car at all times.*

MONTAGNE NOIRE★

Michelin map 82 fold 20 and 83 folds 11 and 12 or 235 folds 35, 36 and 40

The Montagne Noire, or Black Mountain, forms the southwest tip of the Massif Central. It is separated from the Agout massif (Sidobre and the Lacaune and Espinouse ranges) by the furrow formed by the Thoré which is extended by the valleys of the Jaur and the upper Orb.

There is a strong contrast between its northern slope, which rises steeply above the Thoré, and its southern slope, which drops gently down to the Lauragais and Minervois plains, in sight of the Pyrenees. The steep northern slope culminates in the Pic de Nore (alt 1 210m/3 970ft).

This very diversified relief transforms the winds that arrive here: the west winds, laden with rain, become violent and dry when they reach the Bas Languedoc plain; the "marine" wind from the east, with a high moisture content, becomes the dry southerly wind *(autan)* bringing the thunderstorms of Haut Languedoc. This explains why rainfall (in the Montagne Noire is more than 1m/33in per year.

Vegetation – The northern slopes, where most rain falls, are covered with dark forests (oak, beech, fir, spruce), while the southern slopes are Mediterranean in appearance, rugged and with scant vegetation including a mixture of *garrigue*, gorse, sweet chestnut trees, vines and olive trees.

Way of life on the Montagne Noire – Only a relatively meagre income can be brought in by raising stock or growing crops here, and it has been many years since anyone earned a living weaving wool and hemp. The gold mines in Salsigne are still operational, and marble is mined at Caunes-Minervois, but the main industrial activity is concentrated in the Thoré valley, where it grew up under the impetus of Mazamet.

The Montagne Noire's greatest wealth nowadays lies in its abundant reserves of water and its beautiful countryside.

HARNESSED WATER

Round tour from Revel *114km/71mi – allow 5hr – see local map*

Revel – Revel lies on the edge of the Montagne Noire and the Lauragais region. It is the birthplace of **Vincent Auriol**, President of the French Republic from 1947 to 1954.

Designed as a *bastide*, it has a geometric street layout around a central square surrounded by covered arcades or *garlandes*. The 14C **covered market** still has its original timber roof and its belfry (renovated in the 19C). The manufacture of furniture, cabinet making, marquetry, bronze work, gold-plating and lacquer work are the town's main activities.

★ **Bassin de St-Ferréol** – This reservoir stretches for 70ha/173 acres between wooded hillsides; the retaining dam is 800m/about half a mile long. This magnificent lake is ideal for sailing and swimming, and its shores make a pleasant place for a stroll. Located on the side of the Montagne Noire towards the Atlantic ocean, it is the main supply reservoir for the Canal du Midi.

The St-Ferréol reservoir itself is fed by the Lampy reservoir and a supply channel from the Montagne Noire *(Rigole de la Montagne)*, formed by diverting water from the Alzeau.

The park here has a number of waterfalls and a water spray 20m/66ft high. The road runs alongside the Laudot through green and pleasant countryside.

After Les Cammazes, take the road on the left to the dam.

Cammazes Dam – The 90ha/220 acre reservoir retained by this 70m/230ft high arch dam is not one of the several that supply the Canal du Midi. It instead supplies 116 towns and villages with drinking water and irrigates the entire Lauragais plain east of Toulouse. Footpaths lead down to the edge of the Sor.

Return to D 629.

Saissac – The village sits above the Vernassonne ravine which is dominated by the ruins of a 14C castle. A small road, skirting the village to the north, offers an attractive view of this picturesque site.

To appreciate the panorama over a wider area, go up to the platform of the largest tower in the old curtain wall. The tower houses a **museum** ⊙ displaying various objects and tools evoking the history of Saissac and the traditional crafts practised there.

Take D 4 to the west of Saissac, then turn right onto D 324.

Bassin du Lampy – This 1 672 000m³/60 000 000ft³ reservoir on the Lampy flows into the Montagne Noire channel from the Alzeau offtake to the St-Ferréol reservoir. A pleasant footpath runs alongside the channel for 23km/14.5mi as far as the village of Les Cammazes.

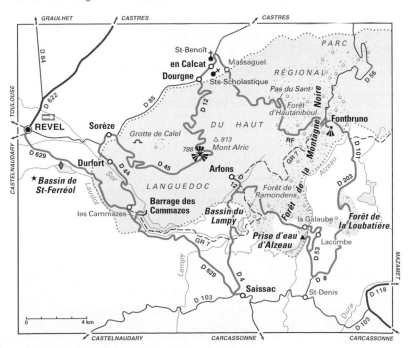

The reservoir was built from 1778 to 1782 to supply the Canal du Midi, after the Robine de Narbonne branch canal was opened. Magnificent beech groves, criss-crossed with shady paths, make the Bassin du Lampy a popular place for a walk.

Return to D 4.

Arfons – Once the property of the Knights Hospitaller of St John of Jerusalem or of Malta, Arfons is now a peaceful mountain village with slate-roofed houses. Surrounded by forests, it is the point of departure for a number of delightful walks *(GR 7 waymarked footpath)*.
On the corner of a house in the main street is a lovely 14C stone statue of the Virgin Mary.

Retrace your steps and after 1.5km/1mi, take the road to La Galaube on the left.

Forêt domaniale de la Montagne Noire – This 3 650ha/9 000 acre forest, consisting mainly of beech and fir trees, includes the Romondes and Hautaniboul forests. The road crosses the Alzeau at La Galaube in a lovely woodland setting.

After the bridge, continue to Lacombe, go through the village, take the direction St-Denis and, after 1.5km/1mi, turn right and follow the road to the Alzeau channel.

Prise d'eau d'Alzeau – A monument put up in memory of Pierre-Paul Riquet, who designed and built the Canal du Midi, retraces the various stages of construction of the canal. It marks the beginning of the Rigole de la Montagne, the channel which collects the waters of the Alzeau, the Vernassonne and the Lampy and takes them to the Laudot which then supplies the St-Ferréol reservoir.
The **Poste des Thommasses** *(south of Revel, on D 624)* catches the waters from St-Ferréol and the Sor, themselves diverted from Montcrouzet via a channel through Revel. The waters caught in this way are then sent on to the Seuil de Naurouze.

Return to D 53 and take it to the right towards St-Denis; then turn left onto D 8, then D 203.

Forêt de la Loubatière – The D 203 makes a particularly pleasant drive through the forest, winding through beech trees, the forest's predominant variety, as well as oak and fir.

Fontbruno – The war memorial to the Montagne Noire resistance forces stands here above a crypt. There is an attractive view of the plain.

Just past the monument, turn left into the forest of Hautaniboul.

The forest road comes to a pass, the **Pas du Sant**, at the intersection of three roads.

Take D 14 to the left, and after Massaguel turn left again onto D 85 to St-Ferréol.

En Calcat – Two Benedictine abbeys were established here by Father Romain Banquet on his personal estate. The **Monastère de St-Benoît**, for men only, was consecrated in 1896 and is still an active community. The artistic work carried out by the monks includes a workshop which produces cartoons for Dom Robert tapestries, which are then made in Aubusson, as well as crafts such as pottery, stained glass and zither-making.
A little further on the left, is the **Abbaye Ste-Scholastique** (founded in 1890), occupied by a contemplative order of nuns (weaving and binding workshops).

Carry on to Dourgne; in the village, take D 12 to the left towards Arfons.

Dourgne – The village makes its living quarrying slate and stone.

After 10km/6mi take the track on the right.

Mont Alric viewing table – Alt 788m/2 585ft. The view to the west stretches as far as the Revel plain, while the Pyrenees can be seen in the south. In the foreground, to the east, is Mont Alric (alt 813m/2 667ft).

Return to D 12, then take D 45 to the right.

Sorèze – The village developed in the 8C around an abbey, the only remains of which is the majestic 13C octagonal **bell-tower**.
The abbey's famous **college** ⊘, founded in the 17C by Benedictine monks, became a royal military school during the reign of Louis XVI. Bought back by the Dominicans in 1854, its first head was Father Lacordaire, who died there in 1861. The famous preacher is buried in the parish church in the village, and there is a statue of him, in white marble, in the front playground of the village school. Sorèze was selected as one of the centres for the Parc naturel régional du Haut Languedoc.

On leaving Sorèze, take the first road on the left which rejoins the D 44.

Durfort – At the threshold of the deeply incised Sor valley, Durfort has always been a centre of copper-smithing. Craftsmen continue this industry today, with copper-smiths working with the last tilt-hammer (15C) still in operation to produce various objects from copper. There is a **copper museum** ⊙ in one of the old copper-smith's houses.

The road narrows before entering the isolated gorge of the Sor. Between two steep valley sides, the Sor gushes along as a torrent.

The road rejoins D 629 offering attractive glimpses of the gorge, before returning to Revel.

★ **Round tour from Mazamet** *105km/66mi – allow 5hr – local map below*

The itinerary described below gives a good idea of the variety of relief of the Montagne Noire with its steep northern slopes, forest-covered crests and southern slopes, the **Cabardès**, criss-crossed by rivers scarcely visible at the bottom of deep gorges in which Mediterranean flora grows.

Mazamet – In the 5C, the Visigoths built **Hautpoul** clinging to a hilltop site to protect it from would-be attackers. Nonetheless, Simon de Montfort managed to storm the stronghold in 1212 and the Wars of Religion finished off what he left standing. In the valley below, the textile industry expanded, thanks to the supply of pure water from the Arnette ideal for washing wool. With the advent of machinery, the river was harnessed to provide the necessary power to drive it. The inhabitants of Hautpoul were thus persuaded to abandon their hilltop site to found Mazamet.

With the neighbouring plains producing valuable dyestuffs such as woad, madder and saffron, the nearby Montagne Noire specialising in sheep rearing and the Arnette and Thoré providing an abundant supply of water, it is hardly surprising that Mazamet had become a major centre for the wool industry by the 18C. In 1851, the company of Houlès Père et Fils et Cormouls imported sheepskins from Buenos Aires and stripped them of their wool. This opened up a new branch of the industry for obtaining "pulled wool": wool is loosened (with soft water or chemical products) and removed from sheeps' pelts (as opposed to wool obtained from fleeces sheared off living animals) and cleaned, then handed over to the textile industry for carding, combing, spinning and weaving; the sheepskins are sent to be dressed in the *mégisseries* or tawing workshops. Modern Mazamet is still a thriving centre for producing pulled wool and for dressing pelts, importing sheepskins mainly from Australia, South Africa and Argentina, and exporting wool to Italy and skins to Spain, Belgium, Italy and the USA.

In the town centre, the **Maison Fuzier** ⊙ houses a **museum on the Cathars**, retracing the history of Catharism and of the ruined castles which abound in this region. The museum also has an exhibition on the various types of local burial procedure dating back to earliest times.

Just northwest of Mazamet, in Aussillon-Plaine, there is the church of **Sacré-Cœur**, built in 1959 (lead statue of the Virgin and Child; sanctuary tapestry woven by Simone Prouvé; Dom Ephrem stained glass window in baptistery).

Leave Mazamet to the southwest, on D 118 signposted Carcassonne.

The road twists its way uphill in a series of hairpin bends. After 3km/2mi, stop at **Plo de la Bise** lookout point, from where there is a good view of the ruins of Hautpoul and the thriving town of Mazamet.

Continue along D 118 then turn right into a small road which leads to the Lac des Montagnés.

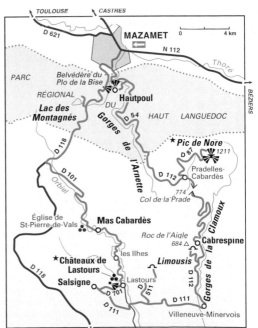

Châteaux de Lastours

Lac des Montagnés – Set against a backdrop of hills and woodland, this beautiful manmade lake, the reservoir which supplies Mazamet with water, is popular with anglers and ramblers.

Carry on along D 118, then take D 101 to the left towards Mas-Cabardès.

This very picturesque road goes down in between wooded slopes overlooked by impressive rocks. On the right, by a bend in the road at the bottom of a valley, stand the ruins of the Gothic chapel of St-Pierre-de-Vals.

Mas-Cabardès – The village stands proudly below the ruins of its fortified castle.

The narrow streets lead to the **church** ⊘ whose belfry, topped by an octagonal tower, still has a somewhat Romanesque appearance, even though it dates from the 15C. The church itself was rebuilt in the 16C, over a 14C building. Remains of this are to be found inside *(on the left of the entrance)*: a Romanesque capital and a low relief. In the Lady Chapel, to the left of the chancel, note the beautiful 14C stone Virgin and Child and a gilt wood altarpiece.

Going down the street to the left of the church brings you to a junction with a second street, where there is a 16C stone cross. This is adorned with a carving of a shuttle, emblem of weavers and witness to the textile industry in the Orbiel valley.

Continue along the same road and 2km/1mi after Les Ilhes, leave the car in the parking laybys provided on the right at the foot of the cliff on which the Châteaux de Lastours stand.

★ **Châteaux de Lastours** ⊘ – *Departure from the village centre, at the "Accueil Village".*

The ruins of four castles stand in this rugged setting on a rocky ridge between the deep valleys of the Orbiel and the Grésillou. They look particularly attractive in the light of late afternoon or evening, which enhances the golden colour of the stone. The castles, called Cabaret, Tour Régine, Fleur d'Espine and Quertinheux, made up the **Cabaret** fortress in the 12C. Their lord, Pierre-Roger de Cabaret, was an ardent defender of the Cathar cause. During the **Albigensian Crusade**, Simon de Montfort was forced to withdraw from these stern walls in 1210, whereas both Minerve and then Termes (southeast of Carcassonne) capitulated. Refugees came to seek protection at Cabaret which resisted every attack. Simon de Montfort only took possession of it in 1211 after the voluntary surrender of Pierre-Roger de Cabaret.

For a particularly beautiful **view** of the Châteaux de Lastours ruins, their slender silhouettes rising harmoniously from the hillside dotted with tapering cypresses (and wild irises in the spring), drive up to the viewpoint on the opposite side of Grésillou valley *(in Lastours, take D 701 right towards Salsigne then, at the top of the hill, turn right into a road which leads around a housing estate and on to the viewpoint).*

Go back to the Salsigne road.

The roads leads through *garrigue* countryside dotted with broom.

Salsigne – Mining has been the source of livelihood in this area for centuries. Roman and Saracen invaders extracted iron, copper, lead and silver. In 1892, gold was discovered here. At present, there are mining concessions at Salsigne, Lastours and Villanière. Since 1924, they have extracted 10.5 million tonnes of ore which has produced 92 tonnes of gold, 240 tonnes of silver, 30 000 tonnes of copper and 400 000 tonnes of arsenic. Since 1992, the mine has produced gold and silver only.

From Salsigne, follow the signs to the Grotte de Limousis.

Grotte de Limousis ⊘ – The entrance to this cave is set in arid, bare limestone countryside where only vines and olive trees grow. Discovered in 1811, the cave comprises a series of chambers extending for about 660m/2 170ft, in which curiously shaped concretions alternate with mirrors of limpid water. In the final chamber, an enormous **chandelier★** of remarkably white aragonite crystals, 10m/33ft in circumference, is the main feature of the cave.

Return on D 511 to D 111 and there, follow the signs to Villeneuve-Minervois. Go through the village, which earns a living mainly from wine-growing, and take D 112 towards Cabrespine.

Gorges de la Clamoux – These gorges show the striking contrast between the two slopes of Montagne Noire. As far as Cabrespine, the road runs along the floor of the valley, covered with orchards and vineyards.

Take a small road on the left which climbs steeply to the Gouffre de Cabrespine.

Gouffre de Cabrespine ⊘ – The upper part of this chasm consists of a huge network of subterranean galleries drained by the river Clamoux, which disappears underground by Cabrespine to re-emerge 7km/4mi further west in the Orbiel valley. The chasm has been described as "gigantic" and its dimensions fully justify this epithet. In the chasm proper, the "Salle des Éboulis" (chamber of fallen earth), the cavern reaches 250m/820ft in height. The tour of the cave follows a long balconied walkway, from which there is a spectacular overall view, while the concretions adorning the walls of the cavern can be appreciated from closer up. These form characteristic features such as solidified calcite flows coloured differently by mineral oxides, stalactites and stalagmites some of which have joined to form tall and slender columns, mini-shrubs or dazzling curtains of aragonite crystals, eccentrics apparently defying the laws of gravity and many more. The tour ends in the "Salles rouges" (red galleries) and the "Salle aux cristaux" (crystal gallery).

Return to D 112.

The road reaches Cabrespine, overlooked by the Roc de l'Aigle to the left, then winds rapidly up a series of hairpin bends between groves of chestnut trees, overlooking deep ravines in the bottom of which a few tiny hamlets are huddled.

At the Col de la Prade, the road crosses the watershed, leaving the Mediterranean slopes for those facing the Atlantic.

At Pradelles-Cabardès, take D 87 to the right towards the Pic de Nore.

★ Pic de Nore – Alt 1 210m/3 970ft. The highest point in the Montagne Noire, the Pic de Nore towers above the surrounding gently undulating countryside, which is covered with heathland. Not far from the television transmitter station, a viewing table offers a **panorama★** which reaches easily from the Lacaune, Espinouse and Corbières mountains, to Mont Canigou, the Carlit massif and the Midi de Bigorre summit.

Return to Pradelles-Cabardès and turn towards Mazamet.

Gorges de l'Arnette – These gorges, once they are on the outskirts of Mazamet, are dotted with factories, mainly specialising in loosening wool from sheepskins and the production of pulled wool.

Hautpoul – Built on a spur which bears the ruins of its castle and church, this hamlet was the original site of Mazamet. Its setting, directly above the Arnette gorges, offers an attractive **view★** of Mazamet and the Thoré valley. The **Maison de l'Artisanat** ⊘ (craft centre) is a good departure point for rambles in the Montagne Noire.

Respect the life of the countryside.
Drive carefully on country roads.
Protect wildlife, plants and trees.

MONTAUBAN*

Conurbation 53 010
Michelin maps 79 folds 17 and 18 or 235 fold 22

On the boundary between the hillsides of Bas Quercy and the rich alluvial plains of the Garonne and the Tarn, the old *bastide* of Montauban, built with a geometric street layout, is an important crossroads and a good point of departure for excursions into the Aveyron gorges. It is an active market-town, selling fruit and vegetables from market gardens from all over the region.

The almost exclusive use of pink brick lends the buildings here a distinctive character, found in most of the towns in Bas Quercy and the Toulouse area.

HISTORICAL NOTES

A powerful stronghold – In the 8C, there were already several communities on the site of the modern suburb of Moustier, on a hillside overlooking the Tescou. A Benedictine monastery was later established, around which a village called Montauriol grew up. However, it was not until the 12C that the present town was founded. Fed up with being exploited by the Abbot of Montauriol and the neighbouring feudal lords, the town's inhabitants sought help and protection from their overlord, the Count of Toulouse, who founded a *bastide*, or fortified walled town, in 1144 on a plateau overlooking the east bank of the Tarn to which he accorded a very liberal town charter. Attracted by the advantages this new town offered, the inhabitants of Montauriol flocked there, contributing to its rapid expansion. Its name, *Mons albanus,* later became Montauban.

A Citadel of Protestantism – By 1561, most of the town had espoused Reformism; the two town consuls were Calvinists and encouraged the inhabitants to pillage churches and convents. Catholic reaction, led by Charles IX, failed to check the general trend in favour of new ideas. At the time of the peace treaty of St-Germain in 1570, Montauban was known to be a safe refuge for Protestants. Henri of Navarre reinforced its fortifications, and it was on this site that the general meeting of all the reformed churches in France was held on three occasions. But the accession of Louis XIII heralded a "Catholic reconquest". In 1621, Montauban was besieged by an army of 20 000 men, under the command of the king himself and the royal favourite, de Luynes. The townspeople put up a magnificent resistance, repelling three assaults. After three months, on the king's order to abandon the fight, the Catholic army withdrew. But success was to be short-lived, and when La Rochelle fell in 1628, Montauban, the last bastion of Protestantism, saw Louis XIII's army marching on it once again. This time, the town opened its gates without a fight and acclaimed the king and Cardinal Richelieu. The fortifications were destroyed, but the Huguenots were granted a taste of royal clemency.

FAMOUS LOCAL ARTISTS

A master draughtsman – Born in Montauban in 1780, the son of a minor painter and craftsman who gave him a solid grounding in music and painting until the age of 17, Ingres attended the studio of the painter Roques in Toulouse before being drawn to Paris where he became the pupil of David. After winning second prize in the Prix de Rome at the age of 21, he spent nearly twenty years in Italy before moving to Paris where he opened a studio and founded a school. His greatest talent lay in draughtsmanship. He achieved a purity and precision of line which verges on technical perfection, while at the same time imbuing his works with extraordinary personality, often sensuality, in the composition of numerous portraits and studies frequently executed in pencil. Well before his death at the age of 85, Ingres had won considerable recognition and glory. He remained very attached to his home town and bequeathed it a major part of his work, now housed in the museum which bears his name.

A great sculptor – Also born in Montauban, Bourdelle (1861-1929) owes much to his master, Rodin. In his compositions – busts or sculpted groups – he combines strong energetic poses with simplicity of line and the evocation of noble sentiment. *Héraklès Archer,* in the Musée Bourdelle in Paris, is one of his most impressive works.

★ MUSÉE INGRES ⊙

The museum occupies the old bishop's palace, built in 1664 on the site of two castles. The first castle, the "Château-bas", was built in the 12C by the Count of Toulouse. Demolished in 1229, it was replaced a century later by another fortress, built on the orders of the Black Prince, of which a few rooms still remain. The current palace was bought by the municipality when the diocese was suppressed during the Revolution and converted to a museum in 1843. It is an imposing, sobre pink brick edifice consisting of a main building flanked by two pavilions.

1st floor – Given over to the work of Ingres, this floor is the main attraction of the museum. French-style ceilings and marquetry floors provide a choice backdrop for the collection of the master's oeuvre.

After a room devoted to Ingres' work in the classical tradition, including his admirable canvas of *Jesus among the Doctors*, completed at the age of 82, a large room contains numerous sketches, academic studies, **portraits** – of Gilbert, Madame Gonse, Belvèze – and *Ossian's Dream*, a huge canvas executed in 1812 for Napoleon's bedchamber in Rome. Note also *Ruggiero freeing Angelica*, an oval copy of the original in the Louvre. Works by David, Chassériau, Géricault and Delacroix complete the exhibition. Carry on into the drawing rooms of the old bishop's palace to see a glass display case containing the master's personal mementoes – his paintbox and famous violin – as well as a selection of his 4 000 **drawings**, the highlight of the museum, displayed in rotation.

2nd floor – This contains excellent works by primitive schools and paintings from the 14C to 18C, mostly bequeathed by Ingres. In the 1st room, a glass case contains Italian works from the 15C; the 3rd room is particularly rich in beautiful paintings from the 17C Flemish (Jordaens, Van Dyck), Dutch and Spanish (José de Ribera) schools. Louis XV and Louis XVI style furniture complements the exhibition. From the windows there is a bird's eye view of the Tarn and the Pont-Vieux.

Ground floor – A huge room is devoted to **Bourdelle**, tracing the evolution of this great sculptor's art. Works on display include a patinated plaster version of his *Héraklès Archer*, busts of Beethoven, Rodin, Léon Cladel and Ingres as well as bronzes such as *The Night* and *Rembrandt in Old Age*.

A gallery is devoted to the works of painter Armand Cambon (1819-85).

Basement – In the surviving part of the 14C castle, seven interestingly vaulted rooms on two floors are devoted to regional archeology, local history, the applied arts and temporary exhibitions.

The former Guard Room, known as the Black Prince's Room, contains medieval lapidary collections and has two beautiful 15C chimneypieces adorned with the arms of Cahors. The Jean-Chandos room displays bronzes, antique terracotta pieces and a Gallo-Roman **mosaic** found at Labastide-du-Temple northwest of Montauban. The main works of **Desnoyer** (1894-1972), a painter born in Montauban, are on display in one of the galleries. Thanks to generous donations, a beautiful collection of **regional earthenware** has been put together (Montauban, Auvillar). Opposite the Musée Ingres, on the edge of Square du Général-Picquart, stands the admirable bronze **The Last of the Centaurs Dies**★ (**B**), a powerful, compact sculpture by Bourdelle (1914) and, near the Pont-Vieux, on Quai de Montmurat, the 1870 War Memorial (**D**), showing the artist's architectural capacities.

★ PLACE NATIONALE

It was to replace the wooden roofs or *couverts* above the galleries, destroyed by two fires in 1614 and 1649, that the arcades were rebuilt in brick in the 17C. There is now a double set of arcades around the square, vaulted with pointed or rounded arches. The fanciful detail and warm tones of the brick soften what would otherwise be a rather austere effect without destroying the stylistic homogeneity. The pink brick houses surrounding this beautiful square have high façades divided into bays by pilasters, which are connected at each corner by a canted portico. On the corner of Rue Malcousinat, there is a drapers' measure on the first pillar. Every morning the square comes to life with a busy, colourful market.

Beneath the arcades on Place Nationale

Anger/IMAGES TOULOUSE

★OLD TOWN

Montauban's historical town centre has recently been restored. The best way of exploring it is on foot. Selected highlights are given below.

Rue de la République – At no 23 there is an attractive courtyard with multi-storey arcades on three sides.

Place Franklin-Roosevelt – Next to the building with caryatids, a partially vaulted alley (Passage du Vieux-Palais) linking two Renaissance courtyards leads to Rue de la République, emerging at no 25.

Rue des Carmes – At no 24, the Hôtel Mila de Cabarieu features a red brick portico with depressed arcades, an interesting architectural composition.

Rue de l'Hôtel de Ville – One of the interesting houses lining this street is the Hôtel Sermet-Deymie (late 18C), a typical example with its entrance doorway flanked by four Ionic columns.

Rue Cambon – Hôtel Lefranc de Pompignan (**E**) boasts a handsome brick doorway★. In the courtyard at no 12 *(go right up to the railing to see)* there is an elegant wooden gallery supported by a stone colonnade.

Place Léon Bourjade – From the terrace of the brasserie there is a good view of the Pont-Vieux spanning the Tarn.

Collège des Jésuites (**F**) – This austere building, built in the late 17C and recently restored, houses the Maison de la Culture, an information centre on local events and entertainment.

ADDITIONAL SIGHTS

Pont-Vieux – When approached from the west bank of the Tarn, the old bridge gives a good view of the former bishop's palace and, beyond it, numerous 17C town residences and the elegant tower of St-Jacques.
Built in brick in the 14C by the architects Étienne de Ferrières and Mathieu de Verdun, on the orders of Philip the Fair, the Pont-Vieux is 205m/672ft long and spans the Tarn in seven arches resting on piers protected by cut-waters; its arches are divided up by small arcades so that floodwaters can pass through more easily. Contemporary with the Pont Valentré in Cahors, it too was fortified.

Église St-Jacques – Dominating the town, this fortified church, dedicated to St James, still bears traces on the tower façade of cannonballs fired during the 1621 siege. After the Catholic reconquest, in 1629, the church where Louis XIII was to be solemnly received in 1632 was raised to the rank of cathedral, a prerogative it was to keep until 1739. Resting on a machicolated square tower,

MONTAUBAN

Nationale (Pl.)
République (R. de la) 63
Résistance (R. de la) 64

Bourdelle (Pl.) 4
Bourjade (Pl. L.) 6
Cambon (R.) 9
Carmes (R. des) 10
Comédie (R. de la) 13
Consul-Dupuy
  (Allée du) 14
Coq (Pl. du) 16
Dr. Lacaze (R. du) 19
Guibert (Pl.) 29
Hôtel-de-Ville
  (R. de l') 31
Lafon (R. Mary) 32
Lagrange (R. L.) 35
Malcousinat (R.) 36
Martyrs (Carrefour des) ... 46
Michelet (R.) 51
Midi-Pyrénées (Bd.) 52
Monet (R. J.) 53
Montmurat (Quai de) 54
Mortarieu
  (Allées de) 56
Notre-Dame (R.) 60
Piquard
  (Square du Gén.) 62
Roosevelt (Pl. F.) 66
Sapiac (Pont de) 68
Verdun (Q. de) 71
22-Septembre
  (Pl. du) 76

B Bronze du Dernier centaure mourant
D Monument aux Combattants
E Hôtel Lefranc de Pompignan
F Collège des Jésuites
   (Maison de la culture)
M Ancienne Cour des Aides (Musées)

the **belfry** dates from the late 13C. It is built of brick on an octagonal plan and has three rows of windows. The nave, flanked by side chapels, was renovated in the 15C and had rib vaulting added in the 18C.

Cathédrale Notre-Dame ⊙ – The cathedral is a classical building of vast proportions. The façade, framed by two square towers, has an imposing peristyle supporting colossal statues of the four Evangelists, copies of the originals which are to be found inside the cathedral *(by the entrance)*.

The chancel is very deep and the crossing surmounted by a dome on pendentives is decorated with the theological virtues. In the north arm of the transept is a famous painting by Ingres, the **Vow of Louis XIII**. The king, in the foreground, clothed in a rich mantle decorated with fleur-de-lis, is turning towards the Virgin Mary, who is holding the Infant Jesus in her arms, and handing her his kingdom symbolised by a sceptre and crown *(painting can be illuminated; light switch to the right towards middle of church)*.

Ancienne Cour des Aides (M) – This beautiful 17C building, which once housed the Court of Excise Taxes, houses two museums.

Musée du Terroir ⊙ – On the ground floor of this regional folk museum, local society Escolo Carsinol presents a display on daily life in Bas Quercy. Most traditional crafts are represented by tools, instruments and model figures. One of the rooms is a reconstruction of the inside of a peasant home during the 19C, complete with inhabitants.

Musée d'Histoire naturelle et de Préhistoire ⊙ – On the 2nd floor, several rooms contain a variety of zoological exhibits and, in particular, a very large ornithological collection – 4 000 items, only some of which are displayed, including exotic birds such as parrots, humming birds and birds of Paradise. There is also a paleontological section featuring a large number of vertebrates from the Tertiary Era.

►► **Lafrançaise** – *17km/10mi northwest (D 927)*. Good view from church terrace. Bathing at nearby lake.

►► **Villemur-sur-Tarn** – *23km/14mi southeast (D 21)*. Former stronghold with remains of its fortifications, the Vieux-Moulin tower.

MONT-LOUIS★

Population 200
Michelin maps 86 fold 16 or 235 folds 51, 55 – Local map see La CERDAGNE

Built 1 600m/5 200ft above sea level on a hillock commanding a view of the threshold of the Perche and the valleys of the Cerdagne to the west, the Capcir to the north and the Conflent to the east, Mont-Louis was originally a fortified town founded in 1679 by Vauban, who had observed and perfectly understood its strategic importance, to defend the new borders laid down in the **Treaty of the Pyrenees**. This treaty, signed more than twenty years earlier in November 1659, on Pheasant Island in the Bidassoa river *(see Michelin Green Guide Atlantic Coast)*, put an end to the hostilities between France and Spain. One of the territories which Spain relinquished to France was Roussillon.

Thus Mont-Louis, because of its geographical and strategic importance, became an excellent border stronghold... which was never needed! Now, a mobile defence and commando training centre has been set up in the citadel (1681), which lends itself perfectly to guerilla warfare.

This austere fortress town pays tribute to General Dagobert *(in the church square)*, a master in the art of mountain warfare who in 1793, during the dark hours of the invasion of Roussillon, drove the Spaniards out of the Cerdagne, and to General Gilles (1904-61) another military figure who was a native of the town.

The fortified town – This consists of a citadel and a lower town, built entirely within the ramparts. The citadel has a square layout, with cut-off corners extended by bastions. Three demilunes protect the curtain walls.

As the town, named after Louis XIV, the reigning monarch during its construction, was never besieged, the ramparts, the main gatehouse (Porte de France), the bastions and the watchtowers have remained intact.

The southern slopes offer views of the Perche threshold and Cambras d'Aze.

Solar furnace ⊙ (Four solaire) – The solar furnace was installed in 1953. The concentrating panel, refurbished in 1980, consists of 860 parabolic mirrors and the heliostat of 546 flat mirrors. The structure focusses the sun's rays into its centre where temperatures can reach up to 3 000-3 500°C/5 400-6 300°F. Since July 1993 it has been put to commercial (rather than research) use.

Lac des Bouillouses

EXCURSIONS

Planès – *6.5km/4mi south on the road to Cabanasse and St-Pierre-dels-Forçats. Leave the car in front of the Mairie-École in Planès and take the path on the right to the church.* A small cemetery around the church offers a beautiful **view** of the Carlit massif. The tiny **church**★ has a curious ground plan in the shape of a sort of five-pointed star, the "rays" of which are formed by alternately pointed or blunted semi-circular apsidal chapels. The central dome rests on three semidomes.

The origins of this monument have given rise to intense speculation over the years, as its structure was extremely rare in the medieval western world. Local tradition attributes it to the Saracens, hence the church was known locally as *la mesquita* or mosque. It is probably a Romanesque building inspired by the symbol of the Holy Trinity.

★ **Lac des Bouillouses** – *14km/8.5mi to the northwest – about 1hr. Leave Mont-Louis on the road to Quillan (D 118); 300m/330yd after a bridge over the Têt, turn left onto D 60.*

After 8km/5mi, the road leaves the bottom of the wooded furrow formed by the Têt to climb up to the threshold which marks the lower terrace of the Bouillouses plateau. A dam has turned this mountain lake (alt 2 070m/6 790ft) into a reservoir containing 17.5 million m³/618 million ft³, which supplies water to the irrigation canals and hydroelectric plants in the Têt valley.

The worn-down, rather bleak Bouillouses plateau is dotted with about twenty small lakes and pools, apart from the Lac de Bouillouses itself, which are of glacial origin, at an altitude of more than 2 000m/6 560ft, within the natural amphitheatre lying between the Carlit, Péric and Aude peaks.

Route du col de MONTMIRAT★★

Michelin map 80 folds 5 and 6 or 240 folds 2 and 6
Local map see Mont LOZÈRE

The Montmirat pass road, at the far eastern edge of the Causse de Sauveterre, is a picturesque way of beginning a trip south to explore the Tarn gorges.

FROM MENDE TO FLORAC *39km/24mi – allow 1hr 30min*

★ **Mende** – *See MENDE.*
Leave Mende on ③ on the town plan.
The N 88 runs along beside the Lot between the steep wooded slopes of the Mende and Changefège *causses.*

Balsièges – To the south of this village tower the cliffs of the Causse de Sauveterre. High up on the skyline stand two huge limestone rocks, one of which is known as the "lion of Balsièges" because of its shape.
In Balsièges, turn left onto N 106 towards Florac.

The road goes up the Bramon valley, which gradually widens to reveal views of the foothills of Mont Lozère in the distance and of the "Truc de Balduc", a small, steep-sided *causse*. After the hamlet of Molines, the road climbs towards the Montmirat pass giving lovely views of the surrounding countryside as it goes.

★ **Col de Montmirat** – Alt 1 046m/3 432ft. The pass cuts between the granite of Mont Lozère and the limestone of the Causse de Sauveterre. To the south there is a vast **panorama**★: in the foreground lie the *valats* or little troughs along which water drains down into the Tarn; beyond these loom the cliff edges of the Causse Méjean; further left are the Cévennes ridges; and on a clear day the summit of Mont Aigoual can be seen.

After a spectacular cliff-edge route downhill, keep left past the road leading along the **Tarn gorge**★★★ to the right. The Rochefort rock comes into sight as the road reaches the outskirts of Florac.

Florac – *See FLORAC.*

MONTPELLIER★★

Conurbation 248 303
Michelin map 83 fold 7 or 240 fold 23

Bathed in uniquely Mediterranean light Montpellier, capital of Languedoc-Roussillon, owes much of its charm to its beautiful historical districts and superb gardens juxtaposed with modern buildings which bear witness to the dynamic character of this large administrative centre and university city.

HISTORICAL NOTES

The Middle Ages – Unlike neighbouring Nîmes, Béziers and Narbonne, Montpellier did not enter the historical arena until about the 10C. Two villages formed the beginnings of the future major conurbation. Montpellieret, a dependency of the Bishop of Maguelone, and Montpellier, owned by the lords of Guilhem.

In 1204, after the marriage of Marie de Montpellier (daughter of Guilhem VIII) to Peter of Aragon, Montpellier became a Spanish enclave and remained so until 1349 when John III of Majorca sold it to the King of France for 120 000 *écus*.

After that, the town developed quickly and played an important role in trade with the Levant. Its spice and dyestuff merchants were familiar with the therapeutic values of the products they sold; some of the more educated among them read translations of Hippocrates and were thus able to share their knowledge with scholars of medical science. This was how the first "schools" of medicine were created. These became a university in the early 13C and were later joined by law and art faculties. A bull issued by Pope Nicolas IV, recognising these establishments, was the basis for the founding charter of the **University of Montpellier**. A number of prestigious scholars were to be attracted to study here, among them **Rabelais**, who completed his studies in 1530, graduating as a doctor of medicine. The end of the 14C was marked by several disasters (bubonic plague, famine, etc.). To ward off ill fortune, the town decided to make a **giant candle** as long as its fortified curtain wall (3 888m/ 12 752ft); it was a soft candle, coiled around a cylinder, which was unwound as the wax burnt, in front of the altar to Our Lady. In the

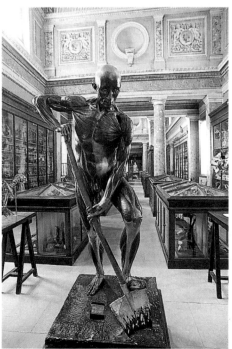

Montpellier's medical history on display in the museum of anatomy

243

middle of the 15C, trade began to flourish once again and Montpellier became one of the centres of economic activity of **Jacques Cœur**, King Charles VII's treasurer.

The union of Provence with France in 1481 struck Montpellier a harsh blow, since Marseille then became the main port for Levantine trade.

Montpellier, capital city – In the 16C, the Reformation arrived in Montpellier, and Protestants and Catholics in turn became masters of the town. After becoming a Protestant fief, the town was the scene of violent confrontations; most of the churches and convents were destroyed. In 1622, the royal armies of Louis XIII laid siege to the fortifications of Montpellier, which capitulated after three months. Richelieu then had the citadel built to keep watch over the rebel city. Some of the Protestants left the town, selling up their affairs to the "good people of Montpellier".

Louis XIV made Montpellier the administrative capital of Bas Languedoc, and factories were set up there at the same time as the university, under royal patronage, continued to expand. From 1593 on, the botany professorship had a botanical garden at its disposal.

The now prosperous town carried out extensive projects to embellishment itself. Well-known architects, such as **d'Aviler** who had studied in Rome, and the **Giral** family (Étienne, with his brother Jean and son Jean-Antoine) vied with each other to display their talent. They built the Promenade du Peyrou, the Esplanade and fountains, while at the same time working for rich financiers and senior civil servants for whom they designed the superb town mansions which can be seen in the historic town centre of Montpellier.

Modern Montpellier – After the Revolution, the town had to forego its role as the capital of Languedoc to become the simple *préfecture* of the Hérault *département*. Only the University and the retail trade, especially that of wine, remained significant.

OUT AND ABOUT IN MONTPELLIER

Guided tours – These are a particularly good way of visiting the inner courtyards of the private *hôtels*, which for the most part are otherwise closed to the public. Tours leave from the Triangle Bas tourist office. There is a tour of the historic town centre at 3pm on Wednesdays and Saturdays during term time, and every day during school holidays. Minimum group size: 5. The tourist office also offers quarterly programmes of tours on a particular theme, which begin at 2.30pm. ☎ 04 67 58 67 58.

Out on the town – Good places to go and soak up a little atmosphere are the Place de la Comédie, a lively square with plenty of *brasseries*, cinemas, theatres etc., Place Jean-Jaurès, Rue de l'Université and the surrounding streets, in the vast setting provided by the Polygone, and on the Esplanade de l'Europe, at the far east end of the Antigone district.

Entertainment – Montpellier and the local area have all sorts of festivals and other forms of entertainment on offer.

Festival de Radio-France et de Montpellier: concerts of classical music, opera and jazz. ☎ 04 67 61 66 81.

Festival International Montpellier-Danse: dance shows at the Opéra Berlioz, the Opéra Comédie, in the courtyard of the old Ursuline convent and on Place de la Comédie. ☎ 04 67 60 83 60.

Festival du Cinéma méditerranéen: local films in the Corum and at the Centre Rabelais. ☎ 04 67 66 36 36.

Opéra Berlioz (Le Corum): Esplanade Charles-de-Gaulle. ☎ 04 67 60 19 99.

Opéra Comédie: Place de la Comédie. ☎ 04 67 60 19 99.

Centre dramatique national: Domaine de Grammont *(east of town on D 24)*, avenue A.-Einstein. ☎ 04 67 58 08 13.

Zénith: Domaine de Grammont, avenue A.-Einstein. ☎ 04 67 64 50 00.

Markets – Every morning there are food markets in the town centre in: Halles Castellane, Halles Laissac, Place de la Comédie, Plan Cabannes. On Tuesdays and Saturdays there is a market of organic products in Place des Arceaux. On the third and last Saturdays of the month there is a market of secondhand books, antiques and bric-à-brac in the area around the church of Ste-Anne. On Sunday mornings there is a rural market on Avenue Samuel-Champlain in the Antigone. In La Paillade, the suburb to the west of the town centre, there is a flower market every Tuesday and a flea market every Sunday (Esplanade de la Mosson).

With the return of the French from North Africa after 1962, the city found a renewed dynamism. To the west of the city a new residential suburb grew up, La Paillade, currently home to more than 25 000 people.

To expand the sphere of its economic activity and tourist industry, Montpellier has created five *pôles*: Euromédecine, with its numerous research laboratories and pharmaceutical companies; Agropolis to the north of the city, home to farm-produce industries; Antenna, with its various radio and television production centres; Héliopolis, which regroups businesses concerned with the tourist and leisure industries; and Informatique, for information technology, which has in fact been represented in the region since 1965 when IBM set up a plant here. In view of Montpellier's role as administrative capital, almost three quarters of the city's working inhabitants are employed in tertiary industries. The high speed (TGV) rail link means that Montpellier is only just over four hours away from Paris.

Evidence of the dynamism of this city is provided more than anything else by the wealth of construction projects designed by contemporary architects which have been commissioned in recent years. To the north of the historic town centre is the Corum, a conference and concert centre; to the east, the Antigone district, linked to old Montpellier by the Triangle and Polygone shopping centres. Other projects are underway, including that of Port-Marianne in the south, as further evidence of Montpellier's ambitions in the field of urban planning.

Throughout the year, the city hosts numerous events, including Montpellier-Danse, the Radio France and Montpellier Festival, and fairs such as the Foire Internationale and the Congrès Euromédicine.

★★HISTORIC MONTPELLIER *3hr*

Since the courtyards of most of the hôtels are generally closed to the public, visitors are strongly recommended to go on one of the guided tours organised by the tourist office.

Between the Place de la Comédie and the Peyrou Arc de Triomphe, on either side of Rue Foch, lie the historic districts of Montpellier, with their narrow, winding streets, the last vestiges of the original medieval town.

Lining the streets are superb 17C and 18C private mansions, or *hôtels*, with their main façades and remarkable staircases hidden from the public eye in inner courtyards.

Place de la Comédie (FY) – This lively square at the heart of Montpellier links the city's old districts with the new. The 19C façade of the theatre serves as a backdrop to a fountain of the Three Graces, by sculptor Étienne d'Antoine. The ovoid area of paving around the fountain is a reminder of the old egg-shaped terreplein (levelled off earth embankment, often where guns were positioned) which earned Place de la Comédie the nickname *l'œuf* ("the egg").

Place de la Comédie is continued to the north by the **Esplanade (FY)**, a beautiful promenade lined with plane-trees where Montpellier residents come in summer to stroll among the terrace cafés or listen to musicians playing in the bandstands. Closing off the view at the far end is the **Corum (FX)**.

To the east **(CU)** lie the paving of the **Triangle** and the **Polygone** complex (shopping centre, administrative buildings, including the town hall).

Take Rue de la Loge.

The name of this street is a reminder of the all powerful merchants' lodge in the 15C.

Turn left into Rue Jacques-Cœur.

Hôtel des Trésoriers de France ⊙ **(FY M²)** – *No 7*. This private mansion has been known by various names depending on who owned it at any particular time. It was called the Hôtel Jacques-Cœur when the King's treasurer was living there in the 15C – the vaulted cellars and polychrome coffered ceilings which adorn some of the rooms date from this period. In the 17C it became the Hôtel des Trésoriers de France, after the resident senior magistrates in charge of administering the royal estates in Languedoc. These dignitaries had the grand three-flight staircase built along with the majestic façade overlooking the courtyard with its superimposed colonnades. Finally, the name Lunaret by which it has also been known is in memory of Henri de Lunaret who bequeathed it to the local archeological society (Société Archéologique de Montpellier).

★ **Musée languedocien** – *On the ground floor*. The medieval room in this local museum houses a collection of Romanesque sculpture, including the Virgin Mary and the Three Wise Men from the abbey of Fontcaude (Aude), capitals from the cloisters of St-Guilhem-le-Désert, and three inscriptions in Arabic.

On the 1st floor. In the Gothic Robert St-Jean room, there is a Vias lead font (13C), a rare wooden vessel and a collection of 13C and 14C ceramic ware. The main ceremonial hall, hung with 17C Flemish tapestries, houses a painting by the Fontainbleau School, two beautiful Languedoc cabinets, and a Coronelli celestial globe. The yellow room successfully evokes the spirit of the 18C with marquetry furniture and collections of Sèvres, Meissen and East India Company porcelain. The next room contains ceramic ware from various places (Moustiers-Ste-Marie, Marseille and Delft), and the room adjoining that 16C-18C faïence from Montpellier displayed in pretty Rococo glass cases. Go through the apartments which used to be the Lunaret family's to get to the second floor.

MONTPELLIER

Polygone (Le) .... **CU**

Anatole-France (R.) ...... **BU** 3

Antonelli (Av. Prof. E.) **CDV** 5
Arceaux (Bd des) ...... **AU** 7
Bazille (R. F.) .... **BCV** 12
Blum (R. Léon) ...... **CU** 13
Broussonnet (R. A.) .... **AT** 18
Chancel (Av.) .... **AT** 25

Citadelle (Allée) .... **CU** 26
Clapiès (R.) .... **AU** 28
Comte (R. A.) .... **AU** 29
Délicieux (R. B.) .... **CT** 31
États-du-Languedoc (Av.) **CU** 35
Fabre de Morlhon (Bd) . **BV** 36

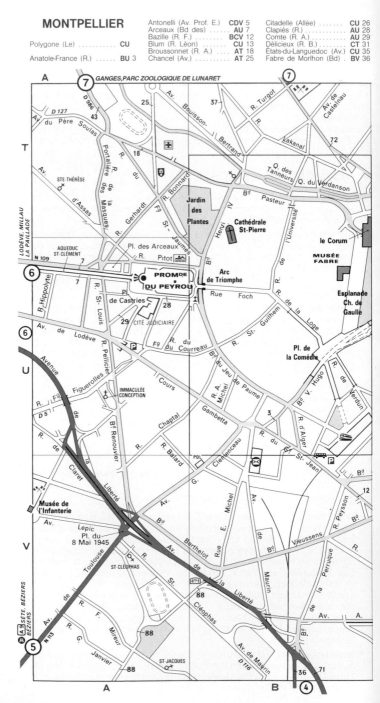

On the 2nd floor. This floor is devoted to prehistory and archeological collections (Etruscan and Greek vases, Egyptian statues, Gallo-Roman sculptures). In the department on folk art and tradition, curious bridle attachments for mules illustrate 16C to 18C Cévennes craftsmanship.

To the right of the *hôtel* stands the **Chapelle des Pénitents Blancs (FY)**, once the church of Ste-Foy, which was rebuilt in the 17C and which features a doorway with a triangular pediment.

Take the Rue Valedeau and the Rue Collot.

South of the Place Jean-Jaurès, a flight of steps leads to the **crypt of Notre-Dame-des-Tables** ⊙ **(FY B)**, the name of which recalls the tables set up around the church by money-changers in the Middle Ages. The church was destroyed in the Revolution.

Fg-Boutonnet (R.)	**BT** 37	Leclerc (Av. du Mar.) ... **CV** 58
Fg-de-Nîmes (R.)	**CT** 40	Millénaire (Pl. du) ..... **CU** 62
Flahault (Av. Ch.)	**AT** 43	Nombre-d'Or (Pl. du) .. **CU** 64
Fontaine-de-Lattes (R.)	**CU** 44	Olivier (R. A.) .... **CU** 66
Henri-II-de-		Pont-de-Lattes (R. du).. **CU** 69
Montmorency (Allée) . **CU** 51		Pont-Juvénal (Av.) .... **CDU** 70
Près-d'Arènes		
(Av. des) .... **BV** 71		
Proudhon (R.) .... **BT** 72		
René (R. H.) .... **CV** 73		
Villeneuve-		
d'Angoulême (Av.) . **ABV** 88		

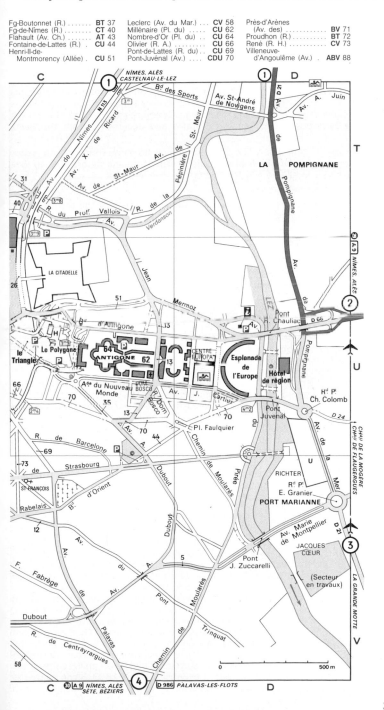

In memory of the original sanctuary, the name Notre-Dame-des-Tables was transferred to the chapel of the Jesuit college built in the 18C by Giral, part of which now houses the Musée Fabre.

Rue de la Petite-Loge, north of the square, leads to Place Pétrarque.

On the right, at the entrance to Rue Embouque-d'Or, which has been restored, stands the Hôtel de Manse, and opposite, **Hôtel Baschy du Cayla (FY L)**, with its Louis XV façade, next to Hôtel de Varennes.

Hôtel de Manse ⊙ **(FY D)** – *4, rue Embouque-d'Or*. The Count of Manse, who was treasurer to the King of France, had Italian artists design this interior façade with its double colonnade forming the bays of a beautiful staircase called the "Manse's Steps".

★ **Hôtel de Varennes** ⊙ **(FY M¹)** – *2, place Pétrarque*. An archway leads to several Gothic rooms with intersecting ribs. One of these rooms contains Romanesque columns and capitals from the original church of Notre-Dame-des-Tables; gemel windows and castle doors have been incorporated into the walls, forming a very harmonious whole. The 14C **Salle Pétrarque**, with its ribbed vaulting, is used by the city of Montpellier for receptions.

Musée du Vieux Montpellier ⊙ – *1st floor*. This museum of local history contains a selection of engravings, portraits of the town's leading citizens, old maps and religious objects, including the Virgin Mary reliquary from the church of Notre-Dame-des-Tables, penitents' staffs and documents from the Revolution.

Musée Fougau ⊙ – *2nd floor*. The museum derives its name from the Languedoc expression *lou fougau* (the hearth). Objects, furniture and decors give an idea of popular 19C local arts and traditions.

Turn right into Rue de l'Aiguillerie.

As this street's name ("needle factory") suggests, this was the town's street for arts and crafts in the Middle Ages. Some of the shops still have their beautiful 14C and 15C vaulted roofs.

Take Rue Montpellieret on the right.

Hôtel Sabatier d'Espeyran ⊙ **(FY Z)** – This 19C private town house is an excellent example of a wealthy Second Empire mansion.

The entrance to the Musée Fabre is in Boulevard Sarrail.

★★ **Musée Fabre** ⊙ **(FY)** – The museum was founded in 1825 thanks to the generosity of the Montpellier painter **François-Xavier Fabre** (1766-1837). Fabre studied under David and spent many years in Italy where he inherited the superb collection of the Countess of Albany, a legacy to her from the poet Vittorio Alfieri. Fabre donated the collection of books, paintings, drawings and etchings to the city of Montpellier.

In 1836, the original collection was enhanced by the Antoine Valedeau bequest consisting of Flemish and Dutch works, then in 1868 by the Alfred Bruyas collection. The latter, a banker's son, and a friend of Courbet and numerous other painters of the same generation, owned a large collection of contemporary works.

Originally housed in the 19C Hôtel de Massilian, the museum was extended in 1878 by the addition of a wing running along the Rue Montpellieret, and in 1981 by the addition of some rooms from the neighbouring former Jesuit college.

The collections include a series of Greek and European ceramic ware (including 17C and 18C Montpellier apothecary's pots), works from the English (Reynolds), Spanish (Zurbarán and a stunning *St Mary of Egypt* by Ribera), Italian (Veronese, Allori, Il Guercino, Domenichino and Cagnacci), Dutch and Flemish (Jan Steen, Metsu, Ruysdael, Rubens, Teniers the Younger) schools. The 17C and 18C French schools are represented by numerous masterpieces by S Bourdon *(Man with Black Ribbons)*, Poussin, Dughet, Vouet, La Hyre, Ranc *(Vertumnus and Pomona)*, Vincent, David *(Hector, Portrait of Doctor Alphonse Leroy)*, a large collection of works by Greuze *(Le Petit Paresseux, Twelfth Night Cake, Morning Prayer)* as well as sculptures by Houdon *(Summer, Winter)*, Lemoyne and Pajou.

Early 19C French painting is particularly well represented thanks to the Alfred Bruyas collection, as well as by works by the *luminophiles* (light-lovers), the nickname given to Languedoc painters who tried to capture on canvas the superb light of their region. Next to portraits of Bruyas (19 in all) painted by his friends Delacroix, Cabanel and Courbet, are world-famous works by Delacroix *(Algerian women in their room, Fantasia)*, Courbet (including *La Rencontre ou Bonjour Monsieur Courbet*, a highly original self-portrait, *Les Baigneuses*, which scandalised the public at the 1853 Salon with the "indecency" of the bathers, and *Ambrussum Roman Bridge*, which then had two arches), and Montpellier artist Frédéric Bazille *(View of the Village, La Toilette, The Ramparts of Aigues-Mortes* and *Black Woman with Peonies).*

Among sculptures by Bourdelle, Maillol and Richier are works by Van Dongen *(Portrait of Fernande Olivier),* De Staël, Marquet, Dufy, Soulages, Vieira da Silva, Viallat and Montpellier artist Vincent Bioulès *(Square in Aix-en-Provence, Homage to Auguste Chabaud).*

Return to Rue de l'Aiguillerie going north around the Musée Fabre, then turn right into Rue de la Carbonnerie.

Hôtel Baudon de Mauny (FY E) – *1, rue de la Carbonnerie.* This house features an elegant Louis XVI façade decorated with garlands of flowers facing onto the street.

Rue du Cannau (FY) – This street is lined with classical town houses: at no 1, **Hôtel de Roquemaure** with a door studded with nailhead stones and boasting fluted

Musée Fabre – *View of the Village* by Frédéric Bazille

Musée Fabre, Montpellier

pilasters; at no 3, **Hôtel d'Avèze**; at no 6, **Hôtel de Beaulac**; at no 8, **Hôtel Deydé** featuring architectural innovations introduced by d'Avilar in the late 17C – a depressed arch and a triangular pediment.

Turn back and take Rue Delpech to Place du Marché-aux-Fleurs, with its modern fountain.

At the north-east corner of the square, **Hôtel de Mirman (FY F** – *closed to the public)* is named after the treasurer Jean de Mirman, who bought it in 1632.

Turn back and take Rue de Girone on the left, then Rue Fournarié.

Hôtel de Solas (FY K) – *1, rue Fournarié.* This 17C town house features a Louis XIII door. Note the plasterwork on the porch ceiling.

Hôtel d'Uston (FY K) – *3, rue Fournarié.* This house dates from the first half of the 18C. The archway of the door is decorated with wreaths (with a female figure on the keystone) and the pediment with cherubs framing a vase of flowers.

Carry on along Rue Cambacérès which leads to Place Chabaneau.

Place Chabaneau (EY 24) – The façade of the *préfecture,* which overlooks the square, is that of the former Hôtel de Ganges built in the 17C by Cardinal de Bonzy and given by him to his friend the Countess of Ganges. The charming Cybele fountain dates from the 18C.

Return to Rue de la Vieille-Intendance.

At no 9 is **Hôtel de la Vieille Intendance (EY Q)**, which has been inhabited by many famous people including Lamoignon de Basville, Intendant of Languedoc, and later the philosopher Auguste Comte and the writer Paul Valéry.

Place de la Canourgue (EY) – In the 17C, this square was the centre of Montpellier, and numerous *hôtels* still remain around the garden with its Unicorn fountain, the last of three fountains designed to distribute water supplied by the St-Clément aqueduct.

From the square, there is a view down onto the cathedral of St-Pierre.

Hôtel Richer de Belleval (EY N) – *Annexe of the law courts.* For a long time, this housed the town hall. The square courtyard is decorated with busts and balustrades typical of the late 18C.

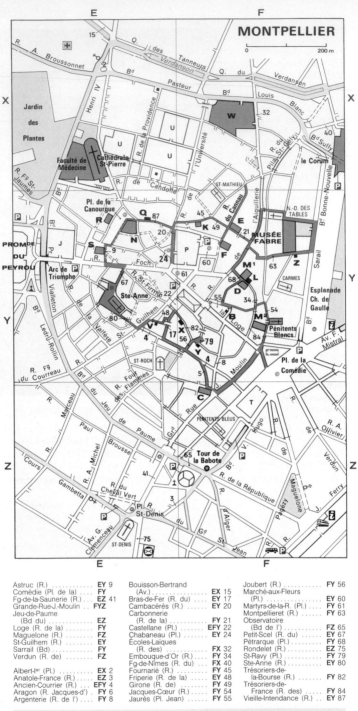

MONTPELLIER

Astruc (R.)	**EY** 9	Bouisson-Bertrand		Joubert (R.)	**FY** 56
Comédie (Pl. de la)	**FY**	(Av.)	**EX** 15	Marché-aux-Fleurs	
Fg-de-la-Saunerie (R.)	**EZ** 41	Bras-de-Fer (R. du)	**EY** 17	(Pl.)	**EY** 60
Grande-Rue-J.-Moulin	**FYZ**	Cambacérès (R.)	**EY** 20	Martyrs-de-la-R. (Pl.)	**FY** 61
Jeu-de-Paume		Carbonnerie		Montpellieret (R.)	**FY** 63
(Bd du)	**EZ**	(R. de la)	**FY** 21	Observatoire	
Loge (R. de la)	**FY**	Castellane (Pl.)	**EFY** 22	(Bd de l')	**FZ** 65
Maguelone (R.)	**FZ**	Chabaneau (Pl.)	**EY** 24	Petit-Scel (R. du)	**EY** 67
St-Guilhem (R.)	**EY**	Écoles-Laïques		Pétrarque (Pl.)	**FY** 68
Sarrail (Bd)	**FY**	(R. des)	**FX** 32	Rondelet (R.)	**EZ** 75
Verdun (R. de)	**FZ**	Embouque-d'Or (R.)	**FY** 34	St-Ravy (Pl.)	**FY** 79
		Fg-de-Nîmes (R. du)	**FX** 40	Ste-Anne (R.)	**EY** 80
Albert-Ier (Pl.)	**EX** 2	Fournarié (R.)	**FY** 45	Trésoriers-de-	
Anatole-France (R.)	**EZ** 3	Friperie (R. de la)	**EY** 48	la-Bourse (R.)	**FY** 82
Ancien-Courrier (R.)	**EFY** 4	Girone (R. de)	**FY** 49	Trésoriers-de-	
Aragon (R. Jacques-d')	**FY** 6	Jacques-Cœur (R.)	**FY** 54	France (R. des)	**FY** 84
Argenterie (R. de l')	**FY** 8	Jaurès (Pl. Jean)	**FY** 55	Vieille-Intendance (R.)	**EY** 87

B	Crypte N.-D.-des-Tables	**M²**	Hôtel des Trésoriers de France :
C	Hôtel St-Côme		Musée languedocien
D	Hôtel de Manse	**N**	Hôtel Richer de Belleval
E	Hôtel Baudon de Mauny	**Q**	Hôtel de la Vieille Intendance
F	Hôtel de Mirman	**R**	Hôtel de Cambacérès-Murles
K	Hôtels de Solas et d'Uston	**S**	Hôtel du Sarret
L	Hôtel Baschy du Cayla	**V**	Hôtel de Montcalm
M¹	Hôtel de Varennes :	**W**	Ancien couvent des Ursulines
	Musée du Vieux Montpellier,	**X**	Hôtel des Trésoriers de la Bourse
	Musée Fougau	**Y**	Salle St-Ravy
		Z	Hôtel Sabatier d'Espeyran

*Travel with **Michelin Maps** (scale 1: 200 000) which are revised regularly.*

Hôtel de Cambacérès-Murles (EY R) – This house's façade, by Giral, shows the richness and elegance of 18C ornamentation – beautifully curved and shaped wrought iron work, grotesque masks etc.

Hôtel du Sarret (EY S) – This is known as the Maison de la Coquille ("shell house") because of its squinches, a real architectural feat in which part of the building itself is supported on part of the vault. One of the squinches spans a corner on the street while the other, inside the courtyard, is beneath a corner tower.

Take Rue Astruc and cross Rue Foch.

This leads to the district known as **Ancien Courrier**, the oldest part of Montpellier, its narrow pedestrian streets lined with luxury boutiques.

From Rue Foch, take Rue du Petit-Scel.

The 19C **church of Ste-Anne (EY)**, surmounted by a high bell-tower and now deconsecrated, houses temporary exhibitions.
Opposite the church porch, stand the remains of a small building, which has been rebuilt here. Its early 17C decor is in Antique style.

Take Rue St-Anne and Rue St-Guilhem to Rue de la Friperie.

At no 5, **Hôtel de Montcalm (EY V)** has a beautiful hollow spiral staircase.

Take Rue du Bras-de-Fer left, then Rue des Trésoriers-de-la-Bourse right.

★ **Hôtel des Trésoriers de la Bourse (FY X)** – *4, rue des Trésoriers-de-la-Bourse.*
Also called Hôtel Rodez-Benavent, this town house by architect Jean Giral features an impressive open staircase in which sloping balustrades and rampant arches follow the line of the flights of steps, making an interesting contrast with the level balustrades and round arches framing the landings on either side. The façade overlooking the courtyard is decorated with delightful little cupids.
A second courtyard offers the peace and tranquillity of a large garden whose rear wall is decorated with flame ornaments.

Go back to Rue du Bras-de-Fer.

The narrow **Rue du Bras-de-Fer (EY 17)** is a medieval street spanned by a pointed archway. It leads down to **Rue de l'Ancien-Courrier★ (EFY 4)**, once called Rue des Relais-de-Poste and now lined with art galleries and elegant boutiques.

Turn left into Rue Joubert which leads to Place St-Ravy.

Place St-Ravy (FY 79) still boasts the remains (Gothic windows) of the Palace of the Kings of Majorca.
The **Salle St-Ravy (FY Y)**, in which temporary exhibitions are held, has beautiful vaulting decorated with keystones.

Return to Rue de l'Ancien-Courrier and take Rue Jacques-d'Aragon.

Hôtel St-Côme ⊙ **(FZ C)** – Now the Chamber of Commerce, this town house was built in the 18C by Jean-Antoine Giral thanks to a donation by François Gigot de Lapeyronie, surgeon to Louis XV, who bequeathed part of his fortune to the surgeons of Montpellier so that they could build an anatomical theatre similar to that in Paris.
The building facing the street is decorated with a double colonnade. The other building houses the famous polygonal anatomical theatre, under a superb dome with oculi and lanterns letting in a flood of light.

Return to Place de la Comédie via the busy Rue Jean-Moulin.

★★ PROMENADE DU PEYROU (AU, EY) *1hr*

An eventful history – In 1688, the town council decided to create a promenade in the highest-lying part of Montpellier to act as a framework for a monumental statue of Louis XIV. The architect d'Aviler designed a terrace with a view of the whole city and surrounding countryside. All that was missing was the statue which, although cast in Paris in 1692, did not reach its final location until 1718 after a long and arduous journey which took it from Le Havre to Bordeaux, then on to the Canal du Midi, and during which a number of misadventures befell it, not the least of which was falling into the Garonne. No trouble was too great, to the extent that a channel was even cut through the Frontignan lagoons so that the statue could be transported from the Mediterranean to Montpellier. Having finally made it to its destination, the statue was destroyed during the Revolution. It was replaced by the present replica in 1838. In the meantime, the Promenade du Peyrou had undergone a change of appearance.

The construction of the St-Clément aqueduct (1753 to 1766) by the engineer Pitot meant that the layout of the Promenade du Peyrou had to be altered. This task was entrusted to Jean-Antoine Giral and his nephew Jacques Donnat. Giral designed the ravishing **Château d'eau**, a water tower in the form of a small temple decorated with columns built to hide the aqueduct. By 1773, Promenade du Peyrou looked as it does today.

Tour – The promenade consists of two levels of terraces. The upper terrace, adorned with the equestrian statue of Louis XIV, affords a sweeping **view**★ of the Garrigues and Cévennes to the

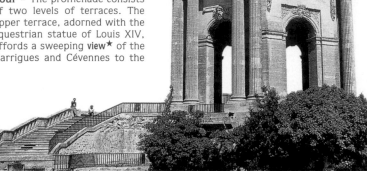

Château d'eau in the Peyrou

north, and the Mediterranean and, on a fine day, Mont Canigou in the distance to the south. Monumental flights of steps lead to the lower terraces decorated with wrought iron railings made after sketches by Giral. The most original feature of the Promenade du Peyrou is the ensemble of the Château d'eau and St-Clément aqueduct, 880m/2 890ft long and 22m/72ft high. The aqueduct's two levels of arcades were inspired by the Roman Pont du Gard *(east of Nîmes)*. It brings in water from Lez spring to the Château d'eau, which in turn is connected to three fountains built in the town centre at the same time: the fountain of the Three Graces *(Place de la Comédie)*, the Cybele fountain *(Place Chabaneau)* and the Unicorn fountain *(Place de la Canourgue)*. Promenade des Arceaux beneath the arches is transformed into a flea market on Saturdays.

The Arc de Triomphe (EY) – Built in the late 17C, the arch is decorated with low reliefs depicting the victories of Louis XIV and major events from his reign. Towards the city: to the north, the linking of two seas by the Canal du Midi, and to the south, the revocation of the Edict of Nantes; towards the Promenade du Peyrou: to the north, Louis XIV as Hercules being crowned by Victory, and to the south, the capture of Namur in 1692 and the United Provinces of the Netherlands kneeling before Louis XIV.

★THE ANTIGONE DISTRICT (CDU) *45min*

Behind the Polygone shopping centre and office complex, the new Antigone district is the boldly designed creation of Catalan architect, **Ricardo Bofill**.

Covering the 40ha/100 acres of the old polygonal army exercise ground, this vast neo-Classical housing project combines prefabrication technology (the prestressed concrete has been given the grain and colour of stone) with rigorously harmonious design on a gigantic scale. Behind a profusion of entablatures, pediments, pilasters and columns are low-income housing, public facilities and local shops, arranged around numerous squares and patios. The architect's quest for harmony has manifested itself in the smallest details, from the design of the paving to the street lighting.

Place du Nombre-d'Or, built to proportions based on an Antique architectural concept, is symmetrically composed of smooth curves and setback features around a vast area of ground planted with trees. The continuation of this square is formed by **Place du Millénaire**, a long mall lined with cypresses, Place de Thessalie then Place du Péloponnèse. The almost 1km/half a mile long vista, which stretches from the "Échelles de la ville" *(flights of steps backing onto the Polygone)*, past the **Esplanade de l'Europe**, with its crescent-shaped buildings, to the **Hôtel de Région**, with its glass walls reflected in the Lez, which has been converted into a dock for Port Juvénal at this point.

ADDITIONAL SIGHTS

Cathédrale St-Pierre (EX) – The cathedral, towering up like a fortress, is made to seem even more massive than it is by the adjacent façade of the Faculty of Medicine which prolongs it. It is the only church in Montpellier which was not completely destroyed during the Wars of Religion.

The former chapel of the college of St-Benoît (14C) was promoted to the rank of cathedral in the 16C when the diocesan seat was transferred from Maguelone to Montpellier, and restored in the 17C and again in the 19C. The building has nonetheless retained its original character.

Although built in the Gothic style, the cathedral is reminiscent of the single-nave Romanesque churches along the coast. The porch consists of two 14C towers, in front of a vault resting on the façade. Inside, the chancel and transept, rebuilt in the 19C, contrast with the austere 14C nave. The altar and the ambo (pulpit) in the pre-chancel, as well as the altar and tabernacle door in the sacrament chapel, left of the chancel, are the work of sculptor Philippe Koeppelin. The 18C organ case was made by Jean-François Lépine.

Faculté de Médecine (EX) – The Montpellier Faculty of Medicine occupies a former Benedictine monastery, founded in the 14C at the orders of Pope Urban V. The building was renovated in the 18C; most notably the façade, which was reworked by Giral and crowned with machicolations. Two bronze statues, depicting the Montpellier doctors Barthez and Lapeyronie, stand guard at the entrance.

The busts in the hall also depict famous doctors. From the courtyard, there is a view of the west side of the cathedral and the anatomical theatre built in the early 18C.

★ **Musée Atger** ⊘ – *1st floor, access (signposted) via the Houdan staircase.*

This museum is devoted mainly to the collection of drawings bequeathed by Xavier Atger (1758-1833) who was at the Faculty of Medicine from 1813 to 1833, and includes works by artists from the south of France, representing the 17C and 18C French school (Bourdon, Puget, Mignard, Rigaud, Lebrun, Subleyras, Natoire, Vernet, Fragonard, J.-M. Vien), the 16C, 17C and 18C Italian school (Tiepolo) and the 17C and 18C Flemish school (Velvet Bruegel, Van Dyck, Rubens, Martin de Vos).

Musée d'anatomie ⊘ – *1st floor, access signposted.*

The museum of anatomy is housed in an enormous room and comprises exhibits of normal and pathological anatomy.

Le Corum ⊘ **(FX)** – Designed by the architect Claude Vasconi, this vast elongated complex made of concrete and red granite from Finland, closes off the long gap made by the Esplanade. Its modular structures can host several conferences at once, as well as exhibitions and various other events. The Corum's main feature is the **Opéra Berlioz**, with excellent acoustics, designed to seat 2 000 spectators. The **view** from the **terrace** ⊘ encompasses the roofs of the city, the cathedral of St-Pierre, the former Jesuit college, and the dazzling white spire of the church of Ste-Anne.

Post-modern architecture in the Antigone district

Ancien couvent des Ursulines (FX W) – The buildings of this former 17C Ursuline convent, which was extended in the 19C to be used as a prison, have been restored to their original appearance. The convent now houses the Centre chorégraphique Montpellier-Languedoc-Roussillon and various cultural events.

Tour de la Babote (FZ) – This tower, recently unearthed and restored, was one of 25 towers in the 12C curtain wall. The lower part dates from this period, while the upper part was built in the 18C to house the observatory of the Académie Royale des Sciences. In 1832, Chappe's semaphore visual telegraph was installed. The building now serves as the headquarters of an astronomy society *(Société astronomique de l'Hérault)*.

Jardin des Plantes ⊘ **(EX)** – The botanical gardens, the oldest in France, founded in 1593 by Henri IV and laid out by Richer de Belleval, initially stretched as far as the Peyrou. They were created for the Montpellier Faculty of Botany and for the study of medicinal plants. The gardens contain both temperate and tropical hothouses, and are home to various species of Mediterranean tree, such as nettle tree, holm-oak and mock privet (phillyrea). A large ginkgo biloba (maidenhair tree), planted in 1795, is a graft from the first ginkgo plant introduced to France by Antoine Gouan.

The southern part is occupied by a botanical garden containing 3 000 species – set up following the principles of natural classification of plants based on their anatomy laid down by the botanist Augustin Pyrame de **Candolle** in the early 19C. An orangery occupies one end.

The busts of famous naturalists from the Montpellier faculty occupy the length of the garden.

►► **Musée de l'Infanterie** ⊘ **(AV)** – Museum on the French Infantry.

THE MONTPELLIER "FOLLIES"

Dotted around the outskirts of Montpellier are a number of elegant "follies", built as summer residences in the 18C by aristocrats and wealthier bourgeois citizens of the city. Some have been swallowed up by suburbs as the city continues to expand, while others – about thirty or so – are still surrounded by acres of vineyards. Those outside the city suburbs provide particularly charming examples of old country mansions, set in pretty gardens, often with lakes and fountains.

East of Montpellier – *Round tour of 9km/6mi*

From the city centre, follow the signs to the "Montpellier-Méditerranée" airport. After the bridge over the Lez, take the road to Mauguio (D 24). The Château de Flaugergues is situated about 2km/1mi down the road, on the right, in the Millénaire district.

★ **Château de Flau-gergues** ⊘ – This estate on a hillock overlooking the plain was purchased by Étienne de Flau-gergues, Montpellier financier and advisor to the Parlement de Toulouse, in 1696. The château has quite a plain façade on three levels which gives onto terraces and French style gardens. It is the oldest of the Montpellier "follies" and is built in the style of an Italian villa. To the southwest stretches the park, in which many rare varieties of tree are planted. Inside the château, a monumental

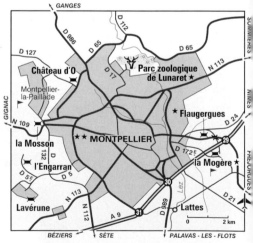

staircase, with a vaulted ceiling adorned with pendant keystones, is hung with a set of magnificent 17C Brussels tapestries depicting the life of Moses. The various rooms contain beautiful furniture as well as engravings and antique paintings. Flaugergues exudes the charm of a house that has been home to the same family for many years.

The tour of the château ends with an opportunity to taste some of the wine produced on the estate.

Rejoin the road to Mauguio, heading right, and drive past the Château de Flaugergues and under the motorway to get to the Château de la Mogère.

★ **Château de la Mogère** ⓥ – Designed by Jean Giral, this elegant early-18C folly, renovated at the end of the 18C, has a harmonious façade surmounted by a pediment which is outlined against a backdrop of pine trees. In the park, a beautiful Italian style Baroque fountain is decorated with shell motifs and surmounted by groups of cherubs. Inside the château are numerous family portraits, furniture and paintings from the 18C. (A Brueghel, Hyacinthe Rigaud, Louis David, Jouvenet). The great hall is decorated with delicate plasterwork.

Return to the city centre on the D 172^E.

West of Montpellier – *Round tour of 22km/14mi*

From the city centre take the road to Ganges (D 986) for 6km/4mi, then turn left towards Celleneuve, and then right onto D 127. A little further on, two lion-topped pillars indicate the turnoff to Château d'O.

Château d'O ⓥ – The 18C building is surrounded by a very beautiful park, decorated with statues from Château de La Mosson. Owned by the Conseil Général de l'Hérault, the château is used as a theatre during the *Printemps des Comédiens* festival *(see Calendar of events at the end of the guide).*

Carry on to Celleneuve. Follow signs to Juvignac, then turn left into the road leading to the Château de La Mosson.

Château de La Mosson – This was the most sumptuous residence in the Montpellier area. It was built from 1728 to 1729 by a very rich banker, Joseph Bonnier, who was made Baron de La Mosson. The pediment on the garden façade was sculpted by the Lorraine artist, Adam. The park was decorated with beautiful statues which have now been dispersed. Only the Baroque fountain is a reminder of the originally lavish decoration of the park, which is now a public park.

Return to N 109 and take the first road on the left towards Lavérune.

Before long, the road is passing through vineyard country.

Château de l'Engarran – Beyond the superb wrought-iron entrance gate from the Château de La Mosson stands a Louis XV style building.

Carry on towards Lavérune. The Château de Lavérune is on the far west side of the village.

Château de Lavérune – This imposing 17C-18C building in the middle of a park full of cypresses, plane trees, magnolias and sweet chestnut trees was once the residence of the bishops of Montpellier. The first floor houses the **Musée Hofer-Bury**, which displays a collection of paintings and sculptures by contemporary artists in temporary exhibitions. Artists whose work is featured here include Henri de Jordan, Gérard and Bernard Calvet, Roger Bonafé, Vincent Bioulès and Wang Wei-Xin. On the ground floor there is an Italian style music room decorated with a wrought iron balustrade and ornate plasterwork.
To the east of the château is a 16C gateway, which looks as if it was part of some fortifications, despite the vermiculated bosses with which it is adorned (the side facing the church doorway).

Take D 5 back to the city centre.

EXCURSIONS

★ **Parc zoologique de Lunaret** ⓥ – *6km/4mi north of the Hôpitaux-Facultés district. Leave town on Avenue Bouisson-Bertrand (**ABT**) and take the road to Mende.*
In this vast 80ha/200 acre park bequeathed to the town by Henri de Lunaret, the animals are kept relatively at liberty in a setting of *garrigues* and undergrowth. The zoo is a very pleasant place for a stroll, with the opportunity of watching zebras, bison, elk, alpacas, moufflons, wolves etc, as well as exotic birds in aviaries.

Lattes – *6km/4mi south of Montpellier. Leave by ④ on the town plan.*
In 1963, the small town of Lattes rediscovered the archeological site of Lattara which, for eight centuries (from 6C BC to 3C AD) was a thriving port, handling Mediterranean trade. Situated at the delta of the Lez, it supplied the hinterland, particularly Sextantio, as Castelnau-le-Lez was known in Antiquity. The local people imported wine, oil, luxury ceramic ware and manufactured articles and exported the region's traditional resources in exchange – freshwater fish, wool and pelts, resin, mineral ore, etc. However, although excellent for trade, the town's site surrounded by marshes led to problems and more particularly gradual subsidence. Stratigraphic study has revealed that a total of twelve towns were built one on top of the other. The rising water table effectively meant that the town had to be raised by 20-30cm/8-12in every 50 years (two towns were also

destroyed by fire in about 550 and 50 BC). The numerous remains have shown that, after a period of apparently free trade between the Etruscans and Greeks, the port became a redistribution centre for Marseille trade until the Phocean city fell in 49 BC. Having served as a river port during Gallo-Roman times, the site was abandoned when an increase in rainfall caused the port to silt up and the water table to rise.

Musée archéologique Henri-Prades ⊘ – *Leave Lattes to the southeast on D 132 towards Pérols.*

This archeological museum housed in the old farmhouse of the painter Bazille displays temporary exhibitions on the 1st floor (local archeological collections) and, on the 2nd floor and mezzanine, local discoveries. In this part of the museum, there is an exhibition on the conversion of the site into a town during the second Iron Age and the creation of the port, as well as daily life in Lattara (house, furniture, kitchen; large collections of ceramic and glass ware), funerary arrangements (steles and funerary furniture) and the port of Lattara itself.

Finally, part of the museum is devoted to the site after the port had been abandoned, including a display on the 3C and 4C necropolis of St-Michel in which 76 tombs were discovered.

⚓ **Palavas-les-Flots** – *12km/7mi south of Montpellier. Leave on ④ on the town plan.*

Located at the mouth of the river Lez, now a canal, this fishing port has a charming, lively historical district. Palavas was transformed into a seaside resort

Musée Albert Dubout, Palavas-les-Flots

Les vacances by cartoonist Albert Dubout

highly popular with Montpellier families, who flocked here armed with their picnic lunches and shrimping nets every Sunday, by the opening of a railway line in 1872 – the *petit train*, immortalised by the famous cartoonist Albert Dubout (1905-76), who lived at Palavas-les-Flots for many years, and now replaced by the **Petit train Albert Dubout** ⊘ designed to resemble its cartoon equivalent. For years, Palavas was the only beach on this stretch of the coast, until the Languedoc-Roussillon shoreline was developed for tourism and the neighbouring resorts of Grande-Motte and Carnon-Plage built. The *joutes nautiques* held in Palavas are very popular.

Musée Albert-Dubout ⊘ – *Access on foot from the east bank along Quai des Arènes or by boat.* This museum in memory of the cartoonist occupies the Ballestras redoubt, a reconstruction of an 18C fortified tower built in the middle of Levant lagoon. Besides his boldly executed and amusing illustrations of Montpellier holiday-makers, Dubout also drew numerous scenes of bull-fighting, a sport of which he was a life-long fan. From the terrace, there is a **panoramic view** from Mont St-Clair to the gulf of Aigues-Mortes.

Not far from Palavas is **Maguelone★** with the remains of its interesting **cathedral.**

Chaos de MONTPELLIER-LE-VIEUX★★★

Michelin map 80 fold 14 or 240 fold 10 – 18km/11mi northeast of Millau
Local maps see Vallée de la DOURBIE and Les GRANDS CAUSSES

The *chaos* of Montpellier-le-Vieux is an extraordinary collection of rock formations, created by erosion and rainwater streaming over dolomite, which covers 120ha/300 acres of the Causse Noir. It was given its name by shepherds bringing their flocks from the Languedoc to summer pastures, who caught sight of this gigantic jumble of rocks which looked for all the world as if it were a vast ruined city.

Until 1870, this mass of rocky outcrops overgrown with dense forest was considered by local inhabitants to be a cursed city and the haunt of the devil himself. Any adventurous sheep or goats who strayed there would vanish into the night, devoured by the numerous wolves which roamed the site. Eventually the area was cleared of these undesirable residents and of some of its trees, so that the tumbledown "city" of rocks could be seen.

"Ruined city" of natural rock formations

Montpellier-le-Vieux was discovered in 1883 by J and L de Malafosse and De Barbeyrac-Saint-Maurice, who were amazed at this intricate maze of alleyways, arches and corbelled ledges. In 1885, E-A Martel mapped the site.

Getting there – The entrance (ticket booth) to Montpellier-le-Vieux lies at the end of a private road leading from the hamlet of Maubert for 1.5km/1mi, past a viewing table and into a car park. To get to Maubert:

– from Millau, take D 110 (16km/10mi);

– from Rozier or from Peyreleau, take D 29 and then D 110 off to the right (10km/6mi);

– from Nant, take D 991 to la Roque-Ste-Marguerite, from which you take a very narrow road up past the church heading north of the village and then turn left onto D 110 (26km/16mi).

There is also a footpath leading up from la Roque-Ste-Marguerite *(1hr 30min each way)*.

TOUR ⊙

On foot – The site can be explored along several waymarked footpaths (coloured plastic markers on the ground):

– a walk to the "Belvédère" and back *(waymarked in blue – 30min; not very taxing)*

– the Grand Tour *(waymarked in red – 1hr 30min; some quite steep ups and downs)*

– a walk to the "Camparolié" *(waymarked in yellow – 15min from the "Porte de Mycènes")* with a possible extension to la Roque Ste-Marguerite.

– the tour of the "Lac" *(waymarked in orange – 30min from the "Cénotaphe")*

By tourist train – The *Petit Train Vert*, a rubber-wheeled train service, follows a route well away from the footpaths, enabling visitors to reach the heart of the site and see some of its finest rocks without undue exertion:

– to the "Belvédère" *(40min)*

– to the "Porte de Mycènes" *(1hr)* with a short walk within everyone's capacity

– the "Circuit Jaune" *(1hr 30min)* part of which is on foot along a footpath

Selected features – Montpellier-le-Vieux is such an unusual and captivating place, in a beautiful natural setting, that many tourists may wish to spend longer than the minimum time recommended for a visit *(but beware of getting lost by straying from the waymarked paths)*. The hours spent wandering among the rocks in this peaceful place, in the shade of pines and oak trees, past craggy columns and massive walls will leave any nature lover feeling refreshed, and it will be a day to remember.

Almost all the rock formations of Montpellier-le-Vieux have earned nicknames in keeping with their shape or outline: Skittle, Crocodile, Mycaenae Gate, Sphinx, Bear's Head etc.

The "Douminal" – From the top of this natural tower of rock overlooking four irregularly shaped cirques ("le Lac", "les Amats", "les Rouquettes", "la Millière"), separated by tall rocky crests and surrounded by the cliffs of the Causse Noir, there is an extensive view. To the north lies the "Rocher de la Croix" (Cross) and, on the right, the Cirque du Lac thick with pine trees (in the distance, the sharply defined outline of the cliffs lining the Tarn gorge can be seen); to the south, lies the Dourbie valley and the scenic ridge road of the Causse du Larzac; to the west, is the Cirque des Rouquettes; and to the east, the Chaos de Roquesaltes.

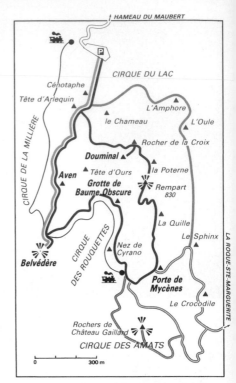

Having negotiated its way round the "Poterne" (Postern) the footpath almost immediately reveals another spectacular view of the whole site from the "Rempart" (Rampart; alt 830m/2 723ft). Then the path leads down towards the Cirque des Amats and the "Porte de Mycènes" (Mycaenae Gate).

The "Porte de Mycènes" – To Martel, the Mycaenae Gate evoked the celebrated Gate of Lions of Ancient Greece. Its sheer size and the height of its natural arch (12m/39ft) make it one of the most original phenomena of Montpellier-le-Vieux.

After crossing a culvert, the path leads to the "Baume Obscure" grotto where Martel discovered the bones of cave-bears. To the left of the mouth of the grotto there is a glimpse of the "Nez de Cyrano" (Cyrano de Bergerac's famously large nose). Then the footpath leads up to the "Belvédère".

The "Belvédère" (Viewpoint) – There is a view over the Cirque des Rouquettes, around which the path has just led, of the sunken valley of the Dourbie to the south, and the Cirque de la Millière to the north.

The path winds back towards the beginning of the various circuits, skirting along the Cirque de la Millière at mid-height. On the right, about 200m/220yd on from the "Belvédère", is a yawning chasm the "Aven".

The "Aven" (Chasm) – This drops to a depth of 53m/174ft.

From here, the footpath leads straight back to the car park.

The key on the inside front cover explains the abbreviations and symbols used in the text or on the maps.

MONTSÉGUR★

Michelin map 86 fold 5 or 235 fold 46 – 12km/7.5mi south of Lavelanet

The holocaust of the Cathar church is vividly recalled by the Montségur crag – the setting for the final episode of the Albigensian Crusade which brought about the political downfall of Languedoc at the hands of the Capetian dynasty. High up on this rocky peak (alt 1 216m/3 989ft) stand the ruins of a castle.

HISTORICAL NOTES

In 1204 a second castle was built at Montségur to replace a fortress of unknown date. It was occupied by about a hundred men under the command of Pierre-Roger de Mirepoix and beyond its ramparts by a community of Cathar refugees with their bishop, deacons and *parfaits*. The prestige of the place, and the pilgrimages it drew to it, found no favour with either the Roman Catholic Church or the French monarchy.

When, in 1242, Blanche de Castille and the clergy heard the news of the massacre of members of the Inquisition at Avignonet by a band of men from Montségur, the fate of the citadel was sealed.

The seneschal of Carcassonne and the archbishop of Narbonne were ordered to lay the fortress to siege, which they duly began in July 1243. It is thought that the Roman Catholic armies numbered about 10 000 men!

Under cover of the long winter nights, patrols of experienced mountain dwellers scaled the steep cliff (more easily than knights would have done) and, bypassing the fortress to the east, gained a foothold on the upper plateau. A huge ballista, taken up in separate pieces and then assembled on site, breached the castle walls with rock projectiles dug out from an open quarry on the mountainside.

Pierre-Roger de Mirepoix then surrendered on condition his garrison was spared. A truce was made lasting from 1 to 15 March 1244. The Cathars, who had not agreed to it, did not take advantage of this respite to try and escape their fate by recanting or taking flight. On the morning of 16 March, 207 of them came down the mountain and climbed onto a gigantic pyre. The self-assurance of the martyrs, and the mystery surrounding the safe hiding place of their "treasure", still fascinate scholars and all those who are true to the tradition of Occitania or who follow sects that promote Cathar philosophy.

In 1245, the new lord of Mirepoix, Guy de Lévis II, came to live there and swore allegiance to the king. A third castle was built towards the middle or end of the 13C; nothing is left of the castle that still stood in 1244.

Strategically placed, facing the Cerdagne, between France and Aragon, it made an ideal stronghold for observation and defence. It is the ruins of this castle that modern visitors explore.

CHÂTEAU ⊘

Leave the car in the car park along D 9. 1hr 30min there and back along a steep rocky footpath.

Before climbing the sheer face of the crag itself, the path passes the stele erected in 1960 "to those martyred in the name of pure Christian love".

The castle occupies a **site★★** on the top of towering cliffs more than a thousand feet high and offering a remarkable panorama over the ranges of the Plantaurel, the deep valley of the Aude and the massif of St-Barthélemy.

The fortress, in the shape of a pentagon, follows the outline of the plateau on the summit. It is reached through a gate on the south side.

Around the inner courtyard, various buildings (dwelling places, annexes) backed onto the ramparts.

In the past, access to the keep from the ramparts was through a doorway level with the first floor. Inside, a staircase led to the lower room, which was used for defence and as a storeroom. Nowadays, it is reached by walking round

Montségur perched on its rocky crag

through the north gate of the curtain wall and through an opening overlooking the old water tank. In this room at the summer solstice, sunbeams shine in through two arrow slits and straight out through the arrow slits opposite.

Northwest of the foot of the keep, the remains of the "Cathar village" are being excavated.

MONTSÉGUR VILLAGE

This lies at the foot of the rock in the valley of the Lasset. In the town hall *(mairie)* there is an **archeological museum** ⊙, housing the discoveries of the excavations undertaken since 1956: a large amount of furniture from the 13C and tools have enabled experts to trace occupation of the Montségur crag back to Neolithic times.

The museum also contains information on Cathar philosophy.

Cirque de MOURÈZE★★

Michelin map 83 fold 5 or 240 fold 22 – 8km/5mi west of Clermont-l'Hérault

The Cirque de Mourèze lies concealed between the valleys of the Orb and the Hérault, on the south side of Liausson mountain. This vast jumble of dolomitic rocks forms a natural amphitheatre covering over 340ha/840 acres, with significant differences in height (varying from 170m/557ft to 526m/1 725ft). It rests on the Jurassic rock strata of Liausson mountain and is delimited by the green valley of the Petite Dourbie to the south.

TOUR *allow 45min*

The village – The picturesque old village of Mourèze, with its narrow streets, its little houses with outside staircases and its red marble fountain, lies at the foot of a sheer rock face, the top of which is home to a castle.

In the Romanesque church, which has been heavily restored, there is a 15C apse.

★★ **The cirque** – The cirque is surrounded by enormous boulders. A number of waymarked footpaths lead through fresh, green nooks and crannies in between rocks which have been eroded into the strangest shapes – a Sphinx, a Camel, a Damsel, a Sleeping Lion and many more. There are also the "Fairies" and numerous other weird rocks resembling ruins which are particularly eyecatching in the light of the beginning and close of day.

Parc des Courtinals ⊙ – Situated east of the cirque and covering a surface of 40ha/98 acres, Courtinals park is an ancient Gallic settlement, which was inhabited as early as the Middle Neolithic Age until about 450 BC (end of the Bronze Age and first Iron Age). It is almost surrounded by a high barrier of rocks, at the foot of which there are natural cavities once used for storing silex and pottery.

Along the archeological and botanical trail, there are several sites of Iron Age huts, one of which has been reconstructed.

From the viewpoint *(viewing table)*, there is an **overall view** of the dolomitic cirque.

NAJAC★

Population 766
Michelin map 79 fold 20 or 235 fold 19

Situated on a conical peak enclosed in a meander of the Aveyron, on the boundary of Rouergue and Quercy, the ancient village of Najac occupies a remarkable **site**★★. The ruins of the fortified castle tower above the slate rooftops of the village.

Two large holiday villages *(villages de vacances)* in the vicinity contribute to the lively local atmosphere. The D 239, to the east, offers the best overall **view**★ of Najac: the narrow, sinuous street of houses following the line of the ridge on which it stands, while the turrets of the fortress which once held a superb strategic position loom on top of a rocky outcrop.

Najac and the Albigensian heresy – Bertrand de Saint-Gilles, son of the Count of Toulouse Raymond IV, ordered the construction of the first castle and made Najac the administrative centre for the province of Rouergue. In 1182, Philippe Auguste endorsed Najac as the fief of his vassal, the Count of Toulouse Raymond V de Saint-Gilles. Three years later, the English seized the fortress and signed an alliance there with the King of Aragon against the Count of Toulouse. In 1196 Najac became once more the fief of the Count of Toulouse Raymond VI. Soon after 1200, the Cathar heresy took root in Najac.

After being destroyed by the troops of Simon de Montfort, the castle was rebuilt by Alphonse de Poitiers, brother of St Louis and husband of the Count of Toulouse's daughter, Jeanne. The inhabitants, accused of being heretics, were punished by being forced to build the church.

The village – The castle ruins are reached through the Place du Faubourg, with covered arcades, and down the main street lined with mainly 13C-16C houses. On the way there are two fountains with basins; the second one is carved from an enormous monolithic slab of granite dated 1344 and bearing the arms of Blanche de Castille.

★ Fortress ⊘ – A castle had originally been built by Bertrand de Saint-Gilles. It was replaced by this fortress, a masterpiece of 13C military architecture, which keeps watch over the valley of the Aveyron. At the time, a large garrison lived in the village which numbered more than 2 000 inhabitants.

Of the three original curtain walls there still remain considerable fortifications flanked by large round towers. The castle itself, built partly from pale-coloured sandstone, is protected by thick walls and is shaped like a trapezium. The most impregnable of the towers, on the southeast, was the keep.

Having passed the successive curtain walls through the postern gates, visitors reach the terrace of the keep. This gives a magnificent **view★** over the fortress, the rows of village houses, the pretty Aveyron valley and the church built between the castle and the river, at the heart of the original village.

Church – In spite of additions, this is an interesting Gothic building. The west front is adorned at the top with a rose window. Inside, the single nave ends with a flat chevet. On the left of the nave is an unusual 14C wrought-iron structure in which "the candle of Our Lady" (Easter candle) was kept. In the chancel note the original altar (14C) made from a vast slab of fine sandstone; a Crucifix by the 15C Spanish school; two 15C statues: the Virgin Mary and St John; and also a fine 16C polychrome wood statue of St Peter seated.

NARBONNE★

Population 45 849
Michelin map 83 fold 14 or 240 folds 29 and 30 – Local map see Les CORBIÈRES

Narbonne, which has been in its time the ancient capital of Gallia Narbonensis, the residence of the Visigoth monarchy and an archiepiscopal seat, is now a lively Mediterranean city playing an important role as a wine producing centre and a road and rail junction. Its municipal, military and religious architecture, the treasures in its museums, the charm of the river banks of the Robine, and its shaded boulevards all contribute to its appeal to visitors.

HISTORICAL NOTES

A sea port – Narbonne may well have served as a harbour and market for a 7C BC Gallic settlement on the Montlaures hill to the north of the modern city. The town of "Colonia Narbo Martius", established in 118 BC by decree of the Roman Senate, became a strategic crossroads along the Via Domitia as well as a flourishing port. It exported oil, linen, wood, hemp, the cheeses and meat from the Cévennes so much appreciated by the Romans, and later on sigillated earthenware. Most of the river shipping business, however, was centred on the Italian, Iberian and then Gallic wine trade. During this period the city expanded dramatically and was embellished with magnificent buildings (Capitoline temple, forum).

A capital city – In 27 BC Narbonne gave its name to the Roman province created by Augustus. It was "the most beautiful", according to Martial, and, together with Lyon, the most densely populated city of Gaul. Cicero proclaimed Narbonensis to be "the boulevard of the Latin world".

The Roman Empire was then crushed by Barbarian invasions. After the sack of Rome in 410 by the Visigoths, Narbonne became their capital. Later, it fell to the Saracens; in 759 after a long siege Pépin the Short recaptured it.

Charlemagne created the duchy of Gothie with Narbonne as the capital. It was divided into several seigneurial estates: the City, with the cathedral and the archbishopric, belonging to the archbishop; the town, with the basilica of St-Paul-Serge, headed by the Viscount; and the New Town, left to the Jews. Municipal administration was carried out by Consuls.

In the 12C a troubadour, Bertrand de Bar, wrote a *chanson de geste* called "Aimeri de Narbonne", depicting the city, and the great ships made with iron nails, the richly laden galleys to which the city's inhabitants owed their wealth.

From the 14C, the change in course of the Aude, the havoc wrought by the Hundred Years War and plague, and the departure of the Jews caused Narbonne to decline.

The arrest of Cinq-Mars and de Thou (1642) – As a young man, Cinq-Mars, chief equerry of France, managed to win the friendship of Louis XIII. Carried away by his success, he attempted to overthrow Cardinal Richelieu. His friend de Thou, a Counsellor of State, was party to his plans. Together with the entire French aristocracy, Cinq-Mars took part in the siege of Perpignan, which was then held by the Spaniards; however, he struck up negotiations with Spain.

The Cardinal, who lay sick in Narbonne – where in fact he was to draw up his famous last testament, obtained the text of the agreement Cinq-Mars had made with the enemy and had Cinq-Mars arrested. De Thou was also seized. The two friends were tried at Lyon and beheaded on 12 September 1642.

From the bridge (Pont-des-Marchands) leading off Cours Mirabeau (**BY**) a passenger barge runs along the Canal de la Robine as far as Port-la-Nouvelle. This trip through the Narbonne lagoons includes a stop at Île-Ste-Lucie, a protected natural site. Allow one day. Operates May to October. ☎ 05 68 49 12 40.

Silting-up, decline and renewal – Until the 14C, Narbonne had been a maritime city; but gradually alluvial river deposits and sand silted up the bay. On the banks of the present lagoon of Bages and Sigean, the remains of the ancient maritime bay, there are many salt marshes. At the time of the Revolution, Narbonne numbered only a few thousand inhabitants, and it was stripped of its status as archbishopric.

Nowadays, the high level of wine-producing in the area has once more made the city a dynamic centre of economic activity, and new areas of town are being developed.

★★ CATHÉDRALE ST-JUST ⊙ (BX) *30min*

The present cathedral is the fourth church built on this site since the reign of Constantine. The first stone was laid on 3 April 1272; it had been sent from Rome by Pope Clement IV, a former archbishop of the city. In 1332, the radiating chancel had been completed in the same style as the great cathedrals of northern France, but building the nave and the transept would have involved breaching the ancient rampart which still served in troubled medieval times, so this was postponed...and had just been begun by the 18C.

Exterior – Note in particular the chevet with its High Gothic lancets, the great arches surmounted by merlons with arrow slits overlooking the terraces of the ambulatory, the flying buttresses with two arches, the turrets and the powerful defensive buttresses, and the lofty north and south towers. A visitor facing the wall bounding the choir will be impressed by the sturdiness of the 18C pillars on which the transept and the first 2 vaults of the nave would have rested, and which surround the **Cour St-Eutrope**. From this courtyard, the **terraces** ⊙ and the **north tower** ⊙ can be reached, both of which give an interesting **view★** over the flying buttresses of the cathedral, the Archbishops' palace and the city.

From the 18C **Jardin des Archevêques**, there is a fine view of the flying buttresses, the south tower of the cathedral and the Synodes building, flanked by two round towers.

Palais des Archevêques and Cathédrale St-Just

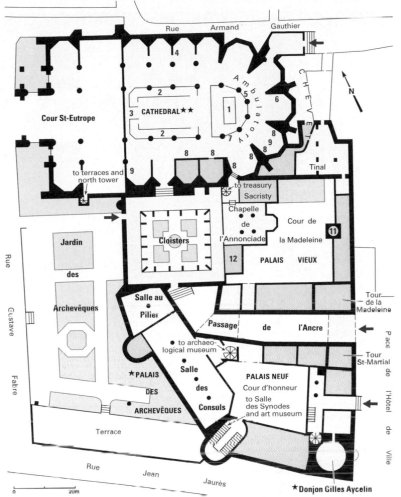

1 - High altar (1694), with baldachin and Corinthian columns, designed by J. Hardouin-Mansart.
On either side of the altar the first few pillars of the chancel are adorned with very old mural paintings.

2 - 18C choir stalls

3 - Organ case in two parts (18C)

4 - Marble funerary statue of the Chevalier de La Borde (17C)

5 - Renaissance tomb of Cardinal Briçonnet in white marble

6 - In 1981, a high relief depicting the Redemption was discovered in this chapel

7 - Flamboyant Gothic tomb of Cardinal Pierre de Jugie

8 - Aubusson and Gobelins tapestries from the 17 and 19C

9 - This chapel houses a beautiful alabaster statue of the Virgin and Child (14C), normally on display in chapel 6

10 - Late 15C polychrome stone Entombment from Bavaria

Cloisters - 14C. The cloisters are at the foot of the south side of the cathedral; note the high Gothic vaulting of the galleries and, overlooking the courtyard, the gargoyles carved amongst the buttresses.

Interior - Inside, the strikingly well-proportioned chancel was the only part to be completed. The height of its vaulting (41m/134ft) is exceeded only by that in the cathedrals of Amiens (42m/137ft) and Beauvais (48m/157ft).
The supporting structure of the chancel exhibits great architectural purity: large arches beneath a triforium, in which the colonnettes are an extension of the lancets of the great windows.
The cathedral chancel comprises four bays, surrounded by an ambulatory and radiating chapels. In it are numerous works of art *(see diagram)*. The five chapels, the tall windows in the apse and the second tall window on the right still feature some fine 14C stained glass.

15C tapestry in the cathedral

The chapel of the Annonciade, outside, dating from the 15C, was the old chapter-house; opposite the entrance there is a fine painting by Nicolas Tournier (17C), *Tobias and the Angel*.

Treasury ⊘ – The treasury is in a room above the chapel of the Annonciade, in which the vaulting creates an unusual acoustic.

It includes illuminated manuscripts and, together with other church plate, a fine gilt chalice (1561). The most remarkable exhibit is a magnificent late-15C Flemish tapestry depicting the **Creation★★**, woven in silk and gold thread. The subtlety of the colours, the skill of the design, and the expression of the three figures of the Holy Trinity, creating the elements and man, make this an exceptionally beautiful composition. It is the only one remaining from a set of 10 donated to the chapter by the archbishop François Fouquet.

Note also a fine late-10C carved ivory missal plaque and marriage casket in rock crystal with antique intaglio decoration, which was used as a reliquary.

★PALAIS DES ARCHEVÊQUES ⊘ (BX) *2hr*

NB the visit to the cathedral and cloisters can also be made by following the directions displayed in the precinct "Palais des Archevêques – Cathédrale", leaving from Place de l'Hôtel-de-Ville.

The façade of the Archbishops' Palace overlooks the lively **Place de l'Hôtel-de-Ville**, at the heart of the city. It has three square towers: framing the Passage de l'Ancre, the Tour de la Madeleine (the oldest) and Tour St-Martial; and further to the left the Donjon Gilles-Aycelin. Between the last two, Viollet-le-Duc built the present Hôtel de Ville (town hall) in a neo-Gothic style.

The Archbishops' Palace, originally a modest ecclesiastical residence, is now an example of religious, military and civil architecture bearing the imprint of centuries: the 12C Old Palace, the 13C Madeleine and Gilles-Aycelin towers, the 14C St-Martial tower and New Palace, the 17C archbishops' suite and the 19C façade of the Hôtel de Ville. There are fine interior courtyards in the Old Palace, north of the Passage de l'Ancre, and in the New Palace, to the south.

Passage de l'Ancre – This almost fortified street with its impressive walls leads to the Place de l'Hôtel-de-Ville between the St-Martial and Madeleine towers.

Salle au Pilier – This fine 14C room, with its vaulting supported by a huge central pillar, houses a collection of Romanesque capitals, the recumbent figure of Viscountess Algayette (13C) and Visigothic and Carolingian inscriptions and low reliefs.

Palais Vieux (Old Palace) – The Old Palace consists of two main buildings flanking the Madeleine tower. To the east, a square staircase tower divides a Romanesque façade pierced by arcades (**11**). The Madeleine tower has a Romanesque door, originally from elsewhere, on the upper floor and to the south a façade pierced with Romanesque, Gothic and Renaissance windows. Other monuments stand around Madeleine courtyard: the square Carolingian bell-tower of the church of

St-Théodard (**12**), the apse of the Annonciade chapel overlooked to the north by the imposing cathedral chevet, and the 14C Tinal (the canons' old storeroom) which has recently been restored.

Palais Neuf (New Palace) – The New Palace complex surrounds the cour d'honneur (or Cour du Palais Neuf) and comprises the façade over the courtyard of the Town Hall, the Gilles-Aycelin keep, the St-Martial tower, the Synodes building and the north and south wings.

Salle des Consuls – This room on the ground floor of the Synodes building is supported on part of the old Roman fortified city wall. The room has a fine central row of pillars.

★★ **Archeological Museum** ⓥ – Narbonne undoubtedly possesses one of the finest collections of **Roman paintings**★★ in France. Most come from the archeological excavations at Clos de la Lombarde (north part of the ancient town) and the frescoes and floor coverings testify to the style in which the homes of the rich in Narbo Martius were decorated in the first two centuries AD. After an introduction to the architecture of a Gallo-Roman house (exhibition of building materials, reconstruction of a deposit of various painted plasters) and an explanation of the techniques of mural painting in the days of Antiquity, the museum visit leads into an area containing various examples of painted and mosaic decors. The style best represented in Narbonne is the Fourth Pompeian style (late 1C AD). The walls are generally divided into three tiers: the bottom imitation marble, the middle on the whole mythological scenes framed in elaborate floral borders and the top window-like panels divided by ornate columns creating the effect of a sort of architectural perspective. They feature stylised

motifs, hunting or pastoral scenes and garlands, on a red or white background. Various kinds of openwork border are displayed together on a stand (palm leaf motifs, arcs of a circle). The most famous decor of this type is the **painting of a Genie** which adorned the triclinium (dining room) of the villa: to the right, above the entablature of an aedicula, is a bust of Apollo wreathed in laurel; to the left is a Genie carrying a horn of plenty and a libations dish, accompanied by a winged Victory, damaged, brandishing a shield. Decorating a coffered section in a ceiling is a Maenad, or female follower of Bacchus, holding a beribboned thyrsus (wand tipped with a pine cone, an ancient fertility symbol). Most of the mosaics are in black and white and are inspired by works of this kind made in Pompeii. These are either marble inlaid on a black background (middle of 1C), or geometrical motifs (strapwork, squares, loz-

Cartier/IMAGES TOULOUSE

Roman painting

enges etc). One example of a mosaic of marble inlaid on a black background features a shield of triangles framed in strapwork of two interlaced strands. In La Madeleine upper chapel is a display of artefacts discovered during excavations of the oppidum at Montlaurès. These include some 14C frescoes (Annunciation). The following rooms contain a large collection of stone fragments evoking the institutions, daily life, religious practices and commercial activities of Roman Narbonne: note a milestone, a 1C Drunken Silenus, a late 1C Roman Diana with a "bee-hive" hairstyle, the sarcophagus of the "Amours vendangeurs" (grape-picking cupids) (3C), a wooden and lead anchor discovered in Port-la-Nautique, stelae and funerary cippi, one of which is dedicated to a baker. In La Madeleine lower room, objects of note include a superb pagan mosaic, various sarcophagi decorated with narrative scenes or fluting and a 5C dedicatory lintel from the early cathedral built here by Bishop Rustique.

The Tinal, linked to the archeological museum, houses prehistoric collections.

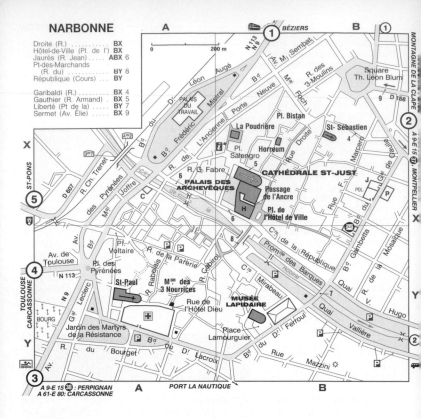

Salle des Synodes – *Courtyard of the New Palace*. This room is reached via a large staircase with balusters built in 1628 by archbishop Louis de Vervins. This is where the States General of Languedoc met, and it contains four fine Aubusson tapestries.

★ **Museum of Art and History** ⊘ – *In the same building as the Salle des Synodes, on the 2nd floor.*

This museum occupies the old episcopal apartments where Louis XIII stayed during the siege of Perpignan in spring 1642.

Next to the **audience room**, where several portraits of archbishops hang, is the **King's bedchamber** which boasts a fine coffered ceiling depicting the nine Muses and, on the floor, a Roman mosaic with geometrical motifs in wonderfully preserved colours; on the walls there are 17C paintings (portraits by Rigaud and Mignard).

In the **great gallery**, there is a fine display of pharmacists' jars made of Montpellier *faïence*; also on display are several 16C and 17C Flemish and Italian paintings.

The **faience room** contains an impressive collection of glazed earthenware pieces from some of the greatest French faience manufacturers (Montpellier, Narbonne, Marseille, Moustiers-Ste-Marie and Strasbourg).

In the **Grand Salon** hang Beauvais tapestries inspired by the *Fables* of La Fontaine and several interesting paintings, for example the *Adoration of the Shepherds* by Philippe de Champaigne. In the semicircle at the end of the Grand Salon, there is a white marble bust of Louis XIV by Coysevox.

The tour ends with a room of 19C and 20C art, including works by Pradier, Louis Garneray, Falguière, D de Montfreid and Maurice Marinot.

★ **Donjon Gilles-Aycelin** ⊘ – This fortified tower with its rusticated walls stands on the remains of the Gallo-Roman rampart which once protected the heart of the old town. It represented the archbishops' power as opposed to that of the viscounts, who occupied a building on the other side of Place de l'Hôtel-de-Ville. It is a fine example of a late 13C keep and its interior is very well appointed.

On the ground floor there is an interesting dome-vaulted room, on the 1st floor the Gilles-Aycelin room, and on the 3rd floor the guard room surrounded by defensive alcoves. From the sentinel path on the platform *(162 steps)*, the **panorama**★ stretches over Narbonne and the cathedral, the surrounding plain and away across La Clape summit, the Corbières and the coastal lagoons as far as the Pyrenees on the horizon.

ADDITIONAL SIGHTS

Basilique St-Paul ⊘ **(AY)** – This basilica was built on the site of a 4C and 5C necropolis near the tomb of the city's first archbishop. Inside, near the south door, stands a font famed for the curious little sculpted frog which adorns it. The chancel★, which was begun in 1224, is notable for the height of its supporting structure (large arcades, double triforium, tall windows), its vaults in the style of Champagne and its overall elegance. The perspective of the nave is broken by three massive basket-handle arches. Beneath the great organ, two early Christian sarcophagi are embedded in the wall; a third is used as a lintel.

Paleo-Christian crypt ⊘ – *Entrance through the north door of the basilica*. This formed part of the sizeable necropolis founded in the early 4C during the reign of Constantine. The remains of an edifice composed of a square room and an apse constitute a crypt which houses six sarcophagi. Of these the most interesting are one which is decorated with acroters, another with foliage in the Aquitaine style, and a third in white marble reminiscent of pagan sarcophagi.

Maison des Trois-Nourrices (AY) – Legend has it that it was in this 16C house that Cinq-Mars was arrested. It owes its unusual name ("House of the Three Wet Nurses") to the generous curves of the caryatids supporting the lintel of a magnificent Renaissance window.

★ **Lapidary Museum** ⊘ **(BY)** – This is in the deconsecrated 13C church of Notre-Dame-de-la-Mourguié, attached to a priory which was linked to the Benedictine abbey of St-Victor in Marseille in 1086. The exterior looks magnificent with its projecting buttresses and crenellated chevet. Inside, the vast nave is covered by a visible roof structure supported by pointed transverse arches.

Crammed into four rows, a collection of almost 1 300 antique inscriptions, with steles, lintels, busts, sarcophagi and huge carved blocks of stone, most of them from the city ramparts, recalls the prestigious past of the ancient capital of Gallia Narbonensis.

Banks of the Robine (BY) – The Robine canal links the Sallèles-d'Aude junction canal to Port-la-Nouvelle. The plane trees along its course, the Pont des Marchands and the colourful pedestrian street which spans it, the footbridge and the Promenade des Barques, all make it the ideal place for a leisurely stroll.

►► **La Poudrière (BX)** – 17C powder magazine which houses temporary exhibitions.

►► **Horreum** ⊘ **(BX)** – Roman warehouse.

►► **Place Bistan (BX)** – Remnants of a 1C temple on the site of the Antique forum and capitol.

►► **Église St-Sébastien** ⊘ **(BX)** – 15C church with 17C extensions, according to legend on the site of the saint's birthplace. In the chapel of Ste-Thérèse: *Ecstasy of St Theresa* by Mignard.

MONTAGNE DE LA CLAPE

Round tour of 53km/33ml. Allow 3hr. Leave town on ② on the town plan, then take D 168 on the left towards Narbonne-Plage.

The 214m/702ft high limestone massif of La Clape towers above the sea, the coastal lagoons round Gruissan and the vine-covered lower valley of the Aude. The steep and winding road offers splendid views over the cliffs and slopes of La Clape.

⌂ **Narbonne-Plage** – This resort stretching along the coast is typical of the traditional Languedoc seaside resorts. There is sailing and water-skiing here. *From Narbonne-Plage, carry on to St-Pierre-sur-Mer.*

St-Pierre-sur-Mer – Family seaside resort. The chasm of l'Oeil-Doux to the north is a curious natural phenomenon. It is 100m/328ft wide and contains a salt water lake 70m/229ft deep into which the sea surges.

⌂ **Gruissan** – *See GRUISSAN.*

Leave Gruissan, turn right and immediately on the left take a little road signposted Notre-Dame des Auzils.

Cimetière marin – *See GRUISSAN: Excursion.*

Follow the little road across the lower slopes of La Clape. On reaching D 32, turn right to Narbonne. At Ricardelle, take a steep, narrow little road on the right.

Coffre de Pech Redon – This marks the summit of La Clape mountain. From it, there is a scenic view over the lagoons and Narbonne with the cathedral of St-Just and the Archbishops' Palace rising above the city's skyline.

Turn back and return to Narbonne on D 32.

EXCURSIONS

★★ **Fontfroide Abbey** – *14km/8.5mi to the southwest on ④ on the town plan, N 113, then left on D 613. Description under Abbaye de FONTFROIDE.*

★ **Sigean African Safari Park** – *17km/10.5mi south on ③ on the town plan, N 9. Description under Réserve africaine de SIGEAN.*

Étang de Bages et de Sigean – *29km/18mi south. Description of lagoon under Les CORBIÈRES.*

Terra Vinea ⊙ – *18km/11mi. Leave Narbonne on ③, N 9 towards Perpignan. After 15km/9.5mi, turn right onto d 611ᴬ, then left towards Portel-des-Corbières (follow signposts to Terra Vinea).*

A botanical footpath leads to the entrance to a disused gypsum quarry, now converted into maturation cellars for a group of local vineyards – Peyriac-sur-Mer, Portel and Sigean – known under the name Rocbère. The trail leads along the old quarrying galleries, lined with casks and various tools of the wine-grower's trade. A Gallo-Roman villa with its baths, cellar and atrium recalls life in the days of Antiquity, when wine was transported along the Via Domitia. The visit ends at an underground lake and then back to the reception area, where it is possible to taste some of the products of the estate.

Sallèles d'Aude – *11km/6.5mi north. Leave Narbonne north on D 13. At Cuxac-d'Aude, take D 1118 to the left as far as Sallèles d'Aude, or follow the signs to "Musée des Potiers" on D 1626, which follows the junction canal. Cross the bridge to get to the car park.*

Extensive excavations northeast of this small wine-growing centre near the ancient capital of Roman Narbonensis brought to light numerous pottery fragments in 1968. Since then, continued work has enabled an important Gallo-Roman centre for making earthenware, in particular **amphorae**, to be displayed in situ to the public.

The texts of Martial and Pliny the Elder testify to the high quality of wines produced in southern Gaul – especially Marseille, Béziers and Vienne – during Roman occupation. One of the most famous grape varieties at that time was *amineum*. In order to transport these wines, which were in demand from well beyond the boundaries of Gaul, flat-bottomed, pot-bellied amphorae of the "Gauloise 4" type with a capacity of about 26l/just under 6gal(UK) were used. Study of the sites in which fragments of such amphorae have been found have revealed that the wines were transported not only to the countries of the eastern Mediterranean but also to the very northern limits of the Roman Empire, via the Rhine and Danube rivers.

★ **Amphoralis-Musée des Potiers gallo-romains** ⊙ – *1hr. Take D 1626 northeast of town and follow the signs to "Musée des Potiers".* The central section of the modern museum building houses an exhibition on the craft of making amphorae, which was both varied and prolific, lasting from 1C to 14C AD. Open-sided structures here and there reveal the site of the excavations, comprising the workshop area around a dozen or so kilns, settling vessels, workshops with towers in which clay was made and various other utilitarian buildings. The open clay quarry is nearby. Besides the excavations, the tour includes displays on the sorts of earthenware produced at Sallèles-d'Aude (domestic ceramic ware, building materials, wine amphorae), firing techniques (models of kilns), daily life and trade under the Roman Empire.

The reconstruction of a children's necropolis (the oldest bodies were of 9-month-old babies), discovered in part of the workshop area, sheds light on funerary rituals observed in the Gallo-Roman world in 1C BC. To the north of the site are the remains of an aqueduct (early 2C) which brought water across the plain to Narbonne.

Ginestas – *17km/10.5mi to the northwest. Leave town on ⑤ on the town plan, D 607; after crossing the Canal du Midi, turn left.*

In this village surrounded by vineyards there is a dimly lit **church** ⊙ containing some fine works of art: a 17C altarpiece in gilded wood, the statue of Notre-Dame-des-Vals, a very simply made Virgin and Child and a 15C naïve polychrome statue of St Anne.

Le Somail – *2km/1.2mi east of Ginestas.* The Canal du Midi flows through this peaceful hamlet, where there is a **Musée de la Chapellerie** ⊙ (Headdress Museum): hats and headdresses from all over the world from 1885 to the present.

The Michelin Green Guide France.
A selection of the most unusual and the most typical sights along the main tourist routes.

Seuil de NAUROUZE

Modern motorists may find it hard to imagine that this "pass" (alt 194m/636ft) represented a major obstacle for civil engineers prior to Riquet, responsible for the successful design and construction of a canal linking the Atlantic and the Mediterranean.

CANAL DU MIDI

The idea of building a canal to link the Atlantic and the Mediterranean dates back to the Romans. François I, Henri IV and Richelieu all commissioned studies to this end, none of which bore fruit. Finally **Pierre-Paul Riquet**, baron of Bonrepos (1604-80) and state tax-farmer for Languedoc, successfully carried out the project, at his own expense. The construction of the port at Sète in Riquet's lifetime, and the opening of the canal from the Rhône to Sète and of the Garonne lateral canal in the 19C crowned his efforts.

A solo achievement – When the construction of a canal linking "the two seas" was first dreamt of, the Seuil de Naurouze was an insurmountable obstacle. After meticulously studying the site, Riquet, a man of imagination, found a solution: the Seuil de Naurouze was the site of a spring – the Fontaine de la Grave (no longer extant after the construction work) – whose waters divided into two streams, one flowing west and the other east; all that would be necessary would be to increase the flow of this spring in order to feed the canal and its locks on either side of the watershed. Riquet decided to tap the waters draining from the Montagne Noire. With the help of a hydraulic engineer from Revel, he harnessed the waters of the Alzeau, the Vernassonne, the Lampy and the Sor, directing them along two channels, the Rigole de la Montagne to the St-Ferréol reservoir, and then the Rigole de la Plaine to Naurouze.

In 1662, he succeeded in interesting Colbert in his project and was granted the necessary authorisation for it in 1666. Over a period of fourteen years, 10 000-12 000 workmen were employed. Into this massive undertaking, Riquet sank money representing a third of the total cost of the project, namely 5 million *livres*, burdening himself with debts and sacrificing his daughters' dowries. He died exhausted in 1680, six months before the opening of the Canal du Midi. Under the Restoration his descendants regained their rights to a share of the profit from the canal and in 1897 they agreed to sell the canal to the state, since when it has been administered as a public enterprise.

Heritage and future projects – Riquet's 240km/150mi long canal begins at Toulouse at the Port de l'Embouchure, the end of the Garonne lateral and runs into the Thau lagoon, at the Port des Onglous. It incorporates 91 locks, but there is a reach of 54km/33.5mi (a day's journey by boat) between Argens-Minervois and Béziers.

Commercial traffic now no longer uses the canal, since its locks, which at the time were designed for the ships most commonly in use on the Mediterranean, cannot accommodate any vessel longer than 30m/98ft. Modernisation of the canal began on the section between Toulouse and Villefranche-de-Lauragais (43km/26.5mi). This historic canal follows a most attractive course, with numerous tight bends, locks with oval or round basins, elegant brick bridges, and reaches of water bordered, on the Mediterranean slopes, with plane trees, cypresses and umbrella pines.

After a century of decline, passenger traffic, which before the age of the railway was transported by light "stage boats" travelling at 11km/7mi per hour, has been picking up with the advent of riverboat tourism – numerous companies for hiring houseboats and or going on river cruises have been set up.

SIGHTS

Riquet's Obelisk – *Reached via D 218, to the south, turning off N 113 at Labastide d'Anjou.*
The obelisk, built in 1825 by Riquet's descendants, stands in an enclosure on a natural pedestal formed by the "stones of Naurouze", between the Naurouze pass (N 113) and the canal. It is surrounded by a double ring of fine, stately cedar trees. Local legend has it that when the cracks in the stones close up, society will sink into debauchery and the world will end.

Montferrand – *1km/0.6mi to the northwest. Leave the car south of the village, by N 113, at the side of a chapel next to a churchyard with cypresses growing in it.*
In a room adjoining the chapel, there are discs inscribed with crosses, and Chi Rho monograms – the monogram of Christ drawn with an X and a P intertwined, often accompanied by the letters alpha and omega, the first and last letters of the Greek alphabet. The Chi Rho monogram is frequently seen in southwest France on the tympanum of Romanesque chapels. Since the Middle Ages, this motif has been part of the symbolic repertory of the guilds and is known as "Solomon's Clock".
North of the chapel, an ancient necropolis testifies to the great length of time that this site has been used as a final resting place, and thus to how long the area has been inhabited by humans.

Port Lauragais – Centre Pierre-Paul Riquet ⊘ – *At Avignonet-Lauragais, take D 80 to Baraigne. From A 61 motorway: rest area (aire de repos) halfway between Villefranche-de-Lauragais and Castelnaudary (accessible from either direction).*
Situated at the end of a peninsula that juts out into Port Lauragais, the Centre Pierre-Paul Riquet was inspired by the architecture of the old dry docks of the canal. Beneath the roof extension is a harbourmaster's office to welcome boats passing through. Inside the centre, there is an exhibition space devoted to the construction of the Canal du Midi and temporary displays on related subjects. At the entrance, a fountain by sculptor Sylvain Brino depicts the water supply system of the canal and the functioning of its locks.

For the benefit of yachtsmen, there is some documentation on the canal giving information and practical advice (see Practical information at the end of the guide).

Cirque de NAVACELLES★★★

Michelin map 80 fold 16 or 240 fold 18
Local maps see Les GRANDS CAUSSES and Vallée de l'HÉRAULT

The Cirque de Navacelles is the most impressive natural feature of the Vis valley, which cuts between the *causses* of Blandas on the north and Larzac on the south. The cirque is formed by an immense, magnificent meander, deeply embedded in almost vertical walls of rock. The meander, which once encircled a little promontory, was abandoned by the river Vis which broke through the neck of a loop, just where the village of Navacelles had established itself. The flat valley floor has remained quite moist.

FROM BLANDAS
TO LA BAUME-AURIOL
13km/8mi – allow 1hr 15min

Take the D 713 which branches off the D 158 to reach the edge of the Blandas *causse*.

Belvédère Nord – Alt 613m/ 2 011ft. From this viewing point on the north edge of the plateau there is an interesting view over the cirque and the Vis canyon. The long Séranne chain can be seen on the horizon.

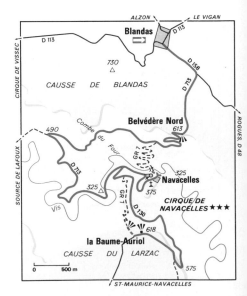

Didillon/CAMPAGNE CAMPAGNE

Cirque de Navacelles

The clearly marked road winds down one or two hairpin bends at the top of the cliff, then forms a large loop round the Combe du Four, before dropping steeply down to the floor of the cirque and on to the village of Navacelles perched on and around a rocky outcrop.

Navacelles – This little village 325m/1 066ft above sea level has a pretty single-arched bridge over the Vis.
The D 130 climbs up the south face of the canyon.

La Baume-Auriol – Alt 618m/2 037ft. From north of the farm, there is a magnificent view of the cirque. The canyon looks splendid as it cuts tight meanders between narrow strips of land edged by steep cliffs on the upstream side. In the distance, the Lingas and Lesperou mountains are silhouetted against the skyline.
A little further on, there is a viewpoint on the right.

Every year
the Michelin Red Guide France
revises the town plans:

  – through routes, by-passes, new streets, one-way systems, car parks
  – the exact location of hotels, restaurants, public buildings...
Current information for easy driving in towns.

271

Grotte de NIAUX**

This cave in the Vicdessos valley is famous for its remarkably well preserved prehistoric wall drawings.

Take a road uphill just past the exit from the village of Niaux.

Entrance porch – This houses a huge metal structure by Italian architect Fuksas. On entering the cave's vast entrance porch, 678m/2 224ft above sea level, the extent of the glacial erosion that occurred many thousands of years ago in the massif of the Cap de la Lesse, where the cave is situated, becomes immediately clear. Successive glaciers at times submerged the valley and completely covered the massif. The immense volume of water would then surge into crevices and wear down the rock, enlarging the cave and its entrance to their enormous size.

With time, the level of the valley floor became lower; the river now flows alongside the D 8, about 100m/328ft below it. The valley has a cross-section characteristic of a glaciated valley, with a flat floor, enclosed by steep terraces and slopes.

R. Delon/CASTELET

Prehistoric cave-wall drawings

Cave ⊙ – *Tickets must be reserved during high season.* The cave consists of vast, high chambers and long passageways leading, 775m/850yd from the entrance, to a kind of natural rotunda known as the "Salon Noir" ("Black Chamber") with walls decorated with the outlines of bison, horses, deer and ibex seen in profile. These drawings executed during the Magdalenian period (11 000 BC) using manganese oxides convey a vision of the world typical of the hunting populations of western Europe at the end of the Paleolithic Age. Many are of an exceptionally high standard and testify to a well-developed technical skill in the art of animal drawing.

*The current edition of the annual **Michelin Red Guide France***
offers a selection of pleasant and quiet hotels in convenient locations.
Their amenities are included (swimming pools, tennis courts,
private beaches and gardens...)
as well as their dates of annual closure.

The selection also includes establishments which offer excellent cuisine: carefully prepared meals at reasonable prices, Michelin stars for good cooking.

*The current annual **Michelin Camping Caravaning France** lists the facilities offered by many campsites (shops, bars, restaurants, laundries, games rooms, tennis courts, miniature golf courses, playgrounds, swimming pools...).*

Chaos de NÎMES-LE-VIEUX★

Michelin map 80 southwest of fold 6 or 240 fold 10

Seen from a distance, the **Chaos de Nîmes-le-Vieux** rises like a ruined city from the bare expanse of the Causse Méjean. It is said that during the Wars of Religion, the royal armies in pursuit of Protestants were sadly disappointed on their arrival here, having thought that they had at last reached their goal, "Nîmes".

Getting there ⊙ – *The group of rock formations is reached via the Col de Perjuret where the Aigoual massif and the Causse Méjean meet. From the pass, head either towards Veygalier or to l'Hom or Gally, or park the car.*

From Veygalier – In Veygalier, an attractive village typical of the *causse*, a house has been converted to display an **exhibition** on the geology of the *causse*. From here a trail leads off through "streets" of stone overlooked by strangely shaped rock formations 10-50m/30-160ft high. From the hill above Veygalier, there are fine views over the cirque bristling with dolomitic rocks, where the stone houses blend in with their curious surroundings.

From l'Hom or Gally – An interesting discovery trail has been laid by the Parc National des Cévennes. The different "explanation tables" enable visitors to appreciate the originality of this natural environment so typical of the Causses.

*Every year
the* Michelin Red Guide France
*revises its selection of starred restaurants
which also mentions culinary specialities and local wines.*

*It also includes a selection of simpler restaurants
offering carefully prepared dishes which are
often regional specialities at a reasonable price.*

It is well worth buying the current edition.

PENNE

Population 507
Michelin map 79 fold 19 or 235 fold 22 – Local map see ST-ANTONIN-NOBLE-VAL

This old village, overlooked by its castle ruins, occupies the most remarkable **site★**, perched on the tip of a bulbous rocky outcrop rising sheer from the south bank of the Aveyron and somewhat precariously overhanging the river on one of the prettiest reaches of its course. There are good views of the village from the roads approaching it from the north (D 33) and south (D 133).
The intricate outline of the powerful medieval fortress with its jagged walls, in some cases poised on the very edge of the rock seemingly defying the laws of gravity, rises above the flat roofs of the village houses.

Village – *Park the car by the side of the road (D 9), at the entrance to the village.*
A narrow street leads to the church, where the belfry spanning a pointed arched gateway marks the entrance to the fortified village. The chancel of the church lost its bastion-like appearance in the 17C, when the main doorway was opened.
From the belfry, a pretty little street lined with old houses leads up to the castle, then down to Peyrière gate on the opposite side of the village. The 17C plague cross, harking back to a scourge that hit Penne on several occasions, marks the beginning of the steep footpath that leads up the rockface to the castle ruins.

Château – The castle's site ensured it a leading role throughout the history of Quercy. At the time of the Albigensian Crusade, it became the stake in the bloody wars fought between the lord of Penne, rallying to the cause of the Cathar "heretics", and the followers of Simon de Montfort. Later, during the Hundred Years War, it passed back and forwards several times between the hands of English and local troops. It finally fell into ruins in the 19C.
From the tip of the promontory, there is a good **view★** of the towers and jagged walls of the castle, the village of Penne and the Aveyron valley.

PERPIGNAN★★

Conurbation 157 873
Michelin map 86 fold 19 or 235 folds 48 and 52 or 240 fold 41

Perpignan, once the capital city of the Counts of Roussillon and the Kings of Majorca, is an outlying post of Catalan civilization north of the Pyrenees and a lively commercial city, which owes its economic growth to the export of fruit, vegetables and wine from the plain or hillsides.

Extending beyond the ramparts built by Vauban, the demolition of which was begun in 1904, the city developed at a safe distance from the Têt. Administration, business and the expanding university ensured the rapid growth of a city, which before 1914 numbered only 39 000 inhabitants.

In the 13C, the city profited from the great upsurge in trade between the south of France, the coast of North Africa and the Levant stimulated by the Crusades. In 1276, Perpignan became the capital of Roussillon as part of the estates of the kingdom of Majorca. Its main activity at this time was the preparation and dyeing of cloth from the large cloth manufacturing cities of Europe.

The second Catalan city – After the kingdom of Majorca had ceased to be in 1344, Roussillon and Cerdagne were integrated into the princedom of Catalonia which, in the 14C and 15C, constituted a kind of autonomous federation at the heart of the State of Aragon. Catalan "Corts" sat at Barcelona, head of the federation, but delegated a "Deputation" to Perpignan. Between the two slopes of the Pyrenees, a commercial, cultural and linguistic community came into being.

In 1463, Louis XI put 700 men-at-arms at the disposal of King John II of Aragon to help him defeat the Catalans; with his usual great common sense, he rewarded himself by taking possession of Perpignan and Roussillon. However, the inhabitants fanned the flames of their nostalgia for Catalan autonomy, and rebellious feeling ran high. 10 years later, John of Aragon returned to Perpignan, but after an all-too-brief period of neutrality, hostilities with France broke out once more and French armies besieged the city. In spite of famine, the people of Perpignan put up fierce resistance (for many years afterwards, they were known as "rat eaters"). They surrendered only when ordered to do so by the king of Aragon, who gave the city the title of "Fidelissima" (most faithful). In 1493, Charles VII, who wished to have a free hand in Italy, sought to win the friendship of Spain, so he gave the province of Roussillon back to the Roman Catholic monarchs Ferdinand and Isabella. Perpignan represented to them the key to Spain, and they made it one of the most heavily fortified cities in Europe. In the 17C, Cardinal Richelieu, methodically implementing his policy of creating natural frontiers, seized the opportunity offered in 1640 by a Catalan rebellion against the government of Madrid and signed an alliance with them; the following year, Louis XIII became Count of Barcelona.

The final siege of Perpignan – However, since a Spanish garrison was holding Perpignan, the city was laid to siege. Louis XIII arrived in person at the city walls with the élite of the French army (Cardinal Richelieu, who was ill, stayed in Narbonne). In the event, the siege was nothing to be proud of; the population, latently hostile towards its defenders, died of hunger, and the Spanish garrison, itself in a desperate state, finally surrendered on 9 September 1642, with full battle honours.

OUT AND ABOUT IN PERPIGNAN

Guided tours of the city – These take place in season, June to September from Monday to Saturday. Meet in front of the tourist office, Place A. Lanoux, at 9.30am for a tour of the churches, or 3.30pm for a tour of Old Perpignan. For details call ☎ 05 68 66 30 30.

Eating and drinking out – Place Arago is one of the liveliest spots in town in the evening: try going for a drink at **Grand Café de la Paix** or, further off on Quai Vauban, eating a meal at Art Deco brasserie **Le Vauban**. **Café Catalan** on Place Verdun is a favourite haunt for local residents. Opposite the Loge de Mer is **Grand Café de la Bourse** which stays open until late at night. "Trendy" bars (somewhere between a bar and a disco) include **Républic'Café** (all-night rock music) on Place République, **Corto Maltaise** on Avenue du Général-Leclerc (**ABY**) and **Bodega Los Toros** on Rue des Fabriques-d'En-Nadal.

Shopping – There are two markets: one held daily on Place de la République, and one on Saturdays and Sunday mornings only on Place Cassanyes (**CZ**). Part of the city centre is a pedestrian zone in which there are several clothes boutiques (begin from Rue Mailly – **BZ**). Avenue Général-de-Gaulle (**AZ**) is lined by a variety of shops in a much busier area of town.

Souvenirs from Perpignan include Catalan espadrilles, from Guitard Fils, 34 boulevard Clemenceau, or as a more expensive alternative the famous Perpignan garnets from Jacques Creuzet-Romeu, 9 rue Fontfroide, or from Michel Gourgot, 15 rue des Trois-Journées.

Richelieu, on the verge of death, was overjoyed. After the execution of Cinq-Mars and de Thou, he wrote to the king: "Sire, your men are in Perpignan and your enemies are dead."

The treaty of the Pyrenees ratified the reunification of Roussillon with the French crown, and Perpignan became French once and for all.

FROM THE PALAIS DES ROIS DE MAJORQUE TO LE CASTILLET *3hr*

★ **Palais des rois de Majorque** ⊙ **(Palace of the Kings of Majorca) (BZ)** – When the Kings of Majorca came to the throne in 1276, Perpignan did not have a suitably grand residence to offer its new overlords, so a palace was built south of the town, on the hill of Puig del Rey.

The palace, once the mainland seat of the short-lived dynasty of Majorca (1276-1344), is enclosed by the citadel of Perpignan dating from the French occupation under Louis XI, and also by subsequent fortifications undertaken under Charles V and Philip II. It is gradually beginning to recover its original character.

Seal of the Kings of Majorca

A vaulted slope leads across the red brick ramparts to a pleasant Mediterranean garden. Pass beneath a tower to the west, the **tour de l'Homage**, to get to the square-shaped main courtyard *(in summer this is the setting for the theatre festival "Estivales")*, open on the east and west sides with two storeys of arcades, in which the decoration fuses Romanesque and Gothic elements in a manner typical of the transitional style of southern France. Note the texture of the masonry on the walls, where smooth pebbles alternate with courses of solid brick *(cayrou)*.

On the first floor of the south wing, the **great hall of Majorca** has a chimneypiece with three fireplaces. Beyond it, the Queen's suite has a superb ceiling painted with the Catalan colours (green and red).

The most splendid part of the building is the **chapel-keep** of Ste-Croix rising above the east wing. It comprises two sanctuaries built one above the other in the 14C by Jaime II of Majorca; their exterior architecture is in a French-inspired High Gothic style, whereas the interior is decorated in a manner typical of the Mediterranean.

The lower "Queen's" chapel, with its green ceramic flooring, shows traces of Gothic polychrome painting – on the blind windows and the squinches – and contains a fine 15C Virgin and Child.

The upper chapel, taller and narrower, is entered through a **fine Romanesque doorway★** decorated with stripes of alternate blue and pink marble around the doorway arch. A fine Catalan Crucifix stands on the altar and the squinches are decorated in the same way as the doorway.

Musée Hyacinthe-Rigaud ⊙ **(BZ M¹)** – This museum is located in the hôtel de Lazerme, a 17C mansion, and bears the name of the famous artist from Perpignan, **Hyacinthe Rigaud** (1659-1743). His portraits, which were mainly ceremonial, earned him such a high reputation that to satisfy his patrons, Louis XIV and the royal court, he had to open a studio. His fame spread far and wide. The prized possession of the museum, the *Portrait of the Cardinal de Bouillon* was said by Voltaire to be "A masterpiece equal to the finest masterpieces by Rubens". Along with other works by the portraitist, Catalan Gothic paintings are displayed, among which is the famous 15C altarpiece of the Trinity.

Contemporary art is represented by such prestigious names as, among others, Maillol, Dufy, Picasso, Alechinsky, Appel. Hispanic art and the art of South America also hold an important place in the museum.

Place Arago (BZ 5) – This lively, pleasant square adorned with palm trees and magnolias and bordered with cafés attracts crowds of people. In the centre stands the statue of the famous physician and astronomer François Arago (1786-1853). This extraordinary personality was fired not only with a love of research and a zeal for popularising scientific knowledge – he was admitted to the Académie des Sciences at the age of 23 – but also a passion for politics. He was a member of the provisional government of 1848.

Palais de la Députation (BY B) – During the reign of the Kings of Aragon this 15C palace was the seat of the permanent commission or *députation* representing the Catalan "Corts". Note the huge, typically Aragonese archstones of the doorway, the fine masonry of the ashlar façade and the bays resting on very slender stone columns.

Opposite the Palais de la Députation, take a little detour down the small Rue des Fabriques d'En Nabot **(BY 24)**, once at the heart of the district des **parayres** (the cloth finishers who in the 13C and 14C formed the first

PERPIGNAN

Alsace-Lorraine (R. d') . . **BY** 2
Arago (Pl.) . . . . **BZ** 5
Argenterie (R. de l') . . . . **BY** 6
Barre (R. de la) . . . . **BY** 7
Clemenceau (Bd G.) . . . **BY**
Louis-Blanc (R.) . . . . **BY** 34
Marchands (R. des) . . . . **BY** 35
Mirabeau (R.) . . . . **BY** 37
Péri (Pl. Gabriel) . . . . **BZ** 39
Théâtre (R. du) . . . . **BZ** 47

Anciens Combattants
  d'Indochine (Pl. des) . **BY** 3
Ange (R. de l') . . . . **BZ** 4
Bartissol (R. E.) . . . . **BY** 8
Batello (Quai F.) . . . . **BY** 9
Carnot (Quai Sadi) . . . . . **BY** 20
Castillet (R. du) . . . . **BY** 21
Cloche d'Or (R. de la) . **BYZ** 22
Côte des Carmes
  (R.) . . . . **CZ** 23
Fabriques
  d'En Nabot (R. des) . **BY** 24
Fabriques d'En Nadal
  (R. des) . . . . **BY** 25
Fontaine-Neuve (R.) . . . . **CZ** 26
Fonfroide (R.) . . . . **BY** 27
Gambetta (Pl.) . . . . **BY** 28
Grande-la-Monnaie (R.) . **BZ** 31
Lattre-de-Tassigny
  (Quai de) . . . . **BZ** 32
Loge (R. et pl. de la) . . **BY** 33
Mermoz (Av. J.) . . . . **CZ** 36
Payra (R. J.) . . . . **BY** 38
Petite-la-Monnaie (R.) . . **BZ** 40
Porte-d'Assaut (R.) . . . . . **BZ** 41
Remparts-la-Réal
  (R. des) . . . . **BZ** 42
République (R. de la) . . **BZ** 43
Résistance (Pl. de la) . . **BY** 44
Rigaud (Pl.) . . . . **BZ** 45
St-Jean (R.) . . . . **BY** 46
Trois-Journées (R. des) . **BY** 48
Vauban (Quai) . . . . **BY** 49
Verdun (Pl. de) . . . . **BY** 50
Victoire (Pl. de la) . . . . . **BY** 51
Vielledent (R. J.) . . . . . . **CZ** 52
Waldeck-Rousseau
  (R.) . . . . **CZ** 55

B Palais
      de la Députation
D Maison Julia
E Loge de Mer
H Hôtel de ville
L Chapelle
      du Dévot Christ
M¹ Musée
      Hyacinthe-Rigaud
N Campo Santo

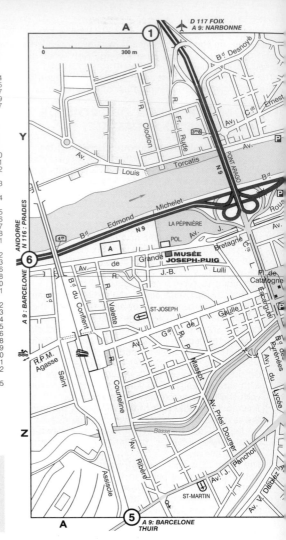

guild of Perpignan). The **Maison Julia★** (**BY D**) at no 2 is one of the few well preserved *hôtels* of Perpignan, possessing a patio with 14C Gothic arcades.

★ **Hôtel de Ville** ⊙ (**BY H**) – The wrought-iron railings date from the 18C. In the arcaded courtyard stands a bronze by Maillol: *La Méditerranée* (a subjet of which he did several copies – see BANYULS-SUR-MER). On the façade of the building, three bronze arms, which are said to symbolize the "hands" or estates of the population required to elect the five consuls, were in fact originally designed to hold torches.
Inside, the Salle des Mariages (Marriage Hall) has a fine 15C coffered ceiling.

Place de la Loge (**BY 33**) – This square (with a statue by Maillol: *Venus*) and the pedestrianised Rue de la Loge, paved in pink marble, form the lively centre of town life. Here, in summer, the *sardana* is danced several times a week.

★ **Loge de Mer** (**BY E**) – This fine Gothic building, dating from 1397 and refurbished and extended in the 16C, once housed a commercial tribunal in charge of ruling on claims relating to maritime trade. It now houses a fast-food restaurant.
The weather vane shaped like a galleon on one of the corners of the building symbolizes the maritime activities of the Roussillon merchants.

★ **Cathédrale St-Jean** ⊙ (**BCY**) – The main church was begun in 1324 by Sancho, second king of Majorca, but was not consecrated until 1509.
A passage on the left leads to the old sanctuary of St-Jean-le-Vieux, where there is a remaining marble Romanesque doorway, on which the central pendentive is decorated with a Christ figure wearing a stern and powerful expression.
The oblong façade of the basilica is constructed from courses of pebbles alternating with bricks. It is flanked on the right by a square tower with a fine 18C wrought-iron campanile housing a 15C bell.

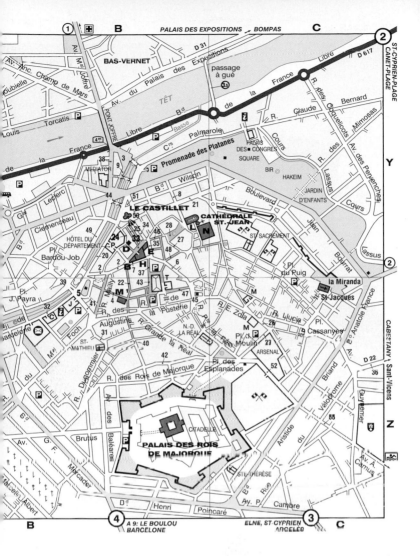

The impressive single nave rests on robust interior buttresses separating the chapels. One of the most interesting features of the cathedral of St-Jean is its sumptuous 16 and 17C altarpieces, particularly that of the high altar and those in the chapels on the left (Ste-Eulalie, Ste-Julie, St-Pierre). In the south apsidal chapel, there is the polychrome altarpiece of the Vierge de la Mangrane (Our Lady of the Pomegranate).

In the central alcove of the white marble high altar stands a statue of St John the Baptist, patron saint of Perpignan: the effigy of the saint and the drapery of the royal arms of Aragon and Catalonia (gold and red) represent the city's coat of arms.

At the entrance to the north arm of the transept is the 17C tomb of Bishop Louis de Montmort. The 16C monumental organ has been restored; its painted shutters have been placed on either side of the doorway to the right. Dating from 1504, they depict the baptism of Christ and Herod's feast.

Beneath the organ case, a passage leads to the Romanesque chapel of Notre-Dame-dels-Correchs, in which there lies a recumbent effigy of King Sancho, donated in 1971 by the town of Palma, and, at the far end, a collection of antique reliquaries behind wrought-iron grilles.

By the exit from the cathedral through the doorway on the south side, there is a separate chapel (**BY L**) which houses a poignant, even harrowing, early-14C carved wooden Crucifix known as the **Dévôt Christ★**, probably a Rhenish work.

Campo Santo ⊘ (**BCY N**) – Situated south of the cathedral, the Campo Santo is a vast square graveyard dating from the early 14C, which, thanks to careful restoration work, is beginning to recover its original appearance. It exhibits great architectural unity with its pointed funeral alcoves and marble recesses, set into walls adorned with pebbles and courses of brick. It is one of the oldest surviving medieval churchyards in France.

Le Castillet, Perpignan

★ **Le Castillet** (**BY**) – This monument, an emblem of Perpignan, which survived the demolition of the ramparts, dominates the Place de la Victoire. Its two towers are crowned with exceptionally tall crenellations and machicolations; note the windows with wrought-iron grilles.

To the original brick construction, begun in 1368, a gate dedicated to Notre-Dame (Our Lady) was added in 1483. During the reign of Louis XI, Le Castillet kept enemies from outside at bay and intimidated the townspeople, should they turn rebellious.

Casa Pairal ⊙ – Catalan folk museum: furniture, implements, ecclesiastical art, costumes, a fine cross with the instruments of the Passion ("Aux Outrages"). From the top of the turret *(142 steps)*, there is an attractive **view** over the city's monuments, the Canigou and the Albères to the south, and the Corbières to the north.

ADDITIONAL SIGHTS

Promenade des Platanes (**BCY**) – This wide avenue is lined with plane trees and adorned with fountains. Palm trees grow along the side avenues.

La Miranda (**CZ**) – This is a small public park on the site of the old fortifications, behind the church of St-Jacques. It is principally given over to the plantlife of the *garrigues* and shrubs which are either native or have been introduced to the region (pomegranates, olives, aloes etc).

Église St-Jacques ⊙ (**CZ**) – The church began life as a sanctuary in the 14C in an old district on top of the ramparts inhabited by gardeners and weavers. Beneath the south porch there is a large cross with the instruments of the Passion.

The south apsidal chapel contains several works of art: a 14C Crucifix, a 15C statue of St James placed above a baptismal font which is still supplied by a spring, and a large Weavers' altarpiece (late 15C) depicting scenes from the life of the Virgin Mary.

At the west end of the nave, a vast chapel added in the 18C was reserved for the brotherhood of La Sanch ("of the precious Blood"). Since 1416, this penitents' brotherhood, formed to give comfort to those condemned to death, has performed a solemn procession on Maundy Thursday, carrying its *misteris* to the singing of hymns. This procession now takes place on Good Friday.

★ **Musée numismatique Joseph-Puig** ⊙ **(AY)** – Part of the Villa "Les Tilleuls" (1907) has been converted into a museum, at the donor's request, to display the numismatic collection bequeathed by Joseph Puig to his native city of Perpignan. There are 1 500 permanent exhibits, out of a collection of 35 000. There is a room for temporary exhibitions. With the aid of Fresnel lenses, visitors can see the mainly Catalan coins minted in Valence, Barcelona, Perpignan or Majorca, and also coins from Roussillon (after the Treaty of the Pyrenees) or from Mediterranean countries (Rome, Greece, Egypt). The collection of medals includes those of the Arago family, mother and son, struck by David d'Angers. Exceptional exhibits such as the double gold ducat depicting Ferdinand II of Aragon, or some Gallic gold staters copied from ancient Greece complete this well presented collection tracing the history of numismatics.

> ### Christmas in Perpignan
>
> Christmas celebrations are very much part of the Catalan tradition which holds sway in Perpignan. A number of Nativity crib scenes are set up in different parts of town, and various street entertainments are organised, such as carol singing in Catalan. A Christmas market is held on Place Gambetta. Instead of Santa Claus's grotto, local children have little presents hidden for them under a log, the Caga Tio, around which they sing and dance.
>
> *Further details from the tourist office,* ☎ *05 68 66 30 30.*

Centre d'artisanat et d'art Sant Vicens ⊙ – *Get there via Boulevard Kennedy or Avenue Jean-Mermoz (east of town plan, D 22).*
Ceramic ware designed by Jean Lurçat and Jean Picart le Doux, among others. Exhibition and sale of ceramics by Roussillon artists. Attractive gardens.

EXCURSIONS

Cabestany – *5km/3mi on D 22 to the southeast.* Inside the church of Notre-Dame-des-Anges, on the wall of the chapel on the right is a famous Romanesque **tympanum**★, the work of a 12C travelling sculptor, the master of Cabestany, depicting the resurrection of the Virgin Mary, her Ascension and her Glory between Christ and St Thomas to whom she had sent her girdle.

Mas Palégry ⊙ – *7km/4mi on N 114 to the south, then take a little road on the right to Villeneuve-de-la-Raho.* Situated amongst vineyards, Mas Palégry is the setting for an **Aviation museum** (planes and models). Amongst the models on display are the Republic RF84F "Thunderflash" and a De Havilland "Vampire".

ROUSSILLON PLAIN
Round tour of 93km/57.5mi allow 1 day

Leave Perpignan on ⑤, D 612A.

Toulouges – On the south side and at the east end of the church, two plaques and a stele commemorate the Synod of 1027 and the Council of 1064-66 which implemented the "Truce of God", one of a number of peace-keeping measures introduced in medieval western Europe. Outside the apse stands a missionary Cross (1782) displaying the instruments of the Passion.

Thuir – This is known mainly for its wine cellars, the **caves Byrrh** ⊙.
The "Cellier des Aspres" also contains information on the development of crafts in neighbouring villages.

Take D 48, to the west.

D'après photo Léo Pélissier

Cross and instruments of the Passion

The road climbs the slopes of the Aspre. Suddenly, at the end of a small valley, the medieval village of Castelnou comes into sight with Mont Canigou rising in the background, making a wonderful **view**★.

Castelnou – This fortified village was the seat of the military administration of the Counts of Besalù in the north of the Pyrenees. Its tiny paved streets are clustered around the foot of the feudal **castle** ⊙, restored in the 19C. Artists and craftsmen vie with each other among the local population.
The *garrigue* on the slopes becomes sparser, and there is an impressive view south over Roussillon, the Albères and the sea.

Église de Fontcouverte – The church lies off the beaten track, in a churchyard in the shade of a large oak tree. It is a beautiful isolated **site**★ overlooking the plain. Straight after the church, by the side of the road to Ille, there is a stopping place beneath the chestnut trees.

Ille-sur-Têt – This little town in the plain is situated between the Têt and its tributary the Boulès. It is an important fruit and vegetable market and departure point of the Conflent road to Prades and the Aspres road to Amélie-les-Bains. The church boasts an imposing Baroque façade. In town there is a medieval sculpture – "les Enamourats" – on the corner of Rue des Carmes and Rue Deljat, and a magnificent 15C sculpted Gothic cross on Place del Ram.
The Hospice St-Jacques (16C and 18C main building) houses the **Hospici d'Illa** ⊙ with a permanent exhibition of Romanesque and Baroque paintings, sculpture and gold and silver plate displayed in a series of alcoves on the ground and first floors. Some 11C frescoes from the church at Casesnoves are on display in the sacristy. The centre also runs Catalan cooking workshops. At the end of the garden, there is the Romanesque church of La Rodona (11C, 12C and 14C) with a pointed arch doorway.

The centre organises visits to some of the other Catalan Baroque churches of the region, at Espira-de-Conflent, Joch and Finestret for example.

The Carmelite church, built in the 17C, houses a collection of paintings from the studio of the Guerras, a family of Baroque artists from Perpignan. At the eastern entrance to the town, on the Perpignan road, the fire station houses a museum on the local fire brigade, the **Musée du Sapeur-Pompier** ⊙. It displays fire prevention equipment from the Napoleonic Empire to date.
The road north of town (D 21), after passing the river, bends back into a little valley dominated by amazing geological formations consisting of earth pillars (*cheminées de fées* or "fairies' chimneys"), columns of soft rock capped with

The Organ Pipes of Ille-sur-Têt set against the Canigou peak hard conglomerate, known as the "**Organ Pipes** ⊙" *(les Orgues)*. These phenomena are grouped on two sites, one of which, to the east, is accessible to the public. It is a wonderful cirque with craggy white walls, in the centre of which stands an impressive earth pillar known as "the Sybil". Further west, towards Montalba, more formations of a deeper ochre colour can be seen to the left of the road. 1km/0.6mi higher, after a series of bends, a **lookout point** *(viewing table)* takes in the site of the "Organ Pipes", with Ille-sur-Têt on the horizon.

Turn back to carry on to Bélesta on D 21.

The road follows a gorge cut into the granite.

Bélesta – This remarkable village perched on a rocky outcrop rising up out of the surrounding vineyards used to be a border-town between the kingdoms of Aragon and France. The town has been of interest for some time to archeologists who have found numerous prehistoric remains in the galleries of the Caune de Bélesta *(excavations in progress)*. Most interestingly, in 1983 they discovered a collective grave dating from roughly 6 000 years ago (Middle Neolithic) which contained a collection of 28 ceramic items, as well as the remains of 32 people.

Château-Musée ⊙ – *Park the car near the wine cooperative or the post office.* The medieval fortress which towers above the town houses archeological collections. These are well presented in four main sections. First, visitors are introduced to techniques and materials used nowadays in archeological excavation work (in particular, pollen analysis enabling specialists to make deductions about climate and vegetation). Then they are taken into an identical reconstruction of the Bélesta excavations, showing the square site of the dig, and the collective grave enveloped in a damp atmosphere. The following room contains a display of the ceramic ware that was found with the bones: vases, bowls, cauldrons and basins all in perfect condition. Three dioramas depict daily life in the cave: milling, carving bones and metalwork. A display on the history of Bélesta gives information on the pre-Romanesque site of St-Barthélemy-de-Jonquerolles and the fortress in which the museum is housed. From the terrace, there is a good **panorama** of the village and the Fenouillèdes uplands.

Take the pass road to the Col de la Bataille.

The Château de Caladroi soon comes into view in the middle of a park planted with tropical trees. A very pleasant stretch of road along the crest between the valleys of the Têt and the Agly leads to the Col and then to the hermitage of Força Réal.

Ermitage de Força Réal – The summit, 507m/1 663ft above sea level at its highest point, forms a bastion towering above the Roussillon. On it are a 17C chapel and a telecommunications station.

There is an impressive **panorama**★★ over the plain, the coast from Cap Leucate to Cap Béar, the Albères and the Canigou. To the northwest, the sharp peaks of Bugarach and the outcrop of rock on which the ruined castle of Quéribus stands loom up on the skyline from the ridge of the southern Corbières.

The contrast between the Têt valley, with its chequerboard of market gardens outlined by straight rows of trees, and the Agly valley, completely covered by vineyards, is striking.

Go back down to the pass, and from there on to **Estagel**, native village of François Arago who is commemorated by a bust – the work of David d'Angers – in the town hall.

On the D 117, just past a long right-hand bend and just before the entrance to Cases-de-Pène, stands the hermitage of **Notre-Dame-de-Pène** perched high above: the tiny white gable of the chapel can scarcely be distinguished from the pedestal of grey cliffs that have been excavated to make a large quarry.

Rivesaltes – This town on the south bank of the Agly is one of the wine-producing capitals of the Roussillon, famous in particular for its sweet aperitif wines.

It is the native town of **Maréchal Joffre** (1852-1931), Commander in Chief of the French forces on the western front during the First World War, the "Victor of the Marne" who won himself the reputation for keeping a cool head under pressure and being equal to any challenge. An equestrian statue of him stands on the avenue which bears his name, which is bordered with plane trees. Since 1987, there has been a **museum** ⊙ in the house where Joffre was born (11, rue du Maréchal-Joffre), devoted to his life and career.

Return to Perpignan on D 117 alongside the airport.

Château de PEYREPERTUSE★★★

Michelin map 86 fold 8 or 235 fold 48 or 240 fold 37
Local map see Les CORBIÈRES

The craggy outline of the ruined fortress of Peyrepertuse, one of the "five sons of Carcassonne", on a crest in the Corbières, standing boldly atop its rocky base, only properly comes into view when seen from the outskirts of Rouffiac, to the north. Peyrepertuse is one of the finest examples of a medieval fortress in the Corbières. Recent discoveries reveal that the Peyrepertuse outcrop has been occupied since Roman times (numerous fragments of amphorae and pieces of brick have been found).

TOUR ⊘ *allow 2hr*

Get there from Duilhac: 3.5km/2mi up a steep, narrow road.

The road, signposted at the southern approach to the village, climbs towards the south face of the outcrop. From that side, all that can be seen of the fortress are a few jagged or crumbling fragments which tend to blend in with the rock face.

From the car park and ticket office, follow a path along the north face, which leads up to the entrance of the castle.

Visitors should have a good head for heights and take great care while exploring the castle, particularly if there is a strong wind (frequently the case on this exposed site). During the summer, visitors would be wise to equip themselves with drinking water and something to protect themselves from the sun.

Peyrepertuse comprises two adjacent but separate castles, on the east (Peyrepertuse) and west (St-Georges) ends of the ridge, and measures 300m/984ft at its longest point. The higher, Château St-Georges, has never been accessible to horses, or even mules.

Peyrepertuse

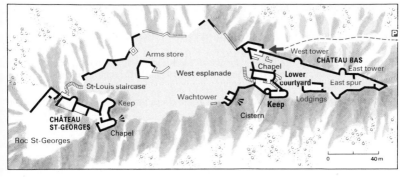

Château Bas - This lower castle is the actual feudal fortress. It was surrendered in 1240, apparently without a fight, to the Seneschal of Carcassonne acting in the name of the king, Louis IX, after Trencavel junior's failure to recapture Carcassonne by siege. The Château Bas stands on the tip of the promontory which tapers into the shape of a ship's prow.

Keep - *Enter through the tall door.* The old keep, the heart of the castle, is quadrilateral in shape. All that can be seen from the courtyard is the front flanked by a round tower (the cistern).
The finishing touches were added to the building in the 12C and 13C by attaching a fortified chapel *(left-hand wall)* to the original chapel with curtain walls which closed off the short walls of the courtyard.

Lower courtyard - The line of the enclosure adopts the triangular shape of the tapering end of the ridge. It is complete only on the north face, where it has a substantial curtain wall, with two round towers – the Tour Ouest and Tour Est – without a wall on the inside of the curtain wall, making them open facing the courtyard.
At the south end, it was only protected by a simple parapet, which has been reconstructed.
Going back towards the entrance to the castle, note the east side of the keep, which was completely redesigned in the 13C, with semicircular towers linked by a crenellated curtain wall.

Château St-Georges - *Cross the west esplanade towards the Roc St-Georges.*
At the north end of the precipice, an isolated watch tower gives a view of Quéribus through a gaping hole. An impressive flight of steps cut into the rock, known as the "St-Louis" staircase, leads up to the castle ruins. This is dangerous in strong winds *(use the chains which serve as a handrail).*
At an altitude of 796m/2 611ft, this royal fortress towers over the lower castle by about 60m/197ft. It was built in a single go on the highest point of the mountain, after Languedoc had been made part of the French royal estate. The tall walls of large bond which are still standing are interesting more for their lofty site than their actual construction.

East of the castle *(head left from the top of "St-Louis" staircase)* is a prominent outcrop, the site of the old chapel, overlooking the lower castle. There are **views** over the whole fortified complex and of its panoramic setting: the Verdouble valley, the ruined castle of Quéribus, and the Mediterranean on the horizon.

PEYRUSSE-LE-ROC★

Population 288
Michelin map 79 fold 10 or 235 fold 15 – 15km/9mi southwest of Capdenac

Situated on the basalt plateaux separating the Aveyron and Lot valleys, Peyrusse fortress kept watch over the Audierne valley. It had an eventful past, as can be seen from the remains of its old buildings. Conquered in 767 by Pépin the Short, united by Charlemagne with the kingdom of Aquitaine, handed over to England in 1152 after the divorce of Louis VII and Eleanor of Aquitaine, ancient Petrucia was the capital of the bailiwick until the 18C. During certain periods, it could number more than 3 000 inhabitants, and it prospered, largely due to its silver mines. These were no longer mined, once a competing version of the metal arrived from America in the 18C. Having lost its raison d'être, the fortified lower town was abandoned. This was the moment when the present village of Peyrusse-le-Roc started to evolve on the plateau.

Place St-Georges – Fine medieval 15C stone cross where a Virgin and Child can be seen beneath a canopy.

Porte du Château – This castle gate is the remains of the medieval curtain wall.

Church – Built in the 18C, it is noted for its large single nave with five bays and its vaulting supported by square pillars. 15C Pietà, sculptures and frescoes by Henri Vernhes, a local artist.

Place de Treize-Vents – In the Middle Ages, this square was the site of the castle of the lords of Peyrusse. All that is now left of it is a room which was used as a prison and a tower (the church bell-tower) which houses a small **archeological museum** ⓥ.

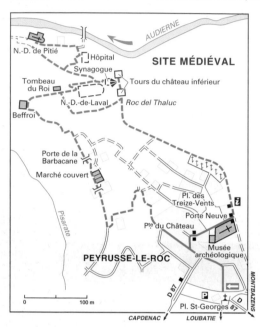

SITE MÉDIÉVAL ⓥ

(Medieval Ruins)

1hr 30min

Go through the Porte Neuve and the fortifications to the left of the church. The footpath on the left leads to the site; beyond the graveyard, bear right (stairway).

Roc del Thaluc – *Take the metal steps (particular care needed on some sections).* From this rock, crowned with the two square towers of the lower castle (*château inférieur*) and over-looking the Audiernes valley 150m/1 614ft below, it is easy to understand the role played by Peyrusse as an important strategic look-out position during troubled medieval times.

Follow the footpath to the bottom of the valley.

Tombeau du Roi – A chapel houses this richly sculpted royal mauseolum probably dating from the 14C.

Notre-Dame-de-Laval – All that remains of this old parish church, directly beneath the two towers of the Roc del Thaluc, are the imposing Gothic arches of the collapsed nave, vestiges of the five south side chapels and of the three-sided chancel standing against a rock, and the remnants of a tomb, with recumbent figure, on the left.

Synagogue – Jews are supposed to have taken refuge here in the 13C, however, it may possibly be the base of a tower which was part of the lower castle.

Hôpital des Anglais – 13C. This "English Hospital" still features its fine round exterior chimney.

Notre-Dame-de-Pitié – 1874. This chapel on the riverbank was built on the site of an old oratory.

Beffroi – This tall square tower is the old bell-tower of Notre-Dame-de-Laval; together with the Porte de la Barbacane (gateway with a fine Gothic relieving arch), it protected the town to the northwest. On the way back to the village, on the left, are some vaulted cellars (known as the *marché couvert* or covered market).

Michelin Route Planning on Internet www.michelin-travel.com.

Michelin, your companion on the road, invites you to visit our Web site and discover European route planning on the Internet.

Whether you just want to know the distance between two points, or need a detailed itinerary, for a holiday or on business, we provide all the information necessary for accurate travel planning.

PÉZENAS★

Population 7 613
Michelin map 83 fold 15 or 240 fold 26

This little town, once called "Piscenae", is built in a fertile plain covered in vineyards. Pézenas prides itself on its past, reflected in its interesting little streets and its mansions unchanged since the 17C. Vidal de La Blache, founder of the French college of geography, was born here in 1845.

A wool market – A fortified town at the time of the Romans, Pézenas was even then an important trading centre for woollen cloth. After it had become part of the royal estate in 1261, its trade fairs expanded. They took place three times a year. Everything possible was done to ensure their success: the merchandise was duty-free for thirty days; the merchants could not be arrested for debt; and by order of the king, local lords had to protect them on their travels. In exchange for these favours, the town paid the royal treasury a fee of 2 500 *livres*.

The "Versailles" of the Languedoc – For the first time, in 1456, the States General of Languedoc met at Pézenas. The town later became the residence of the governors of Languedoc: the Montmorencys, then the Contis. Armand de Bourbon, Prince de Conti, transformed Pézenas into the "Versailles", or royal court, of the Languedoc. Once settled on the estate of La Grange des Prés, where the beauty of the splendid gardens, flower beds and fountains was legendary, he surrounded himself with a court of aristocrats, artists and writers. Each session of the States General was celebrated with lavish entertainments.

Molière at Pézenas – During one of these celebrations, Molière, attracted by the town's reputation, came to Pézenas with his Illustrious Theatre in 1650. In 1653, having been permitted to put on a performance for Conti himself, he was such a success that the great lord gave him the title of "Actor to His Supreme Highness the Prince of Conti".

J. Boyer/IMAGES TOULOUSE

Market day in Pézenas

Molière also gave performances for the public, in the covered square. His repertoire comprised plays from the Italian commedia dell'arte and farces he had written himself. He lived with the other players at the Bât d'Argent hostelry (44 rue Conti), and every day from the barbershop of his friend Gély he would observe people, taking stock of their peculiarities, which he later put to use in his plays. Molière often returned to Pézenas between 1653 and 1656. The nomadic part of his life then came to an end, as he settled in Paris. The death of Armand de Bourbon in 1666 marked the end of Pézenas's heyday.

★★OLD PÉZENAS (X) *2hr*

Old mansions, or *hôtels*, with elegant balconies and ornate doorways, and workshops, now occupied by craftsmen and artists, follow one after the other along streets with evocative names: Rue de la Foire, Triperie-Vieille, Fromagerie-Vieille (Fair, Old Tripe Shop, Old Cheese Shop). In summer, during the "Mirondela dels Arts", the town really comes to life; local crafts are displayed, and folk festivals, theatre performances and concerts take place.

Leave from Place du 14-Juillet.

PÉZENAS
VIEILLE VILLE

Conti (R.) X
Jaurès (Cours Jean) X
République (Pl. de la) .... X 23
Trois-Six (Pl. des) .... X 28

Alliès (R. A.-P.) .... X 2
Béranger (R.) .... X 4
Château (R. du) .... X 6
Ducros (Impasse S.) ...... X 10
Fromagerie-Vieille
  (Impasse) .... X 13
Juiverie (R. de la) .... X 16
Juvenel (R. des) .... X 17
Litanies (R. des) .... X 18
Montmorency (R.) .... X 22
Sabatier (R. A.) .... X 25
Triperie-Vieille (R.) .... X 27
Zola (R. E.) .... X 32

F Hôtel Flottes de Sébasan
K Hôtel Plantavit de la Pause
M Musée Vulliod-St-Germain
N Maison des Pauvres
R Ilôt des prisons
S Hôtel de Carrion-Nizas
V Commanderie
   de St-Jean-de-Jérusalem

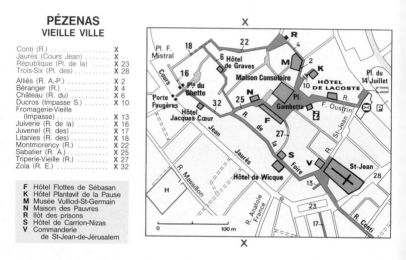

Place du 14-Juillet – In an area of garden there is a statue of Molière, by Injalbert (1845-1933).

★ **Hôtel de Lacoste** – This early-16C mansion has a very fine staircase and galleries with Gothic arches.

Place Gambetta – This square, once known as "Place-au-bled" ("village square"), has retained its medieval structure.
On the left is Gély's old barbershop *(which now houses the tourist information office)* where Molière liked to go.
On the right, stands the **Consular House**; its 18C façade with pediment and wrought ironwork conceals the main building, which dates from 1552. The States General of Languedoc often met there; a particularly memorable session was held in 1632, at which the rebellion of Henry II of Montmorency against the king was hatched. At the far end of the square, there is the Rue **Triperie-Vieille (27)**, once lined with market stalls. Further down, at no 11, in a courtyard at the end of a vaulted passageway, is a fine early 17C stairwell.
At the corner of Place Gambetta and Rue Alfred Sabatier stands the **Hôtel Flottes de Sébasan (F)** with a wide 16C façade; the right side was altered in the 18C (windows and ironwork), but retained its Renaissance (1511) corner niche which houses a 19C statue of St Roch. A plaque records that Queen Anne of Austria slept in the mansion in 1660.
Take Rue A.-P.-Alliès on the right.
Immediately on the right, in the Impasse Simon-Ducros, note the fine 17C **doorway** of the Hôtel de Plantavit de la Pause **(K)**. At no 3 rue Alliès is the Hôtel de Saint-Germain, home to the Musée Vulliod-St-Germain.
Take Rue Béranger on the left (17C house) which leads into Rue de Montmorency.

Rue Montmorency (22) – On the right stand the watch towers of the **ilôt des prisons (R)**. On the way back up the street, note on the left a 17C faïence **Pietà**, and on the right the gateway from the curtain walls of the old castle demolished on Cardinal Richelieu's orders, after the rebellion of Henry II of Montmorency. Just before the Rue du Château is the **Rue des Litanies (18)** which was one of the two axes of the Ghetto.

Rue du Château (6) – The beautiful ogee doorway of the **Hôtel de Graves** dates from the 16C.

Rue Alfred-Sabatier (25) – At no 12 the **Maison des Pauvres** (almshouse) possesses a fine staircase and 18C wrought ironwork.

Rue Émile-Zola (32) – At no 7 the **Hôtel Jacques Cœur** features a façade adorned with culs-de-lampe in the shape of little figures. It is the only 15C mansion in Pézenas decorated in this way, and is probably the work of Franco-Flemish artists sent by the king's Superintendent of Finance.
At the end of this street the **Porte du Ghetto** opens into **Rue de la Juiverie (16)**, two names which indicate the past role of this district.
On the left, the **Porte Faugères**, which leads into Cours Jean-Jaurès, was once part of the old 14C ramparts.
Retrace your steps.

Rue de la Foire – Once known as Rue Droite (roughly meaning "main street"), this street was the setting for fairs and processions. At no 16, there is a carved lintel representing some charming child musicians.

Hôtel de Wicque – An elegant Renaissance façade surmounts an art gallery. The passage on the left leads to a courtyard in the same style with the original windows and carved medallions.
Opposite stands the **Hôtel de Carrion-Nizas (S)** with a 17C doorway.

Collégiale St-Jean ⊙ – This church was built in the 18C on the site of an old Templars' church which collapsed under the weight of its bell tower in 1733. It was designed by Avignon architect Jean-Baptiste Franque and contains a white marble statue attributed to Coustou *(Lady Chapel on the left of the chancel)*.

Commanderie de St-Jean-de-Jérusalem (V) – The commandery features two well preserved early-17C façades with their mullioned windows. A corner turret is supported by a masonry buttress.
In the Impasse de la Fromagerie-Vieille there is a fine 17C doorway.
This is where this tour leaves the old town centre to carry on into the *faubourg* ("suburb") which grew up in the 17C and 18C around the Rue Conti. This road can be taken from the other side of the Place de la République.

Rue Conti (Z) – Many private mansions were built along this street, which, in the 17C, was also full of inns and shops. At no 30, the **Hôtel de Conti (Z X)** features a façade, renovated in the 18C, with Louis XV balconies and wrought iron window sills.

★ **Hôtel d'Alfonce** ⊙ **(Z)** – *No 32, rue Conti.* This fine 17C building, one of the best preserved in Pézenas, was used by Molière from November 1655 to February 1656. In the entrance courtyard is a pretty interior terrace adorned with balustrades. The façade overlooking the second courtyard has a portico surmounted by two tiers of loggias. On the right, there is a fine 15C spiral staircase.
Carry on along the Rue de Conti, past the **Hostellerie du Griffon d'Or** *(no 36)*, before going into the courtyard of the **Hostellerie du Bât d'Argent** *(no 44)*, which houses several craftsmen (potters, painters, leatherworkers etc).

Hôtel d'Alfonce (17C)

L.-Y. Loirat/EXPLORER

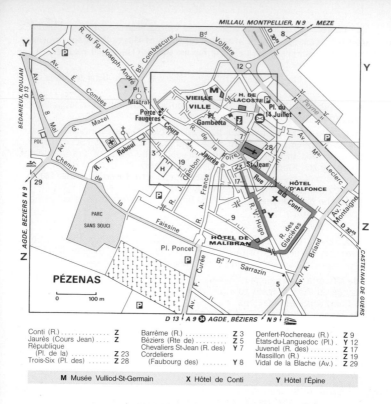

Conti (R.)	Z	Barrème (R.)	Z 3	Denfert-Rochereau (R.)	Z 9	
Jaurès (Cours Jean)	Z	Béziers (Rte de)	Z 5	États-du-Languedoc (Pl.)	Y 12	
République		Chevaliers St-Jean (R. des)	Y 7	Juvenel (R. des)	Z 17	
(Pl. de la)	Z 23	Cordeliers		Massillon (R.)	Z 19	
Trois-Six (Pl. des)	Z 28	(Faubourg des)	Y 8	Vidal de la Blache (Av.)	Z 29	

M Musée Vulliod-St-Germain   **X** Hôtel de Conti   **Y** Hôtel l'Épine

Turn right into Rue des Glacières, cross Rue Victor-Hugo and climb a flight of steps opposite.

★ **Hôtel Malibran** (**Z**) – This mansion's magnificent 18C façade is embellished with fine windows surmounted by masks representing smiling women, while the balconies are supported by garlands of leaves. The door leads straight to an interior 17C staircase supported by two tiers of superimposed columns.

Go back to Rue Victor-Hugo; at no 11 is the fine façade of the **Hôtel l'Épine** (**Z Y**) (18C).

Return to Place de la République along Rue de Juvenel.

Every Shrove Tuesday and first Sunday in July, the inhabitants of Pézenas commemorate the birth of a foal (poulain) to King Louis VIII's favourite mare here in their town in 1226. The celebrations take the form of a parade in which nine men dress up as the foal (like a pantomime horse) and prance through town to a musical accompaniment.

ADDITIONAL SIGHTS

Musée Vulliod-St-Germain ⊙ (**X M**) – The collections of this museum are displayed in the Hôtel de Saint-Germain, a fine 16C building, the exterior of which was renovated in the 18C, and the interior in the 19C.

On the ground floor, next to the entrance hall which contains tombstones and some sculptures from different buildings in the town, there is a reconstruction of a rustic Pézenas interior.

On the first floor, a group of Aubusson tapestries depict the Triumph of Alexander. Among the 16C, 17C and 18C furniture is a fine Louis XIII wardrobe with carved panels representing the four horsemen of the Apocalypse. A neighbouring room has been given over to Molière memorabilia.

The upper floor contains a collection of earthenware and pharmacist's jars.

There is an audiovisual presentation on the history of Pézenas and the time Molière stayed here.

Rue Henri-Reboul (**Z**) – The former Rue des Capucins was built in the 17C, when Pézenas started to expand beyond the medieval town walls.

On the left, coming from Cours Jean-Jaurès, stands the façade of the 16C chapel of the Pénitents Noirs, converted into a theatre in 1804.

At no 13, the façade of the Hôtel de Montmorency, once the residence of the governor of Languedoc, has a very fine 17C door with a pediment flanked with scrolls.

Further down, the **Hôtel de Guers de Paulhan** (now a hospital) also features an interesting 17C doorway.

Cours Jean-Jaurès (X) – The Cours Jean-Jaurès was constructed by Henry II of Montmorency who wished to extend the town beyond its fortified walls. At the time it was called le Quay, and it supplanted the Rue de la Foire as the town's main centre of activity. Aristocratic mansions were built facing south, the back of the house opening on to Rue de la Foire. These mansions can be entered through vaulted passageways leading into courtyards with attractive open staircases. The plain façades are sometimes decorated with masks. The most interesting buildings are at no 18, the **Hôtel de Landes de Saint-Palais**, no 20, the **Hôtel de Grasset** and, on the other side of the road, no 33, the **Hôtel de Latudes**.

►► **Abbaye de Valmagne★** – *14km/9mi northeast. See Abbaye de VALMAGNE.*

Clive Pies

The little pies *(petits pâtés)* of Pézenas are a culinary speciality of Indo-British origin made with sweet and spicy minced meat. In 1768, Lord Clive, accompanied by his Indian cooks, stayed in the town and in the nearby Château du Larzac. Before returning to Market Drayton in England, the cooks gave the Pézenas bakers and confectioners the recipe for the spicy little pies shaped like cotton reels. It was forgotten during the 19C, but has been rediscovered today, thanks to the research of keen gastronomes. In England, the little pies known as "Clive Pies" are made with minced mutton, brown sugar, sultanas and curry; in Pézenas, glacé lemon zest is used instead of sultanas.

Le PONT-DE-MONTVERT

Population 305
Michelin map 80 fold 6 or 240 fold 7 – Local map see Mont LOZÈRE

The tall grey houses of Le Pont-de-Montvert stand on either bank of the Tarn, which is spanned by a 17C humpbacked bridge surmounted by a toll tower.

The death of the Abbot of Chayla – This abbot, in charge of Roman Catholic operations in the Cévennes, was staying in Le Pont-de-Montvert and holding prisoner there some Protestants he had managed to capture. On 24 July 1702, two members of the Protestant movement, Abraham Mazel and Esprit Séguier, decided to secure the release of their fellows. The expedition they mounted to this effect resulted in the death of the Abbot of Chayla, who was caught whilst trying to make good his escape through the village (his body was thrown into the river from the old hump-backed bridge over the Tarn), and sparked off the Camisard uprising.

SIGHTS

Maison du Mont Lozère ⊘ – This centre is the headquarters of the Écomusée du Mont Lozère, an open-air museum set up by the Parc national des Cévennes. A large polygonal building houses an exhibition on the natural and human history of Mont Lozère, and an overnight shelter *(gîte)* for ramblers.

Sentier de l'Hermet – *6km/4mi from the Tour de l'Horloge, the clock tower in the centre of Le Pont-de-Montvert.*
This footpath *(allow 3hr there and back)*, which includes 12 observation points, reveals the landscapes, flora and fauna of the Tarn gorge, the traditional architecture of L'Hermet hamlet, various types of shepherds' huts and a panorama of the south face of Mont Lozère.

EXCURSIONS

★ **Mas Camargues** – *12km/7.5mi east of Le Pont-de-Montvert. Take the D 20 towards Bleymard and turn right on leaving Le Pont-de-Montvert.*
The tiny road *(narrow, so passing is difficult, especially in high season)* passes through countryside bare of pasture, and heathland scattered with rocks.

L'Hôpital – This hamlet was a commandery for the Knights Hospitallers of St John of Jerusalem. One or two summer visitors have bought and are restoring some of its granite buildings and the Écomusée has had the old-style thatched roofs put back on the water mill and the old grange.

The GR 7 footpath which crosses L'Hôpital leads to Pont-du-Tarn.

Pont-du-Tarn – *1hr on foot there and back from L'Hôpital.* The GR 7 follows the old Margeride sheep trail, making a very pleasant walk with lovely views of the surrounding Tarn plain, named thus as the young river flows across this plateau. A pretty bridge spans the river as it threads its way through polished rocks at the foot of the Commandeur woods.

★ **Mas Camargues** – This family mansion is surprisingly large and has an unusually regular façade made of hewn blocks of granite. It has been restored by the Parc national des Cévennes. An **observation trail** has been laid out around it to explain various aspects of farming in this region – sheepfold, mill, small canal, reservoir – and the surrounding countryside (jumbles of granite boulders, beech groves). *A guide to the observation trail is on sale here and in the information centres of the Parc national des Cévennes.*

It is possible to walk on as far as **Bellecoste** *(1km/0.6mi)*, an interesting example of rural architecture with a communal oven and a traditional thatched shepherd's house.

Farms of Troubat and Aubaret – *8km/5mi east of Le Pont-de-Montvert. Take D 998 towards Génolhac, then turn left to Masméjan.*

Ferme de Troubat ⊙ – This old farmstead in rose-coloured granite has been restored by the Parc national des Cévennes and has a stable-barn, bread oven, mill and threshing area.

Ferme-fortifiée de l'Aubaret – This fortified farm on the Margeride sheep trail is dwarfed by the massive *chaos* of rocks behind it. The farm's sturdy pink granite walls have mullioned windows.

Cascade des Rûnes – *11km/7mi west. From Le Pont-de-Montvert take the road to Florac, then turn right onto D 35 towards Fraissinet-de-Lozère.* This road lined with ash trees gives some pretty views of the Tarn valley. South of Rûnes, a footpath *(45min on foot there and back)* leads to a lovely waterfall in the Mirals, which drops 58m/190ft.

PRADES

Population 6 009
Michelin map 86 folds 17 and 18 or 235 fold 52 – Local map see Le CANIGOU

Prades, lying at the foot of the Canigou, in the midst of orchards, became home to the cellist Pablo Casals (1876-1973) from 1950. The great concerts of the music festivals take place in the abbey of St-Michel-de-Cuxa.

In the old district around the church, the kerbstones, the gutters and the door sills are frequently made of pink marble from the Conflent.

Église St-Pierre – The church, rebuilt in the 17C, has nonetheless conserved its typical southern French Romanesque bell-tower. An unexpected wealth of furnishings adorns the interior. In the chancel, the Baroque **altarpiece** (1696-

A cellist's happy whim

In 1939, **Pablo Casals** fled the Franco regime in his native country, choosing to live in exile in Prades and thus not abandoning his beloved Catalonia altogether. For ten years this world-famous cellist, a committed pacifist, refused to play in public as a sign of protest. He relented at last in 1950, founding a festival which he dedicated to Bach, firmly stipulating, however, that the festival should take place in his adopted home town. Since then, Prades has become a major venue for chamber music. Every year, between 25 July and 15 August, some of the world's leading chamber musicians convene here to teach 150 outstandingly talented music students. Twenty five concerts are given at the abbey of St-Michel-de-Cuxa, the church of St-Pierre in Prades and some of the other particularly beautiful churches in the region.

Pablo Casals

99) by the Catalan sculptor Joseph Sunyer includes over one hundred carved figures and narrates in 6 sculpted scenes the life of the Apostle Peter, whose statue occupies the centre of the composition. Other Baroque works are on view in side chapels: St-Gaudérique altarpiece (1714), probably from Sunyer's workshop; Trinity altarpiece sculpted by Louis Generès (1655); St-Benoît altarpiece in carved and gilded wood and decorated with paintings on canvas dating from the 16C. In the north transept, note a 16C figure of Christ in black wood and an 18C processional Virgin Mary with a typical Catalan feature – a carved and gilded canopy, known as a *cadireta*, over the statue.

EXCURSIONS

Marcevol – *Round tour 35km/21mi – allow 2hr*

Take D 619, the road to Molitg, as far as Catllar where you should fork right onto D 24.

★ **Eus** – This is a pretty village in which the houses extend down the hillside on the sunny side of the valley amongst granite and broom, enclosed between the large 18C church above and the Romanesque chapel of St-Vincent with its graveyard on the valley floor below.
It is interesting to walk around the ruins of the fortified town, near the church. Through gaps in the walls, there are fine views of the Canigou and the Conflent plain.

Carry on along D 35, leaving the Marquixanes bridge over the Têt to the right.

Marcevol – A tiny village peopled by shepherds and wine growers. Further downhill, an old priory of the canons of St-Sépulcre, perched alone on a grassy hillock overlooking the Conflent, opposite the Canigou, features a portal and a Romanesque window of pink and white marble. The panels still have their scroll hinges, a motif typical of Romanesque wrought ironwork in the Conflent and the Vallespir.
The priory houses the Marcevol **Association du Monastir** ⊙. Founded in 1972, it organises courses and meetings all the year round.

Some distance (5km/3mi) beyond Marcevol, take D 13 on the right, which, after passing through a granite gorge where rockroses are in bloom in early summer, leads back to the Têt valley.

Return to Prades on N 116.

Mosset – *24km/14mi north, on D 619 and D 14 – allow 1hr*

Molitg-les-Bains – This spa is set in the wooded ravine of the Castellane, a sheltered site with meadows, footpaths and a lake. Skin diseases and respiratory ailments are treated thoro.

Mosset – The old fortified village stretches out on the crest as if to close off the valley.

Bambouseraie de PRAFRANCE★

Michelin map 80 fold 17 or 240 fold 14 southwest of Alès

This exotic **bamboo** plantation, not what one would expect in the heart of the Cévennes, was founded in 1855 by Eugène Mazel, who came from the Cévennes area. When Mazel was in the Far East studying the mulberry trees essential for silkworm breeding, he became fascinated by bamboos and brought back some cuttings. At Prafrance, where they reaped the benefits of a soil enriched by the alluvial deposits of the Gardon, a high water table and a suitable micro-climate, the bamboo forest soon became a spectacular jungle.

TOUR ⊙ *1hr 30min*

This park of about 40ha/100 acres has a magnificent avenue running right through it of 20m/65ft tall bamboos and Californian sequoias. Another avenue, lined with palm trees, boasts a superb Virginian tulip tree. A leisurely stroll round the gardens reveals a Laotian bamboo village, a musical village and a building known as the "farm", constructed on the site of an earlier Templars' commandery (an indicator shows the level reached by the floodwaters of the Gardon d'Anduze on 30 September 1958). The arboretum is planted with trees from Japan, China and America, amongst which are magnolias, banana trees, tropical conifers and the remarkable "ginkgo biloba" or "maidenhair tree", so-called because of the bright gold of its leaves in autumn. The

Bamboo forest

greenhouses are particularly interesting during the blossom season. In the water garden, home to Japanese carp, lotuses and Egyptian papyrus plants flourish.

The bamboo plantation at Prafrance covers about 10ha/25 acres and comprises more than a hundred varieties, of which the most widely represented is that of the *phyllostachys,* medium or giant-sized bamboos, some of which can grow to as much as 35m/115ft tall. A bamboo grows from 30-35cm/12-14in a day, soon reaching its final height, but it takes three years to thicken to the consistency of wood. In Asia, it is used for ladders, irrigation pipes, scaffolding, the construction of houses, etc. Certain bamboos, easily recognisable by their yellow trunks, are used for making musical instruments. The rhizomes (underground stems) are transformed into basket or umbrella handles. The exotic scenery of Prafrance has been used as a set for several films, for example *The Wages of Fear* and *The Heroes are Tired.*

The Bambouseraie even supplies fresh foliage for the panda in the Berlin zoological gardens.

PRATS-DE-MOLLO★

Population 1 102
Michelin map 86, folds 17 and 18 or 235 folds 55, 56 or 240 fold 45

Prats-de-Mollo lies in the broad upper valley of the Tech overlooked by the close-cropped slopes of the Costabonne massif and the Canigou. It combines the character of a walled fortress town designed by Vauban with the charm of a lively, Catalan mountain town.

SIGHTS

Enter the town through Porte de France and follow the shopping street of the same name.

Opposite the Place d'Armes, climb the steps up the Rue de la Croix-de-Mission, overlooked by a Cross and Instruments of the Passion.

Church – A Romanesque church, of which only the crenellated bell-tower remains, predated the present build-

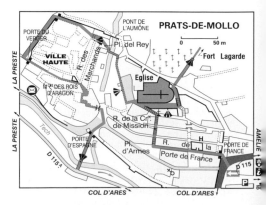

ing which has a Gothic structure, despite dating from the 17C. The 13C portal has scrolled hinges. A curious votive offering has been stuck in the wall to the right – a whale rib more than 2m/6ft long. In the chapel facing the door stands the statue of Notre-Dame-du-Coral, a copy of the 13C statue worshipped in the old shepherds' sanctuary of the same name situated near the Col d'Ares. The Baroque altarpiece on the high altar, nearly 10m/32ft tall and which was covered in gold leaf in 1745, depicts the life and the martyrdom of Sts Justa and Rufina of Andalusia, patron saints of the town.

Go along the south side of the church and take a fortified rampart walk round the chevet. Leave the precinct and walk uphill for about 100m/110yd towards Fort Lagarde.

Turn round for a good view of the roof and upper sections of the church.

Fort Lagarde – The fortress was built in 1692 on a rocky spur overlooking the town, and at the centre of the site there are now the remains of the old castle. A redoubt, halfway between the fort and the town, stood guard over the path that linked the two. Take the steps up the side of the curtain wall to get to the fort.

Return to the church portal and take the street to the right.

In sight of the almshouse, go down the steps on the left and follow the street as it runs along below the almshouse gardens. There is an attractive view of the upper town and the hills in the background; the Mir tower and the Costabonne summit can be seen at the far end of the valley. Cross the torrent over the fortified bridge, just downstream of the old humpbacked bridge of La Guilhème, to get to the upper town.

Church of Ste-Juste-et-Ste-Rufine, Prats-de-Mollo

Cancanaque/IMAGES TOULOUSE

★ **Upper Town** (Ville haute or Ville d'amoun) – Place del Rey, where an old house once belonging to the military Engineers stands, was the site of one of the residences of the Counts of Besalù, who, in the 12C, reigned over one of the pieces of land which formed part of the patchwork of Catalan territory. Where Rue des Marchands leads off to the left, take a carved stairway up to the right. From the top of the steps, there is a fine view of the church towering above the lower town.

Continue along the curtain wall. Leave the town through a modern gateway, and return to it through the next one round (a gatehouse), the "Porte du Verger".

The street leads to a crossroads, overlooked by a house in the shape of a ship's prow; some people think this was once a palace of the Kings of Aragon, and others think that it once housed the trade union of the weavers' guild. High quality cloth and linen were once produced in the Haut-Vallespir region. An alleyway leads downhill to the exit from the upper town.

Go through the Porte d'Espagne onto the footbridge over the Tech, from where there is a good view of the south side of the town.

LA PRESTE

Leaving Prats-de-Mollo to the northwest, the D 115ᴬ leads, after 8km/5mi, to the spa town of La Preste (alt 1 130m/3 707ft). It has five springs (temperature 44°C/111°F) which are recommended for the cure of infections of the colon. Napoléon III had this road up to the spa built. As he was unwell, he had intended to follow a course of hydrotherapy at the spa, but the war of 1870 intervened and he was forced to abandon the idea.

The Michelin on-line route planning service is available on a pay-per-route basis, or you may opt for a subscription package. This option affords you multiple route plans at considerable savings.

Plan your next trip in minutes with Michelin on Internet: ***www.michelin-travel.com.***

Bon voyage !

Château de QUÉRIBUS★

Michelin map 86 fold 8 or 235 fold 48 and 240 fold 37
Local map see Les CORBIÈRES

These castle ruins are reached by taking the D 123 south from the village of Cucugnan and then, just before the Grau de Maury, turning left up a very steep road. From the car park and ticket office a footpath leads up to the castle (30min steep climb each way). Great care is needed in windy weather particularly, when you will also need to hold onto the handrail to get through the small east doorway leading into the castle compound (steps).

As late as 1241, the castle of **Quéribus** ⊘ was providing refuge for Cathar deacons. When it was besieged in 1255, 11 years after the fall of Montségur, in what was to be the last military operation of the Albigensian Crusade, the castle appears not to have been taken by a full-scale assault. Quéribus was then made a royal fortress. It stood on the frontier between France and Aragon, with the role of observing and defending the plain of Roussillon.

Quéribus

★★ Site – The castle occupies a spectacular site, perched 729m/2 391ft above sea level on top of a rocky outcrop, looking for all the world like a "thimble on a finger". From the castle terraces, which are unsafe in strong winds, there is a splendid all-round **view★★** of the Roussillon plain, the Mediterranean, the Albères and the Canigou, the Puigmal and Carlit massifs. To the northwest, in clear weather, the ruins of Peyrepertuse castle can be seen on the other side of the valley.

Interior – The castle is a fascinating place to visit, as inside it has an intriguing maze of winding passages, doorways and flights of steps to be explored. Here and there, arrow slits give glimpses of the outside world. The most impressive part of the interior is the high **Gothic hall★** with vaulting resting on a central pillar. Its unusual layout and lighting have given rise, as at Montségur, to interpretations linked to solar symbolism. However, almost nothing remains of the original castle which was completely transformed to meet the changing needs of the artillery.

RODEZ★

Population 24 701
Michelin map 80 fold 2 or 235 fold 16

Once the capital of the Rouergue, Rodez is situated on the borders of two very different regions, the dry Causses plateaux and the well-watered Ségala hills. The old town stands on a hill some 120m/393ft above the Aveyron river bed.

Divided loyalties – In the Middle Ages, the town was shared between two masters. The bishops, who for a long time were the more powerful, occupied the Cité; the counts ruled the Bourg.

These two adjacent areas were separated by tall fortifications, and for many centuries, the rivalry between the two prompted endless fighting between the inhabitants. The two main squares, Place de la Cité and Place du Bourg, reflect the town's former duality.

When Henri IV became king, the Comté de Rodez was united with the French crown; the bishops promptly took advantage of this, styling themselves Bishops and Counts of Rodez and adding a count's coronet to their coat of arms.

★★ CATHÉDRALE NOTRE-DAME (Y) *1hr*

The red sandstone cathedral was begun in 1277 after the collapse, a year earlier, of the choir and bell-tower of the previous building. Half a century later, the apse and two bays of the chancel had been completed, by the 14C a transept and two bays of the nave, and by the 15C the whole building was finished.

Exterior – The west front overlooking the Place d'Armes has a forbidding, fortress-like appearance. The lower half of the wall is quite bare, with no porch and only the occasional arrow slit. It has massive buttresses, turrets with windows cut at an angle and two plain, unadorned towers. This austere façade, built outside the city wall, acted as an advance bastion the better to defend the city. Only the upper part between the two towers, which was completed in the 17C, is decorated in the Renaissance style with a classical pediment.

Go round the church to the left.

The late-15C north door, known as the Portail de l'Évêché (bishop's doorway), opens beneath three rows of archivolts and a pointed arch; sculptures, sadly damaged, depict the Nativity, the Adoration of the Shepherds and the Magi, and the Presentation in the Temple on the lintel, and, on the tympanum, the Coronation of the Virgin.

The magnificent **bell-tower★★★**, which interestingly stands apart from the cathedral, was built on top of a solid 14C tower; it is 87m/285ft high and comprises six tiers. The third tier, built in the 16C, is decorated with large window openings with distinctive tracery; the fourth, octagonal in shape, has statues of the Apostles adorning the niches in between the window openings; the fifth is elaborately decorated with turrets, Flamboyant arcades and pinnacles. On the top tier, which has a terrace with a balustrade, a dome and a lantern light, stands a statue of the Virgin Mary.

The interest of the apse lies in the way the terrace roofs of its chapels and ambulatory support doublespan flying buttresses, which in turn receive the thrust from the upper walls of the chancel level with the springing line of the vaulting.

On the south door, the work of Jacques Maurel (late 15C), note the elegant windows adorning the tympanum.

Interior – The elegance of the Gothic style is apparent in the soaring elevation of the chancel with its delicate lancet windows, in the finesse of the pillars in the nave, barely perceptibly moulded at the level of the capitals, and in the height of the great arches surmounted by a triforium which reproduces the same pattern as that of the upper windows. The beauty of the great nave and its vast side aisles, flanked with well-lit side chapels, is best appreciated standing behind the parish altar, at the far west end of the nave.

The **choir stalls★** are by André Sulpice (15C), and the furnishing of the choir was modelled on that of St-Aphrodise in Béziers; 62 tall stalls beneath Gothic oak canopies, as well as a remarkable stall for the bishop surmounted by a little pyramid and an angel (restored in the 19C) displaying the coat of arms of Bertrand de Chalençon,

Bell-tower of the cathedral of Notre-Dame

bishop of Rodez. The skilfully crafted, amusing scenes on the misericords are well worth a closer look.

The third side chapel off the south side aisle is closed off by a fine 16C **stone screen★**, unfortunately with badly damaged carved decoration. The pillars were decorated with twelve statues of sibyls, the prophetesses of Antiquity who, according to Christian tradition, foretold the coming of the Messiah. Only four of these statues are left, together with an Ecce Homo on the inside of the screen. This chapel also contains a Renaissance altar (1523), surmounted by a large altarpiece depicting an Entombment, three little Resurrection scenes, and Christ leaving the Tomb; sadly, the faces were very crudely repainted at the end of the 19C.

In the next chapel along, there is a fine 15C altarpiece: "Christ in the Garden of Olives". The large and richly decorated **rood screen★** (1470) was moved into the south arm of the transept, because it blocked the view of the nave. The **organ case★**, in the north arm of the transept, is a superb piece of 17C carved woodwork (height 20.5m/67ft).

On the high altar stands a fine statue of the Virgin and Child (late 14C). The choir *(choir stalls described above)* is surrounded by an ambulatory with chapels leading off it; in the first bay of the side aisles of the choir are two beautiful marble sarcophagi and an early 15C Entombment; the chapels contain the tombs of several bishops of Rodez, including, in the axial chapel, the particularly interesting tomb of bishop Gilbert de Cantobre (d 1349), surmounted by a Romanesque marble altar-table with scalloped decoration. The Renaissance chapel at the entrance to the sacristy is also of interest.

OLD RODEZ

The old part of town, which formed part of the bishops' estate, lies around the cathedral. Several interesting houses and mansions still remain.

Leave the cathedral through the north door; cross the Rue Frayssinous and enter the courtyard of the bishops' palace.

Palais épiscopal (Y) – The courtyard of the bishops' palace offers the best **view** of the bell-tower of Notre-Dame. There is an interesting staircase with a double revolution, which dates from the late 17C and was partially restored in the 19C.

Turn right; take the Boulevard d'Estourmel alongside the terraces of the bishop's palace.

Tour Corbières (Y) and **Tour Raynalde** (Y) – These two 15C towers are the vestiges of the walls and the 30 towers which once fortified the town.

Opposite the portal of the church of Sacré-Cœur, take the stairway leading to the Impasse Cambon.

Hôtel Delauro (Y) – This 16C and 17C mansion, once a canon's residence, now belongs to an association – the Compagnons du Devoir – who restored it.

Return to Rue Frayssinous and carry on to Place de la Cité.

Place de la Cité (Y) – At the east end stands the bronze statue of an illustrious local hero, Monseigneur Affre, Archbishop of Paris, who was killed on the barricades of Faubourg St-Antoine on 25 June 1848 whilst attempting to make peace.

Take the Rue de Bonald then the Rue de l'Embergue past beautiful old houses, antique shops and craft workshops. Between these two streets lies the **Espace public des Embergues**, an Italian style square or piazza full of cafés and restaurants in summer.

Cross the Place de la Cité diagonally and follow Rue du Touat, until it intersects with Rue Bosc.

RODEZ

Cité (Pl. de la)	Y
Neuve (Rue)	YZ
Touat (R. du)	YZ
Armagnac (R. d')	Z 2
Blanc (R. L.)	Z 3
Bosc (R.)	Y 4
Cabrières (R.)	Y 5
Calvé (Pl. Emma)	Y 6
Corbière (Rue)	Z 7
Estaing (Place d')	Y 8
Foch (Pl. Mar.)	Z 10
Frayssinous (Rue)	Y 12
Galy (Bd)	Z 13
Gambetta (Bd)	Y 14
Gaulle (Pl. Ch.-de-)	Z 16
Madeleine (Pl. de la)	Z 18
Pénavayre (Rue)	Z 19
République (Bd de la)	Y 20
Rozier (Pl. A.)	Y 22
St-Cyrice (R.)	Y 23
St-Étienne (Carrefour)	Z 26
Terral (R. du)	Y 27
Villaret (Rue)	Z 28

E Maison de Guitard dite Tour des Anglais
F Maison de Benoît
L Maison de l'Annonciation
P Préfecture et Hôtel du Département

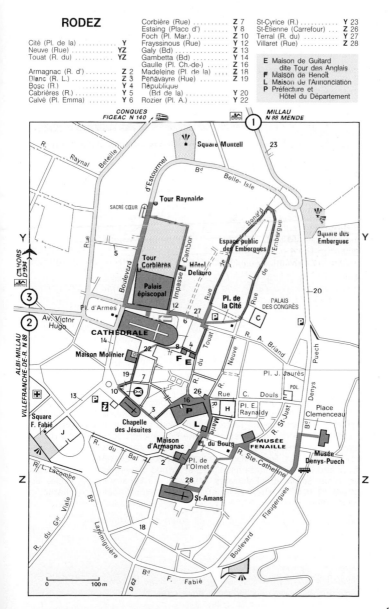

Maison de Guitard dite Tour des Anglais (Y E) – This 14C house (also known as the Tower of the English) features a massive fortified tower and fine gemel windows. The Guitards were rich bankers of the 14C.

Maison de Benoît (Y F) – *Place d'Estaing*. A Gothic gallery runs along two sides of the courtyard *(private)* of this Renaissance house.

Maison Molinier (Y) – *2, Rue Penavayre*. This old 15C canon's house stands behind an enclosing wall surmounted by a gallery and two Gothic loggias (15C).

Carry on along Rue Penavayre and turn right.

Jesuit Chapel (Z) – This 17C Baroque chapel is now used as a conference and exhibition centre. Known as the "Chapelle Foch", because the future Maréchal Foch went to school at the *lycée* next to it, it contains a massive altarpiece and some fine **wooden galleries★** decorated with frescoes of a more naturalistic style than would normally be expected in a Jesuit chapel.

Walk back along Rue Louis-Blanc and round the handsome 18C mansion which now houses the Préfecture (Z P).

Place du Bourg (Z) – This square, once the centre of the old town known as the Bourg, frequented by counts and merchants alike, is still a busy shopping area surrounded by pedestrian precincts lined with shops. There are some old houses on the square.

Maison de l'Annonciation (Z L) – This 16C house is named after the low relief of the Annonciation on the corner turret.

Maison dite d'Armagnac (Z) – *4, place de l'Olmet*. The façade of this fine 16C mansion is adorned with charming medallions depicting the counts and countesses of Rodez.
From Place de l'Olmet, a 16C house which now houses a chemist's can be seen in the Rue d'Armagnac.

Église St-Amans (Z) – This church was built in the 12C, but the exterior was completely restored in the 18C. Inside, it has some of the original fine Romanesque capitals. The choir and the ambulatory are hung with 16C tapestries. In the baptismal chapel there is an unusual statue of the Trinity in polychrome stone.

★ **Musée Fenaille** ⊘ **(Z)** – In two 14C and 16C mansions collections of prehistoric exhibits and archeological finds from the Gallo-Roman and Merovingian periods are on display, together with medieval and Renaissance sculpture, antique furniture, religious objets d'art, and illuminated manuscripts. Note in particular the **menhir-statues★** from the south of the Aveyron which date from late prehistory (the most famous is that of "St Sernin"), a very fine 16C Virgin of the Annonciation and a collection of ceramic ware from the Graufesenque pottery.

Turn back the way you came and take Rue Ste-Catherine on the left, then Boulevard Denys-Puech.

Musée Denys-Puech ⊘ **(Z)** – Founded in 1910 by the sculptor **Denys Puech** (1854-1942), born in the Aveyron, this museum contains both permanent collections of 19C and 20C art, and temporary exhibitions on contemporary art (works by Denys Puech and other artists from the Aveyron).
Since its renovation in 1989, the museum has displayed a monumental work by François Morellet entitled "Integration" on the two gable walls of the building.

Tour of the town – From its site on a hill, Rodez offers numerous points of view of the surrounding countryside. The boulevards built on the line of the old ramparts make it possible to make a round tour of town by car (outside peak times). Leave from Place d'Armes and take Boulevard Estourmel. To the right, the remains of the ramparts (16C) and terraces of the episcopal palace lead to Corbières tower (14C). **Square Monteil (Y)** gives a good view of Comtal *causse* and the Aubrac and Cantal mountains. There are good views to the north and west of town from **Square des Embergues (Y)**, which has a viewing table. **Square François-Fabié (Y)**, in which there is a memorial to the local poet of this name, gives views of the Ségala region.

▶▶ **Haras** ⊘ – *Rue Eugène-Loup*, ② *on town plan*. Stud farm.

*The **Michelin Maps** for this region are shown in the diagram on page 1.*

The text refers to the maps which, owing to their scale or coverage, are the clearest and most appropriate in each case.

ROQUEFORT-SUR-SOULZON★

Population 789
Michelin map 80 fold 14 or 240 folds 13, 14
Local map see Les GRANDS CAUSSES

The name of this market town between Millau and St-Affrique has become synonymous with one of the most famous and widely appreciated of French cheeses, succulent blue Roquefort. However, not a sign of Roquefort's main economic activity is to be seen in the town itself, for production of the cheese takes place underground.

Roquefort cheese – Strict boundaries define the area of production of ewes' milk and the region of caves in which Roquefort cheese is matured. French law decrees that only ewe's-milk cheese produced within these boundaries may be labelled "Roquefort". As an official label of origin *(appellation d'origine)*, "Roquefort" is probably one of the oldest in France – since Roquefort is known to have been appreciated in Rome by Pliny and in Aix-la-Chapelle (Aachen) by Charlemagne. The cheese's official status was confirmed by statute under the law of the Ancien Régime, both by royal charters and in decrees passed by the Languedoc parliament, and, in modern times, by the application of the 1919 generic law on labelling, then the establishment of a special law on 26 July 1925, followed by a decree of 22 October 1979.

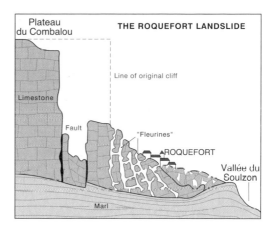

The region of production of ewe's milk has progressively expanded north up to the Lot valley, west to the Montagne Noire, and south and southeast beyond the Grands Causses into the mountains of the Hérault region and the foothills of the Cévennes. Roquefort cheese is made exclusively from full-fat, untreated ewe's milk, neither homogenised nor pasteurised, in dairies located where the milk is drawn.

In the dairies, the milk is first made into a cheese in which the curd has been mixed with a natural mould, *Penicillium roqueforti*, which comes from the caves at Combalou. The rounds of cheese are transported to Roquefort for maturation.

★ **The Roquefort caves** ⚲ – Above the town of Roquefort, which lies at the foot of the cliff, is a little limestone plateau known as "Combalou", the north-east side of which collapsed when it slipped on its clay sub-stratum. These special conditions gave rise to natural caves between the displaced rocks, in which temperature and humidity are constant and ideal for curing cheese, hence their attraction for the very first makers of Roquefort.

Roquefort cheese maturing underground in caves

After the cheese has been made in the dairy, the rounds are set out in long rows on oak shelves in the specially adapted natural cellars. A gradual maturing process gets under way, carefully monitored by experts. Aided by the cold, damp air circulating from the *fleurines*, narrow natural chimneys at ground level, the *Penicillium roqueforti* mould grows, and the cheese takes on its characteristic blue-green veining. A minimum maturation of three months is necessary for a good Roquefort. Annual production is about 20 000 tonnes. Exports, mainly to the U.S.A. and the European Union countries, represent about 15 % of output.

Rocher St-Pierre - *169 steps.*
This rock (alt 650m/2 132ft) against the Combalou cliff offers a **view**★ *(viewing table)* as far as the Lévézou mountains to the left, over the Soulzon valley and Tournemire cirque to the right, opposite to the tabular cliffs of the Causse du Larzac, and of the town of Roquefort at the foot of the cliff.
Note the ruins of the first village church, an 11C Romanesque chapel.

Musée de Préhistoire ⊙ – This museum displays objects found in excavations (pottery, bronze and copper utensils etc) which show that there were periods when the Roquefort and Causses regions were quite densely populated between the beginning of the Neolithic period and the Gallo-Roman era.

Sentier des Echelles – *5km/3mi, allow 2hr.* At the exit from the village (alt 630m/2 067ft), this leads to the Combalou plateau (alt 791m/2 595ft), from which there is a **panoramic view**.

Plages du ROUSSILLON

Michelin map 86 folds 10 and 20 or 240 folds 34, 38, 42 and 46
Local map see La CÔTE VERMEILLE

The stretch of Mediterranean coast described in this guide offers visitors a serene vista of great expanses of sea, shore and vineyards.
Strung out all along this part of the coast lie numerous saltwater lagoons, cut off from the sea by slender sand bars and only connected with it by occasional channels. Because it lacked any proper facilities, the Roussillon coast for years avoided attracting any large-scale tourism, despite its vast sandy beaches, exceptionally sunny weather and inviting blue sea.
A state programme was launched in 1963 and has now largely been completed, for developing and marketing the Languedoc and Roussillon coast as a major tourist attraction. From 1968, this plan was put into action by remodelling the sand bars of Leucate lagoon. This previously deserted stretch of coast, rapidly becoming waterlogged and silted up, now boasts two brand new seaside resorts – Port-Leucate and Port-Barcarès. Before construction work began, a coastal highway was built, which was however not connected to the existing coastal road network, in order to protect the fragile natural environment of this stretch of coast. A campaign was mounted to rid the lagoons of their mosquitoes, land was cultivated and a water supply was set up, opening the way for builders, property developers and holiday camp sponsors. Along the Roussillon coast visitors are now able to enjoy a new type of holiday, combining the colourful variety and lively atmosphere of the resorts, each one designed and built to have its own particular style, with the exploration of a coastal hinterland still redolent with tradition.
The traditional resorts have also been included in the development scheme. The most immediately noticeable improvement is their improved access to the sea: yachting marinas have been built at Collioure, Banyuls and Port-Vendres among other places. The Roussillon resorts, both old and new, benefit from being close to the coastal lagoons. The parks, lawns and gardens which have been planted are lovingly protected from sea spray and continually watered (mainly at Port-Barcarès) to keep them looking fresh and green.

FROM CAP LEUCATE TO ARGELÈS-PLAGE

The development of new tourist resorts along the beaches on this section of the Golfe du Lion accentuates the contrast between the lower-lying sandy coast and the rocky, deeply indented coast further south *(described under La CÔTE VERMEILLE).*

★ **Cap Leucate** – The cliffs of the cape close off the north end of the lagoon of Leucate or Salses. They offer fine views over the whole of the Golfe du Lion.

Sémaphore du Cap – From the lookout point by the signal station on the cape, there is a **view**★ along the coast, from Languedoc to the Albères.

La Franqui – This small seaside resort can be reached on foot *(1hr 30min there and back)* along the cliff path which runs from the signal station to Cap Leucate. The writer Henry de Monfreid (1879-1974), born in Leucate, used to enjoy coming to stay here.

⌂ **Port-Leucate and Port-Barcarès** – The urban planners of these resorts had 750ha/1 853 acres at their disposal. They sought to cater for the modern preference for swimming in natural settings, rather than manmade pools, and demand for sports facilities, as well as combining self-catering tourist accommodation with conventional hotel facilities. The resorts have been laid out with large residential areas of buildings grouped together. The concept of a seafront has been abandoned; access to the beach is via no-through roads.

Sunsets along this part of the coast have something of Greece about them, when the Corbières can be seen tinged with violet rising behind the dark, metallic waters of Leucate lagoon.

The new harbour complex of Port-Leucate and Port-Barcarès constitutes the largest marina on the French Mediterranean coast. It is a major centre for yachting and water-skiing. A stretch of water about 10km/6mi long, unconnected with the sea or the Leucate lagoon, forms a pool free of waves, from which tributary channels flow to supply the marinas.

⌂ **Port-Barcarès** – The **Lydia**★ ⊘, a ship which was deliberately run aground in 1967, is the main attraction of the new Roussillon shoreline (disco and casino). Just by the *Lydia*, along an esplanade by the sea, the **Allée des Arts** *(signposted)* hosts a small display of contemporary sculpture including the "Soleillonautes", totem poles sculpted from the trunks of trees from Gabon. The resort's park is a lovely place for a walk. A modern thalassotherapy centre treats patients suffering from ailments such as overwork, depression and rheumatism.

The next three resorts to the south, which have been patronised for many years by local swimmers, were included in the coastal development scheme. Changes include improving access for boats.

⌂⌂ **Canet-Plage** – This long-established seaside haunt of the inhabitants of Perpignan owes its lively atmosphere to its busy marina (yachts), its sports facilities and the activities of its casino. Interesting museums include the **Aquarium** ⊘, with local and tropical species, the **Musée de l'Auto** ⊘, with a collection

St-Cyprien

Thomas/IMAGES PHOTOTHÈQUE

of restored motor cars covering the period from 1907 to 1989, the **Musée du Bateau** ⊙, with more than a hundred model boats, and the **Musée du Jouet**★ ⊙, displaying toys from all over the world in a historical perspective (the oldest exhibits are ancient Egyptian dolls).

Canet lagoon, covering 956ha/3.7sq mi, has been designated a protected natural environment. A village of fishermen's huts made of plaited reeds is still to be seen on the banks of the lagoon. A footpath (4km/2.5mi) enables visitors to discover some of the lagoon's flora and fauna (including numerous species of bird).

⌂⌂ **St-Cyprien** – This seaside resort was redesigned as part of the development project. The hub of activity has shifted to the district around the new harbour, where the urban planners found some free space to put up buildings of 5 to 10 storeys. This marina, the second most important of Mediterranean France, has been extended in such a way that it is possible to visit it on foot, along the quays. There is also a Catalan village to be explored.

⌂⌂⌂ **Argelès-Plage** – About sixty camp sites and canvas villages within a radius of 5km/3mi make this resort the camping capital of Europe. Argelès-Plage marks the point where the lower Roussillon coast (Plage Nord, Plage des Pins) runs into the first few rocky creeks of the Côte Vermeille (the Racou). The immediate hinterland still has its irrigated gardens, and orchards in which the most delicate of fruit trees thrive, along with nettle trees and eucalyptus. In summer, tens of thousands of holiday makers descend on the resort looking for fun.

Casa de les Albères ⊙ – Situated at the heart of the old town of **Argelès-sur-Mer**, this Catalan museum of folk art and traditions displays tools used for trades once commonly plyed in the Albères: cork (bottle-top) making, barrel manufacture, wine making, and also the fabrication of espadrilles (rope-soled sandals) and toys made from the wood of nettle trees.

ST-ANTONIN-NOBLE-VAL★

Population 1 867
Michelin map 79 fold 18 or 235 fold 19

Towering on the opposite bank of the River Aveyron above St-Antonin, a pretty, old town on the borders of the Quercy, Albigeois and Rouergue regions, is a sheer wall of whitish rock known as the Roc d'Anglars. The town's houses, with virtually flat roofs covered in half-cylindrical tiles faded by the sun, are built in gentle tiers on the north bank of the river.

So delightful was the setting of the Gallo-Roman settlement, forerunner of the present town, that it was given the name "glorious valley" *(noble val)*. An oratory founded by St Antonin, who came to convert this part of the Rouergue, was replaced in the 8C by an abbey.

The town developed rapidly during the Middle Ages, due to trade in cloth, fur and leather, as can be seen by the 13C, 14C and 15C houses which were once the residences of wealthy merchants.

A local troubadour – The viscount of St-Antonin, Ramon Jordan, born in 1150, ranks among the most gifted troubadours of his age. His poetry quivers with passion, but a pure, chaste version of it in keeping with the idea of the "chivalrous love" he declared to Adelais, wife of the lord of Penne. While he was away fighting in the Crusades, however, unfounded rumours that he had been killed began to spread. The emotional strain on Adelais was so great that she shut herself away in a nunnery. Jordan returned safe and sound, but on learning that he would never be able to see his beloved again, he lost all his joy and energy, all desire to sing and even all interest in horse-riding. He too chose to end his life as a recluse.

Defeat by Montfort – St-Antonin, which at the beginning of the 13C tended to sympathise with the Cathars and made no secret of its allegiance to the Count of Toulouse, fell victim in its turn to the ravages of the Albigensian Crusade, led by Simon de Montfort. The townspeople, finding themselves surrounded, made a tentative foray, but were vigorously repelled and, as the chronicler Guilhem Peyre (author of *The Song of the Crusade*) drily recorded, "had hardly a chance to draw breath" before their attackers sacked the town. Those of the defeated who had sought refuge in the monastery were only permitted to return to their homes once they had been stripped of all their clothes.

SIGHTS

★ **Ancien hôtel de ville** – This mansion was built in 1125 for a rich, newly ennobled townsman, Pons de Granholet, and is one of the oldest examples of civil architecture in France. In the 14C, it was the consuls' residence. Viollet-le-Duc restored it in the 19C, adding a square belfry crowned by a machicolated loggia in the Tuscan style, based on a project he presented in 1845. The building now houses a museum.

The façade is composed of two storeys. The gallery of colonnettes on the first storey is decorated with two pillars bearing statues of King Solomon and of **Adam and Eve**; the second storey is divided by three sets of twin windows.

Musée ⊙ – The museum contains prehistoric collections and is particularly rich in material from the Magdalenian Period. One room covers local traditions and folklore.

Rue Guilhem Peyre – This street leads off from beneath the belfry of the old town hall. It used to be the grand route taken by all processions. On the right there is what used to be the Royal Barracks, known as the "English Barracks", and in a bend in the road a splendid 13-16C mansion.

Rue des Grandes Boucheries – The Maison du Roy, now a restaurant, has five large pointed arches looking in at ground floor level, and the same number of twin windows on the first floor, with youthful faces adorning the capitals.

Ancien Couvent des Génovéfains – Built in 1751, this convent of the Order of St Genevieve is now home to the town hall and the tourist office.

Croix de la Halle – In front of the solid pillars of the covered market, there is a strange lollipop-shaped 14C **Cross**, carved on both sides. This rare piece of work would once have stood at the entrance to or in the middle of the town graveyard.

The rooftops of St-Antonin-Noble-Val

Rue Pélisserie – There are 13-14C houses redolent of the former wealth of master tanners and furriers all along this street.

Rue Rive-Valat – A little canal spanned by bridges flows along this street; it is one of many tributaries of the River Bonnière which were dug during the Middle Ages to provide a main drainage system and water for the tanneries. These have open top floors, which are used to store and dry skins.

Rue Droite – Two houses stand out because of their interesting carved keystones: the late 15C **Maison de l'Amour** (House of Love) where a man and woman are depicted chastely touching lips, and the Maison du Repentir (House of Repentance) where, in contrast, two faces are shown turned away from one another. About halfway along the street, there is a beautiful double-corbelled façade, decorated with half-timbering interspersed with slightly golden porous limestone and wooden mullions.

303

★ ① GORGES DE L'AVEYRON

Round trip of 50km/30mi – allow 3hr

Leave St-Antonin south, crossing the bridge over the Aveyron and turning right onto D 115 which runs alongside the river, following the course of the old railway line.
After 2.5km/1.5mi turn left onto a steeply climbing, narrow road up to the top of the cliffs *(signposted "corniche")*. This picturesque **scenic route★★** leads through the hamlet of Viel-Four with its pantiled roofs. Shortly after going through a tunnel there is a viewpoint by the edge of the road, above a sheer drop, from which there is a marvellous view of the Aveyron cutting between tall rocky cliffs. As the road drops back towards the river, the picturesque hamlet of **Brousses** comes into sight.

At Cazals, cross the river and turn left.

The road (D 173) begins to climb again immediately, heading through farming country, giving good views of the Aveyron's meanders and the valley floor covered with peach and apple orchards and fields divided by rows of poplar trees.

Cross back to the south bank of the Aveyron.

Penne - *See PENNE.*

Leave Penne to the south on D 9 which gives some excellent **views★** of the village. The road scales the edge of the plateau before crossing a region of sparse vegetation in which stunted bushes are interspersed with a few vines.
Then it drops into the valley once more heading through a landscape of lofty wooded hillsides on which bare rock is frequently in evidence.

★ **Bruniquel** - *See BRUNIQUEL.*
Cross the Aveyron and follow the road along the north bank to Montricoux.

Montricoux - *See BRUNIQUEL: Excursion.*
Take D 958 back to St-Antonin.

This road runs through the forest of La Garrigue, giving glimpses of the Aveyron below and to the right. The final stretch before St-Antonin is once again a spectacular cliff road overlooking the river.

② UPPER AVEYRON VALLEY

Round trip of 50km/30mi –allow 2hr

Leave St-Antonin north on D 19 towards Caylus.

Château de Cas ⓥ – This castle was built in the 12C and modified in the 14C and 16C. It housed a Templar commandery in the 13C before becoming the property of the powerful Cardaillac family, then passing into the hands of the Lastic Saint-Jals. This solid white stone building contains a number of interesting furnished rooms.

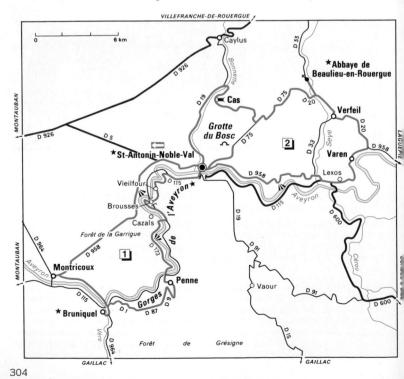

★ **Abbaye de Beaulieu-en-Rouergue** – *See Abbaye de BEAULIEU-EN-ROUERGUE.*

Verfeil – This small fortified town in the Seye valley has some charming old houses, their façades bright with flowers in season, around its covered market which has been rebuilt in stone. Inside the church, there is a gilded wooden high altar decorated with narrative scenes and a 17C wooden Crucifix which comes from the old abbey at Beaulieu.

Varen – *See VAREN.*

Just before arriving at Lexos the road passes a huge cement works. 2km/1mi past Lexos turn right onto D 33, then left onto a road signposted "St-Antonin par le coteau".

The road climbs steeply up the hillside, giving frequent views of the Aveyron valley, to which it returns after a winding descent. The river, lined by a row of poplars, flows at the foot of cliffs to which scrubby vegetation clings here and there. Shortly before St-Antonin, road and river are forced to squeeze through a narrow gap between rocky cliffs.

Grotte du Bosc ⊙ – The galleries of this cave, once the bed of an underground river which has dried up, lead back underneath the plateau between the Aveyron and Bonnette valleys for some 200m/220yd. Numerous stalactites and eccentrics adorn the cave. There is a museum of mineralogy and prehistory in the reception area.

ST-FÉLIX-LAURAGAIS

Population 1 177
Michelin map 82 fold 19 or 235 fold 35

St-Félix, in a pretty **site**★ overlooking the Lauragais plain, passed into history (or legend, as some see it) when the Cathars held a council here to set up their Church.

Déodat de Séverac – St-Félix prides itself on being the birthplace of this composer (1873-1921) of melodies evoking the beauty of nature and the countryside. Debussy said of De Séverac's music that "it smelt good". A pupil of Vincent d'Indy and Magnard at the Schola Cantorum in Paris, Déodat de Séverac was also profoundly influenced by Debussy's work. There are few composers who were able to draw so much inspiration from their native soil: *Song of the Earth, In the Languedoc, On Holiday (Le Chant de la Terre, En Languedoc, En Vacances)* are ranked by many as among the finest pieces of music written for the piano this century.

SIGHTS

Castle – There is a pleasant walkway round this 14-15C castle, which affords fine views to the east over the Montagne Noire with Revel at its foot. To the north, the belfry of St-Julia and, high up, the castle of Montgey can be seen. Not without reason did the Revolutionaries rename St-Félix "Bellevue".

Church – This collegiate church dates from the 14C and was rebuilt at the beginning of the 17C. To the right of the church stands the sober façade of the chapter-house.
To the left of the church doorway, a well has been hollowed out of the wall. Legend has it that it is as deep as the bell-tower is high (42m/137ft). The bell-tower is in the Toulouse style: octagonal, with two tiers of openings with mitre arches.

Walk – Not far from the church a vaulted passageway leads to an area where there is a view to the west over peaceful countryside with hills and cypresses.

LE LAURAGAIS

This little area of Languedoc grew wealthy in the 16C from the cultivation of dyer's woad. Nowadays, the plain is given over to the cultivation of wheat, barley and rape seed, and stock raising (cattle, sheep and poultry). An offshoot of poultry rearing has been the installation of factories for the manufacture of feather duvets.
Heading north from St-Félix, the D 67 brings you to **St-Julia**, an old fortified "free" town with some ramparts and a church which has an unusual bell-tower. A few miles northeast of St-Julia *(via Auvezines)*, on a hill, stands the massive castle of **Montgey** ⊙, a medieval fortress captured by Simon de Montfort in 1211. It was modified in the 15C and 17C. A Renaissance doorway leads into the castle, in which there is a large room with a chimneypiece by the Fontainebleau school.
South of St-Félix is the castle of **Montmaur**, a huge 16C edifice, rebuilt in the 17C and flanked by corner towers. Above the door is a stone statue of the Virgin Mary.

ST-GUILHEM-LE-DÉSERT*

Population 190
Michelin map 83 fold 6 or 240 fold 18 – Local map see Vallée de l'HÉRAULT

This pretty little village is built around an old abbey, in a delightful **site**★, at the mouth of untamed river gorges, where the Verdus flows into the Hérault. It owes much of the story of its origins to legend, related in the 12C *chanson de geste* by Guillaume d'Orange.

Childhood friends – Guilhem, the maternal grandson of Charles Martel (famous for his successful intervention in the Saracen advance in the early 8C), was born in about 755. He was brought up with Pépin the Short's sons and was soon noted for his skilful handling of weapons, his intelligence and his piety. The young princes were very attached to him; his friendship with one of them, Charles, the future Charlemagne, was to last until his death.

In 768 Charlemagne came to the throne. Guilhem was one of his most valiant officers; he conquered Aquitaine and became its governor. Attempted Saracen invasions gave him the opportunity of winning further victories at Nîmes, Orange and Narbonne, and earned him the title of Prince of Orange. His final victory was in Barcelona. On his return to France, he was 48, and his wife, whom he had loved dearly, was dead. From this point on, the great warrior decided to dedicate himself to a quest for solitude. He delegated the government of Orange to his son and went to Paris to inform the king of his decision.

The relic of the True Cross – Charlemagne, however, had no desire to be parted from his childhood friend, whom he kept on with him as his advisor. Guilhem accompanied the emperor to Rome, where a priest called Zacharius gave Charles a remarkable relic – "a 3 inch long piece of the sacred wood of the Cross, placed by St Helena in the church of Jerusalem".

On his return once more to France, Guilhem, who was inspecting his estate in the Lodève region, discovered the Gellone valley. This remote place struck him as ideal for a holy retreat. On the advice of his friend Benoît d'Aniane, he had a monastery built there, in which he settled with some monks. After being recalled once more by Charlemagne to assist in the sharing out of property, Guilhem finally took leave of his sovereign lord; the two men embraced each other in tears. Charles gave Guilhem the relic of the Cross, which was placed in the abbey church. Guilhem returned to his monastery. For another year, he busied himself with further work on the abbey, laying out gardens, building a water supply and improving access. Then turning his back on worldly things for good, the war hero retreated to his cell and spent the rest of his life in fasting and prayer until he died in 812. He is buried in the abbey church.

The abbey of St-Guilhem – After Guilhem's death, the monastery of Gellone became an important place of pilgrimage. Pilgrims came in great numbers to pray before the relic of the Cross and the tomb of St Guilhem. The abbey was also a recommended stopping place on the pilgrimage route to Santiago de Compostela.

St-Guilhem-le-Désert

By the 12C and 13C, the monastery was home to more than a hundred monks and the village of Gellone was renamed St-Guilhem-le-Désert. However, its initially gradual decline was accelerated when in the 15C the king decreed that the abbot would be appointed by him instead of being elected by the monks. The abbey took on a brief new lease of life in the 18C when monks from the community of St-Maur settled there, and restored and rebuilt the buildings. They stayed until the Revolution, by which time there were only six monks in residence.

★ ABBEY CHURCH

30min

All that remains of the abbey founded in 804 by Guilhem is the abbey church, which was built in the 11C and deconsecrated during the Revolution, when the monastic buildings were demolished and the sculptures in the cloisters dispersed throughout the region. Since December 1978, a community of Carmelite nuns has restored some life to the abbey.

Abbey church

The large church doorway adorned with archivolts, which leads off a square shaded by a magnificent plane tree, is surmounted by a 15C bell-tower. The colonnettes on the engaged doorposts and the inlaid medallions are Gallo-Roman fragments. This doorway leads into the narthex *(lo gimel)*, in which the intersecting rib vaulting dates from the end of the 12C.

Interior – The 11C nave is austere in design. The baptismal font, at the far end of the north aisle on the left, comes from the parish church of St-Laurent. The apse and the transept were added at the end of the 11C and do not share the proportions of the rest of the building. The oven-vaulted apse is decorated with seven great arches. On either side are niches in the walls, displaying on the left the reliquary of St Guilhem, complete with his bones, and on the right the fragment of the True Cross given by Charlemagne. This relic is carried in the procession in the village square which takes place every year in May.

Beneath the sanctuary lies the **crypt**, which originally contained St Guilhem's tomb. It is a remnant of the original church.

The organ is the work of J P Cavaillé and was played for the first time in 1789. It is decorated with angel musicians.

Cloisters – *Entrance through the door in the south arm of the transept.* Only the north and west galleries on the ground floor remain of the two-storeyed cloisters. They are decorated with gemel windows in which the arches are supported on very crudely executed capitals.

Some of the sculptures and columns from the upper cloister, which were bought by the collector George Grey Barnard in 1906, have made it possible to reconstruct an approximation of the cloisters in the famous Cloisters Museum in New York *(see Michelin Green Guide New York City)*.

Museum ⊙ – This is in the refectory, a vast tufa building in which the vaulting was rebuilt in the 17C. It contains sculpture work from the abbey and a photographic archive on the history of the abbey.

Note the early Christian (6C) grey marble sarcophagus, said to have housed the remains of St Guilhem's sisters. The front shows Christ with the Apostles, the sides Adam and Eve being tempted by the serpent and the three young Hebrews in the fiery furnace, and the lid Daniel in the lions' den.

Another sarcophagus in white marble (4C) is said to be that of St Guilhem.

★ **Chevet** – *To see this, walk round the church to the left.* From the alley lined with old houses, the rich decoration of the chevet can really be appreciated. On either side of the chevet are two apsidal chapels. It features three windows and a series of tiny arched openings separated by slender colonnettes surmounted with curious capitals, the whole of which is embellished by a frieze of cog-tooth indentations echoing that of the doorway.

ADDITIONAL SIGHTS

Village – Narrow winding streets lead through St-Guilhem to Place de la Liberté, the square onto which the abbey's west doorway opens. There are one or two fine medieval façades with twin or Gothic arched windows lining the square. More such residences are to be seen in the streets leading off from the west and north of the square (rue du Bout-du-Monde and rue du Font-du-Portal).

Castle – *1hr on foot there and back. From the church, take rue du Bout-du-Monde and follow the red and white flashes of the long-distance footpath (GR).* This footpath passes under one of the gates of the old curtain wall, then offers good views over the Cirque de l'Infernet.

After reaching the top of the ridge, leave the GR to follow the steep path to the right leading to the castle (great care is needed).

From the ruins of this castle perched high up, there is a good **view**★ over St-Guilhem and the Verdus gorges.

Viewpoint – *Walk back down to the village, crossing D 4.* At the foot of a stairway immediately after the Hôtel Fonzes, there is a very unusual view of the Hérault flowing in a sunken channel between steep limestone banks pockmarked with numerous large rounded hollows.

ST-JEAN-DU-GARD

Population 2 441
Michelin map 80 fold 17 or 240 folds 11 and 15 – Local map see FLORAC

This little town typical of its kind in the south of France, with its narrow Grand'Rue lined with tall houses, stands on the north bank of the Gardon, surrounded by orchards. The Gardon de St-Jean, as this stretch of the river is known, is subject to sudden flooding caused by torrential rainfall from the rapid cooling of clouds from the Mediterranean when they come into contact with the mountains of the Cévennes.

Every Tuesday St-Jean is the scene of a very lively market.

In 1958, the picturesque **old humpback bridge** over the Gardon was partially destroyed. This bridge, with six semicircular arches of unequal height resting on piers protected by buttresses, has now been reconstructed. The Romanesque style clock tower rises above the rooftops of the old town.

★ **Musée des vallées cévenoles** ⊙ – Located in an old 17C inn, this museum covers the history of the daily life and traditions of the inhabitants of this part of the Cévennes. The collections of everyday objects, tools, documents, photographs and so forth have been brought together by the inhabitants of St-Jean.

There are displays on various themes: agricultural implements used in the cultivation of cereal crops, vines and chestnut trees; objects used in the rearing of sheep, goats and bees; the different types of porterage practised in this mountainous region – on the backs of man or mule etc; information on the problems caused by water. A special place has been allotted to the two main traditional local activities: the cultivation of chestnut trees and silkworm farming.

The **chestnut tree**, almost a "tree of life" for local people, has been the basis of the Cévennes economy. Its wood was used in construction and for furniture, its leaves for feeding cattle; strips of its wood were used for basket making and its fruit could be part of any meal. Chestnuts were gathered with various implements, some of which are on display here, for example the *grata*, a three-pronged fork. They were put to dry in a little building, the **clède**, consisting of two rooms built on top of one another. The constant heat of a fire on the ground floor dried the chestnuts on the first floor. The dehydrated skins were then split with *solas*, curious shoes with iron points, or the chestnuts were placed in a sack which was then beaten against a wooden block or, later, put into cylindrical machines with large-pronged rakes inside. The white chestnut kernels were then stored for family consumption throughout the year, some were sold, and the waste was fed to the livestock, in particular to the pigs.

Silkworm farming developed throughout the Cévennes from 1709 onwards, when the chestnut trees, which had been destroyed during a particularly hard winter, were replaced with mulberry trees. These soon became the main source of wealth in the region; the era of the "tree of life" gave way to the "tree of gold".

The eggs laid by the silkworm moth, or *bombyx*, were put in a warm place to incubate, either in little sachets which women hung in their bosom, or in artificial incubators. After the eggs had hatched, the silkworms were put on a tiered stand until they had sloughed off their skin for the third time (they need to do this four times). They were then placed in the *magnanerie*, a room situated at the top of the house, with four corner chimneys to maintain a constant temperature. This is the stage when the silkworm is most hungry: 1 000kg/2 200lb of mulberry leaves are needed to rear 25g/1oz of eggs. Just before pupation, a bed of heather is put into the room to give the silkworms something to cling to as they spin their cocoon. The finished cocoon consists of a continuous silken thread. Until the end of the 18C, production of silk thread was more or less a cottage industry, then there was an increase in the number of spinning mills. Each cocoon produces 500 to 1 000m/550 to 1 100yds of silk thread, sometimes more. To obtain this, the pupa inside is suffocated in steam, and then the cocoon beaten in boiling water. This process dislodges the end of the thread so that it can then be unravelled. The thread is wound round a spool, while the cocoon is unravelled. The Cévennes spinning mills used to supply the great silk workshops of Nîmes and Lyon.

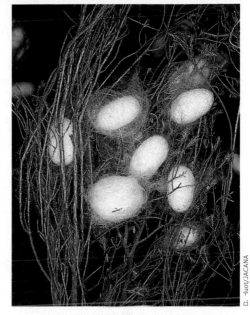

D. Huot/JACANA

Silkworm pupae

"Voyage dans le temps ⊙**"** - *Avenue de la Résistance, opposite the station for the Cévennes steam train.*
This exhibition of old vehicles, horse-drawn or motorised, traces the history of locomotion since 1850. Among the vehicles shown in their historical context are an 1853 stagecoach, an 1870 mailcoach and American automobiles of the 1960s.

Atlantide Parc ⊙ - *Avenue de la Résistance, south bank of the Gardon.*
Set in old-fashioned décors, these aquariums display a great variety of tropical aquatic fauna. The artificial river, into which a foaming waterfall tumbles, adds an exotic touch.

EXCURSIONS

★★★ **Corniche des Cévennes** - *Leave St-Jean on D 907, to the northwest; after 2km/1mi, take D 260. Route described from the opposite direction under Corniche des CÉVENNES.*

★★ **Route du Col de l'Asclier** - *44km/27mi. See Col de l'ASCLIER.*

Cévennes Steam Train ⊙ - The steam railway which, from 1905 to 1960, ran between the stations of St-Jean-du-Gard, Générargues and Anduze has been reopened as a tourist attraction. The railway follows or crosses the Gardons of St-Jean, Mialet and Anduze, passes through the Prafrance bamboo plantation and, after a long tunnel, arrives at Anduze opposite the "Porte des Cévennes".

MICHELIN GREEN GUIDES

   Architecture
   Fine Art
   Ancient monuments
   History
   Geography
   Picturesque scenery
   Scenic routes
   Touring programmes
   Places to stay
   Plans of towns and buildings

A collection of regional guides for France.

Pic ST-LOUP★★

Michelin map 80 fold 17 or 240 fold 19

St-Loup peak marks the highest point (658m/2 158ft) of a long ridge above the Montpellier Garrigues. Its limestone strata rise almost vertically, making a dramatic break in the monotonous plains surrounding it.

Getting there – *Take D 113. Park the car at Cazevieille (east of the village) and follow the directions to St-Loup. The wide stone path leads up to a Calvary. From there, take a little winding footpath which climbs up to the chapel and observatory. Allow 2hr 30min there and back.*

★★ **Panorama** – From St-Loup peak, there is a magnificent panorama of the surrounding countryside. The north face drops straight down into a ravine which separates St-Loup peak from the rocky ridge of the Hortus mountain; beyond, to the northwest and the north, the view embraces the Cévennes. To the east lie the ruins of Montferrand, the Nîmes plain and, beyond the Rhône valley, Mont Ventoux, the Alpilles and the Luberon; to the southeast is the Camargue; to the south, the Montpellier plain and the Mediterranean with its string of coastal lagoons; to the southwest, the Causse de Viols and, on the horizon, the Canigou and the Corbières; to the west, the mountains of Celette, Labat and Suque and, beyond them, the Séranne.

ST-MARTIN-DU-CANIGOU★★

Michelin maps 86 fold 17 or 235 fold 52
3km/2mi south of Vernet-les-Bains – Local map see Le CANIGOU

This abbey perched in its eagle's eyrie 1 055m/3 460ft above sea level is one of the prime sights to be seen in the area around Vernet-les-Bains.

Getting there ⊙ – *Park the car in Casteil, then follow a steep road uphill – a little over 1hr on foot there and back. The abbey can also be reached by Jeep – see the Practical information section at the end of the guide.*

Abbey ⊙ – The abbey, built on a rocky pinnacle at an altitude of 1 094m/3 589ft, grew up around the monastic community that was originally founded here in the 11C. After falling into disuse at the Revolution, it was restored from 1902 to 1932 by Msgr de Carsalade du Pont, bishop of Perpignan, and extended from 1952 to 1972.

Cloisters – At the beginning of the 20C, all that remained of the cloisters was three galleries with somewhat crude semicircular arcades. Restoration work included rebuilding a south gallery, overlooking the ravine, using the marble capitals from an upper storey which was no longer extant.

Abbey of St-Martin-du-Canigou

310

Churches – The lower church (10C), dedicated to "Notre-Dame-sous-Terre" in accordance with an old Christian tradition, forms the crypt of the upper church (11C). The latter, consisting of three successive naves with parallel barrel vaults, conveys an impression of great age with its rugged, simply carved capitals. A statue of St Gaudérique is a reminder that, following the theft of some relics, the abbey became an important meeting place for Catalan peasants. A capital from the old cloisters has been used as the base for the high altar. Depicted on it are two scenes from the life of St Martin.

On the north side of the choir stands a bell-tower crowned with a crenellated platform. Near the church, two tombs have been hollowed out of the rock: the

Highest peaks in the Pyrenees:	
ANETO *(in Spain)*	3 404m/11 169ft
VIGNEMALE	3 298m/10 821ft
CARLIT	2 921m/9 584ft
MIDI	2 877m/9 439ft
CANIGOU	2 784m/9 134ft
ANIE	2 504m/8 216ft
RHUNE	900m/2 953ft

tomb of the founder, Count Guifred de Cerdagne, which he dug out with his own hands, and that of one of his wives.

Site – *To appreciate the originality of St-Martin's site, after reaching the abbey (30min on foot there and back) take a stairway to the left (itinerary No. 9) which climbs into the woods. Just past the water outlet turn right.*
From here, there is an impressive view of the abbey, which lies in the shadow of the Canigou until late in the morning. Its site dominating the Casteil and Vernet valleys is most striking.

Abbaye de ST-MICHEL-DE-CUXA★

Michelin maps 86 folds 17 and 18 or 235 fold 52
3km/2mi south of Prades – Local map see Le CANIGOU

The elegant crenellated tower of the abbey of St-Michel-de-Cuxa rises from one of the valleys at the foot of the Canigou. After a series of misfortunes, the abbey is once again the seat of Catalan culture north of the Pyrenees. Every summer, it is the venue for the "Journées romanes" and for the concerts of the Prades festival. There have been four successive churches in Cuxa. The last, which is the present church, was consecrated in 974. Founded under the protection of the counts of Cerdagne-Conflent, with St Michael as its patron saint, the abbey won renown largely due to abbot Garin. A great traveller and man of action, Garin can be compared to Gerbert, the most erudite man of his time who became Pope Sylvester II. The Doge of Venice, Pietro Orseolo, retired to the abbey with St Romuald, founder of the Camaldoli order, and died there "in the odour of sanctity".

In the 11C, the abbot Oliba, a keen builder related to the counts of Cerdagne-Conflent, developed the great Catalan monasteries: Montserrat, Ripoll and St-Michel. He enlarged the chancel of the abbey church by adding a square ambulatory to it and chapels opening off it, built two bell-towers in the Lombard style and hollowed out the underground chapel of La Crèche. He arranged for some of his monks to settle in St-Martin-du-Canigou.

After a long period of decline, the abbey of St-Michel was abandoned, then sold during the Revolution. Its works of art disappeared and the cloister galleries were dismantled. In 1907, the American sculptor George Grey Barnard found and bought over half of the original capitals. They were bought in 1925 by the New York Metropolitan Museum which undertook the restoration of the cloisters by adding new elements carved in the same Pyrenean marble. Since 1938, the cloisters of St-Michel-de-Cuxa have stood in the midst of a park, on the hillside overlooking the Hudson valley.

From 1952, considerable work has been undertaken in Cuxa: the abbey church was restored and some of the cloister galleries were put back in place by using parts which had been recovered (it is not certain whether these are in their original position). Since 1965, the abbey has been occupied by Benedictine monks subordinate to Montserrat.

TOUR ⏱ *allow 45min*

First walk round the outside of the buildings to see the abbey church's fine Romanesque **bell-tower★**, with four tiers of twinned bays, surmounted by round windows and crenellations.

Crypt of the Vierge de la Crèche – Located at the centre of an underground sanctuary, which has managed to escape destruction or alterations since the 11C, this circular chapel has a vaulted ceiling supported by a single central pillar. Despite its lack of ornamentation, it exudes elegance. The chapel, dedicated to the "Virgin Mary of the Crib", was reserved for Marian worship.

St-Michel-de-Cuxa

Abbey church – The church has retained very little of its original appearance. It is entered through a doorway reconstructed from a single archway, the remains of a gallery put up in the 12C at the far end of the nave. The nave is one of the very rare surviving examples of pre-Romanesque art in France, exemplified here by the horseshoe or "Visigothic" arch which can be seen in part of the transept standing out against later construction. Covered once more by a timber-framed roof, the central nave ends in a rectangular apse. The pointed vaulting in the chancel dates from the 14C. Each of the two side aisles can be entered through three semi-circular arches.

★ **Cloisters** – These consist of arches and capitals found in Prades or in private ownership and recovered. The arches of the gallery adjacent to the church and those of most of the west gallery and the front of the east gallery have all been used to reconstruct almost half of the cloisters. The sculpture on the capitals (12C) is distinguished by the absence of any religious theme in the motifs; only the decoration itself seemed to matter to the artist.

In the west building (10C), the history of the abbey is retraced in an exhibition of documents, photographs and a model.

Arcs de ST-PIERRE★

Michelin map 80 southwest of fold 5 or 240 fold 10
Local map see Gorges du TARN

The "Arcs de St-Pierre" is a mass of eroded rock formations resembling ruins on the Causse Méjean.

Getting there – *There are two possible ways to get to the Arcs de St-Pierre:*
1) On D 63 which branches off D 986 at Hures-la-Parade; after 3km/2mi, take the little road on the right to St-Pierre-des-Tripiers. 1km/0.6mi past this village, take the small unsurfaced road, again to the right, opposite the junction for La Viale.
2) Up the steep, narrow hairpin road off D 996, from Le Truel towards St-Pierre-des-Tripiers, in the Jonte valley. Level with the junction for La Viale, take the small unsurfaced road to the left.

Tour – *1hr 30min on foot there and back.* Take the footpath downhill *(waymarked in red)* to the **Grande Place**. In the middle of this rocky amphitheatre stands a 10m/32ft high monolithic column. The footpath climbs to the left, up to the grotto of **La Baumelle**.
Dry-stone walls, which for a long time were kept up by shepherds who brought their sheep here, can still be seen. A small natural arch stands near the entrance to the grotto.

After returning to the Grande Place, follow the waymarked path leading from it to the **Caverne de l'Homme mort** ("Dead Man's Cave"); fifty skeletons similar to that of Cro-Magnon man were discovered here; most of them had been cut into pieces with flint.

Further along, on the left, huge boulders come into sight with shapes that have earned them evocative names such as **Poule de Houdan** ("Houdan's hen") or **La République** (looking for all the world as if it is wearing the Republicans' cap of liberty). The path bends to the left and, after about 300m, leads to the site of a **prehistoric village** of which only sections of ruined walls are left, some of them half buried. The cavities still visible in the rock face have been identified by historians as notches for fixing roof beams.

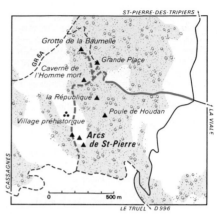

Finally the path arrives at the **Arcs de St-Pierre** themselves, three natural arches, the first of which, with its overhanging spur, is regarded as one of the finest in the Causses. The second, very regular, opens out onto a space wooded with slender pine trees soaring towards the light. Some of them have been bent or broken by wind or rough weather, since the soil on the Causse Méjean is never very deep. The third arch has a huge vault.

Consult the Index to find an individual town or sight.

STE-ÉNIMIE★

Population 473
Michelin map 80 fold 5 or 240 fold 6
Local maps see les GRANDS CAUSSES and Gorges du TARN

The village of Ste-Énimie lies in terraced rows below the steep cliffs bordering a loop of the Tarn, where the canyon is at its narrowest. The canyon walls form a passageway 500-600m/1 640-1 968ft deep and 1.8km/just over a mile wide. The floor of the gorge is covered in greenery. The retaining walls, which can still be seen on the steeply sloping sides of the Tarn gorges, indicate the extent of the work accomplished by local inhabitants over the centuries. On these terraces, rising in tiers from the banks of the Tarn, vines, almond, walnut, cherry and peach trees were cultivated. The massive exodus of the local population since the Second World War has resulted in the vineyards and orchards largely falling fallow. From the D 986, 5km/3mi before reaching Ste-Énimie coming from Mende, there is a fine view over the village and its surroundings.

Until the Revolution, Ste-Énimie was an important trade centre. Nowadays, tourism has given local economy a tremendous boost.

When in spate, the Tarn rises to impressive levels at Ste-Énimie. In the church, near the holy water stoup, a mark records the level reached on 29 September 1900. The altar was swimming in water. The most recent exceptionally high flood levels were in 1965 and 1982.

The legend of St Énimie – Énimie was a Merovingian princess, the daughter of Clotaire II and sister of King Dagobert. All the noblemen at court were in love with her, as she was exceptionally beautiful; however, she rejected every proposal of marriage, as she wanted to dedicate herself to God. The king refused to contemplate this idea and betrothed Énimie to one of his barons. The young girl promptly went down with leprosy, and her suitor abandoned her. Every known remedy was tried, but in vain. One day, in a vision, an angel ordered Énimie to leave for the Gévaudan, where a spring would restore her to her previous beauty.

Accompanied by a large retinue, after a long and arduous journey, she reached a place where sick people came to bathe (the present Bagnols-les-Bains). She was going to stay there, but the angel appeared and told her to continue on her way. At last, in a deep valley miles from anywhere, she was told by shepherds of a nearby spring, the Source de Burle. The princess dived into the waters which forthwith miraculously cleansed her of all symptoms of the disease. Overjoyed, she set off on her way home with her retinue. But no sooner had she left the valley, than the symptoms of leprosy returned. She went back to the spring and was miraculously cured once more. Every time she tried to leave the valley, the disease returned.

She therefore realised this must be a divine sign and decided to settle in Burle. From then on, she lived in a cave with her goddaughter, doing good works for all those around her, founding a nunnery, and fighting with the devil who undermined her good works and destroyed the convent walls as fast as they were being built. She managed to drive him out *(see Pas de Souci, p 330)*. St Hilaire, bishop of Mende, having heard the marvellous stories about Énimie, came to visit her and invested her as abbess of Burle convent. She died in around 628, having achieved a reputation for her saintliness.

She was buried in the cave-hermitage in a fine silver reliquary, and the area soon became a place of pilgrimage where many miracles are said to have occurred. Beneath the rock on which the monastery stood, there is a small village.

SIGHTS

A leisurely stroll through the pretty little streets of Ste-Énimie is a good way to discover the village's charm.

Convent (Ancien Monastère) – *Entrance off Place du Plot. Follow the arrows to the chapter-house. Go through a vaulted room, climb a flight of steps in front of the crypt and walk past a sports ground. The chapter-house is at the far end.* Of the convent, a Romanesque chapter-house is still extant. Around the site of the convent are the ruins of some old fortifications.

"Le Vieux Logis" ⊘ – This museum, which is located in a room with an alcove, hearth, table and various utensils, gives an idea of the local way of life of days gone by.

Place au Beurre and Halle au Blé – This square at the heart of the old village features an attractive old house, while the corn market contains an old wheat measure.

Church – This dates from the 12C and has undergone several transformations. The fine oven-vault of the apse and the 14C stone statue of St Anne are particularly interesting. Modern ceramic panels, by Henri Constans, depict the legend of St Énimie.

Source de Burle – The spring is due to the resurgence of rainwater which has fallen on the Causse de Sauveterre. These are the spring waters which are said to have cured St Énimie of leprosy.

EXCURSIONS

Viewpoint from the cave-hermitage – *45min on foot there and back from Ste-Énimie along a footpath (located behind the Gîtes St-Vincent); or 3km/2mi along D 986 towards Mende, then 30min on foot there and back.*
At the entrance to the **cave** ⊘, two rocks hollowed out into the shape of armchairs were said to have been used by St Énimie.
Adjacent to the chapel, which occupies the saint's cave itself, is a platform bearing a cross named the Croix de St-Jean. From here, there is a remarkable view over the Tarn and the town.

★★ **Viewpoints over the Tarn gorges** – *6.5km/4mi. Leave Ste-Énimie on D 986 to the south.*

The road crosses the Tarn and, climbing onto the Causse Méjean, offers extraordinary views over the Tarn gorges and the cirques of St-Chély and Pougnadoires, which justify a visit to this headland beyond the gorges.

Fort de SALSES★★

Michelin maps 86 fold 9 or 235 fold 48 or 240 fold 37
16km/10mi north of Perpignan – Local map see Les CORBIÈRES

Salses fortress was built in the 15C, on the Roman road from Narbonne to Spain, known as the "Via Domitia", at the strategic point where the waters of coastal lagoons are almost lapping at the foot of the Corbières mountains. It is a unique example in France of Spanish medieval military architecture adapted by Vauban in the 17C to meet the demands of modern artillery.

Rising above the surrounding vineyards, this half-buried fortress, which was saved from destruction by the sheer offputting thickness of its masonry, is surprisingly big. The colour of the brickwork, bronzed by the sun, blends harmoniously with the golden sheen of the stonework, mainly of pink sandstone.

Fort de Salses

Hannibal's passage – In 218 BC, Hannibal made plans to cross Gaul and invade Italy. Legend has it that after following the same route as Hercules, he had to cross the Perthus, then the threshold of Salses which links Roussillon to the plains of Bas Languedoc. Rome immediately sent five venerable senators, as emissaries, to ask the Gauls to resist the Carthaginians' advance. There was uproar among the Gauls, who were incensed that they should be expected to wage war on their own soil in order to prevent fighting in Italy. Hannibal passed himself off as "a guest" and signed the treaty of Elne, a clause of which stated that if the local inhabitants had grounds for complaint from his soldiers, their grievances would be judged by him or by his officers, whereas if the Carthaginians had any disagreements with local people, the dispute would be settled by the local womenfolk

The Romans remembered this episode with bitterness. When they occupied Gaul, they built a camp at Salses and linked it by a road suitable for vehicles to the Perthus pass.

A Spanish fortress – After Roussillon had been restored to Spain in 1493, Ferdinand of Aragon gathered his troops in the province and in 1497 had this fortress built in record time by his gunner-engineer Ramirez. The stronghold was designed to house a garrison of 1 500 men and to withstand attack by newly evolving artillery.

When Richelieu undertook to reconquer Roussillon, Salses became the focus of a bitter struggle. The French seized the fort in July 1639, but lost it again in January 1640. Finally, it was decided to attack from land and sea simultaneously; Maillé-Brézé was at the head of the fleet. The governor of Salses, learning of the fall of Perpignan, resigned himself to surrendering with full battle honours.

At the end of September 1642, the garrison returned to Spain.

In 1691, Vauban made some improvements and ordered the demolition of superstructures that were decorative rather than useful as a defence. However the line of fortifications between France and Spain was determined from then on by the new "natural" frontier of the Pyrenees, bringing the military role of the Fort de Salses to an end.

TOUR ⏱ *1hr*

The fortress has an oblong ground plan and is laid out around a central courtyard – the old parade ground. This is reached through a redoubt, a demi-lune outwork and three drawbridges.

The visit starts on the upper parts of the **interior curtain wall**. Various cunning devices are in evidence, such as the rounded top of the curtain walls, an unusual feature added in the 15C and designed to make bullets ricochet off and to discourage climbers, and the polygonal layout of the counterscarp (wall on the outside of the moat), which enabled those being besieged to make their shots ricochet into the corners. The scarp (wall on the inside of the moat) averages 9m/29ft in thickness.

The buildings inside the interior curtain wall were used as a barracks and a blockhouse. The vaulted basement around the central courtyard housed the stables (about 300 horses), above which ran large vaulted galleries to protect against fire and missiles; one of these, in the east wing, was used as a chapel. The "**redoubt**" in the keep is then reached; it is separated from the central courtyard by an interior moat and a high wall with a spur. In it were located the cowshed, the bakery and, adjacent to it, a room with basins.

The **keep** itself is divided into five storeys alternately with ceilings or vaulted. Originally designed as the governor's residence, it was used as a powder magazine in the 19C. Zigzag passages, designed so as to be protected by the gunfire of the look-outs, as in the large bunkers of the Second World War, and drawbridges for footsoldiers only were its ultimate defences.

Plateau de SAULT*

Michelin maps 86 fold 6 or 235 folds 46 and 47

This high-lying, windswept plateau, at an average altitude of 1 000m/3 280ft, is the last bastion of the limestone Pyrenees east of St-Barthélemy peak. The cliffs along the edge of it facing the plain and the gorges with which it is scored lend it a certain bleakness, accentuated by the harsh climate. The main resource and principal attraction of this region is the forest.

Aude firs – This species, well adapted to the chalky soil and severe climate of the area, is the glory of forests such as Comus, La Plaine, La Bunague, Comefroide, Picaussel and Callong.

★★ FORESTS OF COMUS AND LA PLAINE

Round tour from Belcaire *97km/60mi – allow 4hr*

This trip includes a large stretch of the **Route du Sapin de l'Aude**, a drive through woodland where there are conifers over 50m/160ft tall.

Belcaire – This village is situated on the D 613, 1 002m/3 287ft above sea level. Leave Belcaire on the Ax-les-Thermes road, which climbs to the Col des Sept-Frères, before reaching the upper valley of the Hers, where despite the harsh climate there was once terrace cultivation on the slopes.

After the dry Hers valley, which narrows into a sort of funnel, the road goes through Comus and gets to the Gorges de la Frau.

★ **Gorges de la Frau** – *1hr 30min on foot there and back.* Park the car at the entrance to a wide forest track climbing a tributary valley and walk down the old road, once used for moving livestock from one pasture to another, or for transporting firewood. The path runs along at the foot of yellow-tinged limestone cliffs. After a 45min walk, turn back at the point where the valley makes a sharp bend.

Return to Comus and take the road to the left.

The steeply climbing road leads into the pine forest.

At the Col de la Gargante, take the steep road straight ahead and then to the right which is signposted *"belvédère à 600m"*.

★★ **Belvédère du Pas de l'Ours** – *15min on foot there and back.* From the lookout point, there is a magnificent view of the Gorges de la Frau; 700m/2 296ft lower down are the Montségur outcrop and the Tabe mountain; beyond these, and much higher up, the white patches of the Trimouns quarry can be seen.

Return to the Col de la Gargante, head back and take the road to the right to La Benague.

★ **Pas de l'Ours** – The road runs along a rocky cliff above the Gorges de la Frau. On the way down the road makes a broad sweep to the left.

Leave the car in a bend on the right, by the Langarail drinking troughs.

★ **Langarail pastures** – *45min on foot there and back.* As its name suggests, this is a rural site. Follow the stony track until the bumpy stretch from which there is a **view** to the north, beyond the Belesta forest as far as the foothills of the chain towards the Lauragais.

The forest road leads to La Benague where there is a road to the right. This leads to the D 613 on the left, which runs along the Sault plateau.

Level with Belvis, there is a road to the right leading into and along the left side of the Rebenty valley.

Défilé de Joucou – The road through this ravine follows a series of tunnels and overhangs.

Joucou – This village lies well sheltered in the broad part of the valley, gathered around an old abbey.

Marsa – *Downstream from Joucou.* A village which is dominated by the curious openwork belfry-wall of its Romanesque church.

Turn back.

The road runs back up through the **Rebenty gorge**, then upstream of the Joucou ravine, where it slips beneath the impressive overhangs of the **Able defile**.

Niort – The village church has an interesting belfry-wall. The surrounding woodland is dotted with rocky outcrops.

La Fajolle – *Upstream of Niort.* A typical Pyrenean mountain village. The impressively large stocks of firewood are evidence of the harsh winters.

Turn back. Just before Niort, take the road on the left back to Belcaire via the Col des Sept-Frères.

FROM MONTSEGUR TO QUILLAN *40km/24mi – allow half a day*

Montségur is reached on D 9 (south of Lavelanet).

The road runs down into the Touyre valley, the centre of industry in the Pays d'Olmes. After Villeneuve-d'Olmes (textiles), and Montferrier where the mountain landscape becomes more rugged, the road climbs towards Montségur. The castle appears at each bend on the hilly route along the edge of the St-Barthélemy massif.

★ **Château de Montségur** – *See Château de MONTSÉGUR.*

The road leaves the coomb of Montségur – look back for a view of the jagged crest of the Soularac peak – along a rocky gorge, on the east side of the rock of Montségur.

Beyond Fougax village, before the Hers disappears into a gorge, a backward look will provide a final, breathtaking **view**★★ of Montségur on its rock, which seen from this aspect looks like a needlepoint of rock against the backdrop of the St-Barthélemy massif.

Intermittent fountain of Fontestorbes – Fontestorbes spring, which emerges from a rocky cave in the Hers valley, is the resurgence of water which has soaked into the chalky soil of part of Sault plateau. When water levels are low, the spring becomes intermittent (usually from mid July to end of November). This happens whenever the rate of flow falls below 1 040 litre/229gal per second; the phenomenon recurs regularly initially every hour and eventually increasing to every hour and a half. The flow varies from 100 to 1 800 litre (22-396gal) per second. When it is not in full flow, visitors can walk to the end of the cave *(ramp)*.

Beyond Bélesta, the road along the foot of the wooded edge of Sault plateau gives, from the Babourade pass, a distant view ahead over the Corbières and the thrusting rocky summit of the Pic de Bugarach (alt 1 230m/4 035ft), the highest point of the massif.

Puivert – The valley in which Puivert lies is surprisingly green and fresh-looking after the wooded hills of Sault plateau. It was still under water until 1279, when the lake suddenly overflowed, with disastrous consequences for Chalabre and Mirepoix downriver. There is now a small reservoir south of the village. The local museum, the **Musée du Quercorb** ⊘, contains displays on local history, traditions and livelihoods. On the second floor there is an interesting collection of casts of medieval musical instruments originally part of the ornamentation of the castle.

Puivert **castle** ⊘ *(east of the village)* was captured during the crusades of 1210, and given by Simon de Montfort to Lambert de Thury, before being handed back to the lords of Bruyères-le-Châtel (near Arpajon), who from then on settled in the region and enlarged the castle. All that remains of the castle which dates from before the siege of 1210 is a few sections of wall to the west. Of the 14C new castle, part of which was destroyed *(excavations in progress)*, a square tower-gate decorated with the Bruyères lion on a coat of arms and a 35m/115ft high keep are still standing. Visitors can see one of the lower rooms of the keep, with barrel vaulting, the chapel, with ogive vaulting and a "piscina" (or basin for ablutions) set into the wall, and finally the "Minstrels'" room in which ogive vaulting rests on culs-de-lampe carved to depict musicians playing their instruments (bagpipes, tambourine, viol, lute etc), evoking the splendour of court life at Puivert during the age of the troubadours.

After Puivert, the road passes over less rugged plateaux and finally runs for a stretch above the Aude valley. After giving a vista over the valley and the Razès, the road crosses the Portel pass before winding downhill towards Quillan.

Quillan – *See Haute vallée de l'AUDE.*

Prieuré de SERRABONE★★

Michelin maps 86 fold 18 or 235 fold 52 or 240 fold 41

The steep, winding road up to Serrabone, in the rather bleak part of Roussillon known as Les Aspres, does not at any stage give so much as a glimpse of the Romanesque priory which lies at the end of it.

TOUR ⊙ *allow 30min*

The exterior of the priory has an impressive, if somewhat forbidding, appearance with its rugged architectural style and dark schist stonework. The building is modest, with no frivolity – probably to blend in better with the severity of its surroundings, so it is all the more surprising therefore to discover that the interior features a wealth of sculpted ornamentation.

Entrance to the church is through the south gallery.

Tribune

★ **South gallery** – 12C. Overlooking the ravine, the gallery was used as a covered walkway by the regular Augustine canons. The carved capitals show traces of oriental influence, as is usual with Romanesque sculpture in Roussillon. There is a significant difference, artistically, between the interior capitals, which do not differ much from those of the tribune, and the exterior capitals in low relief, which are indisputably the work of less accomplished craftsmen.

Church – The nave dates from the 11C, the chancel, transept and the north side aisle are 12C. The church contains a pink marble **tribune★★** with impressively rich ornamentation. The ten columns and two oblong pillars supporting the six intersecting ribs are adorned with capitals representing, in a stylised manner, rampant animals: eagles, griffons, floral motifs, angels and above all lions – which feature in every carving, since the role played by these beasts in the Bible, mythology and fables was so great. The most remarkable decoration is to be found in the delicate ornamentation of the three archivolts, incised in the marble, and the corner stones adorned with flowers, for all the world as if they were embroidered onto the stone.

The **"Carte Inter-Sites"** *(price: 20F, sold at sites)* is a reduced price entrance ticket to the 17 monuments, museums and sites which make up the Catalan cultural network called "Terre catalane": museum at Tautavel, castle-museum at Bélesta, archeological footpath at Eyne, museum at Ste-Léocadie, cloisters and Musée Terrus at Elne, castle at Castelnou, priory at Serrabone, abbey of St-Michel-de-Cuxa, palace of the kings of Majorca at Perpignan, fort at Salses, ramparts at Villefranche-de-Conflent, Fort Lagarde at Prats-de-Mollo, centre of sacred art and "organ pipe" rock formations at Ille-sur-Têt, modern art museum at Céret, royal castle at Collioure. ☎ 04 68 22 05 07.

SÈTE★

Conurbation 63 833
Michelin maps 83 fold 16 or 240 fold 27

Sète was built on the slopes and at the foot of Mont St-Clair, a limestone outcrop 175m/541ft high, at the edge of the Thau lagoon. Once an island, it is linked to the mainland by two narrow sand spits.
The new town, east and northeast of Mont St-Clair, runs right up to the sea itself and is divided up by several canals.
A fine sandy **beach** stretches over 15km/9mi west from Sète as far as Cap d'Agde.

Birthplace of poets – Paul Valéry (1871-1945) paid tribute to his native town of Sète, when he said that he had been born in one of the places he would have chosen had he had the choice. In 1925, he wrote to Sète town council, which had congratulated him on his election to the Académie Française, "It seems to me that all my work reflects my roots." In *Charmes*, published in 1922, the poet celebrated the marine cemetery where he was to be buried in July 1945. At the foot of this peaceful setting, the sea can be seen spreading away to the horizon like a vast flat roof. This is the first stanza of the poem, in the Cecil Day Lewis translation:

> *This quiet roof, where dove-sails saunter by*
> *Between the pines, the tombs, throbs visibly.*
> *Impartial noon patterns the sea in flame -*
> *That sea for ever starting and re-starting.*
> *When thought has had its hour, oh how rewarding*
> *Are the long vistas of celestial calm!*

Another famous native of Sète, the singer-songwriter **Georges Brassens** (1921-81) sang about his place of birth in his *Supplique pour être enterré à la plage de Sète (Request to be buried on Sète beach)*.

LIFE IN SÈTE

Its commercial, fishing and sailing ports make Sète a lively maritime centre.
It is the leading fishing port on the French Mediterranean coast and the second most important freight port. The Sète area (including Frontignan, la Peyrade and Balaruc) forms a dynamic economic centre in the Bas Languedoc plain which is devoted primarily to wine growing. Many of the industrial activities are linked to its function as a port: chemical industry (fertilizer), cement works, sawmills, food industries (preserving olives, condiments and fish).

Local festivities – Since it was founded in 1666, Sète has been the scene of the famous *joutes nautiques* (jousting in boats). *See the chapter on Practical information at the end of the guide.*

The "Joutes nautiques" Two boats, one red and one blue, are each fitted with a raised platform, the *tintaine*, which protrudes from the stern of the boat by 3m/10ft above the water. Ten rowers propel the boats towards each other. The jousters, dressed in white with their chests protected by a shield, stand on the platform armed with a 3m/10ft long three-pronged lance. Each of them tries to dislodge his opponent. The loser falls into the water to the sound of laughter and jeers, while the winner preens himself, leaning on his spear, to loud applause. At the prow of each boat, there is an oboe and a drum playing the 300 year old music of the jousts. The joust tournaments are particularly well attended on the day of St-Louis in August (25).

The "Grand Pardon de la St-Pierre" On the festival of St Peter, the statue of the patron saint of fishermen is borne by boat from St-Louis church to the fishing harbour, where, after it has been placed in a trawler decorated with flowers, it is blessed: the flowers are then thrown out to sea in memory of those lost at sea.

Theatre Festival – Since 1960, this lively event has taken place in the Théâtre Jean-Vilar, an open-air theatre with more than 2 000 seats, located in an old fort built by Vauban in a pleasant setting near the sea, below the marine cemetery.

Sète canal seen from the air

THE PORT

Excavations on the Barrou headland, north of Mont St-Clair, reveal that the island of Sète was inhabited in the Gallo-Roman period. However, the town itself was founded in the 17C when Colbert decided to have a port constructed, a project which had already been envisaged by Henri IV, making Sète the outlet on the Mediterranean for the Canal des Deux-Mers. Building started on 29 July 1666. Henceforth, the town's development progressed hand in hand with that of its port. From 1669, **Pierre-Paul Riquet**, architect of the Canal du Midi, was made responsible for the completion of the project. At that time, Sète consisted only of a few fishermen's huts. To stimulate expansion, in 1673 Louis XIV gave permission for "everyone to build houses, sell and produce any goods with exemption from tax duty". Before very long the town had become a thriving commercial and industrial centre. Meanwhile, Riquet supervised the building of the two jetties protecting the outer harbour, and of the Sète canal linking Thau lagoon to the sea.

Nevertheless, the town and port grew slowly during the 18C, with Montpellier, a major trade centre, controlling commercial activities in Sète. It was not until the 19C that Sète embarked upon its golden age. To prevent silting up, a freestanding jetty or breakwater was built in 1821, which, running parallel to the shore, protected the entrance to the port. The construction of the new harbour basin and the maritime canal was begun in 1839, while the railway companies linked Sète to the PLM network and to the Midi network. By about 1840 Sète was the fifth most important French port. After the conquest of Algeria, Sète, which specialised in the wine trade, found its main outlets in North Africa.

The modern industrial and commercial port – Decline in the North African wine trade, following the declaration of independence for Algeria in 1962, coupled with a drop in trade of petrochemicals meant that the port had to discover new outlets. Sète is nonetheless now the second most important port on the French Mediterranean coast (handling almost 4 million tonnes of merchandise in 1991). The three main areas of its activity are the handling of bulk goods (mineral ores, coal, raw materials, animal foodstuffs, exotic timbers, raw paper), passenger and container traffic to North and West Africa, South America, the French Caribbean and Australia, and storage.

VIEUX PORT (**ABZ**) *45min*

The old port, with its picturesque fishing boats and yachts, is the most interesting part of Sète port.
The **Marine** is lined with fish and seafood restaurants, with terraces overlooking the Sète canal. **Motorboat excursions** in the harbour or the Thau lagoon, and **fishing expeditions** ⊙ are available.
A little further down, fishermen and bystanders are summoned by the "**criée éléctrique**" (electronic auction) when the boats come in.
From the Quai de l'Aspirant-Herber, there is a fine view over the town lying in tiers up Mont St-Clair. It is worth taking a stroll round the other basins and the canals as well.

★ MONT ST-CLAIR *allow half a day – local map p 322*

From Promenade Maréchal-Leclerc (via ② on the town plan), carry on along Avenue du Tennis and take the right fork into Montée des Pierres Blanches.

A trip to the Mont St-Clair will leave visitors with one of the best of their memories of Sète. This hill, once covered by pine forests and oaks, rises 175m/574ft above sea level and forms an ideal viewpoint from which to appreciate the surrounding area.

Parc panoramique des Pierres Blanches – This park is well covered by waymarked footpaths and makes a pleasant place for a stroll exploring the area. From the viewing table, there is a wide **view★** over the west end of the Thau lagoon, the lower Hérault plains, the open sea, the Promenade de la Corniche and the beach.

Chapelle Notre-Dame-de-la-Salette – Mont St-Clair is named after a saint who was venerated here as early as the Middle Ages. In the 17C, a hermitage still existed near the small fort of "la Montmorencette" built by the duke of Montmorency as a defence against Barbary pirates. But when the duke rebelled, the king had the fort dismantled and a former blockhouse transformed into an expiatory chapel. In 1864, it was dedicated to Notre-Dame-de-la-Salette. It is a centre of pilgrimage all year round, but especially on 19 September.

Viewpoints – From the esplanade opposite the chapel, where a large cross is lit up every night, there is a splendid **view★** of Sète, the east end of the Thau lagoon, the Garrigues, the Cévennes, St-Loup peak, the Gardiole mountain and the coast itself with its necklace of lagoons and small towns. From the top of Mont St-Clair, the whole of the surrounding countryside, including the intricacies of the port, appears spread out like a map.

A viewing tower on the presbytery terrace gives a marvellous **panorama**★★. While the foreground reflects light and colour, shapes in the distance blend into hazy tints. On a clear day, the view extends over the lagoons and the sea as far as the Pyrenees, to the southwest, and the Alpilles, to the east.

Carry on along the Chemin de St-Clair which drops steeply downhill.

On the right lies the cliff-top cemetery celebrated by Paul Valéry and the museum dedicated to him.

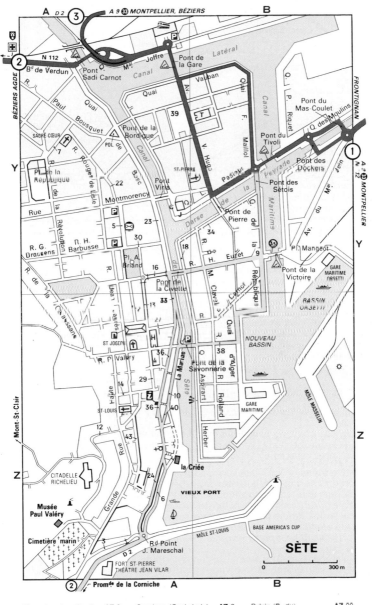

SÈTE

Alsace-Lorraine (R d')	**AZ** 2	
Euzet (R. H.)	**BY**	
Gambetta (R.)	**AZ** 13	
Gaulle (R. Général de)	**AY** 16	
Mistral (R. F.)	**AZ** 27	
Roustan (Gd R.-Mario)	**AZ** 36	
Arabes (Rampe des)	**AZ** 3	
Blum (Pl. L.)	**AZ** 4	
Casanova (Bd D.)	**AY** 5	
Consigne (Quai de la)	**AZ** 6	
Danton (R.)	**AY** 7	
Delille (Pl.)	**BY** 9	
Durand (Quai Gén.)	**AZ** 10	
Franklin (R.)	**AZ** 12	
Garenne (R.)	**AZ** 14	
Guignon (Quai N.)	**AY** 18	
Jardins (R. des)	**AY** 22	
Lattre-de-Tassigny (Quai Mar.-de-)	**AY** 23	
Marty (Prom. J.-B.)	**AZ** 24	
Palais (R. du)	**AZ** 29	
Péri (R. G.)	**AY** 30	
Résistance (Quai de la)	**AZ** 33	
Rhin-et-Danube (Quai)	**BY** 34	
Savonnerie (R. de la)	**BZ** 38	
Stalingrad (Pl.)	**AY** 39	
Valéry (Rampe P.)	**AZ** 40	
Villaret-Joyeuse (R.)	**AZ** 43	

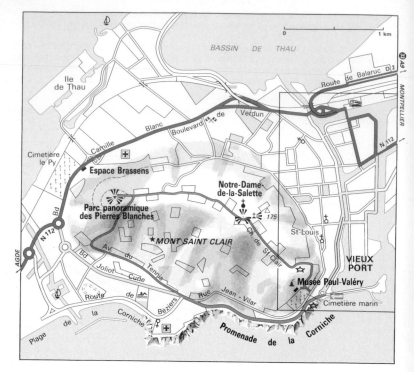

Musée Paul-Valéry ⊘ (**AZ**) – Facing the sea and very close to the "**cimetière marin**" where Paul Valéry *(in the upper part)* and Jean Vilar *(in the lower part)* are buried, the museum contains many documents on the history of Sète. The various rooms are separated by movable panels to enable variation in the layout of the exhibitions. On the ground floor are archeological remains from excavations in the Barrou and literature on the nautical jousts; these lively, colourful games have been a source of inspiration to painters and, over the centuries, have made use of a variety of costumes, of which the history can be traced from 1666 to 1891. On the first floor, a room is devoted to Paul Valéry, from his childhood in Sète onwards. A poet and a philosopher, Valéry could also express himself admirably through drawing, sculpture and painting.

Return to Sète along the Grande-Rue-Haute.

At the foot of Mont St-Clair

Promenade de la Corniche – *Leave on* ② *(N 112 to Béziers and Agde) on the town plan.*
This busy road, leading to a fine sandy **beach**, the Plage de la Corniche, situated 2km/1mi from the centre of town, cuts around the foot of the Mont St-Clair with its slopes covered by villas.

Espace Brassens ⊘ – *67, boulevard Camille-Blanc.* This museum traces the life and work of the singer-songwriter from Sète, Georges Brassens (1921-81) in an interesting and original exhibition combining audio-visual input (visitors wear headphones) with visual displays (posters, photographs, newspaper articles etc). Brassens wrote simple (and sometimes irreverent) lyrics and melodies, which he sang to a guitar accompaniment, evoking eternal themes such as friendship *(Chanson pour l'Auvergnat)*, love *(Je me suis fait tout petit)* or death *(Pauvre Martin)*.
The display retraces Brassens's childhood in Sète, his arrival in Paris and his early successes, as well as the work of writers who inspired him (*Ballade des Dames au temps jadis* by Villon, *Il n'y a pas d'amour heureux* by Aragon). There is a short video of a selection of songs he recorded in Bobino, including many of his best-known numbers, which may get quite a few feet tapping.
Georges Brassens is buried in Le Py cemetery, which is to be found opposite the museum.

EXCURSIONS

★ **Abbaye de Valmagne** – *25km/15.5mi northeast. See Abbaye de VALMAGNE.*

Bassin de Thau – *See Bassin de THAU.*

SÉVÉRAC-LE-CHÂTEAU*

Population 2 486

Michelin maps 80 fold 4 or 240 fold 6 – Local map see Les GRANDS CAUSSES

This village, which was once fortified, stands on an isolated hillock in the valley watered by the Aveyron and its tributaries. It is overlooked by a sheer outcrop of rock bearing the remains of an imposing castle. Benefiting from its position as a major road and rail junction, Sévérac's main economic activities are furniture manufacture and the mechanical engineering industry.

The Sévérac barony – This barony, one of the oldest and most powerful in France, numbers among its ranks **Amaury de Sévérac** (1365-1427), a Maréchal de France, who became lord of the castle in 1416. Before being appointed chamberlain to the Dauphin (the future Charles VII), he won a reputation for being a true *condottiere*, Rouergue-style, taking part in countless daring feats of arms. At the age of 26, he brought back to France the army of his cousin, Jean d'Armagnac, killed in action in Lombardy. In 1421, he was made a Maréchal de France. He was assassinated in 1427 at the Château de Gages, northeast of Rodez, dying without issue.

With the death of Maréchal Amaury de Sévérac, the older branch of the barons of Sévérac died out. From 1300, another branch of the family established itself at Entraygues, then at St-Félix-Lauragais – the composer Déodat de Sévérac (1873-1921) is a famous descendant of this line. Another is **Louis d'Arpajon**, a famous warrior but murderous husband, who inherited the seigniory of Sévérac-le-Château. In 1637, his bravery and talent won him appointment as a general and, later on, as count of Rodez. His favour was further increased, when he went to the assistance of the Order of Malta, at war with the Turks. The marquisate of Sévérac was made a duchy, and Louis was made a minister of State. Among his guests at his Paris mansion was Cyrano de Bergerac. In fact, it was while returning to the duke's that the writer received his fatal blow on the head from a log. In 1663, at the peak of his glorious career, Arpajon retired to end his days at his château, studying philosophy and tending to his estate.

In 1622, he had married Gloriande de Thémines, who had been his intended since birth. Gloriande, who was very proud of her "valiant lord", transformed the castle into a suitably magnificent setting for the many lavish entertainments put on there. Her mother-in-law, an austere Calvinist and a convert to Catholicism, never forgave her this extravagance. For years, Louis d'Arpajon resisted the pressure of his mother's slanders. In 1632, a son was born. The entire family, in league with Louis's mother against his wife, contrived to make him believe that the son was not his. Crazed with jealousy, he killed his alleged rival and imprisoned his wife. When the time came for a customary pilgrimage to Notre-Dame-de-Ceignac, Gloriande was permitted to set out on the journey. However, her litter was ambushed in a forest by armed men, who held her down while her wrists and ankles were cut. Her body was returned to the castle, with its wounds carefully bandaged, and nobody dared to question the "official" version of events stating that she had died of a massive heart attack.

Sévérac-le-Château

SIGHTS

Château ⊙ – A 17C entrance gate leads into the main courtyard. Older buildings (13C and 14C) can be seen on the north side: remnants of curtain walls, three watch-towers and a chapel. On the south side are the Renaissance façade and the remains of a monumental double flight of stairs.

From the terrace, to the east of the main courtyard, there is a view of the town of Sévérac, the upper Aveyron valley, the Causses de Sévérac and Sauveterre, the foothills of the Cévennes and, further to the right, the Lévézou.

From the far west side of the courtyard, there is an extensive view over the Aveyron valley, with, in the distance, the outline of Loupiac castle flanked by four round towers.

Picturesque houses – In the little streets leading to the château are some picturesque old houses (15C-16C), with pretty window frames, their corbelled turrets and upper storeys overhanging the street.

EXCURSION

►► **Château de Vezins** ⊙ – *21km/13mi southwest.* Interesting castle which well reflects its architectural evolution over the centuries (12C-19C).

Le SIDOBRE★

Michelin maps 83 folds 1 and 2 or 235 folds 31 and 32

To the east of Castres lies the Sidobre, a granite plateau delimited by the river Agout, cutting through a deep gorge, and its tributary, the Durenque.

This massif, which falls within the perimeter of the Parc naturel régional du Haut Languedoc, is interesting for two reasons. On the one hand, it is pitted with huge quarries, at times with rather unfortunate consequences for the landscape, which are evidence of its economic importance. It is one of the most important deposits in Europe, and part of the product of the quarries is worked and polished locally for tombstones, monuments etc. On the other hand, the plateau offers tourists fascinatingly unusual landscapes of granite rocks sculpted into ball shapes by erosion. Enormous rounded boulders, balanced on top of each other, rivers of rocks and the **compayrés** – heaps of rocks formed by isolated blocks shifted by the running water beneath them – make it a renowned tourist attraction.

ROUND TOUR FROM CASTRES *53km/33mi – allow 3hr*

★ **Castres** – *See CASTRES.*

Leave Castres on D 622 to Brassac (② on the town plan under CASTRES). Turn right at the hamlet of La Fontasse.

Chaos de St-Dominique – This river of rocks, in a pleasant wooded setting, covers the real river Lézert for a stretch of some 4km/2.5mi *(rocks are slippery in rainy weather).*

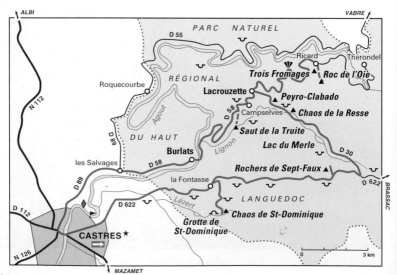

Grotte de St-Dominique – *15min on foot there and back. Accessible to those without reduced mobility.* Go along the north bank of the river, then cross it. The cave overlooks a glade and once gave shelter, if not to St Dominic himself, to one his distant disciples being hunted down during the Revolution.

Return to D 622 and head back towards Brassac. After 5km/3mi, just past a café, turn left then in the hamlet of Loustalou stop at the café-tabac "Au rocher tremblant".

Rocher de Sept-Faux – This is the finest example of a rocking-stone in the Sidobre. Two blocks poised on top of one another, weighing 900 tonnes, can be rocked by simply pressing on a wooden lever.

Return to the Brassac road and turn left towards Lacrouzette.

Lac du Merle – Large rounded blocks of rock break the surface of this fine lake, which is fed by the waters of the Lignon and surrounded by forests.

Chaos de la Resse (or "River of Rocks") – The roar of the Lignon, which is totally covered by this chaotic heap of rocks, is clearly audible to those nearby.

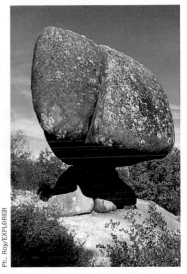

Ph. Roy/EXPLORER

Peyro Clabado

Peyro Clabado – The Peyro Clabado rock is the most impressive sight in the Sidobre. An enormous granite boulder, with an estimated weight of 780 tonnes, is balanced on a tiny pedestal of rocks. By an accident of nature, a corner of the boulder is wedged between the pedestal and the rock, ensuring the stability of the whole structure.

Lacrouzette – Most of the inhabitants of this small town earn their living from mining or working granite.

From Lacrouzette, take D 58 to Thérondel.

This splendid road gives bird's-eye views of the Agout valley.

Stop at the village of Ricard. Go through it on foot to take the footpath to the Trois Fromages and Roc de l'Oie.

Trois Fromages; Roc de l'Oie – *45min on foot there and back. Follow the red and white flashes marking the GR footpath, a pleasant walk through the woods.*

The rock known as Trois Fromages ("three cheeses") is a single boulder fractured by erosion into three rounded fragments.

Further on, the Roc de l'Oie, seen from the path coming from Crémaussel, bears a striking resemblance to a goose – hence its name.

Return to D 58 and follow signposts to Lacrouzette and Burlats. About 2km/1mi past Lacrouzette, after the turnoff to Campselves, a little road is signposted to the left.

Legend has it that in those long-gone days when animals could talk, there was once a goose who lived in a cave with a tyrannical owner who would only allow her to go out at night-time to brood, insisting that she had to be back inside by daybreak. One morning, however, the sun had long since risen by the time the unfortunate goose made it back to her cave, and as punishment, her master turned her and the egg on which she was sitting to stone.

Saut de la Truite – *Stop near the river Lignon and take a footpath to the right of the torrent. 10min on foot there and back as far as the foot of the waterfall.* At the level of this gushing waterfall, the surrounding landscape, which has been fresh and green up to now, becomes more arid.

Burlats – At the point where the road leaves the Agout gorge stand the remains of a Benedictine abbey founded in the 10C, decorated with Romanesque doorways, capitals and mouldings and mullioned windows. Next to these is the **Pavillon d'Adélaïde**, a fine Romanesque house with beautiful windows, home in the 12C to Adélaïde de Toulouse and her court, where troubadours sang of courtly love.

Return to Castres via les Salvages and D 89.

Réserve africaine de SIGEAN★

Michelin maps 86 folds 9 and 10 or 240 fold 33
7km/4.5mi northwest of Sigean – Local map see Les CORBIÈRES

This 260ha/642 acre **safari park** ⊘ owes much of its unique character to the wild landscape of coastal Languedoc, with its *garrigues* dotted with lagoons, and to the fact that for each species large areas have been set aside, which resemble their original native environment as closely as possible.

Visit by car – *30min. Please observe the safety instructions displayed at the entrance.* The route for visitors in cars goes through four areas, reserved for free ranging animals: lions, Tibetan bears (recognizable by the white V on their chests), white rhinoceros, zebras, ostriches, marabou storks and a species of antelope with spiral horns.

Visit on foot – *2hr. Start from the central car parks, inside the safari park.* Walking round the safari park, visitors will come across the fauna of various continents – elephants, dromedaries, antelopes, zebras, cheetahs, alligators – and, near the lagoon of L'Oeil de Ca, birdlife such as pink flamingoes, cranes, ducks, white storks, sacred ibis, macaws, swans and pelicans.

Three observation posts enable those visitors who are quiet and patient enough to observe various types of antelope from the African plains: oryx, springboks, gnus, impalas, white-faced damaliscus, water bucks, South African elks.

Teissedre/IMAGES TOULOUSE

Pink flamingos at Sigean safari park

TARASCON-SUR-ARIÈGE

Population 3 532
Michelin maps 86 folds 4 and 5or 235 fold 46 – Local map see FOIX: Excursions

Tarascon lies in an accessible, sheltered **site** in the centre of the Ariège valley floor. The surrounding chalk cliffs, carved out by the river's passage, and the tributary river Vicdessos add to the charm of the site. The town, dominated by the Castella tower, was home to the last blast furnace in the Pyrenees, until this was closed down in 1932. Nowadays, production at the Sabart factory (aluminium, electrodes) ensures that Tarascon's metallurgical tradition does not die out. The town is a major centre in the Pyrenees for speleological experts (mainly engaged in studies of the Neolithic period), as well as amateur enthusiasts, seeking to unravel the mysteries contained in the many caves which pepper the slopes at this confluence of river valleys, called **Sabarthès** in the Middle Ages.

★★PARC PYRÉNÉEN DE L'ART PRÉHISTORIQUE ⊘

This museum of prehistoric art is located in a beautiful mountain setting at Lacombe on the road to Banat *(northwest of Tarascon)*. It is devoted to cave wall paintings, a particularly common feature in the Ariège *département* which boasts some dozen decorated caves, including the famous example at Niaux. A resolutely contemporary building beside a lake houses the **Grand Atelier**, where visitors wearing infrared helmets go round an initiatory exhibition in the half-dark.

In the entrance corridor, drops of water falling on steel cylinders evoke the passage of time, while the history of art since its origins unfolds on screens on the walls. A reconstruction of the Dune des Pas gallery from the Clastres network at Niaux, a section not open to the public, shows the poignant imprint of children's feet in the ground made thousands of years ago. From the same part of the subterranean network, the skilfully executed sketches of a weasel and a horse have been reproduced on a neighbouring wall. The next part of the visit is a short film on methods of excavation and dating used by archeologists with an overview of cave wall art from all over the world. A scale model (1:100) of the Clastres network illustrates the path taken by the prehistoric artists as they searched for the right place to adorn with their images of animals. The exhibition also covers themes such as painted symbols, carved weapons and jewellery, other carvings and techniques used by artists of the Magdalenian period. At the end of the exhibition there is a life-size reproduction of the Salon Noir at Niaux, its walls decorated with paintings of horses, ibex and bison and carved symbols. It is the work of Renaud Sanson, the artist responsible for Lascaux II at Montignac in the Dordogne, and in fact shows the images more complete than they are in reality. Using photographic evidence revealed in ultraviolet light, the artist has reconstituted the drawings as they were before deposits of calcite built up and obscured parts of them.

The visit can be continued outside in a specially landscaped setting focussing on water and rock features such as the "Torrent of tracks", "Panorama of the hunt" with its sculpted bison, "Labyrinth of sounds" and "Pyrenean meadow" giving an idea of the plantlife that would have been around in the Magdalenian period.

There are restaurant facilities and a souvenir shop and bookshop.

SABARTHÈS CAVES

★★ **Grotte de Niaux** – *Turn left off N 20 onto D 8. See Grotte de NIAUX.*

Grotte de la Vache ⊙ – *Carry on along D 8 and turn right towards Alliat.* This cave was occupied at the end of the Magdalenian period and consists of two galleries, one of which is called Monique, explored up until 1967. There is a display of weapons, tools and, most interestingly, carved or sculpted artefacts (on bone or animal horn) which reveal something of life 13 000 years ago.

Grotte de Bédeilhac ⊙ – *Past Tarascon-sur-Ariège, northwest along D 618.* This cave has a huge entrance (36m wide by 25m high/118ft by 82ft, large enough to allow a plane to take off and land during a film that was shot here once). From the entrance, go past an enormous stalagmite (120m/394ft circumference) to the end gallery. The prehistoric drawings inside the cave, dating from the Magdalenian period, were discovered in 1906. Over the last 15 000 years the cave roof has remained water-tight, ensuring that the paintings of animals and the rock carvings (some of which even adorn the floor of the cave) are well preserved. The artists used the texture of the rock itself to give added expression to their work (large bison, beautiful deer, horses).

Grotte de Lombrives – *See Grotte de LOMBRIVES.*

Gorges du TARN ★★★

Michelin maps 80 folds 4 to 6 or 240 folds 6 and 10
Local map see below and Les GRANDS CAUSSES

The Tarn gorges are one of the most spectacular sights in the Causses region. Stretching over more than 50km/30mi, they offer a seemingly endless succession of admirable landscapes and sites.

GEOGRAPHICAL NOTES

The course of the Tarn – The Tarn rises in the uplands of Mont Lozère, at an altitude of 1 575m/5 167ft, and gushes turbulently down the Cévennes slopes. On its way, it picks up many tributaries, notably the Tarnon near Florac.

The Tarn then reaches the Causses region. Its course is now determined by a series of rifts which it has deepened into canyons. In this limestone region, not a single one of its tributaries flows above ground until Le Rozier. It is fed solely by forty resurgent springs from the Causse Méjean or Causse de Sauveterre, of which only three form small rivers over a distance of a few hundred metres. Most of them flow into the Tarn as waterfalls.

Appearance of the valley – Since the subsoil of the *causse* is composed of limestone, dolomite and marl, none of which resists erosion to the same degree, the valleys and gorges cut into it differ in appearance. The compact strata of limestone and dolomite, eroded or weakened from within, break off in whole chunks, forming lines of cliffs or rocky stumps. Being less resistant, limestone in narrow strata and marl disintegrate into scree slopes. The valley profile becomes more complex and varies according to the arrangement of the rock strata. At times the tall, sheer rock face towers abruptly above the scree slopes (**1** – *see diagram*), at others they encase the

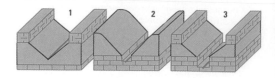

river bed itself in a superb corridor (**2**), occasionally overhanging it. At yet others, cliffs form the lower and upper tiers of the canyon sides, separated by scree slopes often covered by trees (**3**).

At its floor, the Tarn gorge is between 30 and 500m/98 and 1 640ft wide; at the top of the walls of the gorge the switchback roads of the Causses are separated by a gap of over 2km/1.2mi; in three places, however, this distance is no greater than 1 200m/1 312yd.

Human presence – In this gorge, where the sun beats down in summer, towns or villages – which are at risk from flash floods when the river is in spate – are few and far between. Those that there are occupy the mouth of dried-up river valleys, or ravines, or the spots where the Tarn valley widens. The slopes surrounding such settlements are thick with orchards and vines.

The density of human habitation in certain parts of the gorge contrasts with the lack of habitation on the Causses. This may come as a surprise to visitors who have travelled for miles on the plateaux, without encountering so much as a single hamlet. In many places, on the banks of the Tarn or perched high up on the valley sides, stand ruined castles which, in the Middle Ages, mostly harboured bands of robbers. The lively atmosphere of the gorges is enhanced by the number of sports and recreation facilities that have been set up, enabling large numbers of people – and especially the young – to indulge in amusements such as: canoeing, potholing, rock climbing etc. Leisure centres can be found in, among other places, Florac, Ispagnac, Ste-Énimie, le Rozier-Peyreleau, Meyrueis (Jonte gorges), and, further downstream, in Millau, St-Rome-du-Tarn, Trébas, and Albi-Aigulèze.

MAKING THE MOST OF THE TARN GORGES

There are three possibilities open to tourists for exploring the Tarn gorges, which might also be combined: driving along the scenic Tarn gorge road; taking boat trips along the most spectacular stretch of the valley; or striding out along the footpaths on the high cliffs of the Causse Méjean. Needless to say, the quickest or easiest of these is far from being the most exhilarating.

The D 907, which runs along the entire stretch of the gorges, reveals to view a magnificent landscape of castles, lookout points and picturesque villages. The road has now been widened, and parking areas built, so that driving along it is easier, but unfortunately at the cost of the charm of certain sites.

Travelling along the gorges by boat or canoe means that the cliffs can be seen close up and reveals, on the right-hand side of the gorge (travelling downstream), views otherwise hidden from the road, which runs too close to the cliff. A boat trip is the only means of obtaining a good view of the "Détroits" and the Cirque de Baumes, two of the most beautiful spectacles in the canyon.

However, the most breathtaking landscapes and the closest contact with the rocky cliffs are reserved for those who take up the challenge of an exploration on foot which will leave them with the impression that they have actually formed for a while a part of this natural grandeur.

Those in search of a break from their everyday surroundings will be spoilt for choice in this region, which is rich in both spectacular natural settings and unusual manmade attractions. The wonders of the Aven Armand and the caves of Clamouse, Dargilan, Desmoiselles and Trabuc, among others, lie below ground level, which itself features amazing phenomena such as the Bramabiau waterfall and chasm, the weird limestone rock formations of the Chaos de Montpellier-le-Vieux and the Chaos de Nîmes-le-Vieux, and the breathtaking cirques of Mourèze and Navacelles, as well as the Prafrance bamboo plantation, the Gévaudan wolf reserve and many more...

☐ THE TARN GORGES ROAD

The scenic road, D 907bis, runs along the floor of the gorge, on the right bank of the Tarn. It makes a pretty journey which is never monotonous owing to the constantly changing appearance of the gorge, tinted with different hues depending on the time of day. Late afternoon, when the sun's slanting rays shed a golden light upon the cliffs, shows the canyon at the height of its splendour.

From Florac to Ste-Énimie *30km/18mi – about 1hr 30min – see local map*

All along this road, there are one or two houses which are still roofed with the heavy schist slabs known as *lauzes*; the roof ridge is made of slabs laid out like the sails of a windmill, which is evidence of the proximity of the Cévennes.

Florac – *See FLORAC.*

The N 106 heads north along the Tarn valley bordered to the east by the Cévennes and to the west by the cliffs of the Causse Méjean which tower above the river bed by 500m/1 640ft.

Within sight of the village of Biesset, on the opposite bank of the Tarn, leave the road to Mende via Montmirat pass to the right and take D 907bis to the left, which runs along the north bank of the river.

Level with Ispagnac, the Tarn makes a sharp meander; this is where the canyon really begins, as a gigantic defile 400-600m/1 300-2 000ft deep separating the Méjean and the Sauveterre *causses.*

Ispagnac – At the mouth of the Tarn canyon, the little dip in which Ispagnac lies, sheltered from the north and northwest winds and basking in a mild climate which has always been renowned, is planted with orchards and vineyards. The cultivation of strawberries is also developing here. This "garden of Lozère", which once attracted the nobility of Lozère, is now a summer holiday resort.

Ispagnac **church**, dating from the 11C and 12C, is entered through a Romanesque doorway beneath a fine rose window. The interior, with three naves, is notable mainly for its chancel and capitals. Above the transept crossing, an octagonal bell-tower rises from a dome. The other bell-tower was built recently. A button to the right of the entrance switches on a 15min recorded guided tour with music. The building is adjacent to a priory which still bears traces of fortifications. Note also the gate of the old castle and several 14C Gothic houses with their fine casement windows.

1km/0.6mi after Ispagnac, bear left.

Quézac – At Quézac a Gothic **bridge** spans the Tarn. Pope Urban V, born in Grizac in the Lozere, thought of building it to enable pilgrims to reach the sanctuary he had founded in Quézac; his successor carried out the project. The bridge, demolished during the Wars of Religion, was rebuilt in the early 17C by the bishop of Mende, following the original plan.

A narrow street, lined with old houses, leads to **Quézac** church, built on the same site where a statue of the Virgin Mary, which attracts numerous pilgrims, was discovered in 1050. A 16C porch leads into the church. Inside, the keystones and some of the capitals are embellished with the arms of Pope Urban V. A major pilgrimage takes place in September.

Return to D 907bis.

Between Molines and Blajoux stand two castles.

First, on the right bank, is the **Château de Rocheblave** (16C) – with its distinctive machicolations – overlooked by the ruins of a 12C manor and by a curious limestone needle. Further down, on the left bank, stands the **Château de Charbonnières** (16C), situated downstream of Montbrun village.

★ **Castelbouc** – *On the south bank of the Tarn.* The strange site of Castelbouc ("Goat's castle") can be seen from the road. The name is said to date from the Crusades. A lord, who stayed at home with the womenfolk, died of his complacency. The story goes that when his soul left his body, an enormous billy goat was seen in the sky above the castle, which after that became known as Castelbouc. It was demolished in the 16C to drive out its occupants who were fleecing the inhabitants of the valley.

The ruins of Castelbouc castle stand on a steep rock, 60m/196ft high, which overhangs a little village, nestling in a hollow of the rock, with the backs of its houses against the cliff.

A very powerful resurgent spring gushes out of three apertures, two in a cave, and one in the village. Its catchment area extends over 10km/6mi to the south, beneath the Causse Méjean to Hures chasm.

Shortly afterwards, to the left of the road, Prades castle comes into view.

Château de Prades ⊙ – Perched on a rocky spur overhanging the Tarn, this castle was built in the early 13C to protect Ste-Énimie abbey and to defend access to the gorges. At the outset, it belonged to the bishops of Mende then, from 1280 to the Revolution, to the priors of Ste-Énimie abbey. In 1581, it distinguished itself by resisting the attacks of the Protestant troops of Captain Merle.

A tour of the fortifications and the rooms vaulted with intersecting ribs, all of them embellished with monumental fireplaces, gives an insight into the lifestyle of the lords who lived there.

★ **Ste-Énimie** – *See STE-ÉNIMIE.*

From Ste-Énimie to Le Rozier *60km/ 37mi - allow 2hr 30min - see local map*

★ **Ste-Énimie** - *See STE-ÉNIMIE.*

Leave Ste-Énimie on D 907bis to the south.

★ **Cirque de St-Chély** - The pretty village of St-Chély stands on the south bank of the Tarn at the threshold of the huge desolate cirque of St-Chély with its superb cliffs, at the foot of the Causse Méjean.

Cross to the other bank of the Tarn to see the Romanesque church with its pretty square belfry, the communal bread oven on the square, the old houses (Renaissance doors and chimneys) still full of character, and the fine orchards.

Two resurgent springs tumble into the Tarn as waterfalls. The source of one is in Cénaret cave at the mouth of which stands a chapel (12C).

Fine caves nearby, particularly the Grotte du Grand-Duc with its galleries extending to 150m/490ft, may be of interest to tourists.

★ **Cirque de Pougnadoires** - The houses in Pougnadoires village are embedded in the rock. The village is built against the colossal cliffs of the Pougnadoires cirque, pocked with caves. The reddish hue of the rocks indicates the presence of dolomite.

★ **Château de la Caze** - This 15C château *(hôtel-restaurant)* stands in a romantic setting on the banks of the Tarn.

It was built during the reign of Charles VIII, by François Alamand, a former prior of Ste-Énimie. He gave it to his niece, Soubeyrane Alamand, on her marriage to the baron of Montclar.

The château is still remembered for the eight young girls who inhabited it, known as the "Nymphs of the Tarn", who were so beautiful that all the squires in the neighbourhood were in love with them.

The backdrop of leafy trees, ancient stones and overhanging rocks looks like something out of a fairy-tale.

On the far bank, further to the south, the ruins of Haute-Rive castle appear above a village with fine traditional houses of grey and golden stone, which have been well restored.

La Malène - *See La MALÈNE.*

★★ **Rocs des Hourtous et du Serre** - *See La MALÈNE: Excursions.*

On leaving La Malène, the road runs through some narrow straits known as the **Détroits**★★ *(see* ② *below)*. A **viewpoint**, on the left, offers a good view over this the narrowest part of the gorge.

Further down, the road passes round the foot of the **Cirque des Baumes**★★ *(see* ② *below)*.

Pas de Souci - At this point, the Tarn disappears beneath a chaotic heap of enormous boulders – the result of two rock slides *(soussitch* in dialect), the most recent being due to the earthquake of 580.

A more poetic legend ascribes the origin of this pile of boulders to the following: the devil fled over the rocks along the cliff above the Tarn, with St Énimie in

hot pursuit. When the saint realised she would never catch up with the devil, she called to the rocks for help. In answer to her prayer, a colossal rock slide occurred. One particularly huge rock, Roque Sourde, hurled itself onto Satan with full force. However, the Evil One, though badly bruised, slipped into a crevice in the river bed and returned to Hell.

Climb down to the edge of the river bank *(15min there and back, rocky path quite steep and overgrown)* for a view of the massive Roque Sourde which fell without shattering. 150m/492ft higher up, the 80m/262ft tall needle, Roche Aiguille, towers towards the abyss. Take care if crossing the Tarn by stepping from one rock to the other, as the slippery surface of the rocks and the strength of the rushing torrent can make this dangerous.

A climb *(steps; 15min there and back)* to the **viewpoint** ⊙ on **Roque Sourde** will give a bird's eye view of the Pas de Souci.

Les Vignes – This village lies at a crossroads, in a broad part of the valley well exposed to any sunshine.

Leave Les Vignes by car, on D 995, a cliff road with tight hairpin bends. After 5km/3mi, take D 46 to the right which runs across the Causse de Sauveterre and, at St-Georges-de-Lévéjac, turn right once more.

★★★ **Point Sublime** – From the Point Sublime, there is a splendid view over the Tarn gorge, from the Détroits to the Pas de Souci and the Roche Aiguille. At the foot of the little plateau which overlooks the Tarn from a height of more than 400m/1 312ft, lies the magnificent, deepset Cirque de Baumes, with its colossal limestone cliffs.

Return to Les Vignes and the Tarn gorge road.

After the village, the road reveals some fine views along the gorge. Soon, flanking the Causse Méjean, the last remaining ruins of **Château de Blanquefort** can be seen clinging tenaciously to a large rock.

Further along, the huge Cinglegros *(see 3 below)* rock looms into sight, jutting up starkly detached from the Causse Méjean. On the right bank, cliffs at the edge of the Causse de Sauveterre slope away from the Tarn, forming the St-Marcellin cirque.

Then, on the left, appears Capluc rock, recognisable by the cross surmounting it. Like the prow of a ship at the end of the Causse Méjean, it overlooks the confluence of the Tarn and Jonte rivers.

Finally, having crossed a bridge over the river adorned with a monument in honour of Édouard-Alfred Martel, the road comes to Le Rozier.

Le Rozier – *See Gorges de la JONTE.*

② BOAT OR CANOE TRIPS

Boat trip from La Malène to the Cirque des Baumes ⊙ – *It is advisable to make this trip in the morning, since this section of the canyon is at its best in the morning light.*

The waters of the Tarn, which gush along turbulently in some places while flowing almost imperceptibly in others, are tremendously clear; even in the deepest stretches of the river, it is still possible to see the pebbles of the river bed.

★★ **Les Détroits** – This is the most spectacular, and the narrowest, section of the Tarn gorges. The boat passes in front of an opening known as the Grotte de la Momie ("mummy's cave"), then carries on into a magnificent ravine between two tall,

Teissèdre/IMAGES PHOTOTHÈQUE

Rapids on the river Tarn

sheer cliffs which plunge abruptly into the river. The higher cliff towers in tiers to over 400m/1 312ft above the Tarn. The impressive effect of the limestone walls hemming in the river is heightened by their colourfulness.

★★ **Cirque des Baumes** – Downriver from the Détroits, the Tarn gorge widens, flowing into the splendid Cirque des Baumes (*baume* means cave). The surrounding rock faces are resplendent with colour: predominantly red, but also tinges of white, black, blue grey, and yellow. Clusters of trees and brushwood blend in green and dark tones.

The boats stop at Baumes-Hautes.

Canoe trips down the Tarn – These can be undertaken by any canoeist with some experience of fast-flowing rivers.

During the summer months, the water level between Florac and Ste-Énimie may be too low for trips to be possible. Apart from a few passages of rapids, the journey from Ste-Énimie to the Pas de Souci is easy. The short stretch of river from here to the Pont des Vignes is very dangerous, so canoes will have to be carried overland. The stretch from Pont des Vignes to Le Rozier is quite turbulent; care should be taken negotiating some of the rapids.

Keen explorers of gorges, leaving from La Malène in the morning, could take a picnic, linger on a beach in the Détroits, have a swim, lunch by the river and explore the gorges further during the afternoon, on foot or by canoe.

③ RAMBLES

There are numerous rambles possible in the gorges or on the *causses;* the three described below are among the most interesting.

Other possibilities include walking beneath the line of the cliffs from the foot of the Rocher de Cinglegros to the Pas de l'Arc, or along the top of the cliffs from the Pas des Trois Fondus to the Baousse del Biel, or finally across the "hinterland" of the *causse* itself from Le Bindous to La Bourgarie via Volcégure.

★★★ Corniches du Causse Méjean

Round tour from Le Rozier - allow 7hr. See also Les GRANDS CAUSSES.

This remarkably well laid out and well maintained footpath should present few difficulties, although there are one or two particularly spectacular clifftop passages which require great care. Take enough food and water for one day. Behind the church in Le Rozier, take the footpath which leads off from the junction of two roads.

Capluc - Half an hour's climb brings ramblers to the pretty little hamlet of Capluc, now deserted.

Rocher de Capluc - *Not recommended to those who suffer from vertigo.*
Bear left towards Capluc rock, easily identified by the metal cross on top of it. The rock forms the far end of a promontory at the southwest edge of the Causse Méjean. At the top of a flight of stone steps, to the right, there is a house leaning against the rock face which is entered through a doorway with a three-pointed arch. Take a metal ramp and another flight of stone steps up to the terrace around the rock. From here there is a dizzying climb to the summit of the rock up metal ladders. But the reward at the top is an exhilarating view plunging down to Peyreleau and the confluence of the Jonte and Tarn rivers. Opposite, there is a fine view of the villages of Liaucous and Mostuéjouls perched high on the cliff.

Return to Capluc.

Climb to the Col de Francbouteille - 200m/220yd past the hamlet of Capluc, there are two ways of reaching the Francbouteille pass.
The path known as the "Ravin des Echos" *(accessible to all capabilities),* which runs along a section of the GR 6^A footpath, winds gently uphill, offering fine views of the *causse.*
The Jacques-Brunet path *(steep, with vertiginous sections),* which is reached up a flight of steps, climbs through juniper bushes, boxwood and pine. It threads its way between little chimneys, reaches the top of a crest from which there is a magnificent view of the Tarn and Jonte canyons, then carries on along the slope overlooking the Tarn. It skirts the "Enclume" (Anvil) standing detached from the magnificent surrounding rock walls. After a passage through cool undergrowth from which there are numerous views of the Tarn valley, the path reaches the pass.

Col de Francbouteille - This pass is still also known as the "pass of the two canyons". It is marked by a stele dedicated to the Club Alpin. The Francbouteille rock looms, to the right, like the prow of a colossal ship.

Follow the arrows to the GR 6^A footpath.

Soon, Teil spring comes into view on the left. Springs are few and far between on the plateau of Causse Méjean, and this one is much appreciated by hikers.

At the Col de Cassagnes, leave the Martel footpath leading to Cinglegros rock (see below) to the left, and bear right towards the isolated village of Cassagnes.

The footpath crosses the *causse;* only the cry of the griffon vulture, recently reintroduced to the Causse Méjean, breaks the monotonous silence. Leave a pine plantation to the right to follow the footpath along the cliffs overlooking the Jonte gorge.

Belvédère du Vertige - After about an hour's walk, there is a lookout point with a protective handrail, which gives an impressive view over the Jonte canyon, with the river flowing more than 400m/1 300ft below. A short distance upstream, the viewpoints called the "Terrasses" can be seen far below as pinpricks beside the valley road. In the foreground, an enormous rock stands completely detached from the cliff.

Pas du Loup; Vase de Chine; Vase de Sèvres - The footpath runs in front of a cave, once used as a sheep pen, then between two natural bridges. The steep descent, barred in the middle by a grille to stop the sheep from leaping into the ravine, is called Pas du Loup ("wolf's tread"). Immediately after negotiating this, two enormous monoliths - the Vase de Chine, at the mouth of the ravine, and then the Vase de Sèvres - come into sight, an incalculable reward for all the effort spent trying to reach them. From each of these monoliths,

there is a good view of the other. In the distance, Peyreleau and Le Rozier, Capluc rock, and the cliffs of the Causse Noir above the south bank of the Jonte can be seen.

Return to the footpath which drops downhill amid a group of extraordinarily jagged dolomitic rocks. Leave the footpath to the Col de Francbouteille to the right, and return to Capluc and Le Rozier along the Ravin des Echos and Brèche Magnifique paths.

Rocher de Cinglegros *Round tour from Le Rozier – one day on foot*

This ramble is recommended only for those with a good level of fitness and concentration, and who do not suffer from vertigo.
Follow the route of the Corniches du Causse Méjean described above as far as the Col de Cassagnes, then turn left to Cinglegros rock.

This well laid out path offers excellent views of the cliffs overhanging the west bank of the Tarn opposite. After about 20min walk, a natural **lookout point** made of rocks provides a view down into an impressive ravine. Then, the footpath reaches the source of the Sartane (sometimes dried up), and immediately after this it gets wider. Again, to the left of the path, there is a small spring – the source of the Bindous.

At the next fork, leave the path to Volcégure to the right to take the path to the left through the undergrowth, towards the Pas des Trois Fondus. Before long, a stretch of path leads downhill to a terrace, from which there is a gratifying view of the Cinglegros gap.

Take the steep path downhill to the left.

The **Pas des Trois Fondus** leads down to the floor of the ravine where Cinglegros stands in splendid isolation. First there are two metal ladders, followed by a series of cramp-irons fixed into the rock face, and finally some steps cut into the rock.

A footpath leads through the undergrowth to the foot of the rock. The aids installed for climbing to the summit are very well maintained, and the ascent is most impressive. It is made up of nine metal ladders with six handrails, steps cut into the rock face and cramp-irons fixed to the rock in between. Once at the summit, relax and take a well-earned leisurely stroll on the terrace, from which there is an incomparable view over the Tarn gorges.

Return to base along a footpath leading down to the hamlet of Plaisance, then to Le Rozier on the path to La Sablière.

Corniche du Tarn *Round tour from Le Rozier – 21km/13mi by car, then 3hr 30min on foot*

From Le Rozier, take the road along the Tarn gorges (D 907) as far as Les Vignes, described in the opposite direction under **1** *above. Turn right towards Florac. The steep road climbs in a series of hairpin bends above the gorge. Turn towards La Bourgarie and park the car there.*

At the end of the hamlet, follow the path waymarked in red. It passes in front of the Bout du Monde ("End of the World") spring. Soon after, at a fork, the right-hand path leads down to the Pas de l'Arc.

Pas de l'Arc – This is a natural pointed arch, formed by erosion of the rock.
Turn back to the fork and then continue to Baousso del Biel.

Baousso del Biel – This opening, measuring 40m/131ft up to the arch roof, is the largest natural arch in the region.
The path reaches the point where the arch merges with the plateau. Several hundred yards after this bridge, follow the path up to the left to reach the abandoned farm of Volcégure.

From here, a forest footpath (GR 6A) leads back to La Bourgarie.

Musée de TAUTAVEL★★

Michelin maps 86 southwest of fold 9 or 235 fold 48 or 240 fold 37
9km/5mi north of Estagel – Local map see Les CORBIÈRES

Tautavel, a little village in the Corbières, on the banks of the Verdouble, has become a major centre of prehistory due to the discovery in the area of objects which have proved to be of vital significance in the study of the origins of human life.

In the **Caune de l'Arago** (a karstic cavity 40m/131ft long by 10-15m/32-49ft wide, west of D 9 to Vingrau), fragments of human skull, some of the oldest ever to be found in Europe, were excavated in 1971 and later in 1979. With the aid of these, the appearance of "Tautavel man" was reconstructed. This prehistoric hunter lived in the Roussillon plain about 450 000 years ago *(see Introduction, p 32)*.

The significant archeological finds recorded on the various strata of habitation (which are still being excavated) have provided evidence that this refuge, about 100m/300ft above the Tautavel plain, was occupied alternately by prehistoric men and animals between 700 000 and 100 000 BC.

CENTRE EUROPÉEN DE PRÉHISTOIRE ⊘ *allow 1hr 30min*

The **European Centre of Prehistory** is devoted to the evolution of man and his environment (based on the significant discoveries made in the Caune de l'Arago and surrounding area). This vast museum makes use of the latest technology and state-of-the-art scenography to take visitors on a journey far back in time, in search of their earliest origins. The rooms are laid out round a patio with a sculpture by Raymond Moretti dedicated to Tautavel

/Musée de Tautavel

Prehistoric hunting scene

man; they are equipped with interactive control panels and video screens which give information on several themes: man's place in the universe, the first tools found on the terraces of the rivers along the Roussillon coastline, the geological formation of the cave and its contents (a stratographic section shows the strata of no interest and those of archeological interest), climatic variations and the corresponding types of fauna, and the tools used by Tautavel man.

A whole floor is devoted to the visual and auditory evocation of life in the Lower Paleolithic age. Besides several very realistic dioramas showing hunting scenes and wall mounted graphics tracing the evolution of the landscape in the Roussillon plain, the main attraction is the **life-size reproduction** of the Caune de l'Arago, made with castings of the ceiling and walls of the original cave. Standing at the back of the cave, visitors can watch film extracts of scenes depicting various stages of the cave's occupation: first there are prehistoric men returning from the hunt, hacking up and eating the game they have just caught; then a bear is seen going into hibernation in his lair; finally the progressive transformation of the cave to its present form is shown. A room with a large picture window and a viewing table overlooks the plateaux of Devèze and the Caune d'Arague. The Caune de l'Arago is hollowed out of the cliffs of the latter, above the Gouleyroux gorge.

The following room displays fragments of skull and a reconstitution of the skeleton of Tautavel man. The **skull** itself consists of the face, frontal and parietal bones of the same roughly twenty year old man; the other parts are castings of discoveries from other sites.

The **reconstituted skeleton of Tautavel man**, one of the oldest human species known to date outside Africa, gives an idea of his stature: upright and about 1.65m/5ft tall. His lower limbs moved in a different way from ours. He was related to Homo Erectus and preceded Neanderthal man by about 300 000 years.

Tautavel is home to the European Centre of Prehistoric Research where specialists work from an interdisciplinary viewpoint.

Bassin de THAU

Michelin maps 83 fold 16 or 240 folds 26 and 27

The Bassin de Thau covers an area of 8 000ha/19 768 acres and is the largest lagoon on the Languedoc coast. It is separated from the sea by the isthmus of Onglous (Sète beach). Its shores are home to a whole range of activities: to the east is a busy industrial complex; to the south, the offshore sand bar is a beach; while on the north shore several villages which once made their living from fishing now specialise in oyster and mussel farming. For many years, the fishermen led an isolated life in their reed huts, before gathering together in villages, such as Marseillan or Mèze.

Oyster beds on Thau lagoon

Boat trips – These enable visitors to take a closer look at the oyster and mussel farming concerns in the lagoon.

Oyster and mussel farming – In the Mediterranean, two types of **oyster** are bred – flat oysters *(huîtres plates)* and concave or deep-shelled oysters *(huîtres "creuses")*. Of the two, the *"creuses"* tend to be richer and fleshier, with a less delicate flavour than the *plates*. Oysters raised in the Thau lagoon are marketed as "**huîtres de Bouzigues**", after the village where oyster farming in the lagoon began. The oysters are fixed with cement onto lines or poles, and then immersed in the lagoon until they reach the required size.

In **mussel** farming, the very young mussels *(naissain* – measuring less than 2cm/1in) are hung in clusters along ropes and nets to form huge garlands which are then immersed in the lagoon for maturation and fattening.

ROUND TOUR FROM SÈTE   *74km/45mi – allow 4hr*

★ **Sète** – *See SÈTE.*

Leave Sète on ③ on the town plan under SÈTE, skirt the east shore of the Thau lagoon, and head towards Balaruc-les-Bains.

‡‡ **Balaruc-les-Bains, Balaruc-le-Vieux** – *See BALARUC-LES-BAINS.*

From Balaruc-le-Vieux, take D 2 and rejoin N 113 towards Gigean. From there follow the signs to St-Félix-de-Montceau.

Ancienne abbaye de St-Félix-de-Montceau ⊘ – The remains of this old Benedictine abbey, built in the 11C and 13C, occupy a wonderful hilltop site from which there is an extensive **panorama**★ over the plain and the Thau lagoon. The ruins show that a Romanesque chapel coexisted with a Gothic church, in which the seven-sided chevet was lit through three twin windows.

From Gigean rejoin N 113 towards Béziers.

Bouzigues   In this quiet little village, which is a centre of oyster and mussel farming, the **Musée de l'étang de Thau** ⊘, located on the quay of the fishing harbour, contains a wealth of information about the local inhabitants' main livelihood. With the aid of attractive displays, the museum retraces the evolution of fishing techniques and shellfish breeding (oyster and mussel farm of the 1950s, a fishermen's "shop", aquariums stocked with aquatic life from the lagoon, video film).

Return to N 113 and turn right to Loupian.

Loupian – This small wine-growing village on a Gallo-Roman site still has the remains of its medieval ramparts (14C fortified gateway) and its castle, built in the 16C. Unusually, it is also home to two churches, one Romanesque and one Gothic. The church of **St-Hippolyte** ⊘, the old castle chapel dating from the 12C, was fortified and incorporated into the town ramparts. Inside, the church features a barrel-vaulted nave and an interesting arrangement of the keystones in the apse. The church houses various artefacts discovered in a nearby **Gallo-Roman villa** ⊘ *(on D 158E towards Mèze),* where excavations have brought to light 4C-5C polychrome mosaics which once adorned a luxurious residence on a 4ha/10 acre estate. The majestic 14C church of **Ste-Cécile** ⊘, in beautiful ochre stone, has very pronounced buttresses and a wide single nave with ribbed vaulting terminating in a polygonal apse typical of Languedoc Gothic style.

Rejoin N 113 to Mèze.

Mèze – This town, which is an important centre for oyster and mussel farming, attracts many tourists around the harbour and in the narrow little streets. Its Gothic church dates from the 15C. The **station de lagunage** ⊘ (lagoon research station) displays interesting examples of aquaculture (films and photographic exhibitions) and possesses an **aquarium** with various tropical fish. The tour includes a demonstration of recycling plastic materials.

Return to N 113 towards Béziers then take D 51 towards Agde to the left.

Marseillan – This lovely old fishing village was probably founded in the 6C BC by fishermen from Massalia (Ancient Marseille) and is still home to many fishermen. Marseillan harbour is a pleasant port of call for inland pleasure boats. Near the harbour are the **chais de Noilly-Prat** ⊘, where the famous aperitifs of this name are made. The guided tour of the plant takes visitors through the process of making dry vermouth (developed in 1813 by Joseph Noilly) and dessert wines *(vins doux naturels).* The Noilly Prat process characteristically includes ageing the blend of Picpoul and Clairette grape varieties in 600 litre/132gal wooden casks left out in the open to brave blazing sunshine and heavy rainstorms alike. 6km/3mi further round, on the Mediterranean coast, is **Marseillan-Plage** with miles and miles of sandy beach.

Return to Sète along the offshore sand bar, which makes up Sète beach. Once arrived at the cliffs at the other end, why not follow the panoramic tour of Mont St-Clair (described under SÈTE)?

TOULOUSE★★★

Conurbation 650 336
Michelin maps 82 fold 8 or 235 fold 30

Once the capital of all the regions united by the Occitanian dialects *(langues d'oc)*, Toulouse is now the sixth most important city in France.

The city's busy industrial life centres around the aeronautical construction industry, to which numerous high-tech industries have appended themselves. Toulouse is also home to a first-rate university and scientific research laboratories.

Besides its economic strength, the many and varied cultural opportunities – music, theatres, museums – and leisure facilities Toulouse has to offer play a great part in making it the worthy capital of the Midi-Pyrénées region.

In June 1993, an underground rail network *(métro)* was inaugurated in Toulouse, to help ease traffic congestion in the city centre.

A "red-brick" city – Brick, the only construction material available in any sufficient quantity in the alluvial plain of the Garonne, has long predominated in the buildings of Toulouse, lending the city its unique style and beauty. Bathed in Mediterranean light, Toulouse façades can take on a variety of hues depending on the time of day, ranging from scorching red to dusky pink or even violet. As brick is so light and mortar adheres to it easily, the master-masons of Toulouse were able to construct extravagantly wide vaults spanning a single nave.

Full of life – The lively, welcoming atmosphere that characterises Toulouse continues well into the early hours. It is influenced in part by the high proportion of students resident here and the good-humoured nature of local people as a whole.

The hub of the city's activity is its squares and the fairly considerable length of Rue Alsace-Lorraine, which links the noisy, popular Place Esquirol to the markets on the boulevards and the shops of the neighbouring streets, ranging from luxury boutiques installed in elegant old town houses to department stores.

Evening reveals the full charm of Place Wilson, all green and pink around a central fountain dedicated to the poet Godolin (pronounced "Goodoolee"), reputedly the last of the troubadours and the first poet in the Occitanian tongue (1580-1649). Many local residents enjoy coming to this square for an apéritif on one of the café terraces.

THE RIVER GARONNE

Between leaving the Pyrenees and reaching Agen, France's fourth longest river the Garonne flows rapidly across an alluvial plain interspersed with corridors with terraced sides on which orchards, ploughed fields or woodland can be seen.

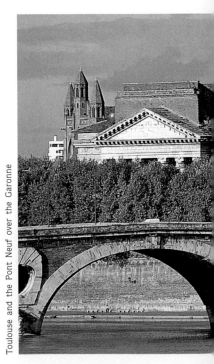

Toulouse and the Pont Neuf over the Garonne

Goods and passengers were transported on the river, mainly down-river of Toulouse to Bordeaux and back, from the mid 17C onwards. These trips were not without their dangers, with boats frequently capsizing or passengers drowning. In the early 19C, the introduction of steam boats increased the popularity of this form of transport; however this was to be short-lived due to the advent of rail travel, despite the opening of the Garonne side canal in 1856 creating a clear reach from the Canal du Midi to Bordeaux. Nowadays the canal holds its own thanks to modernisation of its course and that of the Canal du Midi so that they can accommodate vessels with a larger draught.

Moderation of the river's flow has always been a concern, particularly along the Garonne's middle reach, where the spring flood tides augmented by rivers draining off the Massif Central, such as the Tarn, can cause catastrophic flooding (1930). In the absence of any efficient way of straightening out the riverbed, the river has been tamed to some extent by the building of dams creating reservoirs used for hydroelectric power and water sports. From the 18C, plantations of poplar trees were one way of earning income from land prone to being flooded; the timber was used for carpentry and paper-making. The resulting elegant rows of poplars along the river's banks make a beautiful sight with their curtains of leaves reflecting in the water.

HISTORICAL NOTES

From Celtic to "Capitoul" rule – The ancient settlement of the Volcae, a branch of Celtic invaders, was probably situated in Vieille-Toulouse (9km/5mi south), but moved site and expanded into a large city which Rome made the intellectual centre of Gallia Narbonensis. In the 3C, it was converted to Christianity and became the third most important city in Gaul. Visigothic capital in the 5C, it then passed into the hands of the Franks.

After Charlemagne, Toulouse was ruled by counts, but it was far enough removed from the seat of Frankish power to keep a large degree of autonomy. From the 9C to the 13C, under the dynasty of the counts Raymond, the court of Toulouse was one of the most gracious and magnificent in Europe. The city was administered by consuls or *capitouls*, whom the count would systematically consult concerning the defence of the city or any negotiation with neighbouring feudal lords. By the time the city passed under the rule of the French crown in 1271, only 12 *capitouls* remained. A parliament, established in 1420 and reinstated in 1443, supervised law and finance.

The administration of the *capitouls* meant that the merchants of Toulouse had the possibility of becoming members of the aristocracy (to mark their rise in station, the new-fledged noblemen would adorn their mansion with a turret).

The Albigensian crisis – In the early 13C, the estates of the count of Toulouse and his vassals extended from Marmande, on the border with the territory of the king of England, duke of Aquitaine, as far as the marquisate of Provence, which was to become the Comtat Venaissin, under the hegemony of the Holy Roman Empire. However, the administration of the counts was weak compared to that of the Capetian monarchy. Nowhere was this more true than in the Haut Languedoc, and it was here that the Cathar heresy first caught hold and began to spread.

The fight against this heresy strongly advocated by the Papacy was initially confined to ecclesiastical sanctions – personal excommunication, papal interdicts on entire provinces, suspension of bishops – then took the form of sermons by the official clergy. The mission of St Dominic of Guzman and his friars seemed to be meeting with the most success, but, in 1208, the papal legate, Pierre de Castelnau, was

assassinated in St-Gilles *(see Michelin Green Guide Provence)*. Pope Innocent III immediately retaliated by excommunicating the count of Toulouse, Raymond VI, accused of complicity, and by calling for a crusade against the heretics. Philippe-Auguste, king of France, declined the invitation.

The crusade (1209-18) – The new crusaders, whether soldiers or clergy, were for the most part from the north of France (from the Paris region, Champagne, Burgundy), Flanders and also Germany, and were now awarded the same spiritual rewards as if they had volunteered for a crusade to the Holy Land: absolution for past sins, indulgences etc. They were certainly motivated by a sincere desire to serve the Church, but the opportunity of conquering new lands from discredited lords, who had rebelled against the orthodox religion, must also have played some part in their enthusiasm for the cause. Furthermore, feudal law required them to serve for only forty days.

After the massacre at Béziers and the fall of Carcassonne (1209), Simon de Montfort, now head of the crusade, seized the Trencavel viscounty. Toulouse was gradually overrun with refugees. At Muret, the insanely suicidal conduct of the Paladin King Peter II of Aragon, one of Cathar Languedoc's faithful allies, led to a resounding defeat for the forces of Raymond VI of Toulouse at the hands of de Montfort's troops (1213).

At the Pamiers Assizes (1212), de Montfort's companions in arms, among them Guy de Lévis, had been awarded confiscated territories, and the clergy had acquired numerous privileges. However, Toulouse remained steadfastly loyal to its count Raymond VI and resolutely settled down behind the city walls to withstand a siege. In June 1218, while laying siege to the city for a second time, Simon de Montfort was killed by a projectile from a ballista.

The Capetian involvement (1224-1229) – The barons' crusade fell apart. Amaury, son of Simon de Montfort, was hounded by Raymond VII, who had inherited Toulouse, and abandoned the south of France, yielding his rights to Louis VIII, king of France (1224).

However, on the diplomatic front, the count of Toulouse was playing a losing game. Barred from meetings between the court of St Louis and the cardinal de Saint-Ange, one of the most renowned diplomats of the Vatican, exposed to the relentless hostility of the episcopate and demoralised by the "scorched earth" policy carried out by the king's lieutenant on his lands, Raymond agreed to enter into negotiations. On Maundy Thursday, 12 April 1229, he came as a penitent to the parvis of Notre-Dame cathedral in Paris and swore to observe the clauses of the treaty, known as Treaty of Paris (or of Meaux). The count was awarded Haut Languedoc – but as a temporary possession only. His only daughter Jeanne was

Arènes Rom. (Av.)	**AU** 3
Babinet (R. J.)	**AV** 6
Barcelone (Allée de)	**BU** 8
Barrière de Paris	**BT** 10
Billières (Av. E.)	**BU** 13
Bonnefoy (R. du Fg)	**BCT** 15
Brienne (Allée de)	**BU** 22
Catalans (Pont des)	**BU** 29
Delacourtie (Bd)	**BV** 40
Demoiselles (Allée)	**BU** 42
Déodat de Sév. (Bd)	**BV** 43
Desbals (R. H.)	**BV** 45
Dillon (Cours)	**BU** 46
Dr-Baylac (Pl. du)	**AU** 47
Embouchure (Bd)	**BU** 52
États-Unis (Av. des)	**BT** 55
Fer-à-Cheval (Pl. du)	**BU** 56
Fitte (Allée Ch. de)	**BU** 59
Gare (Bd de la)	**BU** 65

Gde-Bretagne (Av. de)	**AU** 67
Griffoul-Dorval (Bd)	**BU** 72
Japon (R. du)	**BU** 77
Julien (Av. Jules)	**BV** 80
Kœnigs (Allée G.)	**BU** 81
Langer (Av. M.)	**BV** 84
Lascrosses (Bd)	**BU** 86
Lombez (Av. de)	**AU** 88
Lyon (Av. de)	**BU** 89
Male (Pl. E.)	**BU** 93
Marquette (Bd de la)	**BU** 97
Matabiau (Bd)	**BU** 101
Minimes (Av. des)	**BT** 104
Minimes (Bd des)	**BU** 105
Mirail (Av. du)	**AV** 106
Muret (Av. de)	**BV** 107
Patte d'Oie (Pl.)	**BU** 110
Pompidou (Allée)	**BU** 118
Pont de Guilheméry (R.)	**BCU** 119
Pujol (Av. C.)	**CU** 121
Récollets (Bd des)	**BV** 123
République (R. de la)	**BU** 124
Revel (Rte de)	**CV** 125
Riquet (Bd)	**BU** 120
St-Étienne (Port)	**BCU** 133
St-Sauveur (Port)	**BCU** 135
St-Simon (Rte de)	**AV** 136
Sarrault (Allée M.)	**BU** 138
Ségoffin (Av. V.)	**BV** 140
Séjourné (Av. P.)	**BV** 141
Serres (Av. Honoré)	**BU** 143
Trentin (Bd Silvio)	**BT** 148
URSS (Av. de l')	**BV** 154
Vauquelin (R. L.-N.)	**AV** 156

K Galerie municipale du Château d'eau

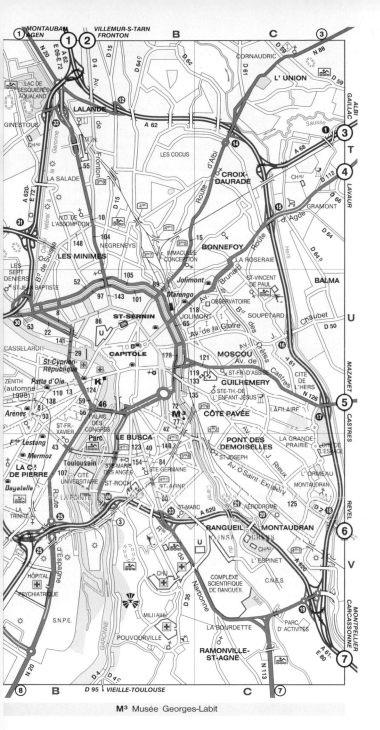

M³ Musée Georges-Labit

married to Alphonse de Poitiers, brother of St Louis. It was decreed that, unless there was any issue from this marriage, Toulouse would revert to the French crown on the death of the couple. Raymond undertook to dismantle the ramparts of Toulouse, and to support for the next 10 years "four doctors of divinity, two of canon law, six of the arts and two masters of grammar", a pool of academic expertise which marked the birth of the university of Toulouse. In 1271, the shrewdness of the French negotiators paid off, as Alphonse and Jeanne died without issue within three days of each other. Forthwith, the whole of Languedoc came under the jurisdiction of the French crown.

The oldest academy in France - After the turmoil of the Albigensian conflict, Toulouse once more became a centre of artistic and literary creativity. In 1324, seven eminent citizens desiring to preserve the *langue d'Oc* founded the "Compagnie du Gai-Savoir", one of the oldest literary societies in Europe. Every year on 3 May, the best poets were awarded the prize of a golden flower. Ronsard and Victor Hugo were honoured in this way, as was poet, playwright and revolutionary journalist Philippe-Nazaire-François Fabre (1755-94), author of the Republican calendar and the popular song "Il pleut, il pleut, bergère", who immortalised his prize by changing his pen-name to **Fabre d'Églantine** (wild rose). In 1694, Louis XIV raised the society to the status of **Académie des Jeux floraux**.

The dyer's woad boom – In the 15C, the trade in **dyer's woad** launched the merchants of Toulouse onto the scene of international commerce, with London and Antwerp among the main outlets. Clever speculation enabled families like the Bernuys and the Assézats to lead the life of princes. Sumptuous palatial mansions were built during this period, symbolising the tremendous wealth and power of these "dyer's woad tycoons". The thriving city of Toulouse, which had been largely medieval in appearance, underwent harmonious changes influenced by Italian architectural style, in particular that of the Florentine revival. However, with the introduction of indigo into Europe and the outbreak of the Wars of Religion, the boom collapsed after 1560 and recession set in.

No head is too great... – **Henri de Montmorency**, governor of Languedoc, "first Christian baron" and member of the most illustrious family of France, was renowned for his courage, good looks and generosity and soon became well-loved in his adopted province. In 1632, he was persuaded by Gaston d'Orléans, brother of Louis XIII, to take up arms in the rebellion of the nobility against Cardinal Richelieu, a decision that was to cost him dear. Both Orléans and Montmorency were defeated at Castelnaudary, where Montmorency fought valiantly, sustaining more than a dozen wounds, before being taken prisoner. He was condemned to death by the parliament at Toulouse.

Nobody could believe that such a popular and high ranking figure would be executed, but the king, who had come in person to Toulouse with Cardinal Richelieu, turned a deaf ear to the pleas of the family, the court and the people, claiming that as king he could not afford to show favour to any particular individual. He did however graciously concede that the condemned man could be beheaded inside the Capitole, instead of in the market place. On the specially constructed scaffold in the interior courtyard, at the foot of the statue of Henri IV, the 37 year old duke met his death with all the dignity befitting a noble lord. When his head was shown to the crowd in front of the Capitole, there were howls of vengeance levelled at the cardinal.

Violets

The violet, originally from Parma in Italy, is thought to have been introduced to Toulouse during the 19C by French soldiers who had fought in Napoleon's Italian campaign. It was enthusiastically received by the people of Toulouse, and became the most sought-after item at florists', perfume-makers' and confectioners' (the famous crystallized violets). At the beginning of the century, some 600 000 bouquets a year were being sent to the capital, northern Europe and even Canada. Sadly, disease and mildew soon got the better of this delicate winter plant with its tiny purple flowers. However, from 1985, scientists began research into ways of saving the plant. Ten years later, they succeeded in cultivating it under glass. Nowadays, the greenhouses of Lalande, north of Toulouse, are once again fragrant with the scent of this pretty flower and Toulouse has had its emblem restored to it.

TOULOUSE, CAPITAL OF THE AERONAUTICAL INDUSTRY

"La Ligne" – During the interwar period, Toulouse became the departure point for France's first ever scheduled airline, thanks to the efforts of industrialists such as P Latécoère, administrators such as D Daurat, and pilots such as Mermoz, Saint-Exupéry and Guillaumet.

25 December 1918: first trial flight from Toulouse to Barcelona.

1 September 1919: official inauguration of the first air mail service between France and Morocco. Military aircraft, with hardly any modification, linked Toulouse-Montaudran with Rabat, stopping at Barcelona, Alicante, Malaga and Tangiers.

1 June 1925: aircraft reach Dakar. Pioneering pilots operate routes to and in South America.

12 May 1930: first commercial South Atlantic crossing by a crew comprising Mermoz, Dabry and Gimié, making an air link between France and South America a reality.

21 April 1949: maiden flight of the Leduc 010, prototype of high-speed aircraft.

The post-war period – After the Second World War, four important projects helped to relaunch the French aeronautical industry. Two military aircraft (Transall, Breguet Atlantic) and two civil aircraft (Caravelle, Concorde) enabled French engineers and research consultants to hone their talents as aircraft designers and to develop teamwork with their British and German counterparts.

Dumas/IMAGES PHOTOTHÈQUE

Flight simulator in an Airbus 340

1 May 1959: maiden flight of the Caravelle on the Paris-Athens-Istanbul route.

2 March 1969: first test flight of "Concorde 001", the first supersonic airliner, piloted by André Turcat.

Despite their technological sophistication, the two civil aircraft projects did not attract the expected industrial interest. The commercial and financial problems of Concorde were to serve as lessons for the Airbus project.

1 January 1970: founding of Aérospatiale, amalgamation of Nord-Aviation, Sud-Aviation and Sereb.

The success of Airbus – A product of European ambition (initially Anglo-French, then Franco-German from 1969, and Franco-Spanish after 1987), Airbus Industrie has in twenty years become the second most important civil aviation manufacturer in the world, enabling the old world to develop a complete range of aeroplanes seating 150 to 300, starting with one successful model, the A 300. The project was realised largely due to the tenacity of three men, Roger Béteille, project co-ordinator of the Airbus project, Henri Ziegler, managing director of Airbus Industrie, and Franz-Joseph Strauss, president of the supervisory council, who transformed it from a seemingly foolhardy venture to a world class enterprise, with a presence on every continent.

State-of-the-art technology – The success of Airbus Industrie is due mainly to a willingness to produce airliners which always meet the airlines' needs. It is also the result of an impressive series of technological innovations, such as electronic flight control, advanced aerodynamics, design for a two-man cockpit with innovative flight management systems.

Concurrently with the development of Airbus, Franco-American collaboration between Snecma and General Electric has resulted, in 1981, in the production of the CFM-56 engine, one of the most popular aircraft engines in the world.

Usine Clément-Ader ⊘ – *In the suburb of Colomiers west of Toulouse. Take the N 124 towards Auch (⑩ on town plan), leave at junction 3 signposted Colomiers, and follow signs to Usine Clément-Ader/Aérospatiale. The factory is opposite the British Aerospace plant and has a large model of Concorde outside it.*

This factory, measuring 500m/0.3mi long by 200m/656ft wide, is where the A 330/A 340 range of long-range aircraft are assembled. Besides the commentary during the guided tour, a projection room, scale models and literature in the Clément-Ader room explain the Airbus programme. As the factory was designed to accommodate guided tours, there is a footbridge from which visitors can look down onto the aircraft assembly area.

TOWN CENTRE

★★★ Basilique St-Sernin ⊘ (DX)

This is the most famous and most magnificent of the great Romanesque pilgrimage churches in the south of France, and one which can also boast the largest collection of holy relics. The site was home, in the late 4C, to a basilica containing the body of St Sernin (or Saturninus). This Apostle from the Languedoc, the first bishop of Toulouse, was martyred in 250 by being tied to the legs of a bull he had refused to sacrifice to pagan gods, which dragged him down a flight of stone steps.

OUT AND ABOUT IN TOULOUSE

Tourist information – The tourist office is located in the Donjon du Capitole, ☏ 05 61 11 02 22. A monthly publication in French, *Culture Toulouse*, gives the programme of cultural events.

Guided tours – These are organised by the tourist office and cover the city's artistic heritage in a series of walks on certain themes. Combined tickets known as "passports" allow visitors to participate in 2 to 5 walks during their stay in Toulouse.

Parking and public transport – Toulouse has a "Park and Ride" scheme, with free car parks at either end of the métro system. Free parking spaces are often to be found around the university (for those who arrive early) from where it is only a short walk to the city centre. Multi-storey car parks are to be found underneath Place du Capitole, Place St-Georges, Place Esquirol, Place St-Étienne, and on Place des Carmes. The city has an extensive public transport system, including a métro line and numerous bus services, some of which run at night. As well as tickets for individual journeys, day tickets and season tickets are available. Details from Espace Transport, 7, place Esquirol or Allô Semvat, ☏ 05 61 41 70 70.

Views – There are good views of the city to be seen from the cafeteria terrace (access to customers only) of Nouvelles Galeries department store in rues Lapeyrouse/Alsace-Lorraine and from the top of the multi-storey car park on Place des Carmes.

Bars and restaurants – Those looking for a pleasant place to sit and have a drink or something to eat need look no further than the main city squares: one of the many pavement cafés around Place du Capitole (**DY**), for example Brasserie **Le Bibent** (fine Baroque ceiling inside); chic Brasserie **Le Capoul** on Place Wilson (**EY**); **Bistrot Van Gogh**, popular with younger clientele, on Place St-Georges (**EY**). There are numerous good places for eating out along the Boulevard de Strasbourg (**EX**). On Place Arnaud-Bernard (**DX**), **Le Ragtime** offers live music and **Le Méchant-loup** has a disco.

Shopping – Main shopping streets include Rue d'Alsace-Lorraine (**DXY**), Rue Croix-Baragnon (**EY**), for more up-market boutiques, and the pedestrian streets Rue St-Rome (**DY**), Rue Baronie and Rue de la Pomme. Toulouse also has two shopping centres: St-Georges in the centre of town and Compans, an ultra-modern complex northwest of town (**BU**).

Markets – St-Aubin market on Sunday mornings has a good selection of fresh fruit and vegetables and poultry from local farms. In winter, a geese, duck and *foie gras* market is held on Place du Salin (**DZ**). Health food products are sold on Place du Capitole on Tuesdays and Saturdays. A trip to the flea-market held around St-Sernin basilica on Sunday mornings is a must. Alternatively, animal lovers may prefer the unusual cat and dog market held on Boulevard Lascrosses (**BU**) on Sundays. There is a covered market on Place des Carmes (**DZ**).

Typical local products – Brebis (Pyrenean sheep's cheese); Roquefort; *confits*; *foie gras*; duck and goose; Toulouse (fresh pork) sausage; *saucisson sec*

Local wines – Fronton (north of Toulouse; red, rosé), Madiran (Gers), Buzet, Cahors, Gaillac (towards Albi; red, rosé, white), St-Mont (Gers; white), Pacherenc (dry white)

With the donation of numerous relics by Charlemagne, the church became a focus for pilgrims from all over Europe, and also a stopping place for pilgrims on their way to Santiago de Compostela. The present building was constructed to meet these growing needs. It was begun in c 1080 and completed in the mid-14C. General restoration was undertaken in 1860 by Viollet-le-Duc. The current programme of repair work is intended to restore the roof to its appearance prior to the work carried out in 1860. The transept arms and the nave are now covered once again by ample overhanging roofs with open galleries *(mirandes)* just beneath the eaves.

Exterior – St-Sernin is constructed from red brick and white stone. On the chevet, begun in the late 11C, stone is much in evidence, whereas the nave is built almost all of brick, which in turn is the only material used in the belfry.

The 11C **chevet** is the oldest part of the building. It is quite spectacularly pretty (especially seen from the Rue St-Bernard), forming a magnificent ensemble of five apsidal chapels and four transept chapels combining with the tiered roofs of the chancel and transept, and the elegant bell-tower rising out of the whole.

The five tiered octagonal **bell-tower** stands majestically above the transept crossing. The three lower tiers are embellished with early 12C Romanesque round arches. The two upper storeys were added 150 years later; the openings, shaped like mitres, are surmounted by little decorative pediments. The spire was added in the 15C.

The doorway known as the **Porte des Comtes**, originally dedicated to St Sernin, opens into the south transept. The capitals on their colonnettes, relatively crudely executed, depict the parable of Lazarus and the Rich Man *(right portal)*, concentrating on the punishments meted out to the latter for his sins of avarice *(left portal, first capital on the left)* and lechery *(left portal, first capital on the right and second capital on the left)*; on either side of the central pillar, the Rich Man asking if he might return to earth to warn his brother is depicted being kept imprisoned in Hell (the repetition of the same motif stresses the eternal duration of the punishment).

To the left of the doorway, in an alcove protected by a metal grille, are four sarcophagi, the coffins of the counts of Toulouse, hence the name of the doorway. Further to the left is a Renaissance arcade, all that remains of the fortified wall which, until the early 19C, surrounded the church, the buildings of the chapter of canons and the adjacent cemeteries.

The Romanesque sculpture on the **Porte Miégeville** (leading into the south side of the nave) set a fashion throughout the south of France. Dating from the early 12C, it conveys expression and movement more vividly than any work of the previous century.

Interior – St-Sernin is the epitome of a major pilgrimage church. It was designed to accommodate large

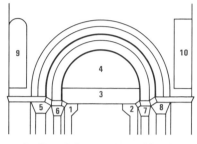

Basilique St-Sernin – Porte Miégeville

1) King David – 2) Two women sitting on lions – 3) The apostles, heads thrown back, watch the Ascension of Christ – 4) Ascension of Christ, surrounded by angels – 5) Massacre of the Innocents – 6) Annunciation and Visitation – 7) Adam and Eve expelled from the Garden of Eden 8) Two lions back to back – 9) St James the Great – 10) St Peter.

congregations, with room for a choir of canons (who used to occupy the cloisters and the buildings to the north of the church, and who were dispersed at the Revolution), and consists of a nave flanked by double side-aisles, a broad transept and a chancel with an ambulatory from which five radiating chapels open off.

For a Romanesque church, St-Sernin is particularly vast, measuring 115m/377ft in length, 64m/210ft in width at the transept and 21m/68ft in height to the roof vault. The nave is most impressive. The view of the chancel, however, is somewhat cut off by the massive pillars of the transept, which were reinforced when the height of the bell-tower was increased.

Imagine a cross-section of the church to appreciate the perfection of its height and proportions. The barrel-vaulted nave is supported by a first set of side-aisles, with ribbed vaulting and surmounted by pretty half-barrel vaulted galleries.

St Saturninus in St-Sernin basilica

TOULOUSE

Alsace-Lorraine (R. d') ... **DXY**
Capitole (Pl. du) .... **DY**
Lafayette (R.) .... **DY**
Metz (R. de) .... **DEY**
Rémusat (R. de) .... **DX**
St-Antoine du T. (R.) ..... **EY**
St-Rome (R.) .... **DY**
Wilson (Pl. Prés.) .... **EY**

Arnaud-Bernard (R. d') .... **DX** 4
Astorg (R. d') .... **EY** 5
Baour-Lormian (R.) .... **DY** 7
Baronie (R.) .... **DY** 9
Boulbonne (R.) .... **EY** 18

Bouquières (R.) .... **EZ** 19
Bourse (Pl. de la) .... **DY** 20
Cantegril (R.) .... **EY** 23
Cartailhac (R. E.) .... **DX** 26
Chaîne (R. de la) .... **DX** 31
Cujas (R.) .... **DY** 36
Daurade (Quai de la) ..... **DY** 38
Esquirol (Pl.) .... **DY** 54
Fonderie (R. de la) .... **DZ** 60
Frères Lion (R.) .... **EY** 62
Henry-de-Gorsse (R.) ..... **DZ** 76
Jules-Chalande (R.) ...... **DY** 79
Lapeyrouse (R.) .... **EY** 85
Magre (R. Genty) .... **DY** 91
Malcousinat (R.) .... **DY** 92
Marchands (R. des) .... **DY** 95
Mercié (R. Antonin) ...... **DEY** 103

Pélissier (R. du Lieut-Col.) . **EY** 112
Peyras (R.) .... **DY** 113
Pleau (R. de la) .... **EZ** 114
Poids-de-l'Huile (R.) ..... **DY** 115
Polinaires (R. des) .... **DZ** 116
Pomme (R. de la) .... **DEY** 117
Riguepels (R.) .... **EY** 127
Romiguières (R.) .... **DY** 129
St-Michel (Grande-Rue) ... **DZ** 134
Ste-Ursule (R.) .... **DY** 137
Sémard (Bd Pierre) .... **EX** 142
Suau (R. Jean) .... **DY** 146
Temporières (R.) .... **DY** 147
Trinité (R. de la) .... **DY** 149
Vélane (R.) .... **EZ** 155
3-Journées (R. des) ...... **EY** 162
3-Piliers (R. des) .... **DX** 164

C Hôtel de Fumel
     (Chambre de Commerce)
D Basilique N.-D.-de-la-Daurade

E Hôtel Béringuier-Maynier
L Tour Pierre Séguy

M¹ Musée du Vieux Toulouse
R Tour de Sarta

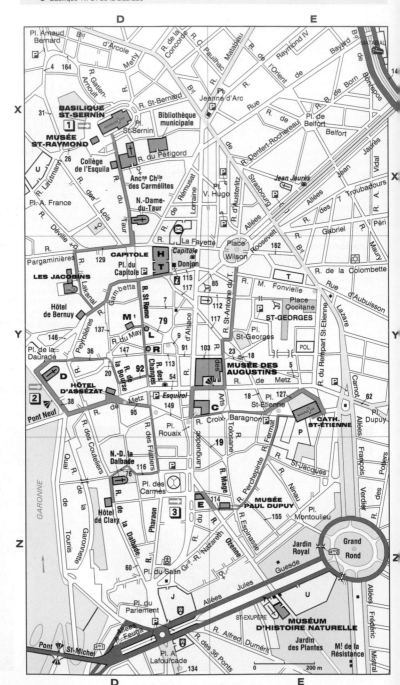

The first side-aisles themselves rest on a second, slightly lower set of side-aisles, again with ribbed vaulting but supported by buttresses. In this way, all of the elements which make up this enormous building combine to ensure its solidity.

Chancel – Beneath the dome of the transept crossing, there is a fine table of Pyrenean marble from the old Romanesque altar signed by Bernard Gilduin and consecrated in 1096 by Pope Urban II.

Transept – The vast transept is laid out as three aisles with east-facing chapels. The capitals of the tribune gallery and the Romanesque mural paintings are worthy of attention. In the north transept, two groups of Romanesque mural paintings have been uncovered *(fairly damaged)*. On the west wall of the first bay is a scene of the Resurrection: from bottom to top, the Holy Women at the tomb with the angel, two Old Testament prophets, Christ in glory between the Virgin Mary and St John the Baptist; on the roof vault: the Lamb of God is shown being presented by the angels (the same scene is depicted on the roof vault of the transept's second chapel).

One of the south transept chapels is dedicated to the Virgin Mary (note the 14C statue of "Notre-Dame-la-Belle"); on the chapel's oven-vault are frescoes one above each other mingling the theme of the Virgin seated "in Majesty" (13C) with the Coronation of the Virgin.

Ambulatory and Crypt ⊘ – Numerous altarpieces and reliquaries on display in the ambulatory have led to its being known as the Corps Saints, or Holy Relics, since the 17C. Carved, gilded and painted wooden caskets contain the remains of St Asciscle, St Victoria, St Hilary and St Papoul, among others.

On the wall curving round the outside of the crypt are seven impressive late-11C **low reliefs**★★ in St-Béat marble from the studio of Bernard Gilduin: Christ in Majesty, with the symbols of the Evangelists, surrounded by angels and Apostles. The crypt itself is in two parts: the upper hexagonal part has a painted keystone on its vault and contains the reliquary of St Saturninus (13C); the lower crypt has ogive vaulting supported on a central pillar, and contains various reliquary chests and statues of the Apostles (14C).

Upper part – The capitals may be admired from the galleries.

The walks recommended below cover the heart of the city. Allow at least one full day.

1 From St-Sernin to Place de la Daurade

★★ **Musée St-Raymond** ⊘ (DX) – *Restoration work in progress.* This is the archeological museum of Toulouse. Since 1891, it has occupied one of the buildings of the old College St-Raymond, rebuilt in 1523 by Louis Privat and restored 1868-71 by Viollet-le-Duc. From the gardens, there are good views of St-Sernin.

The collection of Roman sculpture is remarkably well displayed; there are thousands of artefacts in bronze, iron, ivory, bone, glass, wood and earthenware, from a variety of sources. The museum also contains a good collection of keys and bronze figures and the finest set of Imperial portraits in France. An area is given over to the applied arts, from the origins of mankind to the year 1000. Other interesting displays include a very large collection of Ancient and medieval coins, sculpture, inscriptions, Christian lamps, liturgical vases and jewellery.

Collège de l'Esquila (DX) – This opens off no 69 rue du Taur through a doorway decorated with bosses, a Renaissance work by Toulouse sculptor N. Bachelier.

Ancienne chapelle des Carmelites ⊘ (DX) – *Go down Rue du Périgord.* The decoration of this chapel – woodwork and paintings commemorating the Carmelite order (by the Toulouse painter Despax) – is a fine example of 18C art.

Église Notre-Dame-du-Taur (DX) – This church, known as St-Sernin-du-Taur until the 16C, replaced the sanctuary erected where the martyr saint was buried. The gable wall of the façade, flanked by octagonal towers and decorated with mitre arches, is characteristic of the region, where it served as a model for numerous country churches. The bell-tower is crenellated and topped by a triangular gable. The church is a catalogue of the various decorative devices to which brick lends itself, such as diamond-shaped windows and dogtooth friezes. Inside, the church houses a 16C wooden statue, dressed in a red brocade dress, of the Virgin Mary (Notre-Dame-du-Rempart), which is so darkened with age as to be almost black. The statue was moved here from the Porte Villeneuve in 1785.

★★ **Les Jacobins** ⊘ (DY) – In 1215, St Dominic, alarmed by the spread of the Albigensian heresy, founded the Order of Preachers (Dominican Order). The first Dominican monastery was founded in Toulouse in 1216; the friars reached Paris a year later and set up a community in a chapel dedicated to St James the Great

(St Jacques in French), from which they acquired the name of "Jacobins". The construction of the church and the monastery – the first university in Toulouse – was begun in 1230, and continued throughout the 13C and 14C. The buildings suffered badly when they were converted into barracks to house an artillery regiment during the First Empire (Napoleon I), with the church pressed into service as stables.

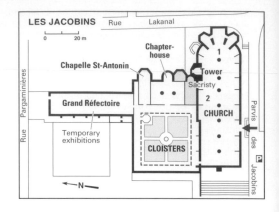

LES JACOBINS   Rue   Lakanal

0   20 m

Chapter-house

Chapelle St-Antonin

Rue Pargaminières

Grand Réfectoire

Tower

Sacristy

CHURCH

Temporary exhibitions

CLOISTERS

Parvis des Jacobins

←N→

Extensive restoration work resulted in the church, cloisters and surviving conventual buildings, including the great sacristy *(closed to the public)*, being restored to their former glory by 1974.

Church – The red brick church is a masterpiece of the southern French Gothic, marking a milestone in the evolution of this style. In 1369, the body of St Thomas Aquinas was placed in the "mother-church" of the Order of Preachers, which had been completed around 1340. The church has a striking exterior, featuring huge relieving arches surmounted by oculi between massive buttresses, and an ornate octagonal bell-tower adorned with mitre arches, which served as a model for the bell-towers of numerous prosperous churches throughout the region. On its completion in 1298, the tower was fitted with the only bell of the Dominican University.

The awesome **main body★★★** of the church, which has two naves, is the result of successive enlargements and additions of further storeys. It reflects the Dominican Order's prestige, its prosperity and its two main aims: the service of God and the preaching of God's word.

On the floor of the church, the ground plan of the original rectangular sanctuary (1234), which was covered by a timber-frame roof, is indicated by 5 black marble slabs (the bases of the old pillars) and by a line of black tiles (the old walls). The church's roof vault, which reaches a height of 28m/91ft up to the keystones, is supported on seven columns. The column at the far east end (**1**) supports the entire fan vaulting of the apse; its 22 ribs, alternately wide and narrow, resemble the branches of a palm tree. As much of the original polychrome painted wall decoration remained, those in charge of the restoration work were able successfully to recreate the atmosphere of the church. Up as far as the sills of the clerestory windows, the walls are decorated with painted imitation brickwork in ochre and pink. Other stripes of contrasting colours are used to emphasize the upward thrust of the engaged colonnettes and the graceful sweep of the ribs on the roof vault.

The stained glass windows were inserted from 1923; the "grisaille" (monotonal) windows round the apse were based on the blind trompe-l'oeil window which backs onto the bell-tower, while the brighter colours of the windows in the nave, by Max Ingrand, were inspired by the two original 14C rose windows on the façade, with "warm" colours predominating on the south side and "cold" on the north.

Since the ceremony for the seventh centenary of the death of St Thomas Aquinas in 1974, the relics of the "saintly doctor" have once more been on display beneath a high altar (**2**) of grey marble, from Prouille.

Cloisters – The north door opens into cloisters adorned with twin colonnettes, typical of Languedoc Gothic (other examples may be found in St-Hilaire in the Corbières and Arles-sur-Tech). It was possible to reconstitute the south and east galleries, which were destroyed in c 1830, by using fragments of work in the same style, which had been found scattered throughout the region.

Chapelle St-Antonin – This chapel, on the left of the chapter-house, was built from 1337 to 1341 as a funeral chapel by friar Dominique Grima, who became bishop of Pamiers (keystone of the arch above the head of Christ of the Apocalypse).

The bones were transferred from tombs in the floor of the nave into an ossuary beneath the raised altar. The chapel is a delicate example of the Gothic style. It was decorated, in 1341, with predominantly blue mural paintings.

The medallions inscribed in the segments of the vault depict the second vision of the Apocalypse: the immaculate Lamb, with its feet resting on the book of seven seals; Christ, ruler of the world, surrounded by the symbols of the Evangelists and the 24 Elders. On the walls, beneath angel-musicians, are two tiers depicting scenes from the fantastic legend of St Antonin of Pamiers which reaches its conclusion on the keystone of the arch of the apse: the martyr's relics are shown being escorted by two white eagles.

Chapter-house – This was built c 1300. Two very slim facetted columns support the roof vault. The graceful apsidal chapel once more boasts colourful mural decoration. Its excellent acoustics make it an ideal setting for concerts, which it hosts during the summer months.

Grand Réfectoire – *Via Rue Pargaminières.* The great refectory (northeast corner of the cloisters) is a vast room, built in 1303, with a timber-frame roof supported on six transverse arches separating the bays. It is open during temporary exhibitions only.

Hôtel de Bernuy (Lycée Pierre-de-Fermat) ⊘ **(DY)** – This mansion was built in two stages in the early 16C. The beautiful main doorway (1 rue Gambetta) blends curves and counter-curves, in typically Gothic style, with medallions. The first courtyard provides an architectural interlude in stone. On the reverse side of the doorway is a sumptuous Renaissance portico complete with loggia, to the right of which is a heavily depressed arch. A passage with ribbed vaulting leads into a second courtyard, in which all the charm of the "red-brick city" is once again in evidence. An octagonal corbelled **staircase turret★**, one of the tallest in Old Toulouse, is lit through windows which neatly follow the angle where two walls meet.

Place du Capitole (DY) – Along the east side of this vast square, the main meeting point for local residents, stretches the majestic façade of the Capitole building. At the centre of the square, inlaid into the paving, is an enormous bronze Occitan cross, surrounded by the signs of the zodiac.

★ **Capitole** ⊘ – *Photograph p 415.* This is the City Hall of Toulouse, named after the *"capitouls"*, or consuls, who used to run the city. The façade overlooking the Place du Capitole dates from the mid 18C. Measuring 128m/420ft in length, it is a fine and colourful example of architectural composition, with the skilful alternating use of brick and stone and the decorative Ionic pilasters. The right wing houses the theatre of Toulouse, refurbished in 1995. In the courtyard, beneath a Renaissance portico, stands a statue of Henri IV erected during his reign. This was the scene of the execution of the duke of Montmorency in 1632 *(see above)* – commemorative plaque on the flagstones.

The staircase, hall and various rooms, most notably the Salle des Illustres dedicated to the most glorious representatives of Toulouse, were decorated with appropriate grandiosity at the time of the Third Republic, by specially commissioned officially approved painters. The hall of mirrors is often used for official functions.

Cross the courtyard and walk diagonally through the gardens to get to the keep *(donjon)*, a remnant of the old 16C Capitole, restored by Viollet-le-Duc (note the slate roof more in keeping with the architecture of northern France) in the 19C. It now houses the tourist office.

Café in the arcades, Place du Capitole

A Toulouse street

Rue St-Rome (**DY**) - *Pedestrian street.* This busy shopping street is part of the old *cardo maximus* (Roman road through town from north to south). At the beginning of the street (no 39) stands the interesting house of Catherine de' Medici's physician (Augier Ferrier). Pierre Séguy's fine Gothic turret (**DY L**) is tucked inside the courtyard of no 4 **Rue Jules-Chalande** (**DY 79**). At no 3 rue St-Rome is an elegant early 17C town house, the Hôtel de Gomère.

Musée du Vieux Toulouse ⊘ (**DY M¹**) - This museum in the Hôtel du May (16-17C) displays collections tracing the history of the city, and local traditional arts and crafts, including ceramic ware.

Rue des Changes (**DY**) - The square known as "Quatre Coins des Changes" is overlooked by the Sarta turret (**R**). Nos 20, 19 and 17 boast some interesting decorative features (timbering, window frames etc), while no 16, the 16C Hôtel d'Astorg et St-Germain, has a façade with a gallery just beneath the eaves - a local feature known as *mirandes* - and a pretty courtyard with timber galleries and diagonally opposed spiral staircases with wooden handrails.

Rue Malcousinat (**DY 92**) - At no 11, the 16C Hôtel de Cheverny, the attractive main building, which is Gothic-Renaissance, is flanked by an austere 15C keep *(press red button on number pad to right of door to get in and see tower).*

Rue de la Bourse (**DY**) - Note at no 15 the Hôtel de Nupces (18C). No 20, the late 15C Hôtel Delfau, is the house of Pierre Del Fau, who hoped to become a *capitoul* - hence the turret - but who never fulfilled his ambition.
The 24m/78m high turret, pierced with five large windows, is quite remarkable. The windows on the second and fifth floors feature an elegant ogee arch shaped lintel.
After walking down the Rue Cujas, carry on to Place de la Daurade.

Basilique Notre-Dame-de-la-Daurade (**DY D**) - The present church, which dates from the 18C, occupies the site of a pagan temple which was converted into a church dedicated to the Virgin Mary in the 5C and a Benedictine monastery. The inhabitants of Toulouse are very attached to this church (pilgrimages to Notre-Dame-la-Noire, a Black Madonna, prayers for the welfare of expectant mothers and ceremonies for the blessing of the flowers awarded to the winners of the Jeux Floraux). It has an interesting façade with a heavy peristyle overlooking the Garonne.

2 From Place de la Daurade to the Hôtel de Clary

Take a short stroll along the Quai de la Daurade, downstream of the Pont Neuf (16-17C), past the fine arts academy (École des Beaux-Arts); there is a good view of the St-Cyprien district (west bank) with its two hospitals, the Hôtel-Dieu and the domed Hospice de la Grave.

Take the Rue de Metz to the left, and bear left again.

Hôtel d'Assézat ⊙ (**DY**) – This, the finest private mansion in Toulouse, was built in 1555-57 according to the plans of Nicolas Bachelier, the greatest Renaissance architect of Toulouse, for the Capitoul d'Assézat, who had made a fortune from trading in dyer's woad.

The façades of the buildings to the left of and opposite the entrance are the earliest example of the use of the classical style in Toulouse, characterised by the three decorative orders – Doric, Ionic, Corinthian – used one above the other, creating a marvellously elegant effect. To add a bit of variety to these façades, the architect introduced rectangular windows beneath relieving arches on the ground and first floors. On the second floor, the lines are reversed, with round-arched windows beneath straight horizontal entablatures.

The sophistication of this design is matched by the elaborate decoration on the two doorways, one with twisted columns and the other adorned with scrolls and garlands. Sculpture underwent a revival in Toulouse at the time of the Renaissance, when stone began to be used again, in conjunction with brick.

On the inside of the façade facing the street, there is an elegant portico with four arcades, surmounted by a gallery. The fourth side was never completed, as Assézat, having converted to the Protestant faith, was driven into exile, a ruined man. The wall is adorned only by a covered gallery resting on graceful consoles.

★ **Fondation Bemberg** – The Hôtel d'Assézat now houses the donation of private art collector **Georges Bemberg**. This impressive collection comprises painting, sculpture and objets d'art from the Renaissance to the 20C.

Old Masters (16-18C) are exhibited on the first floor, which is laid out like a private home. There are paintings by the 18C Venetian school (*vedute* by Canaletto and Guardi), 15C Flemish works such as *Virgin and Child* from the studio of Rogier Van der Weyden and 17C Dutch painting, with *Musicians* by Pieter de Hooch. Displayed with the paintings are 16C objets d'art such as a nautilus and a *grisaille* Limoges enamel plaque depicting Saturn. A gallery of portraits includes paintings (*Venus and Cupid* by Lucas Cranach the Elder, *Charles IX* by François Clouet, *Portrait of a Young Woman with a Ring* by Ambrosius Benson and *Portrait of Antoine de Bourbon* by Franz Pourbus) and 16C sculpture groups. The small room adjoining this contains bronzes from Italy, such as a superb figure of Mars attributed to Jean de Boulogne, alongside Limoges enamels, leatherbound books and paintings by Veronese, Tintoretto and Bassano.

An open gallery overlooking the courtyard leads to the staircase up to the second floor, which is devoted to Modern Masters (19-20C). The collection, in which a high point is the series of paintings by Bonnard, executed in a vibrant palette (*Woman with a Red Cape, Red and Yellow Apples, Still Life with Lemons*), includes works by almost all the great names of the Modern French School, offering an overview of the main movements in paintings from the late 19C to the late 20C: Impressionism, Pointillism, Fauvism. Artists featured include Louis Valtat (*La Lecture*), Paul Gauguin (*Face of a Young Peasant*), Matisse (*View of Antibes*), H. E. Cross (*Canal in Venice*), Eugène Boudin (*Crinolines on the Beach*), Claude Monet (*Boats on the Beach*) and Raoul Dufy (*Kessler Family on Horseback*).

The vaulted rooms in the basement house temporary exhibitions.

Take Rue des Marchands to the right and turn right into Rue des Filatiers, then right again into Rue des Polinaires and Rue H.-de-Gorsse, in which there are some attractive 16C houses. Turn left into Rue de la Dalbade.

Église Notre-Dame-la-Dalbade (**DZ**) – The present church was built in the 16C, on the site of an earlier building, which had white walls. In 1926 the bell-tower fell in, damaging the church, which was subsequently restored, with particular attention paid to its beautiful brickwork. The Renaissance doorway has a ceramic tympanum dating from the 19C.

Rue de la Dalbade (**DZ**) – This street is lined with the elegant mansions of former local dignitaries. Nos 7, 11, 18 and 20 have fine 18C façades. Note no 22, the Hôtel Molinier, which boasts an extravagantly ornate, sculpted doorway (16C) of quite profane inspiration. The **Hôtel de Clary** (**DZ**), at no 25, has a beautiful Renaissance courtyard; its façade, fairly groaning with pillars, festoons and cherubs among other things, caused a sensation when it was put up in the 17C, as it was made of stone, considered the ultimate symbol of the owner's wealth in a city of predominantly brick buildings (hence the other name by which the building is known – the Hôtel de Pierre).

The Hôtel des Chevaliers de St-Jean-de-Jérusalem (nos 30-32), a grand 17C mansion, was the headquarters of the great priory of the Order of Malta (1668).

③ From the Hôtel du Vieux-Raisin to Place Wilson

Hôtel du Vieux-Raisin (Hôtel Béringuier-Maynier) (**DZ E**) – The main building at the back of the courtyard marks the first manifestation of the Italian Renaissance in Toulouse, in the style of the châteaux of the Loire valley (stone as well as brick work). The ornamentation of the wings is much more turbulent in style, verging on the Baroque – windows adorned with caryatids, for example.

Behind the mansion, take Rue Ozenne.

Rue Ozenne (**EZ**) – At no 9 the Hôtel Dahus and Tournoër turret make a handsome 15C architectural group.

Take Rue de la Pleau to the left.

★ **Musée Paul-Dupuy** ⊘ (**EZ**) – This museum is devoted to the applied arts from the Middle Ages to the present: metal and wood work, clock-making, weights and measures, coins, reconstruction of the Jesuit college dispensary (1632). The print room contains some interesting images of Languedoc and the surrounding area.

From the Musée Paul-Dupuy, heading towards Place St-Étienne, take Rues Perchepinte and Fermat which are lined with antiques shops. Leading off to either side of these streets are a number of recently restored streets – Rues Espinasse, Vélane and Ninau – lined with typical old Toulouse houses such as the 16C Hôtel Mansecal in Rue Espinasse and Hôtel d'Ulmo in Rue Ninau.

★ **Cathédrale St-Étienne** (**EY**) – Compared to St-Sernin, the cathedral appears curiously unharmonious in style. It was built over several centuries, from the 11C to the 17C, and combines the Gothic styles of both southern and northern France. As funds ran out, the nave and the upper level of the chancel were left uncompleted. In the 13C, the bishops and the chapter had a rose window inserted into the façade of the original church, which was begun in 1078. Then, in the 15C, a doorway was added. Finally, in the 16C, a rectangular belfry-keep was built, quite unlike the polygonal openwork bell-towers found throughout the region.

Enter through the doorway on the west façade.

Interior – The nave and the chancel are not quite in line with each other and do not give the impression of having been designed as a unit. This is because reconstruction of the church (after Toulouse passed under the rule of the French crown) began with the chancel, without taking the nave, built in 1209, into consideration as it was planned to demolish it. It was eventually

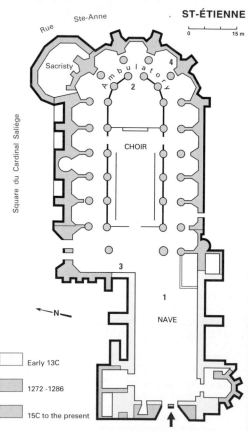

ST-ÉTIENNE

Place St-Etienne

decided to adopt a makeshift solution and link the two, thereby necessitating considerable architectural feats in what should have been the north arm of the transept (note the arrangement of the vault ribs fanning out from the supporting pillar).

The vast single nave, as wide as it is high, is the first manifestation of the southern French Gothic style and gives a good idea of the progress made in architectural techniques: St-Étienne's single vault spans 19m/62ft, and St-Sernin's Romanesque vault a mere 9m/29ft.

The austerity of its walls is alleviated by a fine collection of 16C and 17C tapestries made in Toulouse, tracing the life of St Stephen. On the keystone of the third span of the vault, note the "cross with twelve pearls" (1), the coat of arms of the counts of Toulouse, and later of the province of Languedoc.

The construction of the choir, begun in 1272, came to a halt 45 years later and the building was covered with a timber-frame roof. In 1609, the roof was destroyed by fire and replaced by the present vault, which is only 28m/91ft high, instead of the 37m/121ft anticipated in the original design.

The altarpiece adorning the high altar (2), the choir stalls, the organ case (3), and the stained glass in the five large windows in the apse date from the 17C. In the ambulatory, there are some very old stained-glass windows, notably a 15C window in the chapel immediately to the right of the axial chapel, portraying King Charles VII (wearing a crown and a blue cape with gold fleur-de-lis) and the dauphin Louis, the future Louis XI (depicted kneeling, dressed as a knight). The window is thus known as the "King of France's window" (4).

Leave by the south door and walk round the church to appreciate the robust solidity of the buttresses supporting the chancel, evidence that they were intended to support greater things...

In the middle of Place St-Étienne stands a 16C fountain – the oldest in Toulouse – known as "le Griffoul".

At the far side of Place St-Étienne, take Rue Croix-Baragnon.

Several mansions along Rue Croix-Baragnon have been restored and now house antique shops. No 24 is home to the city's Cultural Centre. From the corner of Rue Tolosane, the façade and tower of the cathedral can be seen looking back, while to the right the tower of Les Augustins rises from among some trees.

Hôtel de Fumel (Palais Consulaire) (DEY C) – This mansion houses the Chamber of Commerce. It features a fine 18C façade, at right angles, overlooking the garden.

No 15 rue Croix-Baragnon, "the oldest house in Toulouse", dating from the 13C, is distinguished by its gemel windows (it is otherwise rather rundown).

Toulouse is more than simply an ensemble of pretty, red-brick buildings and a centre for cassoulet, it is the birthplace of several famous French figures, including Jean-Pierre Rives, champion of the Toulouse rugby team, and Claude Nougaro, a late 20C troubadour. Those familiar with the little round tins of Lajaunie sweets (in aniseed and other flavours) will be interested to know that Lajaunie, a chemist, was also a native of Toulouse.

Turn north into Rue d'Alsace-Lorraine. The entrance to Les Augustins is in Rue de Metz, to the right.

★★ **Musée des Augustins** ⊘ **(DEY)** – This museum is housed in the former Augustinian monastery designed in the southern French Gothic style (14C and 15C), specifically the chapter-house and the great and small cloisters. The building facing Rue d'Alsace-Lorraine was constructed by Darcy in the 19C, following plans by Viollet-le-Duc.

Begin your visit in the charming great cloisters (14C), home to an interesting collection of paleo-Christian archeological exhibits, then the sacristy and the 14C chapel of Notre-Dame de Pitié, where 13C and 14C Gothic sculptures are displayed; and, finally, the chapter-house (late 15C) housing 15C works of art, such as the Pietà des Récollets and the celebrated Virgin and Child known as "Nostre-Dame de Grasse", with its ample, flowing drapery and original stance.

The monastery church is a typical example of southern French Gothic, its chevet with three chapels opening straight into a wide single nave, with no transept. It contains 15C, 16C and 17C paintings on religious themes (Perugino, Rubens, Murillo, Il Guercino, Simon Vouet, Nicolas Tournier etc) and some 16C and 17C sculptures.

Romanesque capital in the Musée des Augustins

In the west wing, the remarkable Toulouse and Languedoc **Romanesque sculptures★★★** (12C), mainly from St-Sernin abbey, La Daurade monastery and the chapter buildings of St-Étienne cathedral, are the most outstanding exhibits of the museum. Because of the numerous pilgrimages and the crusades, Toulouse certainly became a centre of Romanesque culture. The capitals are particularly fine: the wise and foolish Virgins, the story of Job, the death of St John the Baptist etc.

Italian, Flemish and Dutch painting is well represented, as is the French school from the 15C to the 20C. Pride of place is of course given to artists from Toulouse.

At the end of the visit, return to the cloisters where the various types of garden which would have been a feature of medieval monasteries and abbeys have been recreated. From here there is a view of the bell-tower and the nave of the former Augustinian church.

Rue St-Antoine-du-Taur leads to Place du Président-Wilson, the elegant centre of Toulouse.

ADDITIONAL SIGHTS

Bibliothèque municipale (DX) – The city library was founded in 1866, combining the libraries of the local clergy and Collège Royal, which itself had benefited from the confiscation of a dozen or so conventual libraries during the Revolution. The building is the work of Montariol and is a handsome example of 1930s architecture – note in particular the reading room, with its large windows and dome and striking ceiling of coloured glass tiles.

Rue Mage (EZ) – This is one of the best preserved streets in Toulouse, with period houses at nos 20 and 16 (Louis XIV) and no 11 (Louis XIII); the Hôtel d'Espie is an example of French Rococo (Louis XV or Régence style).

Rue Bouquières (EZ 19) – Note the splendid architecture of the Hôtel de Puivert (18C).

Rue Pharaon (DZ) – This really pretty street has a number of interesting features: the Hôtel du Capitoul Marvejol at no 47 (charming courtyard); 18C façades at no 29; turret dating from 1478 at no 21.

★★ Muséum d'Histoire Naturelle ⊘ (EZ) – *Located in the Jardin des Plantes (botanical gardens).* The natural history museum has extensive collections, most notably of ornithological, prehistoric and ethnographical exhibits.

Jardin des Plantes, Jardin Royal et Grand Rond (EZ) – These pretty, well laid out gardens make a very pleasant place for a stroll. At the southern end of the Allée Fréderic-Mistral, in the botanical gardens, stands a **monument to the Résistance** ⊘. An arrangement of lenses ensures that sunlight enters the crypt only on 19 August, the anniversary of the liberation of Toulouse.

Musée Georges-Labit ⊘ (**BU M³**) – *Southeast of city centre; see plan of conurbation.* This museum is located in the Moorish villa in which Georges Labit (1862-99), a citizen of Toulouse and enthusiastic collector of anything to do with the Orient, from India to the Far East, had assembled the artefacts he brought back from his travels. After numerous additions, the museum now displays remarkable collections of sculpture, paintings, textiles, ceramic ware and various other items reflecting the great Oriental civilizations (China, Japan, Cambodia, India, Tibet, Nepal, Thailand), as well as Egyptian antiquity and Coptic art.

Pont St-Michel and the banks of the Garonne (**DZ**) – From St-Michel bridge, a prestressed concrete construction with great simplicity of line, there is an interesting view. On a clear day, from a position between the centre of the bridge and the west bank, the outline of the Pyrenees can be seen far to the south.

From the opposite bank, the view embraces much of the city, from the Jacobins to La Dalbade, and most buildings are easily identifiable. The view of the city is at its best when the warm red tones of the brickwork are set aglow by the rays of the setting sun.

Cours Dillon (**BU 46**) and the west bank of the Garonne are a pleasantly shaded pedestrian zone, from which there are unexpected glimpses of the city.

Galerie municipale du Château d'eau ⊘ (**BU K**) – The red brick tower (1823) at the head of the Pont Neuf on the west bank of the Garonne marks the site of the pumping station which supplied Toulouse's 90 public fountains until about 1855. It was abandoned after 1870, but since 1974 the old water tower has housed a photographic gallery which runs temporary exhibitions and an information centre on the history of photography up to the present. Inside the tower, the old machinery for operating the hydraulic pump is still to be seen.

Parc toulousain (**BV**) – *Southwest of town centre; see plan of conurbation.* This park on an island in the Garonne is home to one indoor and three open-air swimming pools, a sports stadium, and exhibition and conference centres.

CHÂTEAUX AROUND TOULOUSE

There are numerous interesting castles and mansions in the vicinity of Toulouse (although they are privately owned, many are open to the public). Telephone numbers are given below for those interested in details of opening times and admission charges:

Caumont – Renaissance château; ☎ 05 62 07 94 20. *Detailed description in the Michelin Green Guide Pyrénées Aquitaine (in French).*

Fourquevaux – Château-hotel; ☎ 05 62 71 71 03.

Gaudiès – Remains of the late 13C curtain wall; classical south façade; ☎ 05 61 67 10 23.

Larra – 18C château; ☎ 05 61 82 62 51.

Larrazet – Monumental staircase with straight flights of steps; ☎ 05 61 21 68 20.

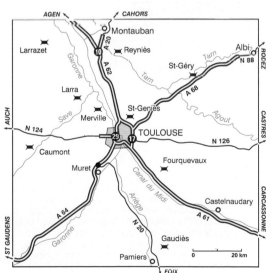

Merville – 18C château; ☎ 05 61 85 15 38.

Reyniès – Exterior open to the public; ☎ 05 63 64 04 02.

St-Geniès – Renaissance château; ☎ 05 61 74 26 45.

St-Géry – 18C château *(not open to the public).*

Grotte de TRABUC★★

Trabuc cave, the largest in the Cévennes, was inhabited in the Neolithic period and used by the Romans at the beginning of our era. More recently, during the Wars of Religion, the Camisards took refuge in its labyrinthine galleries, which proved an excellent hiding place. It was even used as a den by a band of brigands known as the Trabucaires, after the name of the type of gun they used, which in turn became the name by which the cave was known.

It was explored several times in the 19C; the most informative of these expeditions was carried out by Mazauric in 1899. But it is largely due to the investigations of G Vaucher, begun in 1945, that it is possible to visit a significant proportion of the cave. At present, about a dozen kilometres (8mi) of the large galleries have been explored.

The "Hundred thousand soldiers"

TOUR ⏲ *allow 1hr – temperature: 14°C/57°F*

A 40m/130ft long artificial corridor, drilled by miners from Alès 120m/390ft above the natural mouth of the cave, leads into the cave.

The visit reveals such treasures as the Gong chamber, with a great drapery like an elephant's ear which resonates like a gong, the *gours,* or underground lakes or hollows formed by weirs of calcite, the pipe-like concretions in the great corridor, the petrified calcite torrents coloured with oxides known as the "red cascades", and the strangely beautiful aragonite crystallizations, tinted black by manganese. Perhaps the most impressive sight of all is the remarkable underground landscape formed by the "**Hundred thousand soldiers**"★★, extraordinary concretions formed in *gours* reminiscent of the Great Wall of China. Their origin remains a mystery, but they are certainly a magnificent spectacle – the concretions stand only one or two inches high, packed close together, just like an army of footsoldiers besieging a fortified city. On the way back up to ground level, linger a while in the Lake chamber, which contains a beautiful pendant concretion shaped like an enormous butterfly, various jellyfish-shaped concretions, some eccentrics and last but by no means least the underground lake itself – "Midnight lake" – in which the level of the green-tinted waters can vary by about 25m/82ft.

The annual Michelin Red Guide France
offers comprehensive up-to-date information in a compact form.
An ideal companion on holidays, business trips or weekends away.
It is well worth buying the current edition.

Gorges de la TRUYÈRE★★

Michelin maps 76 folds 12 to 14 or 239 folds 41 and 42

Amongst the granite plateaux of upper Auvergne, the river Truyère flows through deeply sunken, narrow, sinuous gorges, in which the landscape is tree-covered and rugged. The gorges constitute one of the finest natural sights of central France. Dams, built as part of a hydroelectric power scheme, have transformed extensive stretches of the river into reservoirs, which have of course altered the appearance of the gorges, happily without spoiling their picturesque character, except when water levels are low. There is no road leading along the entire length of the valley, but many roads cut across it, providing some fine viewpoints over the river and its gorges.

The southwest stretch of the gorge is described below; for the stretch north of Laussac, see the Michelin Green Guide Auvergne – Rhône Valley.

A river captured – The Truyère once flowed north; it was a tributary of the Alagnon and, thus, of the Allier. The trail of alluvial deposits marking the river's upper course can still be seen as far as the outskirts of St-Flour; the further north, the lower their altitude and the smoother the pebbles which mark the old river bed. However, this bed is now abandoned, as the river makes a sharp bend near Garabit, to flow southwest and eventually into the Lot, making it a tributary of the Garonne. This bend is the "elbow of capture" of the upper Truyère by an old tributary of the Lot, which rose to the northeast and carved out a river bed at a lower altitude than that of the Alagnon.

An aftershock of the fold in the earth's crust from which the Pyrenees emerged lifted the plateau on which the river was flowing and split the core foundation of the Massif Central. Powerful eruptions in the Cantal sent streams of lava pouring round the volcanic massif, one of which solidified in the former Truyère valley, contributing to the river's eventual diversion to the southwest. After the Garabit "elbow", the Truyère cuts a deeper course, plunging into winding ravines to restore the balance of its profile, destroyed by the capture.

Truyère river gorge

Hydroelectric projects – The narrow valley cut by the Truyère and the resistance of its granite slopes make it an ideal location for the construction of hydroelectric dams. Moreover, the fact that there were few houses and roads in the valley made it relatively easy to acquire the necessary land and flood it to create huge reservoirs.

Construction work started in 1928. In 1933, the Brommat plant was completed, and in 1934 the Sarrans dam. The reservoir retained by this dam covers the 35km/21mi as far as Lanau bridge. A second large project was completed in 1950: the Couesque dam, retaining a reservoir 13km/8mi long. The Cambeyrac dam, which regulates the flow of the installations upstream was completed in 1957, and the Grandval dam in 1960. The construction, in 1963, of a further dam upstream of Lanau bridge made it possible fully to exploit the difference in altitude between Garabit and Entraygues-sur-Truyère.

Gorges de la TRUYÈRE

Together with other installations on some of its tributaries, such as the Bromme, the Plane, the Goul and the Selves, the Truyère hydroelectric scheme can at present produce 1 634 thousand million kWh a year. To this can be added the 1 150 thousand million kWh produced by the underground plant at Montézic, started up in 1982; this is an energy supply pumping station. All the hydroelectric plants on the Truyère are operated by remote control from the hydraulic control centre at Brive-la-Gaillarde.

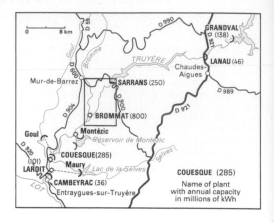

COUESQUE (285)
Name of plant
with annual capacity
in millions of kWh

ROUND TOUR FROM ENTRAYGUES-SUR-TRUYÈRE

128km/79mi – allow half a day

★ **Entraygues-sur-Truyère** – *See ENTRAYGUES-SUR-TRUYÈRE.*
Take D 34 north and cross the Truyère at the Cambeyrac dam.

The road follows the Truyère valley for about 6km/3mi. The **Cambeyrac dam**, which regulates the flow of the river, is the last of the Truyère valley hydroelectric installations, just before the river flows into the Lot. It is 14.5m/47ft high and possesses two 5 150 kW generators. Its annual output is 36 million kWh. In 1988, an additional 10 000 kW generator was installed on the east bank. A little further upstream, after a bend in the river, the Lardit hydroelectric power station can be seen on the opposite bank.

Lardit hydroelectric power station – This energy plant, with an annual output of 105 million kWh, uses water from the Selves and its tributary the Selvet, retained by the Maury dam on the Selves, south of St-Amans-des-Cots. The water is carried to the Lardit power station through a 6km/3mi long tunnel followed since 1985 by a pressure pipeline.

The valley, initially covered with meadows, vineyards and orchards, becomes increasingly rugged as the road travels north.

After Couesque bridge, on the Goul, take a road to the right which runs alongside the Truyère, leading to the Couesque plant and dam.

★ **Couesque dam** – This narrow-vault dam overhanging the river on the downstream side is 60m/196ft high. The reservoir stretches as far as the confluence of the Bromme and the Truyère, where the tail-race from the Brommat underground plant emerges. With a capacity of 56 million m³/1 978 million ft³, the reservoir also stores water from the Goul, brought here along an underground pipe 3.3km/2mi long. The power station, built 300m/330yd downstream of the dam has an annual production of 285 million kWh.

Located in the hydraulic power station, the **Espace Truyère** ⊙ traces the development of the valley's hydroelectric scheme and explains how the various plants work by means of models, presentations and video films.

Return to Couesque bridge and turn right onto D 904 heading north.

As the road leaves the floor of the valley, there are fine views looking back down onto the Goul valley, the deep Truyère gorges, the Couesque dam and its reservoir. The road reaches the plateau and passes the hamlet of **Rouens** on the right. Downhill from the church, there is a scenic view of Couesque reservoir and Phalip bridge.

Continue heading north towards Lacroix-Barrez. Before the village, take D 97 to the right.

The road drops into a deep wooded ravine. In the valley of **Vallon**, there is a fine viewpoint over the Truyère gorges. After skirting the ruined castle of Vallon, perched on a spur above the valley, the road emerges into the magnificent Truyère gorges and crosses the Couesque reservoir on the Phalip suspension bridge.

Shortly after crossing the river, make a hairpin turn to the left onto D 621.

For quite some time, the road follows the southeast bank of the Truyère which has been transformed into a reservoir by the Couesque dam downstream. The road reaches the **underground plant at Montézic**. This energy supply pumping station transforms the surplus electric power of low peak periods, into hydraulic power, which is then stored and redistributed as electric power during times of peak consumption.

Montézic reservoir, situated on the granite Plateau de la Viadène, is formed by two dams on the Plane rivulet. This reservoir, with a surface area of 245ha/605 acres and a capacity of 32.5 million m³/1 165 million ft³, serves as an upper reservoir to that at Couesque and supplies the underground plant through high pressure tunnels. From the power station, set into the heart of the cliff, a low pressure tunnel leads to the Couesque reservoir. The plant is reached along an underground tunnel off D 621 along the Truyère *(no admission to the public)*. Further upstream, the road crosses the Truyère over Valcayles bridge. Near the hamlet of Brézou are the underground plant of Brommat, built of solid granite, and the Rueyres interconnection station which both form part of the **Sarrans-Brommat** hydroelectric scheme. The Barthe (70m/230ft high) and Sarrans dams are also a part of this scheme, which is one of the most important of its kind in France. The combined power of its generators totals 596 200 kW and it produces more than a thousand million kWh per year. The D 900 drops down to the river in a series of hairpin bends and climbs the other bank once more up to the plateau.

At the Croix-l'Évêque crossroads, just before St-Geneviève-sur-Argence, turn left onto D 537 which passes through the hamlet of Orlhaguet. At a wayside cross, turn left onto D 98.

Soon after this, a lookout point provides a view of the tall wall of the Sarrans dam.

★★ **Sarrans dam** – This dam, one of the most important hydroelectric installations in the Massif Central, is 220m/722ft long, 105m/344ft high and 75m/246ft thick at its base. It is a "weight-dam", that is, it resists the force of the water

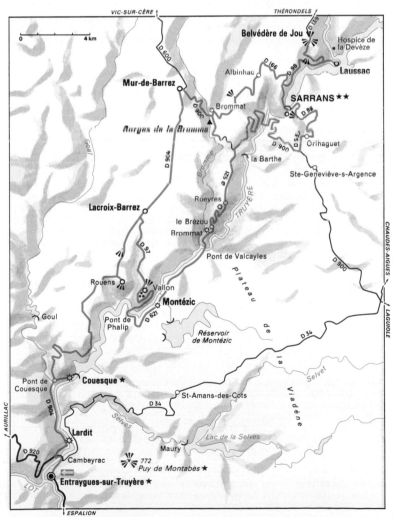

it retains by its sheer mass, but a slight curve on the upstream side acts as a vault. The reservoir is 35km/22mi long, with a surface area of 1 000ha/2 471 acres and a capacity of 296.2 million m³/10 460 million ft³. The **Sarrans plant** at the foot of the dam has four main generators, three of which are 38 500 kW and the fourth 63 500 kW, operated by remote control from Brive-la-Gaillarde.

Having passed the crest of the dam, D 98 runs alongside the reservoir as far as the outskirts of the village of Laussac, which is reached along D 537.

Laussac – The village is built on a promontory which, owing to the flooding of the valley, has become a peninsula.

Rejoin D 98 and turn right.

1.5km/1mi on from the junction, there is a fine view of the reservoir.

Continue along D 98 as far as a crossroads and turn right onto D 139.

Belvédère de Jou – After the hamlet of Jou, there is a panorama of Laussac peninsula, Devèze hospice and Sarrans reservoir.

Return to Laussac along D 98 to the left, and then take D 166 towards Albinhac and Brommat.

The road offers sweeping views of the Barrez countryside, and the Cantal and Aubrac hills. Note the pretty four-sided roofs, covered with limestone slabs arranged like fish scales, typical of the region.

Turn left at Brommat and left again onto D 900 towards St-Geneviève-sur-Argence.

Gorges de la Bromme – The road follows the course of the Bromme, a tributary of the Truyère, for a couple of miles or so, giving a good view of the stream flowing along a deepset, rugged gorge.

Turn back and return to Brommat and continue on the D 900 to Mur-de-Barrez.

Mur-de-Barrez – This pretty little town occupies a volcanic ridge between the valleys of the Goul and the Bromme. From near the ruins of the **castle** there is a good view of the surrounding region: the Cantal mountains, the Bromme valley, the Planèze and the Aubrac mountains. To the east, downhill, are the buildings of the convent of Ste-Claire, surrounded by houses typical of this region, with steeply pitched, four sided roofs. The town's **church** is Gothic in style. It was demolished as far as the transept by Calvinists. Inside, there are some interesting capitals, a 17C altarpiece and keystones, one of which (above the tribune) is shaped like a recumbent figure. Note also the Porte de l'Horloge, a gate which was once part of the town's fortified wall, and a Renaissance mansion decorated with sculpted coats of arms.

Leave Mur-de-Barrez on D 904 heading south.

The straight, level road runs across the Barrez plateau between the Goul and Bromme valleys.

Lacroix-Barrez – This is the native region of Cardinal Verdier, archbishop of Paris, who from 1930 to 1940 had over a hundred churches or chapels built around the capital. At the centre of the village, a monument was erected in 1949 to commemorate the "cardinal of building sites".

3km/2mi after Lacroix-Barrez, the D 904 provides views stretching away to the horizon of the Plateau de la Châtaigneraie to the right and the Plateau de la Viadène to the left.

Return to Entraygues on D 904.

Travelling in this direction, the views down into the Truyère gorge from the road as it cuts along the cliffs are magnificent.

Return to Entraygues-sur-Truyère.

Le VALLESPIR★

Michelin maps 86 folds 18 to 20 or 235 folds 52 and 56 or 240 folds 45 and 46

The Vallespir is the region in the eastern Pyrenees occupied by the Tech valley. Lying upstream of Amélie-les-Bains, this area with its pastoral, highland charm has a most varied, attractive appearance. It is, moreover, an area of geographical interest in that it comprises the most southern communities on French territory. Here, orchards and crops are found only on the floor of the valleys. Instead, there are forests of chestnut trees and beech, and vast expanses of pasture land.

Active industrial concerns and living traditions contribute to the region's unique character. Local festivities provide the best opportunity for watching the region's Catalan inhabitants, although the local colour of such celebrations may seem a little diminished at first by the fact that ever fewer traditional costumes are on show. Anyone fortunate enough to see the *sardana* being danced, or rather celebrated, is unlikely ever to forget the experience.

The crozier and the sword – Wilfred-le-Velu's earldom of Cerdagne was split up in 990 by right of inheritance: Bernard "Taillefer" ("iron-cutter") was given the title of count of Bésalu (a little town in Ampurdan – a plain identical to the Roussillon – south of the Albères) and received the upper Tech valley. After 1111, this family branch died out and its estates passed into the hands of the counts of Barcelona.

In the Middle Ages, the Benedictine abbey of Ste-Marie in Arles-sur-Tech was the most important religious centre in the region. By the end of the 10C, its influence further increased, owing to the transfer of the relics of the martyred Kurdish princes Sts Abdon and Sennen, still widely venerated in the area. The abbots naturally exercised a temporary jurisdiction over numerous estates. The monks, keen to exploit the upper valley of the Tech, founded an agricultural colony which soon became a little town, Prats-de-Mollo, patronised by the kings of Aragon, who appreciated its position and climate, as one of their favourite holiday resorts.

The lords of Serralongue and of Corsavy had castles and watchtowers built, which are still eye-catching.

FROM COL D'ARES TO LE BOULOU 68km/42mi – allow 5hr

★ **Col d'Ares** – Alt 1 513m/4 964ft. Situated on the border, this pass is the gateway to Spain (Ripoll, Vich, Barcelona)

On the way downhill, Mir tower, one of the highest watchtowers in Roussillon, can be seen immediately to the north. Soon afterwards, the chapel of Notre-Dame-de-Coral appears on the right. Further on, Cabrens towers come into view rising above the wooded valleys converging towards Serralongue. On the other side of Seille pass (alt 1 185m/3 887ft), there is a pleasant view of Prats de Mollo, clustered around the foot of Fort Lagarde. The road leads downhill through chestnut groves, in full view of the Canigou massif opposite and the vast meadow-covered foothills of its south face.

★ **Prats-de-Mollo** – See PRATS-DE-MOLLO.

Carry on along D 115.

Baillanouse ravine – The original road, swept away by the catastrophic floods of October 1940, was rebuilt higher up. On the left, a cavity in the side of Puig Cabrès is still visible, from which a huge landslide (6-7 million m³/212 247 million ft³) broke away, blocking the valley to a height of 40m/131ft.

Le Tech   *See ARLES SUR TECH; Excursions.*

1km/0.6mi after Le Tech, take D 44 to the right.

Serralongue – *Walk up to the church.* A nettle tree grows on the esplanade; the wood of this tree was once used for making the famous whips known as *perpignans*.

At the top of the hill stands a ruined *conjurador*, a small building with four apertures above which were alcoves housing the four Evangelists. When the harvest was threatened by storms, the parish priest would come and recite the appropriate prayers to ward off *(conjurer)* the danger, turning towards the storm clouds darkening the horizon as he did so.

Turn back and take the scenic road, D 64, to the right. At Forge-del-Mitg, turn left onto D 3.

The road is well laid out on the "shady" slopes of the Vallespir, covered in luxuriant vegetation (maples, chestnuts) and watered by numerous streams. Looking back and to the left, there is a view of the three Cabrens towers in the distance.

D 3 joins D 115, onto which you turn right.

Arles-sur-Tech – *See ARLES-SUR-TECH.*

After Arles, the road crosses from the north to the south bank of the Tech.

★ **Amélie-les-Bains-Palalda** – *See AMÉLIE-LES-BAINS-PALALDA.*

After Amélie-les-Bains, Palalda immediately comes into view on the left, spread in tiers up the steep bank of the Tech. The D 115, lined here and there with plane trees, leaves the mountainous Vallespir region to enter the Céret-le-Boulou valley.

★ **Céret** – *See CÉRET.*

Take D 618 to rejoin N 9 which leads to Le Boulou.

⊕ **Le Boulou** – *See Le BOULOU.*

Abbaye de VALMAGNE*

Michelin maps 83 fold 16 or 240 fold 26 – 8km/5mi north of Mèze

The great rose-coloured abbey of Valmagne, set in splendid isolation amid a clump of pine trees, rises serenely above the surrounding sea of Languedoc vineyards. The abbey of Valmagne was founded in 1138 by Raymond Trencavel, viscount of Béziers, who entrusted it to Benedictine monks. The monks soon linked up with Cîteaux (1159) and constructed their monastery buildings in accordance with Cistercian rule. From the 12C to the 14C, the abbey was one of the wealthiest in the south of France, housing up to 300 monks. After the Hundred Years War and the Wars of Religion, it gradually fell into ruin. In 1573, one of the commendatory abbots took sides with the Protestants, laying siege to his own abbey and killing all his monks. In the 17C and 18C, one or two wealthy abbots restored the abbey buildings. Cardinal de Bonzi transformed it into a sumptuous palace. However, by the outbreak of the Revolution, decline had set in and only five monks were in residence. Valmagne was sacked, and then sold off. The new owner turned the abbey estate into a commercial vineyard, and his successor, the count of Turenne, devoted his efforts to restoring the abbey buildings to their former elegance.

Since 1975, the Association des Amis de Valmagne has been in charge of the restoration and running of the site. It is possible to taste and buy the wine produced in the abbey grounds.

TOUR ⊙ *allow 1hr*

Church – Begun in the mid 13C and completed in the 14C, the abbey church, with its architecture and soaring nave, is an example of a classic Gothic style, as far removed from the traditions of Languedoc as it is from those of the

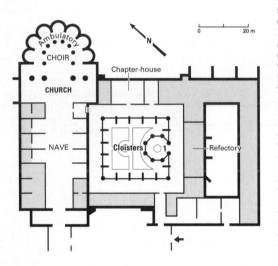

Cistercians. Its dimensions recall those of the cathedrals of northern France (23m/75ft high and 83m/272ft long), as do the façade flanked by towers, the nave supported by flying buttresses, the size and number of the windows in its walls (unfortunately the clerestory windows were blocked up in the 17C) and the semicircular chancel with its great three-pointed arches and ambulatory with radiating chapels. Since the Revolution, the church has been used as a store house for the ageing of wine, which has enabled it to be kept in good repair.

Monastic buildings – These date in part from the founding of the abbey in the 12C, but have been extensively restored since the 13C. The **cloisters**, rebuilt in the 14C, are charming with their golden-coloured stonework. There is a minimum of decoration in the galleries and openings onto the cloister garth. The 12C **chapter-house** is slightly more ornate, however, containing a variety of decoration on the colonnettes and capitals, and the **fountain** (1) is delightful, surmounted by an elegant 18C structure consisting of eight ribs linked by a pendant keystone.

The vast **refectory** *(open only for concerts)* features a remarkable Renaissance chimneypiece.

VAREN

Population 870
Michelin map 79 fold 19 and 235 fold 19 – 16km/10mi east of St-Antonin-Noble-Val
Local map see ST-ANTONIN-NOBLE-VAL

The charming and picturesque old town of Varen stands on the north bank of the Aveyron, its houses clustered around the Romanesque church, which is protected by large-scale defences.

Enter the old part of town from the south. The old fortified gateway, the Porte El-Faoure, leads into a network of narrow streets lined with half-timbered and clay-walled houses with overhanging upper storeys and flat roofs covered with half-cylinder tiles.

Château – This is a massive rectangular keep topped by a machicolated watchpath and flanked by a corbelled turret. It was here that the Lord-Prior of Varen shut himself up when challenging the decisions of the Bishop of Rodez to prove his complete independence. This was brought to an end in 1553 by the Council of Trent which replaced the monks in the Benedictine priory with a more tractable college of 12 canons.

★ **Église St-Pierre** – The church, part of the town's defences, was built at the end of the 11C. Its west face was incorporated into the fortified town wall. The side door was knocked through in 1758 and the present doorway in 1802, when the moats were filled in. The old doorway, which was walled up in the 16C, once led to the old town through the church's east end; two archaic capitals still remain depicting St Michael slaying the dragon *(left)* and Samson opening the lion's jaws *(right)*. A plain square bell-tower rises above the flat chancel between two semicircular apsidal chapels. The south aisle is supported by huge flying buttresses and has numerous windows.

The main body of the building is pure Romanesque in style and consists of a long nave of nine bays separated from the side aisles by square pillars. The chancel and apsidal chapels contain 17C stalls and feature some interesting capitals with plant motifs, tracery, animals and cherubs surrounding the Tree of Life.

VERNET-LES-BAINS★

Population 1 489
Michelin maps 86 fold 17 or 235 fold 51 – Local map see Le CANIGOU

Vernet's **setting**★, at the foot of the wooded lower slopes of the Canigou, on which the bell-tower of St-Martin can be seen, is one of the most refreshing in the eastern Pyrenees. The roar of the Cady torrent in the background lends an unexpectedly mountainous note to this otherwise Mediterranean setting, of which Rudyard Kipling was fond. The thermal spa clinic, which doubles as a rehabilitation centre for those suffering from problems of the neural or motor systems, specialises in the treatment of rheumatism and diseases of the ear, nose and throat.

The narrow sloping streets of Old Vernet, on the east bank of the Cady, are a pleasant place for a stroll.

Vernet-les-Bains

E. Baret

Old town centre – From Place de la République, take Rue J-Mercadet, lined with colourful little houses bright with flowers, up to the top of the hill on which the church stands.

Église St-Saturnin ⊘ – The church's main interest lies in its picturesque site, in full view of the upper Cady cirque and the tower of St-Martin.
The 12C chapel of Notre-Dame-del-Puig, backed onto a fortified castle (reconstructed), is worth a visit for the furniture and various other objects of interest it contains: a font (opposite the entrance), a predella of the Crucifixion which used to be part of an altarpiece painted in the 15C, a Romanesque altar table and an impressive 16C Crucifix hanging in the apse.

EXCURSIONS

★★ **Abbaye de St-Martin-du-Canigou** – *3km/2mi south as far as Casteil. See ST-MARTIN-DU-CANIGOU.*

 ★ **Col de Mantet** – *20km/12.5mi to the southwest – allow 1hr. The cliff road is very steep and narrow (overtaking very difficult) upstream of Py.*
After leaving Vernet to the west, the road (D 27) climbs, from Sahorre on, the Rotja valley first amid apple trees then along a gorge sunk into the granite rock. Above **Py**, a pretty little village 1 023m/3 356ft above sea level, the road scales steep slopes with granite outcrops bristling here and there. After 3.5km/2mi, in a wide bend in the road, a **lookout point★** gives a good view of the village with its red roofs and the Canigou.

The Mantet pass opens up at an altitude of 1 761m/5 777ft, near the evergreen forest of La Ville. On the opposite slope, the strikingly austere site of **Mantet**, an almost deserted village (population 12), can be seen huddled in a dip.

Le VIGAN

Population 4 523
Michelin map 80 fold 16 or 240 fold 14
Local maps see Massif de l'AIGOUAL and Les GRANDS CAUSSES

This little town in the Cévennes, well situated on the southern slope of Mont Aigoual in the Arre valley which, at the confluence of the Souls and the Coudoulous, is particularly fertile, is an industrial centre (hosiery, silk spinning mills).
Le Vigan is the native town of two French heroes, one of whom is more famous than the other, although both are of comparable moral stature: Chevalier d'Assas and Sergent Triaire. The town has had a statue built in memory of each.

Local heroes – **Louis d'Assas** (1733-1760), an aristocrat, was a captain in the regiment of the Chasseurs d'Auvergne, who met an untimely, but heroic death at the battle of Clostercamp during the Hanover campaign. While reconnoitring, he was ambushed by the enemy, but, ignoring their threatening bayonets, he managed to cry out and warn his compatriots of impending attack before being struck down. This heroic act, which had not been officially recognised, was rescued from oblivion by Voltaire in 1768. The house where the Chevalier d'Assas was born is still standing in the Boulevard du Plan d'Auvergne.

Sergent Triaire (b 1771) managed to pack a fair number of daring feats into his military career as a gunner with the Bourgogne regiment. In 1793, he was among the troops fighting the English at Toulon, playing a leading role on the attack on Fort Malbousquet, then he participated in the Italian campaign, holding an abandoned redoubt against the enemy for two hours with only a few helpers. Finally, during action in Egypt, finding himself in the fort at El-Arich as it was overrun by the Turks, he shut himself in the powder magazine and blew the fort and everyone in it sky-high.

SIGHTS

Promenade des Châtaigniers – This pleasant avenue is shaded by enormous, ancient chestnut trees.

Statues of Louis d'Assas and Triaire – The Chevalier's statue is on Place d'Assas, and Triaire's is on Place de l'Hôtel de Ville.

Old Bridge – The bridge, which dates from before the 13C, spans the Arre. There is a good view of it from a platform on the river bank, upstream of the bridge.

 ★ **Musée cévenol** ⊘ – This museum is located in an old 18C silk spinning mill and is almost entirely devoted to the popular crafts and traditions of the Cévennes. The Salle des Métiers displays traditional crafts: basket weaving, wickerwork,

Musée cévenol

gold panning, tinsmithing etc. There are also reconstructions of craftsmen's workshops and a typical Cévennes interior. A room is devoted to André Chamson (1900-83), a writer from the Cévennes, who set some of his novels in the foothills of the Aigoual. The Salle du Temps is devoted to history, from the dawn of time (geology, prehistory) until the time of the Reformation and the 19C, represented by a collection of silk costumes from the Cévennes.

EXCURSIONS

► ► **Col des Mourèzes** – *5km/3mi north.* Good view from pass (alt 560m/1 837ft).

► ► **Arre valley** – *West along D 999.* Pretty river valley; from Bez a tiny winding road leads to the *village perché* of **Esparon**.

VILLEFRANCHE-DE-CONFLENT★

Population 261
Michelin maps 86 fold 17 or 235 fold 51

Villefranche-de-Conflent, which was founded in 1090 by Guillaume Raymond, count of Cerdagne, occupies a remarkable site, on the confluence of the Cady and the Têt, closely surrounded by rock cliffs, which in days gone by provided vantage points for snipers from which people in the village streets were easy prey.

From the time of the treaty of Corbeil (1258), this strategic stronghold acted as a forward bastion of the kingdom of Aragon in the face of the enemy lines of the "five sons of Carcassonne". Villefranche was a fortified town from the start. Its fortifications were improved over the centuries and finally completed in the 17C by Vauban. From the treaty of the Pyrenees (1659) to 1925, it was occupied by a French garrison.

The quarries in the area provided the pink marble enhancing numerous monuments both in the village and throughout Roussillon.

The fair of St-Luc, which was first held in 1303, is evidence of the town's economic importance, particularly in the Middle Ages, derived from the dyeing and selling of cloth.

★THE FORTIFIED TOWN *2hr*

Park the car outside the ramparts, in the car park situated by the confluence of the Têt and the Cady.

Go through the fortified wall at the Porte de France, built in Louis XVI's reign, to the left of the old gateway used by the counts.

Ramparts ⊘ – *Entrance at no 32-34, rue St-Jacques.*
The tour of the ramparts takes in two storeys of galleries one above the other: the lower, dating from the construction of the fortress in the 11C; and the upper, the watch path, dating from the 17C.

In the 13C and 14C, round towers were built adjoining the curtain walls (early 11C-late 12C). Then in the 17C, six bastions were added, which, starting clockwise from the Porte de France, have the following names: Corneilla, Montagne (Mountain), Reine (Queen), Roi (King), Boucherie (Butcher's) and Dauphin.

After returning to the Porte de France, walk through the village along Rue St-Jean (note the 14C wooden statue of St John the Evangelist) with its 13C and 14C houses, many of which still feature their original porches with rounded or pointed arches.

There are some fine wrought-iron shop signs.

Église St-Jacques – The church, which dates from the 12C and 13C, comprises two parallel naves. Enter the church through the doorway with four columns and a cabled archivolt; the capitals are by the school of St-Michel-de-Cuxa.

Watchtower with Fort Liberia in the background

In the left nave, the pink marble font is quite deep, as baptism by total immersion was practised in Catalonia until the 14C. A 14C marble Virgin and Child, Notre-Dame-de-Bon-Succès, is invoked against epidemics; the Child holds a piece of fruit in his right hand, and a bird in his left. Above the altar in the small nave is an altarpiece (1715) dedicated to Notre-Dame-de-Vie by Sunyer.

In the right nave, the central side chapel houses a large 14C Christ on the cross, crafted in the realistic Catalan tradition. The other side chapels contain some interesting Baroque altarpieces.

At the back of the church, as in many Spanish churches, is the west choir, known as the choir of the stalls; these date from the 15C (Flamboyant rosettes on the cheekpieces); on the podium lies a recumbent figure of Christ, a poignant example of 14C popular art. The statue of Joseph of Arimathea was added later.

Porte d'Espagne – This gateway, like the Porte de France, was refurbished as a monumental entrance during Louis XVI's reign.

The machinery for operating the old drawbridge is still in evidence.

★ **Fort Liberia** ⊙ – Overlooked as it is by the Belloc mountain, the town was rather too exposed to attack from any enemy encamped above it. Therefore, from 1679 when he was in charge of the project to fortify the town, Vauban planned to protect it by building a fort.

This fort, equipped with a cistern and powder magazines, clearly illustrates some of Vauban's strategic defensive designs. It was modified during the 19C (the entrance was moved). Most notably, the "stairway of a thousand steps" (there are in fact 734) was built from pink Conflent marble to link the fort to the town by the little fortified St-Pierre bridge over the Têt.

In order to follow the line of the steeply sloping ground, the fortress consists of three sections one above the other. The highest of these, towards the mountain, is shaped like the prow of a ship and protected by a moat. A gallery pierced in the counterscarp reinforces the defences. The pavilion, with a covered balcony, contains a bread oven on the ground floor and in the basement a tiny room in which criminals were incarcerated, in some cases for many years.

As you walk round the fort, note the height of the stone walls surmounted with brick and the wrought-iron rails.

From the fort, there are **wonderful views**★★ of the valleys below and the Canigou.

We recommend taking the "stairway of a thousand steps" back down into the village.

ADDITIONAL SIGHTS

Grotte des Canalettes ⊘ – *Car park 700m/770yd south, below the Vernet road.* The concretions in this cave assume an amazing variety of shapes: petrified calcite torrents, eccentrics. Some of the finest include the Table, a natural hollow *(gour)* which gradually got filled up with calcite, and some dazzling white draperies.

Grotte des Grandes Canalettes ⊘ – This cave forms part of the same network as the Canalettes cave. The reception hall (display of geodes) opens into a manmade gallery leading into an area of petrification, the Fountain chamber, the Cupula corridor, the Balcony chamber, the Lake of Atolls, the "Armandines" (columns with flat platforms) and the Angkor chamber. The Balcony of Shadows, at the end of the tour, overlooks an abyss and borders the chamber of the Red Dome.

Cova Bastera ⊘ – This cave, situated on the Andorra road opposite the ramparts, is at the far end of the Canalettes network. It reveals Vauban's underground fortification system and the various phases of occupation of the site, portrayed in life-size tableaux.

Every year
*the **Michelin Red Guide France***
revises its selection of hotels and restaurants which

– *are pleasant, quiet, secluded;*
– *offer an exceptional, interesting or extensive view;*
– *have a tennis court, swimming pool or private beach;*
– *have a private garden...*

It is worth buying the current edition.

VILLEFRANCHE-DE-ROUERGUE★

Population 12 291
Michelin maps 79 fold 20 or 235 fold 15

On the border of the Rouergue and Quercy regions, the ancient bastide of Villefranche-de-Rouergue, with its rooftops clustered round the foot of the massive tower of Notre-Dame church, lies in the bottom of a valley surrounded by green hills, on the confluence of the Aveyron and the Alzou.

Trade and prosperity – Its situation near the Causse and the Ségala, at the crossroads of major routes used since the days of Antiquity, made Villefranche an important trade centre during the Middle Ages. It was also a stopping place for pilgrims on their way to Santiago de Compostela. In the 15C, Charles V granted the town the right to mint money, and silver and copper mines added to the town's wealth, as it prospered in its function as seat of the Rouergue seneschalsy and capital of Haute Guyenne.

Villefranche is now a centre of the farm-produce and metallurgy (bolts) industries.

SIGHTS

★ **The Bastide** – Villefranche was founded in 1099 by Raymond IV de Saint-Gilles, count of Toulouse, on the south bank of the Aveyron. The town enjoyed a new phase of expansion when, in 1252, Alphonse de Poitiers, brother of St Louis, decided to build a new town on the north bank of the river. This was built with the geometric layout typical of a bastide and completed in 1256. Despite the disagreement between the founder and the bishop of Rodez, who went so far as to excommunicate any newcomers, the town's population soon grew.

With the destruction of its moats, its ramparts and its fortified gates, Villefranche has now lost some of its medieval appearance, although it has kept many of the features of a bastide with its central square and its grid street plan.

★ **Place Notre-Dame** – This fine square, at the heart of the town and always buzzing with life on market days, is framed by houses with covered arcades, some of which have retained their mullioned windows and stone turrets. On one side of the square the tall, solid shape of the old collegiate church can be seen. Go round the arcades *(avoiding the cars)* to take a closer look at the arches and old sculpted doorways. In front of the terrace overlooking the square to the north stands a large ironwork figure of Christ. The whole scene is reminiscent of Spain, which inspired André Malraux to shoot some scenes from his film *L'Espoir (Hope)* here.

Market day in Place Notre-Dame

At the corner of Rue Marcellin-Fabre and the square, there is a lovely 15C half-timbered house facing the street; the central section, which is seven storeys high, houses a staircase lit through mullioned windows. This staircase can be entered through a fine **stone door** on which the lower part of the canopy is adorned with sculpted scrolls and foliage.

On Rue du Sergent-Boriès, south of the square, the first **house** on the right features another fine staircase tower (late 15C), with pilasters and a carved tympanum.

Maison du Président Raynal – This has a fine 15C façade with adjoining windows, on three storeys, in the Romanesque tradition.

Maison Dardennes – *Next to the Maison du Président Raynal.* At the far end of the courtyard, a Renaissance staircase tower features two galleries adorned with sculpted portraits, in vogue at the time of its construction.

★ **Église Notre-Dame** – The construction of this church, which began with the apse in 1260, lasted for over three centuries, with varying degrees of luck. The belfry-porch, 59m/193ft high, bears witness to the rivalry between Villefranche-de-Rouergue and Rodez, with each town intending their cathedral spire to be the highest. As far as can be judged from the massive foundations of its tower, Villefranche must have harboured pretty fierce ambitions; war and lack of money however prevented further efforts, and in 1585 the bell-tower was covered by the present roof. With its powerful corner buttresses adorned with pinnacles, this belfry-porch, beneath which a road passes, resembles a fortress. On the second storey, a balustraded gallery runs all around the sides of the tower, whether set back or protruding, also successfully negotiating the buttresses.

A doorway surmounted by a gable ornamented with openwork leads into the spacious single nave lined with chapels tucked in between the interior buttresses, as was customary in medieval southern French Gothic architecture. In the north arm of the transept, the altar features a marble medallion attributed to the school of Pierre Puget, representing the Visitation. The chancel, into which light is shed through tall narrow windows including two 15C stained-glass windows donated by Charles VII, contains 36 oak stalls from the workshop of André Sulpice (1473-87), which unfortunately were damaged during the Wars of Religion. Note the carving on the panels (the Virgin Mary, the prophets) and on the misericords (mythical animals, figures etc). To the left of the entrance, the font is surrounded by an interesting ironwork railing.

Chapelle des Pénitents Noirs ⓥ – This chapel, which is surmounted by a curious double turret, was built during the 17C to serve as an oratory for the Black Penitent brotherhood. This brotherhood was founded, in 1609, at a time of renewed religious fervour following the Wars of Religion. It attracted up to 200 members and flourished until 1789; it ceased to exist in 1904. The chapel, in the shape of a Greek cross, is decorated with a painted ceiling, the work of a local artist. It contains an 18C altarpiece, in gold leaf, depicting scenes from the Passion. The sacristy contains 18C priestly ornaments, the brotherhood's first register, the great processional cross, together with cowls and staffs decorated with religious scenes which were carried by the Penitents.

★ **Musée Urbain-Cabrol** ⓥ – The collections of Urbain Cabrol on archeology, history, and the popular traditions of Villefranche and the region are on display in an elegant Louis XV mansion.

In front of the museum stands a fine 14C fountain, after which the square has been named.

★ Ancienne Chartreuse St-Sauveur ⊙ – *Get there via ③ on the town plan.* This charterhouse, founded in 1451 by Vézian-Valette, a wealthy local merchant, was built in eight years of continuous effort, which resulted in an almost perfectly consistent Gothic style. At the Revolution, it became public property and would have been demolished, had not the municipality of Villefranche bought it for use as a hospital.

Chapelle des Étrangers – This chapel used to stand outside the charterhouse wall. It housed pilgrims on their way to Santiago de Compostela and was also used for celebrating mass with the local churchgoers. It has fine stellar vaulting.

Great Cloisters – This is one of the largest cloisters in France (66m x 44m/216ft x 144ft). It has strikingly harmonious perspectives. The 13 houses of the Carthusian friars opened out from it. Each comprised four rooms, two on the ground floor, used for storing wood and as a workshop, and two on the upper floor, used as an oratory (known as "Ave Maria") and bedroom. The house was framed by a small garden.

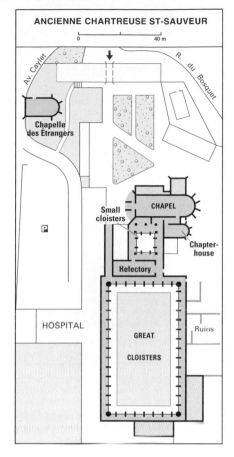

ANCIENNE CHARTREUSE ST-SAUVEUR

Small Cloisters – This is the only authentic "cloisters", in the strictly monastic sense (gallery with communal buildings opening onto it). It is a masterpiece of Flamboyant Gothic, with intersecting rib vaulting adorned with highly ornate keystones, window openings decorated with elegant tracery and culs-de-lampe embellishing the points from which the arches spring. At the entrance to the refectory, a fountain depicting the "Washing of the Feet" is evidence of the influence of the Burgundian school.

Refectory – In accordance with the rule of the order, it was used by the Carthusian friars only on Sundays and for special feast days; it was a vast rectangular room with three bays with intersecting rib vaulting. The stone **pulpit★** with its balustrade decorated in the Flamboyant Gothic style was set into the thickness of the wall. Carthusians never speak in the refectory; every year, they listen to nearly the whole of the Bible, either in church, or during communal meals.

Chapter-house – This is lit through 16C stained glass windows depicting, in the centre, the Shepherds being told of the Birth of Christ, and the founders on either side.

Chapel – A large porch leads into a nave with three bays and a chancel with a polygonal apse. The leaves of the chapel door depict two Carthusian friars bearing the arms of the founders. Other interesting decorative features are the late-15C stalls by the master cabinet-maker André Sulpice, a Louis XV style altar in gilded wood, and a Flamboyant Gothic alcove at the foot of which lie the tombs of the founder and his wife.

*The annual **Michelin Red Guide France** gives the addresses and telephone numbers of main car dealers, tyre specialists, and garages which do general repairs and offer a 24-hour breakdown service. It is well worth buying the current edition.*

Vallée de la VIS*

Michelin maps 80 folds 15 and 16 or 240 folds 14, 15 and 18

The river Vis rises 997m/3 271ft above sea level at the Col des Tempêtes, in the Lingas mountains on the south face of the Aigoual massif. Initially it gushes down the granite slopes as a mountain torrent, but at Alzon it undergoes a change in appearance as it arrives in the limestone countryside of the *causses*.

FROM ALZON TO GANGES 57km/35mi – allow 2hr

Downriver of Alzon, the road (D 814) drops to the floor of the valley, running through woods of oak and fir trees, between valley sides which gradually become steeper. It crosses the river as fords once or twice. Banks of iron-bearing limestone appear, and the remnants of terrace cultivation can be seen. The Vis makes wider and wider meanders on the flat valley floor. The D 113 runs along the floor of the valley to Vissec and crosses a bridge over the river, which is frequently dried up at this point.

Vissec – The aridity of the surrounding countryside, and the bleached white of the rocks lend this remote spot a slightly unsettling character. The village squats in the bottom of the river gorge and consists of two districts, each on an outcrop, one of which is almost completely encircled by the Vis. There is an old castle.

★ **Cirque de Vissec** – During the climb up to Blandas *(gradient 9 %)*, there is a view of the gorge with its bare cliff walls. The Vissec cirque, much less impressive than that of Navacelles, is nonetheless an attractive sight for anyone who loves wild and rugged landscapes. The river's flow picks up downstream of Lafoux spring, a resurgence of the Vis and the Virenque, which "got lost" somewhere back near Alzon.
The road reaches Blandas across the bleak limestone plateau.

★★★ **Cirque de Navacelles** – *See Cirque de NAVACELLES.*

After La Baume-Auriol, the road continues to St-Maurice-Navacelles, where you should turn left towards Ganges.

Further along, the road plunges downhill in a series of hairpin bends, passing the Rau de Fontenilles, heading towards the Vis gorge. At the start of the downhill stretch to Madières, there is a good view of the gorge.

★★ **Gorges de la Vis** – Beyond Madières, the road goes through nursery gardens thick with evergreen trees. It sticks closely to the bank of the Vis, which cuts a pretty course between the tall dolomitic cliffs of the Causse de Blandas, on the left, and the slopes of Séranne mountain, on the right. After the forester's lodge at Grenouillet, scattered vines, mulberry bushes and olive trees can be seen growing to the side of the road. After Claux, note the ruins of the Château de Castelas, which can be seen clinging to a cliff at the mouth of a ravine ahead and to the right.
After Gorniès, a bridge spans the Vis. Look out for a lovely view of **Beauquiniès**, a pretty terraced village, and then of the **Roc de Senescal**, which juts out like a ship's prow from the slope on the left. The valley becomes narrow and rugged, before running into the Hérault gorge. Carry on along the banks of the Hérault to Le Pont and Ganges.

The Via Domitia

The Via Domitia is the oldest of the Roman roads built in Gaul. It was named after the Consul of the Roman province of Gallia Narbonensis, Domitius Ahenobarbus, who had it built in 118-117 BC at the time the province was founded.
Following an ancient route once used by the Ligurians and Iberians, the Via Domitia ran from Beaucaire (Gard) to Le Perthus (Pyrénées-Orientales), forming a communications route between Rome and Spain. Beyond the Rhône, the Via Domitia led into the Via Aurelia. Spanned by bridges and punctuated along its length by milestones marking every Roman mile (1 481.5m) and staging posts, the Via Domitia linked Beaucaire (Ugernum), Nîmes (Nemausus), Béziers (Julia Baeterrae), Narbonne (Narbo Martius) and Perpignan (Ruscino).
Originally intended for military use, to enable Roman legions to reach the furthest outposts of the Empire, Roman roads also aided the transportation of commercial goods and the spread of new ideas.

Michelin Green Guides are revised regularly.
Use the most recent edition to ensure a successful holiday.

Practical
information

Planning your trip

Passport – Visitors entering France must be in possession of a valid national passport. Citizens of one of the European Union countries only need a national identity card. In case of loss or theft report to your country's embassy or consulate and the local police. A leaflet entitled *Get It Right Before You Go*, on the do's and don't's of staying in France, is available from the French Tourist Office.

Visa – No **entry visa** is required for European Union, US, Canadian and New Zealand citizens as long as their stay in France does not exceed 3 months. Australians require a visa and should apply for one at the nearest French consulate. Citizens of other countries, check with a French consulate or travel agent.
US citizens should obtain the booklet *Your Trip Abroad* (US$1.25), which provides useful information on visa requirements, customs regulations, medical care etc. for international travellers. Contact the Superintendent of Documents, PO Box 371954, Pittsburgh, PA 15250-7954, ☎ (202) 512-1800.

Customs – Apply to the Customs Office (UK) for a leaflet entitled *A Guide for Travellers* on customs regulations and the full range of duty-free allowances. The US Customs Service, PO Box 7407, Washington, DC 20044, ☎ (202) 927-5580, offers a free publication *Know Before You Go* for US residents. There are no customs formalities for holidaymakers bringing caravans into France for a stay of less than 6 months. No customs document is necessary for pleasure boats and outboard motors for a stay of less than 6 months, but the registration certificate should be kept on board.

French Tourist Offices – For information, brochures, maps and assistance in planning a trip to France, travellers should contact the official tourist office in their own country:

Australia-New Zealand
French Tourist Office, BNP Building, 12 Castlereagh Street, Sydney, NSW 2000.
☎ (2)-9231-5244, Fax (2)-9231-8682.

Canada
Maison de la France, 1981 Av McGill College, Suite 940, Montreal, QUE H3A 2W9.
☎ (514) 288-4264, Fax (514) 845-4868/(416) 767-6755.

Eire
French Tourist Office, 35 Lower Abbey St, Dublin 1,
☎ (1) 703-40-46, Fax (1) 874-73-24.

United Kingdom
French Tourist Office, 178 Piccadilly, London W1V 0AL,
☎ (0891) 244-123 (France Information Line, £0.50/min),
email *piccadilly@mdlf.demon.co.uk*

United States
France On Call Hotline: ☎ 900-990-0040 (US$0.50/min) for information on hotels, restaurants and transportation.
East Coast: 444 Madison Avenue, 16th floor, New York, NY 10022.
☎ (212) 838-7800, Fax (212) 838-7855.
Mid-West: 676 North Michigan Avenue, Suite 3360, Chicago, IL 60611-2819.
☎ (312) 751-7800, Fax (312) 337-6339.
West Coast: 9454 Wilshire Boulevard, Suite 715, Beverly Hills, CA 90212-2967.
☎ (310) 271-2693, Fax (310) 276-2835.

Travelling to France

By air – The various international and other independent airlines operate services to **Paris** (Roissy-Charles de Gaulle and Orly airports), **Montpellier** and **Toulouse**. Check with your travel agent, however, before booking direct flights, as it is sometimes cheaper to travel via Paris. There are air links from Paris to Montpellier, Béziers-Agde and Toulouse (Air Inter Europe, part of Air France), to Rodez (TAT, charter flights through Nouvelles Frontières (Paris) ☎ 01 42 66 92 00 or (UK) ☎ (0171) 629 7772) and Castres (TAT).
Contact airline companies and travel agents for details of package tour flights with a rail or coach link-up as well as Fly-Drive schemes.

By rail – British Rail and French Railways (SNCF) operate a daily service via the Channel Tunnel on Eurostar in 3hr between **London** (Waterloo International Station, ☎ (0345) 881-881) and **Paris** (Gare du Nord) – bookings and information: ☎ (0990) 330-003. There are trains from **Paris** (Gare de Lyon) to Montpellier (4hr 30min), Paris (Gare Montparnasse) to Toulouse (5hr) and Paris (Gares d'Austerlitz, de Lyon or Montparnasse) to Perpignan (6hr).

There are rail passes offering unlimited travel and group travel tickets offering services for parties. **Eurodomino Rover** tickets for unlimited rail travel over 3, 5 or 10 days are available in the UK, along with other kinds of tickets. Information and bookings, from The Rail Shop (Rail Europe), 179 Piccadilly, London, W1V 0BA, ☎ (0990) 300-003, or British Rail International, PO Box 303, Victoria Station, London SW1V 1JY, ☎ (0990) 848-848, Fax (0171) 839-3341, and from travel agencies. **Eurail pass, Flexipass** and **Saverpass** are just some of the options available in the US for travel in Europe and must be purchased in the US from Eurail USA Inc. ☎ 888 387 2457 (toll free within the USA).

Tickets bought in France must be validated *(composter)* by using the orange automatic date-stamping machines at the platform entrance (failure to do so may result in a fine).

A worthwhile investment is the **Thomas Cook European Rail** timetable, which gives train schedules throughout France (and Europe) as well as useful information on rail travel.

> The French railway company SNCF operates a telephone information, reservation and prepayment service in English from 7am to 10pm (French time). In France call ☎ 08 36 35 35 39 (when calling from outside France, drop the initial 0).

By coach – The region described in this guide can be reached by coach via Paris. Eurolines has services via Avignon and Nîmes to Perpignan (24hr), on the way to Spain. For further information, contact:

London: 52 Grosvenor Gardens, Victoria, London SW1W 0AU, ☎ (01582) 404511 (information), (0990) 143219 (ticket sales).

Paris: 28 Avenue du Général de Gaulle, 93541 Bagnolet. ☎ 01 49 72 51 51.

By car – Drivers from the British Isles can travel to the southwest of France by car, making use of the numerous cross-Channel services (passenger and car-ferries, hovercraft and SeaCat operating across the English Channel and St George's Channel and Le Shuttle via the Channel Tunnel). For details contact travel agencies or:

Brittany Ferries, The Brittany Centre, Wharf Road, Portsmouth, Hants PO2 8RU. ☎ (0990) 360360, Fax (01705) 873237.

Hoverspeed, Western Docks, Dover, Kent CT17 9TG. ☎ (01304) 240241, Fax (01304) 240088.

Irish Ferries, 50 West Norland Street, Dublin 2. ☎ (1) 6-610-511.

P&O European Ferries, Channel House, Channel View Road, Dover, Kent CT17 9TJ. ☎ (0990) 980980, Fax (01304) 223464.

Sally Line, Argyle Centre, York Street, Ramsgate, Kent CT11 9DS. ☎ (0990) 595522, Fax (01843) 589329.

Sea France Ltd, Eastern Dock, Dover, Kent CT16 1JA, ☎ (01304) 212696, Fax (01304) 240033.

Le Shuttle, Customer Services Centre, PO Box 300, Folkestone, Kent CT19 4QW, ☎ (0990) 353535.

Stena Line, Charter House, Park Street, Ashford, Kent TN24 8EX. ☎ (0990) 707070, Fax (01233) 202361.

To choose the most suitable route between one of the ports along the north coast of France and your destination, use the Michelin Motoring Atlas France, Michelin map 911 (which gives travel times and mileage) or Michelin maps from the 1:200 000 series with the yellow covers *(see page 1)*.

Motoring in France

Documents – Nationals of the European Union countries require a full valid **national driving licence**. Nationals of non-EU countries should obtain an **international driving licence** (obtainable in the US from the American Automobile Association, cost for members: US$10, for non-members US$22). Motorists must carry with them the vehicle's **registration papers** (logbook) and a current insurance certificate. A nationality plate of the approved size should be displayed near the registration plate on the back of the vehicle.

Insurance – Insurance cover is compulsory and although an international insurance certificate (green card) is no longer a legal requirement in France for vehicles registered in Great Britain, it is the most effective proof of insurance cover and is internationally recognised by the police and other authorities. Most British insurance policies give the minimum third party cover required in France (check with your insurance company) – but be warned that this amounts to less than it would in the UK. Certain UK motoring organisations (AA, RAC) offer special accident insurance and breakdown service schemes for members (the AA also has a scheme for non-members), and motorists should check available schemes with their own insurance company.

Members of the American Automobile Association should obtain the free brochure Offices To Serve You Abroad. The affiliated organisation for France is the Automobile Club National, 5, rue Auber, 75009 Paris, ☎ 01 44 51 53 99.

Highway code – The minimum age to drive in France is **18 years** old. Traffic drives on the right. It is compulsory for the front-seat and back-seat passengers to wear **seat belts** where they are fitted. Children under the age of 10 should not travel in the front of the car. Full or dipped headlights must be switched on in poor visibility and at night; use side lights only when the vehicle is stationary. Headlight beams should be adjusted for driving on the right. It is illegal to drive with faulty lights in France, so it is advisable to take a spare set of bulbs with you.

In the case of a **breakdown**, a red warning triangle or hazard warning lights are obligatory. Drivers should watch out for unfamiliar road signs and take great care on the road. In built-up areas **priority** must be ceded to vehicles coming **from the right**. However, traffic on main roads outside built-up areas (indicated by a yellow diamond sign) and on roundabouts has priority. Vehicles must come to a complete stop at stop signs and when the lights turn red at road junctions (where they may filter to the right only if indicated by a flashing amber arrow).

The regulations on **drinking and driving** (maximum permissible blood alcohol content: 0.05%) and **speeding** are strictly enforced – usually by an on-the-spot fine and/or confiscation of the vehicle.

Speed limits

Although liable to modification, these are as follows:
- toll motorways *(péage)* 130kph/80mph (110kph/68mph when raining);
- dual carriage roads and motorways without tolls 110kph/68mph (100kph/62mph when raining);
- other roads 90kph/56mph (80kph/50mph when raining) and in towns 50kph/31mph;
- outside lane on motorways during daylight, on level ground and with good visibility, minimum speed limit of 80kph/50mph.

Parking regulations – In town there are zones where parking is either restricted or subject to a fee; tickets should be obtained from the ticket machines (*horodateurs* – small change necessary) and displayed inside the windscreen on the driver's side; failure to display may result in a heavy fine (and, in extreme cases, removal of the offending vehicle!). In some towns there are "blue" parking zones *(zone bleue)* marked by a blue line on the pavement or a blue signpost with a P and a small square underneath. In this particular case motorists should display a cardboard "parking disc", which can be adjusted to display their time of arrival and which allows a stay of up to 1hr 30min (2hr 30min over lunchtime). These discs are on sale in supermarkets or petrol stations (ask for a *disque de stationnement*).

Route planning – The French road network is excellent and includes many motorways. The roads are very busy during the holiday period (particularly weekends in July and August) and to avoid traffic congestion it is advisable to follow the recommended secondary routes (signposted as *Bison Futé* or *Itinéraires bis*). The motorway network includes rest areas *(aires)* every 10-15km/5-10mi and petrol stations, usually with restaurant and shopping complexes attached, about every 40km/25mi, so that long-distance drivers have no excuse not to stop for a rest every now and then.

Tolls – In France, most motorway sections are subject to a toll *(péage)*. This can be expensive especially if you take the motorway all the way south (eg: Calais to Perpignan around 300F for a car). Tolls can be paid in cash or with a credit card (Visa, Mastercard).

Car rental – There are car rental agencies at airports, railway stations and in all large towns throughout France. European cars usually have manual transmission. Those wishing to hire a car with automatic transmission must book it in advance and should bear in mind that cars of this type are only available in large towns and cities. The minimum age for car rental is 21 years, although in some cases motorists under 23 years of age will be able to rent a car only through a travel agent. It is relatively expensive to hire a car in France; Americans in particular will notice the difference and should consider booking a car from home before leaving or taking advantage of Fly-Drive schemes. Drivers between 21 and 25 years old may find that they have to pay an additional fee of 50-100F per day. Those who rent a car before leaving home should make sure that they inform the car hire company that they intend to take the car to France, so that their hire contract includes insurance for the car while on French soil.

Central Reservation in France:

Avis: ☎ 01 46 10 60 60   Europcar: ☎ 01 30 43 82 82
Budget: ☎ 01 46 86 65 65   Hertz: ☎ 01 47 88 51 51
Eurodollar: ☎ 01 49 58 44 44

Petrol

In France 4 different types of petrol (US: gas) are available:

sans plomb 95 – unleaded 95 octane
sans plomb 98 – unleaded 98 octane
super – super leaded
diesel/gazole – diesel

Petrol is more expensive in France compared to the USA and the UK. The French Tourist Office issues a map showing the location of cheaper petrol stations within a mile or so of motorway exits, usually in a hypermarket complex (send an SAE).

Tourist information

Local Tourist Offices – To find the addresses of local tourist offices throughout France, contact the **Fédération Nationale des Comités Départementaux de Tourisme**, 280 boulevard St-Germain, 75007 Paris. ☎ 01 44 11 10 20. Otherwise, contact local tourist offices directly to obtain useful brochures and information:

Comité régional de tourisme **Languedoc-Roussillon**, 20 rue de la République, 34000 Montpellier, ☎ 04 67 22 81 00

Comité régional de tourisme **Midi-Pyrénées**, 54 boulevard de l'Embouchure, BP 2166, 31022 Toulouse Cedex 2, ☎ 05 61 13 55 55

Comité départemental de tourisme de l'**Ariège**, 31 bis avenue du Général-de-Gaulle, BP 143, 09004 Foix Cedex, ☎ 05 61 02 30 70

Comité départemental de tourisme de l'**Aude**, Centre Administratif Départemental, 11855 Carcassonne Cedex 09, ☎ 04 68 11 66 00

Comité départemental de tourisme de l'**Aveyron**, 6 place Jean Jaurès, 12000 Rodez, ☎ 05 65 75 55 75

Comité départemental de tourisme du **Gard**, 3 place des Arènes, BP 122, 30010 Nîmes Cedex, ☎ 04 66 21 02 51

Comité départemental de tourisme de la **Haute-Garonne**, 14 rue Bayard, 31000 Toulouse, ☎ 05 61 99 44 00

Comité départemental de tourisme de l'**Hérault**, avenue des Moulins, BP 3067, 34034 Montpellier Cedex 1, ☎ 04 67 67 71 71

Comité départemental de tourisme du **Lozère**, 14 boulevard Henri-Bourrillon, BP 4, 48001 Mende Cedex, ☎ 04 66 65 60 00

Comité départemental de tourisme des **Pyrénées-Roussillon**, 7 quai de Lattre-de-Tassigny, BP 540, 66005 Perpignan Cedex, ☎ 04 68 34 29 94

Comité départemental de tourisme du **Tarn**, Moulins Albigeois, BP 225, 81006 Albi Cedex, ☎ 05 63 77 32 10

Comité départemental de tourisme du **Tarn-et-Garonne**, 2 boulevard Midi-Pyrénées, 82000 Montauban, ☎ 05 63 63 31 40.

Tourism for the Disabled – Some of the sights described in this guide are accessible to handicapped people and are indicated in the Admission Times and Charges section with the symbol ♿. For further information on museums which are accessible to the handicapped, contact the Direction des Musées de France, Service Accueil des publics spécifiques, 6, rue des Pyramides, 75041 Paris Cedex 01, ☎ 01 40 15 35 88. The **Michelin Red Guide France** and **Michelin Guide Camping Caravaning France** indicate hotels and camp sites with facilities suitable for physically handicapped people. Information is also available from the Comité National Français de Liaison pour la Réadaptation des Handicapés (236bis rue de Tolbiac, 75013 Paris, ☎ 05 53 80 66 66) and the Association France Handicaps (9 rue Luce-de-Lancival, 77340 Pontault-Combault, ☎ 01 60 28 50 12).

Useful organisations in the UK include RADAR (Royal Association for Disability and Rehabilitation, 12 City Forum, 250 City Road, London EC1V 8AF, ☎ (0171) 250-3222, Fax (0171) 2580-0212) and Access Project (39 Bradley Gardens, West Ealing, London W13 8HE), who provide specialised practical information about on such matters as health insurance for disabled travellers.

Accommodation

Places to stay – The **Places to Stay** map *(p 10)* indicates recommended places for overnight stops and can be used in conjunction with the **Michelin Red Guide France**, which lists a selection of hotels and restaurants.

Loisirs Accueil is a booking service which has offices in most French *départements*. For information, contact Réservation Loisirs Accueil, 280 boulevard St-Germain, 75007 Paris, ☎ 01 44 11 10 44, or local tourist offices.

A guide to good-value, family-run hotels, *Logis et Auberges de France*, is available from the French Tourist Office, as are lists of other kinds of accommodation such as hotel-châteaux, bed-and-breakfasts etc.

Rural and self-catering accommodation – The **Fédération nationale des Gîtes de France** is an information service on self-catering accommodation in this region (and all over France). *Gîtes* usually take the form of a cottage or apartment decorated in the local style where visitors can make themselves at home. Contact the Gîtes de France office in Paris: 59, rue St-Lazare, 75439 Paris Cedex 09. ☎ 01 49 70 75 75, or their representative, in the UK, Brittany Ferries *(address above)*.

Gîtes de France, Springfield Books Ltd and FHG Publications/World Leisure Marketing all publish listings of *gîtes* in France with details of how to book, or try contacting the local tourist offices which also send out lists of available properties.

Walkers, climbers, skiers, cyclists and canoeists in search of stop-overs during a trip should consult *Gîtes d'étapes, refuges* by A. and S. Mounaret, published by Éditions La Cadole, 74 rue Albert-Perdreaux, 78140 Vélizy, ☎ 01 34 65 10 40.

Bed and Breakfast – Gîtes de France *(see above)* also publishes a guide to bed and breakfast accommodation *(chambres d'hôtes)* which consists of a room and breakfast at a reasonable price. Various other listings are available, either from bookshops or from the French Tourist Office. Another possibility is the organisation **Café-Couette**, which publishes a *Guide des chambres d'amis* (further details and bookings: 8 rue d'Isly, 75008 Paris, ☎ 01 42 94 92 00).

Youth Hostels (Auberges de jeunesse) – Contact the French youth hostel association:

Paris: Ligue Française pour les Auberges de la Jeunesse, 38 boulevard Raspail, 75007 Paris. ☎ 01 45 48 69 84, Fax 01 45 44 57 47.

Holders of an International Youth Hostel Federation card should contact the International Federation or the French Youth Hostels Association to book a bed.

Hostelling International / American Youth Hostel Association in the US (☎ (202) 783-6161) offers a publication **International Hostel Guide for Europe** (US$13.95) – also available to non-members.

Camping – There are numerous officially graded sites with varying standards of facilities throughout this region of France. The **Michelin Guide Caravaning France** lists a selection of camp sites. An international Camping Carnet for caravans is useful but not compulsory; it may be obtained from motoring organisations or the Camping and Caravanning Club (Greenfield House, Westwood Way, Coventry CV4 8JH, ☎ (01203) 694-995).

General information

Electricity – The electric current is 220 volts. Circular two-pin plugs are the rule. An electrical adaptor may be necessary (these are on sale at most airports).

Medical treatment – First aid, medical advice and chemist's night service rota are available from chemists/drugstores (*pharmacie* identified by a green cross sign). It is advisable to take out comprehensive insurance cover as tourists undergoing medical treatment in French hospitals or clinics have to pay for it themselves. Nationals of non-EU countries should check with their insurance companies about policy limitations. Reimbursement can then be negotiated with the insurance company according to the policy held. All prescription drugs should be clearly labelled; it is recommended to carry a copy of prescriptions. American Express offers its cardholders only a service, "Global Assist", for any medical, legal or personal emergency: ☎ 01 47 16 25 29.

British and Irish citizens should apply to their local post office for **Form E111** (application form included in the brochure *Health Advice for Travellers* available from the post office). Form E111 entitles the holder to urgent medical treatment for accident or unexpected illness in EU countries. A refund of part of the costs of treatment can be obtained on application in person (recommended) or by post to the local French Social Security offices *(Caisse Primaire d'Assurance Maladie)*.

Tipping – Since a service charge is automatically included in the price of meals and accommodation in France, it is not necessary to tip in restaurants and hotels. However taxi drivers, bellboys, doormen, filling station attendants or anybody who has been of assistance are usually tipped at the customer's discretion. Most French people give an extra tip in restaurants and cafés (about 50 *centimes* for a drink and several *francs* for a meal). There is no tipping in theatres.

Currency – There are no restrictions on the amount of currency visitors can take into France. Visitors wishing to export currency in foreign banknotes in excess of the given allocation from France should complete a currency declaration form on arrival.

Notes and coins – *See illustration on p 381*. The unit of currency in France is the French *franc* (F), subdivided into 100 *centimes*. French notes are available for the values 50, 100, 200 and 500 *francs* (the old 20 *franc* note is being phased out). French coins come in the following values: 5, 10, 20, 50 *centimes* (all gold coloured except the 50 *centime* coin which is silver); 1, 2, 5, 10, 20 *francs* (all silver except the 10 and 20 *franc* coins which are silver with a gold border).

Banks and currency exchange – Banks are generally open from 9am to 4.30pm (smaller branches may close for lunch) and are closed on Mondays or Saturdays (except if market day). Some branches are open for limited transactions on Saturdays. Banks close early on the day before a bank holiday.

A passport is necessary as identification when cashing cheques (travellers' or ordinary) in banks. Commission charges vary and hotels usually charge more than banks for cashing cheques for non-residents.

By far the most convenient way of obtaining French currency is the 24hr **cash dispenser** or ATM (*distributeur automatique de billets* in French), found outside many banks and post offices and easily recognisable by the CB (Carte Bleue) logo. Most accept international credit cards (don't forget your PIN) and some even give instructions in English. Note that American Express cards can only be used in dispensers operated by the Crédit Lyonnais bank or by American Express.

A. Ei/MICHELIN

Foreign currency can also be exchanged in major banks, post offices, hotels or private exchange offices found in main cities and near popular tourist attractions.

Credit cards – American Express, Visa, Mastercard/Eurocard and Diners Club are widely accepted in shops, hotels, restaurants and petrol stations. If your card is lost or stolen, call the appropriate 24hr hotline:

      American Express ☎ 01 47 77 72 00
      Visa ☎ 01 42 77 11 90
      Mastercard/Eurocard ☎ 01 45 67 84 84
      Diners Club ☎ 01 47 62 75 50

You should also report any loss or theft to the local police who will issue you with a certificate (useful proof to show the credit card company).

Post – Main post offices open Monday to Friday from 8am to 7pm, and Saturdays from 8am to noon. Smaller branch post offices generally close at lunchtime between noon and 2pm and finish for the day at 4pm. Stamps are

Postage via airmail
UK: letter (20g) 3F
North America: letter (20g) 4.40F
Australia and NZ: letter (20g) 5.20F

also sold in newsagents and cafés that sell cigarettes *(tabac)*. Stamp collectors should ask for *timbres de collection* in any post office (there is often a *philatélie* counter).

Public Holidays – The following are days when museums and other monuments may be closed or may vary their hours of admission:

1 January	New Year's Day *(Jour de l'An)*
	Easter Day and Monday *(Pâques)*
1 May	May Day
8 May	V E Day
	Ascension Day *(Ascension)*
	Whit Sunday and Monday *(Pentecôte)*
14 July	France's National Day (Bastille Day)
15 August	Assumption
1 November	All Saints Day *(Toussaint)*
11 November	Armistice
25 December	Christmas Day *(Noël)*

Time – France is one hour ahead of Greenwich Mean Time (GMT), except between the end of September and the end of October, when it is the same.

When it is **noon in France**, it is

> 3am in Los Angeles
> 6am in New York
> 11am in Dublin
> 11am in London
> 7pm in Perth
> 9pm in Sydney
> 11pm in Auckland

In France time is generally given using the 24hr clock, and "am" and "pm" are not used.

Embassies and Consulates

Australia:	Embassy	4 rue Jean-Rey, 75015 Paris, ☎ 01 40 59 33 00, Fax 01 40 59 33 10
Canada:	Embassy	35 avenue Montaigne, 75008 Paris, ☎ 01 44 43 29 00, Fax 01 44 43 29 99
	Consulate	30 boulevard Strasbourg, 31000 Toulouse, ☎ 05 61 99 30 16
Eire:	Embassy	4 rue Rude, 75016 Paris, ☎ 01 44 17 67 00, Fax 01 45 00 84 17
New Zealand:	Embassy	7 ter rue Léonard-de-Vinci, 75016 Paris, ☎ 01 45 00 24 11, Fax 01 45 01 26 39
UK:	Embassy	35 rue du Faubourg St-Honoré, 75008 Paris, ☎ 01 42 66 91 42, Fax 01 42 66 95 90
	Consulate	16 rue d'Anjou, 75008 Paris, ☎ 01 42 66 06 68 (visas)
	Consulate	Victoria Center, 20 chemin Laporte, 31300 Toulouse, ☎ 05 61 15 02 02
USA:	Embassy	2 avenue Gabriel, 75008 Paris, ☎ 01 43 12 22 22, Fax 01 42 66 97 83
	Consulate	2 rue St-Florentin, 75008 Paris ☎ 01 42 96 14 88

Shopping

Opening hours – Department stores and chain stores are open Monday to Saturday, 9am to 6.30pm-7.30pm. Smaller, more specialised shops may close during the lunch hour. Food stores (grocers, wine merchants and bakeries) are open from 7am to 6.30pm-7.30pm and some open on Sunday mornings. Many food stores close between noon and 2pm and on Mondays. Hypermarkets are usually open until 9pm-10pm.

What to take home – Most of the local products that cry out to be taken home as a souvenir are of the comestible kind. Particular specialities include *foie gras* and *confits* from the southwest, the varied *charcuterie* on offer throughout the region, and sheeps'-milk cheese such as Pyrenean *fromage de brebis* or Roquefort. Besides the wide range of local wines, there are the *vins doux naturels* such as Banyuls and Rivesaltes, full of the flavour of the south of France.
Hand-crafted souvenirs include Laguiole knives.
Travellers from America and Australia should note that they are not allowed to take food and plant products home, so this rules out *foie gras*, French cheeses and candied fruit, for example.
Americans are allowed to take home, tax-free, up to US$400 worth of goods, Canadians up to CND$300, British up to £ 136, Australians up to AUS$400 and New Zealanders up to NZ$700.

Telephoning

Public Telephones – Most public phones in France use prepaid phone cards *(télé-cartes)*. Some telephone booths accept credit cards (Visa, Mastercard/Euro-card; minimum monthly charge 20F). *Télécartes* (50 or 120 units) can be bought in post offices, branches of France Télécom, cafés that sell cigarettes *(tabac)*

and newsagents, and can be used to make calls in France and abroad. Calls can be received at phone boxes where the blue bell sign is shown.

National calls – French telephone numbers have 10 digits. Numbers begin with 01 in Paris and the Paris region; 02 in northwest France; 03 in northeast France; 04 in southeast France and Corsica; 05 in southwest France. The French ringing tone is a series of long tones and the engaged (busy) tone is a series of short beeps.

International calls – To call France from abroad, dial the country code (33) + 9 digit number (omit the initial 0). When calling abroad from France dial 00, followed by the country code, followed by the area code and number of your correspondent.

International dialling codes:

Australia: 61	New Zealand: 64
Canada: 1	United Kingdom: 44
Eire: 353	United States: 1

To use your personal calling card dial:

AT&T: 0 800 99-0011	BT: 0 800 99-0044
MCI: 0 800 99-0019	Mercury: 0 800 99-00 944
Sprint: 0 800 99-0087	Canada Direct: 0 800 99-0016

Telephone rates from a public phone are about 3F/min from France to the UK, and about 4.50F/min from France to the USA and Canada. Cheap rates with 50% extra time are available from private telephones to the UK on weekdays between 9.30pm and 8am, from 2pm on Saturdays and all day on Sundays and holidays. Cheap rates to the USA and Canada are from 2am to noon all week, and to Australia between 9.30pm and 8am Monday to Saturday and all day Sunday.

Toll-free numbers in France begin with 0 800.

Emergency numbers:
Police: 17
Fire (Pompiers): 18
Ambulance (SAMU): 15

Minitel – France Télécom operates a system offering directory enquiries (free of charge up to 3min), travel and entertainment reservations, and other services (cost varies between 0.37F-5.57F/min). These small computer-like terminals can be found in some post offices, hotels and France Télécom agencies and in many French homes. **3614 PAGES E** is the code for directory assistance in English (turn on the unit, dial 3614, hit the "connexion" button when you get the tone, type in "PAGES E", and follow the instructions on the screen). For route planning, use Michelin services **3615 MICHELIN** (tourist and route information) and **3617 MICHELIN** (information sent by **FAX**).

Cellular phones – In France these have numbers which begin with 06. Two-watt (lighter, shorter reach) and eight-watt models are on the market, using the Itinéris (France Télécom) or SFR network. Cell phone rentals (delivery or airport pickup provided):

Ellinas Phone Rental	☎ 01 47 20 70 00
Euro Exaphone	☎ 01 44 09 77 78
Rent a cell Express	☎ 01 53 93 78 00

International information, UK	00.33.12.44
International information, USA/Canada	00.33.12.11
International operator	00.33.12 + country code
Local directory assistance	12

Conversion tables

Weights and measures

1 kilogram (kg)	2.2 pounds (lb)	2.2 pounds
1 metric ton (tn)	1.1 tons	1.1 tons

to convert kilograms to pounds, multiply by 2.2

1 litre (l)	2.1 pints (pt)	1.8 pints
1 litre	0.3 gallon (gal)	0.2 gallon

to convert litres to gallons, multiply by 0.26 (US) or 0.22 (UK)

1 hectare (ha)	2.5 acres	2.5 acres
1 square kilometre (km²)	0.4 square miles (sq mi)	0.4 square miles

to convert hectares to acres, multiply by 2.4

1centimetre (cm)	0.4 inches (in)	0.4 inches
1 metre (m)	3.3 feet (ft) - 39.4 inches - 1.1 yards (yd)	
1 kilometre (km)	0.6 miles (mi)	0.6 miles

to convert metres to feet, multiply by 3.28, kilometres to miles, multiply by 0.6

Clothing

Women	🇪🇺	🇺🇸	🇬🇧		🇪🇺	🇺🇸	🇬🇧	Men
	35	4	2½		40	7½	7	
	36	5	3½		41	8½	8	
	37	6	4½		42	9½	9	
Shoes	38	7	5½		43	10½	10	Shoes
	39	8	6½		44	11½	11	
	40	9	7½		45	12½	12	
	41	10	8½		46	13½	13	
	36	4	8		46	36	36	
	38	6	10		48	38	38	
Dresses &	40	8	12		50	40	40	Suits
Suits	42	12	14		52	42	42	
	44	14	16		54	44	44	
	46	16	18		56	46	48	
	36	08	30		37	14½	14,5	
	38	10	32		38	15	15	
Blouses &	40	12	14		39	15½	15½	Shirts
sweaters	42	14	36		40	15¾	15¾	
	44	16	38		41	16	16	
	46	18	40		42	16½	16½	

Sizes often vary depending on the designer. These equivalents are given for guidance only.

Speed

kph	10	30	50	70	80	90	100	110	120	130
mph	6	19	31	43	50	56	62	68	75	81

Temperature

Celsius (°C)	0°	5°	10°	15°	20°	25°	30°	40°	60°	80°	100°
Fahrenheit (°F)	32°	41°	50°	59°	68°	77°	86°	104°	140°	176°	212°

To convert Celsius into Fahrenheit, multiply °C by 9, divide by 5, and add 32.
To convert Fahrenheit into Celsius, subtract 32 from °F, multiply by 5, and divide by 9.

Notes and coins

500 Francs featuring scientists Pierre and Marie Curie (1858-1906), (1867-1934)

200 Francs featuring engineer Gustave Eiffel (1832-1923)

100 Francs featuring painter Paul Cézanne (1839-1906)

50 Francs featuring pilot and writer Antoine de Saint-Exupéry (1900-1944)

20 Francs   10 Francs   5 Francs   2 Francs

1 Franc   50 Centimes   20 Centimes   10 Centimes   5 Centimes

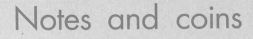

Further reading

An Englishman in the Midi *and* More from an Englishman in the Midi *J P Harris*
A Little Tour in France *H James*
Blue Guide to the Midi-Pyrénées
Cadogan Guide to the South of France *D Facaros and M Pauls*
Footsteps *R Holmes*
High are the Mountains *H Closs*
Hills and the Sea *H Belloc*
Montaillou *E le Roy Ladurie*
The Midi – Languedoc and Roussillon *J Law (John Murray)*
Toulouse-Lautrec: A Life *J Frey (Phoenix)*
Toulouse-Lautrec: The Complete Posters *R Ash (Pavilion)*
Travels with a Donkey *R L Stevenson*
Walks in the Cévennes *(Footpaths of Europe series)*
West of the Rhone *F White*
Wild Flowers of the Mediterranean *D Burnie (Dorling Kindersley)*
Wonderful Cathar Country *J-L Aubarbier et al (Ouest-France)*

Sport and leisure

Beaches – Since the project to clean up and develop the Languedoc coast, vast sandy beaches now stretch invitingly for miles, often sandwiched between the sea and lagoons. The best are to be found between La Grande-Motte and Palavas-les-Flots, from Sète to Cap-d'Agde, and around Cap-d'Agde and Valras.
Bathing conditions are indicated by flags on beaches which are covered by lifeguards (no flags means no lifeguards): green indicates it is safe to bathe and lifeguards are on duty; yellow warns that conditions are not that good, but lifeguards are still in attendance; red means bathing is forbidden as conditions are too dangerous.

Canoeing – The upper and middle valley of the Tarn, and the valleys of the Dourbie, the Orb, the Hérault and the Garonne among others are wonderful places to explore by canoe, with their beautiful scenery, stretches of rapids and tiny beaches ideal as picnic spots. Centres for canoeing have been set up in the Parc régional du Haut-Languedoc.
Various canoeing guides (to different stretches of river etc.) are on sale from the Fédération française de canoë-kayak, 87, quai de la Marne, 94340 Joinville-le-Pont, ☏ 01 45 11 08 50, or the Ligue Midi-Pyrénées de Canoë-Kayak, Z.A. La Tuilerie, 31810 Venerque.

The beach at La Grande-Motte

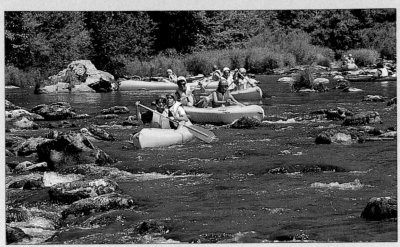

Canoeing for all the family

Inland water sports bases include:

Escapade at **Aguessac**, ☎ 05 65 59 72 03 (Aveyron, map 80 fold 14).

Base nautique du Piolet at **Albi**, ☎ 05 63 45 04 95 (Tarn, map 83 fold 1).

Sports Montagne Loisirs Ozone 3 at Les **Angles**, ☎ 04 68 30 90 21 (Pyrénées-Orientales, map 86 fold 16).

Base nautique du Saut de Sabo at **Arthès**, ☎ 05 63 54 38 40 (Tarn, map 80 fold 11).

Sud Rafting at **Axat**, ☎ 04 68 20 53 73 (Aude, map 86 fold 7).

Carcassonne Canoë-kayak, ☎ 04 68 71 43 94 (Aude, map 83 fold 11).

ASPTT canoë-kayak at **Foix**, ☎ 05 61 65 03 38 (Ariège, Michelin map 86 fold 4).

L'Espace Bleue at **Langogne-Naussac**, ☎ 04 66 69 06 51 (Lozère, map 76 fold 17).

Base Eaux Vives at **Marquixanes**, ☎ 04 68 96 20 33 (Pyrénées-Orientales, map 86 fold 18).

Aquaraid at **Millau**, ☎ 05 65 61 10 00 (Aveyron, map 80 fold 14).

Roc et Canyon at **Millau**, ☎ 05 65 61 17 77 (Aveyron, map 80 fold 14).

Centre Eaux Vives des Ajustons at Le **Monastier**, ☎ 04 66 32 08 35 (Lozère, map 80 fold 5).

Pyrénées Loisirs Nautisme at **Montbel**, ☎ 05 61 68 27 27 (Ariège, map 86 fold 6).

Muret Olympique Canoë kayak at **Muret**, ☎ 05 61 51 38 21 (Haute-Garonne, map 82 fold 17).

Centre International de Séjour Sports Nature at **Quillan**, ☎ 04 68 20 23 79 (Aude, map 86 fold 7).

Canoë Le Moulin at **St-Bauzille-de-Putois**, ☎ 04 67 73 30 73 (Hérault, map 83 fold 5).

Association Le Merlet at **St-Jean-du-Gard**, ☎ 04 66 85 18 19 (Gard, map 80 fold 17).

Lo Capial at **St-Juéry**, ☎ 05 63 45 43 39 (Tarn, map 83 fold 1).

Cercle nautique des Corbières at **Sigean**, ☎ 04 68 48 42 68 (Aude, map 86 fold 10).

Vénerque Eaux Vives, ☎ 05 61 08 09 37 (Haute-Garonne, map 82 fold 18).

Caving – Useful addresses include:

Comité régional de Spéléologie, Midi-Pyrénées, 7, rue André-Citroën, 31300 Balma, ☎ 05 61 11 71 60.

École française de Spéléologie, 23, rue de Nuits, 69004 Lyon, ☎ 04 78 39 43 30.

Fédération française de Spéléologie, 130, rue St-Maur, 75011 Paris, ☎ 01 43 57 56 54.

Cycling – Many tourist offices issue lists of local cycle hire companies. Certain SNCF stations (Agde, Béziers, Carcassonne, Langogne, Marvejols, Millau, Moissac, Montauban and Narbonne) rent various types of bicycle (including cross-country) for anything from half a day to several days; contact the stations themselves or look on the Minitel. The French cycling federation has marked out cycle routes in various areas, graded in difficulty (green is easy; blue is fairly easy; red is difficult; black is very difficult); maps and details can be obtained from the Fédération française de cyclisme, Bâtiment Jean-Monnet, 5 rue de Rome, 93561 Rosny-sous-Bois Cedex, ☎ 01 49 35 69 00.

Freshwater fishing – A brochure called *Pêche en France* is available from the Conseil Supérieur de la Pêche, 134, avenue de Malakoff, 75116 Paris, ☎ 01 45 02 20 20. This can also be obtained from local branches of the Fédérations départementales de Pêche et de Pisciculture (at Albi, Carcassonne, Mende, Montpellier, Nîmes, Perpignan, Rodez and Toulouse). Two-week holiday fishing permits are also available in some areas - contact the local federation for details (or try local fishing tackle shops or tourist offices). For information on fishing regulations in the twenty or so lakes in the Bouillouses area, contact the tourist office in Font-Romeu.

Fly-fishing

Golf – For location, addresses and telephone numbers of golf courses in France, consult the map *Golfs, Les Parcours Français* published by Éditions Plein Sud based on Michelin map 989. Otherwise, contact the Fédération française de Golf, 69 avenue Victor-Hugo, 75783 Paris Cedex 16, ☎ 01 44 17 63 00.

Hang-gliding and paragliding – Useful addresses include:
"Les Aigles du Montcalm", ☎ 05 61 64 87 53.
Association de parapente du Vallespir, Corsavy, ☎ 04 68 83 99 11.
Bar catalan, Prats-de-Mollo, ☎ 04 68 39 70 20.
Le Comité départemental de vol libre de la Lozère, ☎ 04 66 47 04 10.
Delta Club Aude, 64, rue de la République, Céret, ☎ 04 68 87 25 54.
Évasion Vol Libre, La Borie Blanque, 12520 Millau, ☎ 05 65 61 02 03.
Fédération Française de Vol Libre, 4, rue de Suisse, 06000 Nice, ☎ 04 93 88 62 89.
La Ligue Midi-Pyrénées de vol libre, 54 rue des Sept Troubadours, 31000 Toulouse, ☎ 05 62 99 65 60.
Millau Vol Libre, 79, avenue Jean-Jaurès, 12100 Millau, ☎ 05 65 60 83 77.
Parapente Évasion, Les Angles, ☎ 04 68 66 51 31.
"VOLEM", école de parapente d'Espouillouse, ☎ 04 68 30 10 10.

House-boats – House-boats with a capacity for 6 to 8 people enable visitors to get a different perspective on the region from the Canal du Midi, the Canal de la Robine or the Rhône-Sète canal. For boats with a horsepower of less than 10 it is not necessary to have a permit. Nautical maps and plan-guides are available from:
Éditions GRAFOCARTE, 125, rue Jean-Jacques Rousseau, 92132 Issy-les-Moulineaux Cedex, ☎ 01 41 09 19 00.
Éditions du Plaisancier, BP 27, 100, avenue de Gal-Leclerc, 69641 Caliure Cedex, ☎ 04 78 23 31 14.
Voies navigables de France, 175 rue Ludovic Boutleux, 62 408 Béthune Cedex, ☎ 03 21 63 24 22 *(information on river tolls)*.
The Comité Régional du Tourisme de la région Languedoc-Roussillon publishes a brochure called "Tourisme fluvial" in English and French.
Companies from which houseboats can be hired:
Amica Tours, Port Neuf, 34440 Béziers, ☎ 04 67 35 28 70.
Camargue Plaisance, Base fluviale de Carnon, 34280 Carnon, ☎ 04 67 50 77 00.
Crown Blue Line, Port Cassafières, 34420 Portiragnes, ☎ 04 67 90 91 70.
Locaboat Plaisance, Port de Plaisance, 30220 Aigues-Mortes, ☎ 04 66 53 94 50.
Or contact local tourist offices for information.

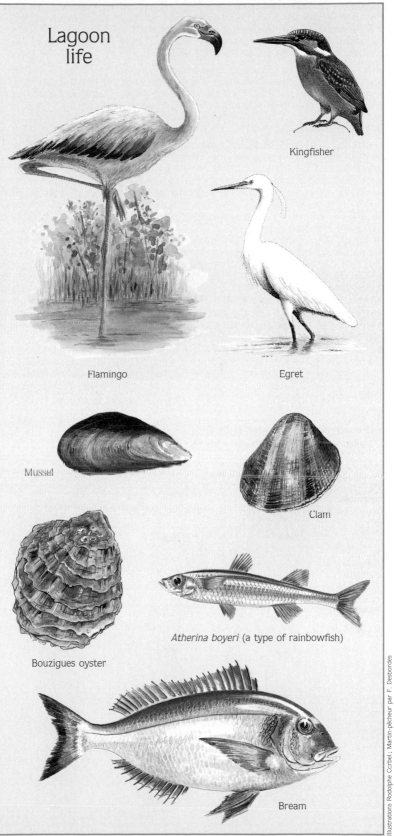

Lagoon life

Kingfisher

Flamingo

Egret

Mussel

Clam

Bouzigues oyster

Atherina boyeri (a type of rainbowfish)

Bream

Illustrations Rodolphe Corbel : Martin-pêcheur par F. Desbordes

Hunting – The Pyrenees attract hunters in search of large game. Some of the mountain resorts are favourite haunts of enthusiasts of rarer species of grouse. October is the season for hunting wood pigeon.

For further information on hunting, contact the St-Hubert Club de France, 10, rue de Lisbonne, 75008 Paris, ☎ 01 45 22 38 90.

Lakes and reservoirs – The main lakes and reservoirs with facilities for swimming and various water sports, and where it is possible to go for walks or picnic on the lake shore, include: Maury, Pareloup, Pont-de-Salars, St-Gervais, Sarrans, Ville-franche-de-Panat, Flagnac, Couesque, Le Goul, Touluch, Golinhac, Castelnau, Pinet, La Jourdanie, La Croux (in the **Aveyron**); Les Camboux (in the **Gard**); La Ravière, Thau, Salagou (in the **Hérault**); Naussac, Villefort (in the **Lozère**).

Rambling – A network of several hundred miles' worth of long-distance footpaths *(sentiers de Grande Randonnée – GR)* covers the Causses, the Cévennes, the Haut Languedoc and the Rouergue. They are waymarked with red and white flashes painted onto rocks, trees etc. There are two further categories of footpath: *sentiers de Grande Randonnée de Pays*, or long-distance footpaths which cover a certain region only; and *sentiers de Petite Randonnée*, or short-distance footpaths. Rambling is an excellent way of benefitting from the fresh air and breathtaking scenery of mountain regions.

The main GR footpaths in the regions covered by this guide are the GR 6 (Alps-Atlantic), the GR 7 (Vosges-Pyrenees) from Mont Aigoual to the Canal du Midi, the GR 10 (Pyrénées – from Banyuls to Mérens-les-Vals, in this guide), the GR 36 from the Aveyron gorge via the Cathar castles to the Canigou, the GR 62 from Meyrueis to Conques, the GR 65 (Way of St James), the GR 66 (around Mont Aigoual), the GR 67 (through the Cévennes), the GR 68 (around Mont Lozère), the GR 70 (route taken by Robert Louis Stevenson through the Cévennes), the GR 71 across the Causse du Larzac and the GR 623 around Toulouse.

The *Topo-guides* series, published by the Fédération française de la Randonnée pédestre, 64, rue de Gergovie, 75014 Paris, ☎ 01 45 45 31 02, provides detailed maps of all the above. Tourist offices in the Tarn gorges provide information on local and short-distance footpaths. The footpath from Florac to Albi (250km/155mi) which follows the banks of the Tarn, can be tackled on foot, by cross-country bike or on horseback.

The Parc national des Cévennes and the Parc naturel régional du Haut-Languedoc also issue leaflets on footpaths in the area. Ramblers can stay overnight in one of the numerous *gîtes d'étape* to be found along the route.

	Carry straight on	Turn right (shown)/left	Wrong way
GR *Long-distance footpaths*			
GRP *Regional long-distance footpath*			
PR *Short-distance footpath*			

The footpaths and waymarkers shown as GR above are reproduced with the kind permission of the FFRP-CNSGR (Fédération Française de la Randonnée Pédestre - Comité National de Sentiers de Grande Randonnée) and are protected by copyright dated 1992. The marks GR are registered trademarks, protected by registration with the INPI (Institut National de Propriété Intellectuelle). The reproduction or other use of the protected information is forbidden without the prior authorisation of the FFRP-CNSGR.

Riding in the Parc national des Cévennes

Association Chamina-Sylva, BP 5, 48300 Langogne, ☎ 04 66 69 00 44, organises a number of walks south of the Massif Central.

For details of rambling in the Pyrenees, contact La Balaguère, 65400 Arrens-Marsous, ☎ 05 62 97 20 21.

In order to get the best out of your walk, you should check the weather forecast before you leave and, regardless of the distance you intend to go or the level of difficulty, take with you a detailed scale map (1:25 000 or 1:50 000), 2-4 pints of water per person, high-energy sweets or candy, water-proof clothing, a warm pullover, sunglasses, suncream and a basic first-aid kit. Make sure to wear proper walking shoes for a blister-free experience!

In the dry, rocky scrubland of the *garrigues* and the *causses*, walkers may come across the odd viper, so it is important to wear stout footwear, preferably with some protection around the ankle. Most of the time the snakes will make themselves scarce as soon as they hear someone coming, so make plenty of noise, and avoid lifting up rocks in case of disturbing a slumbering serpent beneath.

Riding – Details of waymarked bridle-paths and relevant maps contact the nearest Comité départemental de tourisme équestre (CDTE) – list of addresses available from the Délégation nationale de tourisme équestre, 30 avenue d'Iéna, 75116 Paris, ☎ 01 53 67 44 44. Other useful addresses include:

Association régionale pour le tourisme équestre et l'Équitation de loisirs en Languedoc-Roussillon (ATECREL), 14 rue des Logis, Loupian, 34140 Mèze, ☎ 04 67 43 82 50.

Association régionale de tourisme équestre de Midi-Pyrénées (ARTEMIP), 17 avenue Winston-Chruchill, 31100 Toulouse, ☎ 05 61 44 01 45.

Rock-climbing – It is advisable to go with a guide, and beginners should take advantage of the numerous courses available to learn a few basic techniques. Useful addresses include:

Fédération française de la Montagne et de l'Escalade, 10 quai de la Marne, 75019 Paris, ☎ 01 40 18 75 50.

Bureau des Guides St-Girons, ☎ 05 61 66 49 19.

Club Alpin Français d'Ariège-Pyrénées, ☎ 05 61 65 01 09.

Compagnie des Guides des Pyrénées Catalanes at Les Angles (☎ 04 68 04 39 22), Formiguères (☎ 04 68 04 47 35), Font-Romeu (☎ 04 68 30 36 09), Bolquère (☎ 04 68 30 39 66).

Office de la Montagne (Luchon), ☎ 05 61 79 21 21.

Pays d'Accueil at Axat, ☎ 04 68 20 59 61.

Vertical Club de Cerdagne, Osséja, ☎ 04 68 04 52 75.

Sailing – Useful addresses:

Fédération française de Voile, 55, avenue Kléber, 75784 Paris Cedex 16, ☎ 01 44 05 81 00.

Association des ports de plaisance du Languedoc-Roussillon, Capitainerie de la Grande-Motte, ☎ 04 67 56 50 06.

Ligue de Voile du Languedoc-Roussillon, Maison départmentale des Sports, 200, avenue du Père-Soulas, 34094 Montpellier Cedex, ☎ 04 67 41 78 35.

Local sailing centres include: Balaruc-les-Bains, ☎ 04 67 48 55 63; Canet-Perpignan, ☎ 04 68 73 33 95; Carnon, ☎ 04 67 68 16 03; Frontignan, ☎ 04 67 43 38 75; La Grande-Motte, ☎ 04 67 56 62 64; Gruissan,

04 68 49 33 33; Narbonne-Plage, ☎ 04 68 49 70 58; Palavas-les-Flots, ☎ 04 67 68 97 38; Port-Barcarès, ☎ 04 68 86 07 28; Port-Leucate, ☎ 04 68 40 72 66; Le Barrou at Sète, ☎ 04 67 53 55 24.

Skiing – The wide expanses of the Aubrac, Mont Lozère and around the Aigouals summit lend themselves perfectly to cross-country skiing in the winter. Consult the map of Places to Stay on pp 10 and 11.

Further details can be obtained from local tourist offices or:

Comité Régional de Ski des Cévennes, Espace République, 20, rue de la République, 34000 Montpellier, ☎ 04 67 22 94 92.

Office de tourisme, 12210 Laguiole, ☎ 05 65 44 35 94.

Comité départemental de ski en Lozère, 2 place de Gaulle, 48000 Mende, ☎ 04 66 49 12 12.

The snowy slopes of the Ariège and the Catalan Pyrenees are well equipped with facilities for all sorts of snow sports, including some of the more recent activities such as para-skiing or snow motorbikes. To compensate for uneven snowfall, most ski resorts have snow cannon. Cross-country skiing has been practised as a sport in the Pyrenees since 1910, and it is made all the more enjoyable beneath the Mediterranean sunshine of the Capcir and Cerdagne regions. The Capcir in particular is covered by a network of cross-country ski tracks linking all the villages. Further details available from the resorts themselves or the Maison du Capcir, 66210 Matemale, ☎ 04 68 04 49 86, or the Pyrénées catalanes ski de fond, 66210 Matemale, ☎ 04 68 04 32 75.

Information on reception in the **Ariège ski resorts** can be obtained from the Service Loisirs Accueil Ariège Pyrénées. Other useful addresses include: Ariège Pyrénées ski de fond, Hôtel du Département, 09000 Foix, ☎ 05 61 02 09 70; Ski Andorra, avenue Carlemany, 65, 1 r Local 14, Escaldes, Principat d'Andorra, ☎ (376) 864389.

Always bear ski-slope etiquette in mind when out on the piste: never set off without checking that the way uphill and downhill is clear; skiers coming from further up the slope must give way to skiers downhill from them; never ignore signposts; beware of the danger of avalanches on loosely packed snow (especially skiing off-piste). If in any doubt, check the rules at the ski resort before setting off.

SKI RESORTS	Altitude on low slopes	Altitude on top slopes	Ski lifts	Cross-country tracks (km)	No of downhill slopes	Information ☎
Les Angles	1 600	2 400	22	110	29	04 68 04 32 76
Arinsal (Andorra)	1 550	2 560	15	–	23	(376) 38 822
Ascou-Pailhères	1 500	2 000	6	5	15	05 61 64 60 60
Ax-Bonascre-Le Saquet	1 400	2 400	17	–	26	05 61 64 20 64
Camurac	1 350	1 800	7	50	16	04 68 20 70 83
Err-Puigmal 2600	1 850	2 550	9	14	18	04 68 04 72 94
Eyne	1 620	2 350	8	15	24	04 68 04 02 00
Font-Romeu	1 700	2 200	32	80	40	04 68 30 68 30
Formiguères	1 700	2 380	7	114	17	04 68 04 47 35
La Llagonne	1 700	1 850	2	2	2	04 68 04 21 97
Mijanès-Donezan	1 470	1 750	5	50	9	04 61 20 41 37
Les Monts d'Olmes	1 400	2 000	13	–	20	05 61 01 14 14
Pas de la Casa (Andorra)	2 050	2 600	30	10	45	(376) 55 292
Plateau de Beille	1 800	2 000	–	60	–	05 61 64 60 60
Porté-Puymorens	1 615	2 500	–	28	17	04 68 04 82 16
Prats-de-Mollo/La Preste	1 700	1 850	3	–	4	04 68 39 70 83
Puyvalador	1 700	2 400	9	10	12	04 68 04 44 83
Pyrénées 2000	1 700	2 000	9	30	9	04 68 30 12 42
St-Pierre-Dels Forcats/ Cambre d'Aze	1 600	2 400	8	25	12	04 68 04 21 04
Soldeu-El-Tarter (Andorra)	1 710	2 560	23	12	32	(376) 51 144

Getting to know the region

Bullfighting

Many towns in the Languedoc region, especially towards the Camargue, organise bullfights. Besides the famous *corridas* (bullfights) at Béziers in particular, popular events include bull-running, and *courses à la cocarde*, in which *razeteurs* must remove a rosette from between the bull's horns using a small hand-rake.
Local tourist offices will be able to give details of when and where such events are held.

Crafts

These are many and varied throughout the region, including pottery and ceramics, leatherwork, textiles, bell-founding, knife-making, silk and glass ware. Even the smallest village will have at least one craft workshop tucked somewhere in its narrow streets. Some craftsmen run summer workshops; details available from local tourist offices. Other useful addresses include: Coopérative lozérienne des artisans et paysans, 4 rue de l'Ange, 48000 Mende, ☎ 04 66 65 01 57; Maison des métiers d'art, place Gambetta, 34120 Pézenas, ☎ 04 67 98 16 12 (for details of the annual "Mirondela dels Arts" craft fair).

Regional nature parks

The reception and information centre for the **Parc national des Cévennes** is located in the Château de Florac (BP 15, 48400 Florac; ☎ 04 66 49 53 00). It is open all year, whereas the other information centres are only open in season *(see Introduction)*. Useful information on the park includes the Institut Géographique National (IGN) maps at a scale of 1:100 000 or 1:25 000, Topo-guides of the long-distance footpaths which cross the region and the tourist guide "Parc national des Cévennes". The address of the headquarters of the **Parc naturel régional du Haut-Languedoc** is 13 rue du Cloître, 34220 St-Pons-de-Thomières, ☎ 04 67 97 38 22. The open-air sports centre at Mons-la-Trivalle runs courses for all levels (beginner to advanced).
The **Parc naturel régional des Grands Causses** has its main office in Millau, at 71, boulevard de l'Ayrolle, 12101 Millau Cedex, ☎ 05 65 61 35 50.

"Routes historiques"

A number of "Routes historiques", or itineraries on an historical theme, have been set up nationwide to help visitors find out more about France's architectural heritage in its historical context. Each itinerary is described in a leaflet available from tourist offices or from the Caisse nationale des monuments historiques et des sites (CNMHS, 62 rue St-Antoine, 75004 Paris, ☎ 01 44 61 21 50/1). The Routes historiques for the regions described in this guide are:
De l'Homme de Tautavel à Picasso, Route de la Catalogne romane (Romanesque art in Catalonia and Roussillon), Route des Abbayes de Rouergue, Route des Comtes de Toulouse (northeast of Toulouse as far as the Gorges de l'Aveyron), Route du Gévaudan au Golfe du Lion (southeast Languedoc-Roussillon), Route du Pastel au Pays de Cocagne (explores dyer's woad country between Toulouse and Albi), Route Gaston Fébus (from Foix west across the Pyrénées to Orthez), Route historique en Terre catalane (eastern Pyrénées), Route Vauban (retracing Vauban's achievements in Roussillon) and Via Domitia (retracing the old Roman road running from Beaucaire in Provence, via Béziers and Narbonne to Spain across Panissars pass in the Pyrénées).

Rugby

Although both types of rugby are played throughout the Midi, Rugby League is the more common. Every town and village has its team, and passions run high as enthusiastic supporters follow their team's progress in the weekly Sunday matches which take place from October to May.

Spa resorts and sea-water cures

The spa resorts in this region are shown on the map of Places to Stay (p 10).
The Pyrenees are home to numerous mineral and thermal springs, which have made the area prized for its health restoring qualities since Antiquity. The differing properties of the springs mean that a wide range of therapeutic remedies can be offered. The earlier fashion for taking the waters has continued as modern visitors flock to spa resorts to treat a variety of afflictions, mostly respiratory or rheumatic. Pyrenean spas fall into two categories: sulphurated or salt water springs.

Sulphurated springs – These are situated mainly in the central Pyrenees, stretching towards the Mediterranean, from Ax-les-Thermes to Amélie-les-Bains. Their waters can reach temperatures up to 80°C/176°F. Sulphur, highly valued by the Greeks for its medical properties, is present in the form of chloro-sulphates or sodium sulphates. Sulphurated spa waters are used (baths, showers and inhalations) to treat a number of illnesses of the ears, nose, throat and respiratory tract, rheumatism or bone disorders, renal infections and feminine complaints. The main spa resorts in this category are Ax-les-Thermes, Vernet, Molitg, La Preste, Amélie-les-Bains, Bagnols-les-Bains and Balaruc-les-Bains.

Salt water springs – These are to be found along the line of the primary massif. They differ in mineralogical composition from sulphated, or solutions of chalky bicarbonate of soda, known as "sedative" waters, to sodium chlorinated waters. The first type (found at Ussat, Alet, Le Boulou etc.) are used in the treatment of diseases of the nervous system liver and kidneys. The second type, used as baths or showers, can be helpful for gynaecological complaints, skin complaints or infants' diseases.

The **Michelin Red Guide France** indicates the official dates at the beginning and end of the spa season.

Useful addresses: Chaîne thermale du Soleil/Maison du Thermalisme, 32, avenue de l'Opéra, 75002 Paris. ☎ 01 47 42 67 91; Fédération thermale et climatique française, 16, rue de l'Estrapade, 75005 Paris. ☎ 01 43 25 11 85; Eurothermes, 87, avenue du Maine, 75014 Paris, ☎ 01 43 27 12 50.

Sea-water cures – Known as *thalassothérapie* in French, this kind of cure has been increasing in popularity in recent years, despite the fact that it is not considered a proper "medical" cure as spas are (and so is not reimbursed under the French social security system). Sea-water has certain properties which make it useful in beauty treatments and cures for stress, back problems, expectant mothers etc. The two main centres in Languedoc-Roussillon are at **La Grande-Motte** and **Cap-d'Agde**, which cater for cures lasting anything from a day to several weeks, with or without accommodation included.

Fédération Mer et Santé, 60, boulevard de La Tour-Maubourg, 75007 Paris, ☎ 01 47 05 37 51.

Institut de Thalassothérapie, Le Point Zéro, BP 43, 34280 La Grande-Motte, ☎ 04 67 29 13 13.

Thalacap Languedoc, place de la Falaise, 34300 La Cap-d'Agde, ☎ 04 67 26 14 80.

Tourist trains

These are a pleasant and original way of exploring the region and seeing countryside which one might otherwise not reach by car or on foot. In the **Cévennes**, a little steam train runs between Anduze and St-Jean-du-Gard, via Prafrance bamboo plantation and following the course of the rivers Gardon. The beauty of the **Orb valley** can be admired from the tourist train which operates between Bédarieux and Mons-la-Trivalle. The **Gorges d'Héric** can also be explored by train, leaving from Mons-la-Trivalle.

Wine-tasting

Information on visiting winegrowing establishments and local wine cooperatives, many of which offer the opportunity to taste their products (in moderation of course), can be obtained from the Fédération des Interprofessionnels des Vins de Roussillon, 19 avenue de Grande-Bretagne, 66000 Perpignan, ☎ 04 68 51 31 81, or the Maison des Terroirs en Corbières, R.N. 113, 11201 Lézignan, ☎ 04 68 27 73 00, or the Comité Interprofessionnel des Vins de Gaillac, Maison des Vins, Abbaye St-Michel, 81600 Gaillac, ☎ 05 63 57 15 40.

Jean-Hugues Anglade and Béatrice Dalle
in *Betty Blue*

Calendar of events

The list below is a selection of the many events which take place in the regions described in this guide. Visitors are advised to contact local tourist offices for fuller details of musical events, son et lumière shows, arts and crafts fairs etc, especially during July and August.

Sundays from January to the Sunday before Palm Sunday

Limoux . . . . Traditional carnival with 3 parades at 11am, 5pm and 9pm; Sunday before Palm Sunday, at midnight, judgment is passed on the Carnival King followed by an all-night "Blanquette" party.

February

Prats-de-Mollo . . . . "Fête de l'Ours" (bear festival); ☎ 04 68 39 70 83.

Good Friday

Arles-sur-Tech . . . . Evening procession by the Pénitents de la Sanch.

Collioure . . . . Procession by the Penitents' brotherhoods.

Perpignan . . . . Procession by the Pénitents de la Sanch.

Palm Sunday, Easter Day and Easter Monday

St-Félix-Lauragais . . . . "Foire à la Cocagne" (concerts, circus, jugglers, historical pageant); ☎ 05 61 83 01 71.

Sunday near 25 May

Aubrac . . . . "Fête de la transhumance": livestock taken up to summer pastures; ☎ 05 65 48 01 76.

Mid-June to mid-July

Perpignan . . . . "Estivales" (theatre festival).

Last week in June and 1st week in July

Montpellier . . . . "Montpellier-Danse" festival (traditional music and dance); ☎ 04 67 60 83 60.

July

Carcassonne . . . . Festival de la Cité (concerts, theatre, opera, dance etc).

Perpignan and the Roussillon Coast . . . . Festival (concerts of classical music).

Agde . . . . "Joutes nautiques".

July – August

Toulouse . . . . Summer music festival (classical, jazz, folk).

Pézenas . . . . "Mirondela dels Arts".

St-Guilhem-le-Désert . . . . Musical season at the abbey; ☎ 04 67 63 14 99.

1st weekend in July

Sète . . . . Festival of St Peter.

2nd weekend in July

Céret . . . . "Céret de Toros": various events involving bulls (fighting, racing etc.), sardana dancing.

Mid-July to beginning of August

Montpellier . . . . "Festival de Radio-France et de Montpellier Languedoc-Roussillon" (opera, symphonies, chamber music, jazz); ☎ 04 67 02 02 01.

Fridays and Saturdays from end of July to end of August

Foix . . . . Son et lumière show, "Il était une Foix... l'Ariège" (scenes from local history); ☎ 05 61 65 12 12.

Mid-July to end of August

Conques . . . . "Festival de Conques" (music and cinema); ☎ 05 65 72 85 00.

2nd fortnight in July

Sète . . . . Festival de Sète: Mediterranean music; ☎ 04 67 74 32 52.

Castres . . . . Goya festival: Spanish music, dance and theatre; ☎ 05 63 71 56 58.

Carcassonne . . . . Medieval Cité is "set alight" by an evening firework display.

Cordes . . . . "Fête médiévale du Grand Fauconnier" (historical pageant and various other "medieval" entertainments).

3rd weekend in July

Mirepoix . . . . Medieval festival.

3rd week in July

Frontignan . . . . Muscat festival; ☎ 04 67 48 33 94.

End of July

Cap d'Agde . . . . "Fête de la Mer"; ☎ 04 67 26 38 58.

Cordes-sur-Ciel . . . . "Musiques sur Ciel" music festival; ☎ 05 63 56 00 75.

Osséja . . . . International sheep-dog trials; ☎ 04 68 04 53 86.

End of July/Beginning of August

Albi . . . . Music festival.

26 July to 13 August

St-Michel-de-Cuxa-Prades . . . . Pablo Casals festival (concerts in the abbey).

1st Friday in August

Lautrec . . . . Garlic festival.

1st weekend in August

Gaillac . . . . Wine festival.

Banyuls-sur-Mer . . . . Sardana festival.

1st fortnight in August

Carcassonne . . . . "Les Médiévales"; tournament and show with medieval knights on horseback and a son et lumière show.

Amélie-les-Bains . . . . International folklore festival; ☎ 04 68 83 99 44.

Around 15 August (Feast of the Assumption)

Béziers . . . . "Féria"; ☎ 04 67 36 73 73.

La Grande-Motte . . . . Jazz festival; ☎ 04 67 29 03 37.

Penultimate Sunday in August

Céret . . . . International Sardana festival (400 dancers in costume).

End of August

Sète . . . . Festival of St Louis: "joutes nautiques", fireworks displays, swimming across Sète; ☎ 04 67 46 20 68.

August

Bouzigues . . . . Oyster festival.

September

Toulouse . . . . Piano recitals at Les Jacobins.

1st Sunday in September

Mas Soubeyran . . . . "Assemblée du Désert": French Protestant gathering; ☎ 04 66 85 02 72.

8 September

Méritxell . . . . National festival of Andorra.

3rd Sunday in October

Béziers . . . . Festival of new wine (dancing, blessing of new wine etc); ☎ 04 67 31 76 76.

End of October (10 days)

Montpellier . . . . International fair; ☎ 04 67 17 67 17.

7 November

Nasbinals . . . . Horse fair.

Admission times and charges

As admission times and charges are liable to alteration, the information below is given for guidance only. In cases where it has not been possible to obtain up-to-date information, the admission times and charges from the previous edition of the guide have been given in italics.

The information applies to individual adults. Special conditions for groups are common but arrangements should be made in advance. In some cases there is no charge for admission on certain days, eg Wednesdays, Sundays or public holidays.

Churches are usually closed from noon to 2pm; they should not be visited during services, other than to worship. Admission times are indicated if the interior is of special interest. Visitors to chapels are usually accompanied by the key-holder; a donation is welcome.

Most tours are conducted by French-speaking guides but in some cases the term "guided tours" may cover group visiting with recorded commentaries. Some of the larger and more frequented sights may offer guided tours in other languages. The symbol ▲ indicates that tours are given by lecturers from the Historic Monuments Association (Caisse Nationale des Monuments Historiques et Sites). Enquire at the ticket office or book stall. Other aids for foreign visitors are notes, pamphlets or audio guides.

Enquire at the tourist office, ❶ , for local religious holidays, market days etc. Every sight for which there are times and charges is indicated by the symbol ⊙ in the alphabetical section of the guide. The entries are listed in the order in which they appear in the alphabetical section of the guide.

Sights which have comprehensive facilities for the disabled are indicated by the symbol ᵴ below.

A

AGDE
❶ 1 place Molière – 34300 – ☎ 04 67 94 29 68

Guided tours of the town – Contact the tourist office.

Ancienne cathédrale St-Étienne – Open daily (except Sunday afternoons) in summer or for organised tours by the tourist office the rest of the year.

Musée agathois – Open daily (except Tuesdays) 10am to noon and 2pm to 6pm. Closed 1 May. 15 F. ☎ 04 67 94 82 51.

Massif de l'AIGOUAL

Meyrueis – ❶ Tour de l'Horloge, 48150, ☎ 04 66 45 60 33.

Château de Roquedols – The information centre of the Parc national des Cévennes is open in July and August daily (except for Monday mornings and Sunday afternoons) from 9am to 12.30pm and 3pm to 6.30pm. ☎ 04 66 45 62 81.

Mont Aigoual: Exposition Météo-France – Open 10am to 7pm May to September. Free admission. ☎ 04 67 82 60 01.

ALBI
❶ Palais de la Berbie, place Ste-Cécile – 81000 – ☎ 05 63 49 48 80

Guided tours of the town – Contact the tourist office.

Cathédrale Ste-Cécile – Open 8.30am to 6.45pm June to September, 8.30am to 11.45am and 2pm to 5.45pm the rest of the year. There is a small entrance charge to view the choir.

Musée Toulouse-Lautrec – Open 9am to noon and 2pm to 6pm June to September, 10am to noon and 2pm to 6pm in April and May, daily (except Tuesdays) 10am to noon and 2pm to 5pm the rest of the year. Closed 1 January, 1 May, 1 November and 25 December. 24F. ☎ 05 63 49 48 70.

Musée Lapérouse – Open daily (except Tuesdays) 9am to noon and 2pm to 6pm April to September, 10am to noon and 2pm to 5pm the rest of the year. Closed 1 January, 1 May, 1 November and 25 December. Free admission. ☎ 05 63 46 01 87.

Musée de Cire – Open 10am to noon and 2pm to 6pm June to August, 2pm to 5pm the rest of the year. Closed Mondays (except in July and August) and also all January. 15F. ☎ 05 63 54 87 55.

ALBI

Lescure: Église St-Michel – Open in summer. Information from the Mairie.

Notre-Dame-de-la-Drèche: Musée-sacristie – & Open Mondays to Saturdays 9.30am to noon and 2pm to 6pm, Sundays 2pm to 3pm and 4pm to 6pm. Free admission. ☎ 05 63 53 75 00.

ALÈS   🛈 place Gabriel-Péri - 30100 - ☎ 04 66 52 32 15

Cathédrale St-Jean-Baptiste – Open weekdays from 9am to noon and 2pm to 6pm.

Musée du Colombier – Open daily (except Tuesdays) 10am to noon and 2pm to 5pm. Closed public holidays. Free admission. ☎ 04 66 86 30 40.

Musée minéralogique de l'École des Mines – & Guided tour (1hr 30min) Monday to Friday 2pm to 6pm mid-June to mid-September, by appointment the rest of the year. Closed public holidays. 30F.☎ 04 66 78 51 69.

Musée-Bibliothèque Pierre-André-Benoît – Open daily noon to 7pm in July and August, daily (except Mondays and Tuesdays) at the same times the rest of the year. Closed 1 January, 1 May and 25 December and in February. Free admission.☎ 04 66 86 98 69.

Mine-témoin – Guided tour (1hr) 9.30am to 7pm June to August, 9am to 12.30pm and 2pm to 5.30pm the rest of the year. Last admission 1hr 30min before closing time. Closed mid-November to March. 35F, 20F (children aged 6 to 12). ☎ 04 66 30 45 15.

Excursions

Château de Portes – Guided tour (45min) daily (except Mondays) 9am to noon and 3pm to 7pm July to mid-September, week-ends 2pm to 6pm the rest of the year. Closed mid-November to mid-March. 19F. ☎ 04 66 34 35 90.

Château de Rousson – Guided tour (30min) 10am to 7pm in July and August. 25F. ☎ 04 66 85 60 31.

Rousson: Préhistorama – & Open 10am to 7pm June to August, 10am to 6pm in May, 10am to noon and 2pm to 6pm in April and September, daily (except Saturdays) 2pm to 5pm in March and October, Sundays and daily during school holidays 2pm to 5pm in February and November. Closed in January and December. 30F, 18F (children 7 to 14). ☎ 04 66 85 86 96.

Parc ornithologique des Isles – & Open daily 9am to 7pm May to September, 9am to noon and 2pm to 6pm the rest of the year. 30F, 20F (children). ☎ 04 66 25 66 13.

AMÉLIE-LES-BAINS-PALALDA

Palalda Museum – *Open daily (except Tuesdays, and Saturday and Sunday mornings) from 10am to noon and 2pm (3pm on Sundays) to 7pm from May to mid-October, and from 10am to noon and 2pm to 6pm the rest of the year. Closed from mid-December to mid-February. 10F* ☎ *04 68 39 34 90.*

ANDORRA   🛈 1, rue du Docteur Vilanova - Andorra la Vella – ☎ (376) 82 02 14

Casa de la Vall – Guided tour (30min) daily (except Saturdays and Sundays) 9am to 1pm and 3pm to 7pm. Reserve tours one month in advance. Closed 1 January, 14 March, 8 September and 25 December. Free admission. ☎ (376) 82 02 14.

Sant Joan de Caselles – Guided tour daily in July and August, by appointment the rest of the year. ☎ (376) 85 11 15 or 85 11 34.

ANDUZE   🛈 plan de Brie - 30140 – ☎ 04 66 61 98 17

Musée de la musique – Open 10am to 1pm and 3pm to 7pm in July and August, 2pm to 6pm in June, September, during school holidays and every Sunday and public holiday the rest of the year. 28F.☎ 04 66 61 86 60.

Haute vallée de l'ARIÈGE

Pamiers: Notre-Dame-du-Camp – Open daily from 8.30am to noon and 2pm to 7pm.

ARLES-SUR-TECH

El Palau Santa Maria – Open daily (except Mondays) 3pm to 6pm mid-March to October. 15F. ☎ 04 68 83 90 83.

Excursions

St-Laurent-de-Cerdans Museum – Open July and August from 10am to noon and 3pm to 7pm; the rest of the year from 10am to noon and 3pm to 6pm. Closed at weekends from October to April. 10F. ☎ 04 68 39 55 75 or ☎ 04 68 39 50 06.

Gorges de la Fou – Open 10am to 6pm. Closed November to March. 25F. ☎ 04 68 39 12 44 or ☎ 04 68 39 16 21.

Les ASPRES

Prunet-et-Belpuig: Chapelle de la Trinité – Open daily (except Tuesdays) 9am to 6pm.

Haute vallée de l'AUDE

Grottes de l'Aguzou – Active guided tour in the form of a "caving safari" (one day underground) 9am to 5pm. Reservations 24hr or 48hr in advance from the tourist office at Quillan. The charge (not stated) includes overalls and equipment but not the picnic. ☎ 04 68 20 07 78.

Espéraza: Musée de la Chapellerie – ﴾ Open 10am to noon and 2pm to 6pm (7pm June to September). Closed 6 to 25 January. Charges not stated. ☎ 04 68 74 00 75.

Espéraza: Musée des Dinosaures – ﴾ Same times and conditions as the millinery museum. ☎ 04 68 74 26 88.

Couiza: Château – Access permitted to inner court. Closed in January. ☎ 04 68 74 02 80.

Rennes-le-Château: Domaine de l'Abbé Saunière – ﴾ Open 10am to 7pm. 25F. ☎ 04 68 74 31 16.

Rennes-le-Château: Museum – Open April to October 10am to 1pm and 2pm to 7pm, the rest of the year daily (except Mondays) 10am to noon and 2pm to 6pm. 15F. ☎ 04 68 74 14 56.

Alet-les-Bains: Cathedral ruins – Open April to mid-September 9am to noon and 2pm to 6.30pm, the rest of the year 9am to noon and 3pm to 5pm. 10F (15F for a guided tour). ☎ 04 68 69 93 56.

Limoux: Caves de Blanquette – To find the addresses of the winemakers who open their cellars, contact the tourist office or the Syndicat des Vins AOC de Limoux, 20, avenue du Pont-de-France, ☎ 04 68 31 12 83.

AVEN ARMAND

Guided tour (45min) 9.30am to 7pm June to August, 9.30am to noon and 1.30pm to 6pm mid March to May, 9.30am to noon and 1.30pm to 5pm September to 6 November. Closed the rest of the year. 43F, 20F (children). Joint ticket including admission to the Chaos de Montpellier-le-Vieux : 55F, 25F. ☎ 04 66 45 61 31.

Aven Armand

Excursions

Ax-Bonascre-le-Saquet cable-car – Operates daily from 1pm to 5pm. Closed May to July and mid-September to December. Fare costs 35F there and back. ☎ 05 61 64 20 06.

Luzenac: Carrière de talc de Trimouns – *Guided tour (45min) daily (except Sundays) at 10am, 11am, 2pm, 3pm and 4pm in July and August, at 4pm the rest of the year. Closed November to end April and public holidays. 30 F. ☎ 05 61 64 60 60 (Vallées d'Ax tourist office at Luzenac). Visiting cancelled in bad weather; wear warm clothing and take binoculars.*

B

BALARUC-LES-BAINS   🅱 Pavillon Sévigné – 34540 – ☎ 04 67 48 81 46

BANYULS-SUR-MER   🅱 avenue de la République – 66650 – ☎ 04 68 88 31 58

Aquarium – Open 9am to noon and 2pm to 6.30pm (10pm in July and August). 22F, 11F (children 6 to 12). ☎ 04 68 88 73 39.

Caves (Banyuls) – Guided tour (1 hr 15min) 10am to 5.30pm in July and August, 2.30pm and 4pm (also open Sundays and during school holidays to 3.15pm) the rest of the year. Closed Tuesdays, except during school holidays. 40F, 20F (children 6 to 12).☎ 05 61 05 95 06.

La Grande Cave – Guided tour (45min) 9am to 7pm April to October, daily (except Sundays) 9.30am to 12.30pm and 2pm to 6pm the rest of the year. ☎ 04 68 98 36 92.

Cave du Mas Reig – ♿ Guided tour (45min) 9.30am to 7pm June to September, 2pm to 7pm in May. Closed October to April.

Abbaye de BEAULIEU-EN-ROUERGUE

Tour – Guided tours (45min) July and August daily from 10am to noon and 2pm to 6pm (ticket office closes at 11.45am and 5.45pm); April to June and September to October daily (except Tuesdays) at the same times). Closed 1 May. 32F. ☎ 05 63 67 06 84.

BÉZIERS   🅱 29, avenue St-Saëns – 34500 – ☎ 04 67 76 47 00

Guided tours of the town – Contact the tourist office.

Musée du Biterrois – ♿ Open daily (except Mondays) 10am to 7pm in summer, 9am to noon and 2pm to 6pm the rest of the year. Closed 1 January to Easter, 1 May and 25 December. 15F. ☎ 04 67 36 71 01.

Musée des Beaux-Arts – The Hôtel Fabrégat is open daily (except Mondays and Sunday mornings) 9am to noon and 2pm to 6pm, The Hôtel Fayet is open Tuesdays to Fridays 9am to noon and 2pm to 6pm. Closed 1 January to Easter, 1 May and 25 December. 15F. ☎ 04 67 49 04 66.

Basilique St-Aphrodise – Open weekdays only, 9am to noon and 4pm to 6pm. ☎ 04 67 31 03 53.

Excursion

Abbaye de Fontcaude – Open daily (except Sunday mornings) 10am to noon and 2.30pm to 7pm June to September, Mondays, Saturdays and Sundays 2.30pm to 4.30pm (6pm after the change to summer time) October to May, 2.30pm to 4.30pm during school holidays. Closed in January except Sunday afternoons. 15F. ☎ 04 67 38 23 85.

Le BOULOU

Maureillas-las-Illas: Musée du Liège – Open mid-June to mid-September 10.30am to noon and 3.30pm to 7pm, the rest of the year daily (except Tuesdays) 2pm to 5pm. Closed 1 January, 1 May, 1 November and 25 December. 15F. ☎ 04 68 83 15 41 or 04 68 83 48 00.

St-Martin-de-Fenollar: Chapel – Guided tour (30min) 10.30am to noon and 3.30pm to 7pm mid-June to mid-September, daily (except Tuesdays) 2pm to 5pm the rest of the year. Closed 1 January, 1 May, 1 November and 25 December. 15F. ☎ 04 68 87 73 82 or 04 68 83 48 00.

Vallée de la Rome – Guided tours are organised starting from Le Boulou by the Association pour le patrimoine de la vallée de la Rome. They visit, among other things, the Musée du Liège at Maureillas-las-Illas, the chapel at St-Martin-de-Fenollar, the sites at Les Cluses, the fort at Bellegarde and the archeological site at Panissars. Information and registration: Hôtel Le Domitien, route d'Espagne – 66160 Le Boulou. ☎ 04 68 83 49 50.

Les Cluses: Church of St-Nazaire – Open on Mondays from 1.30pm to 5pm, Tuesdays and Fridays from 9am to noon and 1.30pm to 5pm, and Thursdays from 9am to noon. Further details from Les Cluses town hall *(mairie)*.

Fort de Bellegarde – Open 10.30am to 12.30pm and 2.30pm to 7pm July to September. Closed the rest of the year. 15F. ☎ 04 68 83 60 15.

Abîme du BRAMABIAU

Tour (1hr 30min) 9am to 7pm in July and August, 9am to 6pm April to June and in September, 10am to 5pm the rest of the year. Closed mid-November to March. 32F, 12F (children). ☎ 04 67 82 60 78.

BRUNIQUEL

Chateau de Bruniquel – Open (1hr guided tours available) July and August daily from 10am to 12.30pm and 2pm to 7pm; Easter to June and September to 1 November open on Sundays and public holidays from 10am to 12.30pm and 2pm to 6pm, and afternoons only (2pm to 6pm) during the week. 13F (independent visit), 18F (guided tour). ☎ 05 63 67 27 67.

Maison Payrol – Open (guided tours available) July and August daily from 10am to 7pm; April to June and in September daily from 10am to noon and 2pm to 6pm; in March at weekends only from 10am to noon and 2pm to 6pm. 15F. ☎ 05 63 67 26 42.

Excursion

Montricoux: Musée Marcel-Lenoir – & Open (45min guided tours available) Easter to 1 November daily from 10am to 12.30pm and 2.30pm to 7pm. 25F. ☎ 05 63 67 26 48.

C

Le CANIGOU

Access to Le Canigou, from Cornellla-de-Conflent – *Departures in 4 x 4 at 8am and 11am June to September. 100F. Apply to Transports Circuits Touristiques (M. Cullell).* ☎ 04 68 05 63 97.

Access to Le Canigou, from Prades – Apply to M Colas (Excursions La Castellane) ☎ 04 68 05 27 00; or contact Prades tourist office for other options.

Access to Le Canigou, from Vernet-les-Bains – Apply to Villacèque garage on ☎ 04 68 05 51 14, or to Taxi de la Gare on ☎ 04 68 05 62 28, or to Tourisme Excursion on ☎ 04 68 05 54 39; details of other options available from Vernet tourist office.

Le CAPCIR

Les Angles: Zoological park – Open mid-June to mid-September daily from 8am to 7pm; the rest of the year from 9am to 5pm. 45F, 35F (children 4 to 14). ☎ 04 68 04 17 20.

Grotte de Fontrabiouse: Guided tour (1hr) 10am to 7pm mid-June to mid-September, 10am to noon and 1.30pm to 5.30pm during school holidays, 10am to noon and 2pm to 5pm the rest of the year. 30F, 15F (children). ☎ 04 68 30 95 55.

CAP D'AGDE   🛈 BP 544 - Bulle d'accueil - 34305 Cédex - ☎ 04 67 01 04 04

Musée de l'Éphèbe – & Open 9.30am to 12.30pm and 2.30pm to 6.30pm in July and August, daily (except Tuesdays and Sunday mornings) 9am to noon and 2pm to 6pm the rest of the year. 15F. ☎ 04 67 94 69 60.

Aqualand – Open 10am to 7pm from 7 June to 7 September. Closed the rest of the year. 90F, 77F (children under 10). ☎ 04 67 26 85 94.

CARCASSONNE   🛈 15, boulevard Camille-Pelletan - 11000 - ☎ 04 68 25 07 04

Chateau Comtal – Guided tours (45min) in July and August from 9am to 7.30pm, in June and September from 9am to 7pm, in April, May and October from 9.30am to 12.30pm and 2pm to 6pm, and the rest of the year from 10am to 12.30pm and 2pm to 5pm. Closed 1 January, 1 May, 1 and 11 November and 25 December. 32F. ☎ 04 68 25 01 66.

CARCASSONNE

Basilique St-Nazaire – Open from 9am to noon and 2pm to 5pm, 6pm or 7pm depending on the time of year. ☎ 04 68 25 27 65.

Musée des Beaux-Arts – Open daily from 10am to noon and 2pm to 6pm. Closed on public holidays, on Sundays and Mondays between mid-September and mid-June, and on Mondays and Tuesdays between mid-June and mid-September. Free admission. ☎ 04 68 77 73 70.

Excursions

Brousses-et-Villaret: Paper mill – Guided tours (1hr) July to mid-September at 11am, 3pm, 4pm, 5pm and 6pm, the rest of the year Mondays to Fridays at 11am and 4pm and Saturdays, Sundays and public holidays at 11am, 2.30pm, 3.30pm, 4.30pm and 5.30pm. 15F. ☎ 04 68 26 67 43.

Abbaye de Villelongue – Open 10am to noon and 2pm to 6pm May to October. Closed the rest of the year. 15F. ☎ 04 68 76 00 81.

CASTELNAUDARY   🛈 place de la République – 11400 – ☎ 04 68 23 05 73

Église St-Michel – Open in summer. Information from the Mairie.

Musée archéologique du Présidial – Open daily (except Sunday afternoons) 10am to noon and 3pm to 6pm July to September. ☎ 04 68 23 05 73.

Moulin de Cugarel – *Open 15 June to 15 September Mondays to Saturdays 10am to noon and 3pm to 6.30pm, Sundays 3pm to 6pm. ☎ 04 68 23 05 73.*

Excursion

St-Papoul: Abbey – ♿ Guided tour (45min) 10am to 12.30pm and 2pm to 7pm July to September, 10am to noon and 2pm to 6pm the rest of the year. Closed mid-November to April. 20F. ☎ 04 68 94 97 75.

CASTRES   🛈 3, rue Milhau-Ducommun – 81100 – ☎ 05 63 62 63 62

Guided tours of the town – Contact the tourist office.

Passenger boat trips – The "Miredames", a passenger barge restored on the lines of one of the old river boats, runs up the Agoût from the town centre as far as the Gourjade leisure park. Leaves Pont Vieux: 10.30am, 2pm, 3.20pm, 4.40pm and 6pm in July and August; 2pm, 3.20pm, 4.40pm and 6pm in May, June and September; Wednesdays, Saturdays and Sundays to 2pm, 3.20pm and 4.40pm in October. Leaves Gourjade leisure park: 11.20am, 2.45pm, 4pm, 5.20pm and 6.30pm in July and August; 2.45pm, 4pm, 5.20pm and 6.30pm in May, June and September; and on Wednesdays, Saturdays and Sundays at 2.45pm, 4pm and 5.20pm in October. 25F, 10F (children) ☎ 05 63 59 72 30.

Musée Goya – Open 9am (10am Sundays and public holidays) to noon and 2pm to 6pm in July and August, daily (except Mondays) at the same times from April to June and 1 to 21 September, daily (except Mondays) 9am (10am Sundays and public holidays) to noon and 2pm to 5pm the rest of the year. Closed 1 January, 1 May, 1 November and 25 December. 15F. ☎ 05 63 71 59 27.

Centre national and musée Jean-Jaurès – ♿ Same opening times as the musée Goya. 10F. ☎ 05 63 72 01 01.

Hôtel de Viviès: Centre d'Art contemporain – Open 10am to noon and 2pm to 6pm in July and August, daily (except Monday mornings) 10am to noon and 2pm to 6pm and Saturdays and Sundays 3pm to 6pm the rest of the year. Closed public holidays (except 14 July and 15 August). 5F in July and August, free admission the rest of the year. ☎ 05 63 59 30 20.

Château de CASTRIES

Free entry to the terraces and gardens 2.30pm to 5.30pm, guided tours (1hr) of the interior of the château daily (except Mondays) at 2.45pm, 4pm and 5.15pm. Closed mid-December to mid-January. 25F. ☎ 04 67 70 68 66.

Le CAYLAR

Chapelle Notre-Dame-de-Roc-Castel – *Open from Easter to 1 November.* ☎ *04 67 44 50 39.*

La CERDAGNE

Angoustrine: Church – To visit apply to the Mairie or the grocery shop.

Odeillo: Four solaire – ♿ Open 10am to 12.30pm and 1.30pm to 7.30pm in July and August, 10am to 12.30pm and 1.30pm to 5.30pm the rest of the year. Closed mid-November to mid-December and also 1 January and 25 December. 25F. ☎ 04 68 30 77 86.

Hix: Church – Guided tours in July and August, and by prior appointment at the tourist office or town hall the rest of the year. ☎ 04 68 04 55 35.

"Petit train jaune" – Regular service. Leaflets available from SNCF stations in the area. ☎ 08 36 35 35 35.

Odeillo – Solar furnace

CÉRET

🛈 1, avenue G.-Clemenceau (in season) - 66400 - ☎ 04 68 87 00 53

Musée d'Art moderne – ♿ Open 10am to 7pm July to September, daily (except Tuesdays October to April) 10am to 6pm the rest of the year. Closed 1 January, 1 May, 1 November and 25 December. 35F. ☎ 04 68 87 27 76.

Corniche des CÉVENNES

St-Laurent-de-Trèves: Spectacle audiovisuel – Open in July and August from 10am to 7pm; in May, June, September and October daily (except Tuesdays) from 10am to noon and 2pm to 6pm; during Easter and November school holidays daily from 2pm to 6pm. Closed from mid-November until Easter school holidays. 20F. 15F (children). ☎ 04 00 49 53 01.

Grotte de CLAMOUSE

Guided tours (45min) 10am to 7pm in July and August, 10am to 5pm March to June and in September and October, noon to 5pm the rest of the year. 42F, 21F (children 6 to 12). ☎ 04 67 57 71 05.

Grotte de la COCALIÈRE

Guided tour (1hr 15min) 10am to 6pm in July and August, 10am to noon and 2pm to 5pm April to June, September and October. 42F, 22F (children 6 to 12). ☎ 04 66 24 01 57.

COLLIOURE

🛈 place du 18 juin - 66190 - ☎ 04 68 82 15 47

Église Notre-Dame-des-Anges – Open 9am to noon and 3pm to 6pm.

Château Royal – Open 10am to 6pm June to September, 9am to 5pm the rest of the year. Closed 1 January, 1 May, 1 November and 25 December. 20F. ☎ 04 68 82 06 43.

Prieuré de COMBEROUMAL

Open daily. Free admission.

Le CONFLENT

Corneilla-de-Conflent: Église Ste-Marie – Guided tour 10am to noon and 2pm to 6pm. ☎ 04 68 05 64 64.

CONQUES

🛈 12320 - ☎ 05 65 72 85 00

Abbatiale Ste-Foy – Open 8.15am to 11.15am and 12.30pm to 6pm. For guided tours, contact the tourist office.

Treasury – Open 9am to 1pm and 2pm to 7pm in July and August, 9am to noon and 2pm to 6pm the rest of the year. Closed on the mornings of 1 January and 25 December. 28F. ☎ 05 65 72 85 00.

Les CORBIÈRES

Donjon d'Arques – Open 10am to 7pm in July and August, 10am to 6pm in May, June and September, 10am to 5pm the rest of the year. Closed in December, January and February. 25F. ☏ 04 68 69 82 87.

Château de Puilaurens: Open 9am to 7pm April to 11 November, 10am to 4.30pm during the winter holidays. 20F. ☏ 04 68 20 65 26.

Château de Termes – Open 9.30am to 7.30pm in July and August, 10am to 6pm in May, June and September, 10am to 5pm in April and October, weekends and school holidays the rest of the year. Closed in January. 20F. ☏ 04 68 70 09 20.

Peyriac-de-Mer: Musée archéologique – *Apply to the Mairie.* ☏ *04 68 41 49 90.*

Cucugnan: Théâtre Achille-Mir – ♿ Performances given in July and August from 10am to 9pm; in May, June and September from 10am to 8pm; in April and October from 10am to 7pm; in February, March, November and December at weekends and during school holidays from 10am to 6pm. Closed during January and on 25 December. 25F, combined ticket includes entry to Château de Quéribus. ☏ 04 68 45 03 69.

St-Polycarpe: Church – Open 8am to 7pm in summer, 9am to 5pm in winter. ☏ 04 68 31 14 31.

CORDES-SUR-CIEL   🛈 Maison Fonpeyrouse - 81170 - ☏ 05 63 56 00 52

Guided tours of the town – Contact the tourist office.

Shuttle bus to top of hill – Operates in summer daily from 9.30am to 7pm, otherwise by prior arrangement with the tourist office the rest of the year.

Musée d'Art and d'Histoire Charles-Portal – Open 11am to noon and 3pm to 6pm in July and August, Sundays only 3pm to 6pm the rest of the year. Closed from 1 November to Easter. 15F. ☏ 05 63 56 00 52 (tourist office).

Musée de l'Art du sucre – Open 10am to noon and 2.30pm to 6.30pm. Closed in January and also 25 December. 15F. ☏ 05 63 56 02 40.

Musée Yves-Brayer – Open daily (except Tuesdays and Sunday mornings) 10am to noon and 2pm to 6pm. Closed in January. 10F. ☏ 05 63 56 00 40.

"L'univers des cristaux et des pierres précieuses" – Open 10am to 12.30pm and 2pm to 6pm April to mid-November. Closed the rest of the year. 15F. ☏ 05 63 56 09 55.

Église St-Michel – Open during July and August; the rest of the year contact the tourist office.

Palais des Scènes – *Open 10am to noon and 2.30pm to 6pm in July and August, 2.30pm to 6pm April to June. 20F, 15F (children).* ☏ *05 63 56 00 78.*

La Capelette – To visit see the instructions on the door or contact the tourist office or the Mairie in Cordes.

Excursion

Vindrac: Musée de l'Outil et des Métiers anciens – Open daily (except Tuesdays out of season) 10am to 7pm. Closed December to February. 20 F. ☏ 05 63 56 05 77.

Le Cayla: Musée du Cayla – *Guided tour (1hr 30min) daily (except Tuesdays) 10am to noon and 2pm to 6pm May to October, daily (except Mondays and Tuesdays) 2pm to 6pm the rest of the year. Closed public holidays. 10F.* ☏ *05 63 33 90 30.*

Monestiés: Chapelle St-Jacques – Guided tours 10am to noon and 2.30pm to 6.30pm in summer, 10.30am to noon and 2.30pm to 5pm in winter. ☏ 05 63 76 19 17.

La COUVERTOIRADE

Ramparts – *Open June to August from 9.30am to 6.30pm; March to May and September to 11 November from 10am to noon and 2pm to 5.30pm. Closed 12 November to February. 15F.* ☏ *05 65 62 25 81* or ☏ *05 65 62 11 62.*

Church – Open March to November from 9am to 6pm; the rest of the year open at weekends only. If closed, apply to the town hall ☏ 05 65 62 25 81, the historic monuments ticket kiosk ☏ 05 65 62 11 62 or the community centre ☏ 05 65 62 28 06.

D

Grotte de DARGILAN

Guided tour (1hr) 9am to 7pm in July and August, 9am to noon and 1.30pm to 6pm April to June and September, 10am to noon and 1.30pm to 5pm in October, Open only to 3pm during school holidays. 39F, 24F (children). ☎ 04 66 45 60 20.

Grotte des DEMOISELLES

Guided tour (1hr) 9am to 7pm in July and August, 9am to noon and 2pm to 7pm April to June and September, 9.30am to noon and 2pm to 5pm the rest of the year. Closed 1 January and 25 December. 40F, 20F (children 6 to 12). ☎ 04 67 73 70 02.

Grotte de la DEVÈZE

Guided tour (1hr) 10am to 6pm in July and August, 2pm to 5pm April to June and September. Closed in December and January. 35F, 20F (children), combined ticket includes admission to the Musée français de la Spéléologie. ☎ 04 67 97 03 24.

Musée français de la Spéléologie – &. Same opening times and charges as the cave. ☎ 04 67 97 03 24.

E

ELNE

Cathédrale Ste-Eulalie-et-Ste-Julie: Cloisters and museums – Open June to September from 9.30am to 7pm; April, May and October daily from 9.30am to 12.30pm and 2pm to 6pm; the rest of the year daily (except Tuesdays) from 9.30am to noon and 2pm to 5pm. Closed 1 January, 1 May and 25 December. 20F for a ticket including entry to the Musée Terrus. ☎ 04 68 22 70 90.

Musée Terrus – &. Open 9.30am to 6pm 45 June to September, daily (except Tuesdays in May and October) 9.30am to 12.30pm and 2pm to 5.45pm in April, May and October, daily (except Tuesdays) 10am to noon and 2pm to 4.45pm the rest of the year. 10F. ☎ 04 68 22 88 88.

Oppidum d'ENSÉRUNE

Site – Open 9.30am to 7.30pm June to August, 9.30am to 6.30pm in April, May and September, 9.30am to 5.00pm the rest of the year. Closed 1 January, 1 May, 1 and 11 November and 25 December. ☎ 04 67 37 01 23.

Museum – Open 9.30am to 7pm June to August, 10am to noon and 2pm to 6pm in April, May and September, 10am to noon and 2pm to 4pm (4.30pm Sundays) the rest of the year. Closed 1 January, 1 May, 1 and 11 November and 25 December. 25 F. ☎ 04 67 37 01 23.

Nissan-lez-Ensérune: Archeological museum – Guided tours (45min) on Wednesdays from 5pm and on Sunday afternoons. Free admission including tour of the church. ☎ 04 67 37 01 46 or ☎ 04 67 37 14 12.

ESPALION 🛈 Mairie - B.P. 52 - 12500 - ☎ 05 65 44 10 63

Guided tours of the town – Contact the tourist office.

Musée Joseph-Vaylet – Open 10am to noon and 2pm to 6.30pm in July and August, 10am to noon and 2pm to 6pm in June and September, on application the rest of the year. 15F. ☎ 05 65 44 09 18.

Musée du Rouergue – *Open daily (except Saturday mornings) 10am to 12.30pm and 2pm to 7pm in July and August, 2pm to 6pm in September. Closed October to June. 15F. ☎ 05 65 44 19 91.*

Église de Perse – Open in July and August, ask for the key at the Mairie in Espalion the rest of the year.

Excursion

Château de Calmont d'Olt – Open 9am to 7pm in July and August, daily (except Thursdays and Fridays) 10am to noon and 2pm to 6pm in May, June and September. Closed October to April. 20F. ☎ 05 65 44 15 89.

Monts de l'ESPINOUSE

St-Pons-de-Thomières: Old cathedral – Open daily 8am to 6pm. ☎ 04 67 97 06 65 (tourist office).

St-Pons-de-Thomières: Musée de Préhistoire régionale – *Open 10am to noon and 3pm to 6pm mid-June to mid-September, Tuesdays, Thursdays and Fridays 10am to noon , Wednesdays, Saturdays and Sundays 10am to noon and 2.30pm to 5.30pm. 15F. ☎ 04 67 97 22 61.*

Monts de l'ESPINOUSE

Prat d'Alaric – Farm visit July to mid-September. Check actual opening times. Free admission. ☎ 04 67 97 38 22.

Olargues: Museum – Open daily 10am to noon and 4pm to 7pm July to mid-September. 10F. ☎ 04 67 97 88 00 or ☎ 04 67 97 70 79.

ESTAING

🛈 Mairie - 12190 - ☎ 05 65 44 03 22

Château – Access to terrace and the keep daily (except Tuesdays) 9.30am to noon and 2.30pm to 6pm April to September, 9.30am to noon and 2.30pm to 5pm the rest of the year. Access to the keep closed mid-October to Easter.

F

FANJEAUX

Church and treasury – *Open 10.30am to noon and 2pm to 6pm in July and August, Sunday mornings only the rest of the year.*

Les FENOUILLÈDES

Notre-Dame-de-Laval: Hermitage – Open daily in August and on application to the Mairie in Caudiès the rest of the year. ☎ 04 68 59 92 26.

FLORAC

🛈 château de Florac - 48400 - ☎ 04 66 45 01 14

Château (Parc national des Cévennes information centre) – Open 9am to 7pm July to mid-September, 9am to noon and 2pm to 6pm Easter to June and mid-September to 11 November, weekdays only 9am to noon and 2pm to 6pm the rest of the year. Closed 1 January and 25 December. Free entry to the information centre, 20F for the permanent exhibition. ☎ 04 66 49 53 01.

FOIX
🛈 45, cours G.-Fauré - 09000 - ☎ 05 61 65 12 12

Château – Open 9.45am to 6.30pm in July and August, 9.45am to noon and 2pm to 6pm in June and September, 10.30am to noon and 2pm to 5.30pm the rest of the year. Closed Mondays and Tuesdays November to April, 1 January and 25 December. 25F. ☎ 05 61 65 56 05.

Musée départmental de l'Ariège – As for Château.

Abbaye de FONTFROIDE

♿ Guided tour (1hr) 9.30am to 6.30pm 9 July to 31 August, 10am to noon and 2pm to 5pm April to 8 July and in September and October, 10am to noon and 2pm to 4pm the rest of the year. 35F. ☎ 04 68 45 11 08.

Abbaye de Fontfroide

Château de Gaussan – Exterior open to visitors. Mass sung in Latin and Gregorian chant daily at 10am.

FONT-ROMEU

🛈 avenue E.-Brousse - 66122 - ☎ 04 68 30 68 30

Hermitage chapel – Open 10am to noon and 3pm to 6pm 1st Sunday in July to 7 September. The statue of the Virgin is taken up from Odeillo to the Hermitage on Trinity Sunday and returns to Odeillo on the afternoon of 8 September. ☎ 04 68 30 11 18.

FRONTIGNAN

🛈 rue de la Raffinerie - 34110 - ☎ 04 67 48 33 94

Cave coopérative du Muscat – ♿ Guided tour (30min) 9.30am to 1pm and 3.30pm to 7pm June to September, 9.30am to noon and 2pm to 6pm March to May and October to December, daily (except Sundays) 2pm to 6pm the rest of the year. Closed 1 January and 25 December. Free admission. ☎ 04 67 48 12 26.

Musée d'Histoire locale – Open daily (except Tuesdays) 10am to noon and 2.30pm to 6.30pm. Closed December to February and also 1 May. Free admission. ☎ 04 67 48 26 69.

G – H – J

GAILLAC
🛈 place de la Libération - 81600 - ☎ 05 63 57 14 65

Musée des Arts et Traditions populaires – ♿ Open daily (except Tuesdays) 10am to noon and 2pm to 6pm in summer, 2pm to 6pm in winter. Closed 1 January, 1 May, 11 November and 25 December. 15F. ☎ 05 63 41 03 81.

Musée des Beaux-Arts – Same opening times as the Musée des Arts and Traditions populaires and the Musée d'Histoire Naturelle Ph. Thomas. 15F. ☎ 05 63 57 18 25.

Musée d'Histoire Naturelle Philadelphe-Thomas – Same opening times as the Musée des Beaux-Arts and the Musée des Arts and Traditions populaires. 15F. ☎ 05 63 57 36 31.

Excursion

Lisle-sur-Tarn: Musée Raymond-Lafage – *Open daily (except Tuesdays and Saturdays and Sunday mornings) 10am to noon and 2pm to 6pm May to October, Thursdays and Fridays 10am to noon and 2pm to 6pm the rest of the year. Closed public holidays. 10 F.* ☎ *05 63 40 45 45.*

Château de Mauriac: Guided tour (1hr) 3pm to 6pm, Sundays only and daily during school holidays 3pm to 6pm October to April. Closed 1 January and 31 December. 30F. ☎ 05 63 41 71 18.

Les GRANDS CAUSSES

Hyelzas, a traditional Causse farmstead – *Open in July and August from 10am to 8pm; March to June from 10am to noon and 2pm to 7pm; September from 10am to noon and 3pm to 6pm; October on Saturdays only from 11am to noon and 3pm to 5pm. Closed from 5 November to 20 March. 20F, 9F (children).* ☎ 04 66 45 65 25.

GRENADE

Church – Open daily (except Sunday afternoons) 8.30am to noon and 3pm to 5pm. ☎ 05 61 82 61 35.

Vallée de l'HÉRAULT

Géospace Observatoire d'Aniane – Guided tours (1hr) daily (closed Mondays) 10am to noon and 2pm to 6pm in July and August; Sundays 2pm to 5pm during the rest of the year. Closed on public holidays. 30F peak, 10F off peak. For information on thematic evenings and workshops offered, contact Géospace Observatoire d'Aniane, B.P. 22, 34150 Aniane. ☎ 04 67 03 49 49.

Gorges d'HÉRIC

Scenic railway – The small tourist train runs (journey time: 1hr) from the first weekend in April to late October. First departure of the day is at 10.30am from mid-June to mid-September, and at 1.15pm the rest of the year. Fare costs 35F return, or 25F (children). For further information and reservations: ☎ 04 67 97 70 98.

Gorges de la JONTE

Le Rozier: Musée de l'architecture locale – *Open 10am to noon and 3pm to 7pm in July and August; 3pm to 7pm during the 2nd fortnight of June and the 1st week of September; Saturdays, Sundays and public holidays 3pm to 6pm mid-April to mid-June and mid-September to October. 13F.* ☎ *04 66 45 65 25 or* ☎ *04 66 45 66 74.*

L

Rivière souterraine de LABOUICHE

Subterranean gallery – Guided tour (75min) in boat carrying 12 people, 9.30am to 6pm in July and August; 10am to noon and 2pm to 6pm from Whitsun to September; and during school holidays, Sundays and public holidays April to 11 November, 2pm to 5pm April to Whitsun. Last tours at 11.15am and 5.15pm. 42F, 30F (children under 12). ☎ 05 61 65 04 11.

LAGRASSE

Abbey – Open daily (except Sunday mornings) 10.30am to 12.30pm and 2pm to 6.30pm May to September; 2pm to 5pm the rest of the year. Closed November to March. 20F. ☎ 04 68 58 11 58.

LAGUIOLE

place du Foirail - 12210 - ☎ 05 65 44 35 94

Musée du Haut-Rouergue – Open 3pm to 6.30pm in July and August. Donation welcome. ☎ 05 65 44 34 48.

Excursion

Château du Bousquet: Guided tour (1hr 30 min) daily (except Tuesdays) 2.30pm to 6.30pm. 30F. ☎ 05 65 48 41 13.

LAMALOU-LES-BAINS

2, avenue du Dr.-Ménard - 34240 - ☎ 04 67 95 70 91

Guided tours of the spa – Contact the tourist office.

Bédarieux to Mons-la-Trivalle tourist train – ♿ *Runs in July and August daily (except Mondays); in June and September on Fridays, Saturdays and Sundays; in April, May and October on Saturdays and Sundays, and also on 1, 2, 3, 11 and 12 November. Return Bédarieux-Mons-la-Trivalle: 60F, 30F (children).* ☎ *04 67 95 77 00.*

St-Pierre-de-Rhèdes – Guided tour Wednesdays at 2.30pm. Contact the tourist office in Lamalou-les-Bains.

LANGOGNE

15, boulevard des Capucins - 48300 - ☎ 04 66 69 01 38

Filature des Calquières – Guided tours in July and August 10am to 7pm; April to June and September to mid-November 9am to noon and 1.30pm to 6pm; the rest of the year on weekdays only 9am to noon and 1.30pm to 5.30pm. Closed 1 January, 1 May and 25 December. Charge not stated.

Causse du LARZAC

Maison du Larzac – Open 10am to 7pm from end June to mid-September, week-ends at the same times mid-September to mid-October. Free admission. ☎ 05 65 60 43 58 or ☎ 05 65 60 87 67 (out of summer season).

LAVAUR

Cathédrale St-Alain – Open 9am to 7pm (5pm in winter).

Excursion

St-Lieux-les-Lavaur: Tarn tourist steam train – Runs mid-July to August Mondays, Saturdays and Sundays 2.30pm to 6.30pm; Easter to end October Sundays and public holidays at the same times. 25F. ☎ 05 61 47 44 52.

LÉZIGNAN-CORBIÈRES

Musée de la Vigne et du Vin – ♿ Open 9am to 7pm. 25F. ☎ 04 68 27 07 57 or ☎ 04 68 27 37 02.

Excursion

Gasparets: Musée de la Faune – ♿ Open 9.30am to noon and 2pm to 6pm. 30F. ☎ 04 68 27 57 02.

Fabrezan: Musée Charles-Cros – Open daily (except Saturdays and Sundays) 9am to noon and 2pm to 6pm. Free admission. ☎ 04 68 43 61 11.

LODÈVE

7, place de la République - 34700 - ☎ 04 67 88 86 44

Musée Cardinal-de-Fleury – *Open daily (except Mondays) 9am to noon and 2pm to 6pm. Closed public holidays. 20F.* ☎ *04 67 88 86 10.*

Excursions

Prieuré St-Michel-de-Grandmont: *Guided tours (1hr 30min) in July and August at 10.30am, 3pm, 4pm, 5pm and 6pm; Easter to June and in September 10.30am, 3pm and 5pm; the rest of the year Sundays and public holidays only at 3pm. 28F.* ☎ *04 67 44 09 31.*

Grotte de Labeil: Guided tours (45min) mid-June to 10 September 10am to 7pm; mid-March to mid-June and from 11 September to October 11am to 5pm. Visit can be extended by an underground safari (1hr 15min). Bring a change of clothes. 36F, 18F (children). ☎ 04 67 96 49 47.

Grotte de LOMBRIVES

Guided tour (1hr 30min, 3hr or 5hr). Small train departures and tours every 20min in July and August 10am to 7pm; small train departures and tours from Palm Sunday to May and October to mid-November on Saturdays, Sundays, public holidays and during school holidays at 10am, 10.45am then every 45min 2pm to 5.30pm; small train departures and tours every 45min in May from 2pm to 5.30pm. Mid-November to Palm Sunday tours of the cave only on Saturdays, Sundays, public holidays and school holidays from 2pm and 3.30pm. 38F for a 1hr 30min tour, 90F for 3hr and 250F for 5hr; Small access train: 8F. Check other types of tour offered. ☎ 05 61 05 98 40.

Mont LOZÈRE

Chalet du Mont Lozère: Parc national des Cévennes information centre – Open July to mid-September daily 9.30am to 12.30pm and 1.30pm to 6.30pm. ☎ 04 66 48 66 48.

Château de Castanet – *Open mid-June to mid-September 10am to noon and 2pm to 6pm. 15F.* ☎ *04 66 46 81 11.*

Villefort: Parc national des Cévennes information centre – Open in July and August 9am to 12.30pm and 2pm to 7pm; mid-June to mid-September daily (except Sundays) 9am to noon and 2pm to 4pm; the rest of the year weekdays only 9am to noon. ☎ 04 66 46 87 30.

Mas de la Barque: Observation trail – Path open all year. 20F, ticket including visit to the Maison du Mont Lozère, Ferme de Troubat and Mas Camargues path. Descriptive leaflet and ticket obtainable at the Maison du Mont Lozère, and Pont-de-Montvert. ☎ 04 66 45 80 73.

Génolhac: Parc national des Cévennes information centre – Open July to mid-September daily (except Monday mornings and Sunday afternoons) from 9.30am to 12.30pm and 3pm to 7pm; the rest of the year on weekdays (except Wednesdays) from 9am to 11.30am and 2pm to 5pm and Saturdays from 9.30am to 12.30pm. ☎ 04 66 61 18 32.

M

MAGRIN

Château-musée du Pastel – Guided tours (1hr 30min) mid-July to September 10.30am to noon and 3pm to 7pm; Sundays 3pm to 6pm throughout the year. 35F. ☎ 05 63 70 63 82.

Château de Roquevidal: Open Sundays mid-July to mid-September 3pm to 6pm. 20F. The exterior of the château can be visited. ☎ 05 63 41 32 32.

En Olivier: Musée Nostra Terra Occitana – Guided tours (1hr 30min) 10am to 6pm April to December; by appointment the rest of the year. 20F. ☎ 05 63 75 72 93.

Loubens-Lauragais: Château – Open in August on Thursdays, Fridays, Saturdays, Sundays and public holidays from 2.30pm to 6.30pm; May to 11 November on Sundays and public holidays 2.30pm to 6.30pm. 30F. ☎ 05 61 83 12 08.

MAGUELONE

Access to the old cathedral by little train in July and August 10am to 7pm; in May, June and September 10am to 6pm.

Old cathedral – Open 9am to 7pm. June to September, cars must be left in the car park (20F per day, 10F 5pm to 8pm), then visitors continue by the little train. Free admission. ☎ 04 67 50 63 63.

MARVEJOLS

Château de la Baume – *Guided tours (45min) mid-June to mid-September daily 10am to noon and 2pm to 6pm; the rest of the year daily (except Tuesdays) and by appointment 2pm to 5pm. 25F.* ☎ *04 66 32 51 59.*

Parc à loups du Gévaudan – Open June to September 10am to 6pm; 10am to 4.30pm the rest of the year. Closed in January. 33F, 19F (children). ☎ 04 66 32 09 22.

Grotte du MAS-D'AZIL

Cave – Guided tours (45min) June to September and also during the Easter holidays 10am to noon and 2pm to 6pm; in April and May 2pm to 6pm (mornings 10am to noon on Sundays and public holidays); in March, October and November Sundays and public holidays 2pm to 6pm. 30F (child: 15F), combined ticket including visit to the prehistory museum. ☎ 05 61 69 97 71.

Musée de la Préhistoire – Open June to September 10am to noon and 2pm to 6pm; in April and May 2pm to 6pm (also 10am to noon Sundays and public holidays); in March, October and November Sundays and public holidays 10am to noon and 2pm to 6pm. Closed December to February. 30F. ☎ 05 61 69 97 22.

Le MAS SOUBEYRAN

Musée du Désert – Open 9.30am to 6.30pm July to the beginning of September; 9.30am to noon and 2.30pm to 6pm the rest of the year. Closed December to February. 20F. ☎ 04 66 85 02 72.

MENDE

🇭 14, boulevard Bourrillon – 48000 – ☏ 04 66 65 60 01

Guided tours of the town 🅰 – Apply to the Office municipal de la culture.

Musée Ignon-Fabre – Closed for renovation work.

Coopérative des artisans de Lozère – The shop is open in July and August Monday to Saturday 9am to noon and 2pm to 7pm; Tuesday to Saturday at the same times the rest of the year. Closed public holidays.

MILLAU

🇭 avenue Alfred-Merle – B.P 331 – 12103 – ☏ 05 65 60 02 42

Musée de Millau – Open from 10am to noon and 2pm to 6pm. Closed on Sundays from October to March, and also on 1 January, 1 May, 1 and 11 November and 25 December. 25F. ☏ 05 65 59 01 08.

Belfry – *Open in July and August 10am to 11.30am and 3.30pm (4pm Sundays and public holidays) to 6.30pm; in June and September daily (except Sundays) 10am to 11.30am and 3pm to 5.30pm. Closed October to May. 15F. Information from the tourist office.*

Fouilles de la Graufesenque – Guided tours (45min) 9am to noon and 2pm to 6.30pm. Closed 1 January, 1 May, 1 and 11 November, 25 December. 25F. ☏ 05 65 60 11 37.

MINERVE

🇭 Mairie – 34210 – ☏ 04 68 91 81 43

Guided tours of the town – *Contact the tourist office or call ☏ 04 68 46 10 28 or ☏ 04 68 91 12 26.*

Église St-Étienne – Can only be visited as part of a guided tour of the town.

Museum – Open July to mid-September 10.30am to 5.30pm; April to June weekdays 2pm to 5pm (5.30pm Saturdays) and Sundays 11am to 5.30pm; Sundays only 2pm to 5pm the rest of the year. 10F. ☏ 04 67 89 47 98.

Musée Hurepel – ♿ Open 11am to 7pm in July and August, daily (except Mondays April to June) 2pm to 6pm the rest of the year. Closed October to March. 15F. ☏ 04 68 46 10 28.

Chapelle de Centeilles – Open Sundays 3pm to 6pm. Weekdays, guided tours after 5.30pm on application to Mme Lignères (☏ 04 68 91 50 07) or Mlle Chabaud (☏ 04 68 91 45 36).

MOISSAC

🇭 place Durand-de-Breton – 82200 – ☏ 05 63 04 01 85

Centre Marcel-Durliat – Open 10am to noon and 2pm to 6pm. Closed Mondays May to October, Mondays and Tuesdays November to April and also 1 January and 25 December. Free admission. ☏ 05 63 04 41 79.

Abbey Cloisters – ♿ Open in July and August 9am to 7pm (Fridays 9pm to 11pm); mid-March to end June and September to mid-October 9am to noon and 2pm to 6pm; the rest of the year 9am to noon and 2pm to 5pm. Closed 1 January and 25 December. 20F. ☏ 05 63 04 01 85.

Musée moissagais – Open in July and August daily (except Mondays and Sunday mornings) 10am to 12.30pm and 2pm to 7.30pm; mid-March to end June and September to mid-October 10am to 12.30pm and 2pm to 6.30pm; the rest of the year 10am to 12.30pm and 2pm to 5.30pm. Closed 1 January, 1 May and 25 December. 10F. ☏ 05 63 04 03 08.

MONTAGNE NOIRE

Sorèze: Abbey College – Guided tours (1hr) in July and August daily (except Mondays) 11am to 1pm and 3pm to 7pm; April to June and in September and October 2pm to 6pm. Closed the rest of the year. 20F. ☏ 05 63 74 24 68.

Durfort: Copper museum – Open daily (except Tuesdays and Wednesdays) June to September 2pm to 6.30pm. Closed the rest of the year. 10F. The copper-smiths' workshops are open on working days. ☏ 05 63 74 22 77 or ☏ 05 63 74 14 15.

Mazamet: Maison Fuzier – ♿ Open June to August daily (except Mondays and Sundays) 10am to noon and 2pm to 5.30pm. Closed public holidays. Charges not stated. ☏ 05 63 98 12 80.

Mas-Cabardès: Church – Open 9am to noon.

Châteaux de Lastours – Open in July and August 9am to 8pm; April to June and in September 10am to 6pm; in October 10am to 5pm; in February, March, November and December open week-ends and during school holidays at these times. Closed in January and also 25 December. Walking shoes should be worn. 20F. ☏ 04 68 77 56 02.

Grotte de Limousis – Guided tours (1hr) in July and August 10am to 6pm; April to June and in September 10am to noon and 2pm to 6pm. 36F, 20F (children). ☏ 04 68 77 50 26.

Gouffre de Cabrespine – ♿ Guided tours (45min) mid-June to 8 September 10am to 7pm; April to mid-June and in September 10am to noon and 2pm to 6pm; in October 10am to noon and 2pm to 5.30pm; in March and November 2pm to 5.30pm. Closed December to February. 40F, 20F (children). ☎ 04 68 26 14 22. A 5hr underground safari led by cavers available daily by appointment (1 week ahead), cost 220F (groups of 6 to 15 persons). Bring a change of clothes. ☎ 04 67 66 11 11.

Hautpoul: Maison de l'Artisanat – Open in July and August 10am to 7pm; September to December Sundays 2pm to 5pm. Closed January to April and also on public holidays. Free admission. ☎ 05 63 61 45 57.

MONTAUBAN
🖪 ancien collège pl. Prax - 82000 - ☎ 05 63 63 60 60

Musée Ingres – Open in July and August 9.30am to noon and 1.30pm to 6pm; the rest of the year daily (except Sunday mornings mid-October to Palm Sunday and Mondays) 10am to noon and 2pm to 6pm. Closed public holidays. 20F, free admission Wednesdays. ☎ 05 63 22 12 91.

Cathédrale Notre-Dame - Open 8am to noon and 2pm to 7pm Monday to Saturday, and 9am to noon Sundays. ☎ 05 63 63 10 23.

Musée du Terroir – Open daily (except Sundays and Mondays) 10am to noon and 2pm to 6pm. Closed public holidays. 15F, free admission Wednesdays. ☎ 05 63 66 46 34.

Musée d'Histoire naturelle et de Préhistoire – Open daily (except Mondays and Sunday mornings) 10am to noon and 2pm to 6pm. The Prehistory collections are not on display at the moment (probably until end 1998). Closed public holidays. 15F, free admission Wednesdays. ☎ 05 63 22 13 85.

MONT-LOUIS

Four solaire – ♿ Guided tour (30min) in July and August 9.30am to 6.30pm; 10am to 12.30pm and 2pm to 6pm the rest of the year. 25F. ☎ 04 68 04 14 89.

MONTPELLIER
🖪 "Le Triangle" - allée du Tourisme - 34000 - ☎ 04 67 58 67 58

Guided tours of the town – Contact the tourist office.

Hôtel des Trésoriers de France: Musée languedocien – Open daily (except Sundays) in July and August 3pm to 6pm; the rest of the year 2pm to 5pm. Closed public holidays. 20F. ☎ 04 67 52 93 03.

Crypt of Notre-Dame-des-Tables – Temporarily closed to the public for restoration work.

Hotel de Manse – The door opening onto the courtyard is often closed.

Hôtel de Varennes – Open from 8am to 7pm. Guided tours on Wednesdays and Saturdays from 3pm. Closed on public holidays and sometimes during the Radio-France and Montpellier festival. Free admission.

Musée du Vieux Montpellier – Open daily (except Mondays and Sundays) 9.30am to noon and 1.30pm to 5pm. Closed public holidays. Free admission. ☎ 04 67 66 02 94.

Musée Fougau – Open Wednesdays and Thursdays 3pm to 6.30pm. Free admission. ☎ 04 67 60 53 73.

Hôtel Sabatier d'Espeyran – Can be visited by application to the Musée Fabre. ☎ 04 67 14 83 00.

Musée Fabre – ♿ Open daily (except Mondays) 9am to 5.30pm (5pm Saturdays and Sundays). Closed public holidays. 20F. ☎ 04 67 14 83 00.

Hôtel St-Côme – Can be visited as part of a guided tour of the town, subject to numbers. Contact the tourist office.

Musée Atger – Open Mondays, Wednesdays and Fridays 1.30pm to 5pm. Closed in August. ☎ 04 67 66 27 77.

Musée d'Anatomie – ♿ *Open daily (except Saturdays and Sundays) 2.15pm to 5pm. Closed from December 20 to the first Monday in January and also public holidays. Unaccompanied children not admitted.* ☎ *04 67 60 73 71.*

Le Corum – ♿ Guided tours (45min) only on application. Free admission. ☎ 04 67 61 67 61.

Le Corum Terrace – Open 10am to 10pm May to September; 10am to 7pm the rest of the year.

Jardin des Plantes – Open daily (except Mondays) 10am to 7pm April to September, 10am to 5pm the rest of the year. Free admission. 20F (guided tours on application). ☎ 04 67 63 43 22.

Musée de l'Infanterie – ♿ Undergoing restoration work until June 1999. Open daily (except Mondays) 2pm to 6pm. ☎ 04 67 07 21 39.

Montpellier Follies

Château de Flaugergues – Free entry to the park and gardens in July and August 9am to 12.30pm and 2.30pm to 7pm; the rest of the year daily (except Sundays and public holidays) at the same times. Guided tours (1hr) of the interior in July and August daily (except Mondays) 2.30pm to 6.30pm; by appointment the rest of the year. 38F for the full tour, 20F for the outside only. ☎ 04 67 65 51 72.

Château de la Mogère – Free entry to garden and guided tour (1hr) of the interior every afternoon June to September; Saturday and Sunday afternoons and public holidays and weekdays by appointment the rest of the year. 30F. ☎ 04 67 65 72 01.

Château d'O – Access only during cultural exhibitions and events.

Excursions

Parc zoologique de Lunaret – ♿ Open 8am to 7pm in summer, 8am to 5pm in winter. Free admission. ☎ 04 67 63 27 63.

Lattes: Musée archéologique Henri-Prades – ♿ Open daily (except Tuesdays) 10am to noon and 2pm to 5.30pm. Closed 1 January, 1 May, 14 July and 25 December. 15F. ☎ 04 67 99 77 20.

Palavas-les-Flots: Petit train Albert Dubout – Departures every 30min, in July and August 4pm to midnight; in June daily (except Mondays) 2pm to 8pm and in April, May and September 2pm to 7pm. Fare for 30min trip: 20 F, 15 F (children). Round trip to the Cathédrale de Maguelone mornings only, reservation required, mid-June to mid-September. 30F. ☎ 04 67 68 56 41.

Palavas-les-Flots: Musée Albert-Dubout – Open (1hr 30min with boat trip, boarding stage: quai Paul-Cunq) in July and August 4pm to midnight; in May, June and September daily (except Mondays) 2pm to 7pm; in April and October and also during school holidays November to March 2pm to 6pm. 20F, 10F (children). ☎ 04 67 68 56 41 or ☎ 04 67 07 73 82.

Chaos de MONTPELLIER-LE-VIEUX

Open 9.30am to 7pm mid-March to mid-September; 9.30am to 6pm mid-September to 6 November. Closed the rest of the year. 27F, 10F (children under 14). Small train supplement: 15F return, 10F one way only; children: 10F return, 5F one way only. Combined ticket including visit to the Aven Armand: 55F, 25F (children). ☎ 04 66 45 61 31.

MONTSÉGUR

Château – Open April to September 9am to 7pm; mid-February to end March and in October and November from 10am to 6pm. Closed December to mid-February. 25F, combined ticket includes entry to the archeological museum. ☎ 05 61 01 06 94.

Musée archéologique – Open April to September 10am to 1pm and 2pm to 7pm; in February, March, October and November 11am to 5pm. Closed in January and December. 25F, ticket includes entry to the château. ☎ 05 61 01 06 94.

Cirque de MOURÈZE

Parc des Courtinals – Open daily (at weekends only from October to March) 10am to 6pm. Closed in January and February. 20F. ☎ 04 67 96 08 42.

N

NAJAC
🏛 place du Faubourg - 12270 - ☎ 05 65 29 72 05

Fortress – Open June to September 10am to 1pm and 3pm to 6.30pm; in April and May and also on Sundays in October 10am to noon and 2pm to 5pm. 17F. ☎ 05 65 29 71 65.

NARBONNE
🏛 place R.-Salengro - 11100 - ☎ 04 68 65 15 60

Guided tours of the town 🅰 – Information, reservations: Ville de Narbonne, Association Connaître Narbonne, B.P. 823, 11108 Narbonne Cedex. ☎ 04 68 90 30 66.

Cathédrale St-Just – Open 9am to 6pm May to September; 10am to noon and 2pm to 6pm the rest of the year. For guided tours, apply to the Mairie. ☎ 04 68 32 09 52.

Terraces and North Tower – Open daily (except Sundays) 9.30am to 5.30pm mid-June to mid-September, by appointment the rest of the year. Closed 14 July. 10F. ☎ 04 68 32 09 52.

Treasury – Open daily (except Sundays) mid-June to end November 9.30am to 11.30am and 2.15pm to 5.30pm; April to mid-June 2.30pm to 4.30pm; by appointment the rest of the year. Closed public holidays. 10F. ☎ 04 68 32 09 52.

Palais des Archevêques: Salle au Pilier – Open 11am to 6pm mid-June to end September; guided tour (1hr) as part of guided tours of the town the rest of the year.

Archeological Museum – Open May to September 9.30am to 12.15pm and 2pm to 6pm; the rest of the year daily (except Mondays) 10am to noon and 2pm to 5pm. Closed public holidays. 25F. ☎ 04 68 90 30 54.

Museum of Art and History – As for Archeological Museum.

Donjon Gilles-Aycelin – Open May to September 11am to 6pm; the rest of the year 10am to noon and 2pm to 5pm. Closed 1 January, 1 and 11 November, 25 December. 10F. ☎ 04 68 90 30 13.

Basilique St-Paul – ♿ Open 9am to noon and 2pm to 6pm. Closed 1 January, 1 May, 14 July, 1 November and 25 December. ☎ 04 68 42 28 61.

Paleo-Christian crypt – Ask the caretaker to open the entrance grating.

Lapidary Museum – Open 9.30am to 12.15pm and 2pm to 6pm in July and August. Closed 14 July. 25F. ☎ 04 68 90 30 54.

Horreum – Same opening times as the Archeological Museum and the Museum of Art and History.

Église St-Sébastien – Open daily 2pm to 6pm May to September. ☎ 04 68 32 75 87.

Excursions

Terra-Vinea – ♿ Guided tour (1hr 15min) June to September 10am to 8pm (last visit 6.30pm, 5pm in September); in April and May 10am to noon and 2pm to 6.30pm (last visit 5pm); the rest of the year 10am to noon and 2.30pm to 5.30pm (weekdays just one visit at 3.30pm, week-ends last visit 4.45pm). Closed 1 January and 25 December. 30F. ☎ 04 68 48 64 90.

Sallèles-d'Aude: Amphoralis-Musée des Potiers gallo-romains – ♿ Open July to September 10am to noon and 3pm to 7pm; the rest of the year daily (except Mondays) weekdays 2pm to 6pm, week-ends 10am to noon and 2pm to 6pm. Closed 1 May and 25 December. 25F. ☎ 04 68 46 89 48.

Ginestas: Church – Open 9am to noon (11am Sundays). Guided tour on application to the Mairie, ☎ 04 68 46 12 06, or the presbytery, ☎ 04 68 46 27 21.

Le Somail: Musée de la Chapellerie – ♿ Open Monday to Saturday 9am to noon and 2pm to 7pm, Sundays May to September 2.30pm to 7.30pm (2pm to 6pm the rest of the year). 20F. ☎ 04 68 46 19 26.

Seuil de NAUROUZE

Port-Lauraqais: Centre Pierre-Paul Riquet – ♿ Open mid-May to mid-September 9am to 8pm; 10am to 6pm the rest of the year. Free admission. ☎ 05 61 27 14 63.

Grotte de NIAUX

As the number of visitors to the cave is limited to 220 per day (20 per visit), it is essential to book as early as possible (one week in advance during the summer). Guided tour (1hr 15min) every 45min 15 July to September from 8.30am (10am from 9 to 30 September) at 11.30am and 1.30pm to 5pm; the rest of the year at 11am, 3pm and 4.30pm. Closed 1 January and 25 December. 60F, 25F for children 6 to 12. Wear stout shoes, boots in very rainy weather. ☎ 05 61 05 88 37.

Chaos de NÎMES-LE-VIEUX

Open from the Veygalier starting point, all day April to September. 8F, ticket provides access to small museum. Free entry to the Hom or Gailly starting points.

P – Q

PERPIGNAN 🛈 Palais des Congrès, place. A.-Lanoux - 66000 - ☎ 04 68 66 30 30

Guided tours of the town – Apply to the R.O.U.L.O.T.E. 66 organisation, ☎ 04 68 22 25 96.

Palais des rois de Majorque – Open June to September 10am to 6pm; 9am to 5pm the rest of the year. Closed 1 January, 1 May, 1 November and 25 December. 20F. ☎ 04 68 34 48 29.

Musée Hyacinthe-Rigaud – Open daily (except Tuesdays) mid-June to mid-September 9.30am to noon and 2.30pm to 7pm; the rest of the year 9am to noon and 2pm to 6pm. Closed 1 January, 1 and 8 May, 14 July and 25 December. 25F. ☎ 04 68 35 43 40.

Hôtel de ville – Visits to the patio and Marriage Hall Mondays to Fridays 8am to noon and 2pm to 6pm. Closed public holidays.

Cathédrale St-Jean – Open 7.30am to noon and 3pm to 7pm. ☎ 04 68 51 33 72.

Campo Santo – ♿ Open daily (except Tuesdays and Sunday mornings) mid-June to September 9am to noon and 3pm to 7pm; the rest of the year 10am to noon and 2pm to 5pm. Closed 1 January, 1 May and 25 December, and also 28 June to 27 July and 25 August to 15 September because of a festival on the site. ☎ 04 68 66 30 30.

Casa Pairal – Open daily (except Tuesdays) mid-June to mid-September 9.30am to 7pm (5.30pm Sundays); 9am to 6pm (5pm Sundays) the rest of the year. Closed public holidays. 25F. ☎ 04 68 35 42 05.

Église St-Jacques – Follow instructions posted on the door.

Musée numismatique Joseph-Puig – Open Tuesdays to Saturdays 9am to noon and 2pm to 6pm. Closed public holidays. 25F. ☎ 04 68 34 11 70.

Centre d'artisanat d'art Sant Vicens – ♿ Open weekdays 2.30pm to 7pm and week-ends April to December 10am to noon and 2.30pm to 7pm, 2.30pm to 7pm the rest of the year. ☎ 04 68 50 02 18.

Excursions

Mas Palégry: Aviation museum – ♿ Open daily (except Mondays and Sunday mornings) 10am to noon and 3pm (2pm Sundays) to 7pm mid-June to mid-September; on application the rest of the year. 15F. ☎ 04 68 54 08 79.

Thuir: Caves-Byrrh – ♿ Guided tour (45min) in July and August 10am to 11.45am and 2pm to 6.45pm; April to June, in September and October daily (except Sundays in April, May, June and September, Saturdays and Sundays in October) 9am to 11.45am and 2.30pm to 5.45pm; only by appointment the rest of the year. Free admission; wine-tasting at the end of the tour. ☎ 04 68 53 05 42.

Castelnou: Castle – Open mid-June to mid-September 10am to 8pm; April to mid-June 11am to 7pm; in February and March and mid-September to October 11am to 6pm; noon to 5pm the rest of the year. 28F. ☎ 04 68 53 22 91.

Ille-sur-Têt – 🛈 55, avenue Pasteur, 66130, ☎ 04 68 84 02 62.

Guided tours of the town – Apply to the Office de Pole.

Hospici d'Illa – Open in July and August 10am to noon and 3pm to 7pm; the rest of the year daily (except Tuesdays and Saturday and Sunday mornings) 10am to noon and 3pm to 6pm. Closed 1 May. 15F. ☎ 04 68 84 83 96.

Musée du Sapeur-Pompier – Open mid-June to mid-September 10am to 7pm; the rest of the year daily (except Tuesdays) 10am to noon and 2pm to 6pm. 15F. ☎ 04 68 84 03 54 (barracks).

Organ pipes – Open July to September 9.30am to 7.30pm; April to June 10am to 6pm; the rest of the year 10am to 11.45am and 2pm to 4.45pm. Closed 1 January and 25 December. 15F. ☎ 04 68 84 02 62.

Bélesta: Château-musée – Open mid-June to mid-September 10am to noon and 2pm to 7pm; daily (except Tuesdays) 2pm to 5.30pm the rest of the year. Closed mid-November to mid-April. 22F. ☎ 04 68 84 55 55.

Rivesaltes: Maréchal Joffre Museum – Open June to mid-September 8am to noon and 2pm to 6pm; the rest of the year weekdays only and at the same times (closes at 5pm Fridays). 10F. ☎ 04 68 64 24 98.

Château de PEYREPERTUSE

Open 9am to 9pm in July and August; 10am to 8pm in June; 10am to 7pm in April, May and September; 10am to 6pm in February, March and October; 10am to 5pm in November and December. Closed in January. No visiting in stormy weather. Wear stout shoes. 15F. ☎ 04 68 45 03 26.

PEYRUSSE-LE-ROC
🛈 Mairie – 12220 – ☎ 05 65 80 42 98

Archeological Museum – Reorganisation in progress. ☎ 05 65 80 40 02.

Site médiéval – Open daily in July and August. 10F. ☎ 05 65 80 40 02.

PÉZENAS
🛈 place Gambetta – 34120 – ☎ 04 67 98 35 45

Guided tours of the town 🅰 – Contact the Maison du tourisme et de la culture.

Collégiale St-Jean – Open 8am to noon and 3pm to 7pm (10pm Wednesdays and Fridays mid-July to mid-September, 6pm in winter). Guided tours on application to the tourist office.

Hôtel d'Alfonce – ♿ Open 10am to noon and 2pm to 6pm mid-June to mid-September. 10F. ☎ 04 67 98 10 38.

Musée Vulliod-St-Germain – *Open in July and August 10am to noon and 3pm to 7pm; daily (except Sunday mornings and Mondays) 10am to noon and 2pm to 5pm the rest of the year. Closed 1 January and 25 December. 10F.* ☎ 04 67 98 90 59.

Le PONT-DE-MONTVERT

48220 - ☎ 04 66 45 81 94

Maison du Mont Lozère – ♿ Open 10.30am to 12.30pm and 2.30pm to 6.30pm mid-April to September and also during the holidays at All Saints (1 November). 20F, ticket valid for all the Écomusée du Mont Lozère (Ferme de Troubat and Mas Camargues and la Barque trails). ☎ 04 66 45 80 73.

Ferme de Troubat – Open (except Thursdays and Fridays in June and September) 10.30am to 12.30pm and 2.30pm to 6.30pm mid-June to mid-September. 20 F combined ticket including a visit to the Maison du Mont Lozère and the Mas Camargues and la Barque paths. ☎ 04 66 45 80 73.

PRADES

Excursion

Marcevol: Association du Monastir – The priory church is accessible all year 9am to 7pm. To obtain information about the activities of this association, telephone ☎ 04 68 05 24 25.

Bambouseraie de PRAFRANCE

♿ Open April to September 9.30am to 7pm; in March 9.30am to 6pm; for the period October to December enquire about opening times. Closed Mondays and Tuesdays in November and December, and during January and February. 30F, 18F children under 12. ☎ 04 66 61 70 47.

Château de QUÉRIBUS

Open July to August from 9am to 8pm; in May, June and September from 10am to 7pm; in April and October from 10am to 6pm; the rest of the year at weekends and during school holidays from 10am to 5pm. Closed in January. 25F, combined ticket including admission to the virtual image show "Le sermon du Curé de Cucugnan" at the Théâtre Achille Mir at Cucugnan. ☎ 04 68 45 03 69.

R

RODEZ

🛈 place Foch - 12005 - ☎ 05 65 68 02 27

Guided tours of the town – Contact the tourist office.

Musée Fenaille – Closed for renovation work. ☎ 05 65 77 80 85.

Musée Denys-Puech – ♿ Open from 21 June to 20 September Mondays 2pm to 7pm, other days (except Tuesdays and Sunday mornings) 10am to noon and 3pm to 7pm; the rest of the year Mondays 2pm to 7pm, other days (except Tuesdays and Sunday mornings) 10am to noon and 2pm to 6pm. Closed 1 January, 1 May, 1 November and 25 December. 16F, free admission Monday afternoons. ☎ 05 65 42 70 64.

Haras national – ♿ Guided tours (1hr) 10am to 5.30pm. 20F. ☎ 05 65 73 84 00.

ROQUEFORT-SUR-SOULZON

🛈 avenue Lauras - 12250
☎ 05 65 59 93 19

Roquefort Caves – ♿ Guided tours (1hr) 9.30am to 6.30pm 7 July to 24 August; 9.30am to 11.30am and 2pm to 5.15pm the rest of the year. Closed 1 January and 25 December. Wear warm clothes. 15F. ☎ 05 65 59 93 30.

Musée de Préhistoire – Open 9am to 1pm and 2pm to 7pm mid-June to mid-September. Free admission. ☎ 05 65 59 91 95.

Making Roquefort cheese

Muriot/CAMPAGNE CAMPAGNE

Plages du ROUSSILLON

Port-Barcarès: The "Lydia" – Opening times not stated. 25F. ☎ 04 68 35 66 70.

Canet-Plage: Aquarium – ♿ Open in July and August 10am to 8pm; daily (except Tuesdays) 10am to noon and 2pm to 6pm the rest of the year. Closed 1 January. 26F, 16F for children. ☎ 04 68 80 35 07.

Musée de l'Auto – ♿ Same times as for the aquarium. Closed between the Christmas school holidays and the February holidays. 25F, 15F for children. ☎ 04 68 80 35 07.

Musée du Bateau – ♿ Same opening times as the motor museum. ☎ 04 68 80 35 07.

Musée du Jouet – ♿ Same opening times as the motor museum. ☎ 04 68 80 35 07.

Argelès-sur-Mer: Casa de les Albères – Open daily (except Saturday afternoons and Sundays) 9am to noon and 3pm to 6pm. Closed 23 December to 3 January. 10F. ☎ 04 68 81 42 74.

S

ST-ANTONIN-NOBLE-VAL

Ancien Hôtel de ville: Museum – Open (1hr 15min guided tours available) daily (except Tuesdays) July and August from 11am to 1pm and 3.30pm to 7pm; April to June and in September from 3pm to 6pm; the rest of the year by appointment (3 days in advance) to the curator: M. le Conservateur, Maison de l'Ave Maria, 1 rue Del Pebre, 82140 St-Antonin-Noble-Val. Closed 1 January, 1 May and 25 December. 15F. ☎ 03 63 68 23 52.

Upper Aveyron Valley

Chateau de Cas – Guided tours (1hr) mid-June to mid-September daily (except Mondays) from 10am to noon and 2pm to 6pm; April to mid-June and mid-September to October at weekends and on public holidays (other days by appointment) at these times. 25F, 12F (children). ☎ 05 63 67 07 40.

Château du Bosc – Guided tours (45min) in July and August daily from 10am to noon and 2pm to 6pm; Easter to June and in September on Sundays and public holidays from 2pm to 6pm (and during the week by appointment). Closed the rest of the year. 28F. ☎ 05 63 56 03 12.

ST-FÉLIX-LAURAGAIS

ℹ Place Guillaume-de-Nogaret - 31540 - ☎ 05 62 18 96 99

Guided tours of the bastide – Contact the tourist office.

Excursion

Montgey: Castle – Free admission to the park and terraces Sundays and public holidays 3pm to 6pm. ☎ 05 63 75 76 59.

ST-GUILHEM-LE-DÉSERT

ℹ 2, rue de la Font du Portal - 34150 - ☎ 04 67 57 44 33

Abbey Church Museum – Open daily (except Wednesdays) in July and August 11am to noon and 2.30pm to 6.30pm; in June and September 2pm to 6pm; the rest of the year 2pm to 5pm. 10F.

ST-JEAN-DU-GARD

ℹ place Rabaut-St-Étienne B.P. 2 - 30270 - ☎ 04 66 85 32 11

Musée des vallées cévenoles – Open in July and August 10.30am to 7pm; in May, June and September daily (except Mondays and Sunday mornings) 10.30am to 12.30pm and 2pm to 7pm; during school holidays daily (except Mondays and Saturdays); the rest of the year Sundays 2pm to 6pm. Closed 1 January and 25 December. 20F. ☎ 04 66 85 10 48.

"Voyage dans le temps" – ♿ Open mid-June to August daily; April to mid-June Tuesday to Sunday; in September Tuesdays, Thursdays, Saturdays and Sundays; the rest of the year Sundays only. 30F, 25F (children 4 to 14), family concession. ☎ 04 66 85 30 44 (in season) or ☎ 04 66 22 58 64 (out of season).

Atlantide Parc – ♿ Open July to December 9.30am to 8pm; the rest of the year 9.30am to 7pm. 46F, 28F (children 4 to 12). ☎ 04 66 85 32 32.

Cévennes steam train (Train à vapeur des Cévennes) – Runs 4 times a day April to 1 November between Anduze and St-Jean-du-Gard stations with a stop at Bambouseraie de Prafrance: mid-June to August daily; April to mid-June daily (except Mondays); in September Tuesdays, Thursdays, Saturdays and Sundays; in October Saturdays and Sundays. 45F (55F return), children: 33F (38F return). ☎ 04 66 85 13 17 (Gare du T.V.C. to St-Jean-du-Gard).

ST-MARTIN-DU-CANIGOU

Access road closed to vehicles. Access to the abbey is on foot only or by a jeep service. For all information, contact the tourist office at Vernet-les-Bains. ☎ 04 68 05 55 35.

Abbey – Guided tours (45min) mid-June to mid-September daily at 10am, 12.15pm (12.30pm Sundays and public holidays), 2pm, 3pm, 4pm and 5pm; the rest of the year daily at 10am, 12.15pm (12.30pm Sundays and public holidays), 2.30pm, 3.30pm and 4.30pm. Closed Tuesdays October to Easter. 15F. ☎ 04 68 05 50 03.

Abbaye de ST-MICHEL-DE-CUXA

Open daily (except Sunday mornings and religious festivals) 9.30am to 11.50am and 2pm to 6pm (5pm October to April). 15F. ☎ 04 68 96 15 35.

STE-ÉNIMIE   🚹 Mairie
48210 - ☎ 04 66 48 53 44

"Le Vieux Logis" – Open in July and August 10am to 12.30pm and 2pm to 7pm; April to June and in September 10am to noon and 2.30pm to 6pm. Closed October to March. 10F. ☎ 04 66 48 53 44.

Cave – To visit the cave (open the 1st Sunday in October, day of pilgrimage), apply to the presbytery at Ste-Énimie.

Fort de SALSES

Open 9.30am to 12.30pm and 2pm to 6pm. Closed 1 January, 1 May, 1 and 11 November, 25 December. 36F. ☎ *04 68 38 60 13.*

Ste Énimie

Plateau de SAULT

Puivert. Musée du Quercorb – Open July and August from 10am to 7pm; late March to June and in September from 10am to 6pm; the rest of the year at weekends only. Closed in January. 25F. ☎ 04 68 20 80 98.

Puivert: Castle – Open June to September from 8am to 8pm; the rest of the year from 9am to 5pm. 25F. ☎ 04 68 20 81 52.

Prieuré de SERRABONE

Open April to October 10am to 6pm; 10am to 5pm the rest of the year. Closed public holidays. 10F. ☎ *04 68 84 09 30.*

SÈTE   🚹 60, grand'rue Mario Roustan - 34200 - ☎ 04 67 74 71 71

Guided tours of the town – *Contact the tourist office.*

Boat trips – For details, contact Sète Croisières, B.P. 429, 34204 Sète Cedex. ☎ 04 67 46 00 46.

Musée Paul-Valéry – Open in July and August 10am to noon and 2pm to 6pm; the rest of the year daily (except Tuesdays and public holidays) at the same times. Charges not stated. Free admission Wednesdays. ☎ 04 67 46 20 98.

Espace Brassens – ⴼ Open in July and August 10am to noon and 2pm to 7pm; the rest of the year daily (except Mondays October to May) 10am to noon and 2pm to 6pm. Closed 1 January, Easter Day and Monday, 1 and 8 May, 11 November and 25 December. 30F. ☎ 04 67 53 32 77.

SÉVÉRAC-LE-CHÂTEAU   🚹 rue des Douves - 12150 - ☎ 05 65 47 67 31

Château – Open in July and August 9.30am to 8pm; during the 1st fortnight of September 9am to noon and 2pm to 7pm; during the 2nd fortnight of June 9am to noon and 2pm to 6pm. 15F. ☎ 05 65 47 67 31 (tourist office).

Excursions

Château de Vezins – Guided tours (45min) April to October daily (except Wednesdays and Sunday mornings) from 10am to noon and 2pm to 7pm. Closed the rest of the year. 25F. ☎ 05 65 61 87 02.

SÉVÉRAC-LE-CHÂTEAU

Réserve africaine de SIGEAN

Safari Park – ⅃ Open 9am to 6.30pm in summer, 9am to 4pm in winter. 95F, 75F for children. ☎ 04 68 48 20 20.

T

TARASCON-SUR-ARIÈGE

Parc pyrénéen de l'Art préhistorique – ⅃ Open 12 April to August 10am to 6pm; in September and October 10am to 4.30pm. Closed Mondays, Tuesdays, Thursdays and Fridays mid-April to mid-June. 55F, 35F (children 6 to 17). ☎ 05 61 05 10 10.

Excursions

Grotte de la Vache – Guided tours (1hr 15min) in July and August 10am to 5.30pm; the rest of the year daily (except Tuesdays) to 2.30pm and 4pm. Closed October to March. 40F, 20F (children 6 to 12). ☎ 05 61 05 95 06.

Grotte de Bédeilhac – Guided tours (1hr 15min) in July and August from 10am to 5.30pm; the rest of the year from 2.30pm to 4pm (additional tour on Sundays and during school holidays at 3.15pm). Closed on Tuesdays, except those during school holidays. 40F, 20F (children 6 to 12). ☎ 05 61 05 95 06.

Carcanage-Obeillanne/IMAGES PHOTOTHÈQUE

View of the Tarn gorge from the Roc des Hourtous

Gorges du TARN

Château de Prades – Guided tours (45min) all year round. 20F. ☎ 04 42 26 60 75.

Roque Sourde viewpoint – Open Easter to 11 November from 8.30am to 7.30pm. 2F. ☎ 04 66 48 82 00.

Descent from La Malène to the Cirque des Baumes by boat – Guided trip (1hr 15min) by a boatman from April to October. Charge 388F per boat of 4 people, or 97F per seat. We recommend taking the boat trip at 8.30am, as the light in the gorges is at its best at this time. Apply to Bateliers des Gorges du Tarn, 48210 La Malène. ☎ 04 66 48 51 10.

Musée de TAUTAVEL

Centre Européen de Préhistoire – ⅃ Open in July and August 9am to 9pm; April to June and in September 10am to 6pm; the rest of the year 10am to 12.30pm and 2pm to 6pm. Closed mornings 1 January and 25 December. 35F, 17F (children 7 to 14). ☎ 04 68 29 07 76.

Bassin de THAU

Ancienne abbaye de St-Félix-de-Montceau – Open weekends 3pm to 7pm June to August, 2pm to 5pm the rest of the year. Closed in January and February. Free admission. ☎ 04 67 43 34 81.

Bouzigues: Musée de l'étang de Thau – ᬼ Open June to September weekdays 10am to noon and 2pm to 7pm and weekends 10am to 7pm; the rest of the year 10am to noon and 2pm to 6pm October to May, 10am to noon and 2pm to 5pm. Closed 1 January and 25 December. 20F. ☎ 04 67 78 33 57.

Loupian: St-Hippolyte – Guided tour Sundays 3pm to 6pm. ☎ 04 67 43 87 73 (archaeology department of the Syndicat intercommunal de Mèze).Loupian: Gallo-Roman Villa – Temporarily closed for restoration work.

Loupian: Ste-Cécile – Visit on application to the archeology department, Syndicat intercommunal, Maison de la Mer in Mèze. ☎ 04 67 43 87 73.

Mèze: Station de lagunage – ᬼ Open in July and August 10am to 7pm; the rest of the year 2pm to 6pm. 33F, 20F (children). ☎ 04 67 46 64 94.

Marseillan: Chais de Noilly-Prat – Guided tours (45min) May to September 9.30am to noon and 2.30pm to 7pm; the rest of the year 9.30am to noon and 2.30pm to 6pm (5pm in December). Closed 1 May. Free admission, tasting/sales. ☎ 04 67 77 20 15.

TOULOUSE
🛡 Donjon du Capitole - 31000 - ☎ 05 61 11 02 22

Combined tickets are available for the following museums: St-Raymond, Augustins, Paul-Dupuy, Histoire naturelle and Georges-Labit. One at 20F covers entry to three out of the six, and another at 30F covers entry to all six.

Guided tours of the town – Contact the tourist office.

Usine Clément-Ader – Guided tours (1hr 30min) daily (except Sundays) 9am to 11am and 2pm to 4pm (3.30pm Saturdays) on application 10 days in advance to Taxiway, avenue Jean-Monnet, 31770 Colomiers (visitors must have identification papers with them). 55F. ☎ 05 61 15 44 00.

Basilique St-Sernin – Open July to September 9am to 6.30pm (7.30pm Sundays); the rest of the year Mondays to Saturdays 8am to noon and 2pm to 6pm, Sundays 9am to 12.30pm and 2pm to 7pm. ☎ 05 61 21 80 45 or ☎ 05 61 21 70 18.

Crypt – Open July to September Monday to Saturday from 10am to 6pm, Sundays and public holidays from 12.30pm to 6pm; the rest of the year daily (except Sunday mornings) from 10am to 11.30am and 2.30pm to 5pm. 10F. ☎ 05 61 21 80 45.

Musée St-Raymond – ᬼ *Open 10am to 6pm all year, Sundays 2pm to 6pm. 12F.* ☎ *05 61 22 21 85.*

Ancienne chapelle des Carmélites – *Open May to September 10am to 1pm and 2pm to 6pm; the rest of the year 9am to 12.30pm and 1.30pm to 5pm.* ☎ *05 61 29 21 45 (Direction régionale des Affaires culturelles de Midi-Pyrénées).*

Les Jacobins – *Open mid-June to end September weekdays 10am to 6.30pm, Sundays and public holidays 2.30pm to 6.30pm; the rest of the year daily (except Sunday mornings) 10am to noon and 2.30pm to 6pm. 10F.* ☎ *05 61 22 21 92.*

Hôtel de Dernuy (Lycée Pierre-de-Fermat) – Access to the school is permitted on weekdays from 8am to 5pm. Closed week-ends and public holidays.

Toulouse – The Capitole

J.-P. Garcin/DIAF

TOULOUSE

Capitole – Open 8.30am to 5pm, 11am to 7pm week-ends and public holidays. ☎ 05 61 11 02 22.

Musée du Vieux-Toulouse – Open June to September daily (except Sundays and public holidays) 3pm to 6pm. 10F. ☎ 05 61 13 97 24 (during opening times).

Hôtel d'Assézat (Fondation Bemberg) – ⴕ Open daily (except Mondays) 10am to 6pm (9pm Thursdays). Closed 1 January and 25 December. 25F. ☎ 05 61 12 06 89.

Musée Paul-Dupuy – ⴕ Open June to September daily (except Tuesdays) 10am to 6pm; the rest of the year 10am to 5pm. Closed public holidays. 12F or 20F, when there are temporary exhibitions. ☎ 05 61 22 21 75.

Musée des Augustins – Open June to September daily (except Tuesdays) 10am to 6pm (10pm Wednesdays); 10am to 5pm (9pm Wednesdays) the rest of the year. Closed 1 January, 1 May and 25 December. 12F. ☎ 05 61 22 21 82.

Muséum d'Histoire Naturelle – Open daily (except Tuesdays) June to September 10am to 6pm; 10am to 5pm the rest of the year. Closed public holidays. 12F. ☎ 05 61 52 00 14.

Monument to the Résistance – Open from 10am to noon and 2pm to 5pm. Closed weekends and public holidays.

Musée Georges-Labit – Open daily (except Tuesdays) June to September 10am to 6pm; 10am to 5pm the rest of the year. Closed public holidays. 12F. ☎ 05 61 22 21 84.

Galerie municipale du Château d'eau – Open daily (except Tuesdays) 1pm to 7pm. Closed public holidays, except 8 May. 15F. ☎ 05 6177 09 40.

Grotte de TRABUC

Guided tours (1hr) July to 10 September 9.30am to 6.30pm; mid-March to June and 11 September to mid-October 9.30am to noon and 2pm to 6pm; mid-October to November Sundays or by appointment 2pm to 6pm. Closed December to mid-March. 40F, 20F (children). ☎ 04 66 85 03 28. A 5hr underground safari led by cavers is available all year by appointment (1 week in advance), cost per person 220F (6 to 15 people per group). ☎ 04 67 66 11 11.

Gorges de la TRUYÈRE

Couesque dam: Espace Truyère – Guided tours (1hr 30min) July to September daily (except Sundays) 3pm to 7pm; by appointment one week in advance the rest of the year. Free admission. ☎ 05 65 44 56 10 (Entraygues-sur-Truyère tourist office).

V

Abbaye de VALMAGNE

Guided tours (1hr) mid-June to September 10am to noon and 2.30pm to 6.30pm; 2pm to 6pm the rest of the year. Closed 25 December. 25F.

VERNET-LES-BAINS
🖪 place de la Mairie - 66820 - ☎ 04 68 05 55 35

Église St-Saturnin – Open in July and August Mondays, Wednesdays and Fridays 10am to noon and 4pm to 6pm. Also in July and August, guided tours Fridays at 4pm (start from the tourist office). ☎ 04 68 05 55 35.

Le VIGAN
🖪 place du Marché - 30120 - ☎ 04 67 81 01 72

Musée cévenol – *Open April to October daily (except Tuesdays) 10am to noon and 2pm to 6pm; Wednesdays only the rest of the year. Closed 1 May. 14F.* ☎ 04 67 81 06 86.

VILLEFRANCHE-DE-CONFLENT
🖪 place de l'Église (in season) - 66500
☎ 04 68 96 22 96

Guided tours of the town – Apply 1 month in advance to the association "Les Rendez-vous du Patrimoine", 38, rue St-Jean. ☎ 04 68 96 25 64.

Ramparts – Open June to September 10am to 7pm; in April, May, October, November and 20 December to 5 January 10am to 12.30pm and 2pm to 6.30pm; 21 to 31 March 10am to 6pm; 8 February to 21 March 2pm to 6pm; on application during the rest of the year. Closed in January. 20F. ☎ 04 68 96 16 40.

Fort Liberia – Can be reached via the "stairway of a thousand steps", the footpath or in a four-wheel drive, leaving from inside the ramparts to the right of the Porte de France. Fort is open (1hr guided tours available) June to September from 9am to 8pm; the rest of the year from 10am to 6pm. 30F. ☎ 04 68 96 34 01.

Grotte des Canalettes – Guided tours (45min) in July and August 9.30am to 6.30pm; from Palm Sunday to June and September to 11 November 10am to 5.30pm. 30F, 15F for children. ☏ 04 68 05 20 76.

Grotte des Grandes Canalettes – Open mid-June to mid-September 10am to 6pm; March to mid-June and mid-September to November 10am to noon and 2pm to 5pm; the rest of the year Sundays and school holidays 2pm to 5pm. 40F, 20F (children 5 to 12). ☏ 04 68 96 23 11.

Cova Bastera – Open in July and August 10am to 7pm; from Palm Sunday to June and September to 11 November 10am to noon and 2pm to 6pm. 25F. ☏ 04 68 05 20 75.

A street in Villefranche-de-Conflent

VILLEFRANCHE-DE-ROUERGUE

🛈 promenade du Guiraudet – 12200 ☏ 05 65 45 13 18

Guided tours of the town – Contact the tourist office.

Chapelle des Pénitents Noirs – Open July to 28 September 10am to noon and 2pm to 6pm. 20F. ☏ 05 65 45 13 18.

Musée Urbain-Cabrol – Open June to mid-September weekdays 10am to noon and 2pm to 7pm and Saturdays 10am to noon and 3pm to 7pm; the rest of the year daily (except Saturdays and Sundays) 8.30am to noon and 1.30pm to 6pm. Closed public holidays. 10F. ☏ 05 65 45 44 37.

Ancienne chartreuse St-Sauveur – Open July to 28 September 10am to noon and 2pm to 6pm. 20F. ☏ 05 65 45 13 18.

Rugby match between Narbonne and Toulon

Useful French words and phrases

ARCHITECTURAL TERMS

See the ABC of Architecture in the Introduction

SIGHTS

abbaye	abbey	marché	market
beffroi	belfry	monastère	monastery
chapelle	chapel	moulin	windmill
château	castle	musée	museum
cimetière	cemetery	parc	park
cloître	cloisters	place	square
cour	courtyard	pont	bridge
couvent	convent	port	port/harbour
écluse	lock (canal)	porte	gateway
église	church	quai	quay
fontaine	fountain	remparts	ramparts
halle	covered market	rue	street
jardin	garden	statue	statue
mairie	town hall	tour	tower
maison	house		

NATURAL SITES

abîme	chasm	grotte	cave
aven	swallow-hole	lac	lake
barrage	dam	plage	beach
belvédère	viewpoint	rivière	river
cascade	waterfall	ruisseau	stream
col	pass	signal	beacon
corniche	ledge	source	spring
côte	coast, hillside	vallée	valley
forêt	forest		

ON THE ROAD

car park	parking	petrol/gas station	station essence
driving licence	permis de conduire	right	droite
east	Est	south	Sud
garage		toll	péage
(for repairs)	garage	traffic lights	feu tricolore
left	gauche	tyre	pneu
motorway/highway	autoroute	west	Ouest
north	Nord	wheel clamp	sabot
parking meter	horodateur	zebra crossing	passage clouté
petrol/gas	essence		

TIME

today	aujourd'hui	Monday	lundi
tomorrow	demain	Tuesday	mardi
yesterday	hier	Wednesday	mercredi
winter	hiver	Thursday	jeudi
spring	printemps	Friday	vendredi
summer	été	Saturday	samedi
autumn/fall	automne	Sunday	dimanche
week	semaine		

NUMBERS

0	zéro	15	quinze
1	un	16	seize
2	deux	17	dix-sept
3	trois	18	dix-huit
4	quatre	19	dix-neuf
5	cinq	20	vingt
6	six	30	trente
7	sept	40	quarante
8	huit	50	cinquante
9	neuf	60	soixante
10	dix	70	soixante-dix
11	onze	80	quatre-vingt
12	douze	90	quatre-vingt-dix
13	treize	100	cent
14	quatorze	1000	mille

SHOPPING

bank	banque	fishmonger's	poissonnerie
baker's	boulangerie	grocer's	épicerie
big	grand	newsagent,	
butcher's	boucherie	bookshop	librairie
chemist's	pharmacie	open	ouvert
closed	fermé	post office	poste
cough mixture	sirop pour la toux	push	pousser
cough sweets	cachets pour la	pull	tirer
	gorge	shop	magasin
entrance	entrée	small	petit
exit	sortie	stamps	timbres

FOOD AND DRINK

beef	bœuf	lamb	agneau
beer	bière	lunch	déjeuner
butter	beurre	lettuce salad	salade
bread	pain	meat	viande
breakfast	petit-déjeuner	mineral water	eau minérale
cheese	fromage	mixed salad	salade composée
chicken	poulet	orange juice	jus d'orange
dessert	dessert	plate	assiette
dinner	dîner	pork	porc
fish	poisson	restaurant	restaurant
fork	fourchette	red wine	vin rouge
fruit	fruits	salt	sel
sugar	sucre	spoon	cuillère
glass	verre	vegetables	légumes
ice cream	glace	water	de l'eau
ice cubes	glaçons	white wine	vin blanc
ham	jambon	yoghurt	yaourt
knife	couteau		

PERSONAL DOCUMENTS AND TRAVEL

airport	aéroport	shuttle	navette
credit card	carte de crédit	suitcase	valise
customs	douane	train/	billet de train/
passport	passeport	plane ticket	d'avion
platform	voie	wallet	portefeuille
railway station	gare		

CLOTHING

coat	manteau	socks	chaussettes
jumper	pull	stockings	bas
raincoat	imperméable	suit	costume
shirt	chemise	tights	collants
shoes	chaussures	trousers	pantalons

USEFUL PHRASES

goodbye	au revoir	When is the show?	À quelle heure est la représentation?
hello/good morning	bonjour	When is breakfast served?	À quelle heure sert-on le petit-déjeuner?
how	comment		
excuse me	excusez-moi	What does it cost?	Combien cela coûte?
thank you	merci		
yes/no	oui/non	Where can I buy a newspaper in English?	Où puis-je acheter un journal en anglais?
I am sorry	pardon		
why	pourquoi		
when	quand	Where is the nearest petrol/gas station?	Où se trouve la station essence la plus proche?
please	s'il vous plaît		
Do you speak English?	Parlez-vous anglais?		
I don't understand	Je ne comprends pas	Where can I change traveller's cheques?	Où puis-je échanger des traveller's cheques?
Talk slowly	Parlez lentement		
Where's...?	Où est...?	Where are the toilets?	Où sont les toilettes?
When does the ... leave?	À quelle heure part...?		
When does the ... arrive?	À quelle heure arrive...?	Do you accept credit cards?	Acceptez-vous les cartes de crédit?
When does the museum open?	À quelle heure ouvre le musée?		

Index

Agde *Hérault* . . . . Towns, sights and tourist regions followed by the name of the *département*

Toulouse-Lautrec, Henri de . . . People, historical events and subjects

Isolated sights (caves, châteaux, dams, abbeys etc) are listed under their proper name.

A

Abdon and Sennen, Sts 91
Able (Defile) *Aude* 317
Aeronautical industry (Toulouse) 342
Agde *Hérault* 64
Aguilar (Château) *Aude* 148
Aguzou (Gorges) *Aude* 97
Aigoual (Massif) *Gard, Lozère* 65
Aigoual (Mont) *Lozère* 67
Airbus 343
Albères (Monts) *Pyrénées-Orientales* 109
Albi *Tarn* 68
Albigensian Crusades 37, 69, 105, 119, 236, 273, 339
Alès *Gard* 77
Alet-les-Bains *Aude* 98
Aligot 61
Alric (Mont) *Tarn* 234
Alzeau (Prise d'eau) *Tarn* 234
Alzon *Gard* 370
Amboise, Louis d' 69
Amélie-les-Bains-Palalda *Pyrénées-Orientales* 81
Anchovies 142
Andorra (Principality) 82
Andorra la Vella *Andorra* 84
Anduze *Gard* 87
Les Angles *Pyrénées-Orientales* 116
Angoustrine *Pyrénées-Orientales* 134
Aniane *Hérault* 194
Ansignan *Pyrénées-Orientales* 175
Architectural terms 44
Ares (Col) *Pyrénées-Orientales* 361
Arfons *Tarn* 234
Argelès-Plage *Pyrénées-Orientales* 302
Argelès-sur-Mer *Pyrénées-Orientales* 302
Arget (Vallée) *Ariège* 179
Ariège (Haute vallée) *Ariège* 88

Arles-sur-Tech *Pyrénées-Orientales* 91
Armand, Louis 99
Arnette (Gorges) *Tarn* 237
Arpajon, Louis d' 323
Arques (Donjon) *Aude* 148
Arre (Vallée) *Gard* 365
Asclier (Col) *Gard* 92
Les Aspres *Pyrénées-Orientales* 93
Assas, Chevalier Louis d' 364
L'Aubaret (Ferme) *Lozère* 290
Aubrac *Aveyron* 16, 94
Aude (Gorge) *Aude* 97
Aude (Haute vallée) *Aude, Ariège, Pyrénées-Orientales* 96
Auriac (Château) *Aude* 149
Auriol, Vincent 233
Aven Armand *Lozère* 99
Aveyron (Gorges) *Tarn-et-Garonne* 304
Aveyron (Upper valley) *Tarn-et-Garonne* 304
Aviler, Charles d' 51, 244
Ax-Bonascre-le-Saquet *Ariège* 101
Ax-les-Thermes *Ariège* 101

B

Bages et Sigean (Étang) *Aude* 149
Bagnols-les-Bains *Lozère* 211
Baillanouse (Ravine) *Pyrénées-Orientales* 361
Balaruc-les-Bains *Hérault* 103
Balaruc-le-Vieux *Hérault* 103
Balsièges *Lozère* 242
Bamboo 291
Banyuls-sur-Mer *Pyrénées-Orientales* 103
Banyuls wine 103
Baousso del Biel *Lozère* 335
Barre-des-Cévennes *Lozère* 177

Bas Languedoc 27
Bastides 46, 49
La Baume-Auriol *Hérault* 271
Baume (Château) *Lozère* 217
Baumes (Cirque) *Lozère* 332
Béar (Cap) *Pyrénées-Orientales* 158
Beaulieu-en-Rouergue (Abbaye) *Tarn-et-Garonne* 104
Beauquiniès *Hérault* 370
Bédeilhac (Grotte) *Ariège* 327
Bedos (Col) *Aude* 150
Belcaire *Aude* 316
Bélesta *Pyrénées-Orientales* 281
Bellecoste *Lozère* 290
Bellegarde (Fort) *Pyrénées-Orientales* 110
Belpuig (Château) *Pyrénées-Orientales* 94
Belvédère Nord *Gard* 270
Bemberg, Georges 351
Bez-Bedène *Aveyron* 167
Béziers *Hérault* 104
Birds 196
Blacksmiths 179
Blandas *Gard* 270
Blanquefort (Château) *Lozère* 217, 331
Blanquette de Limoux 61
Le Bleymard *Lozère* 211
Bofill, Ricardo 252
Bolquère *Pyrénées-Orientales* 134
Bonascre (Plateau) *Ariège* 101
Bonnecombe (Col) *Lozère* 96
Bonnefon Aveyron 94
Les Bons *Andorra* 85
Bosc (Grotte) *Tarn-et-Garonne* 305
Botanistes (Sentier) 67
Boudou *Tarn-et-Garonne* 232
Bouillac *Tarn-et-Garonne* 192
Bouillouses (Lac) *Pyrénées-Orientales* 242

Le Boulou *Pyrénées-Orientales* 108
Bourdelle, Antoine 238
Bourg-Madame *Pyrénées-Orientales* 133
Bousquet (Château) *Aveyron* 198
Bouzèdes (Belvédère) *Lozère* 212
Bouzigues *Hérault* 337
Bozouls *Aveyron* 111
Bramabiau (Abîme) *Gard* 112
Brameloup *Aveyron* 94
Brassens, Georges 319
Brissac *Hérault* 193
Bromme (Gorges) *Aveyron* 360
Broude, Pierre 94
Brousses *Tarn-et-Garonne* 304
Brunhilda 113
Bruniquel *Tarn-et-Garonne* 113
Bugarach (Pic) *Aude* 151
Burlats *Tarn* 325
Burons 51

C

Cabardès 235
Cabestany *Pyrénées-Orientales* 279
Cabrespine (Gouffre) *Aude* 237
Calmont d'Olt (Château) *Aveyron* 168
Cambeyrac (Dam) *Aveyron* 358
Camisard uprising 220, 289
Cammazes (Dam) *Tarn* 233
Camon *Ariège* 229
Le Can de l'Hospitalet *Lozère* 137
Canet-Plage *Pyrénées-Orientales* 301
Le Canigou *Pyrénées-Orientales* 114
Canigou (Pic) *Pyrénées-Orientales* 115
Canillo *Andorra* 85
Cantobre *Aveyron* 162
Le Capcir *Pyrénées-Orientales* 116
Cap d'Agde *Hérault* 117
Capitouls 339
Capluc *Lozère* 333
Carcassonne *Aude* 119
Carnival 56
Carnon-Plage *Hérault* 187
Carol (Vallée) *Pyrénées-Orientales* 132
Caroux (Mont) *Hérault* 171
Casals, Pablo 290
Cas (Château) *Tarn-et-Garonne* 304

Cassoulet 125
Castanet (Château) *Lozère* 212
Castanet, Bernard de 69
Castelbouc *Lozère* 329
Castelnaudary *Aude* 125
Castelnau-de-Lévis *Tarn* 77
Castelnau-de-Montmiral *Tarn* 185
Castelnau-Lassouts *Aveyron* 168
Castelnou *Pyrénées-Orientales* 280
Castres *Tarn* 126
Castries *Hérault* 130
Catalan architecture 48
Catalan Baroque 50
Catalan cuisine 59
Catalan language 55
Catalan Midsummer 115
Cathar castles 148
Cathars 36, 69, 105, 259, 260
Caudiès-de-Fenouillèdes *Pyrénées-Orientales* 174
Caumont (Château) *Gers* 355
Caune de l'Arago *Pyrénées-Orientales* 335
Causses 16
La Cavalerie *Aveyron* 201
Cavalier, Jean 220
Caves 18
Le Cayla *Tarn* 156
Le Caylar *Hérault* 130
Caylus *Tarn-et-Garonne* 131
Caze (Château) *Lozère* 330
Centeilles (Chapelle) *Hérault* 227
Cerbère *Pyrénées-Orientales* 157
La Cerdagne *Pyrénées-Orientales* 132
Céret *Pyrénées-Orientales* 136
Céret school 136
Cerisier (Gouffre) *Hérault* 195
Cesse (Canyon) *Hérault* 226
Cévennes 20
Cévennes biosphere reserve *Lozère* 209
Cévennes (Corniche) 137
Cévennes (Parc national) 24
Cévennes (Steam train) *Gard* 309
Champ (Château) *Lozère* 211
Charbonnières (Château) *Lozère* 329
Chasms 18
Chasselas 229
Chayla, Abbot of 289

Chestnut tree 22, 308
Chèvre (Grotte) *Lozère* 195
Chioula (Signal) *Ariège* 102
Cinglegros (Rocher) *Lozère* 334
Cinq-Mars 262
Clamouse (Grotte) *Hérault* 138
Clamoux (Gorges) *Aude* 237
Clape (Montagne) *Aude* 267
Climate 23
Clive Pies 289
Cluse Haute (Fort) *Pyrénées-Orientales* 110
Les Cluses *Pyrénées-Orientales* 110
Cocagne, Pays de 213
Cocalière (Grotte) *Gard* 139
Cœur, Jacques 244
Coffre de Pech Redon *Aude* 267
Collioure *Pyrénées-Orientales* 140
Colombières (Gorges) *Hérault* 199
Comberoumal (Prieuré) *Aveyron* 142
Combret, Bernard de 69
Comus (Forest) *Aude* 316
Concorde 343
Le Conflent *Pyrénées-Orientales* 143
Conques *Aveyron* 144
Conques-sur-Orbiel *Aude* 124
Les Corbières *Aude, Pyrénées-Orientales* 147
Cordes-sur-Ciel *Tarn* 153
Corneilla-de-Conflent *Pyrénées-Orientales* 143
Cornusson (Château) *Tarn-et-Garonne* 131
Corps (Moulin) *Aveyron* 162
Corsavy *Pyrénées-Orientales* 92
Cortalets (Chalet-hôtel) *Pyrénées-Orientales* 115
La Cortinada *Andorra* 86
Côte Vermeille *Pyrénées-Orientales* 157
Couesque (Dam) *Aveyron* 358
Couiza *Aude* 98
Coustouges *Pyrénées-Orientales* 91
La Couvertoirade *Aveyron* 158
Crafts 55
Crouzet (Forêt) *Hérault* 171

Crouzette (Route)
Ariège 180
Cubières (Moulin)
Aude 151
Cubières *Aude* 186
Cucugnan *Aude* 151
Les Cuns *Aveyron* 162

D

Dargilan (Grotte)
Lozère 159
Demoiselles (Grotte)
Hérault 161
Déroc (Cascade, Grotte)
Lozère 95
Desnoyer 239
Les Détroits *Lozère* 331
Devèze (Grotte)
Hérault 161
Diable (Pont)
Hérault 194
Dolmens 33, 45
Dolomite 18
Dominic, St 173, 347
Le Donézan *Ariège* 117
Dorres *Pyrénées-*
Orientales 134
Douch *Hérault* 172
Dourbie (Vallée)
Aveyron, Gard 162
Dourgne *Tarn* 234
Dovecots 52
Drailles 67, 94
Dry-stone huts 204
Dubout, Albert 256
Duilhac-sous-Peyreper-
tuse *Aude* 152
Durfort (Château)
Aude 152
Durfort *Tarn* 235
Dyer's woad 213, 342

E

Écrivains Combattants
(Forêt) *Hérault* 172
Elne *Pyrénées-*
Orientales 164
En Calcat *Tarn* 234
L'Engarran (Château)
Hérault 255
Engolasters (Estany)
Andorra 87
Énimie, St 313, 330
En Olivier *Tarn* 214
Ensérune (Oppidum)
Hérault 165
Entraygues-sur-Truyère
Aveyron 166
Envalira (Pass)
Andorra 85
L'Ermitage *Gard* 80
Escala de l'Ours (Road)
Pyrénées-
Orientales 115
Escale (Pas) *Pyrénées-*
Orientales 152

L'Escalette (Pas)
Hérault 202
Espalion *Aveyron* 167
Esparon *Gard* 365
Espéraza *Aude* 98
L'Espérou *Gard* 68
Espinouse (Forêt do-
maniale) *Hérault* 171
Espinouse (Monts)
Hérault 168
Estagel *Pyrénées-*
Orientales 281
Notre-Dame-de-Pène
Pyrénées-
Orientales 281
Estaing *Aveyron* 172
D'Estaing family 172
Eus *Pyrénées-*
Orientales 291
Eyne *Pyrénées-*
Orientales 134

F

*Fabre d'Églantine
(Fabre, Philippe-
Nazaire-François)* 342
*Fabre, François-
Xavier* 248
Fabre, Georges 65
Fabrezan *Aude* 205
Faïsses (Col) 137
Faith, St 144
La Fajolle *Aude* 317
Fanges (Forêt do-
maniale) *Aude* 152
Fanjeaux *Aude* 173
Farrières (Cirque)
Hérault 195
Fauves 140
Fauzan (Grotte)
Hérault 228
Fébus, Gaston 178
Fennel 175
Les Fenouillèdes
Pyrénées-
Orientales 174
Fenouillet *Pyrénées-*
Orientales 174
Finiels (Col, Sommet)
Lozère 210
Flaugergues (Château)
Hérault 254
Florac *Lozère* 175
Foix *Ariège* 177
Foix, Counts of 178
Folklore 56
Fonséranes (Écluses)
Hérault 108
Fontbruno *Tarn* 234
Fontcaude (Abbaye)
Hérault 108
Fontcouverte (Église)
Pyrénées-
Orientales 280
Fontestorbes (Fountain)
Ariège 317
Fontfrède (Pic)
Pyrénées-
Orientales 109
Fontfroide (Abbaye)
Aude 181

Fontfroide (Col)
Hérault 170
Fontmort (Plan)
Lozère 176
Fontpédrouse *Pyrénées-*
Orientales 143
Fontrabiouse (Grotte)
Pyrénées-
Orientales 117
Font-Romeu *Pyrénées-*
Orientales 182
Força Réal (Ermitage)
Pyrénées-
Orientales 281
Forests 22
Formiquères *Pyrénées-*
Orientales 117
Fou (Clue) *Pyrénées-*
Orientales 175
Fou (Gorges) *Pyrénées-*
Orientales 92
Fourquevaux (Château)
Haute-Garonne 355
Fourtou (Col) *Pyrénées-*
Orientales 93
Fraisse-sur-Agout
Hérault 169
Francbouteille (Col)
Lozère 333
La Franqui *Aude* 300
Frau (Gorges) *Ariège,
Aude* 316
French chalk 102
Frontignan *Hérault* 183
Frontignan-Plage
Hérault 183

G

Gaillac *Tarn* 184
Galamus (Gorges)
Pyrénées-
Orientales 185
*Gallo-Roman
pottery* 268
Gally *Lozère* 273
Ganges *Hérault* 193
La Garde-Guérin
Lozère 186
Garonne corridor 28
Garonne, River 338
Garrigues 27
Gasparets *Aude* 204
Gaudiès (Château)
Ariège 355
Gaussan (Château)
Aude 181
Generès, Lluis 50
Génolhac *Gard* 213
Gévaudan *Lozère* 175,
217
Gévaudan, Bête du 22
Gévaudan (Parc à loups)
Lozère 218
Gignac (Pont)
Hérault 194
Ginestas *Aude* 268
Giral family 244
Gisclard (Pont)
Pyrénées-
Orientales 143

Glove-making 224
Gold-panners 179
Golinhac (Dam)
    Aveyron 208
Goya y Luclentes,
    Francisco de 127
La Grande-Motte
    Hérault 187
Grande Pallière
    (Dolmens) 88
Les Grands Causses
    Aveyron 188
Grands Causses (Parc
    naturel régional) 26
Grand-Vabre
    Aveyron 208
Le Grau-d'Agde
    Hérault 64
Grau de Maury Aude,
    Pyrénées-
    Orientales 152
Graufesenque
    potteries 223
Grenade Haute-
    Garonne 192
Gruissan Aude 192
Gruissan-Plage
    Aude 193
Guérin, Maurice et
    Eugénie de 156
Guilhem, St 306
Guinguettes 133

H – I

Hannibal 315
Hat-making 97
Haut Languedoc 28
Haut Languedoc (Parc
    naturel régional) 24
Haut-Minervois
    Hérault 228
Hautpoul Tarn 237
Hérault (Gorges)
    Hérault 194
Hérault (Vallée)
    Hérault 193
Héric Hérault 195
Héric (Gorges)
    Hérault 195
Hix Pyrénées-
    Orientales 135
L'Hom Lozère 273
L'Hôpital Lozère 289
L'Hospitalet Ariège 89
Hospitallers 201
Hourtous (Roc)
    Lozère 216
Hydroelectricity 357
Hyelzas (Causse farm-
    stead) Lozère 190
Ille-sur-Têt Pyrénées-
    Orientales 280
Ingres, Dominique 238
Innocent III, Pope 69
Les Isles (Parc or-
    nithologique) Gard 81
Ispagnac Lozère 329
Izards 101

J – K

Jaurès, Jean 127
Joffre, Maréchal 281
Jonte (Gorges)
    Lozère 195
Jordan, Ramon 302
Jou (Belvédère)
    Aveyron 360
Joucou Aude 317
Joutes nautiques 64
Karst 17

L

Labeil (Grotte et Cirque)
    Hérault 206
Labouiche (Rivière sou-
    terraine) Ariège 197
Lacamp (Plateau)
    Aude 152
Lacapelle-Livron Tarn-et-
    Garonne 131
Lacroix-Barrez
    Aveyron 360
Lacrouzette Tarn 325
Laffon (Tour)
    Ariège 180
La Française Tarn-et-
    Garonne 241
Lagrasse Aude 197
Laguiole Aveyron 198
Lamalou-les-Bains
    Hérault 198
Lampy (Bassin)
    Aude 233
Lanqarail (Pastures)
    Aude 316
Langogne Lozère 199
Languedoc 27
Langue d'Oc 54, 341
Lapérouse, Admiral
    Jean-François de
    Galaup de 76
Lardit (Hydroelectric
    power station)
    Aveyron 358
Laroque-de-Fâ Aude 152
Larra (Château) Haute-
    Garonne 355
Larrazet (Château)
    Tarn-et-Garonne 355
Larzac (Causse)
    Aveyron 200
Larzac (Maison)
    Aveyron 201
Lastours (Châteaux)
    Aude 236
Lattes Hérault 255
Le Lauragais (Region)
    Haute-Garonne,
    Tarn 305
Laussac Aveyron 360
Lauzes 51
Lavaur Tarn 202
Lavérune (Château)
    Hérault 255
Lavognes 17
Lenoir, Marcel 113
Lers (Étang) Ariège 203

Lers (Route du port)
    Ariège 203
Lescure Tarn 77
Leucate (Cap) Aude 300
Lévézou 21
Lézignan-Corbières
    Aude 204
Limousis (Grotte)
    Aude 237
Limoux Aude 99
Lisle-sur-Tarn Tarn 185
La Llagonne Pyrénées-
    Orientales 116
Llech (Gorge) Pyrénées-
    Orientales 116
Llivia Spain 132
Llo Pyrénées-
    Orientales 135
Local words 23
Lodève Hérault 205
Lombrives (Grotte)
    Ariège 207
Lordat Ariège 102
Lot (Gorges)
    Aveyron 208
Lot (Vallée)
    Aveyron 208
Loubatière (Forêt)
    Aude 234
Loubens-Lauragais
    Haute-Garonne 214
Loupian Hérault 337
Lozère (Mont)
    Lozère 209
Lunaret (Parc zoolo-
    gique) Hérault 255
Luzenac Ariège 102

M

Madeloc (Tour)
    Pyrénées-
    Orientales 157
Magrin Tarn 213
Maguelone Hérault 215
Maillol, Aristide 103
Majorca, Kings of 275
La Malène Lozère 216
Mantet Pyrénées-
    Orientales 364
Marcevol Pyrénées-
    Orientales 291
Margeride 16
Mariailles Pyrénées-
    Orientales 114
Marquixanes Pyrénées-
    Orientales 144
Marrous (Col)
    Ariège 179
Marsa Aude 317
Marseillan Hérault 337
Marseillan-Plage
    Hérault 337
Martel, Édouard-
    Alfred 19
Marvejols Lozère 217
Mas-Cabardès Aude 236
Mas Camargues
    Lozère 209, 290
Mas-d'Azil (Grotte)
    Ariège 218

Mas de la Barque *Lozère* 212
Mas Palégry *Pyrénées-Orientales* 279
Mas Raynal *Aveyron* 200
Massat *Ariège* 180
Le Mas Soubeyran *Gard* 219
Maureillas-Las-Illas *Pyrénées-Orientales* 109
Maures (Château) *Pyrénées-Orientales* 110
Mauriac (Château) *Tarn* 185
Maury (Dam) *Aveyron* 167
Mazamet *Tarn* 235
Le Mazel *Lozère* 211
Megaliths 45
Méjean (Causse) *Lozère* 189
Méjean (Corniches du Causse) *Lozère* 333
Mende *Lozère* 221
Menhirs 45
Mercus-Garrabet *Ariège* 90
Mérens (Centrale) *Ariège* 89
Mérens horses 90
Mérens-les-Vals *Ariège* 89
Mérimée, Prosper 119
Meritxell (Chapel of Our Lady) *Andorra* 85
Merle, Captain 222
Merle (Lac) *Tarn* 325
Merville (Château) *Haute-Garonne* 355
Meyrueis *Lozère* 66
Mèze *Hérault* 337
Midi (Canal) *Haute-Garonne, Aude, Hérault* 269
Military architecture 45
Millau *Aveyron* 223
Minerve *Hérault* 226
Minier (Col) 68
Mining 179
Mir, Achille 152
Mirepoix *Ariège* 228
Mogère (Château) *Hérault* 255
Moissac *Tarn-et-Garonne* 229
Molière 285
Molitg-les-Bains *Pyrénées-Orientales* 291
Le Monastier *Lozère* 96
Mondony (Gorges, Vallée) *Pyrénées-Orientales* 82
Monestiés *Tarn* 156
Montabès (Puy) *Aveyron* 167
Montagne Noire *Aude, Tarn* 232
Montagne Noire (Forêt domaniale) *Tarn* 234
Montagnés (Lac) *Tarn* 236

Montauban *Tarn-et-Garonne* 238
Montbrun-des-Corbières *Aude* 205
Montcalm, Marquis de 162
Montézic (Underground plant and reservoir) *Aveyron* 358
Montferrand *Aude* 270
Montferrer *Pyrénées-Orientales* 92
Montfort, Simon de 38, 69
Montgey *Tarn* 305
Mont-Louis *Pyrénées-Orientales* 241
Montmaur *Pyrénées-Orientales* 305
Montmirat (Col) *Lozère* 243
Montmirat (Route du col) *Lozère* 242
Montmorency, Henri de 342
Montolieu *Aude* 124
Montpellier *Hérault* 243
Montpellier Follies *Hérault* 254
Montpellier-le-Vieux (Chaos) *Aveyron* 256
Montricoux *Tarn-et-Garonne* 113
Montségur *Ariège* 258
Mosset *Pyrénées-Orientales* 291
La Mosson (Château) *Hérault* 255
Mourel des Fades (Dolmen) *Hérault* 227
Mourèze (Cirque) *Hérault* 260
Mourèzes (Col) *Gard* 365
Mur-de-Barrez *Aveyron* 360
Muscat wine 183
Mussels 337

N

Najac *Aveyron* 260
Nant *Aveyron* 162
Nantes, Revocation of Edict of 219
Narbonne *Aude* 261
Narbonne-Plage *Aude* 267
Nasbinals *Lozère* 94
Naurouze (Seuil) *Aude* 269
Naussac (Reservoir) *Lozère* 199
Navacelles *Gard* 271
Navacelles (Cirque) *Gard* 270
Niaux (Grotte) *Ariège* 272
Nîmes-le-Vieux (Chaos) *Lozère* 273

Niort *Aude* 317
Nissan-lez-Ensérune *Hérault* 166
Noilly-Prat 337
Noir (Causse) *Aveyron* 190
Nore (Pic) *Aude* 237
Notre-Dame de Capimont *Hérault* 199
Notre-Dame-de-Colombier *Aude* 205
Notre-Dame-de-Consolation *Pyrénées-Orientales* 157
Notre-Dame-de-la-Drèche *Tarn* 77
Notre-Dame-de-Laval *Pyrénées-Orientales* 174
Notre-Dame-des-Auzils (Chapelle) *Aude* 193
Notre-Dame-des-Grâces *Tarn-et-Garonne* 131

O

O (Château) *Hérault* 255
Occitan 54
Odeillo *Pyrénées-Orientales* 134
Oie (Roc) *Tarn* 325
Olargues *Hérault* 170
Olette *Pyrénées-Orientales* 143
Ordino *Andorra* 86
Orlu (Vallée) *Ariège* 101
Osséja *Pyrénées-Orientales* 135
Ouillat (Col) *Pyrénées-Orientales* 111
Ourtigas (Col) *Hérault* 171
Oysters 337

P

Padern *Aude* 149
Palalda *Pyrénées-Orientales* 81
Palavas-les-Flots *Hérault* 256
Pam (Col) *Pyrénées-Orientales* 183
Pamiers *Ariège* 90
Panissars (Site archéologique) *Pyrénées-Orientales* 111
Parisot *Tarn-et-Garonne* 131
Pas de la Casa *Andorra* 86
Pas de l'Arc *Lozère* 335
Pas de l'Ours (Belvédère) *Aude* 316
Pas des Trois Fondus *Lozère* 334
Pas du Loup *Lozère* 333

Pasteur, Louis 78
Pégairolles-de-l'Escalette
  Hérault 202
Péguère (Col)
  Ariège 179
Penne Tarn 273
Perpignan Pyrénées-
  Orientales 274
Le Perthus Pyrénées-
  Orientales 110
Petits Causses 188
Petit train jaune 135
Peyre Auselère
  Ariège 203
Peyrepertuse (Château)
  Aude 282
Peyre (Roc) Lozère 217
Peyriac-de-Mer
  Aude 150
Peyro Clabado
  Tarn 325
Peyrusse-le-Roc
  Aveyron 283
Pézenas Hérault 285
Pierre-Lys (Défilé)
  Aude 97
Pierre Plantée (Col)
  Aveyron, Gard 162
Pilgrimages 144
La Plaine (Forest)
  Aude 316
Planès Pyrénées-
  Orientales 242
Plo de la Bise Tarn 235
Plo des Brus
  Hérault 171
Point Sublime
  Lozère 331
Le Pont-de-Montvert
  Lozère 289
Pont-d'Hérault
  Hérault 93, 193
Pont d'Orbieu Aude 152
Le Pont du Diable
  Ariège 90
Pont-du-Tarn
  Lozère 290
Portal, Charles 154
Port-Barcarès Aude 301
Port (Col) Ariège 180
Portel (Sommet)
  Ariège 180
Porté-Puymorens
  Ariège 89
Portes (Château)
  Gard 80
Port-la-Nouvelle
  Aude 150
Port-Lauragais Haute-
  Garonne 270
Port-Leucate Aude 301
Port-Vendres Pyrénées-
  Orientales 158
Pougnadoires (Cirque)
  Lozère 330
Pradel (Col) Ariège,
  Aude 102
Prades Lozère 290
Prades (Château)
  Lozère 329
Prades-d'Aubrac
  Aveyron 95
Prafrance (Bambou-
  seraie) Gard 291

Prat d'Alaric
  Hérault 169
Prat-Peyrot Gard 68
Prats-de-Mollo Pyrénées-
  Orientales 292
Prehistoric art 326
La Preste Pyrénées-
  Orientales 294
Protestant sites in
  Languedoc 219
Prouille Aude 174
Prunet-et-Belpuig
  Pyrénées-
  Orientales 94
Puéchagut (Forester's
  lodge) 68
Puech, Denys 298
Puigmal 2600 (Centre
  de ski) Pyrénées-
  Orientales 135
Puilaurens (Château)
  Aude 149
Puivert Aude 317
Puymorens (Pass and
  tunnel) Ariège 89
Puyvalador Pyrénées-
  Orientales 117
Py Pyrénées-
  Orientales 364
Pyrène 207
Pyrenees 29
Pyrenees, Treaty
  of 132, 241
Pyrénées 2000
  Pyrénées-
  Orientales 183

Q – R

Quéribus (Château)
  Aude 294
Quézac Lozère 329
Quillan Aude 97
Rabelais, François 243
Rajol (Chaos)
  Aveyron 192
Le Rancié (Mine)
  Ariège 179
Ras del Prat Cabrera
  Pyrénées-
  Orientales 116
Ravège (Lac)
  Hérault 170
Razès (Region) Aude 97
Rebenty (Gorges)
  Aude 317
Rec d'Agout
  Hérault 171
Réderis (Cap) Pyrénées-
  Orientales 157
Redoulade (Col)
  Aude 152
Regional nature
  parks 24
Religious
  architecture 47
Religious festivals 58
Rennes-le-Château
  Aude 98
Resse (Chaos) Tarn 325
Revel Haute-
  Garonne 233

Reyniès (Château) Tarn-
  et-Garonne 355
Rialsesse (Forêt)
  Aude 152
Rigaud, Hyacinthe 275
Riquet, Pierre-Paul 269,
  320
River gorges 18
Rivesaltes Pyrénées-
  Orientales 281
Rivesaltes wine 281
Rocheblave (Château)
  Lozère 329
Rodez Aveyron 295
Rohan, Duc de 77, 87
Roland 220
Romanesque
  architecture 47
Rome (Vallée) Pyrénées-
  Orientales 110
Roquedols (Château) 67
Roquefort-sur-Soulzon
  Aveyron 299
Roquefort cheese 299
Roquelaure (Château)
  Aveyron 168
La Roque-Ste-Margue-
  rite Aveyron 162
Roquesaltes (Chaos)
  Aveyron 191
Roquevidal (Château)
  Tarn 214
Rosis (Église)
  Hérault 172
Rouens Aveyron 358
Roussan, Diane de 193
Roussillon 29
Roussillon (Plages)
  Aude, Pyrénées-
  Orientales 300
Roussillon Plain
  Pyrénées-
  Orientales 279
Rousson Gard 80
Le Rozier Lozère 196
Rugby 56
Rûnes (Cascade)
  Lozère 290

S

Sabarthès (Region)
  Ariège 327
Sabot de Malepeyre
  Lozère 189
Saillagouse Pyrénées-
  Orientales 135
St-André-de-Valborgne
  Lozère 138
St-Antoine-de-Galamus
  (Ermitage) Pyrénées-
  Orientales 186
St-Antonin-Noble-Val
  Tarn-et-Garonne 302
St-Chély (Cirque)
  Lozère 330
St-Clair (Mont)
  Hérault 320
St-Côme-d'Olt
  Aveyron 95
St-Cyprien Pyrénées-
  Orientales 302

St-Dominique (Chaos et Grotte) *Tarn* 324
St-Étienne-d'Issensac (Chapelle) *Hérault* 193
St-Félix-de-Montceau (Ancienne abbaye) *Hérault* 337
St-Félix-Lauragais *Haute-Garonne* 305
St-Ferréol (Bassin) *Haute-Garonne* 233
St-Geniès (Château) *Haute-Garonne* 355
St-Georges (Gorges) *Aude* 97
St-Germain (Chapelle) *Hérault* 227
St-Gervais (Roc) *Lozère* 195
St-Géry (Château) *Tarn* 355
St-Guilhem-le-Désert *Hérault* 306
St-Igne *Tarn-et-Garonne* 131
St-Jean-du-Bruel *Aveyron* 162
St-Jean-du-Gard *Gard* 308
St-Julia *Haute-Garonne* 305
St-Laurent-de-Trèves *Lozère* 137
St-Lieux-les-Lavaur *Tarn* 202
St-Loup (Pic) *Hérault* 310
St-Martin-de-Fenollar (Chapelle) *Pyrénées-Orientales* 110
St-Martin-du-Canigou *Pyrénées-Orientales* 310
St-Michel-de-Cuxa (Abbaye) *Pyrénées-Orientales* 311
St-Michel-de-Grandmont (Prieuré) *Hérault* 206
St-Michel de Mourcairol (Château) *Hérault* 199
St-Michel-de-Rouviac *Aveyron* 162
St-Paul-de-Fenouillet *Pyrénées-Orientales* 175
St-Pierre (Arcs) *Hérault* 312
St-Pierre-de-Bessuéjouls *Aveyron* 168
St-Pierre-de-Rhèdes *Hérault* 198
St-Pierre-sur-Mer *Aude* 267
St-Polycarpe *Aude* 152
St-Pons-de-Thomières *Hérault* 169
St-Roman-de-Tousque *Lozère* 138
St-Véran *Aveyron* 162
Ste-Énimie *Lozère* 313
Ste-Eulalie-de-Cernon *Aveyron* 201

Ste-Léocadie (Table d'orientation) *Pyrénées-Orientales* 135
Saissac *Aude* 233
Sallèles d'Aude *Aude* 268
Salses (Fort) *Pyrénées-Orientales* 314
Salsigne *Aude* 237
La Salvetat-sur-Agout *Hérault* 170
Salvy, St 75
Sant Antoni (Gargantas) *Andorra* 86
Sant Joan de Caselles *Andorra* 85
Saquet (Plateau) *Ariège* 101
Sardana 58
Sarrans (Dam) *Aveyron* 359
Saturninus, St 343
Sault (Plateau) *Aude* 316
Sauveterre *Lozère* 189
Sauveterre (Causse) *Lozère* 189
Secular architecture 51
Ségalas 22
Sègre (Gorge) *Pyrénées-Orientales* 135
Séjourné (Pont) *Pyrénées-Orientales* 143
Senescal (Roc) *Hérault* 370
Sept-Faux (Rocher) *Tarn* 325
Serembarre (Pic) *Ariège* 102
Sereyrède (Col) 67
Sérignan *Hérault* 108
Sernin, St 343
Serrabone (Prieuré) *Pyrénées-Orientales* 318
Serralongue *Pyrénées-Orientales* 361
Serre (Roc) *Lozère* 217
Sète *Hérault* 318
Sévérac, Amaury 323
Séverac, Déodat de 305
Sévérac-le-Château *Aveyron* 323
Le Sidobre *Tarn* 324
Siege warfare 46
Sigean (Réserve africaine) *Aude* 326
Silkworm farming 78, 308
Soldeu El Tarter *Andorra* 85
Le Somail *Aude* 268
Le Somail *Hérault* 169
Sorèze *Tarn* 234
Souci (Pas) *Lozère* 330
Sourde (Roque) *Lozère* 331
Southern French Gothic architecture 49
Speleology 19
Sunyer, Joseph 50

T

Tarascon-sur-Ariège *Ariège* 326
Targasonne (Chaos) *Pyrénées-Orientales* 134
Tarn (Corniche) *Lozère* 335
Tarn (Gorges) *Aveyron, Lozère* 327
Tarn, River 327
Tautavel (Musée) *Pyrénées-Orientales* 335
Tautavel man 32, 335
Le Tech *Pyrénées-Orientales* 92
Templars 201
Termes (Château) *Aude* 149
Terminet (Gorges) *Aude* 153
Terra Vinea *Aude* 268
Thau (Bassin) *Hérault* 336
Thaurac (Plateau) *Hérault* 161
Thommasses (Poste) *Haute-Garonne* 234
Thou, François de 262
Thuès-les-Bains *Pyrénées-Orientales* 143
Thuir *Pyrénées-Orientales* 279
Toulouges *Pyrénées-Orientales* 279
Toulouse *Haute-Garonne* 338
Toulouse-Lautrec, Henri de 70
Trabuc (Grotte) *Gard* 356
Traditional rural architecture 51
Tramontane 23
Tremullas, Lazare 50
Trencavel, Raymond-Roger 119
Trévezel (Gorges) *Gard* 162
Triaire, Sergent 364
Triballe (Col) *Gard* 93
Trois Fromages (Rocher) *Tarn* 325
Trois Termes (Pic) *Pyrénées-Orientales* 111
Troubadours 54
Troubat (Ferme) *Lozère* 209, 290
Truel (Terrasses) *Lozère* 196
Truite (Saut) *Tarn* 325
Truyère (Gorges) *Aveyron* 357
Tuchan *Aude* 153

U – V – W

Underground rivers 18
Usson-les-Bains
    Ariège 117
Vache (Grotte)
    Ariège 327
Valéry, Paul 318
Valira del Nord (Valley)
    Andorra 86
Valira d'Orient (Valley)
    Andorra 85
Le Vallespir Pyrénées-
    Orientales 360
Vallon Aveyron 358
Valmagne (Abbaye)
    Hérault 362
Valmigère Aude 153
Valras-Plage
    Hérault 108
Varen Tarn-et-
    Garonne 362
Vase de Chine
    Lozère 333
Vase de Sèvres
    Lozère 333

Vauban, Sébastien le
    Prestre de 47
Verfeil Tarn-et-
    Garonne 305
Vernaux Ariège 102
Vernet-les-Bains
    Pyrénées-
    Orientales 363
Verte (Route)
    Ariège 179
Vertige (Belvédère)
    Lozère 333
Vésoles (Saut)
    Hérault 169
Veygalier Lozère 273
Vézénobres Gard 81
Vezins (Château)
    Aveyron 324
Via Domitia 370
Vicdessos Ariège 203
Vieillevie Cantal 208
Le Vigan Gard 364
Vigne (Grotte)
    Lozère 195
Les Vignes
    Lozère 331
Villefort
    Lozère 212

Villefranche-de-Conflent
    Pyrénées-
    Orientales 365
Villefranche-de-
    Rouergue
    Aveyron 367
Villelongue (Ancienne
    abbaye) Aude 124
Villemur-sur-Tarn Haute-
    Garonne 241
Villerouge-Termenès
    Aude 149
Vinça Pyrénées-
    Orientales 144
Vindrac Tarn 156
Vins doux naturels 61
Violets 342
Viollet-le-Duc 119
Vis (Gorges) Gard 370
Vis (Vallée) Gard 370
Vissec Gard 370
Voltes (Col) Pyrénées-
    Orientales 115
Weather 23
Wilfred le Velu 132
Wine 60, 148, 184,
    204

Notes